CATO'S LETTERS

Essays on Liberty, Civil and Religious

VOLUME I

A Da Capo Press Reprint Series

CIVIL LIBERTIES IN AMERICAN HISTORY

GENERAL EDITOR: LEONARD W. LEVY

Brandeis University

John Trenchard
Thomas Gordon

CATO'S LETTERS

Essays on Liberty, Civil and Religious, and
Other Important Subjects

Four Volumes in Two

VOLUME I

DA CAPO PRESS · NEW YORK · 1971

A Da Capo Press Reprint Edition

This Da Capo Press edition of *Cato's Letters* is an
unabridged republication in two volumes of the four-volume
sixth edition published in London in 1755.

Library of Congress Catalog Card Number 74-121105

SBN 306-71965-7

Published by Da Capo Press
A Division of Plenum Publishing Corporation
227 West 17th Street, New York, N.Y. 10011

_C A T O_'s
L E T T E R S:

O R,

Essays _on_ Liberty,
Civil and Religious,

And other Important Subjects.

In FOUR VOLUMES.

VOL. I.

The Sixth Edition, _corrected._

_L O N D O N:_

Printed for J. Walthoe, T. and T. Long-
man, C. Hitch and L. Hawes, J. Hodges,
A. Millar, J. and J. Rivington, and
M. Cooper.

M. DCC. LV.

T O

John Milner, *Efq*;

O F

GREAT RUSSEL-STREET,
BLOOMSBURY.

S I R,

 S fhy as I know You to be
of public Notice and Eclat,
let me for once draw, if not
You, your Name at leaft,
from that Recefs which You value in
Propor-

Proportion to the Meafure of Felicity
that You derive from it, and to your
Contempt for the Blaze and Tumult
of Public Life : A Tafte to which I
have the Pleafure of finding my own fo
intirely conformable.

Quiet Paffions and an eafy Mind
conftitute Happinefs ; which is never
found where thefe are not, and muft
ceafe to be, when thefe ceafe to fupport it. Mighty Pomp and Retinue,
glaring Equipages, and the Attendance
of Crowds, are Signs, indeed Burdens,
of Greatnefs, rather than Proofs of Happinefs, which I doubt is leaft felt where
thefe its Appearances are moft feen.
The principal Happinefs which they
feem to bring, is, that other People
think them Marks of it ; and very imperfect muft be that Happinefs which
a Man derives not from what he himfelf

felf feels, but from what another ima-
gines. We may indeed be happy in
our own Dreams, but can never be happy by the Dreams of others.

HAPPIEST of all Men, to me,
feems the private Man ; nor can the
Opinion of ill-judging Crowds make
him lefs happy, becaufe they may
think others more fo. He who can
live alone without Uneafinefs, who
can furvey his paft Life with Pleafure,
who can look back without Compunction or Shame, forward without Fear
or Rebuke ; he, whofe every Day
hath produced fome Good, at leaft
is pafied with Innocence ; the filent
Benefactor, the ready and faithful
Friend ; he who is filled with fecret
Delight, becaufe he feels his Heart
full of Benevolence, who finds Pleafure in Relieving and Affifting ; the
Domeftic

Domeftic Man, perhaps little talked of, perhaps lefs feen, beloved by his Friends, trufted and efteemed by all that know him, often ufeful to fuch as know him not, enjoys fuch high Felicity as the Wealth of King-doms and the Bounty of Kings cannot confer.

IMAGINARY Happinefs is a poor Amends for the want of real. Nor can a better Reafon than this be urged againft envying any Man's Grandeur and State, however mighty it be, how-ever eafy it appear. A great Lot is ever accompanied with many Cares ; and whoever ftands conftantly in the Eyes of the World, will be apt to feel a conftant Concern (perhaps even to Anxiety) how to become his Station and Degree, or how to raife it, or how to keep it from finking. The more he

is

is fet to View, the more glaring will be any Blot in his Character, and the more magnified : Nay, malignant Eyes will be feeing Blots where there are none ; and 'tis certain, that, with all his Grandeur, nay by the Means and Help of his Grandeur, it will be always in the Power of very little People to mortify him, when he can no ways in return hurt them : And thus the leaft Man may become an Overmatch for the greateft.

M E N are more upon a Level than is generally believed ; or rather the Advantage is commonly where 'tis leaft imagined, if we take our Eftimate where it ought to be taken, from the State and Meafure of their Paffions ; fince from this Source their Happinefs or Mifery arifes. Greatnefs accompanied with Vexations, is worfe than an

humble

humble State void of Anxiety; and he who aims not at an elevated Lot, is happier than he, who, having it, fears to lofe it.

HAPPINESS is therefore from within juft as much as is Virtue ; and the virtuous Man enjoys the moft.

IF with this Goodnefs of Mind he be alfo a wife Man, and a Mafter of his Paffions; if to good Senfe he have joined other laudable Accomplifh-ments, a compent Acquaintance with Books, with a thorough Knowledge of the World, and of Mankind ; if he be a benevolent Neighbour, a ufeful Member of Society, perfectly difin-terefted, and juftly efteemed ; if he have ferved and faved great Numbers ; if he be daily protecting the Innocent, daily watching and reftraining the

Guilty

Guilty; his Happineſs muſt be complete, and all his Reflections pleaſing.

WHO this happy Man is, where this amiable Character to be found, is what I pretend not to inform You; though I am perſuaded that few that know You, will aſk that Queſtion. My Purpoſe here is, to deſire your Permiſſion to prefix your Name to the following Edition of CATO's Letters, as well as to what I have ſaid of Mr. TRENCHARD. He eſteemed You as much as one Man cou'd another: You lived in a long Courſe of Intimacy with him : I have long lived, to my great Advantage and Pleaſure, in an equal Courſe of Intimacy with You. You ſaw moſt of theſe Papers before they came out, and many of them were firſt left to

A 5 your

x DEDICATION.

your Perufal and Judgment. You know in a great Meafure which were his, which were mine ; and no Man elfe whofoever was concerned or con-fulted. You know what Motives pro-duced them ; how remote fuch Motives were from Views of Intereft ; and that whilft they continued in full Credit with the Public, they were laid down, purely becaufe it was judged that the Public, after all its terrible Convul-fions, was again become calm and fafe.

You can vouch, that, as thefe Let-ters were the Work of no Faction or Cabal, nor calculated for any lucra-tive or ambitious Ends, or to ferve the Purpofes of any Party whatfoever, but that they attacked Falfhood and Dif-honefty in all Shapes and Parties, with-out temporizing with any, but doing Juftice to all, even to the weakeft and

most

moft unfafhionable, and maintaining the Principles of Liberty againft the Practices of moft Parties; fo they were dropped without any fordid Compofition, and without any Confideration, fave that already mentioned. They had treated of moft of the Subjects important to the World, and meddled with public Meafures and public Men only in great Inftances.

You know that in the Character which I have here given of Mr. TRENCHARD, I have fet him no higher than his own great Abilities and many Virtues fet him ; that his Failings were fmall, his Talents extraordinary, his Probity equal; and that he was one of the worthieft, one of the ableft, one of the moft ufeful Men, that ever any Country was bleffed withal.

You

You know all the Writings which he ever produced, and faw moft of them before they were publifhed. You know that whatever he wrote was occafional, the Effect of prefent Thought, and for immediate Ufe, and that he never laid up Writings in ftore ; an Undertaking quite oppofite to his Turn ; and all his Acquaintance knew that he could never fubmit to fuch a Tafk.

I mention this laft Particular in Juftice to him, that he may not be anfwerable for any Work in which he had no Share. Becaufe I have been told that fome, who knew nothing, or very little of him, perhaps never faw him, have fathered upon him Writings which he never wrote ; from no Kindnefs to him, but purely becaufe they

they were not difpofed to let me be
the Author of a Work which found
fuch favourable Reception from the
World, though it was written feveral
Years after that worthy Man, my
Friend, was dead. You, who are one
of his Executors, and faw all his Papers, know, as the other Executors
perfectly do, that he left no Writings
at all behind him, but two or three
loofe Papers, once intended for CATO's
Letters, and afterwards laid afide;
which Papers of his, with fome of mine
of the fame Sort, you have in your
Hands.

As You have for many Years feen
whatever I intended for the Public,
You know by what Intervals I tranf-
lated TACITUS, and when it was
that I wrote the Difcourfes upon that
Author, fince you perufed both as I
produced

produced them ; and the Difcourfes
prefixed to the firft Volume were not
begun till three Years after his Death ;
nor thofe to the fecond till two Years
after the former. You can therefore
vouch what an abfurd Falfhood they
are guilty of, who would afcribe thefe
Difcourfes to him, to whofe valuable
Name I ever have done, I ever fhall
do, all Honour and exact Juftice. Had
he really written and owned that Work,
'tis more than probable, that the fame
Slanderers would have attributed it to
fomebody elfe.

I should not have once men-
tioned this ridiculous Falfhood, which
You and many others know to be a
complete one in all its Parts, had it
not in fome Meafure concerned the
Public. Let this Detection be the
Punifhment of the little malicious
Minds

Minds who invented it; nor can there be a greater, if they have one honeſt Paſſion remaining, that of Shame or any other, to repreſent them to them-ſelves in their own miſerable Colours, lying, envious, and contemptible. It is a Lot ſufficiently wretched, to be obliged to hate one's ſelf; and to be hardened againſt juſt Shame and Re-morſe, is almoſt as bad. Doubtleſs it were better to have no Soul, than to have a lying and malicious one; bet-ter not to be, than to be a falſe and ſpiteful Being.

Unhappily for theſe undiſcern-ing Slanderers, who, whilſt they mean me a Reproach, make me a Com-pliment, many of the Reflections in the Diſcourſes upon Tacitus, are illuſtrated from Books that have been written, and from Facts that have happened

happened fince Mr. TRENCHARD's
Death, fome of them long fince his
Death.

IT may be proper here to mention
another Miftake which has generally
prevailed ; That a noble Peer of a
neighbouring Nation, now dead, had
a chief, at leaft a confiderable Hand
in CATO's *Letters*.   Though what I
have already faid in this Addrefs to
You abundantly contradicts this Miftake ; yet, for the Satisfaction of the
World, and for the Sake of Truth and
Juftice, I here folemnly aver (and
You well know what I aver to be
ftrictly true) That this noble Perfon
never wrote a Line of thofe Letters,
nor contributed a Thought towards
them,   nor knew who wrote them,
till all the World knew ; nor was
ever confulted about them before or
after,

after, nor ever faw any of them till they were publifhed, except one by Accident.

I AM far from mentioning thus much as any Reflection upon that able and learned Nobleman, who profeffed a Friendfhip for Mr. TRENCHARD and myfelf, and was fo fond of thefe Letters, that, from his great Partiality in fpeaking of them, many People inferred them to be his own. I muft add, that he fent once or twice, or oftener, fome Papers to be publifhed under CATO's Name; but as they were judged too particular, and not to coincide with CATO's Defign, they were not ufed. He afterwards publifhed fome of them in another Form. What heightened the Report of his being the Author of CATO's *Letters,* was, that there then came forth a
public

xviii DEDICATION.

public Print of his Lordfhip, with a
Compliment at the Bottom to him,
as C A T O. I have been told, that
this was officioufly done by Mr. To-
LAND.

M Y Regard for the Memory of
Mr. T R E N C H A R D obliges me to
take Notice alfo of fome Men, who,
fince his Death, have thought fit to
have been very intimate with him;
though, to my Knowledge and yours,
be hardly ever converfed with them,
and always ftrove to fhun them, fuch
of them efpecially as he found to be
void of Veracity.

L E T me add, that thefe Letters
are ftill fo well received by the Public,
that the laft Edition has been long
fince fold off, and for above three

Years

Years paft it was fcarcely poffible to find a Sett of them, unlefs in public Auctions. I mention this, that the prefent Edition may not feem owing to the frequent Quotations made from them in our late Party-hoftilities. I flatter myfelf, that, as thefe Papers contain Truths and Reafons eternally interefting to human Society, they will at all Times be found feafonable and ufeful. They have already furvived all the Clamour and Obloquy of Party, and indeed are no longer confidered as Party-Writings, but as impartial Leffons of Liberty and Virtue. Nor would it be a fmall Recommendation of them to the World (if the World knew You as well as I know You) that they have ever had your Approbation. I am therefore very proud, upon this public Occafion, to declare, that I have long ex-

perienced

perienced your faithful Friendſhip; and
that I am, with very great and very
ſincere Eſteem,

S I R,

Your moſt faithful and

Moſt Humble Servant,

T. GORDON.

THE

THE
PREFACE.

THE following Letters, firſt printed
Weekly, and then moſt of them gathered into Collections from Time to Time,
are now brought all together into Four Volumes. They were begun in *November*, 1720,
with an honeſt and humane Intention, to call
for Publick Juſtice upon the wicked Managers of the late fatal *South-Sea* Scheme ; and
probably helped to procure it, as far as it
was procured ; by raiſing in a Nation, almoſt
ſunk in Deſpair, a Spirit not to be withſtood
by the Arts and Wealth of the powerful
Criminals. They were afterwards carried
on, upon various publick and important
Subjects, for nigh three Years (except a
few Intermiſſions, which will appear by the
Dates) with a very high Reputation ; which
all the Methods taken to decry and miſre-
preſent them could not abate.

The pleaſing or diſpleaſing of any Party
were none of the Ends of theſe Letters,
which,

which, as a Proof of their Impartiality, have pleafed and difpleafed all Parties; nor are any Writers proper to do Juftice to every Party, but fuch as are attached to none. No candid Man can defend any Party in all Particulars; becaufe every Party does, in fome Particulars, Things which cannot be defended; and therefore that Man who goes blindly in all the Steps of his Party, and vindicates all their Proceedings, cannot vindicate himfelf. It is the bafe Office of a Slave, and he who fuftains it breathes improperly *Englifh* Air; that of the *Tuilleries* or the *Divan* would fuit him better.

The ftrongeft Treatife upon the Liberty of the Prefs could not fo well fhew its great Importance to Civil Liberty, as the univerfal good Reception of thefe Papers has done. The Freedom with which they are written has been encouraged and applauded even by thofe who, in other Inftances, are Enemies to all Freedom. But all Men love Liberty for themfelves; and whoever contends for Slavery, would ftill preferve himfelf from the Effects of it. Pride and Intereft fway him, and he is only hard-hearted to all the reft of the World.

The Patrons of Paffive Obedience would do well to confider this, or allow others to confider it for them. Thefe Gentlemen have

never

never failed upon every Occafion to fhew effectually, that their Patience was nothing increafed by their Principles ; and that they always, very candidly and humanely, ex-cluded themfelves from the Confequences of their own Doctrines.   Whatever their Speculations have been, their Practices have ftrongly preached, that no Man will fuffer Injuftice and Violence, when he can help himfelf.

Let us therefore, without regarding the ridiculous, narrow, and difhoneft Notions of felfifh and inconfiftent Men, who fay and do contradictory Things, make general Liberty the Intereft and Choice, as it is certainly the Right of all Mankind ; and brand thofe as Enemies to human Society, who are Ene-mies to equal and impartial Liberty. When-ever fuch Men are Friends to Truth, they are fo from Anger or Chance, and not for her own Sake, or for the Sake of Society.

I am glad, however, that by reading and approving many of *Cato's Letters*, they have been brought to read and approve a general Condemnation of their own Scheme.   It is more than ever they did before ; and I am not without Hopes, that what they have begun in Paffion, may end in Conviction. *Cato* is happy, if he has been the Means of bringing thofe Men to think for themfelves, whofe

whofe Character it has been to let other
Men think for them :—A Character, which
is the higheft Shame, and the greateft Un-
happinefs, of a rational Being. Thefe Papers, having fully opened the Principles of
Liberty and Power, and rendered them
plain to every Underftanding, may perhaps
have their Share in preventing, for the
Time to come, fuch Storms of Zeal for
Nonfenfe and Falfhood, as have thrown the
Three Kingdoms more than once into Convulfions. I hope they have largely helped
to cure and remove thofe monftrous Notions of Government, which have been long
inftilled by the crafty Few into the ignorant Many.

It was no Matter of Wonder that thefe
Letters fhould be ill underftood, and malicioufly applied, by fome, who, having no
Principles of their own, or vile ones, were
apt to wreft *Cato*'s Papers and Principles to
favour their own Prejudices and bafe Wifhes.
But for fuch as have always profeffed to entertain the fame Sentiments of Government
with *Cato*, and yet have been offended with
his Sentiments; as this their Offence was neither his Fault nor Intention, I can only be
forry for their Sakes, that the Principles
which they avowed at all Times fhould difpleafe them at any Time. I am willing to
believe,

believe, that it was not the Doctrine, but the Application, that difobliged them. Nor was *Cato* anfwerable for this; themfelves made it, and often made it wrong. All candid and well-bred Men (if *Cato* may be reckoned in the Number) abhor all Attacks upon the Perfons and private Characters of Men, and all little Stories invented or revived to blacken them, Thefe are cowardly and barbarous Practices; the Work and Ambition of little and malicious Minds: Nor wanted he any fuch low and contemptible Artifices to gain Readers. He attended only to general Reafonings about publick Virtue and Corruption, unbiaffed by Pique or Favour to any Man. In this upright and impartial Purfuit he abufed no Man's Perfon; he courted no Man's Fortune; he dreaded no Man's Refentment.

It was a heavy Charge upon *Cato*, which however wanted not Vouchers (if they were in earneft) that he has fpoken difrefpectfully, nay, infolently, of the King. But this Charge has been only afferted. If it were in the leaft true, I fhould be the firft to own that all the Clamour raifed againft him was juft upon him. But the Papers vindicate themfelves; nor was any Prince ever treated with more fincere Duty and Regard, in any publick or private Writings, than his prefent Majefty has been in thefe. In Point of

Prin-

Principle and Affection, his Majesty never had a better Subject than *Cato* ; and if he have any bad ones, they are not of *Cato*'s making. I know that this Nation cannot be preserved, if this Establishment be destroyed ; and I am still persuaded, that nothing tended more to his Majesty's Advantage and Popularity, or more to the Credit of his Administration, or more to the Security of the Subject, than the pursuing with quick and impartial Vengeance those Men, who were Enemies to all Men, and to his Majesty the most dangerous of all his Enemies ; a Blot and a Curse to the Nation, and the Authors of such Discontents in some, and of such Designs in others, as the worst Men wanted, and the best Men feared.

In answer to those deep Politicians, who have been puzzled to know who were meant by *Cicero* and *Brutus*: Intending to deal candidly with them, and to put them out of Pain and Doubt, I assure them, that *Cicero* and *Brutus* were meant ; that I know no present Characters or Story that will fit theirs ; that these Letters were translated for the Service of Liberty in general ; and that neither Reproof nor Praise was intended by them to any Man living. And if these guessing Sages are in Perplexity about any other Passage in *Cato*'s Letters, it is ten to one but the same Answer will relieve them.

There

There was nothing in thofe Letters analo-
gous to our Affairs ; but as they are extremely fine, full of Virtue and good Senfe,
and the Love of Mankind, it was thought
worth while to put them into *Englijh*, as a
proper Entertainment for *Englijh* Readers.
This was the utmoft and only View ; and it
was at leaft an unkind Miftake to fuppofe
any other.

In one of *Brutus's* Letters it is faid, *We
do not difpute about the Qualifications of a
Mafter ; we will have no Mafter.* This is
far from being ftronger than the Original :
—*Nifi forte non de fervitute, fed de conditione
ferviendi, recufandum eft a nobis.* From
whence fome have inferred, that becaufe
Brutus was againft having a Mafter, therefore *Cato* was againft having a King : A
ftrange Conftruction, and a wild Confequence ! As if the Tranflator of *Brutus's*
Letters were not to follow the Senfe of *Brutus:* Or, as if there were no Difference in
England between a King and a Mafter,
which are juft as oppofite as King and Tyrant. In a neighbouring Country, indeed,
they fay that their Monarch is born Mafter
of the Kingdom ; and I believe they feel it ;
as they do with a Witnefs in *Turky.* But it
is not fo here : I hope it never will be. We
have a King made and limited by the Law.
Brutus having killed one Ufurper, was oppofing

poſing another, overturning by Violence all Law: Where is the Parity, or Room for it?

The ſame Defence is to be made for the Papers that aſſert the Lawfulneſs of killing *Cæſar*. It has been a Queſtion long debated in the World; though I think it admits of little Room for Debate; the only Arguments to be anſwered being Prejudice and Clamour, which are fully anſwered and expoſed in theſe Papers. What is ſaid in them can be only applicable to thoſe who do as *Cæſar* and *Brutus* did; and can no otherwiſe affect our free and legal Government, than by furniſhing real Arguments to defend it. The ſame Principle of Nature and Reaſon that ſupported Liberty at *Rome*, muſt ſupport it here and every where, however the Circumſtances of adjuſting them may vary in different Places; as the Foundations of Tyranny are in all Countries, and at all Times, eſſentially the ſame; namely, too much Force in the Hands of one Man, or of a few unaccountable Magiſtrates, and Power without a Balance: A ſorrowful Circumſtance for any People to fall into. I hope it is no Crime to write againſt ſo great an Evil. The Sum of the Queſtion is, Whether Mankind have a Right to be happy, and to oppoſe their own Deſtruction? And whether any Man has a Right to make them miſerable?

Machiavel

Machiavel puts *Cæsar* upon the fame Foot with the worft and moft deteftable Tyrants, fuch as *Nabis, Phalaris,* and *Dionyfius.* " Nor
" let any Man, *fays he,* deceive himfelf with
" *Cæfar*'s Reputation, by finding him fo ex-
" ceedingly eminent in Hiftory. Thofe who
" cried him up, were either corrupted by
" his Fortune, or terrified by his Power ;
" for whilft his Empire continued, it was
" never permitted to any Man to fay any
" Thing againft him. Doubtlefs if Writers
" had had their Liberty, they could have
" faid as much of him as of *Catiline :* And
" *Cæfar* is much the worft of the two, by
" how much it is worfe to perpetrate a
" wicked Thing, than to defign it. And
" this may be judged by what is faid of
" *Brutus* his Adverfary ; for, not daring to
" fpeak in plain Terms of *Cæfar,* by reafon
" of his Power, they, by a kind of Reverfe,
" magnified his Enemy." He afterwards gives a Summary of the doleful Wafte and crying Miferies brought upon *Rome* and up-on Mankind by the Imperial Wolves his Succeffors ; and adds, that, by fuch a Re-capitulation, " it will appear what mighty
" Obligations *Rome* and *Italy,* and the
" whole World, had to *Cæfar.*"

I fhall fay no more of thefe Papers either in general or particular. I leave the feveral Arguments maintained in them to juftify
them-

themselves, and cannot help thinking that they are supported by the united Force of Experience, Reason, and Nature, It is the Interest of Mankind that they assert ; and it is the Interest of Mankind that they should be true. The Opinion of the World concerning them may be known from hence ; that they have had more Friends and Readers at Home and Abroad than any Paper that ever appeared in it ; nor does it lessen their Praise, that they have also had more Enemies.

Who were the Authors of these Letters, is now, I believe, pretty well known. It is with the utmost Sorrow I say, that one of them is lately dead, and his Death is a Loss to Mankind. To me it is by far the greatest and most shocking that I ever knew ; as he was the best Friend that I ever had ; I may say the first Friend. I found great Credit and Advantage in his Friendship, and shall value myself upon it as long as I live. From the Moment he knew me, 'till the Moment he died, every Part of his Behaviour to me was a Proof of his Affection for me. From a perfect Stranger to him, and without any other Recommendation than a casual Coffee-house Acquaintance, and his own good Opinion, he took me into his Favour and Care, and into as high a Degree of Intimacy as ever was shewn by one Man to another. This was the more remarkable, and did me

the

the greater Honour, for that he was naturally as fhy in making Friendfhips, as he
was eminently conftant to thofe which he
had already made. His Shynefs this way
was founded upon wife and virtuous Confiderations. He knew that in a Number of
Friendfhips, fome would prove fuperficial,
fome deceitful, fome would be neglected ;
and he never profeffed a Friendfhip without a fincere Intentionto be a Friend ; which
he was fatisfied a private Man could not be
to many at once, in Cafes of Exigency and
Trial. Befides, he had found much Bafenefs from, falfe Friends, who, for his beft
Offices, made him vile Returns, He confidered mutual Friends as under mutual Obligations, and he would contract no Obligation which he was not in earneft to difcharge.

This was agreeable to the great Sincerity
of his Soul, which would fuffer him to miflead no Man into Hopes and Expectations
without Grounds. He would let no body
depend upon him in vain. The contrary
Conduct he thought had great Cruelty in it,
as it was founding Confidence upon Deceit,
and abufing the good Faith of thofe who
trufted in us : Hence Hypocrify on one
Side, as foon as it was difcovered, begot
Hatred on the other, and falfe Friendfhip
ended in fincere Enmity : A Violence was
                                                                done

done to a tender Point of Morality, and the
Reputation of him who did it loft and expofed amongft thofe who thought that he had
the moft.

He was indeed fo tender and exact in his
Dealings with all Sorts of Men, that he ufed
to lay his Meaning and Purpofes minutely
before them, and fcorned to gain any Advantage from their miftaking his Intentions.
He told them what he would and would not
do on his Part, and what he expected on
theirs, with the utmoft Accuracy and Open-
nefs.   They at leaft knew the worft ; and
the only Latitude which he referved to himfelf was, to be better than his Word ; but
he would let no Man hope for what he did
not mean. He thought that he never could
be too plain with thofe whom he had to do
with ; and as Men are apt to conftrue Things
moft in own their Favour, he ufed to forefee
and obviate thofe their partial Conftructions,
and to fix every Thing upon full and exprefs
Terms.   He abhorred the mifleading of
Men by artful and equivocal Words ; and
becaufe People are ready to put Meanings
upon a Man's Countenance and Demeanor,
his Sincerity entended even to his Carriage
and Manner ; and though he was very civil
to every body, he ordered it fo, that the
Forms of his Civility appeared to mean no
more than Forms, and could not be miftaken

for

for Marks of Affection, where he had none :
And it is very true, that a Man's Behaviour
may, without one Word said, make Profeffions and Promifes, and he may play the
Knave by a kind Look.

He ufed to fay, and from knowing him
long and intimately I could believe him
when he faid, that he never broke a Promife
nor an Appointment in his Life, in any Inftance where it was practicable to keep them.
If he were to make a Vifit at an Hour, or to
meet a Friend at an Hour, he was always
there before the Hour. He obferved the
fame fevere Punctuality in every other Engagement of his, and had a very ill Opinion
of fuch as did not make every Promife of
every kind a Matter of Morality and Honour. He confidered a Man's Behaviour
in fmaller Matters, as a Specimen of what
he would do in Matters that were greater ;
and that a Principle of Faithfulnefs, or the
Want of it, would fhew itfelf in little as well
as in confiderable Things ; that he who
would try your Patience in the Bufinefs of
an Appointment, would fail you in a Bufinefs of Property ; that one who promifed at
random, and mifled you without an Intention to miflead you, was a trifling Man, and
wanted Honefty, though he had no Treachery, as he who did it with Defign was a
Knave ; that from what Caufe foever they
deceived

deceived you, the Deceit was the fame, and
both were equally to be diftrufted ; that
Punctuality or Remiffnefs, Sincerity or
Perfidioufnefs, runs, generally, through the
Whole of a Man's Life and Actions, and
you need only obferve his Behaviour in one
or two, to know his Behaviour in all ; and
a negligent Man when he is neglected, has
no Reafon to complain, no more than a
falfe Man when he is hated. In many Inftances, Negligence has all the Effects of
Falfhood, and is as far from Virtue, though
not fo near Vice.

As Mr. *Trenchard* was wary and referved
in the Choice of his Friends, fo no fmall
Faults, no fudden Prejudices nor Gufts of
Humour or Paffion, could fhake their Intereft in him, or induce him to part with
them ; nor could any Calumnies, however
artful, nor the moft malicious Tales and In-
fufions, however fpecioufly dreffed up, leffen his Regard for them. In thofe Cafes,
as in all others, he would fee with his own
Eyes, and have full Proof, before he believed or condemned. He knew how eafily
Prejudices and Stories are taken up ; he
knew how apt Malice and Emulation are to
creep into the Heart of Man, and to canker it ; how quickly Reports are framed,
how fuddenly improved ; how eafily an additional Word or Circumftance can tranf-

form

form Good into Evil, and Evil into Good ; and how common it is to add Words and Circumftances, as well as to create Facts. He was aware that too many Men are governed by ill Nature ; that the beft are liable to Prepoffeffions and Mifinformation ; and that if we liften to every fpiteful Tale and Infinuation that Men are prone to utter concerning one another, no two Men in the World could be two Days Friends. He therefore always judged for himfelf, unbiaffed by Paffion or any Man's Authority ; and when he did change, it was Demonftration that changed him. He carried his Tendernefs even to his loweft Servants ; nor could his Steward, who had ferved him many Years, and given him long Proof of great Integrity and good Underftanding, ever determine him to turn away a Servant, 'till he had fatisfied himfelf that he ought to be turned away. He was not affured but his Steward might be prejudiced, notwithftanding his Probity : And the Steward has told me, that he never went with any Complaint to his Mafter, how neceffary foever for him to hear, but he went with fome Uneafinefs and Diffidence.

No Man ever made greater Allowances for human Infirmities, and for the Errors and Follies of Men. This was a Character which he did not bear ; but it is religioufly true.

true.   He knew what feeble Materials human Nature was made of ; perhaps no Man
that ever was born knew it better.   Mankind lay as it were diffected before him ;
and he faw all their Advantages and Deformities, all their Weakneffes, Paffions, Defects, and Exceffes, with prodigious Clear-
nefs, and could defcribe them with prodigious Force.   Man in Society, Man out of
Society, was perfectly known and familiar
to his great and lively Underftanding, and
ftood naked to his Eye, divefted of all the
Advantages, Supplements, and Difguifes of
Art.   His Reafonings upon this Subject, as
upon all others, were admirable, beautiful,
and full of Life.

As to his Indulgence to human Infirmities, he knew that without it every Man
would be an unfociable Creature to another,
fince every Man living has Infirmities ; that
we muft take Men as they are, or not at
all ; that it is but mutual Equity to allow
others what we want and expect to ourfelves ; that as good and ill Qualities are
often blended together, fo they often arife
out of one another : Thus Men of great
Wit and Spirit are often Men of ftrong Paffion and Vehemence ; and the firft makes
Amends for the laft : Thus great Humou-
rifts are generally very honeft Men ; and
weak Men have fometimes great good Nature.

ture. Upon this Foundation no Man lived more eafy and debonair with his Acquaintance, or bore their Failings better. Good Nature and Sincerity was all that he expected of them. But in the Number of natural Infirmities, he never reckoned Falfhood and Knavery, to which he gave no Quarter. Human Weakneffes were invincible ; but no Man was born a Knave : He choofes his own Character, and no fincere Man can love him.

In his Tranfactions with Men, he had a furprifing Talent at bringing them over to his Opinion. His firft Care was that it was fure, and well-grounded, and important ; and then he was a prevailing Advocate : He entered into it with all his Might ; and his Might was irrefiftible. He faw it in its whole Extent, with all the Reafons and all the Difficulties, and could throw both into a thoufand furprifing Lights ; and nothing could efcape him. This a Friend of his ufed to call bringing Heaven and Earth into his Argument. He had indeed a vaft Variety of Images, a Deluge of Language, mighty Perfuafion in his Looks, and great natural Authority. You faw that he was in Earneft ; you faw his excellent Judgment, and you faw his upright Soul.

He had the fame Facility in expofing and taking to Pieces plaufible and deceitful Reafonings. This he did with vaft Quicknefs

and

and Brevity, and with happy Turns of Ridicule. Many a grave Argument, delivered very plaufibly and at large, in good and well-founding Language, he has quite defeated with a fenfible Jeft of three Words, or a pleafant Story not much longer. He had a Promptnefs at Repartee, which few Men ever equalled, and none ever excelled. He faw, with great Suddennefs, the Strength and Weaknefs of Things, their Juftnefs or Ridicule, and had equal Excellence in fhewing either.

The Quicknefs of his Spirit made him fometimes fay Things which were ill taken, and for which, upon Recollection, he himfelf was always forry. But in the Midft of his greateft Heat I never heard him utter a Word that was fhocking or dangerous : So great was his Judgment, and the Guard which he kept over himfelf and over the natural Impetuofity of his Temper. He was naturally a warm Man ; but his Wifdom and Obfervation gave him great Warinefs and Circumfpection in great Affairs ; and never was Man more for moderate and calm Counfels, or more an Enemy to rafh ones. He had fo little of Revenge in his Temper, that his perfonal Refentment never carried him to hurt any Man, or to wifh him Hurt, unlefs from other Caufes he deferved it.

He

He had an immenfe Fund of natural Eloquence, a graceful and perfuafive Manner,
a world of Action, and a Stile ftrong, clear,
figurative, and full of Fire. He attended to
Senfe much more than to the Expreffion ;
and yet his Expreffion was noble. Coming
late into the Houfe of Commons, and being
but one Seffions there, he could not exert
his great Talent that way with Freedom ;
but the few Speeches which he made were
full of excellent ftrong Senfe ; and he was
always heard with much Attention and Refpect. Whether he would have ever come
to have fpoke there with perfect Eafe and
Boldnefs, Time, from which he is now taken away, could only fhew. It is certain,
in that fhort Space he acquired very high
Efteem with all Sorts of Men, and removed
many Prejudices conceived againft him, before he fhewed himfelf in publick. He had
been thought a morofe and impracticable
Man. — An Imputation which nothing but
Ill-will, or Ignorance of his true Character,
could lay upon him. He was one of the
gayeft, pleafanteft Men that ever lived ; an
enchanting Companion, and full of Mirth
and Raillery ; familiar and communicative
to the laft Degree ; eafy, kind-hearted, and
utterly free from all Grimace and Statelinefs.
He was acceffible to all Men. No Man came
more frankly into Conviction ; no Man was

more

more candid in owning his Miftakes; no
Man more ready to do kind and obliging
Offices. He had not one ambitious Thought,
nor a crooked one, nor an envious one. He
had but one View; to be in the Right, and
to do Good ; and he would have heartily
joined with any Man, or any Party of Men,
to have attained it. If he erred, he erred innocently ; for he fincerely walked according
to the beft Light that he had. Is this the
Character, this the Behaviour, of a morofe,
of an impracticable Man? Yet this was the
Character of Mr. *Trenchard*, as many great
and worthy Men, who once believed the
contrary, lived to fee.

He was cordially in the Intereft of Mankind, and of this Nation, and of this Government ; and never found Fault with
publick Meafures, but when he really
thought that they were againft the Publick.
According to the Views which he had of
Things, he judged excellently ; and often
traced Attempts and Events to their firft
true Sources, however difguifed or denied,
by the mere Force of his own ftrong Underftanding. He had an amazing Sagacity
and Compafs of Thinking; and it was fcarce
poffible to impofe Appearances upon him
for Principles : And they who having the
fame good Affections with him, yet fometimes differed in Opinion from him, did it
often

often from the Difference of their Underftandings. They faw not fo far into the
Caufes and Confequences of Things : Few
Men upon Earth did ; very few. His active
and inquifitive Mind, full of Velocity and
Penetration, had not the fame Limits with
thofe of other Men : It was all Lightning,
and diffipated in an Inftant the Doubts and
Darknefs which bewildered the Heads of
others. In a Moment he unravelled the ob-
fcureft Queftions ; in a Moment he faw the
Tendency of Things. I could give many
undeniable Inftances, where every Jot of
the Events which he foretold came to pafs,
and in the Manner that he foretold. Without doubt, he was fometimes miftaken ;
but his Miftakes did him no Difcredit ;
they arofe from no Defect in his Judgment,
and from no Sournefs of Mind.

As he wanted nothing but to fee the Publick profper, he emulated no Man's Greatnefs ; but rejoiced in the Publick Welfare,
whatever Hands conducted it. No Man ever
dreaded publick Evils more, or took them
more to Heart : At one Time they had almoft broke it. The National Confufions,
Diftreffes, and Defpair, which we laboured
under a few Years ago gave him much Anxiety and Sorrow, which preyed upon him,
and endangered his Life fo much, that had
he ftaid in Town a few Days longer, it was
more

more than probable he would never have gone out of it alive. He even dreaded a Revolution ; and the more, beeaufe he faw fome eafy and fecure, who ought to have dreaded it moft. This was no Riddle to him then, and he fanfied that he had lived to fee the Riddle explained to others.

The perfonal Refentment which he bore to a Great Man now dead, for perfonal Injuries, had no Share in the Oppofition which he gave to his Adminiftration, how natural foever it was to believe that it had. He only confidered the Publick in that Oppofition ; which he would have gladly dropped, and changed Oppofition into Affiftance, without any Advantage or Regard to himfelf, if he could have been fatisfied that that Great Man loved his Country as well as he loved Power. Nor did he ever quarrel with any Great Man about fmall Confiderations. On the contrary, he made great Allowances for their Errors, for the Care of their Fortunes and Families, and even for their Ambition, provided their Ambition was honeftly directed, and the Publick was not degraded or neglected, to fatiate their domeftick Pride. He did not vainly expect from Men that Perfection and Heroifm which, he knew, were not to be found in Men ; and he cared not how much Good Minifters did to themfelves, if by it
they

they hurt not their Country. He had two Thing much at heart ; the keeping *England* out of foreign Broils, and paying off the publick Debts. He thought that the one depended upon the other, and that the Fate and Being of the Nation depended upon the laft ; and I believe that few Men who think at all, think him miftaken. For a good while before he died he was eafier, as to thofe Matters, than I had ever known him. He was pleafed with the Calm that we were in, and entertained favourable Hopes and Opinions. Nor is it any Difcredit to the prefent Adminiftration, that Mr. *Trenchard* was more partial to it than I ever knew him to any other. In this he fincerely followed his Judgment; for it is moft certain than he had not one View to himfelf ; nor could any human Confideration have withdrawn him from the publick Intereft. It was hard to miflead him ; impoffible to corrupt him.

No Man was ever more remote from all Thoughts of publick Employments : He was even determined againft them ; yet he would never abfolutely declare that he would at no Time engage in them, becaufe it was barely poffible that he might. So nice and fevere was his Veracity! He had infinite Talents for Bufinefs ; a Head wonderfully turned for Schemes, Trains of Reafoning,

foning, and Variety of Affairs ; extreme
Promptnefs, indefatigable Induftry, a ftrong
Memory, mighty Difpatch, and great
Adroitnefs in applying to the Paffions of
Men. This laft Talent was not generally
known to be his : He was thought a pofitive, uncomplying Man ; and in Matters of
Right and Wrong he was fo. But it is as
true, that he knew perfectly how Mankind
were to be dealt with ; that he could manage their Tempers with great Art, and
bear with all their Humours and Weakneffes with great Patience. He could reafon
or rally, be grave or pleafant, with equal
Succefs ; and make himfelf extremely agreeable to all Sorts of People, without the leaft
Departure from his native Candour and Integrity. As he chiefly loved Privacy and a
domeftick Life, he feldom throwed himfelf
in the Way of Popularity ; but where-ever
he fought it, he had it. One Proof of this
may be learned from the great Town *
where he was chofen into Parliament ; no
Man was ever more beloved and admired
by any Place. He found them full of Prejudices againft him, and left them full of
Affection for him. Very different Kinds
of Men, widely different in Principle, agreed
in loving him equally ; and adore his Me-

---

* Taunton in Somerfetfhire.

mory,

mory, now he is gone. The few four
Men who oppofed him there, owed him
better Things, and themfelves no Credit by
their Oppofition.

In Converfation he was frank, chearful,
and familiar, without Referve ; and entertaining beyond Belief. His Head was fo
clear, ready, and fo full of Knowledge,
that I have often heard him make as ftrong,
fine, and ufeful Difcourfes at his Table, as
ever he wrote in his Clofet ; though I
think he is in the higheft Clafs of Writers
that have appeared in the World. He had
fuch furprizing Images, fuch a happy Way
of conceiving Things, and of putting Words
together, as few Men upon Earth ever had.
He talked without the Pedantry of a Man
who loves to hear himfelf talk, or is fond of
Applaufe. He was always excellent Company ; but the Time of the Day when he
fhined moft, was for three Hours or more
after Dinner : Towards the Evening he was
generally fubject to Indigeftions. The
Time which he chofe to think in, was the
Morning.

He was acceptable Company to Women.
He treated them with great Nicenefs and
Refpect ; he abounded in their own Chit-
Chat, and faid a world of pleafant Things.
He was a tender and obliging Hufband ;
and indeed had uncommon Caufe to be fo,

as

as he well knew, and has fhewn by his Will :
But he had worthy and generous Notions of
the kind Regard which Men owe to Women
in general, efpecially to their Wives; who,
when they are bad, may often thank their
Hufbands.   This was a Theme that he often enlarged upon with great Wifdom. He
was very partial to the Fair Sex, and had a
great deal of Gallantry in his Temper.

He was a friendly Neighbour : He ftudied to live well with every body about him ;
and took a fenfible Pleafure in doing good
Offices. He was an Enemy to Litigioufnefs
and Strife ; and, I think, he told me, that
he never had a Law-Suit in his Life. He
was a kind and generous Landlord ; he never hurried nor diftreffed any of his Tenants
for Rent, and made them frequent, and un-
afked, Abatements. There were yearly Inftances of this. He was exact in performing all his Covenants with them, and never
forgot any Promife that he had made them.
Nor did he ever deny any Tenant any reafonable Favour : But he knew his Eftate
well ; they could not eafily deceive him :
And none but fuch as did fo, or attempted
it, were known to complain.

To his Servants he was a juft and merciful Mafter.   Under him they had good
Ufage and Plenty ; and the worft that they
had to apprehend in his Service, was now
                                              and

and then a paffionate Expreffion. He loved
to fee chearful Faces about him. He was
particularly tender of them in their Sicknefs, and often paid large Bills for their
Cure. For this his Compaffion and Bounty
he had almoft always ill Returns. They
thought that every Kindnefs done them,
was done for their own Sake ; that they
were of fuch Importance to him, that he
could not live without them ; and that
therefore they were entitled to more Wages.
He ufed to obferve, that this Ingratitude
was infeparable from inferior Servants, and
that they always founded fome frefh Claim
upon every Kindnefs which he did them.
From hence he was wont to make many
fine Obfervations upon human Nature, and
particularly upon the Nature of the common Herd of Mankind.

Mr. *Trenchard* had a liberal Education,
and was bred to the Law ; in which, as I
have heard fome of his Cotemporaries fay,
he had made amazing Progrefs. But Politicks and the *Irifh* Truft *, in which he made
a great Figure, though very young, took
him from the Bar ; whither he never had any
Inclination to return. By the Death of an
Uncle, and his Marriage, he was fallen into

---

* He was one of the Commiffioners of the forfeited
Eftates in Ireland in the Reign of King WILLIAM.

an eafy Fortune, with the Profpect of a
much greater.

He was very knowing, but not learned ;
that is, he had not read many Books. Few
Books pleafed him : Where the Matter was
not ftrong, and fine, and laid clofe together, it could not engage his Attention :
He out-ran his Author, and had much
more himfelf to fay upon the Subject. He
faid, that moft Books were but Title Pages,
and in the firft Leaf you faw all ; that of
many Books which were valued, Half might
be thrown away without lofing any Thing.
He knew well the General Hiftory and
State of the World, and its Geography every where. For a Gentleman, he was a good
Mathematician ; he had clear and extenfive
Ideas of the Aftronomical Syftem, of the
Power of Matter and Motion, and of the
Caufes and Production of Things.   He underftood perfectly the Intereft of *England* in
all its Branches, and the Intereft and Pretenfions of the feveral great Powers in *Europe*,
with the State and general Balance of Trade
every where. Upon thefe Subjects, and upon all others that are of Ufe to Mankind, he
could difcoufe with marvellous Force and
Pertinency.   Perhaps no Man living had
thought fo much and fo varioufly.   He had
a bufy and a juft Head, and was Mafter of
any Subject in an Inftant. He chiefly ftudied

Matters

Matters that were of Importance to the World; but loved Poetry, and Things of Amusement, when the Thoughts were just and witty: And no body enjoyed Pleasantries more. He had formerly read the Classicks, and always retained many of their beautiful Passages, particularly from *Horace* and *Lucretius*, and from some of the Speeches in *Lucan*. He admired the Fire and Freedom of the last; as he did *Lucretius* for the Loftiness of his Conceptions: And *Horace* he had almost all by heart. He had the Works of *Cicero* and *Tacitus* in high Esteem: He was not a little pleased when I set about translating the latter. He thought no Author so fit to be read by a free People, like this; as none paints with such Wisdom and Force the shocking Deformities of that Sort of consuming Government, which has rendered almost the whole Earth so thin and wretched.

He had a great Contempt for Logick, and the Learning of the Schools; and used to repeat with much Mirth an Observation of Dr. *Smith*, late Bishop of *Down*, his Tutor. The Doctor used to say, That " Mr. *Tren-* " *chard*'s Talent of Reasoning was owing to " his having been so good a Logician;" a Character for which he was eminent at the University. The Truth was, that his reasoning Head made him excel in the Subtleties

of

of Logick.   Reafon is a Faculty not to be learned, no more than Wit and Penetration. Having as great natural Parts as perhaps any Man was ever born with, he wanted none of the Shew and Affiftance of Art; and many Men, who carry about them mighty Magazines of Learning and Quotation, would have made a poor Figure in Converfation with Mr. *Trenchard.* He highly valued learned Men, when they had good Senfe, and made good Ufe of their Learning : But mere Authorities, and Terms, and the Lumber of Words, were Sport to him ; and he often made good Sport of thofe who excelled in them.   He had endlefs Refources in his own ftrong and ready Underftanding, and ufed to ftrip fuch Men of their Armour of Names and Diftinctions with wonderful Livelinefs and Pleafantry.   Having loft all the Tackle of their Art, they had no Aids from Nature.   Falfe Learning, falfe Gravity, and falfe Argument, never encountered a more fuccefsful Foe.   Extraordinary Learning and extraornary Wit feldom meet in one Man : The Velocity of their Genius renders Men of great Wit incapable of that laborious Patience neceffary to make a Man very learned. *Cicero* and Monfieur *Bayle,* had both, and fo had our *Milton* and *George Buchanan.* I could name others ; but all that I could

mention

mention are only Exceptions from a general
Rule. As to Mr. *Trenchard*, the Character
of *Aper* the *Roman* Orator suits him so much,
that it seems made for him.—Aprum *ingenio potius & vi naturæ quam institutione &
literis famam eloquentiæ consecutum—communi
eruditione imbutus, contemnebat potius literas
quam nesciebat :—Ingeninm ejus nullis aliena-
rum artium inniti videretur.*
Dialog. de Oratoribus.

He was not fond of Writing ; his Fault
lay far on the other Side. He only did it
when he thought it necessary. Even in the
Course of the following Letters, he was
sometimes several Months together without
writing one ; though, upon the Whole, he
wrote as many, within about thirty, as I did.
He wrote many such as I could not write,
and I many such as he would not. But in
this Edition, to satisfy the Curiosity of the
Publick, I have marked his and my own
with the initial Letters of our different
Names at the End of each Paper. To him
it was owing, to his Conversation and strong
Way of Thinking, and to the Protection and
Instruction which he gave me, that I was
capable of writing so many. He was the
best Tutor that I ever had, and to him I
owed more than to the whole World besides.
I will add, with the same Truth, that, but
for me, he never would have engaged in
any

any Weekly Performance whatfoever. From any third Hand there was no Affiftance whatever. I wanted none while I had him, and he fought none while he had me.

His Notions of God were noble and re-fined ; and if he was obnoxious to Bigots, it was for thinking more honourably of the Deity, and for expofing their ftupid, four, and narrow Imaginations about Him. There was more Inftruction in three *extempore* Sen-tences of his upon this Subject, than in threefcore of their ftudied Sermons. He taught you to love God ; they only to dread him. He thought the Gofpel one continu-ed Leffon of Mercy and Peace ; they make it a lafting Warrant for Contention, Seve-rity, and Rage. He believed that thofe Men, who found Pomp and Domination in the felf-denying Example and Precepts of *Jefus Chrift*, were either Madmen, or worfe ——not in earneft ; that fuch as were Ene-mies to Liberty of Confcience, were Enemies to human Society, which is a frail Thing kept together by mutual Neceffities and mutual Indulgencies ; and that, in order to reduce the World to one Opinion, the whole World muft.be reduced to one Man, and all the reft deftroyed.

He faw, with juft Indignation, the mad, chimerical, felfifh, and barbarous Tenets maintained by many of the Clergy, with the
mifchievous

mifchievous Effects and Tendency of thefe
Tenets: He faw, as every Man that has
Eyes may, that for every Advantage which
they have in the World, they are beholden
to Men and Societies ; and he thought it
downright Fraud and Impudence, to claim
as a Gift from God, what all Mankind knew
was the manifeft Bounty of Men, and the
Policy of States, or extorted from them ;
that Ecclefiaftical Jurifdiction and Revenues
could have no other poffible Original ; that
it was a Contradiction to all Truth, to Chriftianity, and to all Civil Government, to
allow them any other ; that the certain Effect of detaching the Priefthood from the
Authority of the Civil Magiftrate, was to
enflave the Civil Magiftrate, and all Men,
to the Priefthood ; that thefe Claims of the
Clergy to Divine Right and Independency,
raifed a Cumbuftion, a Civil Schifm in the
State (the only Schifm dangerous to Society) made the Laity the Property or the
Enemies of the Clergy, and taught the Clergy avowed Ingratitude for every Bounty,
Indulgence, Privilege, and Advantage,
which the Laity, or any Layman, could
beftow upon them ; fince having all from
God, they could confider Laymen only as
Intruders, when Laymen meddled with cele-
ftial Rents, and pretended to give them
what God had given them. I am apt to
think

think that from this Root of fpiritual Pride
proceeds the too common Ingratitude of
Clergymen to their Patrons for very good
Livings. They think it Ufurpation in Laymen to have Church Benefices in their Gift.
Hence their known Abhorrence of Impro-
priations ; and we all know what they
mean, when they find fo much Precipitan-
cy and fo many Errors in the *Reformation*.
It was a terrible Blow to Church Dominion,
and gave the Laity fome of their own
Lands again.

Some will fay, that thefe are only a Number of hot-headed Men amongft the Clergy ; and I fay, that I mean no other : I
only wifh that the cool Heads may be the
Majority. That there are many fuch, I
know and congratulate ; and I honour with
all my Heart the many Bifhops and Doctors, who are fatisfied with the Condition
of the Clergy, and are Friends to Confcience and Civil Liberty ; for both which
fome of them have contended with immortal Succefs.

But whatever Offence the high Claimers
of fpiritual Dominion gave Mr. *Trenchard*,
he was fincerely for preferving the Eftablifhed Church, and would have heartily oppofed
any Attempt to alter it. He was againft all
levelling in Church and State, and fearful
of trying Experiments upon the Conftitution.

tution.   He thought that it was already upon a very good Balance ; and no Man was
more falfly accufed of an Intention to pull
it down.   The Eftablifhment was his Standard ; and he was only for pulling down
thofe who would foar above it, and trample
upon it.   If he offended Churchmen, while
he defended the Legal Church, the Blame
was not his.   He knew of no Authority
that they had, but what the Laws gave them ;
nor can they fhew any other.   The Sanctions
of a Thoufand Synods, the Names and Volumes of Ten Thoufand Fathers, weigh not
one Grain in this Argument.   They are no
more Rules to us, than the Oracles of *Delphos*, no more than a College of *Augurs*.
Acts of Parliament alone conftitute and li-
mit our Church Government, and create
our Clergy ; and upon this Article Mr.
Trenchard only afferted what they themfelves
had fworn.   Perfonally he ufed them with
great Civility where-ever he met them ; and
he was for depriving them of no Part of
their Dignities and Reverfions.   As to their
fpeculative Opinions, when he meddled
with them, he thought that he might
take the fame Liberty to differ with them,
which they took to differ with one another.   For this many of them have treated
his Name very barbaroufly, to their own
Difcredit.   Laymen can fometimes fight,
and

and be Friends again. The Officers and Soldiers of two oppofite Camps, if they meet out of the Way of Battle, can be well-bred and humane to each other, and well-pleafed together, though they are to deftroy one another next Day. But, I know not how it happens, Clerical Heat does not eafily cool ; it rarely knows Moderation or any Bounds, but purfues Men to their Death ; and even after Death it purfues them, when they are no longer fubject to the Laws or Cognizance of Men. It was not more good Policy than it was Juftice in thefe angry Men, to charge Mr. *Trenchard* with Want of Religion ; as it is owning that a Man may be a moft virtuous Man, and an excellent Member of Society, without it. But, as nothing is fo irreligious as the Want of Charity ; fo nothing is more indifcreet.

As paffionate as he was for Liberty, he was not for a Commonwealth in *England.* He neither believed it poffible, nor wifhed for it. He thought that we were better as we were, than any practicable Change could make us ; and feemed to apprehend, that a neighbouring Republick was not far from fome violent Shock. I wifh that he may have been miftaken ; but the Grounds of his Opinion were too plaufible.

I have before owned that he was paffionate ; but he fhewed it only in Inftances where

where it was not worth while to watch and
reftrain his Temper. In Things of Moment, or when he had a Mind not to be
provoked, no Man was more fedate and
calm. I have often feen him laugh a peevifh Man out of his Peevifhnefs, and without being angry, make others very angry.
If he had a Mind to dive into any Man's
Defigns, in which he was very fuccefsful,
or meant to gain any End upon him, it was
impoffible to ruffle him. He was only hafty,
when he was inadvertent. There was a Rapidity and Emotion in his Way of Talking, which fometimes made him thought
warm when he was not. *Etfi vehemens, non-*
dum iratus ; as I think *Tully* fays of himfelf
upon the like Occafion. He was likewife apt
to give quick Anfwers to impertinent Queftions, and to mortify Men who he thought
talked knavifhly. Hence chiefly he was
called a hot Man. Little Things fometimes
provoked him, but great Provocations fet
him a thinking ; and he was capable of
bearing great Loffes, Oppofition, and Difappointments, with fignal Temper and
Firmnefs. He was very merry with thofe
who wrote fcurriloufly againft him, and
laughed heartily at what they thought he
refented moft. Not many Days before he
died, he diverted himfelf with a very abufe-
ful Book written by a Clergyman, and
pointed

pointed perfonally at him ; by a Clergyman highly obliged to his Family, and always treated with great Friendfhip by himfelf.

He had a noble Fortune, of which he took fuch Care as a wife Man fhould. He underftood Hufbandry and Improvements excellently, and every Place where he came was the better for him. But though he was careful to preferve his Eftate, he was no ways anxious to increafe it. He kept a genteel and a plentiful Table, and was pleafed to fee it well filled : He had a great Number of Servants, and daily employed feveral Tradefmen and many Labourers. So that of his whole yearly Income he faved little at the Year's End, not above Two or Three Hundred Pounds. This will appear ftrange to moft People, who generally believed that he faved great Sums : But I know what I fay, and it is plain from the Perfonal Eftate which he has left.

As to his Family, which I mention laft, becaufe it is the laft Thing upon which a wife Man will value himfelf ; it is one of the ancienteft in *England*, and well allied : His Anceftors came over with *William* the *Norman* ; and there has been a good Eftate in the Name ever fince. He left no Child, and his three Sifters are his Heirs. I know but one Family now remaining of the Name, Mr. *George Trenchard's*, of *Dorfetfhire*, a
Member

Member of the Houfe of Commons ; and
I believe the Eftate in both Families is worth
near Ten Thoufand Pounds a Year.

He died of an Ulcer in the Kidneys, after an Illnefs of five Weeks and fome Days ;
and he died like a wife Man, with great Refignation and Calmnefs of Spirit, quite free
from all falfe Fears or pannick Terrors, and
without one Struggle or Convulfion.   The
Day before his Death he talked to me much
and often of an Affair which regarded myfelf; and which, were I to mention it,
would fhew the great Concern and Tendernefs that he had for me.   He died in the
Fifty-fifth Year of his Age.   I faw him
expire, and thefe Hands helped to çlofe his
Eyes ; the faddeft Office that ever they performed.

In his Perfon he was a ftrong, well-fet
Man, but of a fickly Conftitution, and fcarce
ever in perfect Health.   He thought too
much, and with too much Solicitude : This
without doubt impaired, and at laft wore out,
the Springs of Life : The Vigour and Activity of his Head caufed him many bodily
Diforders,   Whatever he did, he did intenfely ; and no Man was ever more turned
for the *hoc agere*.   What *Livy* fays of *Cato*
the Elder, fuits Mr. *Trenchard* extremely ;
——*Verfatile ingenium fic pariter ad omnia
fuit, ut natum ad id unum diceres, quodcunque
ageret.*

ageret. He had a manly Face, and a fair
fanguine Complexion ; regular Features, a
Look of great good Senfe, and a lively
black Eye, fo full of Fire, that feveral
People have told me that they could not
bear to look him in the Face. I have heard
the fame Obfervation made of his Father,
who, by all Accounts, was a Gentleman of
much Wit and Spirit.

To conclude : He had extraordinary Abilities, extraordinary Virtues, and little Failings, and thefe arifing from good Qualities :
He was paffionate from the Quicknefs of his
Parts ; and his Refentments arofe from
Things which his Heart abhorred. I will
end his Character as *Livy* does that of *Cicero.*
The Words are extremely pertinent :——
*Vir magnus, acer, memorabilis fuit, & in
cujus laudes exfequendas,* Cicerone *laudatore
opus fuerit.*   Fragm. Livii.

Thus much, I hope, I may be permitted
to have faid of this great and upright Man,
and my excellent Friend, before the following Work ; and much more I could have
faid. His Character was as little known, as
his Name was much. Many Sorts of Men
and Caufes combined to mifreprefent him.
Some were provoked by his honeft Freedom ; others emulated his Reputation ;
fome traduced him through Prejudice, fome
through Folly. But no good Man that
knew

knew him thoroughly could be his Enemy;
and what Enemies he had, Malice, Mifinformation, or his own Virtue, made.

The World has few fuch Men as Mr.
Trenchard; and few Men in it will be miffed
fo much. His Parts, his Spirit, and his Probity, will be remembered, and perhaps
wanted, when the Prejudices raifed againft
him will be dead and forgotten with the
Paffions that raifed them.

THE

THE
CONTENTS

Of the Four Volumes of

CATO's LETTERS.

CONTENTS of Vol. I.

The CONTENTS.   lxiii

No. 29.

CONTENTS of Vol. II.

CONTENTS of Vol. III.

No. 81.

The CONTENTS of Vol. IV.

lxxii   The CONTENTS.

An APPENDIX, containing
Additional LETTERS, by *CATO.*

CATO's

C A T O's
L E T T E R S.

SATURDAY, *November* 5, 1720. No. 1.

Reasons to prove that we are in no Danger of losing
Gibraltar.

S I R,

A S I have heard, with Concern, the Report of our being in Danger of losing *Gibraltar*, lately revived; so I had no small Pleasure to see, in the Generality of the People, a just Sense of the great Importance of that Place to the Trade and Security of *England*.

All Men, in Truth, shew their Opinion of it, by the Fears which they express about it; and if
we

we fet afide (as unworthy of mention) a few proftitute Hirelings, who go about Coffee-Houfes to
drop, as far as they dare, ftupid and villainous
Reafons for giving it up : I fay, excepting fuch a
contemptible few, I defy thofe, who for vile Ends,
or to make good vile Bargains, would gladly have
ft furrendered, to pick out of all the People of
England, one honeft, rational, and difinterefted
Man, to concur with them in it.

Thank God, in fpite of the Folly of Parties,
and the Arts of Betrayers, we fee in all Men a
fteady, warm and unanimous Spirit for the Prefervation of *Gibraltar* ; and I hope to fee fhortly
the Time, when we fhall, with the fame Franknefs and Unity, exercife our Reafon and our Eye-
fight in other Matters, in which we are at prefent
mifled, either by Infatuation, or falfe Intereft.

There are two Things which furprize me in
the many Apprehenfions which we have had about
Gibraltar.   The firft is, the great Diffidence ma-
nifefted by fuch Fears : Men muft be far gone in
Diftruft, before they could come to fufpect, that
their Superiors could ever grow fo much as indifferent about a Place of fuch Confequence to their
Country ; and to fuppofe them capable of giving
it up, is to fuppofe them capable of giving up
Portfmouth, nay, *England* itfelf.   Such Suppofitions muft therefore be unjuft, and the Height of
Ignorance or Spleen.   Can it be imagined, that
Men of Honour would forfeit their Reputation,
Patriots facrifice a Bulwark of their Country, or
wife Men venture their Heads, by fuch a traiterous, fhameful and dangerous Step.

But, fay fome, perhaps it will be fuffered to
be taken by Surprize ; and then all the Blame
                                                    will

will only reft upon fome obfcure Officer, who may
eafily be given up or kept out of the Way, while
thofe who contrived the Roguery, and felt the Reward of it, will be as loud in their Refentments,
as others who love their Country well enough to
grieve for its Difgrace or its Loffes.

I know, indeed, that all this has been faid more
than once, and fome plaufible Circumftances urged, to fhew that it was not abfolutely ground-
lefs. But, alas, what a poor Plot would here be !
A Farce of Treachery and Nonfenfe, vifible to
the weakeft of Mankind, and only fit to raife Hatred and Contempt towards the wretched Fra-
mers of it. This would be to deal with us as with
a Nation of Ideots, blind and infenfible, who can
neither fee Day-light, nor feel Injuries, nor return
infolent Ufage. No, no, we are not as yet to be
hood-winked by fuch thin Schemes : We can afk,
if need were, a few plain Queftions, which would
eafily puzzle fuch feeble Politicians ; but at prefent
we have no Occafion.

All this, however, fhews how much we are apt
to fufpect foul Play in this, and many other Cafes
of the like Nature ; nor fhall I now malicioufly
enquire, to what prevailing Caufe fuch Diftruft is
to be afcribed.

Another Thing, at which I am apt to wonder,
is, that, confidering how much our Credit is
concern'd to clear ourfelves from the Charge of
any bafe Purpofe, of being willing that *Gibraltar*
fhould be given away, we have not yet done it,
at leaft in any publick and fatisfactory Manner :
The miftaken People will fay, and have faid, that
our Silence is a Confeffion of our Guilt ; and that
if their Cenfures and Suppofitions had not been
juft

juſt, it was in our Power publickly to have con-
futed and removed them ; neither of which we
have done, but ſuffered Them to remain under
painful Fears, and Ourſelves under the Suſpicion
of neither regarding their Intereſt, nor their Eaſe,
nor our own Credit.

Why did you not, ſay they, tell all the World
how much you were wronged, and belied, in a
Declaration, ſaid to the *Regent*'s of *France*,
which expreſly aſſerted, that a Bargain was made
to give away *Gibraltar ?* Why did you not de-
monſtrate, that you were at leaſt as willing to preferve your own Towns, as to conquer Countries
for other People, who are remarkable for doing
you as little Service as they poſſibly can ? Why
did you ſuffer it to be ſuggeſted, with the leaſt
Colour of Probability, that you would rather
throw away what was your own, than not procure
for foreign Allies, at your Expence, what was
none of theirs ? Why do we fight, why conquer,
if we muſt thus condeſcend to implore the Van-
quiſhed, graciouſly to grant Peace to us the Conquerors, for which we will humbly pay them with
Part of our Dominions ? And how came Foreign
States, moſt of them Slaves, to be more in your
Favour, than *Old England*, which is a Nurſery of
Freemen ?

All theſe are malicious Queſtions, though I hope
ground.eſs ; but as they are propoſed by many
Thouſands of his Majeſty's Liege Subjects, in a
modeſt and ſerious Way, methinks it would be a
ſeaſonable Piece of Diſcretion and good Policy, to
prove them groundleſs.

For God's Sake, let us anſwer, if we can anſwer ; and if our Innocence can be ſhewn, as no
doubt

doubt it can, let it be fhewn. It will not even be enough, that *Gibraltar* is never given up, but we ought to purge ourfelves from the Imputation of ever having entertained fo criminal an Intention. If we can do this, it will recover us fome Part of the Credit and Confidence which we have loft by not doing of it. I therefore hope, and humbly propofe, that we may foon fee fome able and fagacious Pen, inftead of making *Panegyricks* upon us, make *Apologies* for us.

In the mean Time, permit me to give here three unanfwerable Reafons why *Gibraltar* cannot either be given up, or taken:

Firft, Becaufe *Secretary Grimaldo* fays it (*).

Secondly, It would make *South-Sea Stock* fall: And,

Thirdly, and *Laftly*, We have wife and honeft Governors.

G   *I am*, &c.

SATURDAY, *November* 12, 1720.   No. 2.

The fatal Effects of the South-Sea *Scheme, and the Neceffity of punifhing the Directors.*

S I R,

THE terrible Circumftances of our *French* Neighbours, under the Plague in fome Places, expecting it in others, and dreading it in all, is a loud Warning to us, to take all Expedients and poffible Precautions againft fuch a formidable Calamity.

* *This Letter was written in* October 1720.

We

We have already had, and ftill have, a Contagion of another Sort, more univerfal, and lefs merciful, than that at *Marfeilles*: The latter has deftroy'd, we are told, about Sixty Thoufand Lives; ours has done worfe, it has render'd a much greater Number of Lives miferable, who want but the Sicknefs to finifh their Calamity; either by rendering it complete, or by putting an End to them and that together.

Indeed, had the Alternative been offered us half a Year ago, I think it would have been a Symptom of Wifdom in us to have chofen rather to fall by the Hand of God, than by the execrable Arts of Stock-Jobbers: That we are fallen, is a forrowful Truth, not only vifible in every Face which you meet, but in the Deftruction of our Trade, the Glory and Riches of our Nation, and the Livelihood of the Poor.

But complaining does not mend the Matter; yet what fenfible Heart can avoid complaining, when he hears his Country, a whole Country, a potent Nation, a Nation happy in its Climate, in its Prince, and in its Laws, groaning under mighty Evils brought upon it by mean and contemptible Hands, and apprehending Evils ftill more mighty? This gives Bitternefs to a humane Spirit, though it fuffer no otherwife than by Sympathy. Is there no Way left of doing ourfelves Juftice, and has the Death of our Profperity extinguifhed all Senfe of our Injuries?

'Tis true, it is both prudent and religious in private Perfons, to ftifle the Notions of Revenge, and calmly to expect Reparation from God and the Law: But Jealoufy and Revenge, in a whole People, when they are abufed, are laudable and

politick

politick Virtues ; without which they will never thrive, never be efteemed. How far they are to carry their Refentments, I do not pronounce : The Meafures of it muft be determined by Circumftances ; but ftill keen Refentment ought to be fhewn, and fome Punifhment, or Punifhments, inflicted. When the Dignity or Intereft of a Nation is at Stake, Mercy may be Cruelty.

To this Spirit of Jealoufy and Revenge, was formerly the *Roman* Commonwealth beholden for the long Prefervation of its Liberty ; the *Venetian* Commonwealth owes its Prefervation to the fame Spirit ; and Liberty will never fubfift long where this Spirit is not : For if any Crimes againft the Publick may be committed with Impunity, Men will be tempted to commit the greateft of all ; I mean, that of making themfelves Mafters of the State ; and where Liberty ends in Servitude, it is owing to this Neglect. *Cæfar* thought that he might do what he had feen *Marius* and *Sylla* do before him, and fo enflaved his Country : Whereas, had They been hanged, he would, perhaps, never have attempted it.

I bring thefe Examples to prove, that Nations fhould be quick in their Refentments, and fevere in their Judgments. As never Nation was more abufed than ours has been of late by the dirty Race of Money-Changers ; fo never Nation could with a better Grace, with more Juftice, or greater Security, take its full Vengeance, than ours can, upon its detefted Foes. Sometimes the Greatnefs and Popularity of the Offenders make ftrict Juftice unadvifeable, becaufe unfafe ; but here it is not fo, you may, at prefent, load every Gallows in *England* with Directors and Stock-Jobbers,
                                                without

without the Affiftance of a Sheriff's Guard, or
fo much as a Sigh from an Old Woman, though
accuftom'd perhaps to fhed Tears at the untimely
Demife of a common Felon or Murderer. A
thoufand Stock-Jobbers, well truffed up, befides
the diverting Sight, would be a cheap Sacrifice to
the Manes of Trade ; it would be one certain Expedient to foften the Rage of the People ; and to
convince them that the future Direction of their
Wealth and Eftates fhall be put into the Hands of
thofe, who will as effectually ftudy to promote
the General Benefit and Publick Good, as others
have, lately, moft infamoufly facrificed Both to
their own private Advantage. Something is certainly due to both the former. The Refurrection
of Honefty and Induftry can never be hoped for,
while this Sort of Vermin is fuffered to crawl a-
bout, tainting our Air, and putting every Thing
out of Courfe ; fubfifting by Lies, and practifing
vile Tricks, low in their Nature, and mifchievous
in their Confequences.

That a Multitude of Families are ruined, and
fuddenly funk from plentiful Circumftances to abject Poverty, is affecting and lamentable ; though
perhaps all owing to their own rafh Confidence in
the Management of known Knaves : That innocent Children, born, as they imagin'd, to fair
Fortunes, and brought up accordingly, muft now
want Bread, or beg it, is a Cataftrophe that muft
pierce every tender Heart, and produce Pity and
Tears : But to fee one's Country labouring under
all the fad Symptoms of Diftrefs, without the
Violence of War, without the diabolical Refinements of able Politicians ; but purely from the
dull Cunning of inferior Rogues, void of Bravery,
                                                void

void of Abilities ; Wretches that would run away in the Field, and be defpifed in Affemblies ; this is what fhould turn Pity into Rage, and Grief into Vengeance.

For a Nation to fuffer itfelf to be ill ufed, is of dangerous Example ; whether thofe that ufe it ill be its Neighbours or its Natives. Patience, in this Cafe, invites frefh Injuries ; and that People, who would not bear many unjuft Burthens, muft not bear one.

A Country, as I faid above, ought to do itfelf Juftice with Speed, as well as with Vigour : Delay has often rendered a Cure impoffible in the Body Politick, as well as in Human Bodies : By Delays, the Edge of Refentment goes off, and the Offender has Leifure to fortify himfelf by new Rogueries.

I would therefore have my Countrymen take Advantage of the Humour that they are in, and make a Virtue of their prefent Anger. Let them roufe the bold Spirit of a free Nation ; and fhew by all lawful and loyal Means, that they who always fcorned to be the Property of Tyrants, will not be the Prey of Stock-Jobbers.

G

I am, &c.

SATUR-

SATURDAY, *November* 19, 1720.   No. 3.

The peſtilent Conduct of the South-Sea *Directors, with the reaſonable Proſpect of publick Juſtice.*

S I R,

A Man robbed in his Houſe, or on the High-way, receives from the Law all poſſible Sa-tisfaction : He has the Reſtitution of his Goods again, where it can be made ; he has the Life of the Offender, if he can be apprehended ; and there is a plentiful Reward given for every ſuch Appre-henſion.   By this ſalutary Method, Vengeance is at once taken for the Crime committed, and a terrible Example made of its Author, to prevent its Repetition.

The Law is the great Rule in every Country, at leaſt in every free Country, by which private Property is aſcertained, and the publick Good, which is the great End of all Laws, is ſecured ; and the religious Obſervance of this Rule, is what alone makes the Difference between good Laws, and none.   The Terror and Sanctity of the Laws are ſhewn by the Execution of them ; and to a Contempt of the Laws, or to a direct diſpenſing with them, have been owing moſt of the Shocks and Revolutions, that we have, for many Ages, ſuſtained in *England.*

Some Laws are, indeed, unwarily made, be-ing procured by Paſſion, Craft, or Surprize ; but ſuch are generally either ſuffered to wax obſolete,

or

or are repealed, as we have feen in many Inftances, and may yet fee in more.

But I fpeak here of thofe Laws which have a
direct and known Tendency to fecure to us what
we have, and to preferve us what we are : A free
People are kept fo, by no other Means than an
equal Diftribution of Property ; every Man, who
has a Share of Property, having a proportionable
Share of Power ; and the firft Seeds of Anarchy,
(which, for the moft part, ends in Tyranny) are
produced from hence, that fome are ungovernably
rich, and many more are miferably poor ; that is,
fome are Mafters of all Means of Oppreffion, and
others want all the Means of Self-defence.

What Progrefs we have lately made in *England*,
towards fuch a bleffed State of Confufion and Mifery, by the Credulity of the People, throwing
their All upon the Mercy of bafe-fpirited, hard-
hearted Villains, mifchievoufly trufted with a Power
to undo them, is too manifeft from the woful Condition that we are in. The Ruin is general, and
every Man has the miferable Confolation to fee
his Neighbour undone : For as to that Clafs of
Ravens, whofe Wealth has coft the Nation its
All, as they are manifeft Enemies to God and
Man, no Man can call them his Neighbours :
They are Rogues of Prey, they are Stock-Jobbers,
they are a Confpiracy of Stock-Jobbers ! A Name
which carries along with it fuch a deteftable and
deadly Image, that it exceeds all human Invention to aggravate it ; nor can Nature, with all her
Variety and Stores, furnifh out any Thing to illuftrate its Deformities ; nay, it gains vifible Advantage by the worft Comparifons that you can
make : Your Terror leffens, when you liken them

to

to Crocodiles and Canibals, who feed, for Hunger, on human Bodies.

These Monsters, therefore, stand single in the
Creation : They are Stock-Jobbers ; they have
served a whole People as *Satan* served *Job* ; and
so far the Devil is injured, by any Analogy that
you can make between him and them.

Well ; but Monsters as they are, what would
you do with them ? The Answer is short and at
hand, Hang them ; for, whatever they deserve, I
would have no new Tortures invented, nor any
new Death devised. In this, I think, I shew
Moderation ; let them only be hanged, but hanged
speedily. As to their Wealth, as it is the manifest
Plunder of the People, let it restored to the
People, and let the Publick be their Heirs ; the
only Method by which the Publick is ever like to
get Millions by them, or indeed any Thing.

But, say some, when did you ever see Rogues
covered with Wealth, brought to the Axe or the
Gallows ? I own that the Example is rare, more
is the Shame of this Nation, which has had such
rich Temptations, and such frequent Opportunities ; we have had publick Guilt in abundance,
God knows, often protected by Party, and often
by Money. Faction on one Side, and Riches on
the other, have, as it were, made a Lane for the
Great Criminals to escape. But all these Escapes,
which are, indeed, our Reproach, cannot give any
Ground to fear a present one.

This Nation has formerly been bought and
sold ; but Arts were used to blind the People's
Eyes, the Effects of the Treachery were not immediately felt ; and we know that the Resentment
of the Vulgar never follows from their Understand-
ing,

ing, or their Reflection, but from their Feeling:
A Pick-pocket may tickle a plain Fellow's Ear,
till he has got his Purse ; but if he feel it going,
he will knock the Thief down.

We have felt our Pockets picked, and we know
who have done it : Vengeance abides them.

I am told, that some of them have the Face to
pretend, that they ought not to be put to Death ;
but we hope that the Legislature will effectually
convince them, that this their Partiality to themselves is groundless : All their Hopes of Safety must
consist in their Money ; and without Question, they
will try to make the Wages of their Villainy protect their Villainy. But I cannot see how any
Sums can save them ; for as they have robbed and
cheated all Men, except their Accomplices, so all
Men are concerned to see Justice done to themselves ; and if the ordinary Channels of Justice
could be stopped by Bags of Money, or by Part-
nership in original Guilt, the enraged, the abused
People, might be prompted by their uppermost
Passion, and having their Resentment heightened
by Disappointment, might, it is to be feared, have
Recourse to extraordinary Ways ; Ways that are
often successful, tho' never justifiable.

Here are no Parties in this Case to disguise
Truth, and obstruct Justice ; the Calamity is general, so is the Resentment : All are Sufferers, All
will be Prosecutors. The Cry for Justice is loud
and united ; if it be baulked, I can prophesy no
Good from so cruel an Omission.

If this mighty, this destructive Guilt, were to
find Impunity, nothing remains, but that every
Villain of a daring and avaricious Spirit may grow
a great Rogue, in order to be a great Man. When
a People

a People can no longer expect Redress of publick and heavy Evils, nor Satisfaction for publick and bitter Injuries, hideous is the Prospect which they have before them. If they will tamely suffer a Fall from Plenty to Beggary, they may soon expect another, and a worse, from That to Slavery: But I hope better Things of *England*.

I have before my Eyes a wise and beneficent Prince, a generous and publick-spirited Parliament, an able and disinterested Ministry; all contending with each other for the Wealth, the Glory, the Liberty of their Country: And I have before my Eyes a brave and honest People, Lovers of Trade and Industry, free of their Money, and well-deserving of the Legislature, passionate for Liberty, and Haters of Chains; but deluded, drained of their Money, and abused beyond Patience, beyond Expression, by mean Sharpers, that swagger in the Plunder of their Country.

Where therefore there is so much Capacity, and there are so many good Dispositions to help us on one Side; such loud and melancholy Calls, for that Help on another Side; such open, such execrable, such publick Crimes, from a Third Quarter; we may hope every Thing from the speedy Meeting of the *King and Parliament*. They are our *Protectors*, and *we trust that they do not bear the Sword in vain*.

I doubt not but many Schemes will be laid before them, some of them designed for a Source of new Rogueries, and to prevent Enquiries into the old ones. It shall be the Business therefore of this Paper, to watch and examine such Schemes; and to condemn them, or recommend them, just as they deserve.

I have,

I have, you fee, taken the Guilt of our Traytors for granted, as I think all Men do : But becaufe they fhall have all fair Play, I undertake
hereafter, if it be found neceffary, to prove it by
an Induction of Particulars.

G   *I am,* &c.

SATURDAY, *November* 26, 1720.   No. 4.

Againft falfe Methods of reftoring Publick Credit.

S I R,

ALL Men are now taught, by miferable Experience, that the Project of the *South-Sea*,
through the hard-hearted Knavery of fome, who
have been in the Direction of it, and through the
Folly or rather Diftraction of the People, has not
anfwered the good and wife Ends defigned by the
Parliament ; but inftead of that, has ruined Thoufands of innocent and well-meaning People, to
glut Harpies and publick Robbers with Millions :
Unhappy Fate of poor *England*, worthy of a better ! For This, Trade has been neglected : For
This, Induftry difcouraged : For This, Credit undone ; and all, that Stock-Jobbers might make
Fortunes, and fmall Sharpers grow mighty Men.

Every one, therefore, feems to agree, that
fomething is neceffary to be done, in a legal Way,
to reftore, once more, our publick Credit. But
it is hoped, we are far from confenting, that any
Thing ought to be done to repair the Loffes. occafioned by Folly and Covetoufnefs, out of the
Eftates of thofe, who always forefaw, who always

ways oppofed this mighty Mifchief; much lefs at the further Expènce of the Honour and Trade of the Nation.

To fet this Matter in a due Light, it is necef-fary to enquire what is meant by the publick Cre-dit of the Nation.

Firft, Credit may be faid to run high, when the Commodities of a Nation find a ready Vent, and are fold at a good Price; and when Dealers may be fafely trufted with them, upon reafonable Affurance of being paid.

Secondly, When Lands and Houfes find ready Purchafers; and when Money is to be borrowed at low Intereft, in order to carry on Trade and Manufacture, at fuch Rates, as may enable us to underfell our Neighbours.

Thirdly, When People think it fafe and advan-tageous to venture large Stocks in Trade and Deal-ing, and do not lock up their Money in Chefts, or hide it under-ground. And,

Fourthly, When Notes, Mortgages, and publick and private Security will pafs for Money, or eafily procure Money, by felling for as much Silver or Gold as they are Security for; which can never happen, but upon a Prefumption that the fame Money may be had for them again.

In all thefe Cafes, 'tis abundantly the Intereft of a Nation, to promote Credit and mutual Con-fidence; and the only poffible Way effectually to do this, is to maintain publick Honour and Ho-nefty; to provide ready Remedies for private In-juftice and Oppreffion; to protect the Innocent and Helplefs from being deftroyed by Fraud and Rapine.

But

But national Credit can never be fupported by lending Money without Security, or drawing in other People to do fo ; by raifing Stocks and Commodities by Artifice and Fraud, to unnatural and imaginary Values ; and confequently, delivering up helplefs Women and Orphans, with the ignorant and unwary, but induftrious Subject, to be devoured by Pick-pockets and Stock-Jobbers ; a Sort of Vermin that are bred and nourifhed in the Corruption of the State.

This is a Method, which, inftead of preferving Publick Credit, deftroys all Property ; turns the Stock and Wealth of a Nation out of its proper Channels ; and, inftead of nourifhing the Body-Politick, produces only Ulcers, Eruptions, and often Epidemical Plague-Sores: It ftarves the Poor, deftroys Manufactures, ruins our Navigation, and raifes Infurrections, &c.

The firft Lofs is always the leaft ; one half of the Nation is ruined already ; I hope we may learn Wit from our Misfortunes, and fave the other half : In order to this, we may expect, that no new Projects will be countenanced or received, which have any Tendency to prejudice Trade, or which caufe Monopolies, or fet up exclufive Companies ; and that no Privileges or Advantages be granted, for which ready Money might be got.

Some People have the Affurance to publifh it, for Example, that a certain Set of Stock-Jobbers, whofe Faith and Modefty are now well known and felt, expect, among other Gifts from the Publick, that the Ifland of *St. Chriftophers* fhould be given them, as a further Expedient to get more Wealth to themfelves, and leave the Nation none.   Now, *St. Chriftophers* is worth Three
Hundred

Hundred Thoufand Pounds Sterling, and will yield fo much : So that to prefent them with this Ifland, would be juft making them a Prefent of Three Hundred Thoufand Pounds ; a Sum almoft fufficient to make the Fortune of an Under *South-Sea* Clerk ; but fuch a Sum as this poor Nation cannot at prefent fpare.

I hope, therefore, that it will no longer be impudently alledged, that by parting with fuch Gifts, we lofe nothing ; fince that alone is worth nothing, for which nothing can be got. But the Cafe is otherwife here ; and from the Nature of our publick Gaming, and the Spirit of the worthy Sharpers who direct it, I dare pronounce before-hand, that every Scheme which they themfelves propofe, to make their Bubble and their Roguery thrive again, will ftill be built upon the farther Expence, upon the farther Lofs and Mifery of thefe unhappy Nations.

If our Money be gone, thank God, our Eyes are left : Sharpened by Experience and Adverfities we can fee through Difguifes, and will be no more amufed with Moon-fhine.

The Nation and Parliament have been abufed, and they will undoubtedly be revenged ; they will not be put off with dark Juggling, with knavifh Projects, to ftifle Refentments, and divert due Vengeance : There is no attending to any new Schemes, till the Publick Robbers are punifhed, with whom there can never be any Accommodation.

To begin then, in the firft place, with the Criminals, will fhew that we are in earneft Champions for Honefty, for Trade, for the Nation, all oppreffed by Money-Leaches. All other Remedies

dies will be Mountebank Remedies : It would be
Madnefs to concert new Schemes, liable to new
Abufes, without firft doing Juftice to the Abufers
of the old ; Impunity for paft Crimes is a Warrant to commit more, efpecially when they are
gainful.

Such mighty Mischiefs as thefe Men have done,
will be but meanly atoned for by fuch infamous
Lives, unlefs their Eftates be alfo confifcated ; and
even thefe, great as they are, will repair but part
of our Misfortunes. But what we can have of
them, let us have ; their Necks and their Money.

To begin with any other Project, they will take
for a Confeffion, that there is a Defign to fave
them ; and to what that muft be owing, we all
know : What farther Evils it may produce, may
even furpafs our Fears, though already terribly
great ; but a Method of Juftice prefently entered
upon, and impartially carried through, will give us
Patience under our Burdens, banifh all our Fears,
give Credit to the Publick Proceedings, and reftore Hope to the almoft defpairing People.

G   *I am,* &c.

A further Call for Vengeance upon the South-Sea *Plunderers, with a Caution against false Patriots.*

S I R,

THIS great Nation, undone by defpicable Stockjobbers and their Abettors, has hitherto quietly groaned under the mercilefs Hands of its Pillagers, and lived for fome Months upon the pure Hopes of Redrefs. We looked towards the Parliament : His Majefty and his Miniftry being abfent, and bufied with the Affairs of this Kingdom Abroad, in the glorious Aims of fettling the Peace of *Europe*, in ftrengthening the Proteftant Intereft.

The firft Part of our Hopes is now almoft accomplifhed, the Parliament are juft upon meeting ; and never, fure, did ever Seffion open with greater Expectation, or with more to do : Every thing is turned topfy-turvy ; and the Nation, thrown into Convulfions, is waiting for the healing Hand of its Reprefentatives.

Many Expedients will, no doubt, be offered without Doors ; calculated, in Appearance, to improve the Stock, but, in Reality, defigned to fave the Directors. This is to begin at the wrong End. To pretend to form Schemes for the encreafing of Credit, before the Deftroyers, the Canibals of Credit, are honeftly and openly hung up to its Manes, is, in fome fort, to confefs, that we had our Inftructions and Politicks from the Criminals

nals themfelves, and our beft and only Reafons out of their Purfes.

Or if we be not thus wicked, we fhould, at beft, be miferably weak to fall into fuch a prepofterous Method ; and whether great and general Calamities have their Root in Roguery or Folly, is all one to a Nation.

In fpite of all the Remedies that can be applied, Multitudes will ftill remain undone beyond all Remedy : Nay, for aught I can fee, there is no practical Remedy at all for what is paft ; fo effectual has been the Roguery on one Side, fo rivetted is the Ruin on the other.

All, therefore, that feems to me to be left, even to the united Wifdom of *Great Britain*, is the Cure of Prevention, to ftop the Progrefs of the Contagion, to take Care that thofe who have already fuffered, fhall fuffer no more, nor make new Sufferers : It is certain, that all Men have fuffered in one Senfe or other, the Criminals excepted. It is hoped that the miferable People will now be honoured with their good Company ; and that the Box on the Ear, which wantonly began from them, will in good earneft be returned to them, and end with them. It is fome Confolation to the Inhabitants of a Village, who have been bit all round by a mad Dog, to fee the Inftrument of the Poifon, and the Author of their Pain and Danger, honeftly hung up, or knocked on the Head.

The prevailing Woe which has long raged, and ftill fits hard and heavy upon us, has certainly fome Authors ; the Directors are generally taken to be thefe Authors ; and if they be duly and publickly punifhed, they will continue to be taken for the only Authors. But if there be nothing done

to

to them, or nothing effectually done, we fhall naturally look farther, and make bold to know, that though they have been Rogues, yet that others had been greater than they ; that others have directed the Directors, and were Partners in the Spoil.

But if they ftand fingle, and are found the only and original Plunderers of their County, they will infallibly be given up to publick and crying Vengeance ; not only by the Rules of Guilt, but of good Policy. A more popular Thing cannot be done, nor indeed fo popular a Thing. The Bleffings of the People, and the univerfal Affections of *Great Britain*, will be fome of the Rewards attending upon thofe who will be the generous Authors of publick Juftice upon the deteftable Authors of publick and intenfe Mifery.

I will never fuppofe that any Men, or even one Man in any publick Station, did by any Means join with Stock-Jobbers to undo their Country ; much lefs enabled Stock-Jobbers, to undo their Country, and fupported them while they were about it. It would be melancholy and terrible, indeed, to imagine that any publick Men, at leaft, any Man concerned in the Finances, or fet over any Part of the publick Money, by which publick Credit is circulated and fuftained, fhould, in Defiance of his publick Truft, put himfelf at the Head of a Confpiracy of Stock-Jobbers, who were, with mercilefs and unclean Hands, rifling the Publick itfelf, engroffing all its Wealth, and deftroying at once all publick and private Faith.

Such unprecedented Treachery, fuch over-grown Guilt, can never be fuppofed. Our Corruptions cannot be yet become fo bold and bare-faced, nor

we

we so tame. The Thing therefore being so very monstrous, must be impossible, whatsoever Suggestions there may be to the contrary ; which, were they true, could not fail of calling down double and conspicuous Punishment upon such a *Verres*.

As to those who lately encouraged the Scheme, out of an honest Purpose to relieve the Publick, and pay off its Debts, they ought, and no doubt will be the first and the most active to revenge the Publick upon those, who, instead of relieving it, have brought the Publick into such doleful and dying Distress.

By this, they will farther evince the Honesty of that Purpose, merit still more to conduct our Affairs ; and their Services will undoubtedly be remembered by the honest Freeholders of *England*, at a proper Season, to their Advantage : Our Eyes are upon them, our Confidence is in them, and we wish them good Success in this great Trial of Integrity and publick Spirit.

I foresee that there will be many loud in their Call for publick Justice, and yet be the first to prevent it. Their Avarice will arm their Tongues with Zeal, and a proper Present disarm it of its Eloquence. However, the Outside of publick Spirit will still be kept on ; they will be sure to cry out to the last for Punishment, for severe Punishment ; but they will be as sure to find Fault with every Expedient proposed for inflicting it. I could name some worthy Patriots, of many Words, and great Weight, who will act this Farce rarely. It will not be the first Time.——What is human Life, but a Masquerade : And what is civil Society, but a Mock-Alliance between Hyprocrify and Credulity ?

Magna & mifera Civitas, eodem Anno tantas Injurias tantumq; Pudorem paffa, inter Vineos, Fabios, Icelos, Afiaticos, varia & pudenda Sorte agebat ; donec fucceffere Mutianus, & Marcellus, & magis alii Homines quam alii Mores.

These are the Words of a great Ancient, fignal for his Wifdom and ftrong Obfervations. Had he lived now, and written in *Englifh*, he would have written thus :

" Oh *London !* Oh *England !* Oh my Coun-
" try ! How great ! And yet how miferable !
" What Reproach, what Calamities, what Ruin,
" haft thou fuftained ? Suftained in the Space of
" One fhort Year ; and lefs than a Year ! Suftain-
" ed from the Dregs of Human Kind ! From Fel-
" lows, vile in their Original ; and as to their Spi-
" rit, Slaves ! What opprobrious Delufions, what
" deadly Revolutions, haft thou fuffered to be
" brought upon thee, by the ignoble Names and
" fervile Hands of *B—t, L—b—t, H—h,* and
" the like Scum of the Vulgar ! And after all this,
" art thou not weary, O my Country ! of thy
" own Shame ? Not yet fatiated with Devaftation
" and Havock ? And wilt thou yet again try the
" old Knavery, managed by new Knaves ?

G   *I am,* &c.

How eafily the People are bubbled by Deceivers.——
Further Caution againft deceitful Remedies for
the Publick Sufferings from the Wicked Execu-
tion of the South-Sea *Scheme.*

S I R,

NO Experience or Sufferings can cure the
World of its Credulity. It has been a Bubble from the Beginning ; nor is it a bit wifer for
this Difcovery, but ftill runs into old Snares, if
they have but new Names, often whether they
have or no.

Self-Love beguiles Men into falfe Hopes, and
they will venture to incur a hundred probable
Evils, to catch one poffible Good ; nay, they run
frequently into diftracting Pains and Expences, to
gain Advantages which are purely imaginary, and
utterly impoffible.

Were the Paffions properly balanced, Men
would act rationally ; but by fuffering one Paffion
to get the better of all the reft, they act madly or
ridiculoufly.

Our prevailing Paffions in *England*, of late,
have been Hope, Avarice, and Ambition ; which
have had fuch a headlong Force upon the People,
that they are become wretched and poor, by a ravenous Appetite to grow great and rich. Our
Fear and Caution were poftponed ; and by a fanguine Struggle for what we had not, we loft what
we had. Could fuch Courage be infpired by
Stock-

Stock-Jobbing? A cowardly Science of mean Tricks and Lies!

Every Adventurer in this mighty Lottery fore-saw that many muft be Lofers, and that what was got by one muft be loft by another; but every Man hoped that Fate would be kinder to him in parti-cular, than to a thoufand others; and fo this mad Hope became general, as are the Calamities which it has produced.

This fhews the little Power that Reafon and Truth have over the Paffions of Men, when they run high. In the late Revolution in the Alley, Figures and Demonftration would have told them, and the Directors could have told them, that it was Phrenzy; that they were purfuing gilded Clouds, the Compofition of Vapour and a little Sunfhine; both fleeting Apparitions! Common Senfe could have told them, that Credit is the moft uncertain and moft fluctuating Thing in the World, efpecially when it is applied to Stock-Jobbing; that it had long before been exalted higher than it could well ftand, even before it was come to Twenty above *Par*; and therefore al-ways tottered, and was always tumbling down at every little Accident and Rumour. A Story of a *Spanifh* Frigate, or of a few Thieves in the dark Dens in the *Highlands*, or the Sicknefs of a foreign Prince, or the Saying of a Broker in a Coffee-Houfe; all, or any of thefe contemptible Caufes were able to reduce that fame Credit into a very flender Figure, and fometimes within her old Bounds: But particularly, they might have feen, that it was now mounted to fuch an outrageous Height, as all the Silver and Gold in *Europe* could not fupport; and therefore, when People came in

any

any confiderable Number to fell, (and to fell was the whole End of their buying) it would have a dreadful Fall, even to the crufhing of the Nation. This has fince dolefully happened : Our Hopes, which were our Ruin, are gone ; and now we behold nothing but the Face of the Mourner.

But in fpite of this Mifchief, produced by Credulity, by manifeft and ill-grounded Creduli-ty, it is much to be feared that fome little Art and big Promifes would make us repeat it, and grow mad again. This feems evident, not only from the Folly and Feeblenefs of human Nature, ever the Prey of Craft, and ever caught with Shadows ; but from our endlefs gaping after new Projects, and our Eagernefs to run into them. We have been bruifed in a Mortar, but we are not wifer ; while one Ruin is yet upon us, we are panting after another, perhaps worked up by the fame Hands, or by other Hands with the fame Views.

O the Weaknefs and Folly of Man ! It is like a Whirlpool, which deftroys and drowns not by Halves, but when a Part is drawn in, the Whole follows.

Surely the Pleafure is as great,
Of being cheated, as to cheat !

Elfe Men would not be fuch Dupes, as every where they are. Whoever would catch Mankind, has nothing to do, but to throw out a Bait to their Paffions, and infallibly they are his Property. This Secret is well known to corrupt Courts, who flatter or frighten their obeying believing Vaffals in-to all the Exceffes of Mifery and Obeifance. By This, Standing Armies have been maintained ; by This, wild Wars have been waged ; by This, an idle,

expenfive,

expenfive, abfurd, and cruel Popifh Hierarchy has been fupported.

Once more, O wretched Man! Thou willing Inftrument of thy own Bondage and Delufion; even Mountebanks know this Secret of cajoling thee, and picking thy Pocket; nay, worfe than Mountebanks, Stock-Jobbers know it.

When a People are undone, it is fome Confolation to reflect, that they had no Hand in their own Ruin, or did all that they could to prevent it, by the beft Counfels that they could take, or by the braveft Defence that they could make. But alas, poor *England!* thou haft not that Confolation: Thou haft not fallen by able Traytors; thou art not the Victim of deep Defign, or artful Treafon; nor art thou the Price of Victory in the Field; neither art thou out-witted by the fubtile Dealers in Myftery and Diftinction, nor in this Inftance deceived by their falfe Alarms.

No, we have no fuch palliating Reflection to reconcile us to our Mifery, or to abate its Pangs: To our deathlefs Shame, we are the Conqueft, the Purchafe of Stock-Jobbers. The *Britifh* Lions crouch to a Neft of Owls! Can we furvive the Remembrance without Revenge?

But all this is complaining, will fome fay; and we want Remedies, rather than Complaints: To bewail our Calamities, is indeed natural; but to extricate ourfelves out of them, is neceffary. Here are Two Hundred Millions of Imaginary Property loft, and at leaft Twenty Millions of Real Property plundered from the Honeft and Induftrious, and given to Sharpers and Pick-pockets: Shall thefe Rooks be fuffered to enjoy it? And fhall the Bubbles be redreffed out of other Mens Eftates, no

ways

ways chargeable with the Mifchief? Or muſt we proſtitute the publick Honour of the Nation to draw in other People (no way concerned) to take the bold Bargains of raſh Men and Dupes off their Hands? But if none of theſe Methods be taken, our Cullies muſt fit down with their Lofs, or the Traytors be forced to difgorge.

If we make new Schemes, or diverfify the old, till Doom's-Day, there will be no paying Twenty Millions without Twenty Millions, or without what is equivalent to Twenty Millions; which will be the fame Thing to the Nation as the parting with Twenty Millions.

The Payment therefore will either be a real Payment or a ſham Payment; and in this Cafe, if *caveat emptor* (let the Buyer look to it) be a good general Rule in the Bufinefs of Bargains and Sale, it will be a good Rule here too.

If we have any State Chymiſts, who have Art enough to make Millions evaporate into Smoak; yet I muſt beg Leave to doubt their Skill at confolidating Smoak into Gold.

I hope that I ſhall not be underſtood, by what I have faid, to oppofe an Attempt to redeem us out of our prefent wretched Condition. On the contrary, I ſhall be the firſt to vote that Man a Statute of Gold, who can ſtrike out an honeſt and ſkilful Expedient for our Recovery, which I own is far paſt my own Skill: I am no Candidate for the Golden Statue.

By all this, I would only caution my Countrymen not to be caught again; let them beware of new Snares. As to the Lofers, they have not a great deal to expect; And I can faỹ no more to
them

them here, than that in the Countries where the Plague rages, the Prefervation of the Whole is the principal Care; the Infected are, for the moft Part, left to take Care of themfelves; and I never heard it fuggefted, that Nine Millions of People ought to be expofed to the mortal Contagion of that Diftemper, to preferve a few Individuals.
G

I am, &c.

SATURDAY, *December* 17, 1720.   No. 7.

Further Cautions about new Schemes for Publick Redrefs.

SIR,

BEware *of the Step,* will be allowed by all Men, who have any Skill in human Affairs, to be a commendable Caution in all Proceedings of Moment. In how many Inftances do we fee, that Things which begin plaufibly, end tragically? People have been often enflaved by Princes created by themfelves for their Protection, often butchered by Armies raifed by themfelves for their Defence. The late *French* King, whenever he was going to fhed the Blood of his People in any wanton War, though undertaken to gratify his Luft of Power, or to exalt his own Houfe, never failed to let them know, in an Edict made on purpofe, that it was all for their Good and Profperity; that is, they were to fuffer Slaughter Abroad, Oppreffion and Famine at Home, purely for their own Advantage and Felicity.

General

General Propositions are, for the moſt Part, dangerous, and intended to ſupport Conſequences, which, at firſt View, they do not ſeem to mean and imply. They are, therefore, generally plauſible in Appearance, to catch Conſent ; from which Conſent, when it is once got, Advantages are taken, which were not foreſeen ; and freſh Articles are added, which were not known to have been deſigned.

In the late long War with *France*, What was more deſirable, what more plauſible, than *Peace ?* A Bleſſing ſo univerſally underſtood to be one, that the loweſt Vulgar wanted no Words nor Perſuaſions to know its Excellency ! And when we were inſulted with this Queſtion, *What, will you not treat ?* To have ſaid, *No*, would have been an Anſwer ſo invidious, that ſcarce any Man durſt make it ; yet all wiſe Men then knew, that to conſent to a Treaty at that Time with *France*, conſidering the Perſons and their Intereſts who were to manage it, was to conſent to a Conſpiracy againſt *England* in particular, and to plot againſt all *Europe* in general : We were ſtunned with the Word *Peace* ; nor could we ſtand it, though we knew it was hatching Treaſon. In ſhort, to Treat, as ſoft a Phraſe as it was, ſignified neither more nor leſs, than to give to old *Lewis* his wicked Will of all *Europe*, and to the *Tories* their *Pretender*.

Take another Inſtance. In the preſent *Spaniſh* War, which, we are aſſured, wants nothing but a Form to conclude it, we cannot forget the loud Atteſtations that were every where given us, *That to declare War was ſufficient alone to end the War, and to frighten the* Spaniards *into a Peace :* And who,

who, among us, would not willingly be at the
Expence of a Piece of Paper, and of the Heralds
Lungs, to fcare a turbulent and enterprizing Court,
as was that of *Philip*, into Moderation and Quiet-
nefs ? But the Obſtinacy of *Spain*, the Length of
that War, our great Charge in Men and Money
to fupport it, and the Condition of our Fleet, worn
in the Service of our Allies, or eaten by Worms
in the *Mediterranean*, are all fufficient Leſſons to
us, how little we ought to have trufted to fuch
Aſſurances, or to the Word of thofe that gave
them.

Take a Third Inſtance. Upon the Eſtabliſh-
ing of the prefent *Eaſt-India* Company, it was rea-
fonably urged, That fuch a Company would be
no other than a Confederacy of cunning Fellows,
againſt fair and general Trading, by monopolizing to a few the fole Traffick and Riches of a
great Continent. To which it was anfwered,
That there was no fuch Defign ; but that every
Man who would fubfcribe his Name in their Books,
and comply with fome eafy Conditions, would be
frankly admitted to fhare in their Trade. But
this was all Hypocrify or Lying ; for no fooner
had the Projectors by fuch petty Pretences to publick Honefty, got the better of Oppofition, and
cooked up their Project, but it was found that
their Trade was impracticable to all but themfelves : Every Trader was obliged to come into
the Joint-Stock ; and all Attempts fince, for the
publick Good, have proved ineffectual againſt fo
formidable a Society.

We have a Fourth Inſtance from the firſt Inſtitution of the *South-Sea*. It was at firſt pretended,
that every Proprietor was to have Six *per Cent.* for

his

his Money, without Trouble or Deductions ; and need not engage in the Trade, unlefs he chofe it. This drew in a great Multitude to vouch for the Scheme, and encourage it ; but in paffing the Bill, it was found that the crafty Managers had lopt off One *per Cent.* to be applied, as they pretended, to carry on the Trade of the Company, and all were obliged to join in the Chimerical Affiento ; by which they have fince pillaged the Proprietors of a Million and a Half.—*See the vaft Advantage of lofing by Trade !* A Secret well known to the Directors !

The Fifth Inftance may be taken from the fame *South-Sea.* What a rare Sugar-Plumb to the Nation was a Scheme fo finely calculated to pay off the Nation's Debts ! What a tempting Bait was here ! Even thofe who faw whither it mif- chievoufly tended, and perceived the deceitful Hook under it, could not ftand the Scorn and Re- bukes of the Many, who fwallowed it without feeing it. What fatal Devaftation and Poverty it has fince produced, by the unparalleled Treache- ry of the Directors, and fome that are worfe than they, the miferable People feel much more fenfi- bly than I can exprefs, pierced as they are with the keen Arrows of mercilefs Villainy, and unre- lenting Diftrefs. We have undone ourfelves to pay our Debts, and our Debts are not paid. What fhall I fay ? We had once Bread, Money, and publick Faith : But now ! What remains to us ? I cannot anfwer.——Our Grief, our Folly, our Loffes, our Difhonour, our cruel Ufage, are too big for Words.

I have faid fo much, to prove how wary we ought to be in going into *new Schemes.* We
ought

ougt at leaft to know the Whole of them, before we confent to a Part. It will alfo behove
us to have an Eye to the Quarter from whence
they come; whether they be Directors, or their
Mafters, and Confederates; or Men of fair and
upright Characters, whofe Souls are honeft, and
their Hands clean. As. to thofe who are known
to have promoted the mighty Cheat, and the Ruin
of their Country; their Infamy is fo glaring, that,
fince they will not have Modefty and Remorfe
enough to hold their Tongues, and to forbear
meddling with the Concerns of a People beggared
by them, we ought to mind no more what. they
fay, than the Judge did the Houfe-breaker, who,
upon his Trial, told his Lordfhip, that he *would
fwear the Peace againft him, for putting him in
fear of his Life.*

The fame may be faid of thofe that are fallen
in with the Guilty, and unexpectedly fpeak the
fame Note. We guefs at their Motives. The
powerful Getters would fave themfelves, by letting
others get as much; and perhaps are glad to divide
their Gains, to efcape Punifhment.

If any Man would be the unfufpected and fair
Author of a new Project, he can recommend it
and himfelf no better, than by fhewing it to be
honeftly confiftent with the Punifhment of our
Million Knaves, the Blood-Suckers of *England.*
A new Scheme, and an Inquifition into the Management of the old one, may both fuccefsfully
go on at the fame Time; and they who fay that
they cannot, do but own that they are afraid they
fhould. Are they confcious to themfelves, that
the Directors may hope to efcape Part of their
Punifhment, by fathering upon others a great
Share

Share of their Guilt, or rather the Power of being guilty?

What mean fome Men by faying, We ought
to extinguifh the Fire, before we inquire into the
Incendiaries? Are They fome of thefe? Or did
they furnifh out Brands to the reft? Or would
they give them Time to run away? The Truth
is, the Houfe is already burned down, many are
burned to Death, all are miferably fcorched: The
Flame has in a manner wafted itfelf; but thofe
that talk thus, feem eager to revive it, by new
Devices to ftir the Embers. All that we can now
do, is to build the Houfe again, if we can; and
hang thofe that fired it, which we are fure we
ought. Befides, we have long known who did
it; they have been taken in the Fact at Noon-
day, and every Day. This Thing was not done
in a Corner, nor at once, nor by one; the Villainy was deliberate, gradual, and open.

Thefe Gentlemen do however confefs, that the
Houfe has been fet on fire; which Confeffion they
would doubtlefs be glad to avoid, if they could:
But the Mifery is forely felt, and all *Europe* are
Witneffes of it. Can they therefore, after an Acknowledgment that the Nation has been burned,
have the Face to be contriving Ways to delay the
Punifhment of the Burners? Has Self-Love no
Share in this? And by the Delay of the Punifhment of others, do they not as good as avow, that
they tremble for themfelves? For my part, I can
fee no Difference in this Cafe, between delaying it,
and fruftrating it.

The Expediénts for retrieving us, if we can be
retrieved, are certainly compatible with Expedients
for revenging us; and the latter will facilitate the
for-

former.   It will give Life to the poor Bankrupt Heart-broken People, if they see that their
Deſtroyers meet due Vengeance, and that they
are like to be no more the Prey of daring Parricides.
    G

I am, &c.

SATURDAY, *December* 24, 1720. No. 8.

*The Arts of able guilty Miniſters to ſave themſelves.—
The wiſe and popular Conduct of Queen* Elizabeth
towards publick Harpies; with the Application.

SIR,

THERE is not in Politicks a more eſtabliſhed
   Rule, than, *That when a corrupt and wicked
Miniſtry intend to pillage a Nation, they make uſe of
vile and contemptible Inſtruments, to gather in their
Plunder, and allow the Miſcreants Part of it; and
when the Cry for Juſtice becomes ſtrong and univerſal,
they always hang up their faithful Rogues.*   By this
Means they ſtop the People's Mouths, and yet
keep the Money.

But they act by no Rule of good Policy, but
are, in Truth, chargeable with Folly, or rather
with Phrenzy, who dream that they can prevent
this Cry, by the Means that firſt raiſed it, and by
Means that will ever produce it.   As well might
they attempt to prevent the ſpreading of a Deluge,
by damming it up; which would prove the direct
Method to make a whole Country its Conqueſt;
for it will then know no Bounds, but bear down
                    Men,

Men, Beafts, and Cities before it ; whereas its
Force and Mifchief are eafily prevented, if proper
Channels be opened for it, and its Torrent be fkil-
fully directed.

The fimple Multitude, when moft provoked,
are eafily appeafed, if they have but Fuel for their
Rage : They will fcarce feel their Miferies, if they
do but fancy that Juftice is done upon the Authors
of their Miferies. And whatever they fuffer ; the
Hanging of a few forry Knaves, who are but the
Working-Tools of a few Greater, will hufh all
the Tumult of their Spirits, and reconcile them to
Patience and Wretchednefs.

The Expedient, therefore, to pleafe them, is
conftantly practifed by all wife Traytors, by all
able Oppreffors. But when, through the Ignorance of their Pillagers, the Courfe of Juftice is
entirely ftopt ; when the abufed and enraged People can have no Remedy, either real or imaginary,
nor one Victim to their Fury, they will naturally
and neceffarily look higher ; and then who can
forefee where their Vengeance will end ?

If a Pirate, who robs upon the Sea, be hanged
for his Robbery, every Body is fatisfied with the
Death of the Offender : But if the Action be
avowed, and he produce a Commiffion, the State
that gave it becomes anfwerable.

All thefe Secrets in Government were excellently underftood by Queen *Elizabeth*'s Miniftry.
Out of her Hiftory I have therefore copied the following Paffage, and the following Speech.

" The Queen, upon her Return from a Pro-
" grefs, held a Parliament at *Weftminfter* ; where-
" in, among other Things, feveral good Laws
" were

" were made for the Relief of the Poor, and of
" maimed and difabled Soldiers and Seamen ; a-
" gainſt fraudulent Guardians and Truſtees ; the
" Cheats and Impoſitions of Clothiers ; and the
" Robberies and Outrages committed upon the
" Borders of the Kingdom towards *Scotland*. But
" whereas great Complaints were made in the
" Lower Houſe, relating to the Engroſſing Prac-
" tice :" (for it ſeems there were ſome, who, under the Colour of Publick Good, but, in Reality,
to the great Damage of the Kingdom, had got
the Queen's Letters Patents, for the ſole Privilege
and Liberty of vending ſome particular Sorts of
Wares :) " The Queen therefore, to foreſtal
" them, publiſhed a Proclamation, declaring thoſe
" Grants to be null and void ; and alſo left them
" to be tried at Common Law. A Method
" which was ſo acceptable to the Lower Houſe,
" that Eighty of that Body were appointed to wait
" upon her Majeſty with their humble Thanks,
" which the Speaker was to preſent in the Name
" of them all. She received them very graci-
" ouſly, and gave her Anſwer in the following
" Speech :

" *Gentlemen*,
" I Owe you my beſt Thanks and Acknowledg-
" ments for your Reſpect towards me ; not
" only for your good Inclination, but thoſe clear
" and publick Expreſſions thereof, which have
" diſcovered themſelves in retrieving me from a
" Miſtake, into which I have been betrayed ;
" not ſo much by the Faults of my Will, as the
" Error of my Judgment. This had unavoidably
" drawn a Blemiſh upon me, (who account the
                                        " Safety

" Safety of my People my chief Happiness) had
" you not made me acquainted with the Practice
" of these lewd Harpies and Horse-Leeches. I
" would sooner lose my Heart or Hand, than
" ever consent to allow such Privilege to En-
" grossers, as may turn to the Detriment of my
" People. I am not so blinded with the Lustre
" of a Crown, as to let the Scale of Justice be
" weighed down by that of an Arbitrary Power.
" The gay Title of a Prince may deceive such
" as know nothing of the Secret of Governing ;
" as a gilded Pill may impose upon the Patient :
" But I am not one of those unwary Princes ;
" for I am very sensible, that I ought to govern
" for the Publick Good, and not to regard my
" own Particular ; and that I stand accountable
" to another, a greater Tribunal. I account
" myself very happy, that, by God's Assistance,
" I have enjoyed so prosperous a Government in
" all Respects ; and that he hath blessed me with
" such Subjects, for whom I could be contented
" to lay down my Crown and Life. I must en-
" treat you, that let Others be guilty of what
" Faults and Misdemeanors soever, they may
" not, through any Misrepresentation, be laid at
" my Door. I hope the Evidence of a good
" Conscience will, in all Respects, bear me out.
" You cannot be ignorant, that the Servants of
" Princes have, too often, an Eye to their own
" Advantage ; that their Faults are often con-
" cealed from their Notice ; and that they can-
" not, if they would, inspect all Things, when
" the Weight and Business of a whole Kingdom
" lies on their Shoulders."

Here

Here is a Speech, worthy of the Occasion, worthy of a wise Prince, worthy of a free People; a Speech that has Truth, and Sense, and Spirit in it. We may be sure from the Franknefs and Vigour of it, that the Ministers who advised it were no Sharers in the Guilt and Oppression of which it complains: If they had, they would have chosen Words more faint and equivocal; they would have shuffled in their Assertions; they would have talked more cowardly; they would have kept off from Particulars: They could not have hid their Guilt and Fears. But here their Boldnefs is the Effect of their Innocence, and prompted by it.

Her Majesty frankly owns, that she was drawn into an Error; but that it was only an Error of her Judgment, she makes manifest by her Alacrity and Forwardnefs to punish those Harpies and Horse-Leeches, who, in her Name, had abused the Publick: She owns it just, that those Engrossers should suffer: She owns that the Art and End of Reigning, is to advance the Publick Good; and when that Good is not attained, she consigns to Punishment those Rooks and Traytors, through whose Fault it is not attained. She owns that she has been abused by her Servants; who, under her Authority, and in the Name of the Law, had sought their own vile Advantages; and she removes from herself all Guilt, by giving up the Guilty.

Happy Queen! happy in her own Qualifications; happy in those of her Counsellors: But wise and good as she was, she could not have talked thus, if her Ministry had been weak or wicked: Had this been her Misfortune, in spite of her Sincerity,

cerity, Wifdom and Refolution, her Speech would have been falfe, faint, and filly. But her Counfellors were able and faithful, and made *England* profper ; and if we except fome Rebellions, and fome Perfecutions, both the Doings of hot-headed Bigots, her People faw nothing during her whole Reign but Felicity and Sunfhine.

This has entailed Bleffings upon her Memory, and Praife upon that of her Counfellors : And, indeed, the Happinefs or Mifery of a People will always be the certain Meafure of the Glory or Infamy of their Rulers, whenever fuch Happinefs or Mifery is evidently deducible from their Management.

The above Paffage out of Queen *Elizabeth*'s Hiftory, I thought not impertinent to our prefent Times : Her People had fuffered from Harpies and Horfe-Leeches : This fhews, that the Corruption had not reached the Court ; the Hands of her Minifters were clean, elfe her Speech would have taken another Turn.

Has *England* fuffered lefs, in this our Day, from Harpies and Horfe-Leeches ? Surely no : — All our Loffes, Pillages, and Oppreffions, fince the Conqueft, do not balance the prefent great Calamity : From a Profufion of all Things, we are reduced to a Want of every Thing : Heaven avert the Peftilence and the Famine ! — I am afraid that the latter begins to be forely felt by many Thoufands of our Poor, and even the Rich complain that they can hardly find Money to buy Bread.

And fhall not our Harpies be given up ? Shall not their Blood and Money make an undone Nation fome fmall Amends for their heavy Depredations

tions

tions and matchlefs Villainy? Certainly they muft: From a Miniftry as able, and as innocent, as that of Queen *Elizabeth*, we may expect the Behaviour and publick Spirit of Queen *Elizabeth's* Miniftry: Having no Part in the Guilt of Harpies, they cannot dread the Vengeance due to Harpies: They have not raifed out of their Country's Calamities, Fortunes great as thofe Calamities; they have no Difcoveries to dread; they have no Guilt to hide; they have not confpired with Harpies.

G

I am, &c.

SATURDAY, *December* 31, 1720.   No. 9.

Againft the projected Union of the Three Great Companies, and againft remitting to the South-Sea *Company any Part of their Debt to the Publick.*

SIR,

THE moft fuccefsful Deluders and Oppreffors of Mankind have always acted in Mafquerade; and when the blackeft Villainies are meant, the moft oppofite Spirit is pretended. Vice acts with Security, and often with Reputation, under the Vail of Virtue.

Hence Atheifts have fet up for the greateft Piety; and, to cover their own real Want of it, have cruelly burned thofe who really had it. The moft mercilefs Tyrants have, in the Midft of Oppreffion, fet up for the Patrons of Liberty; and, while their Hands were deep in Blood, impudently adopted the Title of Clemency; and publick Liberty

berty has almoft always been given up by thofe, who paffed for the Patrons of publick Liberty.

The cheating religious Orders of the Church of *Rome* gain the greateft Wealth, by a Profeffion of the ftricteft Poverty. The Popifh Inquifitors, while they deliver over to the Flames a poor Wretch, already half dead with Fears, Famine, and Torture, befeech and adjure the Civil Magiftrate, who muft fee it done, by the Love of God, and the Bowels of Jefus Chrift, not to hurt his Life or Limb. And our Inquifitors at Home began their *Occafional Bill* with a Declaration for Liberty of Confcience ; though the Purpofe of them, and their Bill, was to deftroy all Liberty of Confcience.

Companies and Joint-Stocks are always eftablifhed for the Encouragement and Benefit of Trade ; though they always happen to marr and cramp Trade. The *Peerage Bill* was to be granted as a Favour to the Commons of *England*, by cutting off the Commons of *England* from all Right to Peerage. And fome People, to fave Charges to *England*, are for giving up *Gibraltar*, which is of fuch Advantage to *England* ; being the Security of all our Trade. *Sweden* was once to be deftroyed, to preferve the Balance of Power in the *North* ; and now *Sweden* muft be defended, for the very fame Reafon.

When certain Chiefs were at mortal Odds, one Side oppofing (at all Adventures) whatever the other projected, it was thought convenient to both Sides to come to Terms ; for one Party wanted to fill their Coffers, and the other to fave their Bacon. However, the Good of the Publick was their fole Aim : They, Good Men ! fought no

perfonal

perfonal Advantages, though they have fince got confiderable ones : But we muft believe their Sayings, notwithftanding their Doings.

Stock-Jobbing too muft be declared againft, whilft the greateft Stock-Jobbing is promoting. Laft Year a *South-Sea* Project was to be eftablifhed to pay off the National Debts ; and now a Project is faid to be in Embryo, to remit the greateft Part of the Debt due to the Nation by the *South-Sea :* And if fo, the whole Nation is to fuffer this general Lofs, out of mere Pity to a fmall Part of the Nation. Twelve Months ago Forty Millions was not too much to be trufted with one Company, high in Credit, and its Reputation hoifted up by publick Authority ; but now, when they are bankrupt and undone, and when their Directors and Undertakers are univerfally hated and detefted, it is to be feared, it feems, that they will become too formidable, if all the Stock fubfcribed into them be continued with them.

There is, therefore, I am told, a Project on Foot, in *Exchange-Alley*, to deliver up the Nation to Three Companies ; and to let them divide us, their Cully, among them. In order to prevail upon thefe Three Great Societies to accept us as a Prefent, to be ufed as they think fit, I humbly prefume that we muft behave ourfelves as follows : We can do no lefs than facrifice the poor half-ftarved Manufacturers to one of them, and oblige ourfelves to lay no Reftraint upon *India* Callicoes, *&c.* We muft alfo confirm the Claufe which makes that Society perpetual. New Trades, more Monopolies, and frefh Privileges, muft be given to another Great and Virtuous Company, which had made fo good Ufe of the Old : And the *Bank of England,*

England, which long preferved its Integrity, muft be brought into the Confpiracy; and without doubt fomething more muft be given them, perhaps the Increafe of their Term.

Now, if this mighty Project, this noble Defign, can be accomplifhed; I fuppofe that every one will fee, or be prevailed upon to fee, the abfolute Neceffity why all paft Errors, and former Management, fhould be forgot; becaufe publick Credit, which depends upon Temper and Moderation, muft not be interrupted by ill-timed Enquiries, nor difturbed by publick Vengeance.—How finely we are to be difpofed of; and how fafe it is to provoke us!

The Projectors of fuch a publick Good muft deferve well from their Country; and I will give City Security, that they fhall be no Lofers by it. Where is the Wonder, or ill Policy of the Plunderers and Difhonourers of the Nation, if the Betrayers of their Truft fhould keep a little ill-begotten Wealth, to preferve the publick Peace? Without doubt, they will give large Shares of their Prey to thofe who have Power to let them keep the reft; and will readily help their Projectors and Coadjutors with their honeft Skill and Endeavours, to form new Projects, to get as much as they have done.

There lives in a certain Kingdom, a certain Gentleman, of no mean Importance there at prefent, who was Agent to one who had the Cuftodium of a forfeited Eftate there, worth Twelve Thoufand Pounds a Year; and when he gave in his Account to his Succeffor, brought the Eftate fome Hundreds of Pounds in Debt to himfelf. The other refented this with fome menacing Expreffions,

ons, but could get no other Anfwer from him, but that he would abide by his Account : *However*, fays he, *if you will be difcreet, I will help you to the Man that helped me to this Account.*

But what now, if, after all, there fhould be a little Jobb in a Corner ; and if any Gentleman, of remarkable Merit, fhould have Amends made for his Services, Sufferings, and Loffes of late Years ? Why, there is nothing uncommon in it ; for, *who will ferve the Lord for nought ?* This certainly can be no Reafon for rejecting a Project, which will reftore publick Credit, fill the Alley again, raife *South-Sea* Stock to Three or Four Hundred, and help the prefent Proprietors to new Bubbles ; without doing any other Mifchief, than that of ruining a few Thoufand Families more, and of not paying off the Nation's Debts.

Thefe, I confefs, are potent Reafons ; and will, without doubt, have their due Weight with all Perfons interefted. But, for myfelf, who am fo unfortunate as often to differ from my Betters, I can find nothing in this Propofal, which has any Tendency to help the prefent Company, or to raife Credit, in any Refpect, or to retrieve us from our Great and National Calamities ; but, on the contrary, to plunge the Publick inevitably into irretrievable Ruin, by making it impoffible, by any Medium in Nature but that of a Spunge, to difcharge our National Burthens : It will, befides, deprive us of our only colourable Pretence, which could juftify or excufe the late dreadful Scheme ; and which, I believe, I may fafely fay, was the only Pretence ever offered to excufe it. I think that it will be Lifting the Three Great Companies, with all the moneyed Intereft in *England*, againft

againſt *England*; and will, at laſt, reduce, and
even force, all Parties not to oppoſe what I dread
to name, and tremble to think of.

The Project abovementioned is calculated, we
are told, for the Advantage of *South-Sea*, and
for the Improvement of their Stock; and, in order
to this, a great Part of that Stock is to be given
away to the *Bank of England*, and to the *Eaſt-
India* Company; without any apparent Conſideration to themſelves, or any other Uſe to the Publick, than the uniting the Three Great Companies in one Intereſt; and conſequently, the forming ſuch a potent Conſpiracy againſt the whole
Kingdom, as nothing but a total Confuſion of
all Things can diſſolve. O Companies, Companies! ye Bane of Honeſty, and Ruin of
Trade; the Market of Jobbers, the Harveſt of
Managers, and the Tools of Knaves, and of
Traytors!

It is propoſed, that the *South-Sea* is to give the
Bank an Hundred and Twenty Pounds for every
Hundred Pound of Stock in the *Bank*; which
Stock is ſaid to be but barely worth Ninety
Pounds; even though we ſhould ſuppoſe that they
had never divided any of their Principal: Which,
whether they have done it or not, no body but
themſelves can know: But at this Rate, however,
they muſt divide, whenever they are paid off by
the Government.

But we are told, that they are to be let alſo into
the Profits of Banking; from which Profits, 'tis
ſaid, that they are enabled to divide Three *per Cent.*
upon the Old Capital, beſides the Five *per Cent.*
paid them by the Government: But, even upon
this Foot, the greater their Capital is, the leſs they
                                                    will

will be able to divide: And confequently, when
Nine Millions are added to their Old Capital, they
will not be able to divide much above One *per Cent.*
which is not the Intereft of the Money paid in
Difference between Ninety, which is the real Value, and an Hundred and Twenty, which is the
nominal Value.

Befides, there is no Probability that the *Bank*
can continue to make, for the future, the fame
Gain of Banking, as heretofore. The Trafficking in publick Tallies, from whence that
Gain chiefly arofe, will be at an End, unlefs
there be new Funds given, and new Debts contracted.

The Contract propofed by thefe People, to be
made with the other Company, is ftill worfe;
for, there they are to give a Hundred and
Twenty Pounds for a Hundred Pound Nominal Stock, which is fufpected to be worth very
little; fome Men being of the Opinion, that the
greateft Part of the Ten *per Cent.* divided for
fome Years paft, has been pocketed out of other
People's Money, borrowed by the Company upon
their Bonds: And yet for this choice Bargain,
they are to give Six Hundred Thoufand Pounds
at prefent, and fubject Nine Hundred Thoufand
Pounds more to be difpofed of according to the
Pleafure, Skill, and Honefty of the prefent Directors. A pretty Sum, and doubtlefs fet apart
to anfwer and accomplifh fome lovely Jobb,
which will appear in proper Time, and by which
the Projectors of the Scheme, I dare fay, will be no
Lofers!

'Tis faid too, that the Trade of this Company
may be enlarged; I fuppofe they mean, by bringing

ing in more *India* Manufactures, to the Ruin of our own.

Now all this we are given to underſtand is for the ſole Benefit of the *South-Sea*; and if they have not Senſe to conceive it aright, a worſe Thing may befall them: We all know, what Directors and their old Patrons carry Halters about their Necks, though they have Millions in their Pockets; and who would not give away a little of other People's Money, to ſave a great deal of their own, with their Lives into the Bargain? — A ſpecial Set of Traytors, to negotiate for the very Being of a Kingdom!

But I muſt tell all theſe Forgers of Schemes, and Inventors of Grievances, that the Nation, exhauſted by paſt Projects, cannot bear new ones, nor furniſh out more Millions to glut more Harpies. The Want of Bread, long felt by the Poor, begins now to be felt by the Rich. The Purſes therefore of the New Conſpirators muſt be filled out of the Extortions and Depredations of the Old, or remain empty: They may rack their Invention, ſift every Topick of Knavery, and toſs and change their Projects as much and as long as they pleaſe; but we know that nothing but plain Honeſty can ever ſave us; and to thoſe who would practiſe Honeſty, plain Speech is beſt. Let us honeſtly hang up thoſe who have deceived and undone us, and let us beware of new Deceivers and new Deſtroyers: Let us, with a Severity equal to our Diſtreſs, examine what the Directors and their Maſters have embezzled, and loſt to their Country, by their mercileſs Villainy, and conſuming Avarice; and let us have the only Satisfaction that they can make us, their Lives,

and

and their Eftates : Let, afterwards, a fair Valuation be made of their prefent Capital, and let all the World know it ; that the Purchafer may buy folid Subftance, and not a fleeting Shadow.   This is the honeft Way to reftore Credit again ; this will prevent the roguifh Part of Stock-Jobbing ; and this will throw the remaining Money into Trade once more.

But what, may fome fay, if we fhould give away from the *South-Sea* Company fome Millions to make new Friends, and to fave our old Friends, fo long as we can make that Company Amends out of the Publick, for fuch a Lofs ? A Thing eafily done ! — It is only giving them back again the Seven Millions already due by them to the Publick ; or at leaft the greateft Part of thofe Seven Millions, as the fame ftand fecured upon Forty Millions ; and if we do this, behold the Advantage that will accrue from it ! We will then be under no Neceffity of hanging our Countrymen, or calling up any to difgorge their honeft Gains : Befides, it is to be hoped that this Propofal will be backed with fuch powerful Motives, as to meet with little Oppofition.

This calls to my Mind a Comparifon, which I have been for fome time very apt to make, between the *French* Projectors and thofe of another Country which I know.   The firft plunder for the Publick ; the other plunder the Publick : The one robs Part of the People for the Whole People ; the other robs the Whole People for a fmall Part of the People.

This Comparifon may be the Subject of another Letter to you, if you think fit to print this.

T   *I am,* &c.

T u e s-

Tuesday, *January* 3, 1720. No. 10.

The Iniquity of late and new Projects about the South-Sea *considered ——— How fatally they affect the Publick.*

S I R,

WHEN we compare one Nation with another, and balance the Power of both, we are not to confider alone the Number of People, or the Wealth diffufed amongft the People ; though Number and Wealth are undoubtedly the firft Elements of Power in a Commonwealth ; no more than we are to confider the mere Extent of Territory, or the mere Fertility of Soil: But we are chiefly to confider, how much of that Wealth can be brought together, how it may be moft frugally managed, and how moft fkilfully applied to the publick Emolument and Defence.

If, in taxing Labour and Manufactures, we exceed a certain Proportion, we difcourage Induftry, and deftroy that Labour and thofe Manufactures. The like may be faid of Trade and Navigation ; they will bear but limited Burthens : And we find by Experience, that when higher Duties are laid, the Product is not encreafed ; but the Trade is loft, or the Goods are run.

Nor can more be extorted from the Gentleman and Freeholder, than he can fpare from the Support of his Family, in a Way fuitable to his former Condition.

When

When Impofitions exceed thefe Bounds, the
Hiftory of all Ages will convince us, that their
Produce is only Bitternefs, Murmurings, univerfal
Difcontents; and their End, generally, Rebellion,
and an Overthrow of the then prefent Eftablifh-
ment, or of public Liberty.

If therefore one State, for Example, poffeffed
of five times as much true, but fcattered, Wealth,
as another State, cannot for all that, from a Defect in its Conftitution, collect fo much from the
People as the poorer State can; or, if when col-
lected, does yet truft the fame to the Difpofal of
Blood-Suckers and Traytors, who intercept the
National Wealth, and divert it to private Purfes;
or if it be appropriated, before it be raifed, to the
Payment of former Debts; or if it be embezzled in
Penfions and Salaries to mercenary Men, for traiterous Ends; then is fuch a State really weaker
than the other poorer State, and lefs capable of defending itfelf againft the other, fo much its inferior
in outward Shew and intrinfick Power.

This was the State of *Spain* for near Two
Hundred Years; *Spain*, the Miftrefs of fo many
Nations, and of a new World, richer in Silver
and Gold than the old; *Spain*, that from terrifying all Chriftendom with Chains, and from
threatening all *Europe* with univerfal Slavery, reduced itfelf, by mortgaging its publick Revenues,
to fuch a defpicable Condition, that we have feen,
in our Days, that once formidable Kingdom contended for by two fmall Armies of Foreigners,
within its own Bowels: In which Conteft the
Natives themfelves were little more than Spectators; as is very juftly obferved by the Author of a
Pamphlet printed laft Year, and written with a

Spirit

Spirit which I pretend not to imitate. Had that Pamphlet been generally read, and well weighed, it would have prevented moft of the Mifchiefs which we now lamentably labour under. It is entitled, *Confiderations upon the State of the Publick Debts in general, and of the Civil Lift in particular.* I would recommend it to the Reading of every one, who is not afhamed of being an honeft Man.

It is certain, that all the powerful Nations of *Europe*, who were Parties in the two laft bloody and expenfive Wars, were reduced, by mortgaging their publick Revenues, to the fame low and abject Condition ; and nothing faved any one of them from all the reft, but that all the reft were in the fame State of Impotence and Diftrefs. They were all miferably weak. That People, therefore, who can fooneft difcharge their publick Burthens, will give Laws to the reft ; and either reduce them to Subjection and Vaffalage, or to a Neceffity of feizing their mortgaged Funds.

There are in the World but two Ways of clearing a Nation of its publick Engagements: The one is, by paying them off ; the other is, not to pay them at all. When the one cannot be practifed, a fmall Skill in Politicks will tell us, that the other muft.

It is a Jeft for any Man to flatter himfelf, that any State will not fave the whole People, by the Ruin of a Part of the People, when the Ruin of a Part is abfolutely neceffary to the Prefervation of the Whole. This Confideration fhould, methinks, be worth the Attention of the Gentlemen Inhabitants of the Alley. In Truth, nothing would exercife their Thoughts more, were it not that every

one

one hopes to save one, by cheating another into a hard and knavish Bargain. Will Men never have done Hoping? They forget how they were caught last Year in the *South-Sea*, with all their Hopes and their Wisdom about them.

It is, doubtless, the last Misfortune to a Nation, to be beholden to a Spunge for the Payment of its Debts ; such a Necessity must be a heavy Necessity, attended with many sorrowful Circumstances, and much sore Distress. Nothing but the certain Fear of foreign Force, or domestick Tyranny, can justify it. But even a great Calamity is eligible, in Comparison of a greater. Every Person, therefore, who is a Creditor to his Country, and has Demands upon the Publick, is nearly concerned to prevent such great and personal, and indeed general Misery ; which cannot be at all prevented, but by putting the National Debts into a Method of being honourably discharged. This is the Concern of every honest Man ; this ought to be the Care of every worthy Citizen ; this will be the Task of every guiltless Great Man.

All innocent Men, throughout the World, find a private Blessing in the general Felicity of the Publick; and none but Mock-Patriots, who foolishly or deliberately can lead Kingdoms into Ruin ; desperate hard-hearted Parricides, who can wantonly suck out the Vitals of their Country, whose Fortunes are often the Plunder of the Publick, whose Creatures are Conspirators, hired against the Publick ; I say, none but such Traytors can find private Joy in publick Confusion, or their own Security in the Slavery of their Country. Those, it is true, who earn Vengeance by committing t'ng mighty Crimes, would, doubtlefs, go on to refemble themfelves, and to avoid it, if they could, by committing Crimes ftill more mighty. If any amongft us fhould be capable of practifing fuch great Wickednefs to get enormous Wealth, fuch Perfons, if not prevented, might ftill practife greater to keep it. A Fox purfued by the full Cry of the Hounds, will run into the Dog-Kennel for Shelter ; as at the Battle of *La Hogue*, the *French* Fleet fled through the Race of *Aldernly*, and ventured Rocks and Shelves, to efcape from the conquering Enemy.

It is a Folly, and indeed an Infatuation, in any Perfons interefted in the Publick Funds, to form any Schemes, or to fall into any Schemes for increafing thofe Funds, or for continuing in them, any longer than is abfolutely neceffary to pay them their Debts: When our neighbouring Nations have cleared theirs, we too muft clear ours, or we are undone. 'Tis faid, indeed, that a Revolution in Government would certainly and effectually do it, and do it at once ; and this I take to be the true Reafon why fo many unthinking Men appear to wifh it ; though I hope it is in vain. God avert fo dreadful a Cataftrophe !

Spain has already difcharged itfelf of its publick Burthens, by a general Sweep: And behold the Effect of this ! It again fhews its Head in the World ; again it carries its Armies into new Countries. *Holland* lies ftill, free from new Broils, and frefh Expence: It politically pleads poverty : It takes all Ways in its Power to recover its Loffes ; and queftionlefs laughs in its Sleeve to fee another Nation grow more mad, and more in Debt every Year; to fee it every Year mortgaging new Revenues,

nues, and every Year engaging in wild Wars, to fupport the Interefts of a State of no Concernment to it.

But the moft terrible Inftance of all, is that of *France:* That Government, though to the Ruin of great Multitudes of other People, has almoft, if not quite, got rid of its Incumbrances and Engagements. The whole Wealth of that great Kingdom is now got into the Hands of the Publick. From which formidable Situation of theirs, is there not Room to fear, that as foon as the prefent Confufion is a little abated, they will renew their Defigns for Empire, and throw *Europe* into Arms again? This is an alarming Reflection! And what do the Gentlemen of the Alley expect from us, under fuch an ill-boding Circumftance? Trade is already burthened as much as it can bear, and perhaps more than it ought to bear: There is fcarce a Commodity that can be taxed, but is already taxed. We are marked, we are mortgaged from Head to Foot. They do not furely expect that the Parliament will give Ten Shillings in the Pound upon Land, or that it could be raifed if they did.

What therefore are we to do in fuch a calamitous Cafe? Are we to fave ourfelves at the Expence of the Gentlemen of the Alley? Or are we to perifh together with them? The Choice is eafy. Can they be fo weak, as to form a pretended Neceffity, to bring their Country into fuch unhappy Circumftances; and yet not fear that wife and honefter Men may take Advantage of a real Neceffity, to get out of fuch unhappy Circumftances?

There is but one Thing to be done, to fave themfelves and their Country together; and that is, is, to put the Debts into a Method of being certainly and speedily paid off. The present Establishment may be saved, though they are undone: But if, through Folly or Knavery, the Establishment sink, they must sink with it. I hope therefore, that they will not be decoyed into any traiterous Designs of desperate Men: Men, whose Characters are but faintly expressed by that of Parricides; Men, who, had they studied the Art of making us miserable, could not have been more accomplished in their Trade, nor boast of compleater Success. Where is our Trade, by which we so long flourished? It is lost. Where is our Publick Faith, once our own Boast, and the Envy of foreign Nations? It is fled; and one Man has no longer any Faith in another. Where is our Money? Where are our current Millions? The People have none. — The most Part find it hard to buy Bread; and many find it impossible. Every Man whom you meet complains that he is undone. All our Coin is engrossed, pocketed by vile Jobbers, their Prompters and Confederates; publick Robbers, who, to keep what they have got, and to escape deserved Punishment, (if such Punishment can possibly be found) would deliver up the Wealth and Power of *England* into the griping and polluted Hands of a new Conspiracy of Stock-Jobbers, worse than the last, by being more numerous and potent. With these they would combine for common Defence, and for publick Destruction; with these, contrive new Ways to enlarge our Miseries, shorten our Enjoyments still more, and grind us still smaller; with these, they would form into such a Confederacy against their common Country, and against common

mon

mon Honefty, as would mock even the Endeavours of a Legiflature to diffolve it.   Good God!
what implacable Men! thus mercilefly bent to ruin
the very Ruins of their Country!

What *Briton*, bleffed with any Senfe of Virtue,
or with common Senfe; what *Englifhman*, animated with a publick Spirit, or with any Spirit,
but muft burn with Rage and Shame, to behold
the Nobles and Gentry of a great Kingdom; Men
of Magnanimity;   Men of Breeding;   Men of
Underftanding, and of Letters; to fee fuch Men
bowing down, like *Jofeph's* Sheaves, before the
Face of a dirty *Stock-Jobber*, and receiving Laws
from Men bred behind Counters, and the Deci-
fion of their Fortunes from Hands ftill dirty with
fweeping Shops!

Surely we fhall never fuffer this to be our Cafe,
and therefore fhall never fee it.   It is ridiculous to
think that a Nation, free as we are, and bold by
being fo, will ever fubmit to fuch Indignities: It
is therefore eafy to forefee, if once we foolifhly
take the firft Step, what will neceffarily be the
next.   One Oppreffion cannot be fupported but
by another, and a greater; and Force and Violence alone can do what Reafon cannot and will
not do.   Thefe Hardfhips will   produce new
Wants, and new Neceffities for Money; which
Money, if fuch Men can have their Will, will
only be to be had from thefe Companies, and from
them only upon hard Conditions, and in Exchange
for new Privileges, ftill tending to the Detriment
of general Trade, and ending in the total Ruin of
the Nation.

The Nation will be provoked in Proportion as
it is diftreffed;   ill Ufage will be returned with
Rage:

Rage: And then, I doubt not, when these Projectors have rendered the People distracted, they will tell us, that it will not be safe to venture them with another Election. They will do every thing in their Power to make the Kingdom disaffected ; and then urge that Disaffection as a good Reason not to trust them.

This Conduct will produce necessarily more and higher Discontents ; Discontents will make Armies necessary ; Armies will inflame those Discontents still more vehemently. I dare think no further.— But sure there is no one who loves King *GEORGE*, and his Government, but will endeavour to prevent these dismal Mischiefs, before it be too late.

No Man living laments the Calamities brought upon his Country, more than I do those brought upon mine: Yet I freely own, that I think the paying off the Nation's Debts, and restoring, by that Means, the Kingdom to its Power, its Grandeur, and its Security again, was an End worth all the Evils which we have yet suffered ; an End which ought, if possible, to have been purchased with greater than we have yet suffered, if it could not otherwise have been purchased. I think that it ought to have been done, though attended with many ill Circumstances ; and might have been done, even upon those hard Terms, with Justice to private Men, and Honour to the Nation. We are not a People without it ; nor is it worth while to dispute about the best Cabbin in a Ship that is sinking.

This Prospect gave me some Pleasure, and some Relief to my Thoughts, made anxious by the melancholy and importunate Clamours of Thousands

fands and Ten Thoufands of my diftreffed Countrymen : But when I was told that a Project was
formed by Men of Figure, Power, and Fortune,
to give back All, and the only Advantage which
we were to reap, or could reap, from fo many Miferies, and which could alone palliate or excufe
fuch a wild and defperate Attempt ; though this
was the only Excufe which was ever offered, or
can yet be fuggefted by the wifeft Men in behalf
of it ; I confefs that I was feized with Horror
and Confufion from fuch News, and could fee nothing before my Eyes but total Defolation and final
Ruin.

To tell us, that this is to be done out of Tendernefs to the Miferable, is adding Contempt to
the Injury : It is infulting our Underftandings,
and playing with the publick Misfortunes; it is
firft to make us Beggars, then to treat us like
Idiots.   With as much Modefty did a grand Monarch, who was known to make himfelf Sport,
for above half a Century, with the Lives of Men,
pretend to ground his Defire of Peace upon a
confcientious Inclination to prevent the Effufion of
Chriftian Blood.

Thofe who have true Compaffion, Virtue, and
Tendernefs, will fhew it upon the propereft Objects ; they will prefer the Security and Welfare of
many Millions to the Security and Welfare of fome
Thoufands, though they fhould be many Thoufands ; efpecially if the latter prove to have been
covetous and unthinking Men, caught in the
Snare which they fpread for others : For by thefe
wild Bargains no Man is undone, but he who intended the Favour of being undone to fomebody
elfe.   Thefe Gentlemen, pretending to fo much
Tender-

Tenderneſs and Compaſſion, will not at leaſt ſacrifice thoſe who always foreſaw the Miſchief, and always oppoſed it, to the Relief of ſuch who contributed to it ; who made corrupt Applications for an early Admittance into the Advantage of the Secret ; who ſwallowed Plumbs in their Imaginations, and ridiculed as Fools or Beggars all that kept at a wiſe and honeſt Diſtance.

Pity and Compaſſion are charming and engaging Sounds, when rightly applied ; but Pity and Compaſſion do not conſiſt in protecting Criminals from Juſtice, and in ſuffering the Devourers of a Nation to go off with the Plunder of a Nation ; nor in oppreſſing the people over again, to make the Loſer Amends : Neither do they conſiſt in giving away the publick Treaſure of Nations to private Men, for no Reaſon, or for very bad Reaſons ; nor in engaging a Kingdom in wild and romantick Expences, to ſerve wild and romantick Purpoſes ; neither do they conſiſt in ſacrificing the Trade and Manufacture of a whole People, and in conſequence the Bread of a whole People, to the deſtructive Intereſts of Societies of Stock-Jobbers, combined with publick Plunderers for mutual Defence.

Our wiſe and diſintereſted Legiſlature mean other Things ; they have told us, that they will not relieve one Part of the diſtreſſed and deluded Bubbles, to the Detriment of others, who have as much Pretence to Relief as themſelves ; and it is impoſſible to imagine that they will give up the unoffending and almoſt deſpairing People (whoſe Intereſts they are choſen to aſſert) to repair the Loſſes of unwary Men, and to put Thirty Millions in the Pockets of Twenty-Stock-Jobbers.

Can

Can it be fuppofed, that the Parliament will refufe to make void hafty and private Bargains, founded in Corruption and Fraud, and made without any one honeft Confideration? And fhall this Refufal be made for the Publick Good? And yet fhall that very Parliament be thought capable of making void a publick Bargain, made for the publick Good, with the greateft Deliberation, and upon the weightieft Motives in the World? Which Bargain was indeed the chief, if not the only Caufe, that drew upon us our prefent great Calamities.

But we are told by the Projectors, that the Company is not able to pay the publick the Sum ftipulated ; and the King muft lofe his Right, where his Right is not to be had. This is impudently as well as ftupidly faid ; for the Security is already in the Hands of the Publick : The Nation owes the Company near Forty Millions, and nothing is neceflary but to ftop the Payment of Seven.

But it is farther urged by the Projectors, that the Company will be undone, if fo much be ftopt from them ; and I aver, that the Nation is undone, if it be not ftopt

Here a very pleafant Obfervation offers itfelf : For this very fame Project, which would mercifully remit to the *South-Sea* Company the Seven Millions due by them to the Publick, is intended to raife a Hundred Pounds of their Capital Stock to Three or Four Hundred Pounds in Value , I will fuppofe only to three Hundred ; and even then their prefent Capital being about Twenty-fix Millions, the whole will be worth about Eighty Millions ; and furely, if the Publick give them

fuch

fuch an immenfe Advantage, they may well afford
to pay the fmall Sum of Seven Millions due to the
Publick out of it. Our own Laws, and the Laws
of every Country in the World, give Precedence
to the Prerogative, in the Bufinefs of Debtor and
Creditor; and always fecure the Debts due to the
Publick, whatever becomes of thofe due to private
Men. Surely we fhall not rejeft the Wifdom of
Nations, and invert the Maxims of Government,
that while we confirm the Bargains of particular
Men, we deftroy thofe made for the Benefit of all
the Men in the Kingdom.

But there is yet fomething more abfurd in this
Projeft: For the Bargain was made with the Old
Company, who were to give Three Millions and
a Half, certain, to the Publick; and about Three
Millions more, if they could purchafe in the An-
nuitants: Which Sum they could have afforded to
the Publick, if they could but have raifed their
Stock Thirty *per Cent.* upon the whole Stock fo
united: But we have, in Faft, feen its imaginary
Value encreafed, at one time, more than Two
Hundred Millions; which has enabled thofe in the
Secret to carry off more than Twenty, if not
Thirty Millions.

Valuing the Stock, at prefent, at two Hundred, which is lefs than the Stock fells for, the old
Capital alone is advanced near Twelve Millions
above its firft Value; and confequently is able to
pay Seven, without the Affiftance of the new Sub-
fcribers: And, if the Projeftors of the Scheme advance the Stock to Three or Four Hundred, as
they pretend that they will; then the firft Con-
traftors, and thofe who ftand in their Places, will
double or treble their Capital; though they alone
were

were to pay the Publick the poor Confideration which has enabled them to do fo.

Hard Fate of poor *England*, to be thus the laft regarded, even in Schemes and Deliberations which purely regard *England!* Private Men, who have been bubbled, are to be pitied ; but muft private Men, who have contributed to the publick Ruin, and their own, be regarded preferably to the Publick ? And muft publick Compaffion be fhewn to private Dupes, rather than to the Publick itfelf?

Poor *England!* What a Name art thou become ! A Name of Infatuation and Mifery ! How art thou fallen ! how plundered ! And thofe that have done it, would, to keep their Spoil, agree to affift others to fqueeze out thy laft Dregs, and to fuck out thy remaining Blood.   How paffive do they think thee ! How tame would they make thee ! An eafy Prey for Devourers ; who, while they hold thee faft, and gripe thee hard with Iron Claws, aggravate thy Mifery, by mocking it, and infolently talk of Compaffion.

What keener Indignities can they do us, than thus to jeft with us, while we are gafping, while we are expiring, in the midft of the Pangs and Convulfions into which they have wantonly and wickedly thrown us !

Odd is that Compaffion which arifes from Guilt and Avarice ; and with how much Modefty would they chriften, with the deluding Title of Pity, that Conduct, which would prove in effect to be only Impunity to the Murderers of our Profperity, and the Manglers of their Country ! Thus would they infult our Underftanding, and deal with us as if we had none.

How

How long fhall we fuffer under this pungent Ufage? this painful Difgrace to our Senfe and our Spirit ? Patience under Indignities, invites frefh Indignities. We fee our Parricides do, as it were, take Pains to invent new Miferies for us.—A hard Tafk ! confidering thofe that they have already accomplifhed. Nay, they act as if they defpaired of making us defperate.

They may be miftaken. And indeed, in the whole String of their Politicks, I could never dif-cover any one Symptom of their Skill in human Nature, except that which they learned from Bro-kers and Pedlars in Stocks.

In Truth, Matters are come to that Pafs, that an Endeavour to make them worfe, may probably make them better : *Res nolunt male adminiftrari.* All Men fuffer ; all Men are alarmed : Refent-ment rages high, and gathers thick from all Quarters ; and though it may feem big with fome terrible Event, yet it may be prevented by Anti-cipation.

Our Eyes are upon the Parliament, and fo are the Eyes of *Europe.* We have begun to conceive Hope from the bold and upright Spirit which ap-pears in our Reprefentatives to right us and to re-venge us. They have, indeed, a great and un-precedented Opportunity given them, of fecuring to themfelves, in the Hearts of all *Englifhmen,* a Monument of grateful Praife and publick Spirit, and of perpetuating that Praife in the Memory of every *Briton,* till Time fhall be no more.

T *and* G.   *I am,* &c.

SATUR-

SATURDAY, *January* 7, 1720.   NO. 11.

*The Justice and Necessity of punishing great Crimes,
though committed against no subsisting Law of the
State.*

SIR,

S *Alus Populi Suprema Lex esto: That the Benefit
and Safety of the People constitutes the Supreme
Law*, is an universal and everlasting Maxim in Government : It can never be altered by municipal
Statutes : No Customs can change, no positive In-
stitutions can abrogate, no Time can efface, this
primary Law of Nature and Nations.   The sole
End of Mens entering into political Societies, was
mutual Protection and Defence ; and whatever
Power does not contribute to those Purposes, is
not Government, but Usurpation.

Every Man in the State of Nature had a Right
to repel Injuries, and to revenge them ; that is, he
had a Right to punish the Authors of those Injuries,
and to prevent their being again committed ; and
this he might do, without declaring before-hand
what Injuries he would punish.   Seeing therefore
that this Right was inherent in every private Man,
it is absurd to suppose that National Legislatures,
to whom every Man's private Power is committed, have not the same Right, and ought not to
exercise it upon proper Occasions.

Crimes being the Objects of Laws, there were
Crimes before there were Laws to punish them ;
and yet from the Beginning they deserved to be
                                   punish-

punifhed by the Perfon affected hy them, or by the Society, and a Number of Men united with him for common Security, though without the Sentence of a common Judge (called by us the Magiftrate) formally appointed to condemn Offenders.

Laws, for the moft Part, do not make Crimes, but fuit and adapt Punifhments to fuch Actions as all Mankind knew to be Crimes before. And though National Governments fhould never enact any pofitive Laws, never annex particular Penalties to known Offences ; yet they would have a Right, and it would be their Duty to punifh thofe Offences according to their beft Difcretion ; much more fo, if the Crimes committed are fo great, that no human Wifdom could forefee that any Man could be wicked and defperate enough to commit them.

Lawyers diftinguifh betwixt *Malum prohibitum* and *Malum in fe* ; that is, between Crimes that are fo in their own Nature, and Crimes that owe their Pravity to a Difobedience to pofitive Laws. Of the former Sort are all thofe Actions, by which one Man hurts another in his Reputation, his Perfon, or his Fortune ; and thofe Actions are ftill more heinous, if they injure, or are intended to injure, the whole Society.

The latter Sort confifts of fuch Crimes as refult from what Legiflatures enact for the particular Benefit of private Societies ; as Laws concerning the Regularity of Trade, the Manner of chufing Magiftrates, Local Orders ; and from fuch pofitive Inftitutions, as receive their Force alone from the Powers that enact them. Now thofe Crimes were not fo before they were declared fo ; and
con-

confequently, no Man before was under any Obligation to avoid them.

It would be very fevere and unjuft to punifh any Man for an undefigned Tranfgreffion of the latter Sort ; that is, for fuch Action as he thought that he might lawfully and honeftly do, and which he had never Notice given him not to do. But to infer from thence, that a Villain may defpife all the Laws of God and Nature, ruin Thoufands of his Fellow-Subjects, and overturn Nations with Impunity, becaufe fuch Villainy was too monftrous for human Forefight and Prevention, is fomething fo abfurd, that I am afhamed to confute it.

This is nothing lefs than afferting, that a Nation has not a Power within itfelf to fave itfelf : That the Whole ought not to preferve the Whole : That particular Men have the Liberty to fubvert the Government which protects them, and yet continue to be protected by that Government which they would deftroy : That they may overturn all Law, and yet efcape by not being within the exprefs Words of any particular Law.

There are Crimes fo monftrous and fhocking, that wife States would not fuffer them to ftand in their Statute Books ; becaufe they would not put fuch an Indignity upon human Nature, as to fuppofe it capable of committing them. They would not mention what they imagined would never be practifed. The Old *Romans*, therefore, had no Law againft *Parricide* ; yet there was no want of Punifhment for *Parricides* from the Want of Law : Thofe black and enormous Criminals were fewed up in a Sack, and thrown into the *Tyber*.

In

In *Holland*, there was no Law againſt Mens Breaking fraudulently ; yet the firſt Man who was known to do ſo, was immediately executed, and his Eſtate divided among his Creditors.

In *England*, 'tis ſaid, there was no Law, till lately, againſt the burning of Ships; yet, if any Man had burned the Royal Navy of *England*, lying at Anchor, ought not his Crime, which it ſeems was not Felony, to have been declared High-Treaſon?

Many Nations have had particular Officers appointed on purpoſe to puniſh uncommon Crimes, which were not within the Reach of ordinary Juſtice.   The *Romans* had a *Dictator* ; a great and extraordinary Magiſtrate, veſted with an extraordinary Power, as he was created on extraordinary Exigencies; and his Commiſſion was limited only by the Publick Good, and conſiſted in a very ſhort Direction, *Nequid detrimenti Reſpublica capiat* ; in *Engliſh, To ſave the State.*

This powerful Officer was once created on purpoſe to put to Death *Spurius Mælius*, for giving *gratis* to the People a large Quantity of Corn, in a Time of Famine.   This Liberality of his was conſtrued by the Senate, an ambitious Bribe to catch the Hearts of the Multitude, in order to ſeize their Liberties. — *Spurius Mælius — prædives, remutilem peſſimo exemplo, pejore conſilio eſt aggreſſus.* He undertook a publick and plauſible Thing, but of ill Example, and with a worſe Deſign.   *Largitiones frumenti facere inſtituit.*   His avowed Pretence was to relieve the Poor ; *Plebemq; hoc munere delinitam, quacunque incederet conſpectus alatusq; ſupra modum hominis privati, ſecum trahere.* He cajoled the People, intending to enſlave them ; and

growing

growing too powerful for a Subject, became terrible to the common Liberty, which is supported by Equality : *Ipse, ut est humanus animus insatiabilis eo quod fortuna spondet, ad altiora & non concessa tendere :* The Mind of Man is restless, and cannot stand still, nor set Bounds to its Pursuits. It is not to be expected that one of our Million Men (and they say that we have several) will sit down and be content with his Millions, though he were allowed to keep them (which God forbid !) He will be making new Pushes for new Acquisitions, having such ample Means in his Hands. *Spurius Mælius* would at first have been content with the Consulate, or Chief Magistracy in Ordinary ; but because he found that even that could not be got without Force, he thought that the same Force would as well carry him higher, and make him King. — *Et quoniam Consulatus quoque eripiendus invitis patribus esset, de Regno agitare.* The Traytor had been suffered to carry a great Point; he had abused the Publick, and deceived the People. The Senate, therefore, take him to Task : and there being no Law subsisting, by which he could be put to Death — *Consules* legibus *constricti, nequaquam* tantum virium *in Magistratu ad eam rem pro* atrocitate *vindicandum quantum animi haberent ;* They therefore create a Dictator, an Officer with Power, for a Time, to suspend Laws, and make Laws. The Occasion was great — *Opus esse non forti solum viro,* sed etiam *LIBERO, EXSOLUTOQUE LEGUM VINCULIS.* L. *Quincius Cincinnatus* was the Man ; a true and brave old *Republican,* who worthily and boldly did his Work, and by the Hands of his Master of the Horse slew the mighty Traytor, impudently imploring

ploring the publick Faith, to which he was a sworn Enemy; and complaining of the Power of Oppreſſion, when the ſhameleſs Villain had been only ſeeking a Power to oppreſs. *Fidem plebis Romanæ implorare*; & opprimi ſe *CONSENSU PATRUM DICERE*. He knew that his Villainies were out of the Reach of the Law, and he did not dream of an extraordinary Method of puniſhing them by the *Roman* Parliament. But he was deceived; and the Dictator tells the People, that being a ſort of an Outlaw, he was not to be proceeded with as with a Citizen of *Rome*: *Nec cum eo tanquam cum Cive agendum fuiſſe.* An unuſual Death was due to his monſtrous Wickedneſs: *Non pro ſcelere id magis quam pro monſtro habendum.* Nor was his Blood alone, ſays the wiſe Dictator, ſufficient to expiate his Guilt, unleſs we alſo pull down his Houſe, where ſuch crying Crimes were firſt conceived; and confiſcate to the publick Uſe his Eſtate and his Treaſures, the Price and Means of the publick Ruin.— And his Eſtate was accordingly given to the Publick — *Nec ſatis eſſe ſanguine ejus expiatum, niſi tecta parieteſq; inter quæ tantum amentiæ conceptum eſſet, diſſiparentur; bonaq; contacta pretiis Regni mercandi* publicarentur; *Jubere itaque Queſtores, vendere ea bona & in publicum redigere:* The Treaſury had them for the Uſe of the Publick.

Thus did the Great, the Wiſe, and the Free *Romans* puniſh this extraordinary Knave, by a Power that was not ordinary. They likewiſe exerted it upon other Occaſions; nor were they the only People that did ſo.

The *Athenians*, grown jealous by having loſt their Liberties, by the Uſurpation of a private, but

but too powerful Citizen, durst never trust this
great Power to any single Magistrate, or even to
a Council. They would not, however, part with
it, but reserved it to the whole Body of the People, agreeably to the Nature of a popular Government. In this jealous State, it was a Crime
to be popular, much more to affect Popularity:
They would not allow a Man to have it in his
Power to enslave his Country. And, indeed, it
is Wisdom in a State, and a Sign that they judge
well, to suppose, that all Men who can enslave
them, will enslave them. Generosity, Self-denial,
and private and personal Virtues, are in Politicks
but mere Names, or rather Cant-Words, that go
for nothing with wise Men, though they may
cheat the Vulgar. The *Athenians* knew this; and
therefore appointed a Method of punishing Great
Men, though they could prove no other Crime
against them but that of being Great Men. This
Punishment was called the *Ostracism*, or the Sentence of a Majority in a Ballot by Oyster-Shells;
by which a suspected Citizen was adjudged to Ba-
nishment for Ten Years. They would not trust
to the Virtue and Moderation of any private Subject, capable, by being great, to be mischievous;
but would rather hurt a private Subject, than endanger the publick Liberty. Worthy Men are
thought to have suffered unjustly by this Ostracism; and it may be true, for aught that I know;
but still it secured the Publick, and long secured it.
Weak and babbling Men, who penetrate no deeper
than Words, may blame this politick Severity in
the Commonwealth of *Athens*; but it is justified,
in that it was politick.

In

In *Venice*, a wife, ancient, and honourable Republick, there is a Council of Ten, which exercifes this extraordinary Power: Every arbitrary Prince in the World exercifes it; and every free State in the World has an undoubted Right to exercife it, though they have never delegated their Power to particular Magiftrates to exercife it for them.

In *England*, indeed, we have not delegated this Power at all, becaufe we very well know who muft have had it, and what Ufe would be made of it. The Legiflature, therefore, has referved this Power to itfelf, and has an undoubted Right to exercife it; and has often done fo upon extraordinary Occafions. It ought indeed to be exercifed but upon extraordinary Occafions. *Jove*'s Thunderbolts were only launched againft fuch as provoked the Thunderbolts of *Jove*.

I fhall, in my next Letter to you, apply thefe general Maxims of Government to our own particular Conftitution, and to the prefent Occafion, which calls aloud for *Jove*'s Help and Thunder.

G

I am, &c.

SATUR-

SATURDAY, *January* 14, 1720.   No. 12.

Of Treason: All Treasons not to be found in Statutes.
—The right of the Legiflature to declare Treasons.

S I R,

TREASON, properly fo called, in *Latin*, *Crimen læfæ Majeftatis*, is in all Countries the fame: It is an Endeavour to fubvert, or to do fome notable Mifchief to the Publick; of which every Man is a Part, and with which he has joined himfelf for mutual Defence, under what Form foever the Adminiftration is exercifed. I own, that leffer Crimes are fometimes called by the fame Name, and fubjeéted to the fame Punifh-ment.

An Attempt to deftroy the Chief Magiftrate of a Commonwealth, or the General of an Army in the Field, or the Governor of a Town during a Siege, are certainly Treafons every where; be-caufe in fuch Attempts, when they fucceed, are often involved the Ruin of States. They alfo are doubtlefs guilty of High Treafon, who, being en-trufted with the Wealth, Security, and Happinefs of Kingdoms, do yet knowingly pervert that Truft, to the Undoing of that People whom they are obliged, by undeferved Rewards, as well as by all the Ties of Religion, Juftice, Honour, and Gratitude, to defend and proteét.

'Tis the fame, if any Number of Men, though in a leffer Truft, or in no Truft at all, fhould deliberately and knowingly deftroy Thoufands of
                                                        their

their Fellow-Subjects, and overturn the Trade
and publick Credit of the Nation, to enrich themfelves and their Accomplices.

These, and Crimes of the like Nature, are
Treasons from the Nature of Things themselves,
antecedent to all Laws that call them so ; and
will be Treasons, though Laws gained by Subor-
nation should call them otherwife : And every
State has a Right to treat those who commit them,
as Traytors and Parricides.   In Truth, there are
as many of these Kinds of Treasons, as there are
different Methods of confpiring against Kingdoms ; and the Criminals, though ever so Great,
deferve Death and Confifcation ; that is, they
ought to be deftroyed by the People whom they
would deftroy.

The great Principle of Self-Prefervation, which
is the firft and fundamental Law of Nature, calls
for this Procedure ;   the Security of Commonwealths depends upon it ;   the very Being of Government makes it neceffary ; and whatever is neceffary to the Publick Safety, is juft.

The Fate of Millions, and the Being of States,
muft not ftand and fall by the Diftinctions of
Monks, coined in Colleges, or by the Chicane of
Petty-Foggers ;   who would bring every thing
within the narrow Verge of their own Knowledge, under their own Jurifdiction and Cognizance ; and would determine all things by the
Rules of Inferior Judicatures, the Gibberifh of
private Practifers, and the Sayings of Old Women, or of thofe who are like Old Women ;
whofe Brains are addled by being long jumbled
and always turned round within the fcanty Circle
of private Courts, not daring to venture at a
                                                          bold

bold and free Thought out of them, however self-evident; like some Carriers Horses, that are used to a Track, and know not how to travel in an open Road.

But Questions of this Kind belong *ad aliud examen*, and ought to be brought before an higher Tribunal: The Legislature are the only proper and safe Judges: What is done against All, should be judged by All. Nor are their Resolutions to be confined by any other Rule than *Quid est utile, quid honestum*, general Justice, and the general Good. Religion, Virtue, common Sense, and the Publick Peace and Felicity, are the only Counsel to be admitted either for the Publick or the Prisoners.

The Conspirators against Mankind ought to know, that no Subterfuges, or Tergiversations; no knavish Subtilties, or Pedantic Quirks of Lawyers; no Evasions, no Skulkings behind known Statutes; no Combinations, or pretended Commissions, shall be able to skreen or protect them from publick Justice. They ought to know, that there is a Power in being that can follow them through all the dark Labyrinths and doubling Meanders; a Power that can crush them to pieces, though they change into all the Shapes of *Proteus*, to avoid the Fury of *Hercules*: a Power, confined by no Limitation, but that of publick Justice and the publick Good; a Power, that does not follow Precedents, but makes them; a Power, which has this for its Principle, that extraordinary Crimes ought not to be tried by ordinary Rules, and that unprecedented Villanies ought to have unprecedented Punishments.

But though in all Governments, this great Power must exist somewhere, yet it can rarely be delegated
gated

gated with Prudence to inferior Magiſtrates ; who, out of Ambition, Revenge, or Faction, or for Bribes and Preferments, or out of Fear and Flattery, or in Concert with the ill Meaſures or ſelfiſh Intrigues of Stateſmen, may pervert ſo dangerous a Truſt to the Deſtruction of thoſe whom it was intended to preſerve.

This particularly has been the Caſe of *England ;* We know by what Means Judges were often made, and from what Conduct they expected farther Preferment, and from whom they looked for Protection : For this Reaſon they were, and ought to be, confined in their Juriſdiction relating to Treaſon, and the Manner of Trying it.

Undoubtedly every Intention manifeſted by Act to deſtroy the Conſtitution and Government, was Treaſon by the Common Law of *England.* ——— But why do I ſay of *England,* ſince it is, and ever was, Treaſon in every Country throughout the World ? This Treaſon equally extends to thoſe, who would ſubvert either Houſe of Parliament, or the Rights and Privileges of the People, as to thoſe who attempt to deſtroy the Perſon of the King, or dethrone him. And indeed, what can be more abſurd, than to ſuppoſe it to be the higheſt Crime to attempt to deſtroy one Man, for no other Reaſon but that he is King; and yet not to ſuppoſe it the higheſt Crime to deſtroy that People for whoſe Benefit alone he was made King, and for whoſe Sake indeed there ever was ſuch a Thing in the World ?

But though this Propoſition was ſelf-evident, and muſt ever be aſſented to as ſoon as mentioned, yet, by the Flattery of Prieſts and ſervile Lawyers, the *Salus Populi,* or Security of the State, ſoon

came

came to fignify only the unbounded Power and
Sovereignty of the Prince ; and it became Treafon
to hinder One, conftituted, and grandly maintained out of the People's Labour and Wealth,
for the publick Safety, from deftroying the publick Safety. Our Anceftors found, by lamentable
Experience, that unworthy Men, preferred by
corrupt Minifters for unworthy Ends, made Treafons free only of the Court ; that the leaft Attempt to oppofe unlimited and unlawful Authority,
was often called Treafon ; and that the higheft
Treafons of all, which were thofe againft the
Commonwealth, might be committed with Impunity, Applaufe, and Rewards.

It was therefore high time to apply an adequate Remedy to an enormous Mifchief, which
ftruck at the whole State, and at the Fortunes
and Lives of every Subject in *England.* The Statute therefore of the 25th of *Edward* III. was
enacted, which enumerates the feveral Species or
Kinds of Treafons, which fhall continue to be
efteemed Treafons, and be adjudged fo by the
King's Juftices ; and are chiefly thofe which relate to the King's Perfon, his Family, and Dignity : Thefe the Parliament thought they might
fafely truft to the Examination of the King's
Judges, under fuch Limitations and Regulations
as the Act prefents.

But it is plain, from the fame Act, that they
did not intend to confine all Treafons to thofe recited there, becaufe it is declared in the following
Words, viz. *If any other Cafe fuppofed Treafon,
not before fpecified, fhall happen before any Juftices,
they fhall ftay Judgment, till the Caufe be fhewed be-*
fore

fore the Parliament, whether it ought to be judged Treafon or not.

So that here is a plain Declaration of the Legiflature (if any Man can poffibly think fuch a Declaration wanting) that other Crimes were Treafon, and ought to be punifhed as Treafon, (though not by the King's Judges) befides thofe recited in the Act; which were, as has been faid, defigned only to extend to Treafons which were committed againft our Lord the King, and his Royal Majefty, as the Act exprefly fays. And 'tis evident, from the whole Tenor of it, that it was intended purely to reftrain the unlimited and exorbitant Jurifdiction affumed by the King's Courts, in declaring Treafons, and facrificing by that Means, whom they pleafed to unlawful Power.

But as to the higheft and moft heinous Treafons of all, fuch as were Treafons againft the Legiflature, and againft the whole Body of the People, for whofe Safety alone there were any Treafons againft the King at all, feeing that their Safety was, in a great meafure, included in his; the Parliament referved the Judgment of every fuch Treafon to themfelves: They did not alter what was Treafon, but the Judges of it. They knew that Treafons againft the Conftitution could feldom be committed but by Minifters and Favourites of Princes, protected by Power, and fheltered by Authority; and that therefore it would be abfurd to truft the Punifhment of fuch potent Knaves, and criminal Favourites, to Judges made by themfelves; Judges, who would neither have Inclination, Figure, or Character, to reach Crimes coun-

tenanced

tenanced, and perhaps authorized, by a *Richard* II.
or *Edward* II.

Such Crimes, therefore, were the proper Objects of the awful Power of a Legiflature; who
will always be fupported by the People whom they
reprefent, when they exert themfelves for the Intereft of that People.   A Power, fo fupported,
can make the loftieft Traytor quake.   It can fetch
corrupt Minifters out of their dark Receffes, and
make their Heads a Victim to publick Vengeance.
Every wife and good King will lend a willing Ear
to their dutiful Remonftrances; he will hearken
to the importunate Cries of·his People, and readily deliver up the Authors of their Mifery.

One great Part of their Care, therefore, has
ever been, to call thofe to an Account, who have
abufed the Favour of their Royal Mafter, and endeavoured to make him little and contemptible to
his People; weakening, by fuch Means, his Authority, and hazarding his Perfon.   This the
People, whom they reprefented, thought they had
a Right to expect and demand from them; and
this Juftice they have often done to their King
and Country.

An excellent *Difcourfe concerning Treafons and
Bills of Attainder* was publifhed foon after his Majefty's Acceffion to the Throne, and fhewed un-
anfwerably, that our Parliaments, in almoft every
Reign fince the Conqueft, claimed and exercifed
this Right, upon extraordinary Occafions; and
none ever, till lately, oppofed it, but the Criminals who were to fuffer by it, and their Party:
Some Gentlemen now living can give the beft
Account, why that Book, and the Cries of every
                                          honeft

honeft Man, had not their defired Effect. I hope
that no Man will be deluded again by any practifing the fame Arts, and for the fame Reafons
too.

The Length of this Letter will not allow me
to draw from all thefe Reafonings upon Treafon
fuch Applications as I promifed in my laft, and
intended in this. I fhall therefore defer thefe Applications to another, and perhaps more proper,
Occafion. In the mean while, I obferve with
Pleafure the noble Spirit fhewn by our Legiflature,
to punifh, with an exemplary Severity, the Murtherers of our Credit, and the publick Enemies of
our Liberty and Profperity. This revives every
drooping Heart, and kindles Joy in every Face,
in fpite of all our Miferies. And this brings Terror, Trembling, and Palenefs upon the Guilty ;
to fee Death and Deftruction purfuing them clofe,
and befetting them hard on every Side. They
are in the Circumftances and the Agonies of the
guilty *Cain*, who juftly feared that every Man
whom he met would kill him, though there was
no Law then in being againft Murther.

T

I am, &c.

SATUR-

SATURDAY, *January* 21, 1720. No. 13.

The Arts of misleading the People by Sounds.

S I R,

IN surveying the State of the World, one is often at a great Loss, whether to ascribe the political Misery of Mankind to their own Folly and Credulity, or to the Knavery and Impudence of their pretended Managers. Both these Causes, in all Appearance, concur to produce the same Evil; and if there were no Bubbles, there would be no Sharpers.

There must certainly be a vast Fund of Stupidity in Human Nature, else Men would not be caught as they are, a Thousand times over, by the same Snare; and while they yet remember their past Misfortunes, go on to court and encourage the Causes to which they were owing, and which will again produce them.

I will own, however, that Government makes more Fools, and more wise Men, than Nature makes; and the Difference between Nation and Nation, in Point of Virtue, Sagacity, and Arms, arises not from the different Genius of the People; which, making very small Allowances for the Difference of Climate, would be the same under the same Regulations; but from the different Genius of their political Constitutions: The one, perhaps, making common Sense dangerous, and Enquiries criminal; cowing the Spirits of Men, and rebuking the Sallies of Virtue; while the other,

at

at the fame time, encourages the Improvement of the Underftanding, rewards the Difcovery of Truth, and cultivates, as a Virtue, the Love of Liberty and of one's Country.

Yet even in Countries where the higheft Liberty is allowed, and the greateft Light fhines, you generally find certain Men, and Bodies of Men, fet apart to miflead the Multitude; who are ever abufed with Words, ever fond of the worft of Things recommended by good Names, and ever abhor the beft Things, and the moft virtuous Actions, disfigured by ill Names. One of the great Arts, therefore, of cheating Men, is, to ftudy the Application and Mifapplication of Sounds—A few loud Words rule the Majority, I had almoft faid, the whole World.

Thus we have heard from our Fathers, and feen in our own Days, that contemptible Infects, born in Poverty, educated by Charity, and often from cleaning their Mafters Shoes, preferred unexpectedly and undefervedly to Offices and Preferments in the Church, have had the Front to call themfelves the Church itfelf, and every one its Enemy, who defpifed their Meannefs, expofed their reverend Knavery, and laughed at their Grimace.

And thus we have been told of the Times, and fome Men now living remember to have feen them, when unworthy Men, who, by Faction and Treachery, by mean Compliances with Power, or by infolently daring of Authority, having raifed themfelves to Wealth and Honours, and to the Power of betraying fome confiderable Truft, have had the provoking Sawcinefs to call themfelves the Government, and their own Rogueries his then Majefty's Meafures; and the next Thing was, to

pro-

pronounce all thofe Enemies to his then Majefty, who would endeavour to refcue their abufed King and finking Country out of their devouring and polluted Claws.

In King *Charles* I.'s Time, the great Earl of *Strafford* and little Archbifhop *Laud* told the Nation, that his Majefty's Meafures were, governing without Parliaments, a Power without Referve in the State, a flaming Popifh Hierarchy in the Church, abfolute and abject Submiffion in the People, and a Barbarian Army of *Irifh* Papifts to fupport and infure all thefe worthy Meafures. But the untimely Death of one of thefe Offenders, and the Imprifonment of the other, broke all thofe fine Meafures.

In the Reign of *Charles* II. Penfionary Parliaments, a general Depravation of Manners, Guards increafed into Armies, and Popifh Religion and a Popifh Succeffor, Popifh Leagues and Proteftant Wars, were called by wicked Men his Majefty's Meafures ; and all honeft Men and good Subjects were called his Majefty's Enemies : And, when that Prince faw that thefe Meafures of his Miniftry created endlefs Jealoufies to his People, and endlefs Uneafinefs to himfelf, and when he refolved to take other Meafures of his own, it is thought that they put a fhort End to all his Meafures.

When King *James* came to the Crown, though, fetting Bigotry apart, he had fome Royal Virtues, being a Prince of Induftry and good Œconomy ; yet he fuffered himfelf to be governed by a Set of Sycophants, many of them as foolifh as they were mifchievous. The Eftablifhment of bare-faced *Romifh* Popery in the Church, and a lawlefs Ty-

ranny

ranny in the Prince, became then his Majefty's
Meafures ; the Minifters, who advifed and promoted them, called themfelves the *Government* ;
and whoever oppofed his Reafon, his Honefty,
and his publick Spirit, againft thofe Traytors to
the Publick, was charged with flying in the Face
of the Government, and oppofing his Majefty's
Meafures. In what thefe Meafures ended, is well
known : They coft his Majefty his Kingdoms,
and made him an honourable Beggar in *France* all
his Life for his daily Bread.

King *William*, when he came to the Crown,
brought with him the Hearts, and Hands, and
the good Wifhes of every honeft Man in *England* ;
and was fupported by thefe Men through a tedious
and expenfive War, unknown to our Anceftors ;
which, when he had finifhed, and the exhaufted
People expected fome Relaxations from their Sufferings, they were given to know by fome Court
Parafites that his Majefty's Meafures was a ftanding Army in Time of Peace, under the Infpection
of Parliaments. This unexpected Spirit in the
Court gave fuch Jealoufy to thofe who were beft
affected to his Majefty's Perfon and Government,
that with Grief I call to mind the Difficulties and
Anxieties which that great Prince felt ever afterwards to the End of his Reign.

As to Queen *Anne*, I fhall fay no more, than
that it is fhrewdly fufpected, that what her Majefty's Miniftry had the Infolence to call *Her Majefty's Meafures, broke her Majefty's Heart.*

Let Mankind therefore learn Experience from
fo many Misfortunes, and bear no longer to hear
the worft Things called by the beft Names ; nor
fuffer hereafter the brighteft and moft confpicuous
Virtues

Virtues of the wifeft and moft beneficent Princes, to be fullied by Actions which they do not countenance, nor even know of. Let them not permit the Vices of the worft of Servants to be laid at the Door of the beft of Mafters.

We, in this Land, are very fure that we are bleffed with the beft King in the World, who defires of his People nothing but their own Greatnefs and Felicity: A Prince, ready to prevent their Wifhes, and to give them more than their Duty ought to fuffer them to afk. Let us fhew our Duty to this our great and benevolent Sovereign; let us endeavour to alleviate his Cares, and eafe him of all ungrateful Burthens; let us take upon ourfelves the heavy Labour of cleanfing the *Augean* Stables, and of cutting off all the *Hydra*'s Heads at once.

The Law tells us, that the King can do no Wrong: And, I thank God, we have a King that would not, if he could. But the greateft Servants to Princes may do Wrong, and often have done it; and the Reprefentatives of the People have an undoubted Right to call them to an Account for it.

In Truth, every private Subject has a Right to watch the Steps of thofe who would betray their Country; nor is he to take their Word about the Motives of their Defigns, but to judge of their Defigns by the Event.

This is the Principle of a *Whig*, this the Doctrine of Liberty; and 'tis as much Knavery to deny this Doctrine, as it is Folly to ridicule it. Some will tell us, that this is fetting up the Mob for Statefmen, and for the Cenfurers of States. The Word *Mob* does not at all move me, on this
Occa-

Occafion, nor weaken the Grounds which I go upon. It is certain, that the whole People, who are the Publick, are the beft Judges, whether Things go ill or well with the Publick. It is true, that they cannot all of them fee diftant Dangers, nor watch the Motions, and guefs the Defigns, of neighbouring States: But every Cobler can judge, as well as a Statefman, whether he can fit peaceably in his Stall; whether he is paid for his Work; whether the Market, where he buys his Victuals, be well provided; and whether a Dragoon, or a Parifh-Officer, comes to him for his Taxes, if he pay any.

Every Man too, even the meaneft, can fee, in a publick and fudden Tranfition from Plenty to Poverty, from Happinefs to Diftrefs, whether the Calamity comes from War, and Famine, and the Hand of God; or from Oppreffion, and Mifmanagement, and the Villainies of Men. In fhort, the People often judge better than their Superiors, and have not fo many Biaffes to judge wrong; and Politicians often rail at the People, chiefly becaufe they have given the People Occafion to rail: Thofe Minifters who cannot make the People their Friends, it is to be fhrewdly fufpected, do not deferve their Friendfhip; it is certain, that much Honefty, and fmall Management, rarely mifs to gain it. As Temporal Felicity is the whole End of Government; fo People will always be pleafed or provoked, as that increafes or abates. This Rule will always hold. You may judge of their Affection, or Difaffection, by the Burthens which they bear, and the Advantages which they enjoy. Here then is a fure Standard for the Government

vernment to judge of the People, and for the People to judge of the Government.

Bleſſed be God, and Thanks to our Sovereign, who has given us a Miniſtry that makes all theſe Cautions unneceſſary; who will baffle all Calumny, and remove all Suſpicion of Guilt from themſelves, (if any ſuch Suſpicion can be) by being foremoſt to purſue the Guilty; and will, doubtleſs, take double Vengeance upon any in publick Authority, (if any ſuch can be found) who ſhall appear to have contributed to our publick Misfortunes; and, in fine, will promote and encourage a rigorous and ſtrict Enquiry, wherever any Suſpicion is given that Enquiry ought to be made.

Such Conduct will diſperſe our Fears, reſtore our Credit, give Bread to our Poor, make Trade and Manufacture flouriſh again; and, in ſome meaſure, compenſate for all our paſt Evils, by giving us a laſting Proſpect of our future Plenty, Peace, and Felicity.

　　T　　　　　　　　　　　　　　*I am,* &c.

SATURDAY, *January* 28, 1720.　No. 14.

The unhappy State of deſpotick Princes, compared with the happy Lot of ſuch as rule by ſettled Laws. — How the latter, by abuſing their Truſt, may forfeit their Crown.

S I R,

THE beſt, the wiſeſt, and the moſt courageous of deſpotick Princes, have frequently lamented the unhappy Condition into which their Greatneſs
　　　　　　　　　　　　　　　　　　　　betrayed

betrayed them. Being often born in Purple, and educated in Pride and Luxury, they feldom can have any Feeling of the Calamities which the reft of the World fuffer. They are, befides, furrounded, for the moft part, by the falfeft, the moft ambitious, and the bafeft of all Men ; with fuch Mens Eyes they muft therefore fee, with fuch Mens Ears they muft likewife hear.

I cannot, in Truth, fee how, in the Nature of Things, it can be otherwife: For the mean Fawning, the fervile Flatteries, the deceitful Correfpondences, the bafe Ingratitude to old Benefactors, and the flavifh Compliances with new Friends, and all the other Arts and Treacheries, which are neceffary to be put in Practice, in order to rife in fuch Courts, or indeed to become Heads of Parties even in free Governments, make it almoft impoffible for a truly great or virtuous Man to attain to thofe Stations.

A good Man will chufe to live in an innocent Obfcurity, and enjoy the internal Satisfaction refulting from a juft Senfe of his own Merit, and Virtue, rather than aim at Greatnefs, by a long Series of unworthy Arts, and ignoble Actions; whilft the ambitious, the cruel, the rapacious, the falfe, the proud, the treacherous Part of Mankind, will be ever thrufting themfelves forward, and endeavouring to fparkle in Courts, as well as in the Eyes of the unthinking Crowd ; and, to make themfelves neceffary, will be continually either flattering or diftreffing Princes.

Nor can it be expected that Men, who have been raifed to Power by fuch execrable Means, fhould ever ufe it to the Benefit of Mankind, or to any good End. They will always proceed in
the

the fame Steps where they began; and use, for the Support of their Greatnefs, the fame vile Meafures by which they acquired their Greatnefs, till they have at length facrificed all Things in Heaven and Earth to their Ambition.

There is a fine Paffage, to this Purpofe, in the fhort Hiftory of the Emperor *Aurelian* by *Vopifcus* : *Et quæritur quidem quæ res malos principes faciat : Jam primum, Licentia, deinde Rerum Copia, Amici improbi, Satellites deteftandi, Eunuchi avariffimi, Aulici vel Stulti vel et Deteftabiles, & (quod negari non poteft) rerum publicarum Ignorantia. Sed ego a Patre meo audivi, Dioclefianum principem, jam privatum, dixiffe, nihil effe difficilius quam bene imperare. Collegunt fe quatuor vel quinque, atque unum confilium ad decipiendum principem capiunt: Dicunt quod probandum fit. Imperator, qui domi claufus eft, vera non novit. Cogitur hoc tantum fcire quod illi loquuntur : Facit Judices quos fieri non oportet ; amovet a Republica quos debebat obtinere. Quid multa ? Ut Dioclefianus ipfe dicebat, bonus, cautus, optimus venditur Imperator.* Hiftor. Auguft. Scriptor. Tom. II. p. 531, 532.

" My Friends, (fays the great Emperor *Dio-*
" *clefian*, to thofe who advifed him to refume the
" Empire) you little know how difficult an Un-
" dertaking it is to perform the Duty of a *Roman*
" Emperor, and to reign well. The few who
" have Accefs to him, will cabal and confpire to-
" gether, and unite in their Counfels to deceive
" and betray him. They will ftudy how to flat-
" ter him, and never tell him what it is their
" Duty to tell him, and what is his Intereft to
" know ; but only what they think will beft pleafe
" him. They will fhut him up, and, as it were,
                                    " imprifon

" imprifon him in his Palace ; and no one fhall
" be admitted to his Ear, but by their Leave,
" and in their Prefence. So that he fhall never
" know the Condition of his Affairs, or be in-
" formed of the Cries of his People, or, indeed,
" of any thing but what they think fit to tell him.
" By their Means he fhall prefer undeferving Men
" to the beft Pofts of the Empire, and difgrace
" the moft worthy of his Subjects, and the moft
" devoted to his Intereft. But why fhould I la-
" bour this Point any more, when even the good,
" the moft difcerning, when the beft and ableft
" Emperors are bought and fold ?

But *Dioclefian* was an arbitrary Prince, whofe
Will was a Law to his Subjects. But it is far
otherwife in limited Monarchies, where the Prince
governs his People by fixed Rules and known Statutes ; and where his faithful States have a Right
to reprefent freely, though humbly, their Grievances to him, and by his Authority to call to Account, and punifh, fuch Betrayers as are before
defcribed.

Happy therefore is that Prince, happy in the
Love of his Subjects, happy in the juft Applaufe
and dutiful Acknowledgment of Millions of his
Fellow-Creatures, who derive their Felicity from
him ! Thrice happy is that People, where the
Conftitution is fo poifed and tempered, and the
Adminiftration fo difpofed and divided into proper
Channels, that the Paffions and Infirmities of the
Prince cannot enter into the Meafures of his Go-
vernment ; where he has in his Power all the
Means of doing Good, and none of doing Ill ;
where all beneficent and gracious Actions are
owned to flow from his Clemency and Goodnefs,
and

and where inferior Machines are anfwerable for all fuch Conduct as may prejudice the Publick.

Such a Government does, in fome Senfe, refemble that of Heaven itfelf, where the Sovereign Difpofer of all Things can neither will nor do any thing but what is juft and good: He is reftrained, by the Excellency of his own Nature, from being the Author of Evil; and will call to a fevere Account all thofe, who would impute their own Unrighteoufnefs to his Orders or Influence.

Such is the Monarchy of *England*, where the Sovereign performs every Act of his Regal Office by his Authority, without the Fatigue and Anxiety of executing the troublefome Parts of it in his Perfon. The Laws are chofen and recommended to him by his Parliament; and afterwards executed by his Judges, and other Minifters of Juftice: His Great Seal is kept by his Chancellor: His Naval Power is under the Direction of his High Admiral: And all Acts of State and Difcretion are prefumed to be done by the Advice of his Council. All which Officers are anfwerable for their Mifbehaviour, and for all Actions done within their feveral Provinces, which they have advifed or could have prevented by giving their Advice, or by making timely and humble Remonftrances; which they are obliged to fhew that they have done.

His Leagues, his Commands, and even his authentick Speeches, are Records. His High Office confifts in approving Laws chofen by common Confent; in executing thofe Laws, and in being the publick Guardian of the publick Safety: And all private Orders, which are inconfiftent with thefe great Duties, are not the Orders of the Crown;

nor

nor are the Actions done in purfuance of them,
the Actions of the King, but the Actions of thofe
that do them.   He can do no Wrong himfelf, nor
give Authority to any one elfe to do Wrong. Every
Act of his muft be lawful, becaufe all unlawful
Acts are not his.   He can give no Commands, as
a Man, which fhall interfere with thofe which he
gives as a King.   His private Will cannot controul
his publick Will.   He commands, as a King, his
Chancellor, and Judges, to act according to his
known Laws; and no private Orders to do otherwife can be valid.

The Nation has ever acted upon thefe Maxims,
and preferved fuch a dutiful Refpect to the Royal
Majefty, as never to fuffer any Guilt to be laid to
him; but has always heaped double Vengeance
upon fuch Mifcreants as would infinuate, that their
Crimes were approved or countenanced by their
Royal Mafter.

Here is all the Precaution which can be taken
by human Wifdom to make a happy Prince and
a happy People.   The Prince is reftrained in nothing, but from doing Mifchief to his Subjects, and
confequently to himfelf; their true Intereft being
ever the fame: And the People can never have
any Motive to refufe juft Allegiance to their Prince,
whilft the Ligaments of the Conftitution are preferved entire; that is, whilft Parliaments are fuffered to meet, and the Courts of Juftice remain
open, and fuch Force is not ufed againft them as
diffolves all Relation.   All the Subjects of fuch a
Prince highly honour, and almoft worfhip, him.
He has a vaft Revenue to fupport the Splendor and
Magnificence of his Court at Home, and his Royal
Dignity Abroad: He has the Power of difpofing
of

of all Offices : All Honours flow from him : His Perfon is facred, and not anfwerable for any Events : He cannot be accountable for any Wrong, which he is incapable of doing ; and thofe who do it, fhall be punifhed by his Authority, even though it be fuppofed poffible that they could, by falfe Mifreprefentations, deceive him far enough to approve it.

The Examples of *Richard* II. who, as our Hiftories tell us, was depofed by the States of his Kingdom; and of the late King *James*, are no Inftances to difprove the Truth of this Affertion : For neither of them was depofed by his People before he firft depofed himfelf. No Champions for Tyranny, or Dogmatizers for unlimited Dominion, have yet afferted, that a Prince may not refign his Crown by the Confent of his People, when he declines to hold it any longer upon the Conditions on which he firft accepted it.

Suppofe a Prince, in any limited Monarchy, fhould make a publick Declaration to the States of his Kingdom, That, " Whereas the Crown de-
" fcended to him by the Laws of that Country,
" and that all the Power which he was poffeffed
" of was conferred upon him by thofe Laws ;
" That he well knew that the Prefervation of
" thofe Laws, which he had fworn to obferve,
" and the general Good of his People, were the
" fole Confiderations of his enjoying that high
" Dignity ; and yet, notwithftanding, he refufed
" to hold it any longer, upon the Terms upon
" which he had firft accepted it, and fworn to
" obferve ; but that he now renounced that Title,
" and would govern them hereafter by his fole
" Will and Pleafure :" I fay, if any fhould do
this,

this, the Advocates for lawlefs Power would do
well to tell us, whether fuch a Prince did not make
as effctual a Renunciaticn and Refignation of his
Government, as if he difabled himfelf, and refigned it for his Eafe, or from the Satiety of.Power.
And if they allow that he may do all this by Words
fpoken to exprefs his Intentions, I fhould be glad
to know, from thefe Men of Diftinctions, why he
may not do it by a Series of Actions, which will
more effectually difcover and, declare his inward
Intentions, and may therefore be more depended
on than any Words can poffibly be ?

I call upon the Two famous Univerfities of this
Land for an Anfwer: And, till I have a full one,
fhall continue to believe, that what was done, in
regard to the Abdication of the late King *James*,
was juft and neceffary to be done upon the fundamental Principles of Government ; and, that all
his Succeffors fince have been rightful and lawful
Kings and Queens of this Realm ; and I particularly glory to fay, that no Prince has ever better
deferved that high Title, than our prefent great
and glorious Sovereign, King *George*.

   T

I am, &c.

SATUR-

SATURDAY, *February* 4, 1720. No. 15.

*Of Freedom of Speech : That the same is inseparable
from Publick Liberty.*

S I R,

WITHOUT Freedom of Thought, there
can be no such Thing as Wisdom ; and no
such Thing as publick Liberty, without Freedom
of Speech : Which is the Right of every Man, as
far as by it he does not hurt and controul the Right
of another ; and this is the only Check which it
ought to suffer, the only Bounds which it ought to
know.

This sacred Privilege is so essential to free Government, that the Security of Property ; and the
Freedom of Speech, always go together ; and in
those wretched Countries where a Man cannot
call his Tongue his own, he can scarce call any
Thing else his own.   Whoever would overthrow
the Liberty of the Nation, must begin by subduing
the Freedom of Speech ; a Thing terrible to publick Traytors.

This Secret was so well known to the Court
of King *Charles* I. that his wicked Ministry procured a Proclamation to forbid the People to talk
of Parliaments, which those Traytors had laid
aside.   To assert the undoubted Right of the Subject, and defend his Majesty's Legal Prerogative,
was called Disaffection, and punished as Sedition.   Nay, People were forbid to talk of Religion in their Families: For the Priests had
                                                combined

combined with the Minifters to cook up Tyranny, and fupprefs Truth and the Law. While the late King *James*, when Duke of *York*, went avowedly to Mafs ; Men were fined, imprifoned, and undone, for faying that he was a Papift : And, that King *Charles* II. might live more fecurely a Papift, there was an Act of Parliament made, declaring it Treafon to fay that he was one.

That Men ought to fpeak well of their Governors, is true, while their Governors deferve to be well fpoken of ; but to do publick Mifchief, without hearing of it, is only the Prerogative and Felicity of Tyranny : A free People will be fhewing that they are fo, by their Freedom of Speech.

The Adminiftration of Government is nothing elfe, but the Attendance of the Truftees of the People upon the Intereft and Affairs of the People. And as it is the Part and Bufinefs of the People, for whofe Sake alone all publick Matters are, or ought to be, tranfacted, to fee whether they be well or ill tranfacted ; fo it is the Intereft, and ought to be the Ambition, of all honeft Magiftrates, to have their Deeds openly examined, and publickly fcanned : Only the wicked Governors of Men dread what is faid of them ; *Audivit* Tiberius *probra queis lacerabitur, atque* perculfus eft. The publick Cenfure was true, elfe he had not felt it bitter.

Freedom of Speech is ever the Symptom, as well as the Effect, of good Government. In old *Rome*, all was left to the Judgment and Pleafure of the People ; who examined the publick Proceedings with fuch Difcretion, and cenfured thofe who adminiftered them with fuch Equity and Mildnefs, that in the Space of Three Hundred Years, not

Five

Five publick Ministers suffered unjustly. Indeed, whenever the Commons proceeded to Violence, the Great Ones had been the Aggressors.

Guilt only dreads Liberty of Speech, which drags it out of its lurking Holes, and exposes its Deformity and Horror to Day-light. *Horatius, Valerius, Cincinnatus,* and other virtuous and un-designing Magistrates of the *Roman* Common-wealth, had nothing to fear from Liberty of Speech. Their virtuous Administration, the more it was examined, the more it brightened and gained by Enquiry. When *Valerius,* in particu-lar, was accused, upon some slight Grounds, of affecting the Diadem ; he, who was the first Mi-nister of *Rome,* did not accuse the People for exa-mining his Conduct, but approved his Innocence in a Speech to them ; he gave such Satisfaction to them, and gained such Popularity to himself, that they gave him a new Name ; *inde cognomen factum Publicolæ est* ; to denote that he was their Favou-rite and their Friend.—*Latæ deinde leges.*—*Ante omnes de provocatione, ADVERSUS MAGI-STRATUS AD POPULUM,* Livii lib. ii. cap. 8.

But Things afterwards took another Turn : *Rome,* with the Loss of its Liberty, lost also its Freedom of Speech ; then Mens Words began to be feared and watched ; then first began the poi-sonous Race of Informers, banished indeed under the righteous Administration of *Titus, Nerva, Trajan, Aurelius,* &c. but encouraged and enriched under the vile Ministry of *Sejanus, Tigellinus, Pal-las,* and *Cleander : Querilibet, quod in secreta nostra non inquirant principes, nisi quos odimus,* says *Pliny* to *Trajan.*

The

The beft Princes have ever encouraged and promoted Freedom of Speech ; they knew that upright Meafures would defend themfelves, and that all upright Men would defend them. *Tacitus*, fpeaking of the Reigns of fome of the Princes above-mention'd, fays with Extafy, *Rara temporum felicitate, ubi fentire quæ velis, & quæ fentias dicere liceat :* A bleffed Time, when you might think what you would, and fpeak what you thought !

The fame was the Opinion and Practice of the wife and virtuous *Timoleon*, the Deliverer of the great City of *Syracufe* from Slavery. He being accufed by *Demœnetus*, a popular Orator, in a full Affembly of the People, of feveral Mifdemeanors committed by him while he was General, gave no other Anfwer, than that *He was highly obliged to the Gods for granting him a Requeft that he had often made to them* ; namely, *That he might live to fee the* Syracufians *enjoy that Liberty of Speech which they now feemed to be Mafters of.*

And that great Commander, *M. Marcellus*, who won more Battles than any *Roman* Captain of his Age, being accufed by the *Syracufians*, while he was now a fourth Time Conful, of having done them Indignities and hoftile Wrongs, contrary to the League, rofe from his Seat in the Senate, as foon as the Charge againft him was opened, and paffing (as a private Man) into the Place where the Accufed were wont to make their Defence, gave free Liberty to the *Syracufians* to impeach him : Which, when they had done, he and they went out of the Court together to attend the Iffue of the Caufe : Nor did he exprefs the leaft Ill-will or Refentment towards thefe his Accufers ; but

being

being acquitted, received their City into his Protection: Had he been guilty, he would neither have shewn such Temper nor Courage.

I doubt not but old *Spencer* and his Son, who were the chief Ministers and Betrayers of *Edward*. II. would have been very glad to have stopped the Mouths of all the honest Men in *England*. They dreaded to be called Traytors, because they were Traytors. And I dare say, Queen *Elizabeth's Walsingham*, who deserved no Reproaches, feared none. Misrepresentation of publick Measures is easily overthrown, by representing publick Measures truly : When they are honest, they ought to be publickly known, that they may be publickly commended ; but if they be knavish or pernicious, they ought to be publickly exposed, in order to be publickly detested.

To assert, that King *James* was a Papist and a Tyrant, was only so far hurtful to him, as it was true of him ; and if the Earl of *Strafford* had not deserved to be impeached, he need not have feared a Bill of Attainder. If our Directors and their Confederates be not such Knaves as the World thinks them, let them prove to all the World, that the World thinks wrong, and that they are guilty of none of those Villainies which all the World lays to their Charge. Others too, who would be thought to have no Part of their Guilt, must, before they are thought innocent, shew that they did all that was in their Power to prevent that Guilt, and to check their Proceedings.

Freedom of Speech is the great Bulwark of Liberty ; they prosper and die together : And it is the Terror of Traytors and Oppressors, and a Barrier against them. It produces excellent Writers,

ters, and encourages Men of fine Genius. *Tacitus* tells us, that the *Roman* Commonwealth bred great and numerous Authors, who writ with equal Boldnefs and Eloquence : But when it was enflaved, thofe great Wits were no more.—*Poftquam bellatum apud Aĉtium ; atque omnem poteftatem ad unum conferri pacis interfuit, magna illa ingenia ceffere.* Tyranny had ufurped the Place of Equality, which is the Soul of Liberty, and deftroyed publick Courage. The Minds of Men, terrified by unjuft Power, degenerated into all the Vilenefe and Methods of Servitude : Abjeĉt Sycophancy and blind Submiffion grew the only Means of Preferment, and indeed of Safety ; Men durft not open their Mouths, but to flatter.

Pliny the Younger obferves, that this Dread of Tyranny had fuch Effeĉt, that the Senate, the great *Roman* Senate, became at laft ftupid and dumb : *Mutam ac fedentariam affentiendi neceffitatem.* Hence, fays he, our Spirit and Genius are ftupified, broken, and funk for ever. And in one of his Epiftles, fpeaking of the Works of his Uncle, he makes an Apology for eight of them, as not written with the fame Vigour which was to be found in the reft ; for that thefe eight were written in the Reign of *Nero*, when the Spirit of Writing was cramped by Fear; *Dubii fermonis oĉto fcripfit fub* Nerone—*cum omne ftudiorum genus paulo liberiùs & ereĉtius periculofum fervitus feciffet.*

All Minifters, therefore, who were Oppreffors, or intended to be Oppreffors, have been loud in their Complaints againft Freedom of Speech, and the Licence of the Prefs ; and always reftrained, or endeavoured to reftrain, both. In confequence of this, they have brow-beaten Writers, punifhed

them

them violently, and againſt Law, and burnt their
Works. By all which they ſhewed how much
Truth alarmed them, and how much they were
at Enmity with Truth.

There is a famous Inſtance of this in *Tacitus :*
He tells us, that *Cremutius Cordus*, having in his
Annals praiſed *Brutus* and *Caſſius*, gave Offence to
Sejanus, Firſt Miniſter, and to ſome inferior Sycophants in the Court of *Tiberius* ; who, conſcious
of their own Characters, took the Praiſe beſtowed
on every worthy *Roman*, to be ſo many Reproaches
pointed at themſelves : They therefore complain
of the Book to the Senate ; which, being now
only the Machine of Tyranny, condemned it to
be burnt.   But this did not prevent its ſpreading.
—*Libros cremandos cenſuere Patres* ; *ſed manſerunt
occultati & editi :* Being cenſured, it was the more
ſought after.   *From hence, ſays Tacitus, we may
wonder at the Stupidity of thoſe Stateſmen, who hope
to extinguiſh, by the Terror of their Power, the Memory of their Actions* ; for quite otherwiſe, *the Puniſhment of good Writers gains Credit to their Writings : Nam contra, punitis ingeniis, gliſcit auctori-
tas.* Nor did ever any Government, who practiſed
impolitick Severity, get any thing by it, but Infamy to themſelves, and Renown to thoſe who
ſuffered under it.   This alſo is an Obſervation of
*Tacitus : Neque aliud reges, qui ea ſævitiæ uſi ſunt,
niſi dedecus ſibi, atque gloriam illis peperere.*

Freedom of Speech, therefore, being of ſuch
infinite Importance to the Preſervation of Liberty,
every one who loves Liberty ought to encourage
Freedom of Speech.   Hence it is that I, living in
a Country of Liberty, and under the beſt Prince
upon Earth, ſhall take this very favourable Opportunity

tunity of ferving Mankind, by warning them of
the hideous Mifchiefs that they will fuffcr, if ever
corrupt and wicked Men fhall hereafter get Poffeffion of any State, and the Power of betraying
their Mafter: And, in order to do this, I will
fhew them by what Steps they will probably proceed to accomplifh their traiterous Ends. This
may be the Subject of my next.

Valerius Maximus tells us, that *Lentulus Mar-
cellinus*, the *Roman* Conful, having complained, in
a popular Affembly, of the overgrown Power of
Pompey ; the whole People anfwered him with a
Shout of Approbation : Upon which the Conful
told them, *Shout on, Gentlemen, fhout on, and ufe
thofe bold Signs of Liberty while you may ; for I do
not know who long they will be allowed you.*

God be thanked, we *Englifhmen* have neither
loft our Liberties, nor are in Danger of lofing
them. Let us always cherifh this matchlefs Bleffing, almoft peculiar to ourfelves ; that our Pofterity may, many Ages hence, afcribe their Freedom to our Zeal. The Defence of Liberty is a
noble, a heavenly Office ; which can only be performed where Liberty is : For, as the fame *Valerius Maximus* obferves, *Quid ergo Libertas fine*
Catone ? *Non magis quam* Cato *fine Libertate.*

G   *I am,* &c.

SATURDAY, *February* 11, 1720. No. 16.

*The Leaders of Parties, their usual Views.—Advice
to all Parties to be no longer misled.*

S I R,

THE wife *Sancho Pancha* defired that his Subjects, in the promifed Ifland, might be all
Blacks, becaufe he would fell them. And this
feems to be the firft modeft, and, as I think, the
only reafonable Defire of the Leaders of all Parties ; for no Man will be at the Expence and Fatigue of Body and Confcience, which is neceffary
to lead a Faction, only to be difturbed and annoyed by them.

A very great Authority * has told us, that
'*Tis worth no Man's Time to ferve a Party, unlefs he
can now and then get good Jobbs by it.* This, I can
fafely fay, has been the conftant Principle and
Practice of every leading Patriot, ever fince I have
been capable of obferving publick Tranfactions ;
the *primum Mobile,* the *Alpha* and *Omega* of all
their Actions : They all profeffed to have in View
only the Publick Good ; yet every one fhewed he
only meant his own ; and all the while the great
as well as little Mob, the *procerum turba Mobi-
lium,* contended as fiercely for their Leaders, as if
their Happinefs or Mifery depended upon the Face,
the Cloaths, or Title of the Perfons who robbed
and betrayed them.   Thus the Highwayman

* This was faid to have been fpoken by a certain
Lord Chancellor in former Times.

faid

faid to the Traveller, *Pray, Sir, leave your Watch
and Money in my Hands* ; *or elfe, by G—, you will
be robbed.*

Pound a Fool in a Mortar, and he comes out
never the wifer ; no Experience will make the
Bulk of Mankind fo, or put them upon their
Guard ; they will be caught over and over again
by the fame Baits and ftale Stratagems : No fooner
is a Party betrayed by one Head, but they rail at
him, and fet up another ; and when this has ferved
them in the fame Manner, they choofe a Third ;
and put full Confidence in every one of them fucceffively, though they all make the fame Ufe of
their Credulity ; that is, put a Price upon their
Calves Heads, and fell them ; which, however,
they have the lefs Reafon to complain of, becaufe
they would have all done the fame.

I affure you, Sir, that I have not the leaft
Hopes in this Letter to make Men honefter, but
I would gladly teach them a little more Wit ;
that is, I would advife any one who is contented
to be fold, that he receive the Money himfelf,
and take good Care of One, whatever becomes
of his Neighbours ; as fome difcreet Perfons have
lately done. Whatever Bargains are ftruck up
amongft the Betrayers of their Country, we muft
find the Money, and pay both Sides. How wife
and advantageous would it then be for us, not to
intereft ourfelves in the Agreements or Squabbles
of ambitious Men, who are building their Fortunes upon our Ruin ? Once upon a Time, a
French Embaffador defired an Audience of the
Grand Vizier, and in pompous *French* Fuftian no-
tified to him, that his Mafter had won a great
Victory over the *Germans* ; to which that wife
Minifter

Minifter anfwered laconically, *What is it to me,
if the whole Herd of Unbelievers, like Dogs, mutually worry one another, fo that my Mafter's Head be
fafe ?*

This Letter of Advice is not intended for thofe
who fhare already in the publick Spoils, or who,
like Jackalls, hunt down the Lion's Prey, that
they may have the picking of the Bones, when
their Mafters are glutted.   But I would perfuade
the poor, the injured, the diftreffed People, to be
no longer the Dupes and Property of Hypocrites
and Traytors.   But very few can fhare in the
Wages of Iniquity, and all the reft muft fuffer ;
the People's Intereft is the publick Intereft ; it
fignifies the fame Thing : Whatever thefe Betrayers of their Country get, the People muft lofe ;
and, what is worfe, muft lofe a great deal more
than the others can get ; for fuch Confpiracies and
Extortions cannot be fuccefsfully carried on, without deftroying or injuring Trade, perverting Juftice, corrupting the Guardians of the publick Liberty, and the almoft total Diffolution of the
Principles of Government.

Few can receive the Advantages arifing from
publick Misfortunes ; and therefore methinks few
fhould defire them.   Indeed, I can eafily fee how
Men of defperate Circumftances, or Men guilty
of defperate Crimes, can find their Account in a
general Confufion of all Things.   I can fee how
thofe Priefts, who aim at Tyranny, can find their
Intereft in the Lofs of publick Liberty, in the
Reftraint of the Prefs, and in introducing a Religion which deftroys Chriftianity : There are Reafons too at hand, why ambitious Men fhould, *per
fas & nefas,* grafp at the Poffeffion of immenfe
Wealth,

Wealth, high Honours, and exorbitant Power: But that the Gentry, the Body of the People in a free Nation, fhould become the Tools and Inftruments of Knaves and Pick-pockets; fhould lift themfelves in their Quarrels, and fight their Battles; and this too, often at the Expence, and by the Violation of good Neighbourhood, near Relation, private Friendfhip: That Men of great Eftates and Quality, for fmall and trifling Confiderations, and fometimes none at all, fhould promote wild, villainous Projects, to the Ruin of themfelves and Country, by making precarious their own Titles to their Lives, Eftates, and Liberties, is fomething fo ftupendous, that it muft be thought impoffible, if daily Experience did not convince us that it is more than poffible.

I have often feen honeft *Tories* foolifhly defending knavifh *Tories*; and untainted *Whigs* protecting corrupt *Whigs*, even in Inftances where they acted againft the Principles of all *Whigs*; and by that Means depreciated *Whiggifm* itfelf, and gave the ftupid Herd Occafion to believe that they had no Principles at all, but were only a factious Combination for Preferment and Power.

It is high Time, at laft, for the Bubbles of all Parties, for *Whigs* and *Tories*, for High Church and Low Church, to come to an *Eclairciffement*, and no longer fuffer themfelves to be bought and fold by their Drivers: Let them ceafe to be Calves and Sheep, and they will not be ufed like Calves and Sheep. If they can be perfuaded now and then to confer Notes, they will find, that for the moft part the Differences between them are not material; that they take only different Meafures to attain the fame Ends; that they have

but

but one common Interest, which is the Interest of their Country ; and that is, to be freed from Oppreſſion, and to puniſh their Oppreſſors : Whoſe Practice, on the contrary, will always be to form Parties, and blow up Factions to mutual Animoſities, that they may find Protection in thoſe Animoſities.

Let us not therefore, for the Time to come, ſuffer ourſelves to be engaged in empty and pernicious Contentions ; which can only tend to make us the Property and Harveſt of Pickpockets : Let us learn to value an honeſt Man of another Party, more than a Knave of our own : Let the only Contention be, who ſhall be moſt ready to ſpew out their own Rogues ; and I will be anſwerable that all other Differences will ſoon be at an End. Indeed, there had been no ſuch Thing as Party now in *England*, if we had not been betrayed by thoſe whom we truſted.

Through the Villainy and knaviſh Deſigns of Leaders, this Nation has loſt ſeveral glorious Opportunities of reſcuing the Conſtitution, and ſettling it upon a firm and ſolid Baſis : Let us not therefore, by the like Practices, loſe the preſent favourable Offer : Let us make Earnings of our Misfortunes, and accept our Calamities as an Opportunity thrown into our Laps by indulgent Providence, to ſave ourſelves ; and not again fooliſhly and ungratefully reject and ſpurn at the Intimations and Invitations of Heaven, to preſerve our Prince and Country.

Machiavel tells us, that no Government can long ſubſiſt, but by recurring often to its firſt Principles ; but this can never be done while Men live at Eaſe and in Luxury ; for then they cannot

be

be perfuaded to fee diftant Dangers, of which they feel no Part. The Conjunctures proper for fuch Reformations, are when Men are awakened by Misfortunes, and frighted with the Approach and near View of prefent Evils ; then they will wifh for Remedies, and their Minds are prepared to receive them, to hear Reafons, and to fall into Meafures propofed by wife Men for their Security.

The great Authority juft quoted informs us what Meafures and Expedients are neceffary to fave a State under fuch Exigencies : He tells us, that as a Tyranny cannot be eftablifhed but by deftroying *Brutus* ; fo a free Government is not to be preferved but by deftroying *Brutus*'s Sons. Let us therefore put on a Refolution equal to the mighty Occafion : Let us exert a Spirit worthy of *Britons*, worthy of Freemen who deferve Liberty. Let us take Advantage of the Opportunity, while Mens Refentments boil high, whilft leffer Animofities feem to be laid afide, and moft Men are fick of Party and Party-Leaders ; and let us, by all proper Methods, exemplarily punifh the Parricides, and avowed Enemies of all Mankind.

Let neither private Acquaintance, perfonal Alliance, or Party Combination, ftand between us and our Duty to our Country : Let all thofe who have a common Intereft in the publick Safety, join in common Meafures to defend the publick Safety : Let us purfue to Difgrace, Deftruction, and even Death, thofe who have brought this Ruin upon us, let them be ever fo great, or ever fo many : Let us ftamp and deep engrave, in Characters legible to all *Europe* at prefent, and to all Pofterity hereafter, what Vengeance is due to Crimes, which have no lefs Objects in View than
the

the Ruin of Nations, and the Deſtruction of Millions : They have made many bold, deſperate, and wicked Attempts to deſtroy us ; let us ſtrike one honeſt and bold Stroke to deſtroy them.

Though the Deſigns of the Conſpirators ſhould be laid as deep as the Center, though they ſhould raiſe Hell itſelf in their Quarrel, and ſhould fetch Legions of Votaries from thence to avow their Proceedings ; yet let us not leave the Purſuit, till we have their Skins and Eſtates : We know, by paſt Experience, that there are thoſe amongſt us, who will be glad to quit the Chaſe, when our Villains, like Beavers, drop what they are uſually hunted for ; but the Nation is now too much provoked, and too much injured, to ſuffer themſelves to be again ſo betrayed.

We have Heaven to direct us, a glorious King to lead us, and a wiſe and faithful Parliament to aſſiſt and protect us : Whilſt we have ſuch a King, and ſuch a Parliament, every worthy *Briton* cries out aloud,

Manus hæc inimica Tyrannis
Enſe petit placidam, ſub libertate quietem.

T   *I am,* &c.

***

What Measures are actually taken by wicked and
desperate Ministers to ruin and enslave their
Country.

S I R,

AS under the best Princes, and the best Servants
to Princes alone, it is safe to speak what is
true of the worst; so, according to my former
Promise to the Publick, I shall take the Advantage
of our excellent King's most gentle Government,
and the virtuous Administration of an uncorrupt
Ministry, to warn Mankind against the Mischiefs
which may hereafter be dreaded from corrupt ones.
It is too true, that every Country in the World
has sometimes groaned under that heavy Misfortune, and our own as much as any; though I
cannot allow it to be true, what Monsieur *de Witt*
has long since observed, that the *English* Court has
always been the most thievish Court in *Europe.*

Few Men have been desperate enough to attack
openly, and barefaced, the Liberties of a free
People. Such avowed Conspirators can rarely succeed: The Attempt would destroy itself. Even
when the Enterprize is begun and visible, the End
must be hid, or denied. It is the Business and
Policy of Traytors, so to disguise their Treason
with plausible Names, and so to recommend it
with popular and bewitching Colours, that they
themselves shall be adored, while their Work is detested, and yet carried on by those that detest it.

Thus

Thus one Nation has been furrendered to another under the fair Name of mutual Alliance : The Fortreffes of a Nation have been given up, or attempted to be given up, under the frugal Notion of faving Charges to a Nation ; and Commonwealths have been trepanned into Slavery, by Troops raifed or increafed to defend them from Slavery.

It may therefore be of Service to the World, to fhew what Meafures have been taken by corrupt Minifters, in fome of our neighbouring Countries, to ruin and enflave the People over whom they prefided ; to fhew by what Steps and Gradations of Mifchief Nations have been undone, and confequently what Methods may be hereafter taken to undo others : And this Subject I rather choofe, becaufe my Countrymen may be the more fenfible of, and know how to value the ineftimable Bleffing of living under the beft Prince, and the beft eftablifhed Government in the Univerfe, where we have none of thefe Things to fear.

Such Traytors will probably endeavour firft to get their Prince into their Poffeffion, and, like *Sejanus*, fhut him up in a little Ifland, or perhaps make him a Prifoner in his Court ; whilft, with full Range, they devour his Dominions, and plunder his Subjects. When he is thus fecluded from the Accefs of his Friends, and the Knowledge of his Affairs, he muft be content with fuch Mifreprefentations as they fhall find expedient to give him. Falfe Cafes will be ftated, to juftify wicked Counfel ; wicked Counfel will be given, to procure unjuft Orders. He will be made to miftake his Foes for his Friends, his Friends for his Foes ; and to believe that his Affairs are in the higheft

higheft Profperity, when they are in the greateft
Diftrefs ; and that publick Matters go on in the
greateft Harmony, when they are in the utmoft
Confufion.

They will be ever contriving and forming wicked and dangerous Projects, to make the People
poor, and themfelves rich ; well knowing that
Dominion follows Property ; that where there are
Wealth and Power, there will be always Crowds
of fervile Dependents ; and that, on the contrary,
Poverty dejects the Mind, fafhions it to Slavery,
and renders it unequal to any generous Undertaking, and incapable of oppofing any bold Ufurpation. They will fquander away the publick Money in wanton Prefents to Minions, and their
Creatures of Pleafure or of Burthen, or in Penfions to mercenary and worthlefs Men and Women, for vile Ends and traiterous Purpofes.

They will engage their Country in ridiculous,
expenfive, fantaftical Wars, to keep the Minds
of Men in continual Hurry and Agitation, and
under conftant Fears and Alarms ; and, by fuch
Means, deprive them both of Leifure and Inclination to look into publick Mifcarriages. Men,
on the contrary, will, inftead of fuch Infpection,
be difpofed to fall into all Meafures offered, feem-
ingly, for their Defence, and will agree to every
wild Demand made by thofe who are betraying
them.

When they have ferved their Ends by fuch
Wars, or have other Motives to make Peace,
they will have no View to the publick Intereft ;
but will often, to procure fuch Peace, deliver
up the Strong-Holds of their Country, or its
Colonies for Trade, to open Enemies, fufpected
                                        Friends,

Friends, or dangerous Neighbours, that they may not be interrupted in their domeftick Defigns.

They will create Parties in the Commonwealth, or keep them up where they already are; and, by playing them by Turns upon each other, will rule both. By making the *Guelfs* afraid of the *Ghibelines*, and thefe afraid of the *Guelfs*, they will make themfelves the Mediums and Balance between the two Factions; and both Factions, in their Turns, the Props of their Authority, and the Inftruments of their Defigns.

They will not fuffer any Men, who have once tafted of Authority, though perfonally their Enemies, and whofe Pofts they enjoy, to be called to an Account for paft Crimes, though ever fo enormous. They will make no fuch Precedents for their own Punifhment; nor cenfure Treafon, which they intend to commit. On the contrary, they will form new Confpiracies, and invent new Fences for their own Impunity and Protection; and endeavour to engage fuch Numbers in their Guilt, as to fet themfelves above all Fear of Punifhment.

They will prefer worthlefs and wicked Men, and not fuffer a Man of Knowledge or Honefty to come near them, or enjoy a Poft under them. They will difgrace Men of Virtue, and ridicule Virtue itfelf, and laugh at Publick Spirit. They will put Men into Employments, without any Regard to the Qualifications for thofe Employments, or indeed to any Qualifications at all, but as they contribute to their Defigns, and fhew a ftupid Alacrity to do what they are bid. They muft be either Fools or Beggars; either void of
Capa-

Capacity to difcover their Intrigues, or of Credit and Inclination to difappoint them.

They will promote Luxury, Idlenefs, and Expence, and a general Depravation of Manners, by their own Example, as well as by Connivance and publick Encouragement.   This will not only divert Mens Thoughts from examining their Behaviour and Politicks, but likewife let them loofe from all the Reftraints of private and publick Virtue.   From Immorality and Exceffes they will fall into Neceffity ; and from thence into a fervile Dependence upon Power.

In order to this, they will bring into Fafhion Gaming, Drunkennefs, Gluttony, and profufe and coftly Drefs.   They will debauch their Country with foreign Vices, and foreign Inftruments of vicious Pleafures ; and will contrive and encourage publick Revels, nightly Difguifes, and debauched Mummeries.

They will, by all practicable Means of Oppreffion, provoke the People to Difaffection ; and then make that Difaffection an Argument for new Oppreffion, for not trufting them any further, and for keeping up Troops ; and, in fine, for depriving them of Liberties and Privileges, to which they are entitled by their Birth, and the Laws of their Country.

If fuch Meafures fhould ever be taken in any free Country, where the People choofe Deputies to reprefent them, then they will endeavour to bribe the Electors in the Choice of their Reprefentatives, and fo to get a Council of their own Creatures ; and where they cannot fucceed with the Electors, they will endeavour to corrupt the Deputies after they are chofen, with the Money given

for

for the publick Defence ; and to draw into the
Perpetration of their Crimes thofe very Men,
from whom the betrayed People expect the Redrefs of their Grievances, and the Punifhment of
thofe Crimes.   And when they have thus made
the Reprefentatives of the People afraid of the
People, and the People afraid of their Reprefentatives ;   then they will endeavour to perfuade
thofe Deputies to feize the Government to themfelves, and not to truft their Principals any longer
with the Power of refenting their Treachery and
Ill-Ufage, and of fending honefter and wifer Men
in their room.

But if the Conftitution fhould be fo ftubbornly
framed, that it will ftill preferve itfelf and the
People's Liberties, in fpite of all villainous Con-
trivances to deftroy both ; then muft the Conftitution itfelf be attacked and broken, becaufe it
will not bend.   There muft be an Endeavour,
under fome Pretence of publick Good, to alter a
Balance of the Government, and to get it into the
fole Power of their Creatures, and of fuch who
will have conftantly an Intereft diftinct from that
of the Body of the People.

But if all thefe Schemes for the Ruin of the
Publick, and their own Impunity, fhould fail
them ; and the worthy Patriots of a free Country
fhould prove obftinate in Defence of their Country,
and refolve to call its Betrayers to a ftrict Account ;
there is then but one thing left for fuch Traytors
to do ; namely, to veer about, and, by joining
with the Enemy of their Prince and Country,
complete their Treafon.

I have fomewhere read of a Favourite and
Firft Minifter to a neighbouring Prince, long fince
                                              dead,

dead, who played his Part fo well, that, though he had, by his evil Counfels, raifed a Rebellion, and a Conteft for the Crown ; yet he preferved himfelf a Refource, whoever got the better : If his old Mafter fucceeded, then this *Achitophel*, by the Help of a baffled Rebellion, ever favourable to Princes, had the Glory of fixing his Mafter in abfolute Power : But, as his brave Rival got the Day, *Achitophel* had the Merit of betraying his old Mafter to plead ; and was accordingly taken into Favour.

Happy therefore, thrice happy, are we, who can be unconcerned Spectators of the Miferies which the greateft Part of *Europe* is reduced to fuffer, having loft their Liberties by the Intrigues and Wickednefs of thofe whom they trufted ; whilft we continue in full Enjoyment of ours, and can be in no Danger of lofing them, while we have fo excellent a King, affifted and obeyed by fo wife a Parliament.

T   *I am,* &c.

SATURDAY, *February* 25, 1720. No. 18.
The terrible Tendency of publick Corruption to ruin a State, exemplified in that of Rome, *and applied to our own.*

SIR,

VENALIS *civitas mox peritura fi emptorum invenias!* "Mercenary City, ripe for Deftruc-
"tion, and juft ready to deliver up thyfelf, and
"all thy Liberties, to the firft Bidder, who is
                                        "able

" able to buy thee !" said the great King *Jugur-tha*, when he was leaving *Rome*. *Rome* the Nurse of Heroes, the Mistress of Nations, the Glory of Empires, and the Source, the Standard, and Pattern of Virtue and Knowledge, and, indeed, of every Thing which ever was praise-worthy and valuable amongst Men, was soon after fallen, fallen Ten Thousand Thousand Fathoms deep in the Abyss of Corruption and Impiety : No more of that publick Spirit appeared, that rendered it amiable, as well as terrible, to the World : It had conquered by its Virtue more than its Arms : It had commanded a willing Subjection from the numerous Nations, who readily acknowledged its superior Genius and natural Right to Empire, and afterwards their own Condition to be graced by the Dignity of such a Mistress.

" But (says the Abbot *Vertot*) about this Time
" another Nation seemed to appear upon the
" Stage : A general Corruption soon spread itself
" through all Degrees of the State : Justice was
" publickly sold in the Tribunals : The Voices of
" the People went to the highest Bidder ; and the
" Consuls, having obtained that great Post by In-
" trigues, or by Bribery, never now made War
" but to enrich themselves with the Spoils of Na-
" tions, and often to plunder those very Provin-
" ces, which their Duty bound them to protect
" and defend.—The Provinces were obliged to
" supply these prodigious Expences : The Gene-
" rals possessed themselves of the Revenues of the
" Commonwealth ; and the State was weakened
" in proportion as its Members became powerful.
" —It was sufficient Colour for rifling the People,
" and

" and laying new Imposts, if they did but give
" thofe Exactions a new Name.

" There arofe on a fudden, and as it were
" by Enchantment, magnificent Palaces, whofe
" Walls, Roofs, and Cielings were all gilded:
" It was not enough that their Beds and Tables
" were all of Silver; that rich Metal muft alfo be
" carved and adorned with *Baffo Relievo's*, per-
" formed by the moft excellent Artifts.—All the
" Money of the State was in the Hands of the
" Great Men, the Publicans, and certain Freed-
" men richer than their Mafters.

He fays, " It would make a Volume to repre-
" fent the Magnificence of their Buildings, the
" Richnefs of their Habits, the Jewels they wore,
" the prodigious Number of Slaves, Freed-men,
" and Clients, by which they were conftantly at-
" tended, and efpecially the Expence and Profu-
" fion of their Tables : They were not contented,
" if, in the midft of Winter, the *Falernian* Wine
" that was prefented them was not ftrewed with
" Rofes ; and cooled in Veffels of Gold in Sum-
" mer : Their Side-Boards groaned under the
" Weight and Load of Plate, both Silver and
" Gold : They valued the Feaft only by the Coft-
" linefs of the Difhes that were ferved up ; Phea-
" fants muft be fetched for them through all the
" Dangers of the Sea; and, to complete their
" Corruption, after the Conqueft of *Afia*, they
" began to introduce Women-Singers and Dancers
" into their Entertainments.

" What Defenders of Liberty, *fays he*, are
" here ?   What an Omen of approaching Sla-
" very ?   None could be greater, than to fee
" Valour lefs regarded in a State than Luxury ?

" to

" to fee the poor Officer languifhing in the ob-
" fcure Honours of a Legion, whilft the Gran-
" dees concealed their Cowardice, and dazzled
" the Eyes of the Publick, by the Magnificence
" of their Equipage, and the Profufion of their
" Expence."

But what did all this Profufion and Magnificence produce ? Pleafure fucceeded in the room
of Temperance, Idlenefs took place of the Love
of Bufinefs, and private Regards extinguifhed that
Love of Liberty, that Zeal and Warmth, which
their Anceftors had fhewn for the Intereft of the
Publick ; Luxury and Pride became fafhionable ;
all Ranks and Orders of Men tried to outvie one
another in Expence and Pomp ; and when, by fo
doing, they had fpent their private Patrimonies,
they endeavoured to make Reprifals upon the Publick ; and, having before fold every thing elfe, at
laft fold their Country.

The publick Treafure was fquandered away,
and divided amongft private Men ; and new Demands made, and new Taxes and Burdens laid
upon the People, to continue and fupport this Ex-
travagance.   Such Conduct in the Great Ones occafioned Murmurings, univerfal Difcontent, and
at laft Civil Wars. The People threw themfelves under different Heads or Leaders of Parties, who all afpired to make themfelves Mafters
of the Commonwealth, and of the publick Liberty ; and, during the Struggle, *Rome* and all
Italy was but one Slaughter-Houfe. Thoufands,
Hundreds of Thoufands, fell Sacrifices to the
Ambition of a few : Rivers of Blood ran in the
publick Streets, and Profcriptions and Maffacres
were efteemed Sport and Paftime ; till at length
                                             Two

Two Thirds of the People were deſtroyed, and the reſt made Slaves to the moſt wicked and contemptible Wretches of Mankind.

Thus ended the greateſt, the nobleſt State that ever adorned the worldly Theatre, that ever the Sun ſaw : It fell a Victim to Ambition and Faction, to baſe and unworthy Men, to Parricides and Traytors ; and every other Nation muſt run the ſame Fortune, expect the ſame fatal Cataſtrophe, who ſuffer themſelves to be debauched with the ſame Vices, and are actuated by the ſame Principles and Paſſions.

I wiſh I could ſay, that the Abbot *Vertot*'s Deſcription of the *Roman* State, in its laſt Declenſion, ſuited no other State in our own Time. I hope that we ourſelves have none of theſe Corruptions and Abuſes to complain of : I am ſure, if we have, that it is high Time to reform them, and to prevent the diſmal Evils which they threaten. It is wild to think that there is any other Way to prevent the Conſequence, without preventing the Corruption, and the Cauſes which produce it : Mankind will be always the ſame, will always act within one Circle ; and when we know what they did a Thouſand Years ago in any Circumſtance, we ſhall know what they will do a Thouſand Years hence in the ſame. This is what is called Experience, the ſureſt Miſtreſs and Leſſon of Wiſdom.

Let us therefore grow wiſe by the Misfortunes of others : Let us make Uſe of the *Roman* Language, as a Vehicle of good Senſe, and uſeful Inſtruction ; and not uſe it like Pedants, Prieſts, and Pedagogues. Let their Virtues and their Vices, and the Puniſhment of them too, be an Example to

us ;

us ; and fo prevent our Miferies from being an
Example to other Nations : Let us avoid the Rocks
upon which they have fuffered Shipwreck, and fet
up Buoys and Sea-marks to warn and guide Pofterity. In fine, let us examine and look narrowly
into every Part of our Conftitution, and fee if any
Corruptions or Abufes have crept or galloped into
it. Let us fearch our Wounds to the Core, without which it is beyond the Power of Surgery to
apply fuitable Remedies.

Our prefent Misfortunes will roufe up our Spirits,
and, as it were, awaken us out of a deep Lethar-
gy. It is true, indeed, that they came upon us like
a Storm of Thunder and Lightning in a clear Sky,
and when the Heavens feemed more ferene ; but the
combuftible Matter was prepared before : Steams
and Exhalations had been long gathering from Bogs
and Jakes ; and though they fome Time feemed
difperfed and far removed by the Heat of a warm
Sun, yet the Firmament was all the while impreg-
nating with Fire and Brimftone ; and now, on a
Sudden, the Clouds thicken, and look black and big
on every Side, and threaten us with a Hurricane.

Let us therefore act the Part of fkilful Pilots,
and call all Hands to labour at the Oars and at the
Ropes : Let us begin with throwing all our Lug-
gage and ufelefs Trumpery over-board ; then let
us lower or take down all fuperfluous Sails, to prevent the Boat from being overfet ; and when we
have done all in our Power to fave the Ship, let
us implore the Affiftance of Heaven ; and I doubt
not but we fhall out-ride the Storm.

Quid times ? Cæfarem *vehis.*—We have King
George on Board, and at the Helm ; the Favourite
of Heaven, and the Darling of all good Men ;
who

who not only gives us full Leave, but encourages and affifts us, to fave ourfelves: He will not, like fome weak Princes amongft his Predeceffors, fkreen guilty Great Men, fuffer the Faults of others to be laid at his Door, nor permit his Authority to be proftituted to patronize Criminals ; nor interpofe and ftand between his People's juft Refentment and the Punifhment of worthlefs Favourites, of which Sort of Cattle he has none ; fo that it is our own Fault if we are not happy, great, and free.

Indeed, we owe that Juftice and Duty to our great Benefactor, as not only fairly and impartially to reprefent to him our Circumftances, and how we came into them ; but to do all in our Power to put our Conftitution on fuch a Bottom, if any thing be wanting to it, that he may have the Honour and Pleafure of reigning over a free and happy People. This will be to make our Gift complete, in prefenting him with a Crown, not befet with any Difficulties ; a glorious Crown, and not to mock him with one of Thorns.

I fhall foon, in fome other Letter, offer my Thoughts from what Sources thefe Mifchiefs have flowed upon us, and what Methods I conceive are effentially neceffary to retrieve them.
T

I am, &c.

SATUR-

SATURDAY, *March* 4, 1720.   No. 19.

The Force of popular Affection and Antipathy to particular Men.—How powerfully it operates, and how far to be regarded.

SIR,

OPINION and Reputation have often the greatest Share in governing the Affairs of the World.   Misled by the great Biass of Superstition, every where found in human Nature, or by Ignorance and Prejudices, proceeding as often from Education itself, as from the Want of it, we often take the Appearance of Things for Things themselves, mistake our own Imaginations for Realities, our Delusions for Certainties and Truth.   A very small Part of Mankind is exempted from the delusive Influence of Omens, Presages, and Prognosticks.

Thefe and the like Superstitions enter into every Scene of private and publick Life : Gamesters throw away the Cards and Dice which they had lost by, and call for others, without any other Preference than that they are not the same : Gardeners pretend to plant Trees in a fortunate Season : Many People will not marry, or do any Business, but on certain Days accounted prosperous : Even Generals have had their fortunate and unfortunate Times and Seasons ; and have often declined coming to Battle, when the Advantage was apparently on their Side, merely because the Day, or Time of the Day, was ill-boding.

Now,

Now, though all the Whimfies of this Kind have no Foundation, but in Opinion; yet they often produce as certain and regular Events, as if the Caufes were adequate in their own Nature to the Events. The Opinion of a Phyfician or a Medicine, does often effect the Cure of a Patient, by giving his Mind fuch Eafe and Acquiefcence as can alone produce Health. The Opinion of a General, or of a Caufe, makes an Army fight with double Vigour; and a Confidence in the Wifdom and Integrity of Governors, makes a Nation exert its utmoft Efforts for its own Security; whereas by a Diftruft of its Rulers, it often finks into an univerfal Indifference and Defpondency. The Change alone of a General, or of a Minifter, has often changed the Fortune and Difpofition of a People, even where there has been no fuperior Endowments in the Succeffor; for if they can be made to believe, that their Misfortunes are owing to the ill Conduct or ill Genius of thofe who command them, the Removal of the fuppofed Caufe of their Misfortunes will infpire them with new Courage and Refolution; which are almoft always rewarded with Succefs and Victory.

From hence the moft famous Legiflators, Princes and Generals have endeavoured to inftill into their Followers an Opinion of their being more than human, as being defcended from, or related to, fome God; or have afferted a familiar Communion with the Gods, a Right to explain their Wills, and to execute their Commands. By thefe Means they obtained an unlimitted Confidence in their Abilities, a cheerful Submiffion to their Authority,

thority, an Aſſurance of Succeſs under their Conduct.

Where perſonal Virtues and Qualifications, by
which the above Pretenſions are ſupported, are
wanting, as in the ſucceſſive Eaſtern Monarchies ;
other Arts are uſed to gain Admiration, to draw
Reverence to the Perſons of their Princes, and
blind Obedience to their Power.   Thoſe ſtately
Tyrants are, for the moſt Part, ſhut up in their
Palaces, where every thing is auguſt about them :
They ſeldom ſhew themſelves abroad to their People ;   and when they do, it is in the moſt awful
and aſtoniſhing Manner, attended by numerous
Guards, richly habited, and armed ; whilſt their
own Perſons are covered with Gold and Pearl,
and glittering with Diamonds ; and perhaps the
Horſes and Elephants they ride on are all in a Blaze
of Gold and precious Stones.

The demure Faces and deep Silence of their
Miniſters and Attendants, contribute to ſpread the
general Awe ;   which is ſtill heightened by the
ſolemn Clangor of Trumpets, and other warlike
Sounds.   All this prepares the gaping and enchanted Multitude to ſwallow, with equal Credulity and
Wonder, the plauſible Stories artfully given out
amongſt them, of the ſublime and celeſtial Qualities of their Emperors, inſomuch that even their
very Images are worſhipped.

Indeed, in Countries where Liberty is eſtabliſh-
ed, and People think for themſelves, all the above
Arts and Pretences would be ridiculous, and ſuch
Farce and Grimace would be laughed at.   The
People have Senſe enough to know, that all this
Profuſion and Wealth are their own Spoils ;   that
they

they muſt labour and want, that others may be idle and abound ; and they will ſee that their Poverty is encreaſed, and their Miſeries aggravated and mocked, by the Pomp and Luxury of their Maſters.

Amongſt ſuch People virtuous and juſt Actions, or the Appearance of virtuous and juſt Actions, are the only Ways of gaining Eſteem, Reverence, and Submiſſion. They muſt ſee, or fanſy they ſee, that the Views and Meaſures of their Governors tend honeſtly and only to the publick Welfare and Proſperity, and they muſt find their own Account in their Obedience.   A Prince who deals thus with his People, can rarely be in Danger from Diſaffected Subjects, or powerful Neighbours ; his faithful People will be his conſtant Guard ; and, finding their own Security in his Government, will be always ready at his Call to take effectual Vengeance upon thoſe who ſhall attempt to oppoſe or undermine his juſt Authority.

However, the wiſeſt and moſt free People are not without their Superſtitions and their Foibles ; and prudent Governors will take Advantage of them, and endeavour to apply them to the publick Benefit. The *Romans* themſelves had their *Dies faſtos & nefaſtos*, their fortunate and unfortunate Generals ; and ſometimes empty Names have been eſteemed Endowments and Merit.   Another *Scipio* was appointed by the *Romans* to demoliſh *Carthage*, which was firſt ſubdued by the Great *Scipio* ; and the *Athenians* called for another *Phormio* for their War at *Lepanto*.

Generals and Miniſters have been oftentimes diſgraced, even by wiſe Nations, for making unfortunate Expeditions, or for unfortunate Conduct in directing the publick Affairs, when there was

no

no Deceit or Want of Virtue, in thofe Generals and Minifters ; for if a Nation or an Army take an univerfal, though an unreafonahle Difguft at one or a few Men, it is ridiculous to bring his or their Intereft in Balance with the Satisfaction and Affections of Millions, or much lefs than Millions. Prudent Princes therefore have been always extremely cautious how they employed Men in any confiderable Station, who were either odious or contemptible, even though it happened that they were innocently and unfortunately fo.

Indeed this can feldom happen ; for a virtuous and modeft Man will never thruft himfelf into the Service of his Prince, nor continue longer in it than he is acceptable to the People : He will know that he can do no real Good to a Country, which will receive no Good at his Hands ; that the publick Jealoufy will mifreprefent his whole Conduct, render his beft Defigns abortive, his beft Actions ufelefs ; that he will be a Clog and a dead Weight upon the Affairs of his Prince ; and that the general Diftafte taken at him, will, by Degrees, make his Prince the Object of general Diftafte.

But when Minifters have defervedly incurred the general Hatred ; when they have been known to have employed their whole Power and Intereft in Oppofition to the Publick Intereft ; when, being trufted with a Nation's Affairs, they have defperately projected, and obftinately purfued, Schemes big with publick Ruin ; when they have weakened the Authority of their Prince to ftrengthen their own, and endangered his Safety for the Security of their own Heads, and the Protection of their Crimes ; when they have thriven by the publick Ruin ;

Ruin ; and, being the known Authors of univerfal Calamities, have become the proper Objects of fuch univerfal Deteftation, as not to have one real Friend in their Country, or one fincere Advocate even amongft the many that they have bribed to be fo : If, after all this, they will go on to brave a Nation which they have before ruined, confidently continue at the Head of Affairs, and obftinately perfift to overturn their King and Country ; this, I fay, is aggravating their Crimes, by an Infolence which no publick Refentment can equal.

This was the Cafe of *England* under the Influence of *Gaveſton* and the two *Spencers* ; and this was the Cafe of the *Netherlands* under the Adminiftration of the Duke of *Alva* ; which Minifters feverally ruined their Mafters and their Country. Nations under fuch woful Conduct, and unlucky Conftellations, are often driven into Revolts, or lofe all Courage to defend themfelves, either againft the Attacks from their native Traytors, or forign Invaders.

This is famoufly verified in the Story of the *Decemviri*, a College of Magiftrates created by the *Romans* for one Year, to compile and eftablifh a Body of Laws. This Term was thought long enough, and undoubtedly was fo ; but thefe defigning Men, under the plaufible Colour of adding Two more Tables to the Ten already finifhed and publifhed got their Sitting prolonged for another Year : Nor at the expiring of that, though the Two Tables were added, did they diffolve themfelves ; but, in Defiance of the People who chofe them, and now every where murmured againft
them,

them, as well as fuffered by them, continued their Authority.

The City of *Rome* faw itfelf under a new Government ; *Deploratur in perpetuum libertas, nec vindex quifquam extitit, aut futurus videtur :* The Conftitution was gone ; and though all Men complained, yet none offered to help. Whilft the *Romans* were thus defpónding at Home, they were defpifed Abroad : The neighbouring Nations were provoked, that Dominion fhould ftill fubfift in a City, where Liberty fubfifted no longer. The *Roman* Territories therefore were invaded by the *Sabines* and the *Æquians.* This terrified the Faction ; but I do not find that it troubled the People, who neither feared nor hated foreign Invaders half fo much as their own domeftick Traytors. The defperate Parricides determined rather to facrifice their Country, than lofe their Places ; fo to War they went, but with miferable Succefs. They managed the War no better than they did the State ; and had no more Credit in the Camp than in the City : The Soldiers would not fight under detefted Leaders, but ran away before the Enemy, and fuffered a fhameful Rout.

Nor did this Lofs and Difgrace, at once unufual and terrible to *Rome,* at all move the Traytors to refign : They went on mifgoverning and debauching, till, the Meafures of their Wickednefs being full, they were driven out of their Pofts by the Vigour of the State, and the Affiftance of the People. The Two chief Traytors were caft into Prifon, the reft into Banifhment.

This foon happily changed the State of Affairs, and the Spirit of the People ; who, having got at
length

length an honeſt Adminiſtration, and Governors
whom they loved and truſted, quickly beat the
Enemy out of the Territories of *Rome*, that very
Enemy, who in other Circumſtances had beaten
them.

G *I am*, &c.

SATURDAY, *March* 11, 1720. No. 20.

*Of publick Juſtice, how neceſſary to the Security and
Well-being of a State, and how deſtructive the
Neglect of it to the* Britiſh *Nation.* Signal In-
ſtances of it.

S I R,

PArcere ſubjectis, & debellare ſuperbos; to pay
well, and hang well, to protect the Innocent,
and puniſh the Oppreſſors, are the Hinges and Ligaments of Government, the chief Ends why Men
enter into Societies. To attain theſe Ends, they
have been content to part with their natural Rights,
a great Share of their Subſtance and Induſtry: To
quit their Equality, and ſubmit themſelves to thoſe
who had before no Right to command them: For
this Millions live willingly in an innocent and
ſafe Obſcurity, to make a few Great Men, and
enable them, at their Expence, to ſhine in Pomp
and Magnificence.

But all this Pageantry is not deſigned for thoſe
who wear it. They carry about them the Dignity
of the Commonwealth: The Honours which they
receive are Honours paid to the Publick, and they
themſelves are only the Pillars and Images upon
which National Trophies are hung; for when
they

they are divefted of thefe *Infignia*, no more Refpect and Homage is due to them, than what refults from their own Virtue and Merit. Yet fuch is the Depravity of human Nature, that few can diftinguifh their own Perfons from the Enfigns and Ornaments which they wear, or their Duty from their Dignity: There feems to be a Judgment upon all Men in certain Stations, that they can never think of the Time when they have been, or may again be, out of them.

A good Magiftrate is the brighteft Character upon Earth, as being moft conducive to the Benefit of Mankind; and a bad one is a greater Monfter than ever Hell engendered: He is an Enemy and Traytor to his own Species. Where there is the greateft Truft, the betraying it is the greateft Treafon. The Fafces, the Judge, and the Executioner, do not make the Crime, but punifh it; and the Crime is never the lefs, though it efcape the Vengeance due to it. *Alexander*, who robbed Kingdoms and States, was a greater Felon than the Pyrate whom he put to Death, though no one was ftrong enough to inflict the fame Punifhment upon him. It is no more juft to rob with Regiments or Squadrons, than by fingle Men or fingle Ships; for unlefs we are determined by the Juftice of the Action, there can be no Criterion, Boundary, or fixed Mark, to know where the Thief ends, and the Hero begins.

Muft little Villains then fumbit to Fate,
That great Ones may enjoy the World in State?

Shall a poor Pick-pocket be hanged for filching away a little loofe Money; and wholefale Thieves, who rob Nations of all that they have, be efteemed
                                        and

and honoured ? Shall a Roguery be fanctified by
the Greatnefs of it ; and Impunity be purchafed,
by deferving the higheft Punifhment ?   This is
inverting the Nature of Things, confounding
Virtue and Vice, and turning the World topfy-
turvy.

Men who are advanced to great Stations, and
are highly honoured and rewarded at the Publick
Coft, ought to look upon themfelves as Creatures
of the Publick, as Machines erected and fet up
for publick Emolument and Safety.   They ought
to reflect, that Thoufands, Ten Thoufands of
their Countrymen, have equal, or perhaps greater,
Qualifications than themfelves ; and that blind
Fortune alone has given them their prefent Diftinction : That the Eftate of the Freeholder, the
Hazard of the Merchant, and the Sweat of the
Labourer, all contribute to their Greatnefs ; and
when once they can fee themfelves in this Mir-
rour, they will think nothing can be too grateful,
nothing too great or too hazardous to be done for
fuch Benefactors.

They will confider, that no uncommon Application, or diftinguifhing Abilities, will juftify this
Superiority ; that many of their Fellow-Subjects,
poffeffing equal Merit, take much more Pains for
much lefs Confiderations ; nay, that the Bufinefs
of their own Employments is moftly executed by
inferior Officers, for fmall Rewards ; and, confequently, that their great Appointments are given
to fecure their Fidelity, and put them far above
and out of the Reach of Bribery and Corruption :
They ought not to have a Thought which is
mean or little : Their Minds are not to be in the
Dirt, whilft their Heads are in the Clouds : They
ought

ought to infuse and infpire Virtue, Refolution, and publick Spirit, into the inactive Mafs, and be illuftrious Examples of every great and noble Quality.

But if they can fink fo low beneath themfelves; if they can fo far defcend from the Dignity of their Characters ; if they can choofe fo to grovel upon the Earth, when they may afcend to the Heavens ; and be fo poor and abject, as to combine and confederate with Pick-pockets and common Rogues; betray their moft folemn Trufts, and employ all their Power and Credit to deftroy that People, whom they have every Motive which Heaven and Earth can fuggeft to protect and defend : Then, I fay, fuch Wretches ought to be the Scorn and Deteftation of every honeft Man ; and new Kinds of Vengeance, new Tortures, and new Engines of Mifery ought to be invented to make their Punifhments as much exceed common Punifhments, as their Crimes exceed thofe of the worft Sort of common Malefactors, and as their Rewards furpafs thofe of the beft and worthieft Citizens in other Stages of Life and Circumftances of Fortune.

There is no Analogy between the Crimes of private Men and thofe of publick Magiftrates : The firft terminate in the Death or Sufferings of fingle Perfons; the others ruin Millions, fubvert the Policy and Œconomy of Nations, and create general Want, and its Confequences, Difcontents, Infurrections, and Civil Wars, at Home ; and often make them a Prey to watchful Enemies Abroad. But amongft the Crimes which regard a State, *Peculatus*, or robbing the Publick, is the greateft ; becaufe upon the careful and frugal Adminiftration

of

of the publick Treasure the very Being of the Commonwealth depends. It is what my Lord *Coke* calls it, *Tutela pacis*, & *firmamentum belli* ; and the embezzling of it is Death by the Civil Law, and ought to be so by all Laws. It is the worst Sort of Treason, as it draws all other Sorts of Treason after it : It disconcerts all the Measures of Government, and lays the Ground-work of Seditions, Rebellions, and all kind of publick Miseries.

But these, as well as all other Crimes which affect the Publick, receive their Aggravation from the Greatness of the Persons who commit them ; not only as their Rewards are larger, and their Temptations less, but as their Example recommends, and, as it were, authorizes and gives a Licence to Wickedness. No one dares to punish another for an Offence which he knows, and the other knows, that he every Day commits himself. One Great Man, who gets an Hundred Thousand Pounds by cheating the Publick, must wink and connive at Ten others who shall wrong it of Ten Thousand Pounds each ; and they at Ten times as many more, who shall defraud it of One Thousand ; and so on in lesser Progression, till the greatest Part of the publick Revenue is swallowed and devoured by great and little Plunderers.

It is therefore of the utmost Importance to the Security and Happiness of any State, to punish, in the most exemplary Manner, all those who are intrusted by it, and betray that Trust : It becomes the Wisdom of a Nation, to give Ten Thousand Pounds to purchase a Head, which cheats it of Six-pence. *Valerius Maximus* calls *Se-*
verity

verity the sure Preserver and Avenger of Liberty :
It is as neceffary for the preventing of Tyranny,
as for the Support of it. After the Death of the
Sons of *Brutus*, executed by the Command of
their own Father, and in his Prefence, we hear
no more of any Confpirators in *Rome* to reftore
the *Tarquins* ; and had *Marius*, *Cæfar*, and other
Corrupters of the People, met with the fame Punifhment, that glorious Commonwealth might
have fubfifted to this Day. Lenity to great
Crimes is an Invitation to greater ; whereas Defpair of Pardon, for the moft part, makes Pardon
ufelefs. If no Mercy were fhewn to the Enemies
of the State, no State would be overturned ; and
if fmall or no Punifhment be inflicted upon them,
no State can be fafe.

Happy, happy had it been for this unhappy
People, if thefe important and effential Maxims
of Government had been duly regarded by our
Legiflators at the *Revolution* ; (and I wifh too, that
the fincere and hearty Endeavours of our prefent
Legiflators to punifh the Betrayers of the late unfortunate Queen had met the defired Succefs :) For
I doubt that all our Misfortunes have flowed from
thefe Sources, and are owing to thefe Difappointments.

All *Europe* faw, and all good Men in it lamented to fee, a mighty Nation brought to the Brink
of Deftruction by weak and contemptible Inftruments ; its Laws fuperfeded, its Courts of Juftice
corrupted, its Legiflature laid afide, its Liberties
fubverted, its Religion overturned, and a new one
almoft introduced, and a violent and defpotick
Government affumed, which was fupported by
Legions and an armed Force : They faw this
brave

brave People rife under the Oppreffion, and, like *Antæus*, gather Strength by their late Fall : They called for the Affiftance of the next Heir to the Crown, to avenge himfelf and them ; and when they had, by his Affiftance, removed the Ufurpation, they rewarded him with the immediate Poffeffion of the Crown. But when they had all the defired Succefs, and fubdued all that they had fought with ; they foon found, that, by the Treachery and Corruption of their Leaders, they had loft all that they had fought for.

Inftead of compleating their Deliverance, and punifhing the Authors of their Calamities, and facrificing them to the Manes of their once loft Liberties ; upon the moft diligent Search, there was not a guilty Perfon to be found ; not One who had contributed to their Misfortunes. Three Kingdoms had been undone by Male-Adminiftration, and no body had a Hand in it. This Tergiverfation gave frefh Heart and Courage to the defpairing Faction : Some imputed it to Weaknefs and Fear ; others to a Confcioufnefs of Guilt for what we had done ; and all cried out aloud, that if there were no Criminals, there could be no Crimes ; whilft all honeft Men ftood amazed and covered with Shame and Confufion at thefe Proceedings.

All the while our new Betrayers rioted in their Sun-fhine, laughed at the unfeafonable Simplicity and Folly of a few Whimficals, who did not know what a Revolution was good for : They would not make a Rod for themfelves : On the contrary, numberlefs were their Projects and Stratagems to amafs Riches, and increafe their Power. They encouraged and protected a general Prodigality

gality and Corruption, and fo brought the Kingdom into the greateft Neceffities ; then took Advantage of thofe Neceffitics : They got publick
Money into their Hands, and then lent that Money to the Publick again for great Premiums, and
at great Intereft, and afterwards fquandered it away
to make Room for new Projects : They made
Bargains for themfelves, by borrowing in one
Capacity what they lent in another ; and, by a
Ufe of their prior Intelligence, and Knowledge
of their own Intentions, they wholly governed
the National Credit, and raifed and depreffed it
at their Pleafure, and as they faw their Advantage ; by which means they beggared the People,
and mortgaged all the Lands and the Stock of the
Kingdom, though not (like the righteons *Jofeph*)
to their Mafter, but to themfelves.

Thus the *Revolution* and the Principles of Liberty ran backwards again. The banifhed *Tarquin* conceived new Hopes, and made new Attempts for a Reftoration : All who had fhared in
the Benefits of the former wicked Adminiftration ;
all thofe who had ever been the avowed Enemies
to an equal Government, and impartial Liberty ;
all the grim Inquifitors, who had affumed an uncontroulable Sovereignty over the free and ungo-
vernable Mind, Men who have ever pretended a
divine Right to Roguery, united in his Intereft :
With thefe joined the Riotous, the Debauched,
the Neceffitous, the poor deluded Bigots, as well
as all fuch who had not received Rewards equal to
their fanfied Merit, and could not bear to fee
others revel in Advantages, which their own Ambition and Covetoufnefs had before fwallowed for
themfelves.

The

This formidable Party combined againſt the new eſtabliſhed Government, made Earnings of the Miſcarriages and Corruptions of thoſe Miſcreants, who, by their vile and mercenary Conduct, betrayed the beſt Prince and beſt Cauſe in the World, and ſeveral times had almoſt overturned the new reſtored Liberty ; but that the Gratitude and perſonal Love of the People to that great Prince, and the freſh and lively Remembrance of the Evils which they had ſuffered, or had been like to have ſuffered, from the abdicated Family, ſtill preſerved him upon the Throne, in ſpite of all Attempts to the contrary. However, proper Advantages were not taken, neither in this nor the following Reign, from the many Defeats of this reſtleſs Faction, to ſettle the *Revolution* upon ſuch a Baſis, as not be ſhaken but together with the Foundations of the Earth. There was always a Lion in the Way ; the Figure or the Number of the Conſpirators, or the Difficulty of Diſcovery, or their Intereſt, Alliance, or Confederacy with Men in Power, were the Reaſons whiſpered ; but the true one was concealed, namely, that one guilty Perſon durſt not heartily proſecute another : The Criminals had Stories to tell, Secrets not to be divulged ; for an innocent and virtuous Man alone dares undertake to bring a great Villain to deſerved Puniſhment : None but a *Brutus* could have deſtroyed *Brutus*'s Sons.

Nothing was ever done to rectify or regulate the Education of Youth, the Source of all our other Evils ; but Schools of Literature were ſuffered to continue under the Direction of the Enemies to all found Literature and publick Virtue : Liberty, being deſerted by her old Friends, fell

of

of courfe into the Hands of her Enemies; and fo Liberty was turned upon Liberty : By thefe Means the Difcontents were fomented, the Evils ftill increafed, and the Confpirators ftill went on. They had now got new Tools to work with, juft forged, and fent glowing hot from the Univerfities : A new Generation arofe and appeared upon the publick Stage, who had never feen or felt the Misfortunes which their Fathers groaned under, nor believed more of them than what they had learned from their Tutors : So that all Things feemed prepared for a new Revolution ; when we were furprized by a Voice from Heaven, which promifed us another Deliverance.

We have at laft, by the bounteous Gift of indulgent Providence, a moft excellent King, and a wife and uncorrupt Parliament ; and yet—But what fhall I fay, or what fhall be left unfaid ?— I will go on.—We have a Prince, I fay, who is poffeffed of every Virtue which can grace and adorn a Crown ; a Parliament too, than whom *England* has never chofen one better difpofed to do all thofe Things which every honeft Man in it wifhed, and called for ; and yet—by the Iniquity of the Times, or the Iniquities of particular Men, we are ftill to expect our Deliverance ; though I hope that we fhall not expect it long.

Publick Corruptions and Abufes have grown upon us : Fees in moft, if not in all, Offices, are immenfely increafed : Places and Employments, which ought not to be fold at all, are fold for treble Values : The Neceffities of the Publick have made greater Impofitions unavoidable, and yet the Publick has run very much in Debt ; and as thofe Debts have been encreafing, and the People growing

ing

ing poor, Salaries have been augmented, and Penfions multiplied ; I mean in the laft Reign, for I hope that there have been no fuch Doings in this.

Our common Rogues now fcorn little Pilferings, and in the Dark ; 'tis all publick Robbery, and at Noon-day ; nor is it, as formerly, for fmall Sums, but for the Ranfom of Kings, and the Pay of Armies : Figures of Hundreds and Thoufands have loft their Ufe in Arithmetick : (*) Plumbs alone are thought worth gathering ; and they no longer fignify Hundreds of Thoufands, but Millions : One Great Man, who is faid in a former Reign to have plundered a Million and a Half, has made his Succeffors think as much to be their Due too: Poffeffion of great Sums is thought to give a Title to thofe Sums ; and the Wealth of Nations is meafured out and divided amongft private Men, not (as by the *Weft-India* Pyrates) with Shovels, but by Waggons.

The Dregs of the People, and the Scum of the Alley, can buy *Italian* and *German* Sovereigns out of their Territories ; and their Levees have been lately crowded with Swarms of dependent Princes, like *Roman* Confuls, and *Eaftern* Monarchs ; and I am told, that fome of them have been feen afcending to, and defcending from, their Chariots, while they leaned upon the Necks of proftrate Grandees. Oh Liberty ! ftop thy Flight. Oh Virtue ! be fomething more than a Name and empty Sound : Return, Oh return ! infpire and affift our illuftrious Legiflators in the great Work which they have fo generoufly undertaken ! Affift, affift, if it be but to fave thofe who have always

(*) A Cant Word, known to mean an Hundred Thoufand Pounds.

devoutly

devoutly worſhipped thee, and have paid conſtant Incenſe at thy Altars.

But what ſhall be done ! Where is the Remedy for all theſe Evils ? We hope for it, we expect it, we ſee it ; and we call for it, from the healing Hands of our moſt gracious King, and his dutiful Parliament. There is a Criſis in the Health of Governments, as well as of private Perſons. When Diſtempers are at.the worſt, they muſt mend, or the Patient die : And when the Caſe is deſperate, bold and reſolute Methods muſt be taken, or he will be ſuffered to die, for fear of his dying.——— What then is the Remedy ?———We muſt begin with letting out ſome of our adulterate and corrupt Blood, one **Drop of** which is enough to contaminate the Ocean : We muſt firſt take full Vengeance of all thoſe whom we can diſcover to be guilty, and uſe them as Citizens do Shopliſters ; that is, make thoſe who are caught pay for all that is ſtolen. Let us not, Oh let us not ſuffer the Sins of all *Iſrael* to be at this Time of Day laid upon the Head of the Scape-Goat !

When we have taken this firſt and neceſſary Step, to prevent an Apoplexy or malignant Eruptions, let us preſcribe ſtrong Emeticks, proper Sudorificks, and effectual Purgatives, to bring up or throw off the noxious Juices and morbifick Matter that oppreſſes us, and ſo wholly to eradicate the Cauſes of our Diſtemper. But, above all, let us avoid the beginning with Lenitives and palliating Medicines, which will only cover and foment our Evils, make them break out more violently, at laſt perhaps turn into dangerous Swellings and epidemical Plague Sores ; and by ſuch Means ſpread a general Infection : Let us not ſuffer any

of

of our great or little Rogues to escape publick Vengeance.

When we have, by these vigorous Methods, removed the peccant Humours which are the Springs and Sources of our Distemper, let us use proper Applications, gentle Remedies, and wholesome Diet, to correct and rectify the Mass of remaining Blood, to invigorate and renew our Constitution, restore it to its first Principles, and make it sound and active again : Let us see where it abounds, and where it wants ; whether the sanguine, the phlegmatick, or the bilious predominates, and reduce them all to a proper Balance : Let us look back and examine strictly, by what Neglect, by what Steps and Gradations of Intemperance or Folly, we are brought into the present Condition, and resolve to avoid them for the future.

Let us try no more Projects, no more knavish Experiments ; let us have no more Quacking, no more to do with Empiricks. Let us act openly and above-board for the publick Interest, and not hang out false Colours, to catch unwary Preys. Let us plainly tell at first what we mean, and all that we mean : If it be honest and advantageous, every good Man will defend it, and assist in it ; if otherwise, it ought not to be defended at all.

This is the Way, and the only Way, to preserve and continue the inestimable Blessing of our present Establishment : Let the People see the Benefit of the Change, and there is no Fear that they will be against their own Interest ; but State-Quacks may harangue and swear till they are black in the Face, before they will persuade any one to believe that he is in perfect Health, who
feels

feels himfelf fick at Heart. Men in fuch Circumftances are always reftlefs, always tumbling
about from Side to Side, changing every Pofture
for prefent Eafe ; and fo often bring Death upon
themfelves, by trying prepofterous Remedies to
avoid it.

T   *I am,* &c.

SATURDAY, *March* 18, 1720. No. 21.

A Letter from John Ketch, *Efq; afferting his
Right to the Necks of the over-grown Brokers.*

SIR,

IN a general Call for Juftice from an injured
Nation, I beg Leave to put in my Voice, being
myfelf an eminent Sufferer in the ill Fate of my
Country, which no otherwife gains than as I do,
by the Exaltation of Rogues. Our Interefts, in
this Refpect, are the fame. And as it would be
very hard that the Blood-fuckers of the People
fhould not make the People fome Amends, by re-
ftoring the Blood that they have fucked ; fo it
would be as hard that I, who am the Finifher of
Juftice, fhould not have Juftice done me.

From my beft Obfervation upon publick Affairs, laft Summer, I promifed myfelf that I
fhould certainly have full Hands this laft Winter ; I therefore applied myfelf with fingular Diligence to gain the utmoft Perfection and Skill in
the Calling wherein God and the Law hath placed me : For, I did not think it at all laudable,

or

or agreeable to a good Confcience, to accept a Poft, without proper Talents and Experience to execute the fame, however cuftomary and common fuch a Practice might be : And therefore, without prefuming to follow the illuftrious Example of my Betters, in this Matter, I thought it became me to become my Poft. In Truth, Sir, if this Maxim had prevailed, where it fhould have prevailed ; and if my Brethren in Place had as well underftood, and as honeftly executed, their feveral Trufts, as I do mine, we fhould have had a very different Face of Things, nor would I have had Occafion for Journeymen.

Thus, Sir, I was firmly and honeftly refolved, that the Execution of Juftice fhould not ftick with me, where-ever elfe it ftuck. Moreover, at a Time when every Thing, but Honefty, bore a double Price, I bought up a great Quantity of Silken Halters, for the fole Ufe and Benefit of any of our topping Pick-pockets, who fhould be found to have noble or genteel Blood about them, *N. B.* This Compliment was not intended for the Directors, who muft expect to wear the fame valedictory Cravat which is worn by fmall Felons, who come under my Hands every Seffion : But I have fet apart a good round Quantity of thefe delicate Silken Turnovers for the Benefit and Decoration of divers worthy Gentlemen, whom I have marked out for my Cuftomers in the ———; whom it would not be good Breeding in me, as yet, to name ; but I hope they will prove rare Chaps.

I did likewife befpeak, at leaft, a Dozen curious Axes, fpick and fpan new, with rare Steel Edges; the fitteft that could be made, for dividing nobly betwixt the Head and the Shoulders of any dignified

and

and illuftrious Cuftomer of mine, who has, either by Birth or by Place, a Right to die at the Eaft End of the Town.

Now, Sir, it unluckily happens, that I cannot pay for any of the Implements of National Juftice, and of my Trade, till I have ufed them : And my Creditors, though they own me to be an honeft Man, yet, wanting Faith in all publick Officers, begin to fear that I fhall never pay for them at all. It is, in Truth, a fenfible Difcouragement to them and me, that I have fo little to do this Winter, when there appear'd fo much to be done in my Way. Sure never poor deferving Hangman had fuch a fhameful Vacation !

As having a Poft, I have confequently the Honour of being a true Member of the Church of *England*, as by Law eftablifhed ; and therefore under thefe Difappointments I comfort myfelf with fome Patience, and more Beer. I have, befides that, this further Confolation, that if our Canary Birds find Wings to efcape me, neither the Blame nor the Shame fhall lie at my Door.

You fee, Sir, I have Merit ; and yet you fee I labour under Difcouragements enough to fcare any Succeffor of mine from accepting this neglected and pennylefs Poft, till he has a fufficient Sum of Money in Hand paid, and a good Penfion for Life, as is ufual upon lefs Occafions, together with ample Provifion for his Children after him.

But, in fpite of all thefe Difcouragements, I am determined to live in Hopes of fome topping Cuftomers before the Seffions is ended : The Publick and I muft certainly get at laft : God knows we have been eminent Sufferers ; we have been defrauded on every Side.

Being

Being bred a Butcher, I can comfort my faid Cuftomers with an Affurance, that I have a delicate and ready Hand at cutting and tying ; fo let them take Heart, the Pain is nothing, and will be foon over ; I am only forry 'tis fo long a coming : No Man can be pleafed with being defrauded of his juft Dues.

I have one Confolation, Sir, which never leaves me ; namely, that though my Poft has not been fo profitable a one as for fome Time paft it fhould have been, yet it has been a fafe one. I doubt not but many of my Brethren in Place would be glad if they could fay as much. I am moreover of Opinion, that my Poft has, for a Year paft, been one of the moft honeft and creditable Pofts in *England* ; nor would I change Circumftances or Character with fome that hold their Heads very high, and may hold them higher ftill before I have done with them. I am fure it cannot be denied, that the Hangman of *London* has for the above Space of Time been a reputable Officer, in Comparifon.————The Truth is, that they have got more Money than I, but I have more Reputation than they ; and I hope foon to go Snacks with fome of them in their Money.

I know that Knaves of State require a great deal of Form and Ceremony before they are committed to my Care ; fo that I am not much furprized, that I have not yet laid my Hands upon certain exalted Criminals. I hope, however, that, when they come, a good Number will come at once. But there is a Parcel of notorious and forry Sinners, called *Brokers* : Fellows of fo little Confequence, that few of them have Reputation enough to ftand Candidates for my Place, were the fame vacant,

vacant, (which God forbid !) and yet Rogues fo fwoln with Guilt, that poor *Derwentwater* and *Kenmure* (my two laft Cuftomers) were Babes and Petty Larceners to them. Now thefe are the Hang-Rogues with whom I would be keeping my Hand in Ufe.

Sir, I have been with Counfel about them, and my Lawyer ftands amazed that I have not had them already : " But, *fays he*, Mr. *Ketch*, I fore-
" faw that the Brokers were only the Pimps of
" great Rogues, who were themfelves the Pimps
" of greater : So that were thefe Vermin to go
" up to *Tyburn*, they would draw many more
" after them, who would likewife draw others.——
" So, depend upon it, the Lion, if it can, will
" fave the Jackall. And hence it proceeds, Mr.
" *Ketch*, that though it be hard, yet it is not
" ftrange, that thofe Rogues, whom all Men
" wifh in your Hands, are not yet there."

He then told me how the Brokers have violated that Act of Parliament, which allows them but Two Shillings and Sixpence for tranfacting a Hundred Pounds Stock, by taking, or rather ex-acting Twenty Shillings, and fometimes Five Pounds. I hope, when I come to ftrip them, or to commute for ftripping them, that I fhall be al-lowed to mete out to them the fame Meafure.

He told me likewife, that during the Reign of Roguery, they fold for no body but the Directors, and their Betters ; whereas they were obliged in Duty to have fold for all Men alike, who employ-ed them. Their Office is an Office of Truft, as well as that of the Directors. They act, or ought to act, under the Reftrictions of an Act of Parlia-ment, under the facred Obligation of an Oath,

and

and under the Ties and Penalties of a Bond ; by all which they are obliged to difcharge their Duty impartially betwixt Man and Man, and for one Man as foon as another. Now it is well known, that they broke their Truft to the Publick ; that they ceafed to be common and indifferent Officers in the Alley ; and yet retaining the Name and Pretence of their Office, (by which they alfo retained the Power of deceiving) they became only Spies and Liars for the Directors and their Managers, and Sellers for them only. They were therefore Criminals of the firft Clafs, and principal Agents in the publick Mifchief ; for, had they not acted thus for one Side alone, the Directors could not have fold out much at high Prices, nor would others have bought in at thofe Prices : So that they are to be confidered not only as the Inftruments of greater Traytors, though in that Character they are liable to be hanged ; but as wilful and deliberate Confederates with thofe Traytors ; and, confequently, merit every Punifhment which thofe higher Traytors merit.

My Counfel faid too, that there were fome Crimes of fo high and malignant a Nature, that, in the Perpetration of them, all Acceffaries were confidered as Principals ; that thofe who held a Man till he was murthered, were Murtherers ; that thofe who voluntarily held a Candle to others, who robbed a Houfe, were themfelves Robbers ; and that in committing of Treafon, all are Traytors who have had a Hand in that Treafon.

He faid, that the Broker were free Agents, independent of all Companies, and no more attached, in Point of Duty, to the *South-Sea*, than

to

to any other; that being *fui juris* (as he called it) they could not excufe their wicked Dealings by the pretended Commands and Authority of any Superiors, as fome of the *South-Sea* Officers might plead, for that the Directors were not their Superiors; that their Rogueries therefore were voluntary and deliberate Rogueries; and that having wilfully finned with the Directors, they ought in Juftice to fuffer with the Directors, and hang with them.

He told me, that having Share of the Gain of Villainy with the Directors, they ought to have their Share of the Halter too. They tranfacted great Sums for themfelves; though the Law, which eftablifhed them, enacts, That they fhall neither Buy nor Sell for themfelves; which is highly reafonable; for how can any Man tranfact honeftly for another, whilft he is felling to him his own Stock?

He faid, that they deceived every Man into his own Ruin; and ruined the Nation, to enrich the Directors and themfelves: They fold their own Stock, and that of the Directors, under falfe and fictitious Names, contrary to the Obligation of their Bond to the City, which obliges them to declare the Name of the Seller to the Buyer, as well as the Name of the Buyer to the Seller; for they knew that no Man would have been willing to buy, had he known that the Brokers and Directors were in hafte to fell. Thus they ufed falfe Dice, and blinded Mens Eyes, to pick their Pockets. " And furely, Mr. *Ketch*, *fays the Counfellor*, " if he who picks a Man's Pocket is to be hanged, " the Rogues that pick the Pockets of the whole " Country, ought to be hanged, drawn, and " quartered."

But

But what was moſt remarkable of all in what the Counſellor told me, and what indeed gives me moſt Heart, is, that unleſs the Brokers are hanged, it will be ſcarce poſſible that any body elſe ſhould be hanged. If this be true, their Doom is certain, and I ſhall be able to ſupport my Squireſhip before *Eaſter :* For, ſurely, we ſhall never ſave mighty Knaves, for the Sake of ſaving little ones ; and if ſo be it is determin'd to gratify the Nation with a competent Store of Hanging and Beheading, certainly we muſt do every thing neceſſary thereunto.

" Now, *ſays my Counſel*, if the Brokers do not
" diſcover the Secrets which they beſt know, but
" which they will never diſcover, if they can
" ſave their Necks and Purſes without doing it ;
" then, I doubt me, Juſtice will be impotent for
" want of Evidence. But if they find that they
" can ſave nothing by their Silence, they will tell
" all to ſave ſomething. They are hardened
" Rogues ; and, by falſe Oaths, and under-hand
" Dealing, will ſkreen all that are as bad as them-
" ſelves ; but gripe them well, and ten to one but
" you ſqueeze the Truth out of them.

" For all which Reaſons, Mr. *Ketch, continued*
" *he,* I hope ſoon to give you Joy of the Brokers,
" as well as of better Cuſtomers."—And ſo he diſmiſſed me, wirhout taking a Fee ; for he told me, that he conſidered me as an eminent Sufferer, by having as yet got nothing, where he wiſhed that I had, before this Time, got a great deal.

This, Sir, is the Subſtance of what paſſed between us ; for which I am ſo much obliged to him, that if ever he falls in my Way, I'll uſe him with the like Generoſity ; and I will owe you,
Mr.

Mr. *Journalist*, the fame Favour, if you will be
fo kind to publifh this.

If you knew me, Sir, you would own that I
have valuable Talents, and am worth your Acquaintance. I am particularly poffeffed of a praifeworthy Induftry, and an ardent Defire of Bufinefs.
—In Truth, I care not to be idle; and yet it
cruelly happens, that I have but one bufy Day in
fix Weeks, and even then I could do twice as
much. Befides, having a tender Heart, it really
affects me with Pity, to be obliged to ftrangle fo
many Innocents every Seffions; poor harmlefs Offenders, that only commit Murthers, and break
open Houfes, and rob Men of Guineas and Half
Crowns; while wholefale Plunderers, and mighty
Rogues of Prey, the avowed Enemies and Hangmen of Honefty, Trade and Truth, the known
Promoters of Villainy, and the mercilefs Authors
of Mifery, Want, aud general Ruin, go on to
ride in Coaches and Six, and to defy a People
whom they have made poor and defperate; potent
Parricides, who have plundered more from this
Kingdom in Six Months than all the private
Thieves and Highwaymen ever did, or could do,
fince the Creation.

Sir, I repeat it, that the hanging of fuch poor
Felons only, as Things now ftand, is, compara-
tively, fhedding innocent Blood: And fo, for the
Eafe of my Mind, I beg that I may have thofe
fent me, whom I may trufs up with a fafe Con-
fcience. My Teeth particularly water, and my
Bowels yearn, at the Name of the Brokers; for
God's Sake, let me have the Brokers.

Upon the Whole, Sir, I have Reafon to hope,
from the prefent Spirit raifed in the Nation, (and,
they

they fay, it is in a great Meafure owing to you, that there is fuch a Spirit raifed :) I fay, I hope foon to have the fingering of the Throats of thefe Traytors, who have fingered all the Money in the Nation. Their own Guilt, and the inceffant Cry of the People, will weigh them down, in fpite of all Arts and Skreens.

N. B. I have a nice Hand at touching a Neck of Quality ; and when any Cuftomers come, I fhall be ready to give you Joy of it, as well as to receive the like from you. Who am,

G   *S I R*,

Your loving Friend,

JOHN KETCH.

SATURDAY, *March* 25, 1721. No. 22.

The Judgment of the People generally found, where not mifled. With the Importance and Probability of bringing over Mr. Knight.

S I R,

FROM the prefent Spirit of this Nation, it is ftill further evident to me, what I have always thought, that the People would conftantly be in the Interefts of Truth and Liberty, were it not for external Delufion and external Force. Take away Terror, and Men never would have been Slaves : Take away Impofture, and Men will never be Dupes nor Bigots. The People, when they are in the Wrong, are generally in the Wrong through Miftake ; and when they come to know it, are apt frankly to correct their own

Faults,

Faults. Of which Candour in them *Machiavel*
has given several Instances, and many more might
be given.

But it is not so with Great Men, and the Leaders of Parties ; who are, for the most Part, in the
Wrong through Ambition, and continue in the
Wrong through Malice. Their Intention is
wicked, and their End criminal ; and they commonly aggravate great Crimes by greater. As
great Dunces as the Governors of Mankind often
are, (and God knows that they are often great
enough) they are never Traytors out of mere Stupidity.

Machiavel says, *That no wise Man needs decline
the Judgment of the People in the Distribution of
Offices and Honours, and such particular Affairs,*
(in which I suppose he includes Punishment) *for
in those Things they are almost infallible.*

I could give many Instances where the People
of *England* have judged and do judge right ; as
they generally would, were they not misled. They
are, particularly, unanimous in their Opinion, that
we ought by no Means to part with *Gibraltar* ; and
this their Opinion is grounded upon the same Reasons that sway the wisest Men in this Matter.

They likewise know, that an *English* War
with *Muscovy* would be downright Madness ; for
that, whatever Advantage the same might be to
other Countries, it would grievously hurt the
Trade and Navy of *England*, without hurting the
Czar.

They know too, that a Squabble between
Spain and the Emperor about *Italy*, could not much
affect *England* ; and that therefore, were we to
go to War with either, upon that Account, as

Things

Things now ftand, it could not be for the Sake of *England.*

They know, that our Men of War might be always as honeftly employed in defending our Trade, by which our Country fubfifts, from the Depredations of Pyrates, as in conquering Kingdoms for thofe to whom the Nation is nothing obliged, or in defending Provinces with which the Nation has nothing to do, and from which it reaps no Advantage.

They know, that it is of great Concernment to any People, that the Heir Apparent to their Crown be bred amongft them ; not only that he may be reconciled, by Habit, to their Cuftoms and Laws, and grow in Love with their Liberties ; but that, at his Acceffion to the Throne, he may not be engroffed and befet by Foreigners, who will be always in the Intereft of another Country ; and, confequently, will be attempting to miflead him into Meafures mifchievous to his Kingdom, and advantageous to themfelves, or their own Nation.

The People know, that thofe are the beft Minifters, who do the moft Good to their Country, or rather the leaft Mifchief : They can feel Mifery and Happinefs, as well as thofe that govern them ; and will always,. in fpite of all Arts, love thofe that do them a fenfible Good, and abhor, as they ought, thofe that load them with Evils. Hence proceeds the Popularity, and the great and unenvied Charaéters, of our prefent Governors ; who, befides the memorable and profperous Projeéts which they have brought to Maturity, for the Good of *Great Britain* and *Ireland*, would likewife have obliged us with another

Prefent,

Prefent (*), but very few Years fince, which
would have completed all the reft, if we had had
the Courtefy to have accepted it.

It is certain, that the People, when left to
themfelves, do generally, if not always, judge
well ; we have juft now a glaring Inftance of it
in the loud and unanimous Call of all Men, that
Mr. *Knight* may be brought over ; I fay, the Call
of all Men, except the Directors and their Accomplices, Nay, the People judge well, as to the
Caufe of his going away ; they more than guefs
for whofe Sake, and by whofe Perfuafion, he
went ; and they are of Opinion, that, were he
here, the Trials of Guilt in the Houfe of Commons would be much fhorter, and the *Tower* of
London ftill more nobly inhabited. I am indeed
furprized that he is not already in *London*, confidering of what Confequence it is to have him here,
both to publick and to private Men.

Whether the Directors and their Mafters fhall
be punifhed or no, is to me one and the fame Queftion, as to afk, Whether you will preferve your
Conftitution or no ; or, Whether you will have
any Conftitution at all ? It is a Contention of Honefty and Innocence with Villainy and Falfhood ;
it is a Difpute whether or no you fhall be a People ;
it is a Struggle, and, if it be baulked, will, in all
Probability, be the laft Struggle for old *Englifh* Liberty. All this is well underftood by the People
of *England*.

Now, though the inferior Knaves are in a fair
Way of being hanged, yet our Top-Traytors,
having tranfacted all their Villainies in the *South-
Sea* with Mr. *Knight* alone, or with Mr. *Knight*

(*) The Peerage Bill.

chiefly,

chiefly, will think themfelves always fafe, fo long
as they can keep him Abroad ; and while he continues Abroad, the Nation's Vengeance can never
be half complete.

As to my own particular, I am fo fanguine in
this Affair, that the very Reafons commonly given
why he will not be brought over, are to me very
good Reafons why he will be brought over : I cannot but wonder to hear any Doubts about it. I am
fure, that thofe who fuggeft fuch Doubts, muft
fuggeft with the fame Breath very terrible Crimes
againft fome very confiderable Men.

The Bufinefs of bringing over Mr. *Knight* is
become the Bufinefs of the Miniftry, and incum-
bent on them only. It is become their Duty to
their Mafter King *GÈORGE*, as they would
preferve entirely to him the Affections of a willing
and contented People, by fhewing them, that
in Confideration of their mighty Wrongs (which
the faid Miniftry did all in their Power to prevent) they fhall have all fair Play for Juftice and
Reftitution. And it is in this Refpect too become
the Duty of the Miniftry to the People, whofe
Humours it is their Bufinefs to watch, whofe Intereft it is their Bufinefs to ftudy, as much as the
Intereft of the King himfelf ; and it muft be
owned, to the Praife of the prefent Set, that they
have conftantly confulted and purfued the one as
much as the other, with equal Skill and Honefty ;
and fo far King and People are equally obliged to
them.

As to the perfonal Interefts of the Minifters
themfelves, I fay nothing, the fame being fuppofed
always firmly linked with the other two ; as
doubtlefs it is at prefent. Let me only add here,
that

that the bringing over Mr. *Knight* is a Duty which they owe to themfelves, their own Characters being intimately concerned in it ; otherwife—

People indeed begin to fay, that the fuppreffing of Evidence ought to be taken for Evidence, as in the Cafe of Mr. *Aiflabie*, who burned the Book which contained the Evidence.   There is a noble Perfon too, faid to be mentioned in the Report of the Committee, not to his Advantage ; but, I thank God, now fully vindicated by Patriots as incorrupt as himfelf, upon the fulleft Proof of his Innocence ; and if his Acquittal did not meet the univerfal Concurrence of all prefent, it could be owing only to Mr. *Knight*'s not being at hand to fpeak what he knew : Had he made his Appearance, there had never been a Divifion upon the Queftion, but all would have been then as unanimous in their Sentiments about that Great Man's Integrity and clean Hands, as all the reft of the Kingdom at prefent are.   However, Reputation is fo nice a Thing, that it cannot be made too clear ; and therefore we are fure of the hearty Affiftance of this illuftrious Patriot to bring over Mr. *Knight*, if poffible, to make his Vindication yet more complete.

It is alfo the Intereft of another Great Perfon, equal to the firft in Power and Innocence, and who, without Doubt, has taken common Meafures with him for the publick Good, and will equally fhare in the grateful Applaufe of good Men, and the Reproach of bad ; for no Degrees of Virtue will put any one beyond the Reach of Envy and Calumny, and therefore we cannot be fure that his ftrenuous and barefaced Protection of innocent and oppreffed Virtue will not be mif-
inter-

interpreted by popular Clamour, which often mif-
applies eftablifhed and well-known Truths ; as,
that no one who has not Part of the Gain, will
adopt Part of the Infamy ; that it is the Property
of Innocence to abhor Guilt in others, as well as
not to practife the fame itfelf, and to punifh as
well as to hate it ; that no Man who is not a
Thief, will be an Advocate for a Thief ; that
Rogues are beft protected by their Fellows ; and
that the ftrongeft Motive which any Man can
have for faving another from the Gallows, is
the Fear of the fame Punifhment for the fame
Crimes : And though thefe, and a Thoufand other
fuch unwarrantable Imputations, ought not, and
have not made the leaft Impreffion upon one confcious of his own Virtue ; yet it is every Man's
Duty, as well as Intereft, to remove the moft
diftant Caufes of Sufpicion from himfelf, when
he can do it confiftent with his publick Duty ;
and therefore we are equally fure of this Great
Man's Endeavours too for bringing over Mr.
Knight.

Even fome of our Legiflators themfelves have
not been free from Calumny, who are all concerned to have their Characters vindicated ; and
therefore we may be fure will, in the higheft manner, refent any Prevarication, or trifling Chicane,
if fuch a Procedure could be poffibly fuppofed in
an Affair of this nice Importance to all *England,*
as well as to many of themfelves.

Nay, the whole Parliament of *England,* who
have generoufly undertaken the Scrutiny of the
late black Knaveries, and the Punifhment of the
Knaves, are nearly concerned to fee Mr. *Knight*
brought over. They find, in their Enquiries, his
Tefti-

Teftimony often referred to, and that the Evidence is not complete without him. They know already a good deal of what he could fay ; and I doubt not but he could fay more than they know. They have once addreffed his Majefty already, about bringing him over ; and I fuppofe will again, if he do not come fpeedily. The Bufinefs of the whole Nation does, as it were, ftand ftill for it ; feeing it is become the Bufinefs and Expectation of the whole Nation.

As to Remoras from Abroad, I cannot fee Room for any.——Quite otherwife ; I always thought it very fortunate for *England*, that Mr. *Knight* fell into the Emperor's Hands ; a Prince, for whom we have done fuch Mighty, fuch Heroick Favours ; for whom we confumed our Fleet in the *Mediterranean*, for whom we guarantie'd *Italy*, for whom we preferved and conquered Kingdoms ; a Prince, in fine, for whofe Service we have wafted Years, Fleets, and Treafures : And can it be alledged or fuppofed, with the Appearance of common Senfe, that this great Prince, the ftrict Friend, old Confederate, and faft Ally of *England* ; a Prince, who has been, as it were, the Ward of *England*, and brought up in its Arms ; fupported by its Intereft and Counfels, protected and aggrandized by its Fleets and Armies, will, againft all the Principles of good Policy, againft all the Ties of Gratitude and Honour, fly in the Face of his Friends and Benefactors, by refufing to deliver up to this Nation and this King, a little Criminal, fmall in his Character, but great in his Crimes and of the utmoft Confequence to *England* in the Purfuit of this great Enquiry, which merits the Confideration,

tion ; and commands the Attention of every *Englifhman*.

We could draw up a long, a very long Lift of good Deeds done, and expenfive Favours fhewn, to the Emperor ; without being afraid of being put out of Countenance by any *German* Catalogue of Returns made us from *Vienna*. Perhaps there may have been fome Courtefies procured fiom thence by *England*; but we would afk, Whether they were intended or procured for *England* ? It feems to me, that this is the firft Time of afking for ourfelves : And fhall we, this firft Time, be denied ? Will fuch an humble Mite be refufed for Millions frankly beftowed, and beftowed beyond all Conjecture and Expectation ? It cannot be ; nor, if it could, ought it to be borne. We know how to fhew, that we have Senfe as well as Power, and Refentment as well as Liberality.

The Emperor therefore cannot be fufpected in this Matter ; I dare fay that he will comply with our Demands, as foon as they are made, whatever they be. He will not put fuch Contempt upon us, who have purchafed more Refpect at his Hands. Befides, it is confidently afferted, that Mr. *Knight* longs to be at Home ; which I am apt to believe : He knows, that the kind Counfel given him, to go away, was not given him for his own Sake ; and has Reafon to fear, that thofe who fent him away, will keep him away. There is *Laudanum* in *Flanders*, as well as in *England* ; and That or a Poignard may thwart his beft Inclinations to return. If that fhould happen, we are at Liberty to think the worft ; and, I doubt, we cannot think too bad. Unhappy Man ! he was not a Knave for himfelf alone ; and I am apt

to

to believe, were he here, that he would honeftly betray thofe Men to the Publick, for whom he wickedly betrayed the Publick.

Thus then, in all likelihood, neither the Emperor nor Mr. *Knight* are to be blamed, if Mr. *Knight* does not return. But, whether he be willing or no, the Emperor has no Right, no Pretence to keep him. Who will then be to blame, if the univerfal Cry of Juftice, and of the Nation, fhould not have its Effect ? The Queftion is eafy, were the Anfwer prudent to give. In Truth, there needs no Anfwer ; all Mankind will know how to folve this Difficulty.

An honourable Meffenger has been gone near Six Weeks, and yet the Commons have Occafion to addrefs his Majefty to know what Anfwer he has fent. Wonderful, in a Cafe that is of fo much Importance, and which requires fo much Expedition, and fo little Ceremony ! I have fometimes thought a Courier muft needs have been difpatched to *England* about it long fince, but that he was way-laid, and murdered by our Confpirators and their Agents upon the Road. This may feem a ftrange Fancy ; but, without being very aged, I have lived long enough to think nothing ftrange. ———I have not been once amazed thefe Six Months.

In the mean time, the Bufinefs of the Committee, which is the Bufinefs of *Great Britain*, is like to ftand ftill. Thofe Gentlemen have done their Duty ; and if their Evidence be not complete, (which however they deny) the Fault is not chargeable on them, but they are anfwerable who keep them from better. This is a Reproach not like to be wiped off, but by bringing over Mr. *Knight* ;
                                                                and

and then, perhaps, they that deserve it may dread a far worse Thing. Here is the Riddle, and the Solution of the Riddle.—There are those amongst us, who, cloathed as they are with Infamy, and cursed and detested by their Fellow-Creatures universally, do yet dread a greater Evil. So precious and prevailing is the Love of Life! Continue me mine, sweet Heaven, upon better Terms, or not at all!

I shall conclude, by repeating an Observation which I have already made in this Letter; namely, that the suppressing the best Evidence, contains in it the strongest Evidence; and those Men will stand condemned, who, in Trials of Innocence and Guilt, stop the Mouths of their Judges, and deprive the Accusers of their Witnesses.

T *and* G   *I am,* &c.

SATURDAY, *April* 1, 1721. No. 23.

A memorable Letter from Brutus *to* Cicero, *with an explanatory Introduction.*

S *I* R,

I AM going to present you, and the Town by your Means, with the most valuable Performance of all Antiquity: It is not likely that it ever had, or ever will have, its Fellow. The Author of it was, perhaps, the most amiable Character, the most accomplished Man, that ever the World saw.

> *Excellent* Brutus ! *of all human Race*
> *The Best !*   COWLEY.

He

He was the Author of that glorious Letter, which I now fend you in *Englifh*. It was written by the greateft Man upon the nobleft Subject; *BRUTUS* upon LIBERTY. It was fent to *Cicero*, and the Occafion this, as I find it very well explained by Monfieur *Soreau*, and prefixed to his *French Tranflation* of *Brutus*'s Letters.

Octavius Cæfar, afterwards called *Auguftus*, having defeated *Mark Anthony* before *Modena*, and by that Means raifed the Siege of that Place, began now to conceive higher Defigns than he had yet fhewn: He had hitherto declared for the Commonwealth, and feemed to act for it; the Senate having trufted him with an Army, by the Perfuafion and Intereft of *Cicero*. But after this Victory over *Anthony*, he began to fet up for himfelf, and to meditate the Revenge of his Uncle, and Father by Adoption, *Julius Cæfar*; and, finally, to pave himfelf a Way for abfolute Monarchy. He knew well, that *Brutus* and *Caffius* would never, while they lived, fuffer him to poffefs what they would not fuffer the firft *Cæfar* to enjoy; and therefore, to fucceed his Uncle, he muft deftroy them.

But *Cicero*, who equally loved and admired *Brutus*, and pretended to great Power over the Mind of the young *Cæfar*, undertook to write to him in Favour of the Patrons of Liberty, who flew his Uncle, to feek their Pardon; efpecially a Pardon for *Brutus*, that he might return to *Rome*, and be there in Safety. This Letter of *Cicero*'s contained in it alfo Thanks to *Octavius* for his Services to the Republick, and was entirely unknown to *Brutus*; but being informed of it by *Atticus*, he took extreme Offence at this Step of *Cicero*'s, which

which feemed to him a Confeffion of Sovereignty in *Octavius*, by not only owning him Mafter of the Lives of the *Romans* in general, but of his too, who was the Deliverer of the *Romans*, and fcorned to owe Life to *Octavius*.

Brutus had another Spirit, and other Views: He remembered the bold and free Words of the Great *Cato*, his Uncle, to thofe of his Friends who offered to procure for him the Mercy of *Cæfar*, by throwing themfelves, on his Behalf, at *Cæfar*'s Feet.—*No*, fays *Cato*, *I fcorn to be beholden to Tyranny. I am as free as* Cæfar; *and fhall I owe my Life to him, who has no Right even to my Submiffion.*

Brutus found Reafon to refent, that *Cicero* fhould, without his Knowledge, thus treat him as a Criminal, and *Cæfar* as a Sovereign, by begging of *Cæfar* Mercy for *Brutus*. That Refentment gave Occafion to this Letter; in which he treats *Octavius* as a raw Lad, and *Cicero* as a weak and fearful Man. The Reafoning through the Whole fhews *Brutus* to have been animated by a moft fublime and glorious Spirit of Virtue and Liberty; and is fo ftupendoufly ftrong, that his Eloquence muft have been great as his Soul; and yet that great Soul was not fo dear to him as his Liberty.

I am, &c.

BRUTUS to *CICERO*.

" I Have feen, by the Favour of *Atticus*, that
" Part which concerns me in your Letter to
" *Octavius*. The Affection which you there ex-
" prefs for my Perfon, and the Pains which you
" take

" take for my Safety, are great; but they give
" me no new Joy : Your kind Offices are be-
" come as habitual for me to receive, as for you
" to beftow ; and, by your daily Difcourfe and
" Actions on my Behalf, I have daily Inftances
" of your generous Regard for myfelf and my
" Reputation.

" However, all this hinders not but that the
" above-mentioned Article of your Letter to
" *Octavius* pierced me with as fenfible a Grief
" as my Soul is capable of feeling.   In thanking
" him for his Services to the Republick, you have
" chofen a Style which fhews fuch Lownefs and
" Submiffion, as do but too clearly declare, that
" you have ftill a Mafter ; and that the old Ty-
" ranny, which we thought deftroyed, is revived
" in a new Tyrant.   What fhall I fay to you
" upon this fad Head ? I am covered with Con-
" fufion for your fhameful Condition, but you
" have brought it upon yourfelf ; and I cannot
" help fhewing you to yourfelf in this wretched
" Circumftance.

" You have petition'd *Octavius* to have Mercy
" upon me, and to fave my Life.—In this you
" intend my Good, but fought my Mifery, and
" a Lot worfe than Death, by faving me from
" it ; fince there is no Kind of Death but is
" more eligible to me than a Life fo faved.   Be
" fo good to recollect a little the Terms of your
" Letter ! and having weighed them as you
" ought, can you deny that they are conceived
" in the low Style of an humble Petition from a
" Slave to his haughty Lord, from a Subject to a
" King ? You tell *Octavius*, that you have a
" Requeft to make him, and hope that he will
                                    " pleafe

" pleafe to grant it ; namely, to fave thofe Citi-
" zens who are efteemed by Men of Condition,
" and beloved by the People of *Rome*. This is
" your honourable Requeft ; but what if he fhould
" not grant it, but refufe to fave us ? Can we
" be faved by no other Expedient ? Certainly, De-
" ftruction itfelf is preferable to Life by his Fa-
" vour !

" I am not, however, fo defponding, as to
" imagine that Heaven is fo offended with the
" *Roman* People, or fo bent upon their Ruin, that
" you fhould thus choofe, in your Prayers, to ap-
" ply rather to *Octavius*, than to the immortal
" Gods, for the Prefervation, I do not fay of the
" Deliverers of the whole Earth, but even for the
" Prefervation of the meaneft *Roman* Citizen. This
" is a high Tone to talk in, but I have Pleafure
" in it : It becomes me to fhew, that I fcorn to
" pray to thofe whom I fcorn to fear.

" Has then *Octavius* Power to fave us, or de-
" ftroy us ? And while you thus own him to
" be a Tyrant, can you yet own yourfelf his
" Friend ? And while you are mine, can you
" defire to fee me in *Rome*, and at the Mercy of
" an Ufurper ? And yet, that this would be my
" Cafe you avow, by imploring from a giddy
" Boy, my Permiffion to return. You have
" been rendering him a World of Thanks, and
" making him many Compliments ; pray, how
" come they to be due to him, if he yet want to
" be petitioned for our Lives, and if our Liberty
" depend upon his Sufferance ? Are we bound to
" think it a Condefcenfion in *Octavius*, that he
" choofes that thefe our Petitions fhould rather
" be made to him than to *Anthony ?* And are
                                        " not

" not fuch low Supplications the proper Addreffes
" to a Tyrant? And yet fhall we, who boldly
" deftroyed one, be ever brought bafely to fup-
" plicate another? And can we, who are the
" Deliverers of the Commonwealth, defcend to
" afk what no Man ought to have it in his Power
" to give?

" Confider the mournful Effects of that Dread
" and Defpondency of yours in our publick Strug-
" gles; in which, however, you have too many
" to keep you in Countenance. The Common-
" wealth has been loft, becaufe it was given for
" loft. Hence *Cæfar* was firft infpired with the
" Luft of Dominion; hence *Mark Anthony*, not
" terrified by the Doom of the Tyrant, pants
" and hurries on to fucceed him in his Tyranny;
" and hence this *Octavius*, this green Ufurper, is
" ftarted into fuch a Pitch of Power, that the
" Chiefs of the Commonwealth, and the Saviours
" of their Country, muft depend for their Breath
" upon his Pleafure.——Yes, we muft owe our
" Lives to the Mercy of a Minor, foftened by
" the Prayers of aged Senators!

" Alas, we are no longer *Romans!* If we
" were, the virtuous Spirit of Liberty would have
" been an eafy Over-match for the traiterous At-
" tempts of the worft of all Men grafping after
" Tyranny; nor would even *Mark Anthony*, the
" rafh and enterprizing *Mark Anthony*, have been
" fo fond of *Cæfar*'s Power, as frightened by
" *Cæfar*'s Fate.

" Remember the important Character which
" you fuftain, the great Poft which you have fill-
" ed: You are a Senator of *Rome*, you have been
" Conful of *Rome*; you have defeated Confpira-
" cies,

" cies, you have deſtroyed Conſpirators. Is not
" *Rome* ſtill as dear to you as ſhe was ? Or, is
" your Courage and Vigilance leſs ? And is not
" the Occaſion greater ? Or, could you ſuppreſs
" great Traytors, and yet tolerate greater ? Re-
" collect what you ought to do, by what you have
" done. Whence proceeded your Enmity to *An-*
" *thony ?* Was it not, that he had an Enmity to
" Liberty, had ſeized violently on the Publick,
" aſſumed the Diſpoſal of Life and Death into his
" own Hands, and ſet up for the ſole Sovereign
" of all Men ? Were not theſe the Reaſons of
" your Enmity, and of your Advice, to combat
" Violence by Violence ; to kill him, rather than
" ſubmit to him ? All this was well. ⸺ But
" why muſt Reſiſtance be dropped, when there is
" a freſh Call for Reſiſtance ? Has your Courage
" failed you ? Or, was it not permitted to *Anthony*
" to enſlave us, but another may ? As if the Na-
" ture of Servitude were changed, by changing
" Names and Perſons. No, — we do not diſ-
" pute about the Qualifications of a Maſter ; we
" will have no Maſter.

" It is certain, that we might, under *Anthony*,
" have had large Shares with him in the Admi-
" niſtration of deſpotick Power ; we might have
" divided its Dignities, ſhone in its Trappings.
" He would have received us gracioufly, and met
" us half way. He knew that either our Con-
" currence or Acquieſcence would have confirmed
" him Monarch of *Rome* ; and at what Price
" would he not have purchaſed either ? But all
" his Arts, all his Temptations, all his Offers,
" were rejected ; Liberty was our Purpoſe, Virtue
" our Rule : our Views were honeſt and univer-
" ſal ;

" fal ; Our Country, and the Caufe of Man-
" kind.

" With *Octavius* himfelf there is ftill a Way
" open for an Accommodation, if we choofe it.
" As eager as the Name of *Cæfar* has made that
" raw Stickler for Empire to deftroy thofe who
" deftroyed *Cæfar* ; yet, doubtlefs, he would give
" us good Articles, to gain our Confent to that
" Power to which he afpires, and to which, I
" fear, he will arrive : Alas ! what is there to
" hinder him ? While we only attend to the
" Love of Life, and the Impulfes of Ambition ;
" while we can purchafe Pofts and Dignities with
" the Price of Liberty, and think Danger more
" dreadful than Slavery, what remains to fave
" us ?

" What was. the End of our killing the Ty-
" rant, but to be free from Tyranny ? ———— A
" ridiculous Motive, and an empty Exploit, if
" our Slavery furvive him ! ———— Oh, who is it
" that makes Liberty his Care? Liberty, which
" ought to be the Care of all Men, as 'tis the
" Benefit and Blefling of all ! For myfelf, ra-
" ther than give it up, I will ftand fingle in its
" Defence. I cannot lofe, but with my Life,
" my Refolution to maintain in Freedom my
" Country, which I have fet free : I have de-
" ftroyed a veteran Tyrant; and fhall I fuffer,
" in a raw Youth, his Heir, a Power to controul
" the Senate, fuperfede the Laws, and put Chains
" on *Rome* ? A Power, which no perfonal Fa-
" vours, nor even the Ties of Blood, could ever
" fanctify to me ; a Power, which I could not
" bear in *Cæfar*; nor, if my Father had ufurped
" it, could I have borne in him.

" Your

" Your Petition to *Octavius* is a Confeffion,
" that we cannot enjoy the Liberty of *Rome* with-
" out his Leave; and can you dream that other
" Citizens are free, where we could not live free?
" Befides, having made your Requeft, how is it
" to be fulfilled? You beg him to give us our
" Lives; and what if he do? Are we therefore
" fafe, becaufe we live? Is there any Safety with-
" out Liberty? or rather, can we poorly live,
" having loft it, and with it our Honour and
" Glory? Is there any Security in living at
" *Romo*, when *Rome* is no longer free? That
" City, great as it is, having no Security of her
" own, can give me none. ———No, I will owe
" mine to my Refolution and my Sword; I can-
" not enjoy Life at the Mercy of another. *Cæfar*'s
" Death alone afcertained my Liberty to me,
" which before was precarious: I fmote him, to
" be fafe. This is a *Roman* Spirit; and whither-
" foever I carry it, every Place will be *Rome* to
" me; who am *Roman* enough to prefer every
" Evil to Chains and Infamy, which to a *Roman*
" are the higheft of all Evils. I thought that we
" had been releafed from thefe mighty Evils, by
" the Death of him who brought them upon us;
" but it feems that we are not; elfe why a fervile
" Petition to a Youth, big with the Name and
" the Ambition of *Cæfar*, for Mercy to thofe Pa-
" triots, who generoufly revenged their Country
" upon that Tyrant, and cleared the World of
" his Tyranny? It was not thus in the Common-
" wealths of *Greece*, where the Children of Ty-
" rants fuffered, equally with their Fathers, the
" Punifhment of Tyranny.

" Can

" Can I then have any Appetite to fee *Rome*?
" Or, can *Rome* be faid to be *Rome*? We have
" flain our Tyrant, we have reftored her ancient
" Liberty : But they are Favours thrown away ;
" fhe is made free in fpite of herfelf; and though
" fhe has feen a great and terrible Tyrant bereft
" of his Grandeur and his Life, by a few of her
" Citizens ; yet, bafely defponding of her own
" Strength, fhe impotently dreads the Name
" of a dead Tyrant, revived in the Perfon of a
" Stripling.

" No more of your Petitions to your young
" *Cæfar*; nor, if you are wife, on
" your own. You have not many Years to live?
" do not be fhewing that you over-rate the fhort
" Remains of an honourable Life, by making
" prepofterous and difhonourable Court to a Boy.
" Take Care that by this Conduct you do not
" eclipfe the Luftre of all your glorious Actions
" againft *Mark Anthony :* Do not turn your Glory
" into Reproach, by giving the Malicious a
" Handle to fay, that Self-Love was the fole
" Motive of your Bitternefs to him ; and that,
" had you not dreaded him, you would not have
" oppofed him : And yet will they not fay this,
" if they fee, that, having declared War againft
" *Anthony*, you notwithftanding leave Life and
" Liberty at the Mercy of *Octavius*, and tolerate
" in him all the Power which the other claimed?
" They will fay that you are not againft having
" a Mafter, only you would not have *Anthony* for
" a Mafter.

" I well approve your Praifes given to *Octavius*
" for his Behaviour thus far ; it is indeed praife-
" worthy ; provided his only Intention has been
" to

" to pull down the Tyranny of *Anthony*, without
" eftablifhing a Tyranny of his own. But if
" you are of Opinion, that *Octavius* is in fuch a
" Situation of Power, that it is neceffary to ap-
" proach him with humble Supplications to fave
" our Lives, and that it is convenient he fhould
" be trufted with this Power ; I can only fay,
" that you lift the Reward of his Merits far above
" his Merits : I thought that all his Services
" were Services done to the Republick ; but you
" have conferred upon him that abfolute and im-
" perial Power which he pretended to recover to
" the Republick.

" If, in your Judgment, *Octavius* has earned
" fuch Laurels and Recompences for making
" War againft *Anthony*'s Tyranny, which was
" only the Effects and Remains of *Cæfar*'s Ty-
" ranny ; to what Diftinctions, to what Rewards,
" would you intitle thofe who exterminated, with
" *Cæfar*, the Tyranny of *Cæfar*, for which they
" felt the Bleffings and Bounty of the *Roman*
" People ! Has this never entered into your
" Thoughts ? Behold here how effectually the
" Terror of Evils to come extinguifhes in the
" Minds of Men all Impreffions of Benefits re-
" ceived ? *Cæfar* is dead, and will never return
" to fhackle or frighten the City of *Rome* ; fo he
" is no more thought of, nor are they who deli-
" vered that City from him. But *Anthony* is ftill
" alive, and ftill in Arms, and ftill terrifies ; and
" fo *Octavius* is adored, who beat *Anthony*. Hence
" it is that *Octavius* is become of fuch potent
" Confequence, that from his Mouth the *Roman*
" People muft expect our Doom, the Doom of
" their Deliverers ! And hence it is too, that
" we

" we (thofe Deliverers) are of fuch humble Con-
" fequence, that he muft be fupplicated to give us
" our Lives !

" I, as I faid, have a Soul, and I have a
" Sword ; and am an Enemy to fuch abject Sup-
" plications ; fo great an Enemy, that I deteft
" thofe that ufe them, and am an avowed Foe
" to him that expects them. I fhall at leaft be
" far away from the odious Company of Slaves ;
" and where-ever I find Liberty, there I will
" find *Rome*. And for you that ftay behind,
" who, not fatiated with many Years, and many
" Honours, can behold Liberty extinct, and
" Virtue, with us, in Exile, and yet are not
" fick of a wretched and precarious Life ; I
" heartily pity you. For myfelf, whofe Soul
" has never ebbed from its conftant Principles, I
" fhall ever be happy in the Confcioufnefs of my
" Virtue ; owing nothing to my Country, to-
" wards which I have faithfully difcharged my
" Duty, I fhall poffefs my Mind in Peace ; and
" find the Reward of well-doing in the Satif-
" faction of having done it. What greater Plea-
" fure does the World afford, than to defpife the
" flippery Uncertainties of Life, and to value that
" only which is only valuable, private Virtue,
" and publick Liberty ; that Liberty, which is
" the Bleffing, and ought to be the Birthright,
" of all Mankind ?

" But ftill, I will never fink with thofe who
" are already falling ; I will never yield with
" thofe who have a Mind to fubmit : I am re-
" folved to be always firm and independent : I
" will try all Expedients, I will exert my ut-
" moft Prowefs, to banifh Servitude, and fet my
" Country

" Country entirely free. If Fortune favour me
" as fhe ought, the Bleffing and Joy will be
" every Man's; but if fhe fails me, and my beft
" Endeavours be thrown away, yet ftill I will
" rejoice fingle; and fo far be too hard for For-
" tune. What, in fhort, can my Life be better
" laid out in, than in continual Schemes, and re-
" peated Efforts, for the common Liberty of my
" Country ?

" As to your Part in this Crifis, my dear *Ci-*
" *cero*, it is my ftrongeft Advice and Requeft to
" you, not to defert yourfelf : Do not diftruft
" your Ability, and your Ability will not. difap-
" point you ; believe you can remedy our heavy
" Evils, and you will remedy them. Our Mife-
" ries want no Encreafe : Prevent, therefore, by
" your Vigilance, any new Acceffion. Former-
" ly, in Quality of Conful, you defeated, with,
" great Boldnefs, and Warmth for Liberty, a
" formidable Confpiracy againft *Rome*, and faved
" the Commonwealth ; and what you did then
" againft *Catiline*, you do ftill againft *Anthony*.
" Thefe Actions of yours have raifed your Re-
" putation high, and fpread it far ; but it will
" be all tarnifhed or loft, if you do not continue
" to fhew an equal Firmnefs upon as great an
" Occafion ; Let this render all the Parts of your
" Life equal, and fecure Immortality to that
" Glory of yours, which ought to be immor-
" tal.

" From thofe, who, like you, have performed
" great Actions, as great or greater are expected :
" By fhewing that they can ferve the Publick,
" they make themfelves its Debtors ; and it is
" apt to exact ftrict Payment, and to ufe them
                                        " feverely

" feverely if they do not pay: But from thefe
" who have performed no fuch Actions, we ex-
" pect none. This is the Difference betwixt the
" Lot of unknown Talents, and of thofe which
" have been tried; and the Condition of the lat-
" ter is no doubt the harder. Hence it is, that
" though, in making Head againft *Anthony*, you
" have merited and received great and juft Praifes,
" yet you have gained no new Admiration: By
" fo doing, you only continued, like a worthy
" Confular, the known Character of a great and
" able Conful. But if now at laft you begin to
" truckle to one as bad as him; if you abate
" ever fo little in that Vigour of Mind, and that
" fteady Courage, by which you expelled him
" from the Senate, and drove him out of *Rome*;
" you will never reap another Harveft of Glory,
" whatever you may deferve; and even your paft
" Laurels will wither, and your paft Renown be
" forgot.

" There is nothing great or noble in Events,
" which are the Fruit of Paffion or Chance:
" True Fame refults only from the fteady Perfe-
" verance of Reafon in the Paths and Purfuits of
" Virtue. The Care, therefore, of the Com-
" monwealth, and the Defence of her Liberties,
" belong to you above all Men, becaufe you have
" done more than all Men for Liberty and the
" Commonwealth: Your great Abilities, your
" known Zeal, your famous Actions, with the
" united Call and Expectation of all Men, are
" your Motives in this great Affair; Would you
" have greater?

" You are not, therefore, to fupplicate *Octavius*
" for our Safety; do a braver Thing, owe it to
" your

" your own Magnanimity. Roufe the *Roman*
" Genius within you; and confider that this
" great and free City, which you more than
" once faved, will always be great and free, pro-
" vided her People do not want worthy Chiefs
" to refift Ufurpation, and exterminate Tray-
" tors.
    G

SATURDAY, *April* 8, 1721. No. 24.

Of the natural Honefty of the People, and their rea-
fonable Demands. How important it is to every
Government to confult their Affections and Interest.

SIR,

I Have obferved, in a former Letter, that the
People, when they are not mifled or corrupted,
generally make a found Judgment of Things.
They have natural Qualifications equal to thofe of
their Superiors; and there is oftener found a great
Genius carrying a Pitch-fork, than carrying a
White Staff. The poor Cook preferred by the
Grand Seignior to be his Firft Vizier, in order to
cure the publick Diforder and Confufion occafioned by the Ignorance, Corruption, and Neglect
of the former Miniftry, made good effectually his
own Promife, and did Credit to his Mafter's
Choice: He remedied the publick Diforders, *and*
proved, fays Sir *Paul Ricaut, an able and excellent*
Minifter of State.

Befides, there are not fuch mighty Talents re-
quifite for Government, as fome, who pretend to
                                          them

them without poffeffing them, would make us believe : Honeft Affections, and common Qualifications, are fufficient ; and the Adminiftration has
been always beft executed, and the publick Liberty
beft preferved, near the Origin and Rife of States,
when plain Honefty and common Senfe alone governed the publick Affairs, and the Morals of Men
were not corrupted with Riches and Luxury, nor
their Underftandings perverted by Subtleties and
Diftinctions.   Great Abilities have, for the moft
part, if not always, been employed to miflead the
honeft, but unwary, Multitude, and to draw them
out of the open and plain Paths of publick Virtue
and publick Good.

The People have no Biafs to be Knaves; the
Security of their Perfons and Property is their
higheft Aim.   No Ambition prompts them ; they
cannot come to be great Lords, and to poffefs
great Titles, and therefore defire none.   No afpiring or unfociable Paffions incite them ; they have
no Rivals for Place, no Competitor to pull down ;
they have no darling Child, Pimp, or Relation, to
raife : they have no Occafion for Diffimulation or
Intrigue ; they can ferve no End by Faction ; they
have no Intereft, but the general Intereft.

The fame can rarely be faid of Great Men,
who, to gratify private Paffion, often bring down
publick Ruin ; who, to fill their private Purfes
with many Thoufands, frequently load the People
with many Millions ; who opprefs for a Miftrefs,
and, to fave a Favourite, deftroy a Nation; who
too often make the Publick fink and give way to
their private Fortune ; and, for a private Pleafure,
create a general Calamity.   Befides, being educated in Debauchery, and pampered in Riot and
Luxury,

Luxury, they have no Senfe of the Misfortunes of other Men, nor Tendernefs for thofe who fuffer them : They have no Notion of Miferies which they do not feel.   There is a Nation in *Europe*, which, within the Space of an Hundred Years laft paft, has been bleffed with Patriots, who, void of every Talent and Inclination to do Good, and even ftinted in their Ability for Roguery, were forced to be beholden, for moft of the Mifchief which they did, to the fuperior Arts and Abilities of humble Rogues and Brokers.

The firft Principles of Power are in the People ; and all the Projects of Men in Power ought to re- fer to the People, to aim folely at their Good, and end in it : And whoever will pretend to govern them without regarding them, will foon repent it. Such Feats of Errantry may do perhaps in *Afia :* but in Countries where the People are free, it is Madnefs to hope to rule them againft their Wills. They will know, that Government is appointed for their Sakes, and will be faucy enough to expect fome Regard and fome Good from their own De- legates.   Thofe Nations who are governed in fpite of themfelves, and in a Manner that bids Defiance to their Opinions, their Interefts, and their Un- derftandings, are either Slaves, or will foon ceafe to be Subjects.

Dominion that is not maintained by the Sword, muft be maintained by Confent ; and in this latter Cafe, what Security can any Man at the Head of Affairs expect, but from purfuing the People's Wel- fare, and feeking their Good-Will ? The Govern- ment of One for the Sake of One, is Tyranny ; and fo is the Government of a Few for the Sake of Themfelves : But Government executed for the

the Good of All, and with the Confent of All, is Liberty ; and the Word *Government* is profaned, and its Meaning abufed, when it fignifies any Thing elfe.

In free Countries the People know all this. They have their Five Senfes in as great Perfection, as have thofe who would treat them as if they had none. They are not wont to hate their Governors, till their Governors deferve to be hated ; and when this happens to be the Cafe, not abfolute Power itfelf, nor the Affections of a Prince invefted with it, can protect or employ Minifters detefted by the People. Even the Grand Seignior, with all his boundlefs Authority, is frequently forced to give up his Firft Minifter (who is fometimes his Son-in-Law, or Brother-in-Law) a Sacrifice to appeafe the People's Rage.

The People, rightly managed, are the beft Friends to Princes ; and, when injured and op-preffed, the moft formidable Enemies. Princes, who have trufted to their Armies or their Nobility, have been often deceived and ruined ; but Princes, who have trufted wholly to the People, have fel-dom been deceived or deferted : The Reafon is, that in all Governments, which are not Violent and Military, the People have more Power than either the Grandees or the Soldiery ; and their Friendfhip is more fincere, as having nothing to defire but Freedom from Oppreffion. And whilft a Prince is thus beloved by his People, it will rarely happen that any can be fo rafh and preci-pitate as to confpire againft him ; and fuch Con-fpiracies have never the intended Succefs : but, as *Machiavel* well obferves, *When the People are dif-fatisfied, and have taken a Prejudice againft their Go-*
vernors,

vernors, there is no Thing nor Person that they ought not to fear.

It is therefore of vast Importance to preserve the Affections of the People even in those Governments where they have no Share in the Administration. The wise States of *Holland* are so apprized of the Truth of this Maxim, that they have preserved themselves and their State by religiously observing it. Their Government consists of many little Aristocracies, where the Magistrates choose each other, and the People have nothing to do ; but in Spirit and Effect it is a Democracy, and the Dispositions and Inclinations of the People have above all Things the greatest Weight in their Counsels. The Jealousy of the People makes a vigilant Magistracy, who are honest out of Fear of provoking them, and, by never doing it, are in great Safety.

But, Thanks be to Heaven and our worthy Ancestors, our Liberties are better secured. We have a Constitution, in which the People have a large Share : They are one Part of the Legislature, and have the sole Power of giving Money ; which includes in it every Thing that they can ask for the publick Good ; and the Representatives, being neither awed nor bribed, will always act for their Country's Interest ; their own being so interwoven with the People's Happiness, that they must stand and fall together.

But what if our Delegates should not be suffered to meet ; or, when met, should be so awed by Force (as formerly in *Denmark*) or so corrupted by Places and Pensions (as in the Reign of *Charles* II) as to be ready to give up publick Liberty, and betray the Interest of their Principals to secure their own ?

own? This we may be fure can never happen under his Majefty's moft juft and gentle Reign: However, it has happened formerly ; and what has been, may be again in future Reigns.

What, in fuch a Cafe, is to be done? What Remedies have our Laws provided againft fo fatal a Mifchief? Muft the People patiently crouch under the heavieft of all Evils? Or has our Conftitution pointed out the Means of Redrefs? It would be abfurd to fuppofe that it has not ; and, in effect, the People have a legal Remedy at hand : It is their undoubted Right, and acknowledged to be fo in the *Bill of Rights* paffed in the Reign of King *Charles* I. and fince, by the Act of Settlement of the Crown at the *Revolution*; humbly to reprefent their publick Grievances, and to petition for Redrefs to thofe whofe Duty it is to right them, or to fee them righted: And it is certain, that in all Countries, the People's Misfortunes are greater or lefs, in Proportion as this Right is encouraged or checked.

It is indeed the beft and the only juft Way that they can take to breathe their Grievances; and whenever this Way has been taken, efpecially when it has been univerfally taken, our Kings have always accepted fo powerful an Application. Our Parliaments too, who are the Keepers and Barriers of our Liberty, have fhewn themfelves ready and willing to receive the modeft Complaints and Reprefentations of their Principals, and to apply quick Remedies to the Grievances contained in them. It has, indeed, been always thought highly imprudent, not to fay dangerous, to refift the general Groans and Entreaties of the People, uttered in this Manner.

This

This has been a Method, which has always had great Weight with good Men, and has been always a great Terror to bad. It has therefore always been encouraged or difcouraged, according to the Innocence or Guilt of Men in Power. A Prince, who minds the Welfare and defires the Affections of his Subjects, cannot wifh for a better Expedient to know how his Servants are approved, and how his Government is liked, than by this Way of countenancing his People in laying their Hearts, their Wifhes, and their Requefts before him; and Minifters never can be averfe to fuch Reprefentations of the Complaints of the People, unlefs they have given the People Occafion to complain.

Titus and *Trajan*, confcious of their own virtuous Adminiftration, and worthy Purpofes, coured Addreffes and Informations of this kind, from their Subjects: They wifely knew, that if the *Roman* People had free Leave to fpeak, they would not take Leave to act; and that, whilft they could have Redrefs, they would not feek Revenge.

None but defperate Parricides will make the People defperate.

G   *I am,* &c.

SATURDAY, *April* 15, 1721.   No. 25.

Confiderations on the deftruEtive Spirit of arbitrary
Power.   With the Bleffings of Liberty, and our
own Conftitution.

S I R,

THE Good of the Governed being the fole End
of Government, they muft be the greateft
and beft Governors, who make their People great
and happy ; and they the worft, who make their
People little, wicked, and miferable.   Power in a
free State, is a Truft committed by All to One or
a Few, to watch for the Security, and purfue the
Intereft, of All : And, when that Security is not
fought, nor that Intereft obtained, we know what
Opinion the People will have of their Governors.

It is the hard Fate of the World, that there
fhould be any Difference in the Views and Interefts
of the Governors and Governed ; and yet it is fo
in moft Countries.   Men who have a Truft frankly
beftowed upon them by the People, too frequently
betray that Truft, become Confpirators againft
their Benefactors, and turn the Sword upon thofe
who gave it ; infomuch that in the greateft Part of
the Earth, People are happy if they can defend
themfelves againft their Defenders.

Let us look round this great World, and behold
what an immenfe Majority of the whole Race of
Men crouch under the Yoke of a few Tyrants,
naturally as low as the meaneft of themfelves, and,
by being Tyrants, worfe than the worft ; who,

as

as Mr. *Sidney* obferves, *ufe their Subjects like Affes and Maftiff Dogs, to work and to fight, to be oppref-fed and killed for them.* Even the good Qualities and Courage of fuch Subjects are their Misfortune, by ftrengthening the wicked Hands of their brutal Mafters, and ftrengthening their own Chains. Tyrants confider their People as their Cattle, and ufe them worfe, as they fear them more. Thus the moft of Mankind are become the wretched Slaves of thofe, who are or fhould be their own Creatures; they maintain their haughty Mafters like Gods, and their haughty Mafters often ufe them like Dogs: A fine Specimen of Gratitude and Duty!

Yet this cruel Spirit in Tyrants is not always owing naturally to the Men, fince they are natu-rally like other Men; but it is owing to the Na-ture of the Dominion which they exercife. Good Laws make a good Prince, if he has a good Un-derftanding; but the beft Men grow mifchievous when they are fet above Laws. *Claudius* was a very harmlefs Man, while he was a private Man; but when he came to be a Tyrant, he proved a bloody one, almoft as bloody as his Nephew and Predeceffor *Caligula*; who had alfo been a very good Subject, but when he came to be the *Roman* Emperor, grew the profeffed Executioner of Man-kind.

There is fomething fo wanton and monftrous in lawlefs Power, that there fcarce ever was a human Spirit that could bear it; and the Mind of Man, which is weak and limited, ought never to be truft-ed with a Power that is boundlefs. The State of Tyranny is a State of War; and where it prevails, inftead of an Intercourfe of Confidence and Affec-tion,

tion, as between a lawful Prince and his Subjects, nothing is to be seen but Jealousy, Mistrust, Fear, and Hatred: An arbitrary Prince and his Slaves often destroy one another, to be safe: They are continually plotting against his Life; he is continually shedding their Blood, and plundering them of their Property.

Cuncta ferit, dum cuncta timet.

I think it was *Justinian*, the Emperor, who said, *Though we are above the Law, yet we live according to the Law:* But, by his Majesty's Favour, there was more Turn than Truth in the Saying; for Princes that think themselves above Law, act almost constantly against all Law; of which Truth *Justinian* himself is a known Instance. Good Princes never think themselves above it.

It is an affecting Observation, that the Power given for the Protection of the World, should, in so many Places, be turned to the Destruction of it. " As if the Law was in Force for their Destruc- " tion, and not for their Preservation; that it " should have Power to kill, but not to protect, " them: A Thing no less horrid, than if the " Sun should burn us without lighting us, or the " Earth serve only to bury, and not feed and nou- " rish us," says Mr. *Waller* in a Speech of his in Parliament.

Despotick Power has defaced the Creation, and laid the World waste. In the finest Countries in *Asia*, formerly full of People, you are now forced to travel by the Compass: There are no Roads, Houses, nor Inhabitants. The Sun is left to scorch up the Grass and Fruits, which it had raised; or the Rain to rot them: The Gifts of
God

God are left to perifh; there being none of his
Creatures, neither Man nor Beaft, left to ufe and
confume them. The Grand Seignior, who (if
we may believe fome fanctified Mouths, not addicted to Lying) is the Vicegerent of Heaven,
fruftrates the Bounty of Heaven ; and, being the
Father of his People, has almoft butchered them
all. Thofe few (comparatively very few) who
have yet furvived the miferable Fate of their Brethren, and are referved for Sacrifices to his Cruelty, as Occafion offers, and his Luft prompts
him, live the ftarving and wretched Property of
ravenous and bloody Bafhaws; whofe Duty to their
Mafter, as well as their own Avarice, obliges them
to keep the People, over whom they prefide, poor
and miferable.

But neither Bafhaws, nor Armies, could keep
that People in fuch abject Slavery, if their Priefts
and Doctors had not made Paffive Obedience a
Principle of their Religion. The holy Name of
God is prophaned, and his Authority belied, to
bind down Wretchednefs upon his Creatures, and
to fecure the Tyrant that does it. The moft confummate of all Wickednefs, and the higheft of all
Evils, are fanctified by the Teachers of Religion,
and made by them a Part of it. Yes, *Turkifh* Slavery is confirmed, and *Turkifh* Tyranny defended,
by Religion !

Sir *Paul Ricaut* tells us, that the *Turks* maintain,
*That the Grand Seignior can never be depofed, or made
accountable for his Crimes, whilft he deftroys carelefly
of his Subjects under a Hundred a Day :* 'Tis made
Martyrdom to die fubmiffively by the Hand of the
Tyrant ; and fome of his higheft Slaves have declared that they wanted only that Honour to complete

plete their Felicity. They hold, that it is their
Duty to fubmit, though their Tyrant *command a
whole Army of them to precipitate themfelves from a
Rock, or to build a Bridge with Piles of their Bodies
for him to pafs a River, or to kill one another to afford
him Paftime and Pleafure.*

Merciful God! Is this Government! And do
fuch Governors govern by Authority from Thee?

It is fcarce credible what Monfieur *de L'Eftoille*
tells us: He fays he travelled in the *Indies* for above
Twenty Days together, through Lanes of People
hanged upon Trees, by Command of the King;
who had ordered above a Hundred Thoufand of
them to be thus murthered and gibbeted, only becaufe two or three Robberies had been committed
amongft them. *Bayle, Reponfe aux Queft. d'un
Provinc.* Tom. I. p. 595.

It is one of the great Evils of Servitude, that
let the Tyranny be ever fo fevere, 'tis always flattered; and the more fevere 'tis, the more 'tis flattered. The Oppreffors of Mankind are flattered
beyond all others; becaufe Fear and Servitude naturally produce, as well as have recourfe to, Flattery, as the beft Means of Self-Prefervation;
whereas Liberty, having no Occafion for it,
fcorns it. Sir *Paul Ricaut* afcribes the Decay of
the *Ottoman* Empire to the Force of Flattery, and
calls the *Turkifh* Court, a Prifon and Banniard of
Slaves.

Old *Muley*, the Lord's Anointed of *Morocco*,
who it feems is ftill alive, is thought to have butchered Forty Thoufand of his Subjects with his
own Hands. — Such a Father is he of his People!
And yet his Right to fhed human Blood being a
genuine Characteriftick of the Church of *Morocco*,

as

as by Law eftablifhed, People are greedy to die by
his Hand; which, they are taught to imagine,
difpatches them forthwith to Paradife : Infomuch
that, though, as I am told, every Time he mounts
his Horfe, he flices off the Head of the Slave that
holds his Stirrup, to fhew that he is as good an
Executioner as he is a Horfeman, yet there is a
conftant Contention among his Slaves, who fhall
be the happy Martyr on that Occafion ; fo that feveral of them crowding to his Stirrup at once, for
the gracious Favour, his Majefty has fometimes
the Honour to cut off Two Heads, and to make
Two Saints, with one Blow.

The Exercife of defpotick Power is the unrelenting War of an armed Tyrant upon his un-
armed Subjects : It is a War of one Side, and in
it there is neither Peace nor Truce. *Tacitus* de-
fcribes it, — *Sæva juffa, continuas accufationes, fal-
laces amicitias, perniciem innocentium :* — " Cruel
" and bloody Orders, continual Accufations,
" faithlefs Friendfhips, and the Deftruction of
" Innocents." In another Place he fays, " That
" *Italy* was one continual Shambles, and moft of
" its fair Cities were defaced or overthrown ;
" *Rome* itfelf was in many Places laid in Afhes,
" with the greateft Part of its magnificent Build-
" ings: Virtue was defpifed, and barefaced De-
" bauchery prevailed. The folitary Iflands were
" filled with illuftrious Exiles, and the very Rocks
" were ftained with Slaughters : But, in the City
" itfelf, Cruelty raged ftill more ; it was dange-
" rous to be Noble, it was a Crime to be Rich,
" it was Capital to have borne Honours, and
" High Treafon to have refufed them ; and for
" Virtue and Merit, they brought fure and fudden
                                        " Deftruc-

" Deſtruction." Theſe were ſome of the Ravages of abſolute Dominion ! And as to the common People, the ſame Author ſays, " They were de-" bauched and diſpirited, and given up to Idle-" neſs and ſeeing Shews." *Plebs ſordida Circo &* *Theatris ſueta.*

>*Oh ! abject State of ſuch as tamely groan*
>*Under a blind Dependency on One !*

   This is a Sort of Government, which is too great and heavy a Curſe for any one to wiſh, even upon thoſe who are fooliſh enough, or wicked enough, to contend for its Lawfulneſs ; or, which is the ſame Thing, for Submiſſion to it : But ſurely, if ever any Man deſerved to feel the mercileſs Gripes of Tyranny, it is he who is an Advocate for it. *Phalaris* acted juſtly, when he hanſelled his Brazen Bull with the Wretch who invented it.

   As arbitrary Power in a ſingle Perſon has made greater Havock in human Nature, and thinned Mankind more, than all the Beaſts of Prey and all the Plagues and Earthquakes that ever were ; let thoſe Men conſider what they have to anſwer for, who would countenance ſuch a monſtrous Evil in the World, or would oppoſe thoſe that would oppoſe it. A Bear, a Lion, or a Tyger, may now and then pick up ſingle Men in a Wood, or a Deſert ; an Earthquake ſometimes may bury a Thouſand or Two Inhabitants in the Ruins of a Town ; and the Peſtilence may once in many Years carry off a much greater Number : But a Tyrant ſhall, out of a wanton perſonal Paſſion, carry Fire and Sword through a whole Continent, and deliver up a Hundred Thouſand of his Fellow
Creatures

Creatures to the Slaughter in one Day, without any Remorfe or further Notice, than that they died for his Glory. I fay nothing of the moral Effect of Tyranny; though 'tis certain that Ignorance, Vice, Poverty, and Vilenefs, always attend it.

He who compares the World now with what it was formerly, how populous once, how thin now; and confiders the Caufe of this doleful Alteration, will find juft Reafon to fear, that Spiritual and Temporal Tyranny, if they go on much longer, will utterly extinguifh the human Race. Of *Turkey* I have fpoken already: The great Continent of *America* is almoft unpeopled, the *Spaniards* having deftroyed, 'tis thought, about Forty Millions of its Natives; and for fome Kingdoms in *Europe*, efpecially towards the North, I do not believe that they have now half the Inhabitants that they had fo lately as a Hundred Years ago.

Bleffed be God, there are ftill fome free Countries in *Europe*, that abound with People and with Plenty, and *England* is the foremoft. This demonftrates the ineftimable Bleffing of Liberty. Can we ever over-rate it, or be too jealous of a Treafure which includes in it almoft all human Felicities? Or can we encourage too much thofe that contend for it, and thofe that promote it? It is the Parent of Virtue, Pleafure, Plenty, and Security; and 'tis innocent, as well as lovely. In all Contentions between Liberty and Power, the latter has almoft conftantly been the Aggreffor. Liberty, if ever it produce any Evils, does alfo cure them: Its worft Effect, Licentioufnefs, never does, and never can, continue long. Anarchy cannot be of much Duration: and where 'tis fo, it is the Child and

and Companion of Tyranny; which is not Government, but a Diffolution of it, as Tyrants are the Enemies of Mankind.

Power is like Fire; it warms, fcorches, or deftroys, according as it is watched, provoked, or increafed. It is as dangerous as ufeful. Its only Rule is the Good of the People; but becaufe it is apt to break its Bounds, in all good Governments nothing, or as little as may be, ought to be left to Chance, or the Humours of Men in Authority: All fhould proceed by fixed and ftated Rules, and upon any Emergency, new Rules fhould be made. This is the Conftitution, and this the Happinefs of *Englifhmen*; as hath been formerly fhewn at large in thefe Letters.

We have a Conftitution that abhors abfolute Power; we have a King that does not defire it; and we are a People that will never fuffer it: No free People will ever fubmit to it, unlefs it fteal upon them by Treachery, or they be driven into it by Violence. But a State can never be too fecure againft this terrible, this laft of all human Evils; which may be brought upon them by many Caufes, even by fome that at firft Sight do not feem to threaten any fuch Thing: And of all thofe Caufes, none feems more boding than a general Diftrefs, which certainly produces general Difcontent, the Parent of Revolutions; and in what fuch a Circumftance of Affairs may end, no Man can ever forefee: Few are brought about without Armies; a Remedy almoft always worfe than the Difeafe. What is got by Soldiers, muft be maintained by Soldiers; and we have, in this Paper, already feen the frightful Image of a Military Government; a Government, which, at
                                                    beft,

beft, is violent and bloody, and eternally inconfiftent with Law and Property.

It is therefore a dreadful Wickednefs to have
any Share in giving Occafion for thofe Difcontents, which are fo apt to burft into Rage and
Confufion. A State fometimes recovers out of a
Convulfion, and gains new Vigour by it ; but it
much oftener expires in it. Heaven preferve me
from ever beholding contending Armies in *England!* They are different Things from what they
once were. Our Armies formerly were only a
Number of the People armed occafionally ; and
Armies of the People are the only Armies which
are not formidable to the People. Hence it is,
that, in the many Revolutions occafioned by the
Strife between the two Royal Houfes of *York* and
Lancafter, there never was any Danger of Slavery
from an armed Force : A fingle Battle decided the
Contention ; and next Day thefe popular Soldiers
went Home, and refumed their ordinary Arms,
the Tools of Hufbandry. But fince that Time
Armies have not been fo eafily parted with ; but
after the Danger was over for which they were
raifed, have often been obftinately kept up, and by
that Means created Dangers ftill as great.

Some Quacks in Politicks may perhaps venture
publick Difturbances, out of an Opinion that
they fhall be able to prevent them by Art, or fupprefs them by Force. But this fhews their Capacity, as well as their Wickednefs : For, not to mention the Malignity of their Hearts, in rifquing publick Ruin, to gratify a private Appetite ; how can
any Event be certainly forefeen, when the Meafure of the Caufe cannot be certainly known ?
They can never afcertain the Degree of Oppofition :

tion; they cannot foreknow what Circumstances may happen, nor into whose Hands Things may fall. *Cicero* did not dream, when he employed *Octavius* for the Commonwealth, that his young Champion for Liberty would ever be the Tyrant of his Country. Who could foresee that *Cromwel* would enslave those whom he was employed to defend? But there is no trusting of Liberty in the Hands of Men, who are obeyed by great Armies.

From hence may be seen what a fatal and crying Crime it would be, in any free Country, to break the Confidence between the Prince and his People. When Loyalty is once turned into Indifference, Indifference will soon be turned into Hatred; Hatred will be returned with Hatred; Resentment may produce Tyranny, and Rage may produce Rebellion. There is no Mischief which this mutual Mistrust and Aversion may not bring forth. They must therefore be the blackest Traytors, who are the first Authors of so terrible an Evil, as are they who would endeavour to protect them.

Henry III. of *Castile* said, *That he feared the Curse of his People more than he did the Arms of his Enemies :* In which Saying he shewed as much Wisdom as Humanity; since, while he was beloved at Home, he had nothing to fear from Abroad, and the Curses of his Subjects were the likeliest Means to bring upon him the Arms of his Enemies.

G *I am,* &c.

The fad Effects of general Corruption, quoted from
Algernon Sidney, *Efq;*

S I R,

I Send you, for the Entertainment of your Readers this Week, two or three Paffages out of
the great *Algernon Sidney:* An Author, who can
never be too much valued or read ; who does Honour to the *Englijh* Nobility, and to the *Englijh*
Name ; who has written better upon Government
than any *Englijhman*, and as well as any Foreigner ;
and who was a Martyr for that Liberty which he
has fo amiably defcribed, and fo nobly defended.
He fell a Sacrifice to the vile and corrupt Court of
our pious *Charles* II. He had afferted the Rights
of Mankind, and fhewed the Odioufnefs of Tyranny ; he had expofed the Abfurdity and Vilenefs
of the facred and fafhionable Doctrines of thofe
Days, Paffive Obedience, and Hereditary Right ;
Doctrines, which give the Lie to common Senfe,
and which would deftroy all common Happinefs
and Security amongft Men ! Doctrines, which
were never practifed by thofe that preached them !
and Doctrines, which are big with Nonfenfe,
Contradiction, Impoffibility, Mifery, Wickednefs,
and Defolation ! Thefe were his Crimes, and
thefe his Glory.

The Book is every way excellent: He had
read and digefted all Hiftory ; and this Performance
of his takes in the whole Bufinefs of Government :
It

It makes us fome Amends for the Lofs of *Cicero*'s Books *de Republica*. Colonel *Sidney* had all the clear and comprehenfive Knowledge, and all the Dignity of Expreffion, of that great Mafter of Eloquence and Politicks; his Love of Liberty was as warm, his Honefty as great, and his Courage greater.

G

" Liberty cannot be preferved, if the Manners
" of the People are corrupted; nor abfolute Mo-
" narchy introduced, where they are fincere:
" Which is fufficient to fhew, that thofe who ma-
" nage free Governments ought always, to the
" utmoft of their Power, to oppofe Corruption,
" becaufe otherwife both they and their Govern-
" ment muft inevitably perifh; and that, on the
" other hand, the abfolute Monarch muft endea-
" vour to introduce it, becaufe he cannot fubfift
" without it. 'Tis alfo fo natural for all fuch
" Monarchs to place Men in Power who pretend
" to love their Perfons, and will depend upon their
" Pleafure, that poffibly 'twould be hard to find
" one in the World who has not made it the Rule
" of his Government: And this is not only the
" Way to Corruption, but the moft dangerous of
" all. For though a good Man may love a good
" Monarch, he will obey him only when he com-
" mands that which is juft; and no one can en-
" gage himfelf blindly to do whatever he is com-
" manded, without renouncing all Virtue and Re-
" ligion; becaufe he knows not whether that
" which fhall be commanded is confiftent with
" each, or directly contrary to the Laws of God
" and Man. But if fuch a Monarch be evil,
" and

" and his Actions such as they are too often found
" to be ; whoever bears an Affection to him, and
" seconds his Designs, declares himself an Enemy
" to all that is good ; and the Advancement of
" such Men to Power, does not only introduce,
" foment, and increase Corruption, but fortifies
" it in such a Manner, that without an entire
" Renovation of that State, it cannot be removed.
" Ill Men may possibly creep into any Govern-
" ment ; but when the worst are placed nearest
" the Throne, and raised to Honours for being
" so, they will with that Force endeavour to draw
" all Men to a Conformity of Spirit with them-
" selves, that it can no otherwise be prevented
" than by destroying them, and the Principle in
" which they live.

" Man naturally follows that which is good,
" or seems to him to be so. Hence it is, that in
" well-governed States, where a Value is put upon
" Virtue, and no one honoured unless for such
" Qualities as are beneficial to the Publick ; Men
" are from the tenderest Years brought up in a
" Belief, that nothing in this World deserves to
" be sought after, but such Honours as are acquired
" by virtuous Actions : By this Means Virtue it-
" self becomes popular, as in *Sparta*, *Rome*, and
" other Places, where Riches (which, with the
" Vanity that follows them, and the Honours
" Men give to them, are the Root of all Evil)
" were either totally banished, or little regarded.
" When no other Advantage attended the greatest
" Riches, than the Opportunity of living more
" sumptuously or deliciously, Men of great Spirits
" slighted them. When *Ariftippus* told *Cleanthes*,
" that if he would go to Court and flatter the
                                                    " Tyrant,

" Tyrant, he need not feek his Supper under a
" Hedge; the Philofopher anfwered, That he
" who could content himfelf with fuch a Supper,
" need not go to Court to flatter the Tyrant.
" *Epaminondas*, *Ariftides*, *Phocion*, and even the
" *Lacedemonian* Kings, found no Inconvenience in
" Poverty, whilft their Virtue was honoured, and
" the richeft Princes in the World feared their
" Valour and Power. It was not difficult for *Curius*,
" *Fabricius*, *Cincinnatus*, or *Emilius Paulus*, to con-
" tent themfelves with the narroweft Fortune,
" when it was no Obftacle to them in the Purfuit
" of thofe Honours which their Virtues deferved.
" 'Twas in vain to think of bribing a Man, who
" fupped upon the Coleworts of his own Garden.
" He could not be gained by Gold, who did not
" think it neceffary. He that could rife from the
" Plough to the Triumphal Chariot, and content-
" edly return thither again, could not be corrupt-
" ed; and he that left the Senfe of his Poverty
" to his Executors, who found not wherewith to
" bury him, might leave *Macedon* and *Greece* to
" the Pillage of his Soldiers, without taking to
" himfelf any Part of the Booty. But when
" Luxury was brought into Fafhion, and they
" came to be honoured who lived magnificently,
" though they had in themfelves no Qualities to
" diftinguifh them from the bafeft of Slaves, the
" moft virtuous Men were expofed to Scorn if
" they were poor; and that Poverty, which had
" been the Mother and Nurfe of their Virtue, grew
" infupportable. The Poet well underftood what
" Effect this Change had upon the World, who faid,
Nullum crimen abeft facinufque libidinis, ex quo
Paupertas Romana perit.   JUVENAL.
                                    " When

" When Riches grew to be neceffary, the Defire
" of them, which is the Spring of all Mifchief,
" followed. They who could not obtain Ho-
" nours by the nobleft Actions, were obliged to
" get Wealth, to purchafe them from Whores or
" Villains, who expofed them to Sale: And when
" they were once entered into this Track, they
" foon learned the Vices of thofe from whom they
" had received their Preferment, and to delight in
" the Ways that had brought to it. When they
" were come to this, nothing could ftop them:
" All Thought and Remembrance of Good was
" extinguifhed. They who had bought the Com-
" mands of Armies or Provinces from *Icelus* or
" *Narciffus*, fought only to draw Money from
" them, to enable them to purchafe higher Dig-
" nities, or gain a more affured Protection from
" thofe Patrons. This brought the Government
" of the World under a moft infamous Traffick;
" and the Treafures arifing from it were, for the
" moft part, diffipated by worfe Vices than the
" Rapine, Violence, and Fraud with which they
" had been gotten. The Authors of thofe Crimes
" had nothing left but their Crimes; and the Ne-
" ceffity of committing more, through the Indi-
" gency into which they were plunged by the Extra-
" vagance of their Expences. Thefe Things are
" infeparable from the Life of a Courtier; for as
" fervile Natures are guided rather by Senfe than
" Reafon, fuch as addict themfelves to the Service
" of Courts, find no other Confolation in their
" Mifery, than what they receive from fenfual
" Pleafures, or fuch Vanities as they put a Value
" upon; and have no other Care than to get
" Money for their Supply, by begging, ftealing,
" bribing,

" bribing, and other infamous Practices. Their
" Offices are more or lefs efteemed, according to
" the Opportunities they afford for the Exercife
" of thefe Virtues; and no Man feeks them for
" any other End than for Gain, nor takes any
" other Way than that which conduces to it.
" The ufual Means of attaining them are, by
" obferving the Prince's Humour, flattering his
" Vices, ferving him in his Pleafures, fomenting
" his Paffions, and by advancing his worft De-
" figns, to create an Opinion in him that they
" love his Perfon, and are entirely addicted to
" his Will. When Valour, Induftry, and Wif-
" dom advanced Men to Offices, it was no eafy
" Matter for a Man to perfuade the Senate he
" had fuch Qualities as were required, if he had
" them not : But when Princes feek only fuch as
" love them, and will do what they command,
" 'tis eafy to impofe upon them ; and becaufe
" none that are good will obey them when they
" command that which is not fo, they are always
" encompaffed by the worft. Thofe who follow
" them only for Reward, are moft liberal in pro-
" feffing Affection to them ; and by that Means
" rife to Places of Authority and Power. The
" Fountain being thus corrupted, nothing that is
" pure can come from it. Thefe mercenary
" Wretches having the Management of Affairs,
" Juftice and Honour are fet at a Price, and the
" moft lucrative Traffick in the World is thereby
" eftablifhed. Eutropius, *when he was a Slave, ufed*
" *to pick Pockets and Locks ; but being made a Mini-*
" *fter, he fold Cities, Armies, and Provinces ;* (*) *and*

(*) —— Nunc uberiore rapina
Peccat in urbe manus. C L A U D.

" *fome*

" *some have undertaken to give probable Reasons to*
" *believe, that* Pallas, *one of* Claudius's *manumised*
" *Slaves, by these Means, brought together more*
" *Wealth in Six Years, than all the* Roman *Dicta-*
" *tors and Consuls had done, from the Expulsion of*
" *the Kings to their Passage into* Asia. The rest
" walked in the same Way, and the same Arts,
" and many of them succeeded in the same Man-
" ner. Their Riches consisted not of Spoils
" taken from Enemies, but were the base Product
" of their own Corruption. They valued no-
" thing but Money, and those who could bribe
" them were sure to be advanced to the highest
" Offices ; and, whatever they did, feared no Pu-
" nishment. Like Effects will ever proceed from
" the like Causes. When Vanity, Luxury, and
" Prodigality are in Fashion, the Desire of Riches
" must necessarily increase in proportion to them :
" And when the Power is in the Hands of base
" mercenary Persons, they will always (to use the
" Courtiers Phrase) make as much Profit of their
" Places as they can. Not only Matters of Fa-
" vour, but of Justice too, will be exposed to
" Sale ; and no Way will be open to Honours
" or Magistracies, but by paying largely for them.
" He that gets an Office by these Means, will
" not execute it *gratis:* He thinks he may sell
" what he has bought ; and would not have en-
" tered by corrupt Ways, if he had not intended
" to deal corruptly : Nay, if a well-meaning Man
" should suffer himself to be so far carried away
" by the Stream of a prevailing Custom, as to
" purchase Honours of such Villains, he would be
" obliged to continue in the same Course, that he
" might gain Riches to procure the Continuance
" of

" of his Benefactor's Protection, or to obtain the
" Favour of such as happen to succeed them.
" And the Corruption thus beginning in the Head,
" muſt neceſſarily diffuſe itſelf into the Members
" of the Commonwealth : Or, if any one (which
" is not to be expected) after having been guilty
" of one Villainy, ſhould reſolve to commit no
" more, it could have no other Effect, than to
" bring him to Ruin ; and he being taken away,
" all Things would return to their former Chan-
" nel.

I am, &c.

SATURDAY, *April* 29, 1721. No. 27.

*General Corruption, how ominous to the Publick, and
how diſcouraging to every virtuous Man. With
its fatal Progreſs whenever encouraged.*

S I R,

SALLUST, or whoever elſe was the Author
of the two Diſcourſes to *Cæſar* about ſettling
the Commonwealth, obſerves to that Emperor,
that thoſe Magiſtrates judge wildly, who would
derive their own Security from the Corruption of
the People ; and therefore make them wicked
Men, to make them good Subjects: *Whereas,* ſays
he, *'tis the Intereſt of a virtuous Prince to make his
People virtuous* ; *for, the Debauched, having thrown
off all Reſtraint, are of all Men the moſt ungovern-
able.*

Pliny tells *Trajan,* That all his Predeceſſors,
except *Nerva* and one or two more, ſtudied how
to

to debauch their People, and how to banifh all Virtue, by introducing all Vices; firft, becaufe they were delighted to fee others like themfelves; fecondly, becaufe the Minds of the *Romans* being depraved by the Tafte and Vices of Slaves, they would bear with greater Tamenefs the Imperial Yoke of Servitude.

Thus did thefe Governors and Enemies of *Rome* deftroy Virtue, to fet up Power. Nor was fuch Policy at all new or ftrange: It was then, and always will be, the direct Road to abfolute Monarchy, which is in its Nature at everlafting Enmity with all Goodnefs and Honefty. The *Roman* Virtue and the *Roman* Liberty expired together; Tyranny and Corruption came upon them almoft hand in hand.

This fhews the Importance of an honeft Magiftracy; nothing certainly is more threatening, or more to be apprehended, than a corrupt one. A Knave in Power is as much to be dreaded, as a Fool with a Firebrand in a Magazine of Powder: You have fcarce a bare Chance for not being blown up.

From the wicked and worthlefs Men, who engroffed all the Places at *Rome* in the latter Days of the Commonwealth, and from the monftrous Prodigalities, infamous Briberies, and endlefs Corruptions, promoted by thefe Men, the fudden Thraldom of that glorious City might eafily have been forefeen. It was fcarce poffible to be honeft, and preferred. *Atticus* would never accept of any Employment, though he was offered the higheft. " This Refufal, *fays Monfieur* Bayle, was doubt- " lefs owing to his Virtue: There was no rifing " to Offices then, but by Means that were infa-

" mous;

" mous ; nor was there any fuch Thing as exe-
" cuting thefe Offices according to the Rules of
" Juftice and the publick Good, without being
" expofed to the Refentment and Violence of
" many and great wicked Men.   He therefore
" chofe to be rather a virtuous private Man, than
" an exalted and publick Rogue.

    " How charming is this Example, but how
" rare ! If all Men were like *Atticus*, there would
" be no Danger of a State of Anarchy.   But as
" to that we may be eafy ; for there will be al-
" ways more Rogues and Rooks at hand to be
" devouring and monopolizing Places, by all pro-
" per vile Means, than there will be Places to be-
" ftow.

    Bayle goes on, and tells us of " a great Travel-
" ler, who being rallied upon his rambling Hu-
" mour, anfwered, That he would ceafe Travel-
" ling, as foon as ever he could find a Country
" where Power and Credit were in the Hands of
" honeft Men, and Preferments went by Merit.
" *Nay then*, fays one who heard him, *you will in-*
" *fallibly die travelling*.

    Corruption, Bribery, and Treachery, were fuch
Ways to Power, as *Atticus* would not tread.
Colonel *Sidney* fays, that " a noble Perfon in his
" Time, who was a great Enemy to Bribery,
" was turned out from a confiderable Poft, as a
" Scandal to the Court ; *For*, faid the principal
" Minifter, *he will make no Profit af his Place ;*
" *and by that Means caft a Scandal upzn thofe that*
" *do*." And *Alexander ab Alexandro* tells a Story of
" a very honeft Man, well fkilled in the Langua-
" ges, who having long ftruggled with Difficulties
" and Poverty, while he trufted in vain to his
                                    " Honefty

" Honefty and Learning, bethought himfelf of a
" contrary Road ; and therefore turning Pimp and
" Pathick, inftantly he profpered, and got great
" Riches, Power, and Places.

Aude aliquid brevibus gyaris & carcere dignum.

Cicero, who lived to fee difmal Days of Ambition and Corruption at *Rome*, was fenfible that he
could do little or no Good with all his Abilities and
his Honefty. " If I faw, *fays he in a Letter to*
" *Lentulus*, if I faw the Commonwealth held and
" governed by corrupt and defperate Men, as
" has happened in my Days and formerly, no
" Motive or Confideration fhould engage me in
" their Interefts ; neither their Bribes could move
" me, nor could Dangers, which often fway
" the boldeft Men, terrify me ; nor could any
" of their Civilities, or any of their Obligations,
" foften me.

Talking, in another Place, of the Senate, then
awed by Power, or governed by Avarice, he fays,
*Aut affentiendum eft nulla cum gravitate paucis aut
fruftra diffentiendum :* That is, You muft either
bafely vote with *Craffus* and *Cæfar*, and one or
two Men more in Power, or vote againft them to
no Purpofe. Thefe great Men did not feek Power,
nor ufe it, to do Good to their Country, which is
the End of Power ; but to themfelves, which is
the Abufe of Power. Where Government is degenerated into Jobbing, it quickly runs into Tyranny and Diffolution : And he who in any Country poffeffes himfelf of a great Poft for the Sake of
gainful Jobbs, as a certain great Perfon once owned
that he did, ought to finifh his laft Jobb under a
Gallows.

It

It is natural and neceffary for thofe that have corrupt Ends, to make ufe of Means that are corrupt, and to hate all Men that are uncorrupt.

I would lay it down as a Rule for all Nations to confider and obferve, That where Bribery is practifed, 'tis a Thoufand to one but Mifchief is intended; and the more Bribery, the more Mifchief. When therefore the People, or their Truftees, are bribed, they would do well to confider, that it is not, it cannot be, for their own Sakes. Honeft and open Defigns, which will bear Light and Examination, are hurt and difcredited by bafe and dark Expedients to bring them about : But, if you would perfuade a Man to be a Rogue, it is natural that Money fhould be your firft Argument ; and therefore, whoever offers me a Bribe, does tacitly acknowledge that he thinks me a Knave.

Tacitus, taking Notice of the woful Decline of Virtue and Liberty, towards the End of the Republick, fays, That the greateft Villainies were committed with Impunity, and Ruin was the Price of Honefty : *Deterrima quæque impune, ac multa honefta exitio fuere.* And indeed, where Corruption and publick Crimes are not carefully oppofed, and feverely punifhed, neither Liberty nor Security can poffibly fubfift.

The immenfe Briberies practifed by *Julius Cæfar*, were fure and terrible Prefages of *Cæfar*'s Tyranny. It is amazing what mighty Sums he gave away : *Caius Curio* alone, one of the Tribunes, was bought into his Intereft, at no fmaller a Price than Half a Million of our Money. Other Magiftrates too had their Shares ; and all were bribed, who would be bribed. We may

cafily

eafily conceive how he came by fuch Sums ; he got them as wickedly as he gave them away. Nor can I call him generous in this vaft Liberality ; fince he purchafed the *Roman* Empire with its own Money, and gave away a Part to get the Whole.

Unjuft and unfrugal Ways of throwing away Money, make wicked and violent Means neceffary to get Money ; and Rapine naturally follows Prodigality. They that wafte publick Money, feldom ftop there, but go a wicked Step farther ; and having firft drained the People, at laft opprefs them. Publick Frauds are therefore very alarming, as they are very big with publick Ruin. What fhall we fay then of other Times, when publick Schemes have been concerted to confound all Property, to put common Honefty out of Countenance, and banifh it from amongft Men ; and when an Appetite for Power was only an Appetite for Mifchief? Dreadful fure was the Profpect! And yet this was the State of *Rome* in thofe Days ; as will be feen further before this Letter is ended.

Nor would it have been any Advantage or Security to *Rome*, though *Cæfar* and his Party had been lefs able Men than in truth they were: Having debauched the People, he did more by Corruption towards enflaving them, than he did by his Parts, as great as they were. It is fomewhere obferved, that to do Good requires fome Parts and Pains ; but any Man may be a Rogue. *The World*, fays the Proverb, *little knows what filly Fellows govern it.* Even the Difficulties of doing Good proceed from the Pravity of fome Mens Nature, ever prone to do Evil ; and fo ftrong is
that

that Pravity, that many Men frequently flight
great Temptations to be honeft, and embrace flight
Temptations to be Knaves.

It is an Obfervation, which every body is capable of making, that a good Character loft is
hardly, if ever, recovered. Now the Reafon of
this is, not fo much from the Malevolence of the
World (often too ready to calumniate) as from the
Inability of a Knave to become honeft : He is, as
it were, doomed to be one : The Biafs of his Spirit
is crooked; and if ever he act honeftly, it is for a
roguifh Reafon. I have known a Man, who,
having wilfully loft all Credit, rejected as wilfully
all Opportunities to regain it, even when thrown
into his Lap. He could not help earning frefh Deteftation, with great Labour ; when he might have
acquired the higheft Renown with the greateft
Eafe. From hence may be feen how dangerous it
is ever to truft a Man who has once been a Knave ;
and hence too may be learned, that from Men
who have done eminent Mifchief, whether publick
or private, greater ftill is to be dreaded. Vice is
a prolifick Thing, and Wickednefs naturally begets Wickednefs.

Olearius, giving an Account of *Mufcovy*, obferves, that " the Great Duke's Court hath this
" in common with thofe of other Princes, that
" Vice takes Place of Virtue, and gets neareft the
" Throne. Thofe who have the Honour to be
" neareft his Perfon, are withal more fubtle, more
" deceitful, and more infolent, than the others
" that have not. They know very well how to
" make their Advantages of the Prince's Favour,
" and look for the greateft Refpects and humbleft
" Submiffions imaginable, from thofe who make
                                    " their

" their Addreſſes to them ; which the others ren-
" der them, as much to avoid the Miſchief they
" might do to them, as for the Good they expect
" from them." This is the Character of a Court,
where one is not much ſurprized nor troubled to
find out Tyranny and Corruption in abundance :
But one is at once amazed and affected with the
mournful Account *Salluſt* gives us of the *Romans* in
his Time ; the *Romans*, who had been ſo virtuous
a People, ſo great and ſo free !

The *Romans*, he ſays, were arrived to that Pitch
of Corruption, that they gloried in Extravagancy
and Rapine, and made Sarcaſms upon Virtue.
Modeſty and a diſintereſted Mind paſſed with them
only for Sloth and Cowardice. Thoſe that were
in Power, neglecting Virtue, and conſpiring againſt
Innocence, preferred only their own Creatures.
Innocentes circumveniunt, ſuos ad honorem tollunt :
Wicked Deeds, and an infamous Character, were
no Bars to the poſſeſſing of Power ; and thoſe
that acted as if Rapine were their Employment,
and Plunder the Perquiſites of their Place, were
not thought unfit for freſh Preferments : *Non fa-
cinus, non probum, aut flagitium obſtat, quo minus
Magiſtratus capiant : quod commodum eſt, trahunt,
rapiunt.* At laſt, their Great Men had no Principle but Rapaciouſneſs, and obſerved no Law but
their Luſt. The whole Commonwealth was become their Prey and their Pillage : *Poſtremo, tanquam urbe capta, libidine ac licentia ſua, pro legibus
utuntur.*

The ſame Author ſays, That it would have
leſſened his Concern, had he ſeen ſuch great
Wickedneſs perpetrated by Men of great Qualities.
But his Grief had not this Mitigation : For, ſays
he,

he, wretched Creatures with little Souls, whofe whole Genius lay in their Tongue, and whofe utmoft Talent and Ability was to prate glibly, exercifed with Infolence that Power which they had acquired by Chance, or by the Sloth of others. *Ac me quidem mediocris dolor angeret, fi virtute partam victoriam more fuo per fervitium exercerent : Sed homines inertiffimi quorum omnis vis virtufque in lingua fita eft, forte, & alterius focordia, dominationem oblatam infolentes agitant.* And for the *Roman* Nobility of that Time, he fays, that, l ke ftupid Statues, their Names and Titles were their only Ornament : *Inertiffimi nobiles, in quibus, ficut in ftatua præter nomen, nihil eft additamenti.* Salluft. ad C. Cæfarem, de repub. ordinand.

We fee what a Market thefe Men made of Power, and what a Degree of Degeneracy they introduced. The End of all was, the utter Lofs of Liberty, and a fettled Tyranny.

G

I am, &c.

SATURDAY, *May* 6, 1721. No. 28.

A Defence of CATO *againft his Defamers.*

To CATO.

S I R,

SEE what it is to be confpicuous! Your Honefty, and the Truths which you tell, have drawn upon you much Envy, and many Lies. You cannot be anfwered; therefore it is fit to abufe abuſe you. Had you kept groveling near the Earth, in Company with moſt other Weekly Writers, you might have lulled the Town aſleep as they do, with great Safety to your Perſon, and without any body's ſaying an unkind Word of you : But you have galloped away ſo faſt and ſo far before them, that it is no Wonder the poor Vermin, conſcious of their own Heavineſs and want of Speed, crawl after you and curſe you. — It is natural, human Sight is offended with Splendor : This is exemplified in a Man looking at the Sun ; he makes all the while a World of wry Mouths and diſtorted Faces.

Conſider yourſelf, Sir, as the Sun to thoſe Authors, who behold you with Agonies, while they behold you with Admiration. Great Minds alone are pleaſed with the Excellencies of others, and vulgar Souls provoked by them. The Mob of Writers is like the Weavers Mob ; all Levellers. This appears by their unmannerly and ſeditious Speeches concerning you, their Monarch. Strange Inſtance of Impudence and Ingratitude ! They live upon you, and ſcold at you. Your Lot is the ſame with that of many other eminent Authors ; you feed Vermin before you are dead.

Your Slanderers, as they are below even Contempt, ſo are they far below all Notice : But it is worth conſidering who ſet them at work ; from whom they receive the Wages of Proſtitution ; and what contradictory Things the poor Creatures are taught to ſay. Scarce a Paper appeared for a conſiderable Time together in which *Cato*'s Letters were not extolled ; and thoſe who did it endeavoured, to the beſt of their Skill, to write after him : But finding that his Labours made theirs uſeleſs,

ufelefs, and that the recommending of publick
Spirit was too mighty a Tafk for humble Hirelings, they fuddenly, and without Ceremony, tack
about, and, by calumniating *Cato*, make themfelves Liars : Such Deference have they for their
Cuftomers, and for themfelves !

It is no Wonder, therefore, that the fame worthy, but waggifh Pens, reprefent him, with the
fame Breath, as an *abandoned Atheift*, and a *bigoted
Prefbyterian* ; while others as plainly prove him a
flaming Jacobite, and an *arrant Republican* ; that is,
one who is high for Monarchy, and one who is
againft all Monarchy.   I could fhew you thefe
pretty Confiftencies in one and the fame Paper.

Cato had defcribed and fhewed the horrid Effects
of publick Confufion, and contended for punifhing
the Authors of our own : Hence *Cato* is reprefented as *an Enemy to Government and Order, and a
Promoter of Confufion.*

Cato had beftowed real and unfeigned Encomiums upon his Majefty, and done all Juftice to
the Abilities and Honefty of his Minifters : Hence
Cato is charged with *cafting Reproaches, and making
Sarcafms upon his Majefty and his Miniftry.*

Cato has writ againft *Turkifh*, *Afiatick*, and all
Sorts of Tyranny : Hence *Cato* is faid to be a *great
Incendiary, and an open Enemy to our Conftitution.*

Cato contends, that great Traytors ought to be
hanged : Hence *Cato* is traduced, as if he *affronted
the Miniftry.*

Cato afferts, that the Good of Mankind is the
End of Government : Hence *Cato* is for *deftroying
all Government.*

Cato lays down certain Rules for farther eftablifhing his Majefty's Throne, and for enfuring to
him

him for ever the Minds of his People : Therefore *Cato is a Jacobite.*

Cato has shewn at large the Blessings of a limited Monarchy, especially of our own : Therefore *Cato is a Republican.*

Cato has shewn the Dreadfulness of popular Insurrections and Fury ; the Misery of Civil Wars, the Uncertainty of their End : Therefore *Cato stirs up the People to Sedition and Rebellion.*

Cato laments, that great Criminals are seldom brought to the Gallows : Hence *Cato* is represented as one that *deserves the Gallows.*

Cato, talking of *Turkey*, observes with Warmth and Concern, that the holy Name of God was belied, and Religion prostituted, to bind down Wretchedness upon his Creatures, and to protect the Tyrant that does it : Therefore *Cato scurrilously reviles the Church of* England.

Cato has shewn the destructive Terms of arbitrary Power, and how it had almost dispeopled the Earth : In answer to this it is said, that *Cato wears a dark Wig.*

Cato has complained, that this great Nation has been abused, cheated, and exhausted ; its Trade ruined ; its Credit destroyed ; its Manufactures discouraged, &c. and affirmed, that Vengeance is due to those Traytors who have done it ; that none but Traytors will protect Traytors ; that publick Honesty and publick Spirit ought to be encouraged, in Opposition to publick Corruption, Bribery, and Rapine ; that there is Regard to be had to the Rights, Privileges, and Tempers of the People : That Standing Armies are dreadful Things ; that a Military Government is violent and bloody : That they are the blackest Traytors, who would

break

break the Confidence between a Prince and his
Subjects : That Great Men mind chiefly the getting of Plumbs ; and that honeft Meafures are the
beft Meafures.   To all which it is replied, That
*Cato is a whimfical unreafonable Man, who talks and
expects ftrange Things* ; and, in fine, that *he dreams
odd Dreams.*

By fuch powerful Arguments is *Cato* anfwered ;
by fuch pretty Arts decried.   *He is really a great
Criminal* ; he afferts the Rights and Property of
the People, and calls for Juftice upon thofe who
would deftroy them.   *He is furely a Jacobite*, who
would not let certain elevated Sages do what they
would, and get what they pleafed.   I would afk,
Whether the obliging, protecting, and avenging,
the injured People, be likely Ways to bring in the
Pretender ? Yet thefe are the Ways which *Cato*
contends for.   Or, whether the deceiving, load-
ing, and fqueezing of the harmlefs People, be natural Ways to make and keep them well affected ?
Yet thefe are the Ways which *Cato* condemns and
expofes.

Being detached from all Parties, eminently guiltlefs of all perfonal Views of his own, and going
upon Principles certainly true in themfelves, certainly beneficent to human Society ; it is no Wonder that he is read and approved by every intelli-
gent Man in *England*, except the Guilty, their
Skreens, Hirelings, and Adherents.   What he
writes, the People feel to be true.   If Men can be
great Knaves, in fpite of Oppofition ; how much
greater would they be, if there were none ? And
if Juftice be oppofed, openly, fhamelefly, and violently oppofed, in fpite of her Champions and Defenders ; fhe muft certainly be deftroyed, if fhe
                                                    had

had none. It is a difmal Reflexion, that Juftice muft fometimes be fought for Inch by Inch, before it can be obtained, and at laft is not half obtained; and that the higher and blacker the Villainy is, the greater is the Security. I hope that this will never be our Cafe; but I could name many a Country whofe Cafe it has been.

I am not furprized that certain tall Traytors are very angry with *Cato*. *Good now hold your Tongue*, faid a Quack to his complaining Patient, under Agonies into which he had been caft by the Doctor's infallible Specifick: *Good now hold your Tongue, and be eafy;* — *leave the Matter to me, and the Matter will go well:* That is, Lie ftill and die, and I will warrant you. Great Grief and Diftrefs will have Utterance, in fpite of Art or Terror.

On *Afcenfion Day*, when the Doge of *Venice* weds the Sea with a Ring, the Admiral, who conducts the Bucentauro, or Veffel in which that Ceremony is performed, does a bold Thing: He pawns his Head to the Senate, to enfure them, againft the Danger and Effects of Tempefts and Storms. But the Thing would ftill be bolder, if he had firft wilfully raifed a Storm, or bored a Hole in the Veffel.

I appeal to the Senfe of the Nation, daily uttered in their Addreffes to the Parliament for Relief and Vengeance; whether *Cato*'s Sentiments be not the fame with theirs; I appeal to the Sufferings, the heavy, melancholy Sufferings of the People, whether either *Cato* or they fpeak thus without Grounds.

The Grounds are too vifible, and their Allegations too true. — Hence the Rage of Guilt, which
is

is more galled by Truth, than Innocence is hurt by Lies: And hence I have heard it obferved, concerning a Set of Worthies, that they do not care what Falfhoods you pub'ifh concerning them, but will never forgive you if you meddle with Facts.

For certain Gentlemen to find Fault with *Cato*'s Letters, is to avow their own Shame. Why was there Occafion given for thofe Letters? Some other Queftions might be afked too, which would difcover frefh Blacknefs in thefe Betrayers, were they not already all over black. Who is it that might have checked, and yet did not check, rampant Rogues laft Summer? And from what Motives proceeded fuch Omiffion? Who is it that openly fkreens open Guilt? Who is it that conceals the Evidence of Guilt? Who is it that brow-beats the Purfuers of Guilt? Who is it that throws Obftacles in the Parliament's Way? Who is it that lengthens out the Procefs? Who is it that ftrives to defeat the Enquiry? Who is it that makes Malecontents, and then reproaches them for being fo?

In vain they fall upon *Cato*, with lying Reproaches, falfe Pictures, and ugly Names: Their Conduct bewrays them; by making him of every Party, they fhew him to be of none; as he has fhewed himfelf to be of none. I thought it, however, not amifs, thus, once for all, to make his Apology, and to fhew what are his Crimes, and who his Enemies. His great Guilt is, that he will not fpare Guilt; and the great Objection to his Writings is, that they cannot be anfwered. Let the Reader judge whether I have mifreprefented

him

him or his Foes, who are no other than the late Directors, their Friends and Confederates.

As to the poor Weekly Journeymen of the Prefs, whofe Principle is the ready Penny, and who, for a Morfel, defile Paper, and blot Reputations without hurting them, they deferve no Refentment. It is their Profeffion to do what they are bid, when they are paid for it. A Church is not the lefs facred, becaufe Curs frequently lift up their Leg againft it, and affront the Wall: It is the Nature of Dogs. They therefore are and ought to be pitied and overlooked; the Bufinefs of this Letter to you being to expofe the falfe and unjuft Cenfures of fome, who bear a greater Figure than fuch harmlefs Weekly Writers, without poffeffing more Honefty.

The Conjectures of thefe Creatures about the Perfon of *Cato* afford Matter of Mirth. They will needs know him, right or wrong. Let them guefs on; whatever they guefs, I will venture to pronounce them Liars, though they fhould guefs truly: Since without being able to do any thing more than guefs, they yet go on to affirm; which no honeft Man would do without competent Evidence. I am,

G   *S I R,*

Your Humble Servant,

PORTIUS.

SATURDAY, *May* 13, 1721. No. 29.

*Reflexions occasioned by an Order of Council for sup-
pressing certain impious Clubs that were never discovered.*

S I R,

I Would willingly propagate and preserve the following Order of Council, as a Monument of
his Majesty's great Zeal for Virtue and Religion.
It is published in the *Gazette* of the 29th of *April*,
in the following Words:

At the Court of St. *James*'s, the 28th Day of
April, 1721.

PRESENT,

The King's Most Excellent Majesty in Council.

" HIS Majesty having received Information,
" which gives great Reason to suspect, that
" there have lately been, and still are, in and
" about the Cities of *London* and *Westminster*,
" certain scandalous Clubs or Societies of young
" Persons, who meet together, and, in the most
" impious and blasphemous Manner, insult the
" most sacred Principles of our Holy Religion,
" affront Almighty God himself, and corrupt the
" Minds and Morals of one another; and being
" resolved to make use of all the Authority com-
" mitted to him by Almighty God, to punish
                                        " such

" fuch enormous Offenders, and to crufh fuch
" fhocking Impieties before they encreafe and draw
" down the Vengeance of God upon this Nation :
" His Majefty has thought fit to command the
" Lord Chancellor, and his Lordfhip is hereby
" required to call together his Majefty's Juftices
" of the Peace of *Middlefex* and *Weftminfter*, and
" ftrictly to enjoin them in the moft effectual
" Manner, that they, and every of them, do
" make the moft diligent and careful Enquiry and
" Search for the Difcovery of any thing of this
" and the like Sort, tending in any wife to the
" Corruption of the Principles and Manners of
" Men ; and to lay before his Lordfhip fuch Dif-
" coveries as from Time to Time may be made,
" to the End that all proper Methods may be
" taken for the utter Suppreffion of all fuch de-
" teftable Practices. His Lordfhip is further di-
" rected to urge them to the due Execution of
" their Office, in detecting and profecuting, with
" Vigour, all Profanenefs, Immorality, and De-
" bauchery, as they value the Bleffing of Al-
" mighty God, as they regard the Happinefs of
" their Country, which cannot fubfift, if Things
" facred and virtuous are trampled upon, and as
" they tender his Majefty's Favour, to which they
" cannot recommend themfelves more effectually,
" than by fhewing the utmoft Zeal upon fo im-
" portant an Occafion ; to which End his Lord-
" fhip is to acquaint them, that as his Majefty for
" himfelf has nothing more at Heart than to re-
" gard the Honour of God, fo impioufly ftruck
" at, and is determined to fhew all Marks of
" Difpleafure and Difcouragement to any who
" may lie even under the Sufpicion of fuch Prac-
" tices ;

" tices ; fo he fhall always account it the greateft
" and moft fubftantial Service they can do to his
" Majefty or his Government, to exert them-
" felves in difcovering any who are guilty of fuch
" Impieties, that they may be openly profecuted,
" and punifhed with the utmoft Severity and
" moft publick Ignominy which the Laws of the
" Land can inflict.

EDWARD SOUTHWELL.

To this it is added, in the fame *Gazette*, " That
" his Majefty has been pleafed to give Orders to
" the principal Officers of his Houfhold, to make
" ftrict and diligent Enquiry, whether any of
" his Majefty's Servants are guilty of the horrid
" Impieties mentioned in the Order of Council
" inferted above, and to make a Report thereof
" to his Majefty."

Thefe Societies muft certainly be as diftracted
as they are impious. I have indeed been in doubt
till now, whether there really were any fuch ; but
I am in no doubt about the Punifhment which
they deferve : I think that it ought to be the moft
fevere that is due to fuch raving Wickednefs,
which is fuch, as neither Youth nor Wine can
excufe, nor indeed extenuate ; and till they are
further punifhed, I think that the darkeft Holes in
Bedlam ought to be their Portion. But outrageous
and godlefs as they are, they do not merit more
Deteftation and Severity, than do thofe who inhumanly give out, that Gentlemen, who abhor
fuch Clubs, are Members of them : The Authors
of fo dreadful a Calumny are much worfe than
Murderers ; becaufe they endeavour to take away
from Men fomething much dearer than Life :

They

They are therefore in the Clafs with Dæmons, and earn fuch mighty Vengeance as God only can inflict.

The above Order of Council is very juft and religious, and of excellent Ufe and Example : So much Zeal cannot ftop at a Club or two of pernicious though private Sinners ; but doubtlefs extends to other Criminals more publick and confiderable, and even more deftructive. The greateft Part of the Wickednefs done by thofe thoughtlefs young Wretches, is done to themfelves, and like to remain with them ; there being little Probability that they will ever make many Profelytes to their aftonifhing Frenzies : Whereas the other great Criminals, for the fole Sake of doing Good to themfelves, have undone almoft every Man in *England*, with *England* itfelf into the Bargain. They fet Three Nations to fale ; and themfelves fixing the Price, were themfelves the Buyers : They purchafed our Happinefs, and paid us in Want and Sorrow. Every good Man is Proof againft the Contagion of Profanenefs ; but Virtue and Goodnefs ftood us in no ftead againft our Money-Monfters, who, having robbed all honeft Men, made a Jeft of Honefty itfelf. Can there be greater Evils under the Sun, than rampant Plunderers, abandoned Corruption, and devouring Calamity ? Or are there any other Evils which thefe do not produce ?

We therefore take it for granted, That *as his Majefty is determined to fhew all Marks of Difpleafure and Difcouragement to any who may even lie under the Sufpicion of fuch* deftructive *Practices ; fo he will always account it the moft fubftantial Ser-*
vice

vice that we *can do to* him *and his Government, to
exert* ourfelves *in difcovering any who are guilty of
fuch* unparalleled Frauds, fuch *National Wickednefs*; *that they may be openly profecuted, and punifhed with the utmoft Severity, and moft publick Ignominy, that the* Legiflature *can inflict.*

And, as " his Majefty has been pleafed to give
" Orders to the Principal Officers of his Houfe-
" hold, to make ftrict and diligent Enquiry, whe-
" ther any of his Majefty's Servants are guilty of
" the horrid Impieties mentioned in the Order of
" Council inferted above, and to make Report
" thereof to his Majefty :" So we may affure ourfelves, that the fame fevere Enquiry has been already made, whether any of thofe in Truft under
his Majefty, or about his Perfon, have ftained
their Hands, difhonoured their Mafter, and provoked Almighty God, by promoting or embarking in any of the horrid and fpreading Mifchiefs
practifed laft Year by the late *South-Sea* Directors,
and their Confederates.

An Enquiry into Religion, and the private Morals of Men, is not inconfiftent with an Enquiry
into Civil and Publick Villainies ; nor can the former ever prove a Bone of Contention to divert
the latter, whatever the Wicked and the Guilty
may hope, and the Honeft and Diftreffed may apprehend. Frefh Objects of Horror and Averfion
cannot leffen our general Deteftation for thofe who
ought to be beyond all others detefted. While
we purfue Wolves and Tygers, and the mightier
Beafts of Prey, who, if they be not deftroyed, will
continue to deftroy, we are not to be diverted by
the Scent of a Fox or Badger, though they may
annoy

annoy a private Neighbourhood, and difpeople Hen-Roofts.

Our publick Virtue is the beft and fureft Proof that we can give of our private Piety : Piety and Juftice are infeparable ; and Prayers faid Ten times a Day, will not atone for a Murder or a Robbery committed once a Month : Appearances go for nothing, when Facts contradict them. The readieft Way therefore to fhew that our Hearts are pure, is to fhew that our Hands are clean, and that we will punifh thofe that have foul ones.

Here is a Teft of our Virtue and Innocence !

Let us hang up publick Rogues, as well as punifh private Blafphemers. The Obfervance of Religion, and the Neglect of Juftice, are Contradictions. Let any Man afk himfelf, Whether a Nation is more hurt by a few giddy, unthinking, young Wretches, talking madly in their Drink ; or by open, deliberate, and publick Depredations committed by a Junto of veteran Knaves, who add to the Injury, and to their own Guilt, by a Shew of Gravity, and a canting Pretence to Religion? The late Directors all pretended to be good Chriftians. I would afk one Queftion more ; namely, Whether it had not been better for *England*, that the late Directors, and their Mafters, had fpent their Nights and their Days in the *Hell Fire-Club*, than in contriving and executing execrable Schemes to ruin *England?* Pray, which of the Two is your greater Enemy, he who robs you of all that you have, but neither curfes nor fwears at you ; or he who only curfes you or himfelf, and takes nothing from you ?

Where Juftice is exactly obferved, Religion will be obferved ; and to pretend to be very ftrict about
the

the Latter, without minding the Former, would
be highly abfurd and ridiculous. Virtue neceffarily
produces Religion, and is itfelf Religion ; and
Profanenefs and Irreligion will ever and neceffarily
follow Corruption, the prolifick Parent of numberlefs Mifchiefs.

Private Profanenefs is not therefore half fo terrible to human Society, as publick Roguery and
publick Robbery. The Happinefs of Mankind is
furely the Caufe of God ; and whenever I hear of
Arrets and Edicts made by Popifh and Tyrannical
Foreign Princes, in Favour of Religion ; I confider them as fo many Mockeries of God, whofe
Creatures they, at the fame Time, grind and deftroy. As confiftently might they pretend great
Zeal for obferving religioufly the Sixth Command,
and yet murder by War and Famine Ten Thoufand of their Subjects a Week.

James Naylor was feverely punifhed for Blafphemy ; Is there any Comparifon, as to their Effects,
between the Crime of *James Naylor*, and the
Crimes of the late Directors, their Seconds, and
Abettors ? *James Naylor* (being himfelf deluded)
mifled a few ignorant People, whofe Error was
their greateft Crime : But our modern Impoftors,
our *South-Sea* Deceivers have actually and wilfully
plundered their Country of near Thirty Millions
of Money, and involved it in univerfal Confufion
and Want.

It is therefore a fenfible Pleafure to us, to behold his Majefty and his Miniftry engaged with
fo much Zeal in vindicating our Property, as well
as our Religion. His Majefty, in particular, has
condefcended, with unparalleled, I am fure uncommon, Goodnefs, to tell the Lord Mayor and Court

of Aldermen, that *he has no Share in the late wicked Management.* This is a Piece of Royal Grace, with which, I believe, never any Subjects were bleſſed before. From hence we may draw a freſh Aſſurance of his Majeſty's Alacrity and Readineſs to puniſh the execrable Authors of that wicked Management, who are alſo the greateſt Enemies to his Crown and Dignity.

" His Majeſty being reſolved to make Uſe of all " the Authority committed to him by Almighty " God, to puniſh ſuch enormous Offenders, and " to cruſh ſuch ſhocking Impieties, before they " encreaſe and draw down the Vengeance of God " upon this Nation :" I ſay, his Majeſty being thus zealous for Religion and the Nation, will never ſuffer the Authors of the greateſt Evil, the higheſt Villainy ever committed in this Nation, to eſcape unpuniſhed. Has ever a heavier Judgment befallen our Nation, than the laſt Year's mercileſs Rapine ? And can there be greater Enemies to God and Man, than the Authors of it ? Monſters who were for plucking up all Virtue and all Property by the Roots. Oh, that their Succeſs had not encreaſed their Guilt ! They acted as if they did not believe that there was a God who judged the World, and as if they defied all human Tribunals, as well as the Divine. Theſe are the Atheiſts terrible to Society ; this is the Atheiſm wofully and univerſally felt. Deſolation and Miſery are the Occupation and Sport of Devils, and they their Vicegerents who promote them.

He who talks profanely of Things ſacred, is a wicked Man, and as ill bred as he is wicked : But he who wantonly fills a Country, a glorious and happy Country, with Want, Woe, and Sorrow ;

what

what Name, what Torture, what Death, does he not deserve ? He is a Destroyer General :———— He is a mad Dog, with Ten Thousand Mouths, who scatters Poison, Wounds, and Death all around him.

I shall conclude in the strong Words of the above Order of Council ; namely, That as we *value the Blessing of Almighty God, as we regard the Happiness of our Country, which cannot subsist, if Things sacred and virtuous* (and such are private Property, publick Faith, and publick Justice) *are trampled upon* ; *and as we tender his Majesty's Favour, to which we cannot recommend* ourselves *more effectually, than by shewing the utmost Zeal upon so important an Occasion :* I say, as we value all these, let us be warm, bold, and active in the Discovery and Punishment of *such enormous Offenders* ; *and to crush such shocking Mischiefs, before they encrease and draw down the Vengeance of God upon this Nation.*

G

I am, &c.

P. S. I, who hate to see the Punishment of any Sort of great Wickedness linger, do here propose an Expedient to come at a Certainty about the blasphemous Clubs * : Let a Reward be publickly offered for the Discovery of any of their Members, to be paid upon their legal Conviction ; and, in the mean Time, let us not cast random Reproaches upon particular Men ; lest, by falling upon the Innocent, they return double upon our- ourselves. It is base and dishonest to feign Crimes

* Upon the strictest Enquiry, it could not be discovered that any such Clubs ever existed, except in common Fame and the above Order of Council.

that

that are not ; and where they really are, it is barbarous and diabolical to father them upon the Guiltlefs : He who charges upon another a Crime that
deferves the Gallows, does, if it prove falfe, pronounce Sentence againft himfelf, and proclaim his
own Right to *Tyburn* : As, on the other Hand,
he who fkreens from the Gallows thofe that deferve it, adopts their Title to the Halter, and ought
to fwing in their room.

Can there be greater Juftice and Impartiality
than this? And I affure you, Sir, I heartily wifh
that they may take place.

SATURDAY, *May* 10, 1721. No. 30.

An excellent Letter from Brutus *to* Atticus ; *with
an explanatory Introduction.*

S I R,

I Send you another excellent Letter of the great
Brutus. They who fay that I forged the laft,
make me as great a Compliment as ever was made
to Man ; fince whoever could write that Letter, is,
without reflecting on my Cotemporaries, certainly
the greateft Man of the Age.

To the former Letter I gave you an hiftorical
Introduction ; I fhall give you another to this, and
own myfelf obliged for it to Monfieur *Soreau.*

Brutus and *Caffius,* after the Death of *Cæfar,*
having left *Rome, Octavius, Cæfar's* Nephew, arrived there : He was no more than Nineteen Years
old ; and the firft Thing of Note that happened
to him, was a Quarrel with *Mark Anthony,* who
treated

treated him like a Child, with Contempt, and indeed was grown infupportable to all the World. *Cicero* and *Anthony* being then declared Enemies, *Octavius* was perfuaded by his Friends to throw himfelf into the Arms of *Cicero*. Hence began their Friendfhip, equally defirable to both : *Cicero* governed the Senate, and *Octavius* had the Hearts of his Uncle's Soldiers, with great Treafure to gain new Friends, and carry on new Defigns. *Mark Anthony* was the common Enemy of both, and of the Republick, which he as outrageoufly attacked, as *Cicero* warmly defended.

This Quarrel gave Occafion to thofe Orations of *Cicero*, called *Philippicks* ; which are eternal Monuments of his Love for his Country, as well as of the marvellous Eloquence of that Great Man.

Cicero and *Octavius* fucceeded ; they got the better of *Mark Anthony*, and drove him out of *Rome*. But, by his Intereft and Activity, he foon gathered fuch a Force, as he thought fufficient to make himfelf Mafter of *Rome* ; which therefore he prepared to attack and poffefs by downright Violence. But *Octavius* having levied, at his own Expence, an Army, compofed moftly of the veteran Troops of *Cæfar*, oppofed the March of *Anthony*, and diverted that dreadful Storm from the City. *Cicero*, who had undertaken the Defence of *Octavius* from his firft Arrival at *Rome*, and laboured to fortify his Caufe by the Authority of the Senate, was not wanting to extol this firft Service of *Octavius* for the Republick. Hence extraordinary Honours were decreed him ; that he fhould be made Proprætor, and in that Quality Commander of the Army ; that a Recompence fhould be given

to

to his Troops ; that he fhould be received into the Number of the Senators ; that he might, before he came of Age, demand all the other greateft Dignities of the Commonwealth ; and even that a Statue fhould be erected to him.

In the mean Time *Anthony*, thus repulfed by *Octavius*, marched into the *Cifalpine Gaul*, to drive from thence *Decimus Brutus*, its Governor, a Kinfman of our *Brutus*, and one of the *Tyrannicides*. That Governor, being unprovided of Forces fufficient to fight *Anthony*, retired into the City of *Modena*, a *Roman* Colony ; and there fhutting himfelf up, expected Succous from the Senate. *Anthony* in the Interim lays Siege to the Place, in hopes that being once Mafter of that City, he would foon be fo of *Gaul*, and afterwards be enabled to return into *Italy*, witn a Power fufficient to conquer *Rome*, where he meant to erect a Dominion as abfolute as was that of *Cæfar*.

That Siege occafioned frefh Meetings of the Senate ; where, in fine, *Mark Anthony* was declared an Enemy to the Commonwealth ; and both the Confuls, *Hirtius* and *Panfa*, were fent with an Army to relieve *Decimus Brutus* : With the Confuls, *Octavius* was likewife fent.

During all thefe Tranfactions, our *Brutus* and *Caffius* having ftaid fome Time in *Italy*, after their leaving *Rome*, were now retired to their Governments, *Brutus* to *Macedonia*, and *Caffius* to *Syria* ; and both were levying Men, and forming Armies, for the Defence of the Commonwealth.

As to *Cicero*, he was now in the Zenith of Power, and governed all Things at *Rome* : He particularly prefided in the Senate, as the moft antient Confular, during the Abfence of the Two Confuls.

Confuls. In this Situation he was wonderfully curious to know what was the Opinion of *Brutus* concerning himfelf and his Adminiftration. It is certain that *Brutus* had his higheft Efteem ; and he thought that if he could procure the Efteem of *Brutus*, it would be an eminent Proof of his own Virtue and Merit, as well as the moft glorious Reward of that Virtue and Merit. *Brutus* had, in all his Letters, been very filent with him upon this Head. *Cicero* therefore makes Ufe of *Atticus*, their common Friend, to fift *Brutus*, and know his Sentiments. As foon, therefore, as it was known at *Rome*, that the Siege of *Modena* was raifed, and *Anthony* defeated by the Two Confuls and *Octavius*, *Atticus* difpatched the News to *Brutus*, and in his Letter founded him about his Thoughts of *Cicero*.

The following Letter is a frank and open Anfwer to that of *Atticus*. In it he juftly condemns *Cicero*'s over violent Hatred to *Mark Anthony*, which betrayed him into as unreafonable an Affection and Deference for *Octavius*, his Champion againft *Anthony*. *Cicero* faw his Error at laft, but faw it too late ; the Power and Credit to which he had raifed *Octavius*, coft him his Life, and *Rome* her Liberty. *Cicero*, who was the Author of all the Greatnefs and Authority of *Octavius*, was by *Octavius* given up to the Rage and Sword of *Mark Anthony*, againft whom *Octavius* had been generoufly defended and fupported by *Cicero* : And *Octavius* enflaved the Commonwealth with thofe very Arms, which the Commonwealth had trufted with him for her Protection. So early had the pious *Auguftus* learned the Arts and Gratitude of an Abfolute Monarch !   *I am*, &c.

BRUTUS

BRUTUS to *ATTICUS*.

" YOU tell me, that *Cicero* wonders why, in
" any of my Letters, I have never difcovered
" to him my Sentiments concerning his Manage-
" ment and Adminiftration at *Rome* ; I therefore
" difcover thofe Sentiments to you, fince you are
" fo earneft to know them.

" I know well the Sincerity and great Upright-
" nefs of *Cicero*'s Intentions : His Paffion for the
" Good of the Commonwealth is indeed evident
" and remarkable. But prudent and wife as he
" is, he has given Proofs of a Zeal which is im-
" prudent, and a Heart that is vain : I leave it to
" you to judge, which of thefe fwayed him,
" when, more forward than well advifed, he drew
" upon himfelf the Hatred of fo terrible a Foe as
" *Mark Anthony.* This he meant for the Good
" of the Commonwealth ; but it has had a con-
" trary Effect, fince by it, inftead of bridling, as
" he propofed, the dangerous Power of *Octavius*,
" he has further animated his Ambition, and rai-
" fed his Aims. Befides, fuch is the fatal Com-
" plaifance of *Cicero* for that Man, that he cannot
" help fpeaking of myfelf and the Patriots of my
" Country, with fevere and bitter Language ;
" which, however, returns double upon himfelf :
" If we have put one Man to Death, he has put
" many. We killed *Cæfar*, and he the Affociates
" of *Catiline.* If therefore *Cafca*, who gave *Cæ-*
" *far* the firft Blow, be a Murderer, as *Cicero*,
" to pleafe *Octavius*, calls him ; *Cicero* himfelf
" is one, and muft confefs himfelf one, and his
" great Enemy *Beftia* is juftified in calling him
" fo.

" How !

" How ! becaufe we have not the Ides of
" *March*, in which we difpatched *Cæfar*, eter-
" nally in our Mouths, as *Cicero* has the Nones
" of *December*, in which he fuppreffed the Con-
" fpiracy of *Catiline*, and which he is for ever
" celebrating upon all Occafions ; does he take
" Advantage of our Modefty and his own Vanity,
" and find from hence more Reafon to blame a
" glorious Deed done by us for Mankind, than
" *Clodius* and *Beftia* had to condemn, as they al-
" ways did, his own fevere Conduct when he was
" Conful ?

" *Cicero* every where boafts, that he fuftained
" the War againft *Anthony* ; yet no body ever faw
" *Cicero* out of a Gown, and Words were his
" Weapons. But let it be fo, that he has de-
" feated *Anthony* ; where is the Victory, if, curing
" one Mifchief, it introduce a worfe ? And what
" avails it to have extinguifhed the Tyranny of
" *Anthony*, if he who has done it erect another in
" its room more terrible, by being more durable ?
" And yet thus will it be if we fuffer it. Thefe
" are Articles in the Conduct of *Cicero*, which
" fhew that it is not the Tyrant nor the Tyranny
" that he fears ; but it is only *Anthony* that he
" fears. If a Man will have a Tyrant, it is all
" one to me, whether he be more or lefs outrage-
" ous ; it is the Thing, it is the having a Tyrant,
" which I dread.

" That *Cicero* is haftening to fet up a Tyrant,
" is plain, from Actions as vifible as fad. *Octavius*
" is all in all ; a Triumph is decreed him ; his
" Troops have Largeffes given them ; he is loaded
" with Flatteries, he is covered with Honours.
" What Shame for *Cicero*, to behold all this, and
" his

" his own abject Posture ! His publick Behaviour,
" and the Speeches and Motions which he makes
" in the Senate, all centering in his Master ; are
" they not a Scandal to the great Figure of that
" great Consular, and a Stain upon the renowned
" Name of *Cicero* ?

" You will read this with Pain, as with Pain I
" write it ; but it is a Task which you have put
" upon me. Besides, I know your Thoughts of
" our publick Affairs, and that desperate and ex-
" traordinary as they are, you think that, con-
" trary to all Appearance, they may be remedied
" by Means that are ordinary. I do not however
" blame you, my dear *Atticus* ; comfort yourself
" with Hope ; it is agreeable to your Age, to the
" Sweetness of your Temper, and to your Re-
" gard for your Children : I do not therefore
" wonder that you are indolent and sanguine ;
" which Disposition of yours appears still farther
" to me, from the Account which my Friend
" *Flavius* gave me of what passed between you
" and him.

" But to return to *Cicero* : Pray where is the
" Difference between him and the servile *Salvi-*
" *denus* ? Could that base Retainer to *Octavius*
" struggle for the Glory of his Master with more
" Labour and Zeal than does *Cicero* ? You will
" say, perhaps, that *Cicero* dreads still the Remains
" of the Civil War. This is wild : Can any one
" dread a beaten Enemy, and yet apprehend no-
" thing from the formidable Power of one who
" commands a great Army, elevated by Victory ?
" nor from the Rashness of a young Man, who
" may conquer the Commonwealth by the Means
" which enabled him to conquer for it ? Does
                                          " *Cicero*

" *Cicero* therefore make this mighty Court to
" *Octavius*, becaufe, having given him fo much,
" he thinks it dangerous not to give him all ! Oh
" the wretched Folly of Cowardice ! thus to leffen
" your own Secury by confulting it ; and to en-
" creafe Tyranny becaufe you fear it ! Is it not
" better to have nothing at all to fear, than thus
" to compound for the Degrees of Fear ?

" The Truth is, we too much dread Poverty,
" Banifhment, and Death ; and our Imagination
" fwells their Terrors beyond Bounds. There
" are greater Evils than thefe ; and *Cicero* is
" miftaken if he thinks that there are not. And
" yet all goes well with him, if he be but hu-
" moured, if his Opinion be regarded, if his Suits
" be granted ; if he be courted and extolled : He
" has no Quarrel to Servitude, provided it be ac-
" companied with Honour and Luftre ; if there
" can be any fuch Thing as Honour and Luftre
" in this loweft, this vileft Lot of human Na-
" ture.

" *Octavius* may indeed call him Father *Cicero*,
" refer every Thing to his Counfel, footh him
" with Praifes, and fhew great Gratitude and
" Fondnefs towards him, while he lofes nothing
" by all this, which is only a fair Outfide and
" fine Words. Facts fpeak the plaineft Truth,
" and they effectually contradict the above Ap-
" pearances. For, can there be a greater Infult
" upon Common-Senfe, than for *Octavius* to take
" for a Father that Man who is no longer in the
" Number of Freemen ?

" Whither then tend all thefe Compliances, all
" this Zeal of *Cicero* for *Octavius* ? Why, only
" to this ; That *Octavius* may be propitious to
" *Cicero.*

" *Cicero.* In this little, worthlefs, fhameful Point
" center all the Actions and Defigns of the Great
" *Cicero !* Hence it is that I value no longer, in
" the Perfon of *Cicero*, thofe Arts and Accom-
" plifhments with which, doubtlefs, his Soul is
" vaftly replenifhed. What is he the better, him-
" felf, for fo many excellent Precepts, fo many
" noble Difcourfes, every where found in his
" Works, concerning publick Liberty, true and'
" folid Glory, the Contempt of Death, Exile,
" and Want ? How much better does *Philippus*
" underftand all thofe fine Rules laid down by
" *Cicero*, than *Cicero* himfelf does, who pays more
" Homage to *Octavius* than *Philippus*, who is
" Father-in-Law to *Octavius*, pays ?

" Let *Cicero* therefore ceafe glorying thus vainly
" in our Grief, which alfo ought to be his : For,
" to repeat what I have already faid, What Ad-
" vantage can we draw from a Victory, which
" only tranflates the pernicious Power of *Mark*
" *Anthony* to a new Ufurper ? And yet, by your
" Letter, I perceive that it is ftill a Doubt whe-
" ther *Mark Anthony* be entirely defeated.

" After all, fince *Cicero* can live a Dependent
" and a Slave, let him live a Dependent and a
" Slave. It ought not to be otherwife, if he can
" thus fhamefully forget his reverend Age, the il-
" luftrious Honours which he has borne, and the
" memorable Parts which he has performed.

" For myfelf, while I live, I will make War
" upon Tyranny ; that is, upon all exorbitant
" Power that lifts Men above the Laws : Nor
" can any Condition of Servitude, however ad-
" vantageous and alluring, divert me from this
" great, this worthy Purpofe : Nor could *Anthony*
" fhake

" fhake it, though he really were, what you fay
" he is, a Man of Worth ; a Character which
" contradicts my conftant Opinion of him. The
" Judgment and Spirit of our Anceftors are mine ;
" they would not have their Father for their Ty-
" rant, nor would I.

    " All this Opennefs to you is the Refult of my
" Affection for you ; nor could I have faid fo
" much, had I not lovéd you as well as *Cicero*
" thinks he is beloved by *Octavius*. That all
" thefe fad Truths affect not you fo much as they
" do me, is my Concern ; efpecially fince to an
" eminent Fondnefs for all your Friends, you have
" added a particular Fondnefs for *Cicero*. As to
" myfelf, I beg you to believe that my Affection
" for him is ftill the fame, though my Efteem of
" him is greatly abated : Nor can I help it, it
" being impoffible to judge ill or well of Men and
" Things, but according as they appear ill or
" well."

    G

* * * * * * * * * * * *
 * * * * * * * * * * * * *
* * * * * * * * * * * * * *

Confiderations on the Weaknefs and Inconfiftencies of human Nature.

S I R,

THE Study of human Nature has, ever fince
I could ftudy any thing, been a principal
Pleafure and Employment of mine; a Study as
ufeful, as the Difcoveries made by it are for the
moft part melancholy.   It cannot but be irkfome
to a good-natured Man, to find that there is nothing fo terrible or mifchievous, but human Nature is capable of it; and yet he who knows little
of human Nature, will never know much of the
Affairs of the World, which every where derive
their Motion and Situation from the Humours and
Paffions of Men.

It fhews the violent Bent of human Nature to
Evil, that even the Chriftian Religion has not been
able to tame the reftlefs Appetites of Men, always
pufhing them into Enormities and Violences, in
direct Oppofition to the Spirit and Declarations of
the Gofpel, which commands us to *do unto all Men
what we would have all Men do unto us.*   The general Practice of the World is an open Contradiction and Contempt of this excellent, this divine
Rule; which alone, were it obferved, would reftore Honefty and Happinefs to Mankind, who, in
their prefent State of Corruption, are for ever dealing treacheroufly or outrageoufly with one another,
out of an ill-judging Fondnefs for themfelves.

Nay,

Nay, the peaceable, the beneficent, the forgiving Chriftian Religion, is made the Caufe of perpetual Hatred, Animofity, Quarrels, Violence, Devaftation, and Oppreffion ; and the Apoftles, in fpite of all their Poverty, Difinbereftednefs, and Love of Mankind, are made to juftify their pretended Succeffors of the Church of *Rome*, in engroffing to themfelves the Wealth and Power of the Earth ; and in bringing Mankind under a Yoke of Servitude, more terrible, more expenfive, and more fevere, than all the Arts and Delufions of Paganifm could ever bring them under : Of fo much more Force with the corrupt World are the deftructive Villainies and Falfifications of Men, than the benevolent and heavenly Precepts of Jefus Chrift.

The Truth is, and it is a melancholy Truth, That where human Laws do not tie Mens Hands from Wickednefs, Religion too feldom does ; and the moft certain Security which we have againft Violence, is the Security of the Laws. Hence it is, that the making of Laws fuppofes all Men naturally wicked ; and the fureft Mark of Virtue is, the Obfervation of Laws that are virtuous : If therefore we would look for Virtue in a Nation, we muft look for it in the Nature of Government ; the Name and Model of their Religion being no certain Symptom nor Caufe of their Virtue. The *Italians* profefs the Chriftian Religion, and the *Turks* are all Infidels ; Are the *Italians* therefore more virtuous than the *Turks* ? I believe no body will fay that they are ; at leaft thofe of them that live under abfolute Princes : On the contrary, it is certain, that as the Subjects of the Great *Turk* are not more miferable

than

than thofe of the *Pope*, fo neither are they more wicked.

Of all the Paffions which belong to human Nature, *Self-love* is the ftrongeft, and the Root of all the reft ; or, rather, all the different Paffions are only feveral Names for the feveral Operations of Self-love. *Self-love*, fays the Duke of *Rochefoucault, is the Love of one's felf, and of every thing elfe for one's own Sake : It makes a Man the Idolater of himfelf, and the Tyrant of others.* He obferves, that Man is a Mixture of Contrarieties ; imperious and fupple, fincere and falfe, fearful and bold, merciful and cruel : He can facrifice every Pleafure to the getting of Riches, and all his Riches to a Pleafure : He is fond of his Prefervation, and yet fometimes eager after his own Deftruction : He can flatter thofe whom he hates, deftroy thofe whom he loves.

This is a Picture of Mankind ; and they who fay it is a falfe one, ought to fhew that they deferve a better. I have fometimes thought, that it was fcarce poffible to affert any thing concerning Mankind, be it ever fo good, or ever fo evil, but it will prove true. They are naturally innocent, yet fall naturally into the Practice of Vice ; the greateft Inftances of Virtue and Villainy are to be found in one and the fame Perfon ; and perhaps one and the fame Motive produces both. The Obfervance or Non-obfervance of a few frivolous Cuftoms fhall unite them in ftrict Friendfhip and Confederacy, or fet them a cutting one another's Throats.

They never regard one another as Men and rational Beings, and upon the Foot of their common Humanity ; but are cemented or divided by

the

the Force of Words and Habits.——Considerations that are a Difgrace to Reafon ! The not being born in the fame Climate, or on this Side fuch a River, or fuch a Mountain, or the not wearing the like Garments, or uttering the like Sounds, or having the fame Thoughts or Tafte, are all fo many Caufes of intenfe Hatred, fometimes of mortal War. Whatever Men think or do, efpecially if they have found a good Name for it, be it ever fo foolifh or bad, is wifeft and beft in their own Eyes : But this is not all ; we will needs be plaguing our Neigbours, if they do not quit upon our Authority their own Thoughts and Practices for ours.

It fills me with Concern, when I confider how Men ufe one another ; and how wretchedly their Paffions are employed : They fcarce ever have proper Objects for their Paffions ; they will hate a Man for what he cannot help, and what does them no Harm ; yet blefs and pray for Villains, that kill and opprefs them. There never was fuch a dreadful Tribunal under the Sun as the *Inquifition* : A Tribunal, againft which the moft innocent is not fafe, to which the moft virtuous Men are moft expofed ; a Tribunal, where all the Malice, all the fagacious Cruelty, all the Bitternefs, and all the Fury and Falfhood of Devils are exerted, and all the Tortures of Hell are imitated and practifed ; yet this very Tribunal is fo dear to the People, though it terrifies them, enflaves them, and deftroys them, that rather than part with it, they would part with all that is left them. Upon the Surrender of *Barcelona*, in the late War, the Inhabitants capitulated, that the *Inquifition* fhould not be taken from them : And even here in *England*,

we

we may remember the Time when Men have been knocked down for faying that they had a Right to defend their Property by Force, when a Tyrant attempted to rob them of it againft Law. To fuch a Pitch of Stupidity and Diftraction are People to be brought by thofe who belie Almighty God, and falfify his Word to fatiate worldly Pride; and fuch Dupes and Furies are Men to one another !

Every thing is fo perverted and abufed, and the beft Things moft, that a very wife Man had but too much Reafon to fay, that *Truth did not fo much Good in the World, as the Appearance and Pretence of it did Evil.* Thus the faving of Mens Souls is fo univerfally underftood to be a great and glorious Bleffing, that for the Sake of it Men have fuffered, and do fuffer, the higheft Mifery and Bondage from the Impoftors who pretend to beftow it, in the dark Parts of the World, which are by far the greateft Parts of the World. And thus Civil Government is the Defence and Security of human Society; yet Dr. *Prideaux* makes it a Doubt, *whether the Benefit which the World receives from Government be fufficient to make Amends for the Calamities which it fuffers from the Follies, Miftakes, and Male-Adminiftration of thofe that manage it.* And thus to come Home to ourfelves, a Project to pay off the Nation's Debts was fo tempting, fo popular and plaufible, that almoft every body came into it; and yet ——The Confequences fpeak themfelves.

The *Roman* Senate could flatter and adore a *Nero* and a *Caligula*; the *Roman* Soldiers could butcher a *Pifo* and a *Pertinax* : It is hard to fay which were the moft guilty, the Senate while they worfhipped

fhipped Tyranny, or the Army while they deftroyed Virtue. So prone are Men to propagate
publick Deftruction for perfonal Advantages and
Security! I can never think without Horror and
Trembling upon that difmal, that bloody Maxim
of *Philip* II. of *Spain*, That *he would rather be
Mafter of a Kingdom ruined, miferable, and quiet ;
than of a Kingdom rich, powerful, and turbulent.* In
purfuance of this Maxim, he made his Kingdom
a Defart, by deftroying and expelling the moft induftrious of its Inhabitants, the *Moors :* But *Philip*
was very devout, and would frequently wafh a Pil-
grim's Feet ; that is, he was very civil and charitable to an idle religious Stroller, and a cruel Enemy to the general Happinefs of Mankind.

This puts me in mind of the Hiftory of *John
Bafilowitz*, Great Duke of *Mufcovy*. *No Hiftory
of his Time but fpeaks of the unheard-of Cruelties
exercifed by him on all Sorts of Perfons through his
whole Reign : They are fo horrid, that never any
Tyrant did the like ; and yet Bifhop* Paulus Jovius
*gives him the Character of a good and devout
Chriftian, though he deferves not to be numbered even
amongft Men : It is true, he would go often to
Church, fay the Service himfelf, fing, and be prefent at Ecclefiaftical Ceremonies, and execute the
Functions of the Monks : But he abufed both God
and Man, and had no Sentiments of Humanity.*
Ambaffadors Travels, p. 73, 74.

What a Medley is here of Devotion and Cruelty in the fame Men! Nor are thefe Examples
fingular. *Louis* XI. of *France* was a falfe, a
wicked, and an oppreffive Prince, and one of the
greateft Bigots that ever lived ; and fome of the
greateft Saints in the *Roman* Calendar were pernicious

cious Villains, and bloody Monfters. No Sect of Bigots, when they are uppermoft, are willing to tolerate another; and all ground their ungodly Severity upon their Zeal for Religion; though their Want of Charity is a Demonftration that they have no Religion. It is certain, that without univerfal Charity and Forbearance, a Man cannot be a Chriftian.

It is wonderful and affecting, to behold how the Ideas of Good and Evil are confounded! The *Turks* place great Devotion in releafing Captive Birds from their Cages, in feeding indigent and mangey Dogs, and building Hofpitals for them, and in paying a religious Reverence to Camels: But at the fame Time that they thus ufe Birds and Beafts like Men and Chriftians, they ufe Men and Chriftians worfe than they do Beafts; and with them it is a lighter Offence to deny Bread to a poor Chriftian, who is famifhed in his Chains, than to the Dogs of the Street, which are fit for nothing but to breed Infection. They will load a poor Chriftian with Irons, cover him with Stripes, and think that they do well and religioufly in it; yet make it a Matter of Confcience not to overload a Beaft of Burthen.

In Popifh Countries, in Cafes where Nature is left to itfelf, as much Compaffion is fhewn for the Diftreffed as in other Places: Even Thieves, Robbers, and Murderers, are accompanied to the Gallows or the Wheel with Sighs and Tears; efpecially of the tender Sex: But when an unhappy Innocent is going to be burned, to be cruelly and flowly burned, for his Sincerity and Piety in fpeaking Truth, and reading the Bible himfelf, or teaching it to others; nothing is to be feen but a
general

general Joy, nor to be heard but loud Cries of
Approbation and Confent ; and all Pity, all Sympathy, is denied in an Inftance which calls for the
higheft.　Tell a *Spanifh* Lady of a Popifh Prieft
hanged in *England* for Sedition or Murder, fhe inftantly falls into Tears and Agonies : Tell her of
a Kinfman of hers burned for denying Tranfubftantiation, fhe gives Glory to God, and feels a
fenfible Joy.

And, in Proteftant Countries, how many Men
are there, who cheat, ftarve, and opprefs all their
Life long, to leave an Eftate at their Death to religious Ufes ?　As if Men were to be Rogues for
God's Sake.　I have heard of a Man, who haveing given half of his Eftate to mend Highways,
for the Good of his Country, faid, that he would
willingly give the other half, that *England* had
never a Ship, nor a Merchant, nor a Diffenter
from the Church, belonging to it.　Strange Inconfiftency !　By one Act of his, two or three Miles
of Caufeway were kept in good Repair, which
was only a Kindnefs to Horfes Hoofs ; by another
Act of his, he would have made all *England* miferable and defolate !

The Hardfhips and Diftreffes of this Year fhew
too manifeftly the Rogueries and Depredations of
the laft : Villainy was let loofe amongft us, and
every Man endeavoured to entrap and ruin another,
to enrich himfelf.　Honefty was brow-beaten and
driven into Corners ; Humanity was extinguifhed ;
all Friendfhip was abolifhed ; and even the Diftinction of Kindred and Ties of Blood were difcarded :
A raging Paffion for immoderate Gain had made
Men univerfally and intenfely hard-hearted : They
were every where devouring one another.　And
yet

yet the Directors and their Accomplices, who were the acting Instruments of all this outrageous Madness and Mischief, set up for wonderfully pious Persons, while they were defying Almighty God, and plundering Men; and they set apart a Fund of Subscriptions for charitable Uses: That is, they mercilesly made a whole People Beggars, and charitably supported a few necessitous and worthless Favourites. I doubt not, but if the Villainy had gone on with Success, they would have had their Names handed down to Posterity with Encomiums; as the Names of other publick Robbers have been! We have Historians and Ode-makers now living, very proper for such a Task. It is certain, that most People did, at one time, believe the Directors to be great and worthy Persons: And an honest Country Clergyman told me last Summer, upon the Road, that Sir *John* was an excellent publick-spirited Person, for that he had beautified his Chancel.

Upon the Whole, we must not judge of one another by our fair Pretensions and best Actions; since the worst Men do some Good, and all Men make fine Professions: But we must judge of Men by the Whole of their Conduct, and the Effects of it. Thorough Honesty requires great and long Proof; since many a Man, long thought honest, has at length proved a Knave. And it is from judging without Proof, or too little, of false Proof, that Mankind continue unhappy.

G

I am, &c.

SATURDAY, *June* 10, 1721.   No. 32.

Reflections upon Libelling.

S I R,

I Defign in this Letter to lay before the Town
fome Thoughts upon Libelling; a Sort of Writing that hurts particular Perfons, without doing
Good to the Publick; and a Sort of Writing
much complained of amongft us at this Time,
with great Ground, but not more than is pretended.

A Libel is not the lefs a Libel for being true.
This may feem a Contradiction; but it is neither
one in Law, or in common Senfe: There are
fome Truths not fit to be told; where, for Example, the Difcovery of a fmall Fault may do
great Mifchief; or where the Difcovery of a
great Fault can do no Good, there ought to be no
Difcovery at all: And to make Faults where there
are none, is ftill worfe.

But this Doctrine only holds true as to private
and perfonal Failings; and it is quite otherwife
when the Crimes of Men come to affect the Publick. Nothing ought to be fo dear to us as our
Country, and nothing ought to come in Compe-
tition with its Interefts. Every Crime againft the
Publick is a great Crime, though there be fome
greater than others. Ignorance and Folly may be
pleaded in Alleviation of private Offences; but
when they come to be publick Offences, they lofe
all Benefit of fuch a Plea: We are then no longer

to

to confider only to what Caufes they are owing, but what Evils they may produce ; and here we fhall readily find, that Folly has overturned States, and private Ignorance been the Parent of publick Confufion.

The expofing therefore of publick Wickednefs, as it is a Duty which every Man owes to Truth and his Country, can never be a Libel in the Nature of Things ; and they who call it fo, make themfelves no Compliment. He who is affronted at the reading of the Ten Commandments, would make the Decalogue a Libel, if he durft ; but he tempts us at the fame Time to form a Judgment of his Life and Morals not at all to his Advantage : Whoever calls publick and neceffary Truths, Libels, does but apprize us of his own Character, and arm us with Caution againft his Defigns. I doubt not but if the late Directors had been above the Parliament, as they once thought themfelves, they would have called the *Votes of the Houfe of Commons* againft them, *falfe and fcandalous Libels.*

Machiavel fays, *Calumny is pernicious, but Accufation beneficial, to a State* ; and he fhews Inftances where States have fuffered or perifhed for not haveing, or for neglecting, the Power to accufe Great Men who were Criminals, or thought to be fo ; and hence grew the Temptation and Cuftom of flandering and reviling, which was the only Remedy that the People had left them : So that the Evil of Calumny was owing to the Want of Juftice, and the People were more blamelefs than thofe whom they reviled ; who, having forced them upon a Licentioufnefs of Speech, did very unkindly chide and punifh them for ufing it. Slander is
certainly

certainly a very bafe and mean Thing : But furely
it cannot be more pernicious to calumniate even
good Men, than not to be able to accufe ill
ones.

I have long thought, that the World are very
much miftaken in their Idea and Diftinction of
Libels. It has been hitherto generally underftood
that there were no other Libels but thofe againft
Magiftrates, and thofe againft private Men : Now,
to me there feems to be a third Sort of Libels, full
as deftructive as any of the former can poffibly be ;
I mean, Libels againft the People. It was otherwife at *Athens* and *Rome* ; where, though particular Men, and even great Men, were often treated
with much Freedom and Severity, when they deferved it ; yet the People, the Body of the People,
were fpoken of with the utmoft Regard and Reverence : *The facred Privileges of the People*, *The inviolable Majefty of the People*, *The awful Authority
of the People*, and *The unappealable Judgment of the
People*, were Phrafes common in thefe wife, great,
and free Cities. Other Modes of Speech are fince
grown fafhionable, and popular Madnefs is now
almoft proverbial : But this Madnefs of theirs,
whenever it happens, is derived from external
Caufes. *Oppreffion*, they fay, *will make a wife
Man mad* ; and Delufion has not lefs Force : But
where there are neither Oppreffors nor Impoftors,
the Judgment of the People in the Bufinefs of
Property, the Prefervation of which is the principal
Bufinefs of Government, does rarely err. Perhaps
they are deftitute of Grimace, Myftery, Refinements, Shrugs, Diffimulation, and Referve, and
the other Accomplifhments of Courtiers : But as
thefe are only Mafks to conceal the Abfence of
                                            Honefty

Honefty and Senfe, the People, who poffefs as
they do the Subftance, have Reafon to defpife fuch
infipid and contemptible Shadows.

Machiavel, in the Chapter where he proves that
a Multitude is wifer and more conftant than a
Prince, complains, that the Credit which the People fhould be in declines daily ; *For*, fays he, *every
Man has Liberty to fpeak what he pleafes againſt
them* ; *but againſt a Prince no Man can talk without a thoufand Apprehenfions and Dangers.* I have
indeed often wondered, that the inveighing againſt
the Intereſt of the People, and calling their Liberties in Queſtion, as has been and is commonly
done among us by old Knaves and young Fools,
has never been made an exprefs Crime.

I muſt own, I know not what Treafon is, if
fapping and betraying the Liberties of a People be
not Treafon, in the eternal and original Nature of
Things. Let it be remembered for whofe Sake
Government is, or could be, appointed ; then let
it be confidered, who are more to be regarded, the
Governors or the Governed. They indeed owe
one another mutual Duties ; but if there be any
Tranfgreffions committed, the Side that is moſt
obliged ought doubtlefs to bear the moſt : And yet
it is fo far otherwife, that almoſt all over the Earth,
the People, for One Injury that they do their Governors, receive Ten Thoufand from them : Nay,
in fome Countries, it is made Death and Damnation, not to bear all the Oppreffions and Cruelties,
which Men made wanton by Power inflict upon
thofe that gave it them.

The Truth is ; If the People are fuffered to keep
their own, it is the moſt that they defire : But
even this is a Happinefs which in few Places falls
to

to their Lot; they are frequently robbed by thofe whom they pay to protect them. I know that it is a general Charge againft the People, that they are turbulent, reftlefs, fickle, and unruly: Than which there can be nothing more untrue; for they are only fo where they are made fo. As to their being fickle, it is fo falfe, that, on the contrary, they have almoft ever a ftrong Bent to received Cuftoms, and as ftrong a Partiality to Names and Families that they have been ufed to: And as to their being turbulent, it is as falfe; fince there is fcarce an Example in an Hundred Years of any People's giving Governors any Uneafinefs, till their Governors had made them uneafy: Nay, for the moft part, they bear many Evils without returning One, and feldom throw off their Burdens fo long as they can ftand under them.

But intending to handle this Subject more at large in another Letter, I return more directly to the Bufinefs of Libels.

As to Libels againft Government, like all others, they are always bafe and unlawful, and often mifchievous; efpecially when Governments are impudently charged with Actions and Defigns of which they are not guilty. It is certain, that we ought not to enter into the private Vices or Weakneffes of Governors, any further than their private Vices enter into their publick Adminiftra-tion; and when they do, it will be impoffible to ftop People's Mouths: They will be provoked, and fhew that they are fo, in fpite of Art and Threats, if they fuffer Hardfhips and Woe from the private Gratifications of their Superiors, from whom they have a Right to expect Eafe and Happinefs; and if they be difappointed, they
will

will be apt to deal very freely with their Characters.

In Truth, moft Libels are purely perfonal; they fly at Men rather than Things; which Proceeding is as injudicious as it is unmanly. It is mean to be quarrelling with Faces, Names, and private Pleafures; Things perfectly indifferent to the World, or Things out of a Man's own Power; and 'tis filly, as it fhews thofe whom we attack, that we attack them not for what they do, but for what they are: And this is to provoke them without mending them. All this therefore is Libelling; an Offence againft which the Laws of almoft every Country, and particularly of our own, have furnifhed a Remedy in proportion to the Confequence and Quality of the Perfon offended. And it is as juft that Reputation fhould be defended by Law, as that Property fhould.

The Praife of Well-doing is the higheft Reward that worthy and difinterefted Men aim at, and it is villainous and ungrateful to rob them of it; and thofe that do it, are Libellers and Slanderers. On the other hand, while Cenfure and Infamy attend Evil-doers, it will be fome Reftraint, if not upon them, yet upon others, from following their Example: But if Men be ever fuffered to do what they pleafe without hearing of it, or being accountable for it; Liberty and Law will be loft, though their Names may remain. And whether acting wickedly with Impunity, or fpeaking falfly with Impunity, be likely to do moft Hurt to human Society and the Peace of the World, I leave all the World to judge: Common Equity fays, that they both ought to be punifhed, though not both alike.

All

All Libels, the higher they aim, the more Malignity they acquire ; and therefore when they ftrike at the Perfon of the Prince, the Meafure of their Guilt is complete. The Office of a Prince is to defend his People and their Properties ; an excellent and a painful Office ; which, where it is executed with Honefty and Diligence, deferves the higheft Applaufe and Reward ; and whoever vilifies and traduces him, is an Enemy to Society and to Mankind, and will be punifhed with the Confent of all who love either. And yet it is fcarce poffible, in a free Country, to punifh by a general Law any Libel fo much as it deferves ; fince fuch a Law, confifting of fo many Branches, and being of fuch vaft Latitude, would make all Writing whatfoever, how innocent foever, and even all Speaking, unfafe. Hence it is, that in *Turkey*, though Printing were permitted, it would be of no Ufe, becaufe no body would dare to make any Ufe of it.

As long as there are fuch Things as Printing and Writing, there will be Libels : It is an Evil arifing out of a much greater Good. And as to thofe who are for locking up the Prefs, becaufe it produces Monfters, they ought to confider that fo do the Sun and the *Nile* ; and that it is fomething better for the World to bear fome particular Inconveniencies arifing from general Bleffings, than to be wholly deprived of Fire and Water.

Of all Sorts of Libels, fcurrilous ones are certainly the moft harmlefs and contemptible : Even Truth fuffers by Ill-Manners ; and Ill-Manners prevent the Effect of Lyes. The Letter in the *Saturday*'s *Poft* of the 27th paft does, I think, exceed all the Scurrilities which I have either heard,

or

or feen, from the Prefs or the Pulpit. The Author of it muft furely be mad : He talks as if Diftraction were in his Head, and a Firebrand in his Hand ; and nothing can be more falfe, than the Infinuations which he makes, and the ugly Refemblances which he would draw.   The Paper is a Heap of Falfhood and Treafon, delivered in the Style and Spirit of *Billingfgate* ; and indeed moft of the Enemies to his Majefty's Perfon, Title, and Government, have got the Faculty of Writing and Talking, as if they had their Education in that Quarter.

However, as bad as that Letter is, (and, I think, there cannot be a worfe) Occafion will never be taken from fcurrilous and traiterous Writing, to deftroy the End of Writing.   We know that in all Times there have been Men lying upon the Watch to ftifle Liberty, under a Pretence of fuppreffing Libels ; like the late King *James*, who, having Occafion for an Army to fupprefs *Monmouth*'s Rebellion, would needs keep it up afterwards ; becaufe, forfooth, other Rebellions might happen, for which he was refolved to give Caufe.

I muft own, that I would rather many Libels fhould efcape, than the Liberty of the Prefs fhould be infringed ; yet no Man in *England* thinks worfe of Libels than I do ; efpecially of fuch as bid open Defiance to the prefent Proteftant Eftablifhment.

Corrupt Men, who have given Occafion for Reproach, by their bafe and dark Practices with the late Directors, being afraid of Truths that affect them from the Prefs, may be defirous of fhutting it up : But honeft Men, with clear Reputations,

putations, which they know foul Mouths cannot hurt, will always be for preferving it open, as a fure Sign of Liberty, and a Caufe of it.

The beft Way to efcape the Virulence of Libels, is not to deferve them ; but as Innocence itfelf is not fecure againft the Malignity of evil Tongues, it is alfo neceffary to punifh them. However, it does not follow that the Prefs is to be funk, for the Errors of the Prefs. No body was ever yet fo ridiculous to propofe a Law for reftraining People from travelling upon the Highway, becaufe fome who ufed the Highway committed Robberies.

It is commonly faid, that no Nation in the World would allow fuch Papers to come Abroad as *England* fuffers ; which is only faying, that no Nation in the World enjoys the *Liberty* which *England* enjoys. In Countries where there is no Liberty, there can be no ill Effects of it. No body is punifhed at *Conftantinople* for Libelling : Nor is there any Diftinction there between the Liberty of the Prefs, and the Licentioufnefs of the Prefs ; a Diftinction ever to be obferved by honeft Men and Freemen.

G.   *I am,* &c.

Satur-

SATURDAY, *June* 17, 1721. No. 33.

Cautions against the natural Encroachments of Power.

SIR,

COnfidering what fort of a Creature Man is, it is fcarce poffible to put him under too many Reftraints, when he is poffeffed of great Power : He may poffibly ufe it well ; but they act moft prudently, who, fuppofing that he would ufe it ill, inclofe him within certain Bounds, and make it terrible to him to exceed them.

Men that are above all Fear, foon grow above all Shame. *Rupto pudore & metu, fua tantum ingenio utebatur*, fays *Tacitus* of *Tiberius*. Even *Nero* had lived a great while inoffenfively, and reigned virtuoufly : But finding at laft that he might do what he would, he let loofe his Appetite for Blood, and committed fuch mighty, fuch monftrous, fuch unnatural Slaughters and Outrages, as none but a Heart bent on the Study of Cruelty could have devifed. The good Counfels of *Seneca* and *Burrhus* were, for fome Time, Checks upon his wolfifh Nature ; and doubtlefs he apprehended, that if he made direct and downright War upon his People, they would ufe Refiftance and make Reprifals : But difcovering, by degrees, that they would bear any thing, and his Soldiers would execute every thing, he grew into an open Defiance with Mankind, and daily and wantonly wallowed in their Blood. Having no other Rival, he feemed to
rival

rival himfelf, and every Day's Wicknefs was blacker than another.

Yet *Nero* was not the worft of all Men : There have been Thoufands as bad as he, and only wanted the fame Opportunity to fhew it. And there actually have been many Princes in the World who have fhed more Blood, and done more Mif- chief to Mankind, than *Nero* did. I could in- ftance in a late One, who deftroyed more Lives than ever *Nero* deftroyed, perhaps an Hundred to One. It makes no Difference, that *Nero* commit- ted Butcheries out of Cruelty, and the other only for his Glory : However the World may be de- ceived by the Change of Names into an Abhor- rence of the One, and an Admiration of the Other ; it is all one to a Nation, when they are to be flaughtered, whether they be flaughtered by the Hangman or by Dragoons, in Prifon or in the Field ; nor is Ambition better than Cruelty, when it begets Mifchief as great.

It is nothing ftrange, that Men, who think themfelves unaccountable, fhould act unacount- ably, and that all Men would be unaccountable if they could : Even thofe who have done nothing to difpleafe, do not know but fome time or other they may ; and no Man cares to be at the entire Mercy of another. Hence it is, that if every Man had his Will, all Men would exercife Dominion, and no Man would fuffer it. It is therefore owing more to the Neceffities of Men, than to their In- clinations, that they have put themfelves under the Reftraint of Laws, and appointed certain Perfons, called Magiftrates, to execute them ; otherwife they would never be executed, fcarce any Man having fuch a Degree of Virtue as willingly to execute

ecute the Laws upon himfelf; but, on the contrary, moft Men thinking them a Grievance, when they come to meddle with themfelves and their Property. *Suarum legum auctor & everfor*, was the Character of *Pompey* : He made Laws when they fuited his Occafions, and broke them when they thwarted his Will. And it is the Character of almoft every Man poffeffed of *Pompey*'s Power : They intend them for a Security to themfelves, and for a Terror to others. This fhews the Diftruft that Men have of Men; and this made a great Philofopher call the *State of Nature, a State of War* ; which Definition is true in a reftrained Senfe, fince human Societies and human Laws are the Effect of Neceffity and Experience : Whereas were all Men left to the boundlefs Liberty which they claim from Nature, every Man would be interfering and quarrelling with another ; every Man would be plundering the Acquifitions of another ; the Labour of one Man would be the Property of another ; Weaknefs would be the Prey of Force ; and one Man's Induftry would be the Caufe of another Man's Idlenefs.

Hence grew the Neceffity of Government ; which was the mutual Contract of a Number of Men, agreeing upon certain Terms of Union and Society, and putting themfelves under Penalties, if they violated thefe Terms, which were called Laws, and put into the Hands of one or more Men to execute. And thus Men quitted Part of their Natural Liberty to acquire Civil Security. But frequently the Remedy proved worfe than the Difeafe ; and human Society had often no Enemies fo great as their own Magiftrates ; who, where-ever they were trufted with too much Power,
always

always abufed it, and grew mifchievous to thofe who made them what they were. *Rome,* while fhe was free (that is, while fhe kept her Magiftrates within due Bounds) could defend herfelf againft all the World, and conquer it : But being enflaved (that is, her Magiftrates having broke their Bounds) fhe could not defend herfelf againft her own fingle Tyrants, nor could they defend her againft her foreign Foes and Invaders ; for by their Madnefs and Cruelties they had deftroyed her Virtue and Spirit, and exhaufted her Strength.   This fhews that thofe Magiftrates that are at abfolute Defiance with a Nation, either cannot fubfift long, or will not fuffer the Nation to fubfift long ; and that mighty Traytors, rather than fall themfelves, will pull down their Country.

What a dreadful Spirit muft that Man poffefs, who can put a private Appetite in balance againft the univerfal Good of his Country, and of Mankind ! *Alexander* and *Cæfar* were that Sort of Men ; they would fet the World on fire, and fpill its Blood, rather than not govern it. *Caligula* knew that he was hated, and deferved to be hated ; but it did not mend him. *Oderint dum metuant,* was his By-word : All that the Monfter aimed at, was to be great and terrible.   Moft of thefe Tyrants died as became them ; and, as they had reigned, by Violence : But that did not mend their Succeffors, who generally earned the Fate of thofe that went before them, before they were warm in their Place. *Invenit etiam æmulos infelix nequitia : Quid fi floreat vigeatque ?* " If unfortunate Villainy thus " finds Rivals, what fhall we fay, when it exalts " its Head and profpers ? "

There

There is no Evil under the Sun but what is to be dreaded from Men, who may do what they pleafe with Impunity : They feldom or never ftop at certain Degrees of Mifchief when they have Power to go farther ; but hurry on from Wickednefs to Wickednefs, as far and as faft as human Malice can prompt human Power. *Ubi femel recto deerratum eft, in præceps pervenitur ——— a rectis in vitia, a vitiis in prava, a pravis in præcipitia,* fays a *Roman* Hiftorian ; who in this fpeaks the Truth, though in other Inftances he tells many Lies ; I mean that bafe Flatterer of Power, *Velleius Paterculus.* So that when we fee any great Mifchief committed with Safety, we may juftly apprehend Mifchiefs ftill greater.

The World is governed by Men, and Men by their Paffions ; which, being boundlefs and infatiable, are always terrible when they are not controuled. Who was ever fatiated with Riches, or furfeited with Power, or tired with Honours ? There is a Tradition concerning *Alexander,* that having penetrated to the Eaftern Ocean, and ravaged as much of this World as he knew, he wept that there was never another World for him to conquer. This, whether true or no, fhews the Spirit of the Man, and indeed of human Nature, whofe Appetites are infinite.

People are ruined by their Ignorance of human Nature ; which Ignorance leads them to Credulity, and too great a Confidence in particular Men. They fondly imagine that he, who, poffeffing a great deal by their Favour, owes them great Gratitude, and all good Offices, will therefore return their Kindnefs : But, alas ! how often are they miftaken in their Favourites and Truftees ; who, the

the more they have given them, are often the more incited to take All, and to return Deftruction for generous Ufage. The common People generally think that great Men have great Minds, and fcorn bafe Actions; which Judgment is fo falfe, that the bafeft and worft of all Actions have been done by great Men : Perhaps they have not picked private Pockets, but they have done worfe; they have often difturbed, deceived, and pillaged the World : And he who is capable of the higheft Mifch'ef, is capable of the meaneft : He who plunders a Country of a Million of Money, would in.fuitable Circumftances fteal a Silver Spoon; and a Conqueror, who fteals and pillages a Kingdom, would, in an humbler Fortune, rifle a Portmanteau, or rob an Orchard.

Political Jealoufy, therefore, in the People, is a neceffary and laudable Paffion. But in a Chief Magiftrate, a Jealoufy of his People is not fo juftifiable, their Ambition being only to preferve themfelves; whereas it is natural for Power to be ftriveing to enlarge itfelf, and to be encroaching upon thofe that have none. The moft laudable Jealoufy of a Magiftrate is to be jealous *for* his People; which will fhew that he loves them, and has ufed them well : But to be jealous *of* them, would denote that he has evil Defigns againft them, and has ufed them ill. The People's Jealoufy tends to preferve Liberty; and the Prince's to deftroy it. *Venice* is a glorious Inftance of the former, and fo is *England*; and all Nations who have loft their Liberty, are melancholy Proofs of the latter.

Power is naturally active, vigilant, and diftruftful; which Qualities in it pufh it upon all Means and Expedients to fortify itfelf, and upon deftroy-

ing

ing all Oppofition, and even all Seeds of Oppofition, and make it reftlefs as long as any Thing
ftands in its Way. It would do what it pleafes,
and have no Check. Now, becaufe Liberty cha-
ftifes and fhortens Power, therefore Power would
extinguifh Liberty; and confequently Liberty has
too much Caufe to be exceeding jealous, and always upon her Defence. Power has many Advantages over her; it has generally numerous
Guards, many Creatures, and much Treafure;
befides, it has more Craft and Experience, lefs
Honefty and Innocence: And whereas Power can,
and for the moft part does, fubfift where Liberty
is not, Liberty cannot fubfift without Power; fo
that fhe has, as it were, the Enemy always at her
Gates.

Some have faid, that Magiftrates being accountable to none but God, ought to know no other
Reftraint. But this Reafoning is as frivolous as it
is wicked; for no good Man cares how many Punifhments and Penalties lie in his Way to an Offence which he does not intend to commit: A
Man who does not mean to commit Murder, is
not forry that Murder is punifhed with Death.
And as to wicked Men, their being accountable
to God, whom they do not fear, is no Security to
us againft their Folly and Malice; and to fay that
we ought to have no Security againft them, is to
infult common Senfe, and give the Lie to the
firft Law of Nature, that of Self-Prefervation.
Human Reafon fays, that there is no Obedience,
no Regard due to thofe Rulers, who govern by
no Rule but their Luft. Such Men are no Rulers;
they are Outlaws; who, being at Defiance with
God and Man, are protected by no Law of God,

or

or of Reafon.   By what Precept, moral or divine,
are we forbid to kill a Wolf, or burn an infected
Ship ? Is it unlawful to prevent Wickednefs and
Mifery, and to refift the Authors of them ? Are
Crimes fanctified by their Greatnefs ? And is he
who robs a Country, and murders Ten Thoufand, lefs a Criminal, then he who fteals fingle
Guineas, and takes away fingle Lives ? Is there
any Sin in preventing, and reftraining, or refifting
the greateft Sin that can be committed, that of
oppreffing and deftroying Mankind by wholefale ?
Sure there never were fuch open, fuch fhamelefs,
fuch felfifh Impoftors, as the Advocates for lawlefs
Power ! It is a damnable Sin to opprefs Them ;
yet it is a damnable Sin to oppofe Them when
They opprefs, or gain by Oppreffion of others !
When they are hurt themfelves ever fo little, or
but think themfelves hurt, they are the loudeft of
all Men in their Complaints, and the moft outrageous in their Behaviour : But when others are
plundered, oppreffed, and butchered, Complaints
are Sedition ; and to feek Redrefs, is Damnation.
Is not this to be the Authors of all Wickednefs
and Falfhood ?

To conclude : Power, without Controul, ap-
pertains to God alone ; and no Man ought to be
trufted with what no Man is equal to.   In Truth
there are fo many Paffions, and Inconfiftencies,
and fo much Selfifhnefs, belonging to human Nature, that we can fcarce be too much upon our
Guard againft each other.   The only Security
which we can have that Men will be honeft, is to
make it their Intereft to be honeft ; and the beft
Defence which we can have againft their being
Knaves, is to make it terrible to them to be
                                        Knaves.

Knaves. As there are many Men wicked in fome Stations, who would be innocent in others; the beft Way is to make Wickednefs unfafe in any Station.

I am, &c.

P. S. This Letter is the Sequel of that upon Human Nature; and both are intended for an Introduction to a Paper which I intend to write upon the Reftraints which all wife Nations put upon their Magiftrates.

G

The End of the FIRST VOLUME.

C A T O's
LETTERS:

O R,

Essays *on* Liberty,

Civil and Religious,

And other Important Subjects.

VOL. II.

The Sixth Edition, *corrected.*

LONDON:

Printed for J. Walthoe, T. and T. Long-
man, C. Hitch and L. Hawes, J. Hodges,
A. Millar, J. and J. Rivington,
J. Ward, and M. Cooper.
M. DCC. LV.

CATO's LETTERS.

VOL. II.

SATURDAY, *June* 24, 1721. No. 34.

Of Flattery.

SIR,

FLATTERY is a poisonous and pernicious Weed, which grows and prevails every where, but most where it does most Harm; I mean in Courts. If few dare speak the Truth to their Superiors, how shall he who has no Superiors ever come to know the Truth? Perhaps there never was an Instance in the World, where a Prince was told the sincere Truth in every Thing which concerned him to know, by any Servant of his. Truth is of a plain, unalterable Nature, and cannot be moulded into fashionable Shapes ; *Truth* is therefore unfit to be a Courtier: But *Falshood*, being the Creature of the Imagination, is capable of bearing all modish and pleasing Forms ; Falshood is therefore an agreeable Gueſt in Palaces. To illuſtrate this, endleſs Examples might be brought ; but unfortunate Princes are the moſt pregnant Examples. *Galba*, when he had loſt all, and nothing remained to him but his Life, which he was alſo ſoon to loſe, had not one about him to tell him his Condition and Danger; ſo cruelly diſhoneſt were his Servants ! Their Flattery prevented the Means of his Preſervation. They therefore were the firſt Murtherers of their Maſter.

Nothing more is neceſſary in order to be flattered, than to be uppermoſt. *Galba* was hated for his Avarice, and deſpiſed for his Age and Severity ; yet, in Complaiſance to an Emperor, Multitudes of People, and particularly of Senators and Gentlemen, addreſſed him to put *Otho* to death, and to baniſh all his Accomplices : And a Rumour being ſpread, that *Otho* was ſlain, the ſame Set of Flatterers ran to the Palace with noiſy Congratulations, and deceitfully complained that Fate had ſnatched the Uſurper from their Vengeance.

What Marks were here of Loyalty to *Galba*'s Perſon, and of Zeal and Firmneſs to his Intereſt ! yet in ſo ſmall a Space as two Hours after, *Otho*'s Power having prevailed in *Rome*, *Otho* had their Hearts and their Acclamations in his Turn, and *Galba*'s Death was demanded of him with the ſame Importunity that the Death of *Otho* had been demanded of *Galba*, and by the ſame Men.

A melan-

A melancholy Leſſon of the vile Fraudulency of Flatterers, and of the Blindneſs of Princes who truſt in them ! Even *Galba*, who was thought Proof againſt Flatterers (*adverſus blandientes incorruptus*) was deceived by them.

The Sieur *Amelot de la Houſſaye*, from whom many of theſe Obſervations are taken, ſays truly, that moſt Princes are better armed againſt Fear than againſt Flattery : Terrors animate them, and Threats whet their Courage ; but Flattery ſoftens their Minds, and corrupts their Manners ; it makes them negligent and idle, and forget their Duty. *Corrupta mens aſſiduis adulationibus*, ſays *Tacitus* of *Domitian*. Beſides, miſtaking Flattery for Complaiſance (which is a Sign of Affection) they think that thoſe who flatter them love them, and from that Deluſion come to truſt and employ their moſt dangerous Enemies. He further ſays, that *Philip* II. of *Spain* was wont to interrupt thoſe who went about to flatter him, by ſaying to them roundly, *Ceaſe trifling, and tell me what it concerns me to know :* Words worthy of all Princes, who are never entertained by their Flatterers but with Things uſeleſs or pernicious. If Princes never heard any Thing but what they ought to know, they would never hear Flatterers.

Flattery is a falſe and ſelfiſh Thing, begot only by Fear or Favour ; and having itſelf only in View, it obſerves no Rule of Equity or Merit, but praiſes and calumniates, juſt according as Men are exalted or depreſſed. *Mezeray* tells us, that as long as *Henry* III. of *France* built magnificent Monaſteries, and plunged himſelf into Monkiſh Devotions, ill-becoming his Dignity, the Monks revered him as a Saint, and called him one : But

no

no fooner was the religious and feditious League formed againft him, but thefe godly Ingrates loaded him with all the Reproaches and ill Names that they could devife ; Tyrant, Hypocrite, Murtherer, and Abominable, were the Titles which they gave him ; and at laft they butchered him as a Heretick : So eafily can Flatterers make one and the fame Man a God or Devil ; and fo true is it that Flatterers love no Man, and only court the Fortunes of Men.   Flattery is venal, and always goes to the beft Bidder ; and it is fervile, and always crouches moft to thofe who are uppermoft, let them be what they will : *Adulationi fœdum crimen fervitutis ineft*.   Moft of the Evil that Princes commit, comes from the Leffcns and Complaifance of Flatterers ; and to fuch moft Princes have owed their Ruin : Few Princes would have done what many of them did, if their falfe Friends had not told them that they might do what they would : We have had many Inftances of this at home, and there have been more abroad.   It would be a great Advantage to Princes, if they would remember that there never was a Prince in the World but was flattered, and never a Prince but was hurt by Flattery, and many uttetly undone by it.   It has made good Princes bad, and bad worfe : By Flattery they have been brought to think themfelves more than Men, and to act worfe than Brutes ; and, in fine, to live and die as Beafts of Prey live and die, in Blood.   Their Flatterers having made them worfe than Men, adored them like Gods : But, as *Pliny* fays, *Principum exitus docuit ne a diis quidem amari nifi quos homines ament.*

Their

Their Bufinefs is to tell their great Patron what
pleafes him, though it deftroy him ; and when
they have deprived him of all his Friends, his Innocence, his Felicity, and his Poffeffions, they
leave him too ; or having ruined his Fortune,
they take away his Life, which is their laft and
beft Civility : For Flattery ends ever in Ingratitude, and often in Treafon ; and for Princes to be
often diftreffed by thofe whom they have obliged
moft, is nothing new.

Flattery is always great in Proportion as its
Patrons are bad. And therefore *Pliny* obferves,
that thofe Emperors who were moft hated, were
likewife moft flattered : For he fays, " that Dif-
" fimulation is more ingenious and artful than
" Sincerity, Slavery than Liberty, Fear than
" Love." Hence Flattery is a Sign of Servitude,
and inconfiftent with Equality, and with Liberty,
the Offspring of Equality. It is indeed one of the
Purpofes of Flattery to make Men worfe ; it gains
by Corruption, and lives upon Credulity, Folly,
and Vice. It is particularly at perpetual Enmity
with Truth ; and Flatterers are like Liars, not to
be believed even when they fpeak Truth. I have
fomewhere heard Flatterers compared to Thieves,
who break into Houfes by Night ; the firft Thing
that they do, is to extinguifh the Lights : So Flatterers, when they have befet a Prince, or any other
Great Man, never fail to keep far from him all
Light and Information.

Flattery is cruel, and gives bloody Counfels ;
and Flatterers are conftant and mercilefs Calum-
niators : Every Word which they do not like, is a
Libel ; every Action that difpleafes them, is Treafon or Sedition : Where there are no Faults, they
create

create them.   The-Crimes objected to the honeſt
and excellent *Thraſea Petus*, were ſuch as theſe:
" That he had never applauded *Nero*, nor en-
" couraged others to applaud him ; that when the
" Senate were running into all the Extravagan-
" cies of Flattery, he would not be preſent, and
" therefore had not been in it for three Years ;
" that he had never ſacrificed for *Nero*'s charming
" Voice; that he would never own Madam *Pop-*
" *pæa* for a Goddeſs, ſhe who had been *Nero*'s
" Miſtreſs, and was then his Wife; that he would
" not vote that a Gentleman who had made ſaty-
" rical Verſes upon *Nero* ſhould be put to Death,
" though he condemned the Man and his Libel ;
" but he contended that no Law made the Of-
" fence Capital ; that they could not, without
" Scandal, and the Imputation of Cruelty, puniſh
" with Death, an Offence for which the Laws
" had already provided a Puniſhment that was
" milder."   Theſe were the honourable and virtuous Crimes of that great and good Man ; but
they were then High Treaſon, and coſt him his
Life.   Memorable are the Words of *Philip de Co-*
mines, ſpeaking of Court Flatterers : " If a Six-
" penny Tax be to be raiſed, they cry it ought
" by all Means to be a Twelve-penny one.   If
" the Prince be offended with any Man, they are
" directly for hanging him.   In other Inſtances,
" they maintain the ſame Character.   Above all
" Things, they adviſe their Maſter to make him-
" ſelf terrible; as they themſelves are proud, fierce,
" and overbearing, in hopes to be dreaded by
" that Means, as if Authority and Place were
" their Inheritance."

As

As all honeſt Truths affect ſuch Men, whatever
is ſaid againſt ill Men, they conſtrue to be ſaid
againſt them : And even when they are praiſed,
they cry they are abuſed, and that ſuch Praiſe is
rank Irony. Now all this is very impolitick :
Good Men neither fear Libels, nor ſuſpect Ap-
plauſes to be Ironies. *Pliny* ſays juſtly to *Trajan*,
" When I ſpeak of your Humanity, Liberality,
" Frugality, Clemency, Vigilance, &c. I have
" no Apprehenſion that your Majeſty will think
" yourſelf reproached with the contrary Vices."
But it was not ſo in ſome preceding Reigns, when
Virtue was dangerous, Truth capital, and every
Book that contained either was burnt, and its Author put to Death : By which violent and unjuſt
Proceedings, they hoped to ſhut up for ever People's Mouths, to aboliſh the Liberty of the Senate,
and utterly to extinguiſh the Memories of good
Men. Not ſatisfied with killing the Authors, they
exerciſed their Rage upon their Works, and appointed a Junto called *Triumviri*, to deſtroy the
Fruits of the greateſt Geniuſes by Fire.

I have ſcarce ever heard of a more groſs or ingenious Piece of Flattery, than that of *Vitellius* to
Caligula, upon the following Occaſion : That
mad Emperor had taken it into his Head to be a
God, and thought he might debauch ſome of the
She-Deities, as well as he had his Siſters ; he
therefore aſked *Vitellius* this Queſtion, *Pray*, Vitellius, ſays he, *have you never ſeen me embrace the
Moon ? O Sir*, ſays the Paraſite, *that is a Myſtery
which none but a God, ſuch as your Majeſty, ought to
reveal. Vitellius* was one of thoſe, *quibus principum
honeſta atque inhoneſta laudare mos eſt* ; who praiſe
every

every Thing that their Prince does, whether good
or bad. Flattery therefore is never at the Height,
till Liberty and Virtue are utterly loft ; and with
the Lofs of Liberty, Shame and Honour are loft.
Tacitus, who never mentions the Woes of his
Country without feeming to feel them, talking of
Sejanus, who having got the whole Adminiftration
into his Hands, was now the chief Idol at *Rome*,
makes *M. Terentius* fay with Indignation, " We
" worfhipped his manumifed Slaves, and profti-
" tuted ourfelves to his former Footmen ; and to
" be acquainted with his Porter, was a mighty
" Honour."

As Flatterers make Tyrants, Tyrants make
Flatterers ; neither is it poffible that any Prince
could be a Tyrant without them : He muft have
fervile Hands to execute his Will, fervile Mouths
to approve it. It was with great Fear that *Nero*
ordered the Murther of his Mother, though he
had wicked Counfellors enough to advife and applaud it ; and when he had done it, he was thun-
der-ftruck and diftracted with Apprehenfions of
the Confequences : But finding Flattery from all
Hands, inftead of Refentment from any, he grew
outrageoufly abandoned, and plunged into all Licentioufnefs and Infamy : Had it not been for
Flatterers, the Middle and End of his Reign
might have been as good as the Beginning, than
which there was fcarce ever a better.

I have faid enough to fhew the Vilenefs and
Mifchief of Flattery ; a Vice which has finally
ruined many Nations, and many Princes, and one
Time or other hurt all. Let us be thankful that
we are not at the cruel Mercy of Flatterers, and
have

have a Prince who we firmly believe will never be led or perverted by them; we hope that he will never have bad Counsel given him, and would reject it, if it were : We know his honest Purposes, and great Moderation; and confess with Gratitude, that during his whole Reign no Outrages have been committed upon the Lives and Fortunes of any of his Subjects; and that the Protection of the Law has been as strong and extensive, as ever it was, or ought to be. I could say more, but I stop here; for the greatest Honour that can be done a Prince, is, to suppose him above Flattery, and to avoid for his Sake the Appearance of it, when we speak to him, or of him.

G   *I am,* &c.

SATURDAY, *July* 1, 1721. No. 35.

Of publick Spirit.

S I R,

*T*HE *Love of one's Country,* or *Publick Spirit,* is a Phrase in every Body's Mouth, but it seldom goes deeper; it is talked of without being felt : Some mention it without having any Ideas at all of it, but only as a fine Thing which every Body likes, and a good Quality which one would not seem to be without.

Others, when they name it, intend only some poor and selfish Gratification of their own : Thus with Great Men, it is Wealth and Empire, to do what they list, and to get what they can; which is direct Faction, or promoting, under Colour of the Publick, those Views which are inconsistent

with

with it. Thus with the Trader and Artificer, it is the encouraging only that Sort of Art or Ware in which he himfelf deals ; and this is Monopoly and Engroffing, ever mifchievous to the Publick.

In Popifh Countries, it is Publick Spirit to build and beautify many Churches, at the Expence of the poor People; who muft alfo maintain, at a further Expence, a long Band of luxurious Ecclefiafticks, to play Tricks in them ; or, in other Words, to keep the Heads and Pockets of their deluded Hearers as empty as they can. It is moreover great Publick Spirit, to adorn an old Skull with Pearl and Diamonds, and to enrich a venerable rotten Tooth with Gold and Emeralds, of a Value fufficient to maintain a City and all its Inhabitants, who yet perhaps are ftarved by doing it. It is likewife very publick-fpirited there, for a Man to ftarve his Family and his Pofterity, to endow a Monaftery, and to feed, or rather gorge, a Fraternity of Reverend Gluttons, profeffed Foes to Truth and Peace, and to the Profperity of the World ; Idlers, maintained to gormandize and deceive. This, forfooth, is Publick Spirit ; to rob the Country of its Hands, to rear up a pernicious and turbulent Mob of Drones, in Principles deftructive of Liberty, and to bring up Enemies to a Country at its own Charges.

In arbitrary Countries, it is Publick Spirit to be blind Slaves to the blind Will of the Prince, and to flaughter or be flaughtered for him at his Pleafure : But in Proteftant free Countries, Publick Spirit is another Thing ; it is to combat Force and Delufion ; it is to reconcile the true Interefts of the Governed and Governors; it is to expofe

Im-

Impoftors, and to refift Oppreffors ; it is to maintain the People in Liberty, Plenty, Eafe, and Security.

This is Publick Spirit ; which contains in it every laudable Paffion, and takes in Parents, Kindred, Friends, Neighbours, and every Thing dear to Mankind ; it is the higheft Virtue, and contains in it almoft all others ; Stedfaftnefs to good Purpofes, Fidelity to one's Truft, Refolution in Difficulties, Defiance of Danger, Contempt of Death, and impartial Benevolence to all Mankind. It is a Paffion to promote univerfal Good, with perfonal Pain, Lofs, and Peril : It is one Man's Care for many, and the Concern of every Man for All.

Confider this Picture, O ye great Patriots and Guardians of the Earth, and try if you refemble it ! Whom have ye exalted for his own Merits, whom caft down for the Sake of your Country? What Advantages have you acquired to your Nation, with Lofs to yourfelves ? And have your People's Loffes never been your Gains ?

Out of *England* thefe Queftions cannot well be anfwered ; nor could they in *England* formerly.

If my Character of Publick Spirit be thought too heroick, at leaft for the living Generation, who are indeed but Babes in that Virtue ; I will readily own, that every Man has a Right and a Call to provide for himfelf, to attend upon his own Affairs, and to ftudy his own Happinefs. All that I contend for is, that this Duty of a Man to himfelf be performed fubfequently to the general Welfare, and confiftently with it. The Affairs of All fhould be minded preferably to the

Affairs

Affairs of One, as every Man is ready to own when his own Particular is embarked with the Whole ; as indeed every Man's will prove to be sooner or later, though for a while some may thrive upon the publick Ruins, but their Fate seldom fails to meet them at last, them or their Posterity.

It is a favourable Sign of Publick Spirit, though not a certain Sign, when the Interest and Reputation of Men rise and increase together ; and there is Policy and Wisdom in it. He who acquires Money in spite of Fame, pays dear for his Avarice, while it returns him Hatred and Curses, as well as Gold ; and to be rich and detested, is to me no pleasing Character. The same holds true in regard to Ambition, and every other Passion, which breaks its Bounds, and makes a Captive of its Owner. It is scarce possible to be a Rogue and be beloved ; and when Men are arrived to an Insensibility of popular Censure and Opinion concerning their Honesty and Dishonesty, it is a Sign that they are at Defiance with the Community where they live, and that the rest ought to be upon their Guard against them ; they do as it were cut themselves off from the Society, and teach the People what to call them.

It is true, that great ill Men never fail to have great Court paid to their Fortunes ; which Court their own Self-Love always construes to be paid to their Persons : But there is a Way to undeceive them, and it often happens ; let them but sink into Meanness, and they will soon find themselves sunk into Contempt, which is the End of Hatred when the Object of Hatred diminishes.

There

There is a Sort of Men found almoſt every where, who having got a Set of gainful and favourite Speculations, are always ready to ſpread and enforce them, and call their doing ſo *Publick Spirit*, though it often turns the World topſy-turvy : Like the mad Monk at *Heidelberg*, who was for knocking every Man on the Head who did not like *Rheniſh* Wine, which it ſeems was his beloved Liquor ; perhaps he thought it was as reaſonable to make all the World ſwallow *Rheniſh*, as to make them ſwallow Tranſubſtantiation.

Opinions, bare Opinions, ſignify no more to the World, than do the ſeveral Taſtes of Men ; and all Mankind muſt be made of one Complexion, of one Size, and of one Age, before they can be all made of the ſame Mind. Thoſe Patrons therefore of dry Dreams, who do Miſchief to the World to make it better, are the Peſts and Diſtreſſers of Mankind, and ſhut themſelves out from all Pretence to the Love of their Country : Sꝛrange Men ! They would force all Men into an abſolute Certainty about abſolute Uncertainties and Contradictions ; they would aſcertain Ambiguities, without removing them ; and plague and puniſh Men for having but five Senſes.

I would aſſert another Propoſition, as true as the laſt, though it may ſeem ſtranger ; namely, That the taking a Thouſand or Ten Thouſand Pounds a Year for the Merit of helping to draw a Hundred Times as much from the People, is not Publick Spirit, whatever Uſe may call it ; and to graſp at All, and put a whole Country in two or three Pockets, is a Sort of Publick Spirit, which I hope in God never to ſee, though there have been Nations who have ſorrowfully felt it.

As

As Liberty can never fubfift without Equality, nor Equality be long preferved without an *Agrarian* Law, or fomething like it ; fo when Mens Riches are become immeafurably or furprizingly great, a People, who regard their own Security, ought to make a ftrict Enquiry how they came by them, and oblige them to take down their own Size, for fear of terrifying the Community, or maftering it. In every Country, and under every Government, particular Men may be too rich.

If the *Romans* had well obferved the *Agrarian* Law, by which the Extent of every Citizen's Eftate was afcertained, fome Citizens could never have rifen fo high as they did above others ; and confe-qently, one Man would never have been fet above the reft, and have eftablifhed, as *Cæfar* did at laft, a Tyranny in that great and glorious State. I have always thought, that an Enquiry into Mens Fortunes, efpecially monftrous Fortunes raifed out of the Publick, like *Milton*'s infernal Palace, as it were in an Inftant, was of more Importance to a Nation, than fome other Enquiries which I have heard of.

But, will fome fay, Is it a Crime to be rich ? Yes, certainly, at the Publick Expence, or to the Danger of the Publick. A Man may be too rich for a Subject; even the Revenues of Kings may be too large. It is one of the Effects of arbitrary Power, that the Prince has too much, and the People too little ; and fuch Inequality may be the Caufe too of arbitrary Power. It is as aftonifhing as it is melancholy, to travel through a whole Country, as one may through many in *Europe*, grafping under endlefs Impofts, groaning under Dragoons and Poverty, and all to make a wanton

and

and luxurious Court, filled for the moft with the worft and vileft of all Men. Good God ! What Hard-heartednefs and Barbarity, to ftarve perhaps half a Province, to make a gay Garden ! And yet fometimes even this grofs Wickednefs is called Publick Spirit, becaufe forfooth a few Workmen and Labourers are maintained out of the Bread and the Blood of half a Million.

In thofe Countries, were the Judgment of the People confulted, Things would go better : But they are defpifed, and efteemed by their Governors happy enough, if they do not eat Grafs ; and having no Reprefentatives, or Share in the Government, they have no Remedy. Such indeed is their Mifery, that their Cafe would be greatly mended, if they could change Conditions with the Beafts of the Field ; for then, being deftined to be eaten, they would be better fed : Such a Misfortune is it to them that their Governors are not *Cannibals !* Oh happy *Britain*, mayeft thou continue ever fo !

For a Conclufion : As the Prefervation of Property is the Source of National Happinefs ; whoever violates Property, or leffens or endangers it, common Senfe fays, that he is an Enemy to his Country ; and Publick Spirit fays, that he fhould feel its Vengeance. As yet in *England*, we can fpeak fuch bold Truths ; and we never dread to fee the Day, when it will be fafer for one Man to be a Traytor, than for another Man, or for a whole People, to call him fo. Where-ever Publick Spirit is found dangerous, fhe will foon be feen dead.

G   *I am*, &c.

Satur-

Of Loyalty.

S I R,

LOYALTY is a very good Word ; but, like moſt others, being wreſted firſt by Deſign, and afterwards by Ignorance and Cuſtom, from its original and virtuous Signification, ·does now frequently bear a very bad one. In an honeſt Senſe, indeed in common Senſe, it means no more than the ſquaring our Actions by the Rules of good Laws, and an Attachment to a Conſtitution ſupported by ſuch : And the *French* Word *Loyauté,* comes from another *French* Word, which ſignifies *Law.*

Other Meanings have ſince been fathered upon that Word, ſuch as it abhors. To bear ſtupidly the wild or deliberate ill Acts of a Tyrant, over-turning all Law, and to aſſiſt him in it, has been impiouſly called *Loyalty* ; though it was all the while on the other Side : As it is the very Office and Genius of Loyalty to defend Law, Virtue, and Property ; and to pull down, as Traytors and Diſloyaliſts, all who aſſault them.

Whoever is lawleſs, is diſloyal ; and to boaſt of Loyalty to Diſloyalty, is ſtrange Nonſenſe ; a Paradox firſt invented by ſolemn and pernicious Pedants, whoſe Trade it is to pervert the Uſe of Words and the Meaning of Things, to abuſe and confound the human Underſtanding, and to miſlead the World into Miſery and Darkneſs.

To

To obey a Prince, who does himself obey the Laws, is confessed on all Hands to be Loyalty : Now, from hence, one would naturally think, that, by every Rule of Reason, it might be inferred, that to obey one who obeys no Law, is a Departure from all Loyalty, and an Outrage committed upon it ; and that both he who commands, and he who obeys, are Outlaws and Disloyalists : And yet these same ungodly Pedants shall maintain it to your Face, that though Loyalty consist in obeying a good Prince, it also consists in the very contrary, and in obeying a wicked Prince ; who,, though he be an Enemy to God, is the Vicegerent of God ; and though he commit all Wickedness, yet does it by Divine Right ; and though it be a Sin to obey him, yet it is a damnable Sin to resist him : In short, that all the Instruments and Partners of his crying Crimes are Loyalists ; and all who defend Law, Virtue, and Mankind, against such Monsters, are Rebels, and assuredly damned, for preventing or resisting Actions which deserve Damnation: And thus Men become Rebels, by acting virtuously against the worst of all Rebels, who are restrained by no Consideration, human or divine.

Was ever such Impudence, Impiety, and Nonsense, broached amongst Pagans ? In Truth, they never would have been broached amongst Christians, had not Sanctity been made a Cloak for those who fold Godliness for Gain, and propagated Imposture at the Price of all that was virtuous and sacred.

Disloyalty is indeed rarely the Crime of Subjects and private Men ; and they who charge it most upon others, are they who practise it most
                                        them-

themfelves. King *Richard* II. and *Edward* II. were the greateft Rebels in *England* in their own Time: The greateft Rebel in all *Italy*, is the Pope. Every lawlefs Prince is a Rebel, and the Grand Seignior is the greateft that is or can be in his own Dominions. It is true, he is bound by no written Law; but in this very Thing he is a Rebel: No Man ought to be exempt from the Ties of Laws; and the higher any Man is, the more Ties he ought to be under. All Power ought to be balanced with equal Reftraints, elfe it will certainly grow mifchievous: He who knows no Law, but his own Luft, feldom obferves any other. Befides, there are fuch Things as the eternal Laws of Mercy, Juftice, and Truth, legible by every Man's natural Reafon, when it is not blinded by Craft; and whoever obferves not thefe, let him be called by what Name he will, is a Rebel to all the World, and it is Loyalty to all the World to purfue him to Deftruction.

Brutus, who expelled the royal and rebellious Race of the *Tarquins*, was the moft loyal Man in *Rome*; and his Sons, who would have reftored them, were the greateft Rebels in *Rome*: The *Roman* People therefore acted juftly, when they rewarded the Father with the Chief Magiftracy; and the Father acted juftly, when he facrificed the Traytors of his own Loins to the Liberties and Refentments of the *Roman* People.

Some play with the Words *Sovereign* and *Subject*, and divert themfelves with the Ridicule of Obedience refifting Command: But their Wit and Reafoning are alike wretched, whether they proceed

ceed from Ignorance or Dishonesty, as they often
do from both ; as if the World were to be guided
by Sound rather than Sense, in Things essential
to its Well-being. The highest and first Sovereignty is in the Laws, of which the Prince has
only the sovereign Execution : In other Words,
it is his Office and Duty to see the Laws obeyed ;
an Employment which implies their Superiority,
and his own Subjection.

A learned Prince, who knew not much of
Government, and practised less than he knew,
did yet own, that a *King is only the chief Servant
of the State.* The Law ought to be the Measure of his Power and Actions, as much as of
any private Man's, and more ; as his Example
is of greater Influence, and as his Opportunities
and Temptations to break them are greater than
any private Man's can be : And the only just
Reason that can be assigned why those Crimes
which are punished with Death in a Subject, have
been often committed with Impunity by a Chief
Magistrate, was, because the Station which he
was in gave him such Strength, and such a
Party, that to have punished him, the Publick
Quiet must have been risqued or shaken : And
as to the inferior great Traytors, the Gain of
their Crimes and Partners of their Guilt protected
them.

Exalted Wickedness is the safest : I could name
an *English* Reign, in which, for above Twenty
Years together, there scarce passed a Week in
which the Prince did not venture his Crown, and
his Ministers forfeit their Heads. And yet not
one of these Forfeitures were exacted : So corrupt
and wicked was the Government, and so tame
and

and acquiefcing were the People,! Indeed the People in every Country deferve the beft Ufage, and
in almoft all meet with the worft : Their Lot is
very hard and unequal : They often pay Millions,
not only in their own Wrong, but frequently to
ftrengthen the Hands of their Oppreffors : And
this they generally do, without fo much as a Tumult ; yet for one of them to coin a Silver Six-
pence, is Death and Confifcation.

Thefe Things are obvious ; yet how little are
they confidered ! It is fafer for a great Man to
rob a Country, than for a poor Man to fteal a
Loaf : But the Wages of Villainy protect Villains, and Juftice is only blind where the Object
is naked.————But thefe are only Complaints,
which, we hope, we *Britons* will never have Caufe
to make.

We have been formerly ftunned with the big
Word *Prerogative,* by thofe who contend for Unlimited Loyalty : Men, who while they referve
to themfelves a Right to be the moft turbulent of
all Subjects, would make all others the tameft
and the blindeft of all Slaves.   But what Prerogative do they mean ? I know no Prerogative in
the Crown, which is not at the fame Time a
certain Privilege of the People, for their Sake
granted, and for their Sake to be exerted : And
where a Prerogative is claimed in Oppofition to
the Rights and Interefts of the People, fo far a
Tyranny is claimed ; Tyranny being nothing elfe
but the Government of one Man, or of a few
Men, over many, againft their Inclination and
Intereft : And where Prerogative is exercifed
more to the Hurt than the Good of the Governed,
it is no longer Prerogative, but Violence and Ufurpation ;

pation ; and therefore in *England* feveral Prerogatives have from Time to Time been taken from the Crown, becaufe the Crown had abufed them.

A certain *Britiſh* King was wont to fay, *That ſo long as he could make Biſhops and Judges, he would have what Law and Goſpel he pleaſed.*——An impious and arbitrary Saying, and a bold one coming from a Prince of ſo mean a Spirit, governing a brave and a free People, who were difgraced by his profufe and ridiculous Reign, which is one of thofe that ſtain our Annals. But for all the Abfurdity of his Government, and the Smallnefs of his Soul, he found himfelf able, by the Affiftance of Sycophants, to multiply and entail many Evils upon thefe Kingdoms. It is certain, that he and fome of his Pofterity found fuch complaifant Bifhops and Judges, that the Religion and Politicks of the Court were generally the Religion and Politicks of *Weftminfter-Hall*, and of *Henry* the VIIth's Chapel : Abfolute Power in the Crown was pleaded and granted in both thofe folemn Places.

So wicked and mercilefs a Thing is Self-Intereft ! Thofe grave Men, who were by Profeffion the Guardians of Truth and Law, gave up both, to keep Preferment, or to acquire it. How little are Men to be trufted, and how little does Religion bind them ! They can break the ſtrongeft Bands, violate the moſt awful Oaths, and commit the moſt horrid, moſt extenfive Treacheries, for the vileft and moſt uncertain Gratifications. I am therefore feldom furprized to hear of the moſt aftoniſhing Things and Events, whether they be publick Depredations and Maffacres,

facres, or private Treacheries and Parricides ;
having my Mind conftantly filled with Examples
that anfwer them, or exceed them, though perhaps they are not exactly of the fame Nature.

It is certain, that thofe Judges, Counfellors,
and Clegy, who have adjudged a difpenfing
and lawlefs Power to Kings, had, each of them,
the Guilt of a Thoufand private Murtherers
upon their Head : They, as it were, figned a
Dead-Warrant for their Country ; and, as much
as in them lay, made themfelves the Authors of
univerfal Barbarity, Slavery, Infamy, and
Wretchednefs ; and of every other Evil and
Wickednefs, which is produced by that great
Source of all Evil and Wickednefs, Arbitrary
Power.

Of this we are fure, that the leaft Publick
Guilt is greater than the greateft Private Guilt :
Let every Man concerned in Publick Truft,
every where, confider this, and examine his own
Heart : Every Step which a publick Man takes,
every Speech which he makes, and every Vote
which he gives, may affect Millions. Whoever
acts in a great Station againft his Confcience,
might perhaps with more Innocence carry a
Dagger, and like Old *Muley* ftab Twenty Men a
Day.

Now were thefe Judges and Counfellors above-
mentioned, Loyalifts ? Yes, doubtlefs, if there
are fuch Things as Loyal Traytors. For, even
fuppofing Loyalty centered wholly in the Perfon
of the Prince, than which nothing can be more
falfe ; yet even here it lofes its Name, fince it is
doing him the higheft Unkindnefs, as it feparates

him

him from his People, and their Hearts from him, and as it tempts him to Evil, loads him with Infamy and Guilt, and leffens his Security ; in Truth, fuch Loyalty is Perfidioufnefs and Flattery, and has coft many Princes their *Lives* and their Kingdoms.

No good Prince will pretend that there is any Loyalty due to him further than he himfelf is loyal to the Law, and obfervant of his People, the Makers of Kings and of Laws.   If any Man, mifled by Sound and Delufion doubt this, let him confider what is the Defign of Magiftracy, and what the Duty of Magiftrates ; and if he has Reafon in him, he will find that his Duty is only due to thofe who perform theirs ; that Protection and Allegiance are reciprocal ; that every Man has a Right to defend what no Man has a Right to take : That the Divine Right of Kings, if they had it, can only warrant them in doing Actions that are Divine, and cannot protect them in Cruelty, Depredation, and Oppreffion : That a Divine Right to act wickedly, is a Contradiction and Blafphemy, as it is *Maledictio Supremi Numinis*, a Reproach upon the Deity, as if he gave any Man a Commiffion to be a Devil : That a King, in Comparifon with the Univerfe, is not fo much as a Mayor of a Town, in Comparifon with a Kingdom ; and that were Mr. Mayor called *King*, it would give him no new Right ; or, if a King were only called *Mr. Mayor*, it would not leffen nor abrogate his old Jurifdiction : That they are both Civil Officers ; and that an Offence in the Leffer is more pardonable than an Offence in the Greater : That the Doctrines of unbroken Hereditary Right, and of blind Obedience, are the Flights and For-

gcries

geries of Flatterers, who belye Heaven, and abufe
Men, to make their own Court to Power, and
that not one of them will ftand the Trial himfelf:
In fine, that Government, honeft and legal Government, is *imperium legum non hominum*, the Authority of Law, and not of Luft.

Thefe are the Principles upon which our Government ftands, the Principles upon which every
free Government muft ftand ; and that we *Britons*
dare tell fuch Truths, and publifh fuch Principles,
is a glorious Proof of our Civil and Religious Freedom : They are Truths which every *Briton* ought
to know, even Children and Servants: They are
eternal Truths, that will remain for ever, though
in too many Countries they are dangerous, or ufelefs, or little known : They are Truths, to which
we are beholden for the prefent Succeffion, and
the prefent mild Adminiftration ; and they are the
Principles of *Englifh* Loyalty, as well as of *Englifh*
Liberty.

Before I have done, I would take Notice of
another Miftake very common concerning Loyalty : It is indeed a Trick, more than a Miftake ;
I mean of thofe who would affert or rather create
a Sort of Loyalty to Minifters, and make every
Thing which they do not like an Offence againft
their Mafter.

How endlefs are the Arts and Inftances of Deceiving! Yet the ftaleft Artifices are ftill new.
The above is a Method which bad Minifters have
ever taken, but which good ones want not : Innocent Minifters will never proftitute the Name and
Authority of the Prince, to protect their own Faults
and Miftakes ; and every wife and indifferent Man
will be for preferving him from the Imputation of
the

the Guilt and Folly of his Servants, who, whenever they are for thrusting in their Master between themselves and the Censure or Odium of their own Actions, do at once acknowledge that their own Actions are evil, and that they would barbarously and ungratefully make a Skreen of their Sovereign, and save themselves upon his Ruin or Disgrace.

What can be more vile, what more disloyal, than this ! Yet who were louder in their Prate about Loyalty, than the worst Ministers have ever been ; even while they were weakening their Master's Hands, creating him Enemies, and setting him at Variance with his People? This is so true, that it has been sometimes impossible to love the Prince without abhorring his Servants, and to serve them without hurting or abusing him. Yet while they were very loyally undoing him, it was forsooth high Disloyalty to resist or expose them. — Whoever would recollect Instances of this, need not go out of *Europe*, nor above Forty Years backwards : And for Instances at Home, as we can find no present ones, we fear none that are future.

G

I am, &c.

SATURDAY, *July* 15, 1721. No. 37.

Character of a good and of an evil Magistrate, quoted from Algernoon Sidney, *Esq,*

S I R,

THE following are the Sentiments of Mr. *Sidney :* I know it is objected that he is a Republican ; and it is dishonestly suggested that I am a Republican, because I commend him as an excellent Writer, and have taken a Passage or two out of him. In answer to this, I shall only take Notice, that the Passages which I take from him are not Republican Passages, unless Virtue and Truth be Republicans : That Mr. *Sidney's* Book, for the Main of it, is eternally true, and agreeable to our own Constitution, which is the best Republick in the World, with a Prince at the Head of it : That our Government is a Thousand Degrees nearer a-kin to a Commonwealth (any Sort of Commonwealth now subsisting, or that ever did subsist in the World) than it is to absolute Monarchy : That for myself, I hope in God never to see any other Form of Government in *England* than that which is now in *England* ; and that if this be the Style and Spirit of a Republican, I glory in it, as much as I despise those who take base Methods to decry my Writings, which are addressed to the common Sense and Experience of Mankind. I hope that it is not yet made Heresy in Politicks, to assert that Two and Two make Four.

G

" The

" The good Magiſtrate ſeeks the Good of the
" People committed to his Care, that he may
" perform the End of his Inſtitution : and know-
" ing that chiefly to conſiſt in Juſtice and Vir-
" tue, he endeavours to plant and propagate them ;
" and by doing this he procures his own Good,
" as well as that of the Publick. He knows
" there is no Safety where there is no Strength,
" no Strength without Union, no Union with-
" out Juſtice, no Juſtice where Faith and Truth
" in accompliſhing publick and private Engage-
" ments is wanting. This he perpetually incul-
" cates ; and thinks it a great Part of his Duty,
" by Precept and Example to educate the Youth
" in a Love of Virtue and Truth, that they
" may be ſeaſoned with them, and filled with
" an Abhorrence of Vice and Falſhood, before
" they attain that Age which is expoſed to the
" moſt violent Temptations, and in which they
" may by their Crimes bring the greateſt Miſ-
" chiefs upon the Publick. He would do all this,
" though it were to his own Prejudice. But as
" good Actions always carry a Reward with
" them, theſe contribute in a high Meaſure to
" his Advantage. By preferring the Intereſt of
" the People before his own, he gains their Af-
" fection, and all that is in their Power comes
" with it ; while he unites them to one another,
" he unites all to himſelf. In leading them to
" Virtue, he encreaſes their Strength, and by
" that Means provides for his own Safety, Glory,
" and Power.

" On the other Side, ſuch as ſeek different
" Ends muſt take different Ways. When a Ma-
" giſtrate fanſies he is not made for the People,
                                        " but

" but the People for him ; that he does not go-
" vern for them, but for himself; that the Peo-
" ple live only to encreafe his Glory, or to fur-
" nifh Matter for his Pleafure ; he does not en-
" quire what he may do for them, but what he
" may draw from them : By this Means he fets
" up an Intereft of Profit, Pleafure, or Pomp in
" himfelf, repugnant to the Good of the Publick,
" for which he is made to be what he is. Thefe
" contrary Ends certainly divide the Nation into
" Parties; and while every one endeavours to
" advance that to which he is addicted, Occa-
" fions of Hatred, for Injuries every Day done,
" or thought to be done, and received, muft ne-
" ceffarily arife. This creates a moft fierce and
" irreconcileable Enmity ; becaufe the Occafions
" are frequent, important, and univerfal, and the
" Caufes thought to be moft juft. The People
" think it to be the greateft of all Crimes to con-
" vert that Power to their Hurt, which was in-
" ftituted for their Good ; and that the Injuftice
" is aggravated by Perjury and Ingratitude, which
" comprehend all Manner of Ill ; and the Ma-
" giftrate gives the Name of Sedition and Rebel-
" lion to whatfoever they do for the Prefervation
" of themfelves and their own Rights. When
" Mens Spirits are thus prepared, a fmall Matter
" fets them on Fire ; but if no Accident happens
" to blow them into a Flame, the Courfe of Ju-
" ftice is certainly interrupted, the publick Affairs
" are neglected; and when any Occafion, whe-
" ther Foreign or Domeftick, arifes, in which
" the Magiftrate ftands in need of the People's
" Affiftance, they whofe Affections are alienated,
" not only fhew an Unwillingnefs to ferve him
                                    " with

" with their Perfons and Eftates, but fear that
" by delivering him from his Diftrefs, they
" ftrengthen their Enemy, and enable him to op-
" prefs them; and he, fanfying his Will to be
" unjuftly oppofed, or his Due more unjuftly de-
" nied, is filled with a Diflike of what he fees,
" and a Fear of worfe for the future. Whilft
" he endeavours to eafe himfelf of the one, and
" to provide againft the other, he ufually encrea-
" fes the Evils of both; and Jealoufies are on
" both Sides multiplied. Every Man knows that
" the Governed are in a great Meafure under the
" Power of the Governor; but as no Man, or
" Number of Men, is willingly fubject to thofe
" that feek their Ruin, fuch as fall into fo great
" a Misfortune, continue no longer under it than
" Force, Fear, or Neceffity may be able to oblige
" them. But fuch a Neceffity can hardly lie
" longer upon a great People, than till the Evil
" be fully difcovered and comprehended, and
" their Virtue, Strength, and Power be united
" to expel it: The ill Magiftrate looks upon all
" Things that may conduce to that End as fo
" many Preparatives to his Ruin; and by the
" Help of thofe who are of his Party, will en-
" deavour to prevent that Union, and diminifh
" that Strength, Virtue, Power and Courage,
" which he knows to be bent againft him. And
" as Truth, faithful Dealing, and Integrity of
" Manners, are Bonds of Union, and Helps to
" Good, he will always, by Tricks, Artifices,
" Cavils, and all Means poffible, endeavour to
" eftablifh Falfhood and Difhonefty; whilft other
" Emiffaries and Inftruments of Iniquity, by cor-
" rupting the Youth, and fuch as can be brought
" to

" to Lewdnefs and Debauchery, bring the Peo-
" ple to fuch a Pafs, that they may neither care
" nor dare to vindicate their Rights ; and that
" thofe who would do it may fo far fufpect each
" other, as not to confer upon, much lefs to join
" in, any Action tending to the public Deli-
" verance.

" This diftinguifhes the good from the bad
" Magiftrate ; the Faithful from the Unfaithful ;
" and thofe that adhere to either, living in the
" fame Principle, muft walk in the fame Ways.
" They who uphold the rightful Power of a juft
" Magiftracy, encourage Virtue and Juftice, and
" teach Men what they ought to do, fuffer, or
" expect from others ; they fix them upon Prin-
" ciples of Honefty, and generally advance every
" thing that tends to the Encreafe of the Valour,
" Strength, Greatnefs, and Happinefs of the Na-
" tion, creating a good Union among them, and
" bringing every Man to an exact Underftand-
" ing of his own and the public Rights. On
" the other Side he that would introduce an ill
" Magiftrate, make one evil who was good, or
" preferve him in the Adminiftration of Inju-
" ftice when he is corrupted, muft always open
" the Way for him by vitiating the People, cor-
" rupting their Manners, deftroying the Validity
" of Oaths, teaching fuch Evafions, Equivoca-
" tions, and Frauds, as are inconfiftent with the
" Thoughts that become Men of Virtue and
" Courage ; and overthrowing the Confidence
" they ought to have in each other, make it im-
" poffible for them to unite amongft themfelves.
" The like Arts muft be ufed with the Magiftrate :
" He cannot be for their Turns, till he is per-
                                    " fuaded

" fuaded to believe he has no Dependence upon,
" and owes no Duty to, the People; that he is of
" himfelf, and not by their Inftitution; that no
" Man ought to enquire into, nor be Judge of,
" his Actions; that all Obedience is due to him,
" whether he be good or bad, wife or foolifh, a
" Father or an Enemy to his Country. This
" being calculated for his perfonal Intereft, he
" muft purfue the fame Defigns, or his Kingdom
" is divided within itfelf, and cannot fubfift. By
" this Means, thofe who flatter his Humour
" come to be accounted his Friends, and the only
" Men that are thought worthy of great Trufts;
" while fuch as are of another Mind are expofed
" to all Perfecution. Thefe are always fuch as
" excel in Virtue, Wifdom, and Greatnefs of
" Spirit: They have Eyes, and they will always
" fee the Way they go; and leaving Fools to be
" guided by implicit Faith, will diftinguifh be-
" tween Good and Evil, and choofe that which is
" beft; they will judge of Men by their Actions,
" and by them difcovering whofe Servant every
" Man is, know whether he is to be obeyed or
" not. Thofe who are ignorant of all Good,
" carelefs, or Enemies to it, take a more com-
" pendious Way: Their flavifh, vicious, and bafe
" Natures, inclining them to feek only private and
" prefent Advantage, they eafily flide into a blind
" Dependence upon one who has Wealth and
" Power; and defiring only to know his Will,
" care not what Injuftice they do, if they may
" be rewarded. They worfhip what they find
" in the Temple, though it be the vileft of Idols;
" and always like that beft which is worft, be-
" caufe it agrees with their Inclinations and Prin-
                                                    " ciples.

" ciples. When a Party comes to be erected upon
" fuch a Foundation, Debauchery, Lewdnefs,
" and Difhonefty are the true Badges of it; fuch
" as wear them are cherifhed; but the principal
" Marks of Favour are referved for them who are
" the moft induftrious in Mifchief, either by fedu-
" cing the People with the Allurements of fenfual
" Pleafures, or corrupting their Underftandings
" with falfe and flavifh Doctrines.

I am, &c.

Saturday, *July* 22, 1721. No. 38.

The Right and Capacity of the People to judge of
Government.

S I R,

THE World has, from Time to Time, been
led into fuch a long Maze of Miftakes, by
thofe who gained by deceiving, that whoever
would inftruct Mankind, muft begin with remove-
ing their Errors ; and if they were every where
honeftly apprized of Truth, and reftored to their
Senfes, there would not remain one Nation of Bigots or Slaves under the Sun : A Happinefs always
to be wifhed, but never expected !

In moft Parts of the Earth there is neither Light
nor Liberty ; and even in the beft Parts of it they
are but little encouraged, and coldly maintained ;
there being, in all Places, many engaged, through
Intereft, in a perpetual Confpiracy againft them.
They

They are the two greateft Civil Bleffings, infeparable in their Interefts, and the mutual Support of
each other; and whoever would deftroy one of
them, muft deftroy both.   Hence it is, that we
every where find Tyranny and Impofture, Ignorance and Slavery, joined together; and Oppreffors and Deceivers mutually aiding and paying conftant Court to each other.   Where-ever Truth is
dangerous, Liberty is precarious.

Of all the Sciences that I know in the World,
that of Government concerns us moft, and is the
eafieft to be known, and yet is the leaft underftood.
Moft of thofe who manage it would make the
lower World believe that there is I know not what
Difficulty and Myftery in it, far above vulgar Underftandings; which Proceeding of theirs is direct
Craft and Impofture: Every Ploughman knows a
good Government from a bad one, from the Effects of it: he knows whether the Fruits of his
Labour be his own, and whether he enjoy them in
Peace and Security: And if he do not know the
Principles of Government, it is for want of Think-
ing and Enquiry, for they lie open to common
Senfe; but People are generally taught not to think
of them at all, or to think wrong of them.

What is Government, but a Truft committed
by All, or the Moft, to One, or a Few, who are
to attend upon the Affairs of All, that every one
may, with the more Security, attend upon his
own? A great and honourable Truft; but too
feldom honourably executed; thofe who poffefs it
having it often more at Heart to encreafe their
Power, than to make it ufeful; and to be terrible,
rather than beneficent.   It is therefore a Truft,
which ought to be bounded with many and ftrong

Reftraints

Reftraints, becaufe Power renders Men wanton, infolent to others, and fond of themfelves. Every Violation therefore of this Truft, where fuch Violation is confiderable, ought to meet with proportionable Punifhment ; and the fmalleft Violation of it ought to meet with fome, becaufe Indulgence to the leaft Faults of Magiftrates may be Cruelty to a whole People.

Honefty, Diligence, and plain Senfe, are the only Talents neceffary for the executing of this Truft ; and the public Good is its only End : As to Refinements and Fineffes, they are often only the falfe Appearances of Wifdom and Parts, and oftener Tricks to hide Guilt and Emptinefs ; and they are generally mean and difhoneft : they are the Arts of Jobbers in Politicks, who, playing their own Game under the publick Cover, fubfift upon poor Shifts and Expedients ; ftarved Politicians, who live from Hand to Mouth, from Day to Day, and following the little Views of Ambition, Avarice, Revenge, and the like perfonal Paffions, are afhamed to avow them, yet want Souls great enough to forfake them ; fmall wicked Statefmen, who make a private Market of the Publick, and deceive it, in order to fell it.

Thefe are the poor Parts which great and good Governors fcorn to play, and cannot play ; their Defigns, like their Stations, being purely publick, are open and undifguifed. They do not confider their People as their Prey, nor lie in Ambufh for their Subjects ; nor dread, and treat and furprize them like Enemies, as all ill Magiftrates do ; who are not Governors, but Jaylors and Spunges, who chain them and fqueeze them, and yet take it very ill if they do but murmur ; which is yet much lefs

than

than a People fo abufed ought to do. There have
been Times and Countries, when publick Minifters and publick Enemies have been the fame
individual Men. What a melancholy Reflection
is this, that the moft terrible and mifchievous
Foes to a Nation fhould be its own Magiftrates!
And yet in every enflaved Country, which is almoft every Country, this is their woful Cafe.

Honefty and Plainnefs go always together, and
the Makers and Multipliers of Myfteries, in the
political Way, are fhrewdly to be fufpected of dark
Defigns. *Cincinnatus* was taken from the Plough
to fave and defend the *Roman* State; an Office
which he executed honeftly and fuccefsfully, without the Grimace and Gains of a Statefman. Nor
did he afterwards continue obftinately at the Head
of Affairs, to form a Party, raife a Fortune, and
fettle himfelf in Power: As he came into it with
univerfal Confent, he refigned it with univerfal
Applaufe.

It feems that Government was not in thofe
Days become a Trade, at leaft a gainful Trade. —
Honeft *Cincinnatus* was but a Farmer: And happy
had it been for the *Romans*, if, when they were
enflaved, they could have taken the Adminiftration
out of the Hands of the Emperors, and their refined Politicians, and committed it to fuch Farmers,
or any Farmers. It is certain, that many of their
Imperial Governors acted more ridiculoufly than a
Board of Ploughmen would have done, and more
barbaroufly than a Club of Butchers could have
done.

But fome have faid, *It is not the Bufinefs of private Men to meddle with Government.* A bold, falfe,
and difhoneft Saying; and whoever fays it, either
knows

knows not what he fays, or cares not, or flavifhly
fpeaks the Senfe of others. It is a Cant now almoft forgot in *England*, and which never prevailed
but when Liberty and the Conftitution were attacked, and never can prevail but upon the like
Occafion.

It is a Vexation to be obliged to anfwer Nonfenfe, and confute Abfurdities : But fince it is and
has been the great Defign of this Paper to maintain
and explain the glorious Principles of Liberty, and
to expofe the Arts of thofe who would darken or
deftroy them ; I fhall here particularly fhew the
Wickednefs and Stupidity of the above Saying ;
which is fit to come from no Mouth but that of a
Tyrant or a Slave, and can never be heard by
any Man of an honeft and free Soul, without
Horror and Indignation : It is, in fhort, a Saying,
which ought to render the Man who utters it for
ever incapable of Place or Credit in a free Country,
as it fhews the Malignity of his Heart, and the
Bafenefs of his Nature, and as it is the pronouncing of a Doom upon our Conftitution. —— A
Crime, or rather a Complication of Crimes, for
which a lafting Infamy ought to be but Part of
the Punifhment.

But to the Falfhood of the Thing : Publick
Truths ought never to be kept Secrets ; and they
who do it, are guilty of a Solæcifm, and a Contradiction : Every Man ought to know what it
concerns All to know. Now, nothing upon Earth
is of a more univerfal Nature than Government ;
and every private Man upon Earth has a Concern
in it, becaufe in it is concerned, and nearly and
immediately concerned, his Virtue, his Property,
and the Security of his Perfon: And where all
                                    thefe

thefe are beft preferved and advanced, the Government is beft adminiftered ; and where they are not, the Government is impotent, wicked, or unfortunate ; and where the Government is fo, the People will be fo, there being always and every where a certain Sympathy and Analogy between the Nature of the Government and the Nature of the People. This holds true in every Inftance. Public Men are the Patterns of Private ; and the Virtues and Vices of the Governors become quickly the Virtues and Vices of the Governed.

Regis ad exemplum totus componitur orbis.

Nor is it Example alone that does it. Ill Governments, fubfifting by Vice and Rapine, are jealous of private Virtue, and Enemies to private Property. *Opes pro crimine* ; *& ob virtutes certiffi-mum exitium.* They muft be wicked and mifchievous to be what they are ; nor are they fecure while any Thing good or valuable is fecure. Hence it is, that to drain, worry, and debauch their Subjects, are the fteady Maxims of their Politicks, their favourite Arts of Reigning. In this wretched Situation the People, to be fafe, muft be poor and lewd : There will be but little Induftry where Property is precarious; fmall Honefty where Virtue is dangerous.

Profufenefs or Frugality, and the like Virtues or Vices, which affect the Publick, will be practifed in the City, if they be practifed in the Court ; and in the Country, if they be in the City. Even *Nero* (that Royal Monfter in Man's Shape) was adored by the common Herd at *Rome*, as much as he was flattered by the Great ; and both the Little and the Great admired, or pretended to
admire,

admire, his Manners, and many to imitate them. *Tacitus* tells us, that thofe Sort of People long lamented him, and rejoiced in the Choice of a Succeffor that refembled him, even the profligate *Otho.*

Good Government does, on the contrary, produce great Virtue, much Happinefs, and many People. *Greece* and *Italy*, while they continued free, were each of them, for the Number of Inhabitants, like one continued City ; for Virtue, Knowledge, and Great Men, they were the Standards of the World ; and that Age and Country that could come neareft to them, has ever fince been reckoned the happieft. Their Government, their Free Government, was the Root of all thefe Advantages, and of all this Felicity and Renown ; and in thefe great and fortunate States the People were the Principals in the Government ; Laws were made by their Judgment and Authority, and by their Voice and Commands were Magiftrates created and condemned. The City of *Rome* could conquer the World ; nor could the great *Perfian* Monarch, the greateft then upon Earth, ftand before the Face of one *Greek* City.

But what are *Greece* and *Italy* now ? *Rome* has in it a Herd of pampered Monks, and a few ftarving Lay Inhabitants ; the *Campania* of *Rome*, the fineft Spot of Earth in *Europe*, is a Defart. And for the modern *Greeks*, they are a few abject contemptible Slaves, kept under Ignorance, Chains, and Vilenefs, by the *Turkifh* Monarch, who keeps a great Part of the Globe intenfely miferable, that he may feem great without being fo.

Such is the Difference between one Government and another, and of fuch important Con-

cernment

cernment is the Nature and Adminiſtration of
Government to a People. And to ſay that private
Men have nothing to do with Government, is to
ſay that private Men have nothing to do with their
own Happineſs and Miſery.

What is the Publick, but the collective Body
of private Men, as every private Man is a Member of the Publick? And as the Whole ought to
be concerned for the Preſervation of every private
Individual, it is the Duty of every Individual to
be concerned for the Whole, in which himſelf is
included.

One Man, or a few Men, have often pretended the Publick, and meant themſelves, and conſulted their own perſonal Intereſt, in Inſtances
eſſential to its Well-being; but the whole People,
by conſulting their own Intereſt, conſult the Publick, and act for the Publick by acting for themſelves: This is particularly the Spirit of our Conſtitution, in which the whole Nation is re-
preſented; and our Records afford Inſtances,
where the Houſe of Commons have declined entering upon a Queſtion of Importance, till they
had gone into the Country, and conſulted their
Principals, the People: So far were they from
thinking that private Men had no Right to meddle with Government. In Truth, our whole
worldly Happineſs and Miſery (abating for Accidents and Diſeaſes) are owing to the Order or
Miſmanagement of Government; and he who
ſays that private Men have no Concern with Government, does wiſely and modeſtly tell us, that
Men have no Concern in that which concerns
them moſt; it is ſaying that People ought not to
concern

concern themfelves whether they be naked or clothed, fed or ftarved, deceived or inftructed, and whether they be protected or deftroyed : What Nonfenfe and Servitude in a free and wife Nation !

For myfelf, who have thought pretty much of thefe Matters, I am of Opinion, that a whole Nation are like to be as much attached to themfelves, as one Man or a few Men are like to be, who may by many Means be detached from the Intereft of a Nation. It is certain that one Man, and feveral Men, may be bribed into an Intereft oppofite to that of the Publick; but it is as certain that a whole Country can never find an Equivalent for itfelf, and confequently a whole Country can never be bribed. It is the eternal Intereft of every Nation, that their Government fhould be good; but they who direct it frequently reafon a contrary Way and find their own Account in Plunder and Oppreffion ; and while the publick Voice is pretended to be declared, by one or a few, for vile and private Ends, the Publick know nothing of what is done, till they feel the terrible Effects of it.

By the **Bill of Rights,** and the Act of Settlement, at the *Revolution*, a Right is afferted to the People of applying to the King and to the Parliament, by Petition and Addrefs, for a Redrefs of publick Grievances and Mifmanagements, when fuch there are, of which They are left to judge ; And the Difference between free and enflaved Countries lies principally here, that in the former, their Magiftrates muft confult the Voice and Intereft of the People ; but in the latter, the private
Will,

Will, Interest, and Pleasure of the Governors, are the sole End and Motives of their Administration.

Such is the Difference between *England* and *Turkey*; which Difference they who say that private Men have no Right to concern themselves with Government, would absolutely destroy; they would convert Magistrates into Bashaws, and introduce Popery into Politicks. The late Revolution stands upon the very opposite Maxim; and that any Man dares to contradict it since the *Revolution*, would be amazing, did we not know that there are, in every Country, Hirelings who would betray it for a Sop.

G   *I am,* &c.

Saturday, *July* 29, 1721. No. 39.

Of the Passions; that they are all alike good or all alike evil, according as they are applied.

S I R,

NOthing is more provoking than to hear Men talk magisterially, and with an Air of Teaching, about Things which they do not understand, or which they have an Interest to have understood wrong. We have, all of us, heard much of the Duty of subduing our Appetites, and extinguishing our Passions, from Men, who by these Phrases shewed at once their Ignorance of human Nature, and yet that they aimed at an absolute Dominion over it.

Wrong

Wrong Heads and knavifh Defigns are frequently found together; and Creatures that you would not truft with laying out Ten Shillings for you in an Inftance where you truft to your own Underftanding, fhall fometimes, by the mere Sound of their Voice, and an unmeaning Diftinction, make themfelves Mafters of your Mind and your Fortune. It is by trufting to thefe that Men come to know fo little of themfelves, and to be fo much the Prey of others as ignorant and more difhoneft. I know no Man fo fit as himfelf to rule himfelf, in Things which purely concern himfelf. How happy would this plain Rule make the World, if they could be brought to obferve it, and to remember that Brown is as virtuous a Colour as Black; that the Almighty poffeffes alike every Quarter of the World; and that in his Sight Fifh and Flefh in Point of Merit and Innocence are the fame! Thefe Things are felf-evident, and yet the Mifery of Mankind is in a great Meafure owing to their Ignorance of them.

The ancient *Stoicks* had many admirable and virtuous Precepts, but their Philofophy was too rigid to be very popular; they taught Men an abfolute Indifference for fenfual Pain and Pleafure; but in this their Doctrine was neither ufeful nor practicable. Men were not to be thus dealt with; they could not ceafe to be Men, nor change Nature for Philofophy. Befides, thefe Teachers being *Pagans*, and arguing only from the Topicks of Wifdom ftrained too high, had no Equivalent to offer to their Difciples for parting with their Appetites and their Senfes. But when fome of their Sophifts came into Chriftianity, and brought along with them the fevere Notions of their Sect, they fpread

and

and recommended the fame with more Succefs, by tacking to thefe their Opinions the Rewards and Terrors of the World to come, which had nothing to do with them : However, they faid that it had, and quickly found Credit enough to make it dangerous to contradict them.

Thefe favourite Dreams of theirs, added to fome Sayings and Paffages of the Gofpel, ill underftood, were vehemently urged, as if they had been fo many certain Paffports to Paradife; and foon turned Mens Brains, and made them really fond of Poverty, Hardfhips, and Mifery, and even of Death itfelf : Enthufiafm conquered Reafon, and inflamed Nature ; and Men, to be devout, grew diftracted.

This came of ftifling the Paffions, and fubduing Nature, as the Phrafe .was. But the Folly and Mifchief of this Doctrine thus extravagantly pufhed, were not greater than its Falfhood : For, as there is no fuch Thing as departing from Nature, without departing from Life, it is certain that they who were remarkable for reftraining fome of their Appetites, were as remarkable for indulging others ; fo that their boafted Mortification was no more than the Exchange of one Paffion for another, and often of a better for a worfe. Thus there are many Saints in the *Romifh* Calendar, who practifed a religious Abftinence from all Sorts of Flefh living or dead, and yet made it the Duty of their Profeffion, and the Bufinefs of their Lives, to ftir up Diffention and War amongft Men, and to promote Slaughter and Defolation : They abftained from Women, and yet were the Authors of infinite Rapes and Adulteries : Their gentle and fanctified Souls would not allow them to kill, much lefs to

eat

eat any Part of an Animal made to be killed and eaten; but they avowedly and pioufly preached up human and Chriftian Butcheries, and have fmiled over the Carcafes of a Nation maffacred at their Inftigation.

It is the Weaknefs and Misfortune of the human Race, that a Man, by the Means of one Virtue, or the Appearance of it, is often able to do a Thoufand Mifchiefs; and it is the Quality of human Nature, that when any one of its Appetites is violently reftrained, others break out into proportionable Exceffes. Thus Men grow rafh and precipitate, by trampling upon Caution and Fear; and thus they become Cowards, by ftifling the Love of Glory: Whereas, if the Appetite for Danger were checked by the Appetite of Self-Prefervation, and the lazy Love of Safety by the Love of Fame, Rafhnefs and Cowardice would be no more.

It is the higheft Stupidity to talk of fubduing the Paffions, in the common Acceptation of that Phrafe; and to rail at them in grofs, is as foolifh. The greateft Evils often proceed from the beft Things abufed, or ill applied; and this is particularly true of the Paffions, which are the conftituent Parts of a Man, and are good or ill as they are managed.

The Exercife therefore of Reafon is nothing elfe, but the indulging or controuling of the Paffions, with an impartial Hand, and giving them all fair Play; it is an equal Adminiftration of the Appetites, by which they are reftrained from outrunning one another: Thus, for Example, if Mens Fears were always as powerful as their Hopes, they would rarely run into Danger; or, if their

Hopes

Hopes balanced their Fears, they would never defpair.

Every one of the leading Paffions is as neceffary as another; all the Difficulty is to keep them well marfhalled : They are only terrible by breaking out of their Ranks , and when they do, they are all alike terrible, though the World generally thinks otherwife. But it is certain, that thofe Paffions to which the kindeft Ideas are annexed, do as much Mifchief when they get out of their Bounds, as do thofe to which we annex the harfheft Ideas ; and Love and Hope, which bear foft and mild Names, are in their Exceffes as active and as formidable Paffions, as are Anger and Revenge, the Names of which are apt to fhock us ; and Anger and Revenge are, in their proper Limits, more defirable Paffions than are Love and Hope out of their proper Limits ; that is, they are all equally good, or all equally evil, juft as they are let loofe or reftrained. A Man who cuts another's Throat out of Love to his Wife, commits the fame Wickednefs as if he did it out of Revenge. Extravagant Joy for the *Reftoration* (which was doubtlefs a great and extraordinary Bleffing) had well nigh coft *England* its Religion and Liberty ; and afterwards the awakening Fears of Popery faved both. No Nation has been more flefhed in Blood than the *Turks* ; principally, becaufe the falfe Hopes of *Mahomet*'s lafcivious Paradife animated them in their Butcheries.

The only Way therefore of dealing with Mankind, is to deal with their Paffions ; and the Founders of all States, and of all Religions, have ever done fo : The firft Elements, or Knowledge of Politicks, is the Knowledge of the Paffions ; and

the

the Art of Governing, is chiefly the Art of applying to the Paffions. When the publick Paffions
(by which I mean every Man's particular Warmth
and Concern about publick Tranfactions and Events)
are well regulated and honeftly employed, this is
called Government, or the Art of Governing;
and when they are knavifhly raifed and ill employed, it is called Faction, which is the gratifying
of private Paffion by publick Means.

And becaufe Paffion and Opinion are fo nearly
related, and have fuch Force upon each other, arbitrary Courts and crafty Churchmen have ever
endeavoured to force, or frighten, or deceive the
People into an Uniformity of Thoughts, efpecially
of Religious Thoughts. —— A Thing tyrannical
and impoffible ! And yet a whole People do often,
through Ignorance or Fear, feem of one Mind ;
and but feem : For, if they come to explain, they
would find their Ideas differ widely, though their
Words agree. Whereas in a well-governed free
State, Diverfity of Speculations is fo far from clog-
ging the publick Good, that it evidently promotes
the fame ; all Men being equally engaged in the
Defence of that, by which all Men are indifferently
protected. So that to attempt to reduce all Men
to one Standard of Thinking, is abfurd in Philofophy, impious in Religion, and Faction in the State.
And though the mortifying of the Appetites be a
very plaufible Phrafe, and, in a reftrained Senfe,
a laudable Thing ; yet he who recommends it to
you does often mean nothing but this, *Make your*
Paffions tame, that I may ride them.

There is fcarce any one of the Paffions but what
is truly laudable when it centers in the Publick,
and makes that its Object. Ambition, Avarice,
Revenge,

Revenge, are all fo many Virtues, when they aim at the general Welfare. I know that it is exceeding hard and rare, for any Man to feparate his Paffions from his own Perfon and Intereft ; but it is certain that there have been fuch Men. *Brutus, Cato, Regulus, Timoleon, Dion,* and *Epaminondas,* were fuch, as were many more ancient *Greeks* and *Romans*; and, I hope, *England* has ftill fome fuch. And though, in purfuing publick Views, Men regard themfelves and their own Advantages ; yet if they regard the Publick more, or their own in Subferviency to the Publick, they may juftly be efteemed virtuous and good.

No Man can be too ambitious of the Glory and Security of his Country, nor too angry at its Misfortunes and ill Uagfe ; nor too revengeful againft thofe that abufe and betray it ; nor too avaricious to enrich it, provided that in doing it he violates not the Rights of others.

Tacitus giving the Character of the Emperor *Galba,* who doubtlefs was an honeft Man, and had many Virtues, after faying that he coveted no Man's Money, and was fparing of his own, adds, that he was folicitous to fave publick Money :——— *Pecuniæ alienæ non appetens, fuæ parcus, publicæ avarus* ; which publick Avarice in him was a publick Virtue, and coft him his Life ; he was not fuffered to reign, becaufe would not lavifh away the publick Money in Bribes ; *Milites a fe eligi, non emi.* So dangerous, and even fatal, was perfonal Virtue in that corrupt State ; and fo hard and impoffible is it, in any State, to ftay the Progrefs of Corruption ! *Galba* would have reformed the *Roman* State : But the Vices of his Predeceffors, and long Ufe, made it impracticable ; and he loft his

Life

Life in the Attempt. The Paffions of Men were detached from the Commonwealth, and placed upon their own perfonal Security or Gain ; and they had no Senfe of the Publick, and as little Knowledge of its Affairs : For that great People, and almoft the whole World had been long the fole Property of a fingle Man, who took Counfel only of his Luft,

G

I am, &c.

SATURDAY, *Auguft* 5, 1721. No. 40.

Confiderations on the reftlefs and felfifh Spirit of Man.

S I R,

IT is melancholy to confider how every Thing in the World is abufed : The Reafon is, that Men having themfelves chiefly in View, confider all Things with an Eye to themfelves only ; and thus it is that general Bleffings ceafe to be fo by being converted into private Property, as is always done where it is fafe or poffible to be done.

Enquiring how it comes to pafs that the beft Things in the World, fuch as Religion, Property, and Power, are made to do fo much Hurt ; I find it to proceed principally from hence, that Men are never fatisfied with their prefent Condition, which is never perfectly happy ; and perfect Happinefs being their chief Aim, and always out of their Reach, they are reftlefly grafping at what they never can attain.

So

So chimerical is the Nature of Man ! his greateft Pleafures are always to come, and therefore never come. His Content cannot poffibly be perfect, becaufe its higheft Objects are conftantly future ; and yet it is the more perfect for their being future. Our higheft Enjoyment is of that which is not : Our Pleafure is Deceit ; and the only real Happinefs that we have is derived from Non-Entities. We are never fatisfied with being juft what we are ; and therefore, though you give us all that we defire, or can conceive, yet we fhall not have done defiring. The prefent Poffeffions give but little Joy, let them be ever fo great ; even as great as can be grafped : It is the Enjoyment to come that is only or moft valued. When we fay, that if fuch a Thing happened, we would be eafy ; we can only mean, or ought only to mean, that we would be more eafy than we are : And in that too we are often miftaken ; for new Acquifitions bring new Wants ; and imaginary Wants are as pungent as real ones. So that there is the fame End of Wifhing as of Living, and Death only can ftill the Appetites.

Publick Bleffings would really be fo to every Man, if every Man would be content with his Share : But every Man would have more ; nor would more fatisfy him, whatever he may think ; but his Defires would rife with his Poffeffions or his Power, and his laft Wifh would be to have All : Nor would the Poffeffion of All quiet the Mind of Man, which the whole World cannot fill. Indeed, he who has moft, wants moft ; and Care, anxious Care, as it is the clofe Companion of Greatnefs, fo it is furtheft from him who has leaft to care for.

I own,

I own, that many have feemed to defpife Riches and Power, and really declined the Means of acquiring them : But they deceived themfelves, if they thought that this Conduct of theirs was owing to a real Contempt for the Things themfelves ; when in Truth it was only a Diflike of the Terms upon which they were to be had. Difinterestedness is often creared by Lazinefs, Pride, or Fear ; and then it is no Virtue. There is not, perhaps, a Man living but would be glad of Wealth and Grandeur, if he could acquire them with Speed, and poffefs them with Eafe ; and almoft all Men would rifk, and do daily rifk, Eafe, Reputation, Life, and All, to come at them. Do we not fee that Men venture being Beggars to be rich, lofe their Reft for the Sake of Quiet, and acquire Infamy to earn Honour ? We live in a Hurry, in order to come at a Refting-place ; and in Crowds to purchafe Solitude. Nor are we the nearer to our End, though the Means fucceed : Human Life is a Life of Expectation and Care ; and he who rejects the Conditions, muft quit it.

Every Paffion, every View that Men have, is felfifh in fome Degree ; but when it does Good to the Publick in its Operation and Confequence, it may be juftly called difinterefted in the ufual Meaning of that Word. So that when we call any Man difinterefted, we fhould intend no more by it, than that the Turn of his Mind is towards the Publick, and that he has placed his own perfonal Glory and Pleafure in ferving it. To ferve his Country is his private Pleafure, Mankind is his Miftrefs ; and he does Good to them by gratifying himfelf.

Difinte-

Difintereftednefs, in any other Senfe than th's, there is none. For Men to act independently of their Paffions, is a Contradiction ! fince their Paf- fions enter into all that they do, and are the Source of it : And the beft Actions which Men perform, often arife from Fear, Vanity, Shame, and the like Caufes. When the Paffions of Men do Good to others, it is called Virtue and Publick Spirit ; and when they do Hurt to others, it is call- ed Selfifhnefs, Difhonefty, Luft, and other Names of Infamy. The Motive of every Man's Con- duct is fetched from within, and has a good or an ill Name according to its Effect upon others ; and fometimes the great Difference between an honeft Man and a Knave, is no other than a Piece of Humour, or a Piece of Chance. As the Paffions of Men, which are only the Motions raifed with- in us by the Motion of Things without us, are foothed or animated by external Caufes, it is hard to determine, whether there be a Man in the World who might not be corrupted by fome Means and Applications ; the Nicety is, to choofe thofe that are proper.

All thefe Difcoveries and Complaints of the Crookednefs and Corruption of human Nature are made with no malignant Intention to break the Bonds of Society ; but they are made to fhew, that as Selfifhnefs is the ftrongeft Biafs of Men, every Man ought to be upon his Guard againft another, that he become not the Prey of another. The too great Confidence which many Men have pla- ced in One, has often ruined Millions. How many forrowful Experiences have we, that Men will be Rogues where they dare ; and that the greateft Opportunities always make the greateft !

Give

Give them what you can, they will ftill want more than you give; and therefore the higheft Trufts are the moft apt to be broken.

Thofe who have talked moft of the Dignity of human Nature, feem to have underftood it but little. Men are fo far from having any Views purely publick and difinterefted, that Government firft arofe from every Man's taking care of himfelf; and Government is never abufed and perverted, but from the fame Caufe. Do we not know that one Man has flaughtered a Million, and overturned Nations, for the gaining of one Point to himfelf? and that almoft all Men would follow Evil, if they found their greateft Advantage or Pleafure in it.

Here therefore lies the Source of all the Evil which Men fuffer from Men, that every Man loves himfelf better than he loves his whole Species, and more or lefs confults himfelf in all that he does. He naturally purfues what is pleafant or profitable in his own Eyes, though in doing it he entail Mifery upon Multitudes. So that we have no other Security againft the Malice and Rapine of each other, but the Security of Laws or our own Force. By Laws Societies fubfift within themfelves; and by Force they defend themfelves againft each other. And as in the Bufinefs of Faith and Leagues between Nation and Nation, Treaties are made by Confent, but kept by Fear and Power; and obferved or violated juft as Intereft, Advantage, and Opportunities invite, without Regard to Faith and good Confcience, which are only Words of Good-breeding, with which Courts compliment one another and themfelves; fo between Subject and Subject, and between Ma-

giftrates

giftrates and Subjects, Concord and Security are preferved by the Terror of Laws, and the Ties of mutual Intereft ; and both Intereft and Terror derive their Strength from the Impulfes of Self-Love.

Thus one Man is only fafe, while it is the Intereft of another to let him alone ; and Men are Knaves or honeft Men, according to the Judgment which they make of their own Intereft and Eafe, and of the Terms upon which they choofe to live in the World. Many Men are honeft, without any Virtue, or indeed a Thought of Honefty ; as many others are Rogues, without any Malice : And both Sorts mean only their own perfonal Avantage ; but take different Roads to arrive at it. This is their great Aim ; and that Conftitution which trufts more than it needs to any Man, or Body of Men, has a terrible Flaw in it, and is big with the Seeds of its own Deftruction. Hence arofe Tyrants, and Tyranny, and Standing Armies : *Marius*, and *Cæfar*, and *Oliver Cromwell.* How prepofteroufly do Men act ! By too great Confidence in one Man, or a few Men, they become Slaves ; and by a general Diftruft of each other, they continue fo !

It may be objected, that fince Men are fuch a wretched Race, made fo by the Apoftafy of *Adam*, they are not worth ferving ; that the moft unhappy of them are but what they themfelves would make others, and therefore their Fate is juft upon them.

In anfwer to this, I readily own what I have b en proving, that Men are very bad where they dare, and that all Men would be Tyrants, and do what they pleafe. But ftill let us preferve Juftice and

and Equality in the World. Why fhould he, who
is bad himfelf, opprefs others who are no worfe
than him ? Befides, the Lot of Humanity being an
unhappy one, it is an honeft Ambition, that of
endeavouring to mend it, to improve Nature by
Virtue, and to mend Mankind by obliging them
to obferve Rules that are good. We do not expect
philofophical Virtue from them ; but only that
they follow Virtue as their Intereft, and find it penal and dangerous to depart from it. And this is
the only Virtue that the World wants, and the
only Virtue that it can truft to.

G   *I am,* &c.

SATURDAY, *Auguft* 19, 1721. No. 41.

The Emperor Galba's *Speech to* Pifo, *with an Introduction.*

S I R,

I Send you a Tranflation of the Speech of the
Emperor *Galba* to *Pifo,* when he adopted him
his Partner and Succeffor in the Empire ; a Speech
full of great Senfe, great Honefty, and noble Sentiments. Indeed *Galba* feems to have come to the
Government with worthy Intentions to mend it.
To reftore the antient Liberty, was impoffible.
Things had run long in another Channel ; People
were accuftomed to the Largeffes and falfe Bounty
of their Princes, to the awful and founding Names
of the *Cæfars,* and to the Luxury, Pomp, and
Tinfel of a Court. The Soldiers would have an
Emperor ; nor could the Senate withftand the
                                                    Soldiers :

Soldiers: The venerable Orders of the Common wealth had been long abolished, her antient Virtues extinct; *Nihil ufquam prifci & integri moris*; and the Commonwealth itfelf was forgot: *Quotus quifque reliquus qui rem publicam vidiffet !* fays *Tacitus*, fpeaking of the End of the Reign of *Auguftus*. In fhort, the Emperor was all in all :——*Illuc cuncta vergere.* The State was overturned, mangled, and changed: The old Laws of Equality were utterly loft in the Imperial Power, and that was fupported by the Sword. There was no Safety but in Servitude ; *Juffa principis afpectare.*—— All the other Magiftrates were but Shadows with fine old Names.

The chief Aim therefore of *Galba*, fince he could not reftore, was to reform. A worthy Attempt, but he failed in it : So irrefiftible was the Tide of Corruption ! Two Things principally obftructed his Defign, and fhortened his Life and Reign ; the Avarice of the Soldiery, and the vile Conduct of his Servants.

As to the Soldiers, he had honeftly, but unfortunately faid, that he *would choofe them, but not buy them* ; a Saying which they never forgave him. Befides, as he practifed himfelf the rigid old *Roman* Difcipline, he would oblige his Army to practife it ; a Thing new to them, and intolerable. They had been long ufed to Luxury and Sloth, and were grown as fond of the Vilenefs and Vices of their Princes, as the old Republican Armies had been of the Temperance, Modefty, and other Virtues of their Commanders : They therefore could not bear the Severity and Frugality of *Galba* ; nor would *Galba* depart from his Temper and his Purpofes. Money would have made

them

them his Friends ; but he would part with none.
The Reflection of the Historian upon this Conduct
of his is fine, but melancholy ;————*Nocuit anti-
quis rigor, & nimia severitas, cui jam pares non su-
mus :* " He was ruined by reviving unseasonably
" the severe Virtue of our Ancestors : Alas ! we
" are no longer equal to it." To conclude this
Head ; the Soldiers butchered an Emperor that
would not bribe them.

As to the Part of *Galba*'s Servants in the Tragedy of their Master, it was no small one : They
made him odious by their own Crimes ; and in
his Name committed Cruelties and Rapine, which
blackened his Character ; and when they had
brought him under a general Dislike, none of his
own good Qualities could recover him his good
Name : *Inviso semel principe, seu bene seu male facta
premunt.* Their Avarice was imputed to him, and
called his : — *Jam offerebant venalia cuncta præ-
potentes liberti.* They were resolved to make the
most of his short Reign ; and by doing so made it
shorter :—*Servorum manus subitis avidæ, & tanquam apud senem festinantes.* He paid dear for their
Wickedness : —*Odio flagitiorum oneratum destrue-
bant.* His Character, in relation to his Friends
and Servants, was, That he was indulgent to
them, if they were good ; and blind to their
Faults, if they were bad. *Ubi in bonos incidisset,
sine reprehensione patiens : Si mali forent, usque ad
culpam ignarus.*

The rest of his Character, taken from *Tacitus,*
from whom I have taken the Whole, is, That
being Seventy Years old, he had lived in Prosperity during five Reigns, more happy in them than
in his own : That he was of a Family Antient,
                                                    Great,

Great, and Noble, and Mafter of great Wealth :
That he had a moderate Capacity, and more Innocence than Abilities : That he neither courted
Fame, nor defpifed it : That he coveted no Man's
Money, was fparing of his own, and folicitous to
fave publick Money : That a Nobleman of his
great Birth and Quality, having lived fo fecurely
in fuch dangerous Times, was a Thing fo furprizing and rare, that his good Fortune paffed for
Wifdom, and his real Indolence for real Art :
That in the Vigour of his Years he acquired great
Renown in the *German* Wars : That being Pro-
conful in *Africa*, he governed that Province, and
afterwards *Spain*, with great Equity : That he
feemed greater than a Subject, while he was but a
Subject; and that, in the Opinion of all Men, he
was equal to the Empire, if he had never been
Emperor.

So much for the Character of *Galba* ; which I
thought neceffary to introduce his Speech to *Pifo*,
who was every way worthy of the Adoption and
of a better Fortune ; which, however, was of
a-piece : He was long an Exile under *Nero*, who
had murdered his Brother *Craffus* ; as had *Claudius*
his Brother *Magnus :* He himfelf was but four
Days *Cæfar*, and then butchered ; as was his eldeft
Brother prefently after him. He was of a noble
Race, both by Father and Mother, and had an
amiable and popular Character for the Severity of
his Manners, and his many Virtues ; and during
the few Days of his higheft Power and Adverfity
he behaved himfelf with great Modefty and Firmnefs, and feemed to make good every Hope concerning him.——But Virtue and Goodnefs were
then pernicious, and we fee what he got by having
them.

them. The whole Story, and particularly his Fate
in it, affects me.

I am, &c.

The Speech of Galba *to* Piso.

"   WEre I, as a private Man, to adopt you for
"   my Son, by Virtue of the Law *Curiata*,
"   in Presence of the Pontifs, according to the or-
"   dinary Usage ; glorious even then would be the
"   Adoption to us both ; as with the Blood of the
"   great *Pompey* and of *Marcus Crassus* my Family
"   would be enriched ; and the Nobility of your
"   House derive fresh Splendor from the signal Lu-
"   stre and Renown of the *Sulpitian* and *Lutacian*
"   Race.   I am now a publick Person, by the uni-
"   ted Consent of Gods and Men called to the
"   Empire ; and of this same Sovereignty, for
"   which our Ancestors contended with Arms, I,
". who by War have obtained it, do offer you the
"   Possession, while you are neither seeking nor
"   pursuing it : A Gift to which I am urged only
"   by the Love of my Country and your own ex-
"   cellent Qualifications.   In this I follow the Ex-
"   ample of the deified *Augustus*, who assumed suc-
"   cessively, for his Partners in Power, first his
"   Sister's Son, *Marcellus* ; next his Son-in-Law,
"   *Agrippa* ; afterwards his Grandsons ; lastly, his
"   Wife's Son *Tiberius*. But *Augustus*, who would
"   entail the Empire upon his own House, in his
"   own House sought a Successor : I choose out of
"   the Commonwealth an Heir to the Common-
"   wealth.   Not that I am reduced to this Choice
"   by any Want of Relations to my Blood, or of
"   Fellow-Commanders in War.   But neither did
" I,

" I, no more than you, arrive at fupreme Power
" by any Efforts of Ambition ; and my thus over-
" looking your Relations, as well as my own, is
" a Proof and Monument with what Sincerity of
" Intention I prefer you to all Men.   You have
" a Brother, in Nobility your Equal, in Age
" your Superior ; a Man worthy of this Fortune ;
" did I not in you find one ftill more worthy.
" Such is your Age, as to be paft the Giddinefs
" and Impetuofity of Youth ; fuch has been your
" Courfe of Life, that nothing in your Conduct,
" thus far, is fubject to Blame.   But hitherto
" you have only had an adverfe Fortune to con-
" tend with.   More dangerous and keen are the
" Stimulations of Profperity, to try the Temper
" of the Soul, and call forth its Weakneffes. For,
" the Strokes of Calamity we ftruggle under and
" bear : By a Flow of Felicity we are utterly
" fubdued and corrupted.

    " You doubtlefs will ftill retain, with your
" ufual Firmnefs, the fame Honour, Faith in
" Friendfhip, Candour and Freedom of Spirit ;
" Endowments which, above all others, adorn
" the Mind of Man.   But the falfe Complaifance
" of others will flacken your Fortitude.   Flattery
" will force its Way to your Heart ; deceitful
" Soothings, the moft peftilent Poifon to every
" honeft Affection, will enchant you ; and to
" his own fordid Gain will every Particular be
" wrefting your Honour and good Inclinations.
" You and I upon this Occafion converfe together
" with Hearts perfectly open and fincere : Others
" will choofe to make their Addreffes to our For-
" tune rather than to us.   Indeed, to deal faith-
" fully with Princes, to reafon them into their
                                    " Duty,

" Duty, is a mighty Talk, and with infinite
" Difficulty performed. But eaſy is the Art of
" cajoling any Prince whatſoever, and in doing
" it the Heart has no Share. Could this immenſe
" Empire ſubſiſt, and be ſwayed without a ſingle
" Ruler, I ſhould glory in reſigning, glory in
" being the firſt Emperor who reſigned the Power
" of the Republick into her own Hands. But
" ſuch, long ſince has been the fatal Situation
" of the State, that all the Good which my old
" Age enables me to do to the *Roman* People, is
" to leave them a good Succeſſor ; nor can you,
" with all your Youth, do more for them than
" afford them in yourſelf a benevolent Prince.
" Under *Tiberius* and *Caligula* and *Claudius*, we
" were all of us no more, the *Roman* World was
" no more, than as the Inheritance of one Fa-
" mily. That the Empire has in me begun to
" be elective, is a Sign of our antient Liberty re-
" vived, and ſome Equivalent for it ; the only
" Liberty we are capable of enjoying. Now the
" *Julian* and *Claudian* Families being extinct, the
" beſt Men are likely, in this Way of Adoption,
" to become the higheſt. To be ſprung from a
" Sovereign Race, is the Effect of Chance, and
" further than this requires no Deliberation or
" Regard. But in the Work of Adoption the
" Judgment is exerciſed, free from Biaſs and Re-
" ſtraint ; and whenever you want to chooſe, you
" are by the general Conſent directed to the Per-
" ſon worthy to be choſen.

" Have always before your Eyes the Example
" of *Nero*, who, ſecure as he was, and ſwelling
" with the Pride of his Race, a long Genealogy of
" the *Cæſars* his Anceſtors, was not in reality de-
" throned

" throned by *Julius Vindex*, the Governor of a
" Province unprovided with Forces, nor by me,
" affifted by one Legion : No, it was his own
" brutal Tyranny, his own beaftly Debaucheries,
" that flung down the Tyrant from riding on the
" Necks of Mankind. Nor was there till then
" any Inftance of an Emperor by publick Sen-
" tence condemned and depofed. We who fuc-
" ceed him by a different Title, by War and by
" publick Approbation and Choice, fhall thence
" reap publick Glory, however the Malignity of
" Particulars may purfue us. Nor muft you be
" alarmed, if while the World itfelf continues in
" this general Uproar, there are two Legions
" which yet remain unreclaimed to Obedience. It
" was my own Lot to be called to an unfettled
" State ; and as to my old Age, the only Ob-
" jection to my Government, it is no longer one,
" fince, when it is known that I have adopted
" you, I fhall feem young in my Succeffor. The
" Lofs of *Nero* will ever be regretted by all the
" moft Profligate and Bad. To us it belongs, to
" you and to me, fo to govern, that he may not
" alfo be regretted by the Good.

" To fay more in this Way of Inftruction,
" the prefent Conjuncture fuffers not ; nor is it
" neceffary ; fince if I have in you made a wor-
" thy Choice, I have anfwered every Purpofe.
" One certain Rule you have to obferve, exceed-
" ing wholefome, as well as exceeding fhort ; fo
" to comport yourfelf towards your Subjects, as,
" were you a Subject, you would wifh your Prince
" to comport towards you. By this Rule you will
" beft diftinguifh the Boundaries of Juftice and
" Iniquity ; beft comprehend the Art of Reigning:
                                            " For,

" For, you muſt remember that it is not with us
" as with other Nations, ſuch as are barbarous
" and tyrannized, where a particular lordly Houſe
" is eſtabliſhed, and where all beſides are Slaves
" without Reſerve. But you are about to govern
" the *Romans*; a People of too little Virtue to
" ſupport complete Liberty, of too much Spirit to
" bear abſolute Bondage.
    G

SATURDAY, *Auguſt* 26, 1721. No. 42.

Conſiderations on the Nature of Laws.

S I R,

THE Miſchiefs that are daily done, and the
Evils that are daily ſuffered in the World, are
ſad Proofs, how much human Malice exceeds human Wiſdom. Law only provides againſt the
Evils which it knows or foreſees ; but when Laws
fail, we muſt have Recourſe to Reaſon and Nature, which are the only Guides in the making of
Laws. *Stirpem juris a natura repertam,* ſays *Cicero*;
there never would have been any Law againſt any
Crime, if Crimes might have been ſafely committed, againſt which there was no Law : For every
Law ſuppoſes ſome Evil, and can only puniſh or
reſtrain the Evils which already exiſt.

But as poſitive Laws, let them be ever ſo full
and perſpicuous, can never entirely prevent the
Arts of crafty Men to evade them, or the Power
of great ones to violate them ; hence new Laws
are daily making, and new Occaſions for more
                                                    are

are daily arifing : So that the utmoft that Wifdom, Virtue, and Law can do, is to leffen or qualify, but never totally abolifh, Vice and Enormity. Law is therefore a Sign of the Corruption of Man ; and many Laws are Signs of the Corruption of a State.

Pofitive Laws deriving their Force from the Law of Nature, by which we are directed to make occafional Rules, which we call Laws, according to the Exigencies of Times, Places, and Perfons, grow obfolete, or ceafe to be, as foon as they ceafe to be neceffary. And it is as much againft the Law of Nature to execute Laws, when the firft Caufe of them ceafes, as it is to make Laws, for which there is no Caufe, or a bad Caufe. This would be to fubject Reafon to Force, and to apply a Penalty where there is no Crime. Law is right Reafon, commanding Things that are good, and forbidding Things that are bad ; it is a Diftinction and Declaration of Things juft and unjuft, and of the Penalties or Advantages annexed to them.

The Violation therefore of Law does not conftitute a Crime where the Law is bad ; but the Violation of what ought to be Law, is a Crime even where there is no Law. The Effence of Right and Wrong does not depend upon Words and Claufes inferted in a Code or a Statute-Book, much lefs upon the Conclufions and Explications of Lawyers ; but upon Reafon and the Nature of Things, antecedent to all Laws. In all Countries Reafon is or ought to be confulted, before Laws are enacted ; and they are always worfe than none, where it is not confulted. Reafon is in fome Degree given to all Men ; and *Cicero* fays, that whoever has Reafon, has right Reafon ; that

Virtue

Viatue is but perfect Reason ; and that all Nations having Reason for their Guide, all Nations are capable of arriving at Virtue.

From this Reasoning of his it would follow, that every People are capable of making Laws, and good Laws ; and that Laws, where they are bad, are gained by Corruption, Faction, Fear, or Surprize ; and are rather their Misfortune, than the Effects of their Folly. The Acts of *Cæsar* were confirmed by the Senate and the People ; but the Senate was awed, and the Tribunes and People were bribed : Arms and Money procured him a Law to declare him lawless. But, as the most pompous Power can never unsettle the everlasting Land-marks between Good and Evil, no more than those between Pleasure and Pain ; *Cæsar* remained still a Rebel to his Country, and his Acts remained wicked and tyrannical.

Let this stand for an Instance, that Laws are not always the Measure of Right and Wrong. And as positive Laws often speak when the Law of Nature is silent, the Law of Nature sometimes speaks when positive Laws say nothing :—*Neque opinione, sed natura constitutum esse jus.* That brave *Roman, Horatius Cocles,* was bound by no written Law to defend the wooden Bridge over the *Tiber,* against a whole Army of *Tuscans* ; nor was there any Law, that I know of, in *Rome,* against Adultery, when the younger *Tarquin* ravished *Lucretia :* And yet the Virtue of *Horatius* was justly rewarded, and the Vileness of *Tarquin* justly punished, by the *Romans.*

It is impossible to devise Laws sufficient to regulate and manage every Occurrence and Circumstance of Life, because they are often produced

and

and diverfified by Caufes that do not appear; and
in every Condition of Life Men muft have, and
will have, great Allowances made to their own
natural Liberty and Difcretion: But every Man,
who confents to the neceffary Terms of Society,
will alfo confent to this Propofition, That *every
Man fhould do all the Good, and prevent all the Evil,
that he can.* This is the Voice of the Law of Nature; and all Men would be happy by it, if all
Men would practife it. This Law leads us to
fee, that the Eftablifhment of Falfhood and Tyranny (by which I mean the Privilege of One or
a Few to miflead and opprefs All) cannot be juftly
called Law, which is the impartial Rule of Good
and Evil, and can never be the Sanction of Evil
alone.

It has been often faid, that Virtue is its own
Reward; and it is very true, not only from the
Pleafure that attends the Confcioufnefs of doing
well, and the Fame that follows it, but in a more
extenfive Senfe, from the Felicity which would
accrue to every Man, if all Men would purfue
Virtue: But as this Truth may appear too general to allure and engage particular Men, who will
have always their own fingle felves moft at Heart,
abftracted from all the reft; therefore in the make-
ing of Laws, the Pleafures and Fears of particular
Men, being the great Engines by which they
are to be governed, muft be confulted: Vice muft
be rendered deteftable and dangerous; Virtue amiable and advantageous. Their Shame and Emulation muft be raifed; their private Profit and
Glory, Peril and Infamy, laid before them. This
is the Meaning of *Tully*, when he fays, *Vitiorum
emen-*

emendatricem legem effe oportet, commendatricemque virtutem.

Rewards and Punifhments therefore conftitute the whole Strength of Laws ; and the Promulgation of Laws, without which they are none, is an Appeal to the Senfe and Intereft of Men, which of the two they will choofe.

The two great Laws of human Society, from whence all the reft derive their Courfe and Obligation, are thofe of Equity and Self-prefervation : By the firft all Men are bound alike not to hurt one another ; by the fecond all Men have a Right alike to defend themfelves : *Nam jure hoc evenit, ut quod quifque ob tutelam corporis fui fecerit, jure feciffe exiftimetur,* fays the Civil Law ; that is, " It " is a Maxim of the Law, that whatever we do " in the Way and for the Ends of Self-defence, " we lawfully do." All the Laws of Society are entirely reciprocal, and no Man ought to be exempt from their Force ; and whoever violates this primary Law of Nature, ought by the Law of Nature to be deftroyed. He who obferves no Law, forfeits all Title to the Protection of Law. It is Wickednefs not to deftroy a Deftroyer ; and all the ill Confequences of Self-defence are chargeable upon him who occafioned them.

Many Mifchiefs are prevented, by deftroying One who fhews a certain Difpofition to commit many. To allow a Licence to any Man to do Evil with Impunity, is to make Vice triumph over Virtue, and Innocence the Prey of the Guilty. If Men be obliged to bear great and publick Evils, when they can upon better Terms oppofe and remove them ; they are obliged, by the fame Logick,

to

to bear the total Deſtruction of Mankind. If any Man may deſtroy whom he pleaſes without Reſiſtance, he may extinguiſh the human Race without Reſiſtance. For, if you ſettle the Bounds of Reſiſtance, you allow it ; and if you do not fix its Bounds, you leave Property at the Mercy of Rapine, and Life in the Hands of Cruelty.

It is ſaid, that the Doctrine of Reſiſtance would deſtroy the Peace of the World : But it may be more truly ſaid, that the contrary Doctrine would deſtroy the World itſelf, as it has already ſome of the beſt Countries in it. I muſt indeed own, that if one Man may deſtroy all, there would be great and laſting Peace when nobody was left to break it.

The Law of Nature does not only allow us, but oblige us, to defend ourſelves. It is our Duty, not only to ourſelves, but to the Society ; *Vitam tibi ipſi ſi negas, multis negas,* ſays *Seneca :* If we ſuffer tamely a lawleſs Attack upon our Property and Fortunes, we encourage it, and involve others in our Doom. And *Cicero* ſays, " He who does " not reſiſt Miſchief when he may, is guilty of " the ſame Crime, as if he had deſerted his Pa- " rents, his Friends, and his Country.

So that the Conduct of Men, who, when they are ill treated, uſe Words rather than Arms, and practiſe Submiſſion rather than Reſiſtance, is owing to a prudential Cauſe, becauſe there is Hazard in Quarrels and War, and their Cauſe may be made worſe by an Endeavour to mend it ; and not to any Confeſſion of Right in thoſe that do them wrong. When Men begin to be wicked, we cannot tell where that Wickedneſs will end ; we have Reaſon to fear the worſt, and provide againſt it.

Such

Such is the Provision made by Laws : They are Checks upon the unruly and partial Appetites of Men, and intended for Terror and Protection. But as there are already Laws sufficient every where to preserve Peace between private Particulars, the great Difficulty has hitherto been to find proper Checks for those who are to check and administer the Laws. To settle therefore a thorough Impartiality in the Laws, both as to their End and Execution, is a Task worthy of human Wisdom, as it would be the Cause and Standard of Civil Felicity. In the Theory nothing is more easy than this Task : Yet who is able to perform it, if they who can will not ?

No Man in Society ought to have any Privilege above the rest, without giving the Society some Equivalent for such his Privilege. Thus Legislators, who compile good Laws, and good Magistrates, who execute them, do, by their honest Attendance upon the Publick, deserve the Privileges and Pay which the Publick allows them ; and Place and Power are the Wages paid by the People to their own Deputies and Agents. Hence it has been well said, that a Chief Magistrate is *major singulis, omnibus minor* :—" He is above the " private Members of the Community ; but the " Community itself is above him."

Where-ever, therefore, the Laws are honestly intended, and equally executed, so as to comprehend in their Penalties and Operation the Great as well and as much as the Small, and hold in awe the Magistrates as much as the Subject, that Government is good, that People are happy.

G   *I am*, &c.

SATURDAY, *September* 2, 1721. No. 43.

The natural Passion of Men for Superiority.

S I R,

ALL Men have an Ambition to be confiderable, and take fuch Ways as their Judgments fuggeft to become fo. Hence proceeds the Appetite of all Men to rife above their Fellows, and the conftant Emulation that always has been, and always will be, in the World, amongft all Sorts of Men. Nature has made them all equal, and moft Men feem well content with the Lot of Parts which Nature has given them; but the Lot of Fortune never thoroughly fatisfies thofe who have the beft.

The firft Spring therefore of Inequality is in human Nature, and the next in the Nature of Society. In order that many may live together in perfect Equality, it is neceffary that fome fhould be above the Many, who otherwife will be ufing Frauds and Violence to get above one another. Some Inequality there muft be; the Danger is, that it be not too great: Where there is abfolute Equality, all Reverence and Awe, two Checks indifpenfible in Society, would be loft; and where Inequality is too great, all Intercourfe and Communication is loft.

Thus in *Turkey*, where there are no natural Links, nor proper Degrees of Subordination in the Chain of their Government, there is a monftrous Gap between the Subject and the Throne. The
Grand

Grand Seignior preferves no Underftanding with his People : Nothing is to be feen but the Terrors of abfolute Monarchy, and the abject Poftures of crouching Slaves. Power does not glide there, as it ought every where, down an even and eafy Channel, with a gentle and regular Defcent ; but pours from a Precipice with dreadful Din, Rapidity, and Violence upon the poor and paffive Valleys below, breaking down all before it, and laying wafte where-ever it comes.

All Men in the World are fond of making a Figure in it. This being the great End of all Men, they take different Roads to come at it, according to their different Capacities, Opinions, Tempers, and Opportunities. No Man would choofe to have any Man his Equal, if he could place himfelf above all Men. All would be *Pompeys*. But though it has fallen to the Share but of few Men to be above all Men ; yet as every Man may, or thinks he may, excel fome Men, there is a perpetual Spur in every Defcendant of *Adam* to be afpiring. Every Man has Self-love, and Self-love is never deferted by Hope.

But this Spirit in every Man of rifing above other Men, as it conftitutes the Happinefs of private Individuals, who take great Complacency in their favourable Opinion of themfelves and their own Abilities ; fo is it the great Caufe of publick and private Evils, Wars, Frauds, Cruelty, and Oppreffion. The Ambition of excelling in every Station by honeft Means, is not only lawful, but laudable, and produces great Good to Society : But as nothing produces Good in this World, but what may, and generally does, produce Evil ; and as Fame, Riches, and Power, may be honeftly

got,

got, but wickedly ufed, it ought to be the Care of Society to provide that fuch Emulation amongft its Members be fo directed and controuled, as to be always beneficial, but never dangerous. But this is a Felicity at which few Nations have arrived, and thofe that had it rarely preferved it long.

It is a nice Point of Wifdom, perhaps too nice for human Judgment, to fix certain and lafting Bounds to this Spirit of Ambition and Emulation amongft Men. To ftop it too foon, fruftrates its Ufe ; and not to ftop it at all, invites its Mifchief. The *Venetians*, by difcouraging it, have never, or very rarely, felt its Advantages ; and the *Athenians* found their *Oftracifm*, an Expedient invented for this very Purpofe, ineffectual to prevent their great Men, who had done great Good to the State, from growing terrible to the State itfelf : *Pericles* in particular, by his Arts, Eloquence, and Popularity, made himfelf Mafter of it, and did almoft what he pleafed in it all his Life ; that fingle Man was fo potent in that free City, that he broke the Power of the *Areopagus*, the Senate of *Athens*, a Court of Magiftrates that balanced the Power of the Populace ; who, being fet free from that Reftraint, ran into all manner of Licentioufnefs and Corruption.

The People of *Athens* became the Subjects of *Pericles* : By having done them much Good, he found Credit enough to deftroy their Government and their Virtue. From the Character of a Benefactor, he ftole into that of a Mafter : So narrow and invifible are the Bounds between the Benefactor and the Betrayer ! *Valerius Maximus* obferves very finely, that " the only Difference be-

" tween *Pififtratus* and *Pericles* was, that the latter
" exercifed by Art the fame Tyranny that the
" other had exercifed by Arms.

Good and Evil thus often flowing from the fame
Root, and Mifchief being frequently introduced
by Merit, it fhews great Difcernment and Virtue
in a People, and a happy Spirit in their Laws, if
they can encourage and employ the Capacity and
Genius of their principal Men, fo as to reap only
the good Fruits of their Services.

This was the Practice and good Fortune of the
old *Romans* for feveral Ages : Virtue was the only
Road to Glory; it was admired, fupported, applauded, and recompenfed ; but they who had
fhewn the greateft found no Sanctuary from it,
when they committed Crimes that deferved none.
This is particularly verified in the Cafes of *Corio-
lanus* and *Manlius Capitolinus*. They were both
brave Men, and had deferved well of their Country; were both, in Recompence, diftinguifhed
with great Honours ; yet were both afterwards
condemned by their Country, the one for a Confpiracy againft it, the other for defpifing its Laws.
Their Services and Crimes were properly feparated
and rewarded.

Emulation therefore, or the Paffion of one Man
to equal or excel another, ought to be encouraged,
with thefe two Reftrictions : Firft, that no Man,
let his Merit be what it will, fhould take his own
Reward ; fecondly, that he fhould have no more
than comes to his Share. *Scipio*, afterwards called
Africanus, was chofen as the greateft and beft Man
in *Rome*, to invade the Territories of *Carthage*;
and he performed it with great Glory to himfelf,
with great Emolument to his Country. He defeated

feated *Hannibal*, and conquered *Carthage*. The
like Praife is alfo due to *Metellus*, *Lucullus*, to *T.
Flaminius*, *Paulus Emilius*, and many other *Roman*
Commanders, who all conquered for their Coun-
try, and were rewarded by their Country with its
Laurels and its Dignities.

Julius Cæfar, being alfo employed by the Com-
monwealth to conquer for it, fucceeded in his
Commiffion; but, as a Reward, took the Com-
monwealth for his Pains: He paid himfelf with
the whole *Roman* World, for having conquered
Part of it. *Alexander* the Great, and moft other
Conquerors, had the fame Modefty, and the fame
Wages; they took All to themfelves.

When Men are left to meafure their own Merit,
and the Reward due to it, they rarely ftint themfelves; all that they can get is the leaft that they
expect: And, to defcend to leffer Inftances, the
World has always abounded in Men, who, though
they deferved Contempt or a Prifon, yet could
never be fatiated with Places and Power. And all
Men who have obferved the Affairs of the World,
will remember and acknowledge, that fometimes
one Man has poffeffed many Pofts, to whom the
publick Suffrage and Confent never gave one.

In my Reflections upon this Subject, I have often
amufed, and even diverted myfelf, with an odd
Imagination; namely, what a wonderful and epidemical Ceffation of Power and Place would en-
fue a fudden and univerfal Removal from thence
of every Man who deferved neither. I fanfied
that I faw the whole Inhabitants of feveral Countries, towards every Quarter of the Sky, gaping
round them for Magiftrates, at leaft for one fingle
Magiftrate, and finding none; and yet even in
this

this State of Anarchy congratulating one another and themselves upon the wonderful Amendment of their Government. I faw all *Afia*, the whole ample Dominions of the *Turk*, and many potent Kingdoms nearer home, all in an abfolute State of Nature : In the large Bofom of the *Romifh* Church, not a Prieft was to be feen ; and in fome Proteftant Countries, the good People were greatly put to it, where to get a Man in a proper Habit to fay publick Prayers. Here in *England*, indeed, I found a different Face of Things, and more Comfort : For, though at prefent we have no Parliament fitting, and though in other Places I faw difmal Solitude, and numberlefs Vacancies ; yet I perceived many worthy Perfons in Church and State doing their Bufinefs, and counting their Gains, with great Attention and Alacrity, but greatly diftreffed how to find new Perfons for old Places.

Imagination apart : I fhall conclude in the Words of a great *Englifh* Writer. It is true that " Con-
" fideration ought to be had of human Frailty ;
" and fome Indulgence may be extended to thofe
" who commit Errors, after having done impor-
" tant Services : But a State cannot fubfift, which
" compenfating evil Actions with good, gives Im-
" punity to dangerous Crimes, in Remembrance
" of any Services whatever. He that does well,
" performs his Duty, and ought always to do fo ;
" Juftice and Prudence concur in this ; and it is
" no lefs juft than profitable, that every Action
" be confidered by itfelf, and fuch a Reward allot-
" ted to it as in Nature and Proportion it beft de-
" ferves.

G   *I am*, &c.

SATUR-

SATURDAY, *September* 9, 1721. No. 44.

Men not ruled by Principle, but by Paſſion.

SIR,

MR. *Bayle*, in the Article of *Epicurus*, ſays, that " Multitudes of Chriſtians believe well, " and live ill: But *Epicurus* and his Followers had, " on the contrary, very ill Opinions, and yet lived " well." The Truth is, the worſt Opinions that are can do but little Harm, when they are impracticable, or when no Advantages are gained by reducing them into Practice ; and the beſt can do but little Good, when they contradict the darling Pleaſures and prevailing Intereſts of Men.

Dry Reaſoning has no Force : If you would have your Doctrine ſuccesſful, you muſt prove it gainful. And as in order to lay down good Rules for well governing the Commonwealth, you muſt firſt know the Commonwealth; ſo in order to perſuade and govern Men, you muſt know what will pleaſe or frighten them. The Good that they do to one another, they do not becauſe it is juſt or commanded ; nor do they forbear mutual Evil, becauſe it is unjuſt or forbid : But theſe Things they do out of Choice or Fear, and both theſe center in themſelves ; for Choice is Pleaſure, and Fear is the Apprehenſion of Pain. So that the beſt Things that Men do, as well as the worſt, are ſelfiſh ; and Self-love is the Parent of Moral Good and Evil.

What Mr. *Selden* ſays of Humility, may be ſaid of every other Virtue. " Humility, *ſays that wiſe*
" *Man,*

" *Man*, is a Virtue that all preach, none practife,
" and yet every body is content to hear: The
" Mafter thinks it good Doctrine for his Servants,
" the Laity for the Clergy, and the Clergy for
" the Laity." Thus we deal with all the Virtues; we leave and recommend the Practice of
them to others, and referve the Advantage and
Praife of them to ourfelves.

All this, and the reft of this Letter, is meant
to fhew that this World is governed by Paffion,
and not by Principle; and it ever will be fo as long
as Men are Men.

There are rarely any Men, never any Body of
Men, but what profefs fome Sort of Religion; and
every Religion profeffes to promote the Peace of
Mankind, the Happinefs of Human Society, and
the Security of the World; and, for Proof of this,
refers to its Principles, Doctrines, and Decifions.
And it is very true, that all Parties in Religion
contend for Submiffion to the State, as long as the
State humours them, or fubmits to them; but their
Obedience and good Humour never hold longer.
All their Principles ply in the Day of Trial, and
are either thrown away, or diftinguifhed away;
which is the fame Thing, though not fo honeft.
Nature is then the beft Guide, and Paffion the
moft popular Preacher.

Men fuit their Tenets to the Circumftances that
they are in, or would be in; and when they have
gained their Point, they forget their Tenets. I could
give Inftances of this from all Sorts of Men, and even
from many whofe Names are great and venerable.

Gregory Nazianzen, that eloquent and eminent
Greek Father, being himfelf Orthodox, contended
for Toleration to the *Arians*, while the *Arians*
were

were uppermoft, and had the Emperor on their
Side : But as foon as Things took a contrary Turn,
and his own Party had the Imperial Power on
their Side, he changed his Stile ; and then it was
unpardonable Boldnefs and a horrible Attempt, for
the *Arians* and *Macedonians* fo much as to meet together to worfhip God their own Way.

St. *Auftin* had the fame Spirit and Inconfiftency :
He was once in the Sentiments of Charity and
Toleration towards Hereticks ; but his Difpute
afterwards with the *Donatifts* fo inflamed him, that
he changed without any Ceremony from White
to Black, and maintained with Violence, that
Hereticks ought to be compelled, perfecuted, and
exterminated.

Thus it is that Men bear witnefs againft themfelves, and practife the Evils which they condemn.
" The *Puritans, fays Mr.* Selden, who will allow
" no Free will at all, but God does all ; yet will
" allow the Subject his Liberty to do, or not to
" do, notwithftanding the King, who is God
" upon Earth : The *Arminians,* who hold that
" we have Free-will, do yet fay, when we come
" to the King, we muft be all Obedience, and
" no Liberty is to be ftood for.

" While *Spain* was the moft renowned Power
" in *Europe*, the *Jefuits, fays Mr.* Bayle, were all
" *Spaniards* ; as well thofe born at *Paris* or *Rome,*
" as thofe born in *Old Caftile.* Ever fince the
" Decay of the Houfe of *Auftria*, and the Eleva-
" tion of *Lewis le Grand*, the *Jefuits* are all *French,*
" at *Rome,* at *Vienna,* at *Madrid,* as well as in
" the College of *Clermont.* In thofe Days the
" Liberties of the *Gallican* Church appeared to
" them not well grounded : They never ceafed
                                        " writing

" writing for the Rights of the Pope againſt thoſe
" of our Kings.   One might fill a Library with
" the Defences compoſed by the Society, and
" condemned by the Parliament and the *Sorbon*. —
" At preſent his Majeſty has not truſtier Pens
" than theirs in his Differences with the Pope.
" It is now the Turn of the Court of *Rome* to
" cenſure the Books of the Reverend Fathers. It
" ſeems the King's Proſperity and Succeſſes have
" afforded them new Lights.

It is with Laymen and Civil Societies, as with
Religi us : They have one Set of Principles when
they are in Power ; another, and a contrary, when
they are out of it.   They that command, and
they that obey, have ſeldom or never the ſame
Motives.   Men change with their Condition, and
Opinions change with Men. And thus is verified
that Maxim of *Rochefoucault*'s, that the Underſtanding is the Dupe or Tool of the Heart ; that
is, our Sentiments follow our Paſſions.

Nor has Religion been ſuffered to mend Nature :
On the contrary, being inſtituted as a Reſtraint,
and an Antidote againſt Sin, it has been, and is
frequently perverted into a Reaſon for Sinning :
Yes, to the Shame and Misfortune of the World,
Men often make War upon Truth, Conſcience,
and Honeſty, in behalf of their Religion ; and
there are others, who, when they have wantonly
wounded Virtue, have Recourſe to Religion for a
Bàlſam.

All Men ſpeak well of Religion, either natural
or revealed, and readily practiſe every Thing in
Religion that is eaſy, indifferent, or advantageous
to them : But in almoſt every Contention between
Religion and the Appetites, the Victory remains
                                                    to

to Nature; that is, Men are never diſhoneſt without Temptation, and rarely honeſt againſt it.

Thus their Principle is Intereſt or Pleaſure; and
when they ſay that they act from Principle, how
can we believe them, unleſs we ſee that they do
it againſt Intereſt? A Proof which they rarely
give us! Had the ſeveral Contracts and Treaties
between Nation and Nation been obſerved, there
would never have been War above once between
any; or had every free Nation obſerved its own
Laws, every free Nation would have continued
free; or, had private Men obſerved the common
Laws of Equity, and thoſe of mutual Compact
between each other, every private Man would
have lived in Peace and Security. But Treaties,
Compacts, and Laws are only ſo far ſtrong as no
body dares break them.

I think it is *Juvenal*, who ſomewhere brings in
a Couple of falſe Witneſſes perjuring themſelves for
Hire; one is a religious Rogue, and believes in
the Gods; the other is an Infidel, who diſbelieves
or deſpiſes them. But though they diſagree in their
Sentiments, they agree in the Thing, with this
very ſmall Difference; the Atheiſt forſwears himſelf boldly without Remorſe; the Believer forſwears himſelf too, but does it with a ſmall Qualm,
which is preſently over.

————— *Vendet perjuria ſumma*
Exigua, Cereris tangens aramque pedemque.

Bayle very humorouſly engages a *Mandarin* of
China, of the Sect of the *Literati*, in a Dialogue
with the *Jeſuits*, and with a *Dutch* Embaſſador:
The *Jeſuits* tell the *Mandarin*, that the Emperor
had no Subjects in his Dominions, whoſe Obedience

dience was fo fecure to him as that of their Con-
verts the Chriftians ; and none whofe Allegiance
was fo precarious as that of the *Literati*, who were
Atheifts.

" Hold, cries the *Mandarin* ; let us not affert
" too much without proving it : What Reafon
" have you to fay that the Submiffion of the Chri-
" ftians to the Orders of the Emperor is more
" certain than that of all his other Subjects ?"
That Book infpired by God, anfwer the Jefuits ; *that
Book, which is the Rule of our Faith, commands us
exprefly to* fubmit ourfelves to the higher Powers :
*Take the Trouble, my Lord, to read in it fuch and
fuch Paffages : Nothing is more clear, nothing fo pre-
cifely determined.*

" But, *fays the* Mandarin *turning to the Embaf-*
" *fador*, are not you in *Europe* divided about the
" Meaning of thefe Paffages ?

" So divided, *replies the* Dutchman, that one
" Room would not contain the Volumes written
" for and againft the Right of Subjects to refift
" and depofe their Prince : And both Sides take
" particular Care in all their Writings to examine
" accurately every Text of Scripture, which the
" Reverend Fathers refer you to.   This Difcuf-
" fion of Texts has therefore begot two Propofi-
" tions, flatly contradicting each other.   One
" Party afferts, that in departing from your Obe-
" dience, you depart from the *Bible :* The other
" fays, they refift with the *Bible* on their Side.
" We have in *Chriftendom* many Inftances of
" Princes attacked by Parties of their Subjects,
" bereft of their Sovereignty, banifhed, beheaded,
" affaffinated, and generally for the Intereft of
" Religion.   Nor is there any End of the Books
                                    " publifhed

" publifhed on this Occafion ; we have every
" Day printed Accufations, and every Day printed
" Apologies ; and both they who accufe and they
" who defend appeal to God, and refer to his
" Word. As to the *Jefuits* in particular, it be-
" comes them the leaft of all Men to talk in this
" Manner ; no Society of Men have ever written
" fo much in behalf of popular Infurrections ; they
" have openly contended for Rebellion, and prac-
" tifed it ; they have been the Authors of Royal
" Affaffinations, and have been turned out of States
" for difturbing them.

" If thefe Things are fo, *concludes the* Manda-
" rin, you Gentlemen of the Order of *Jefus* have
" no Reafon to boaft in behalf of yourfelves and
" your Followers, as if you were better Subjects
" than other Men. This your pretended Article
" of Faith about the Submiffion of the Subject
" is couched fo obfcurely in your Book of facred
" Laws, that you will never find it there when
" you have Occafion for a Rebellion or a Revo-
" lution ; Events which I find are frequent enough
" in your Country.

The fame *Bayle* obferves, that the fame Party
of Chriftians, namely, the *French* Catholicks, who
had maintained, under *Charles* IX. and *Henry* III.
That it was againft all Laws, human and divine,
for Subjects to take Arms againft their Prince, did
alfo maintain, even before the Death of *Henry* III.
That it was agreeable to Laws, human and divine,
to take up Arms againft one's Prince. The other
Party of Chriftians, namely, the Proteftants, were
not more confiftent. They maintained, during
the Reigns of *Charles* IX. and *Henry* III. That
Laws, human and divine, allowed the fmaller Part
of

of the Subjects to arm themfelves againft the greater
Part even with the King at their Head : But after
the Death of *Henry* III. when they had got a
King of their own Religion, they maintained,
That both the Law of God and the Law of Man
forbid even the greater Part of the Subjects to arm
themfelves againft the fmaller Part with the King
at their Head.

It were needlefs to give more Proofs, and endlefs to give all that might be given.   Almoft every
Thing that Men do, is an Evidence that their
Friendfhip for themfelves does effectually extinguifh their Regard for all the reft of their Species ;
and that they adopt or reject Principles, juft as
thefe Principles promote or contradict their Intereft
and Paffions.

Nor are religious or moral Principles the worfe
for being thus ufed ; but Men fhew their own unconquerable Malignity and Selfifhnefs in ufing them
thus.

Upon the Whole, I think it very plain, that if
you feparate from the Principles of Men the Penalties and Advantages which are annexed to them
by Laws human and divine, or which every Man
has annexed to them in his own Mind, you will
hardly leave fuch a Thing as Principle in the
World ; the World is therefore not governed by
Principle.

    G   *I am,* &c.

SATURDAY, *September* 16, 1721. No. 45.
Of the Equality and Inequality of Men.

S I R,

MEN are naturally equal, and none ever rofe above the reft but by Force or Confent : No Man was ever born above all the reft, nor below them all ; and therefore there never was any Man in the World fo good or fo bad, fo high or fo low, but he had his Fellow. Nature is a kind and benevolent Parent; fhe conftitutes no particular Favourites with Endowments and Privileges above the reft ; but for the moft part fends all her Offfpring into the World furnifhed with the Elements of Underftanding and Strength, to provide for themfelves : She gives them Heads to confult their own Security, and Hands to execute their own Counfels; and according to the Ufe that they make of their Faculties, and of the Opportunities that they find, Degrees of Power and Names of Diftinction grow amongft them, and their natural Equality is loft.

Thus Nature, who is their Parent, deals with Men : But Fortune, who is their Nurfe, is not fo benevolent and impartial; fhe acts wantonly and capricioufly, often cruelly; and counterplotting Juftice as well as Nature, frequently fets the Fool above the wife Man, and the Beft below the Worft.

And from hence it is, that the moft Part of the World, attending much more to the noify Conduct and glaring Effects of Fortune, than to the

the quiet and regular Proceedings of Nature, are
miſled in their Judgment upon this Subject : They
confound Fortune with Nature, and too often
aſcribe to natural Merit and Excellency the Works
of Contrivance or Chance.   This however, ſhews
that Reaſon and Equity run in our Heads, while
we endeavour to find a juſt Cauſe for Things that
are not juſt ; and this is the Source of the Reverence which we pay to Men whom Fortune ſometimes lifts on high, though Nature had placed
them below.   The Populace rarely ſee any Creature riſe, but they find a Reaſon for it in his Parts ;
when probably the true one will be found in his
own Baſeneſs, or another Man's Folly.

From the ſame Reaſoning may be ſeen why it
is, that, let who will be at the Head of a Party,
he is always extolled by his Party as ſuperior to
the reſt of Mankind ; and let who will be the
firſt Man of his Country, he will never fail being
complimented by many as the firſt of his Species.
But the Iſſue and their own Behaviour conſtantly
ſhew, that the higheſt are upon a Level with the
reſt, and often with the loweſt.   Men that are
high are almoſt ever ſeen in a falſe Light ; the
moſt Part ſee them at a great Diſtance, and
through a magnifying Medium ; ſome are dazzled
with their Splendor, many are awed by their
Power.   Whatever appears ſhining or terrible, appears great, and is magnified by the Eye and the
Imagination.

That Nature has made Men equal, we know
and feel ; and when People come to think otherwiſe, there is no Exceſs of Folly and Superſti-
tion which they may not be brought to practiſe.
Thus they have made Gods of dead Men, and
paid

paid divine Honours to many while they were yet living : They faw them to be but Men, yet they worfhipped them as Gods. And even they who have not gone quite fo far, have yet, by their wild Notions of Inequality, done as much Mifchief ; they have made Men, and often wicked Men, to be Vice-Gods ; and then made God's Power (falfly fo called) as irrefiftible in the Hands of Men as in his own, and much more frightful.

It is evident to common Senfe, that there ought to be no Inequality in Society, but for the Sake of Society ; but thefe Men have made one Man's Power and Will the Caufe of all Men's Mifery. They gave him as far as they could the Power of God, without obliging him to practife the Mercy and Goodnefs of God.

Thofe that think themfelves furtheft above the reft, are generally by their Education below them all. They are debafed by a Conceit of their Greatnefs : They truft to their Blood ; which, fpeaking naturally, gives them no Advantage ; and neglect their Mind, which alone, by proper Improvements, fets one Man above another. It is not Blood or Nature, but Art or Accident, which makes one Man excel others. *Ariftotle*, therefore, muft either have been in Jeft, when he faid, that he, who naturally excelled all others, ought to govern all ; or faid it to flatter his Pupil and Prince, *Alexander* the Great. It is certain, that fuch a Man never yet was found in the World, and never will be found till the End of it. *Alexander* himfelf, notwithftanding the Greatnefs of his Spirit, and his Conquefts, had in his own Army, and perhaps among the common Soldiers, Men

naturally

naturally as great and brave as himfelf, and many more wife.

Whoever pretends to be naturally fuperior to other Men, claims from Nature what fhe never gave to any Man. He fets up for being more than a Man; a Character with which Nature has nothing to do. She has thrown her Gifts in common amongft us; and as the higheft Offices of Nature fall to the Share of the Mean as well as of the Great, her vileft Offices are performed by the Great as well as by the Mean : Death and Difeafes are the Portion of Kings as well as of Clowns ; and theCorpfe of a Monarch is no more exempted from Stench and Putrefaction, than the Corpfe of a Slave.

Mors æquo pulfat pede.

All the Arts and Endowments of Men to acquire Pre-eminence and Advantages over one another, are fo many Proofs and Confeffions that they have not fuch Pre-eminence and Advantages from Nature ; and all their Pomp, Titles, and Wealth, are Means and Devices to make the World think that they who poffefs them are fuperior in Merit to thofe that want them. But it is not much to the Glory of the upper Part of Mankind, that their boafted and fuperior Merit is often the Work of Heralds, Artificers, and Money ; and that many derive their whole Stock of Fame from Anceftors, who lived an Age or many Ages ago.

The firft Founders of great Families were not always Men of Virtue or Parts ; and where they were fo, thofe that came after them did frequently, and almoft generally, by trufting to their Blood, difgrace their Name. Such is the Folly

of

of the World, and the Inconvenience of Society, to allow Men to be great by Proxy ! An Evil that can scarce ever be cured. The Race of *French* Kings, called by their Hiftorians in Contempt, *Les Rois faineants* and the Succeffion of the *Roman Cæfars*, (in both which, for one good Prince they had ten that were intolerable, either for Folly, or Cruelty, and often for both) might be mentioned as known Proofs of the above Truth ; and every Reader will find in his own Memory many more.

I have been told of a Prince, who, while yet under Age, being reproved by his Governor for doing Things ill or indecent, ufed to anfwer, *Je fuis Roy* ; *I am King* ; as if his Quality had altered the Nature of Things, and he himfelf had been better than other Men, while he acted worfe. But he fpoke from that Spirit which had been inftilled into him from his Cradle. *I am King !* What then, Sir ? The Office of a King is not to do Evil, but to prevent it. You have Royal Blood in your Veins : But the Blood of your Page is, without being Royal, as good as yours ; or, if you doubt, try the Difference in a Couple of Porringers next Time you are ill; and learn from this Confideration and Experiment, that by Nature you are no better than your People, though fubject from your Fortune to be worfe, as many of your Anceftors have been.

If my Father got an Eftate and Title by Law or the Sword, I may by Virtue of his Will or his Patent enjoy his Acquifition ; but if I underftand neither Law nor the Sword, I can derive Honour from neither : My Honour therefore is, in the

Reason of Things purely nominal; and I am still by Nature a *Plebeian*, as all Men are.

There is nothing moral in Blood, or in Title, or in Place: Actions only, and the Causes that produce them, are moral. He therefore is best that does best. Noble Blood prevents neither Folly, nor Lunacy, nor Crimes: but frequently begets or promotes them: And Noblemen, who act infamously, derive no Honour from virtuous Ancestors, whom they dishonour. A Man who does base Things, is not noble; nor great, if he do little Things: A sober Villager is a better Man than a debauched Lord; an honest Mechanick than a knavish Courtier.

—— *Nobilitas sola est atque unica virtus.*

Prima mihi debes animi bona; *sanctus haberi Justitiæque tenax factis, dictisque mereris?*
                                                    Juv. Sat. 8.

We cannot bring more natural Advantages into the World than other Men do; but we can acquire more Virtue in it than we generally acquire. To be great is not in every Man's Power; but to be good is in the Power of all: Thus far every Man may be vpon a Level with another, the Lowest with the Highest: and Men might thus come to be morally as well as naturally equal.

G

I am, &c.

SATURDAY, *September* 23, 1721. No. 46.

Of the false Guises which Men put on, and their ill Effect.

SIR,

MEN are often capable of doing as much, whether it be Good or Evil, by the Appearance of Parts, as by possessing them ; and become really considerable by being thought so. Some, by pretending to great Interest with the Gods, have gained great Interest among Men; and plagued the Earth, to prove themselves Favourites of Heaven : Others grow great at Court, by being thought great in a Party ; and grow at the same time great in a Party, by being thought great at Court : Twice Liars, they meet with the double Wages of Lying.

Thus is the World deceived ; a Thing so easily done, that rarely any Man sets about it but he succeeds in it, let his Parts be ever so scanty or starved. Murderers have passed for Saints, Buffoons for Wits, and solemn Dunces for wise Men.

I have been often provoked to see a whole Assembly, sometimes neither contemptible for Number, nor Figure, nor Sense, give themselves up to the Guidance and Management of a silly ignorant Fellow, important only in Grimace and Assurance : Nay, Parties, potent Parties, generally throw themselves into the Hands and Direction of Men, who, though they chop them and sell them, yet want every Talent for this Sort of Negotiation, but what they possess in the Credulity of those that

trust

truft them. This is the beft Qualification, and it is fufficient. Thefe are the *Sidrophels*, the cunning Men in Parties, as ignorant as thofe in *Moorfields*; they only know more than thofe whom they deceive, by pretending to more.

The Affectation of Wifdom is a prevailing Folly in the World; Men fall naturally into the Practice of it; and it would be pardonable, as it is common, if it went no further than the aiming at a little Notice and Reverence, which every body may be innocently fond of. But when Men feek Credit this Way, in order to betray, and make ufe of their Grimace as a Trap to deceive; when they turn their Admirers into Followers, and their Followers into Money; then appearing Wifdom becomes real Villainy, and thefe Pretenders grow dangerous Impoftors.

And this is what Men frequently get by trufting more to the Underftanding of others than to their own, though often the better of the two; and therefore we find, in many Inftances, that Fools miflead and govern Men of Senfe. In Things where Men know nothing, they are apt to think that others know more than they; and fo blindly truft to bold Pretenfions: And here is the great Caufe and firft Rife of Sharpers and Bubbles of all Denominations, from Demagogues and their Followers, down to Mountebanks and their Mobs.

I think that there is not a more foolifh Figure in the World than a Man affectedly wife: But it is not every body that fees it: and fuch a one is often the Admiration of one Sort of People, and the Jeft of another, at the fame Time. Where we fee much of the Outfide of Wifdom, it is a

fhrewd

fhrewd Sign that there is but little within; becaufe
they who have the leaft often make the greateft
Shew : As the greateft Hypocrites are the loudeft
Prayers.

The Infide of fuch a Man is not worth knowing; and every Man muft have obferved his Outfide : His Words fall from him with an uncommon Weight and Solemnity ; his Gait is ftately
and flow, and his Garb has a Turn in it of Prudence and Gravity, of which he that made it is
the Author, and by that Means becomes a confiderable Inftrument and Artificer of Wifdom.

This will be better illuftrated in the Character
of Lord *Plaufible*, who having long fet up for a
wife Man, and taking Eloquence to be the moft
effectual Sign of Wifdom, is an Orator and a wife
Man in every Circumftance of his Life, and to
every body ; he is eloquent to his Footman, to his
Children, and at his Table.   Lord *Plaufible* never
converfes ; no, talking carelefly as other People
do, would not be wife enough ; he therefore does
not converfe inCompany, but makes Speeches ; he
meditates Speeches in his Clofet, and pronounces
them where he vifits.   Even while he drinks Tea,
or plays at Cards, his Language is lofty and founding; and in his Gait you fee the fame Sublime as
in his Words.   Add to all this, an unrelenting
Gravity in his Looks, only now and then foftened
by a ftudied Smile.   He never laughs without
checking his Mufcles : Mirth would be a Blot
upon his Wifdom ; the good Man only creates
Mirth in others.

Thus he grows important, without fuffering in
his Character for his natural Shallownefs and acquired Folly, unfeen by the Bulk of his Party,
who,

who, being for Underſtanding and Breeding pretty
much in the lower Claſs, think him an Oracle,
and believe him deep in the Counſels and Reverence of Great Men, who uſe him civilly and
laugh at him.

As a Man can hardly be ſeverely juſt and conſtant to the Ways which he approves, without
ſome Degree of Auſtereneſs, or what the World
calls ſo ; it is no Wonder if this Character, always
eſteemed and often beloved, becomes mimicked
by thoſe who have no Pretence to it. But I am
at a Loſs whether it be more provoking or merry,
to ſee Creatures ſetting up for a Severity of Behaviour, without one Grain of Juſtice and Honour
about them ; pretending to Wiſdom, with great
Conceit and Stupidity ; complaiſant in every Step
and Degree of Corruption, yet preſerving a Stiff-
neſs in their Behaviour, as if they were ſo many
rigid *Stoicks*.

> *Quid? Si vultu torvo & pede nudo*
> *Exiguæque togæ ſimulet textore Catonem ;*
> *Virtutemque repræſentet moreſque Catonis.*

There are Mimicks of Wiſdom and Virtue in
all Ages, as well as in that of *Horace*.

A Man may be a Lord, or a Miniſter, or a
conſiderable Man, without declaring War againſt
Gaiety and Eaſineſs. But grave Fellows, who
become grave to gain Importance, are by all Men
of Senſe diſappointed. A wiſe Man may be a
merry Fellow ; and a very ſilly Fellow may be a
very grave Man. The wiſeſt Men of my Acquaintance are the merrieſt Men that I know ;
nor could I ever find what Wiſdom had to do
with an unpleaſing and rebuking Statelineſs, that
contra-

contradicts it.   Mirth, and what thefe folemn
Drones call Folly, is a Piece of Wifdom which
they want Senfe to know and practife.   Befides,
there is a wife Way of playing the Fool, which
wife Men know how to practife, without lofing
their Character.   But your grave Fellows are perhaps afraid of playing the Fool, becaufe they
would do it too naturally ; yet even that would be
better than being thus ridiculoufly wife againft Nature.

Some Mens natural Heavinefs paffes for Wifdom, and they are admired for being Blockheads.
Sometimes forced Gravity does the fame Thing.
Nor is it any thing new to place Wifdom in Grimace ; many of the old Philofophers did the fame,
and made their long Beards, in particular, an eminent Type of it.

—— *Juffit fapientem pafcere barbam.*

Doubtlefs, like others who have lived fince, they
often poffeffed the Sign only.   The Schoolmen
were reckoned deep and wife Men, for talking
unintelligibly, and their Wifdom was Jargon and
Obfcurity.

They that are really wife, need not take much
Pains to be thought fo ; and they that do, are not
really wife.   We cannot live always upon the
Stretch, either of Silence, or of Eloquence, or of
Gaiety : and whoever endeavours it, fhews his
Folly while he feeks Renown.

A Man of great Quality and Age, and of great
Reputation for Wifdom, being once furprized by
a foreign Minifter, while he was at play with his
little Children, was fo far from confeffing any
Shame for being thus caught indulging the Fancy
and

and Fondnefs of a Father, that he told the Ambaffador, who feemed to have found what he did not expect : " Sir, be in no Pain for me ; he " who is accounted a wife Man in the Morning, " will never be reckoned a Fool at Night." This is, no doubt, true of a Man truly wife. But it is as true, that many Men have paffed for wife Men in the Morning, who have been found Fools before Noon.

Men, affectedly wife, need only be examined to be defpifed ; and we find by Experience, that ftarched Gravity creates more Jeft and Laughter amongft Men of Senfe, who are generally frank and pleafant Men, than the moft remarkable Levity and Giddinefs can do. The Reverence therefore paid to fuch Men, if it be real, is conftantly the Effect of Ignorance : We admire them at a Diftance ; but when we fee them a little nearer, we begin to admire at our own Admiration.

But fuch Examination is never like to be very popular, and confequently fuch Difcoveries are not like to be very formidable ; the Multitude will never make them ; there will always be a great deal in refolving to be great and wife, and great Succefs will be ever attending it : *Si populus vult decipi, decipiatur*, is at all Times a fafe Way of Reafoning. And hence Drones and Coxcombs will, by a falfe Shew of Wifdom, be always bidding fair for the Reputation of Wifdom, and often for its Rewards. This is more eafily fhewn, than mended.
      G

                              I am, &c.

SATURDAY, *October* 7, 1721. No. 47.

Of the Frailty and Uncertainty of human Judgment.

S I R,

HUman Judgment is the beft and fureft Guide that we have to follow, in Affairs that are human; and even in Spirituals, where the immediate Word of God interpofes not. But it is fo liable to be corrupted and weighed down by the Biaffes that Paffion, Delufion, and Intereft hang upon it, that we ought never to truft, without Caution and Examination, either to our own or that of others.

Men are hardly ever brought to think themfelves deceived in contending for Points of Intereft or Pleafure. But as it is rare that one Man's Purfuits do not crofs and interfere with the Purfuits of others, and as every Man contends for the Reafonablenefs of his own; though it muft be in the Nature of Things, that they may be both in the Wrong, and only one can be in the Right : Hence it proceeds that Men, who are fo naturally alike, become morally fo unlike, that fometimes there is more Refemblance between a Man and a Wolf, than between one Man and another; and that one and the fame Man is not one and the fame Man in two different Stations.

The Difference therefore between one Man's Judgment and another's, arifes not fo much from the natural Difference between them; though that too, the Structure of their Organs being different,

may

may beget different Sentiments; as from the Difference of their Education, their Situation and Views, and other external Caufes.

Men, who in private Life were juft, modeft, and good, have been obferved, upon their Elevation into high Places, to have left all their virtuous and beneficent Qualities behind them, and to have acted afterwards upon a new Spirit, of Arrogance, Injuftice, and Oppreffion. And yet, perhaps, their latter Actions had as much the Sanction of their own Judgment as their firft.

England could not boaft of a greater Patriot than the great Earl of *Strafford*, while he was yet a private Commoner. No Man expofed better, or more zealoufly, the Encroachments and Oppreffions practifed by the Court upon the Kingdom, or contended more loudly for a Redrefs of Grievances: But he was no fooner got into the Court, but he began openly to counter-act the wholeCourfe of his paft Life : He devifed new Ways of Terror and Oppreffion, heightened all thofe Grievances of which he had complained; and, as the excellent Lord *Falkland* faid of him in the Houfe of Commons, The Oppreffions which he committed were *fo various, fo many, and fo mighty, as were never committed by any Governor in any Government fince* Verres *left* Sicily. But though the two great Parts of his Life, were thus prodigioufly inconfiftent, I do not remember that he ever condemned. the Worft, though he fuffered for it, or recanted the Beft. It is probable, that his Judgment in both Cafes approved his Conduct.

Nor is the Judgment of Men varied by great and confiderable Caufes only ; to the Difgrace of our Reafon we muft own, that little ones do it as

effectu-

effectually. A wife Man ruffled by an Accident, or heated by Liquor, fhall talk and act like a Madman or a Fool; as a Madman, with a little Soothing and Management, fhall talk like a wife Man: And there are Inftances of very able Men, who, having done great Service to their Prince and Country, have undone it all from Motives that are fhameful to mention.——— Perhaps they miffed a Smile from him, when they expected one; or met with a fatyrical Jeft, when they expected none: and thus, piqued by a little real Mirth or fanfied Neglect, they have run into all the Exceffes of Difloyalty and Rebellion, and either ruined their Country, or themfelves and their Families in attempting it. Others, mifled by a gracious Nod, or a Squeeze by the Hand, or a few fair Promifes no better than either, have, by running all the contrary Lengths of Complaifance and Subferviency, done as much Mifchief to their Country, without intending it any, and perhaps thinking that they did it none. There are Examples of the fame Men practifing both thefe Extremes.

So mechanical a Thing is human Judgment! So eafily is the human Machine difconcerted and put out of its Tone! And the Mind fubfifting in it, and acting by it, is calm or ruffled as its Vehicle is fo. But though the various Accidents and Diforders happening to the Body, are the certain Caufes of Diforders and irregular Operations in the Mind; yet Caufes that are internal affect it ftill more; I mean the Stimulations of Ambition, Revenge, Luft, and Avarice. Thefe are the great Caufes of the feveral irregular and vicious Purfuits of Men.

Neither

Neither is it to be expected, that Men difagree-
ing in Intereft, will ever agree in Judgment.
Wrong, with Advantages attending it, will be
turned into Right, Falfhood into Truth ; and, *as
often as Reafon is againft a Man, a Man will be
againft Reafon:* And both Truth and Right, when
they thwart the Interefts and Paffions of Men,
will be ufed like Enemies, and called Names.

It is remarkable that Men, when they differ in
any Thing confiderable, or which they think confiderable, will be apt to differ in almoft every
thing elfe. Their Differences beget Contradiction, Contradiction begets Heat, Heat quickly rifes
into Refentment, Rage, and Ill-will. Thus they
differ in Affections, as they differ in Judgment ;
and the Contention, which began in Pride, ends in
Anger.

The acquiefcing fincerely in the Judgment of
another, without the Concurrence of our own,
and without any Advantage, real or fanfied, mov-
ing us to fuch Acquiefcence, is a Compliment
which I do not know that one Man ever paid to
another: An unanfwerable Argument, why no
Man fhould be provoked at thofe whom he cannot convince; fince they, having Reafons, or
thinking that they have Reafons, on the contrary
Side, as ftrong as his, or ftronger, have as much
Caufe to be provoked with him for not acquiefcing
in theirs. Yet there are but few Debates of Confequence in this World, where the Arguments are
not feconded by Wrath, and often fupplied by it.

But this is not the Way of dealing with Men ;
nor is there any other Way of perfuading them
into your Judgment, but by fhewing it their
Intereft. Their Minds are fo corrupted by their
                                        Appetites,

Appetites, that, generally fpeaking, their Judgment is nothing but their Intereft in Theory ; and
their Intereft is their Judgment reduced into Practice.   This will account for the contradictory
Parts which Men play, and the contrary Parties
that they occafionally choofe.   This ferves them
with Reafons for the unreafonable Things that
they do, turns Roguery into Honefty, Madnefs
into Merit.

In Truth, whenever Men leave their own
Judgment for the Judgment of others, as they
fometimes do, they either do it for Gain, or
Glory, or Pleafure, or for the avoiding of Shame,
or fome fuch Caufe ; all which Motives are Intereft, as is every Thing elfe that they do for their
own Sakes.   Thus Honefty is often only the Fear
of Infamy, and Honour the Appetite of Applaufe:
Thus Men rufh into Danger and Death, to gratify Love or Anger, or to acquire Fame : And
thus they are faithful to their Word and Engagement, to avoid the Reproach of Treachery.

Men are fo apt to link their Approbation to
their Profit and Pleafure, that their Intereft,
though ever fo vile, abfurd, and unjuftifiable, becomes really their Judgment.   I do not think that
human Art and Imagination could have invented
Tenets more falfe and abominable, more chimerical or mifchievous, than are thofe of the *Infallibility of the Pope*, and the *Irrefiftiblenefs of Tyrants* ;
that is, that one Man, living in the hourly Practice of Error, or Vice, or Folly, and often of
them all, fhall judge for the whole Earth, and do
what God has not done ; that is, fafhion the
Minds of all the human Race like his own, and make
them his Sacrifices, where he cannot make them

his Slaves : And that another Man fhall have a di-vine Right to reprefent God and govern Man, by acting againft God and deftroying Man.

Thefe are fuch monftrous Abfurdities, fuch terrible, ridiculous, and inhuman Inventions, as could arife from nothing but Pride and Avarice on one Side, and Fear and Flattery on the other ; and could be defended by nothing but the moft brutifh Force, or the moft abandoned Impudence. Yet we have feen thefe monftrous Abfurdities defended, and God Almighty declared their De-fender ; even Him, who is the God of Mercy and Truth, made, blafphemoufly, the Author of Cruelty and Lies.

In this Light do thefe Things appear to one who confiders them without embarking in them, and receiving any Advantage from them. But thofe who gain or fubfift by them, fee them in a different Light : I doubt not but their Judgment, as they call it, does actually blend with their In-tereft, or for the moft part does ; and therefore they are really in earneft in maintaining it. Folly, Falfhood, and Villainy, are no longer called by their own Names, nor thought to deferve them, by thofe that reap Advantages from them. Even thofe, who have practifed the greateft of all Evils, even that of deftroying God's People, have thought that in doing it they did God good Service. Our bleffed Saviour foretold it ; and his Words have been fulfilling ever fince, and perhaps will be till he return.

Oliver Cromwell fought God in all his Oppref-fions ; and though I am fure that he was an Ufurper, I am not fure that he was a Hypocrite, at leaft all along ; though it is moft probable that he was one

at

at firft.   But he had fo long perfonated a Saint,
that he feems at laft to have thought himfelf one ;
and when he faw his latter End approaching, he
was fo far from fhewing any Compunction for the
Part which he had acted, that he, on the contrary, boafted that he had been the Caufe of much
Good to this Nation; and added fuch Ejacula-
tions and Prayers, as fhewed that he poffeffed his
Mind in Peace, and was not without Confidence
in God.

The Emperor of *Morocco*, than whom a more
inhuman Butcher never lived, makes God the
Author of all his Barbarities; and when he murders a Slave (as he does every Day fome) out of
Wantonnefs or Wrath, he lifts up his Eyes and
fays, *'Tis God that does it :* No Man talks more of
God and Religion, and he certainly thinks himfelf
a moft religious Man.

Let all this ferve to fhew, how little Mens
Judgment is to be trufted when Intereft follows it,
and is probably both the Caufe and the Effect.
Let it abate our Confidence in particular Men,
who may make our Truft in them the Means of
their mifleading us : Let us learn to believe no
Man the more, for that he believes himfelf; fince
Men are as obftinate in Error, efpecially in gainful Error, as they are in Truth; and more fo,
where Truth is not gainful: And laftly, let us
fwallow no Man's Judgments, without judging of
it and him ; and yield up our Reafon to no Man's
Authority, nor our Intereft to any Man's Direction, any farther than Prudence or Neceffity obliges us. Let us remember what the World has ever
got by implicit Faith of any Kind whatfoever.

G   *I am*, &c.

SATUR-

SATURDAY, *October* 14, 1721. No. 48.

*The general unhappy State of the World, from the
Bafeneſs and Iniquity of its Governors in moſt
Countries.*

S I R,

WHILE I have been reading Hiſtory, or confidering the State of human Affairs, how
wofully they are neglected, how fooliſhly managed,
or how wickedly diſconcerted and confounded, in
the moſt and beſt Countries : When I have remembered how large, every where, is the Source
of Miſchief, how eaſily it is ſet a running, and
how plentifully it flows ; how it is daily breaking
into new Channels, and yet none of the old ones
are ever ſuffered to wax dry: I have been apt to
wonder, that the general Condition of Mankind,
though already vaſtly unhappy, is not ſtill worſe.

Pope *Æneas Sylvius* muſt have had ſuch Reflections as theſe, when he ſaid, that *this World did, in
a great Meaſure, govern itſelf.* He had many Examples before his Eyes, how eaſy it was to govern
wretchedly, and yet continue to govern. The
Papacy itſelf might particularly have furniſhed him
with many Examples. It is a Fairy Dominion,
founded upon Non-Entities, Inventions, and Abo-
minations ; ſupported by Lies and Terrors; exerciſed with Cruelty, Craft, and Rapine ; and producing Meanneſs, Deluſion, and Poverty, where-
ever it prevails.

What

What could appear more ftrange, incredible, and fhameful, than to fee a mean Monk, refiding in a Corner of the World, and ruling and plundering it all; living in Crimes, Pride and Folly, and controuling *Chriftendom* by the Sounds of Humility, Holinefs, and Infallibility; fubfifting upon the Spoils and Induftry of Nations, and engaging Nations in a blind Confpiracy againft themfelves, for the Defence of their Oppreffor; pronouncing the Peace of God to Mankind, and animating Mankind to continual Quarrels and Slaughters; declaring himfelf the Vicar of Chrift, and making unrelenting War againft the Followers of Chrift; and, finally, the Father of *Chriftendom*, and the Deftroyer of Chriftians.

All this Villainy and Impudence was obvious to common Senfe, and felt by long Experience. But how little do Men fee, when they are taught to be afraid of their Eye-fight! Even the *Reformation*, one of the greateft Bleffings that ever befel *Europe*, has but partially removed this mighty and enormous Ufurpation. The Root of the Evil ftill remains: and Men are not yet weary of fighting about Words, Subtilties, Chimeras, and about the Shape of their Thoughts and Imagination; a Thing as much out of their own Power, as the Shape of their Limbs, or the Motion of the Winds: The Iffue and Defign of all which is, that their Leaders in Strife reap the Fruits of it, and gather the Spoils, the whole Spoils of thofe Battles, in which Craft only blows the Trumpet, while Ignorance weilds the Sword, and runs all the Danger.

If in this, as in other Wars, none would fight but thofe that are paid, or find their Account in
fighting,

fighting, the Combatants would foon be reduced to a few ; and they too would quickly leave a Field where there was no Booty.

Will the World never learn, that one Man's Corn grows not the worfe, becaufe another Man ufes different Words in his Devotion? That Pride and Anger, Wealth and Power, are of no Religion? And that Religion is infeparable from Charity and Peace?

I am told, that the famous Combuftion raifed fome Years ago at *Hamburgh*, by one *Krumbultz*, a Divine, and in which that free City had like to have perifhed, was occafioned by this momentous Queftion, namely, Whether in the Lord's Prayer we fhould fay, *Our Father*, or, *Father our*. ⸺ A hopeful Point of Debate, to be the Caufe of Civil Diffention, and a true Specimen of the Importance and Confequences of Ecclefiaftical Difputes, and of the Spirit of thofe that manage them !

It is a fhameful Satire upon the Wickednefs of fome, and the Weaknefs of others, thus to endanger the Peace of Society and their own, for the Sake of a Sound ; to be thus eager for Trifles ; thus to concern Heaven and Earth in behalf of Conceits, which of themfelves concern neither: but, as they are generally managed, do both provoke God, and hurt Men.   But fo it will ever be, as long as Men, in Poffeffion of Reverence, find their Ends and Gratifications in fetching knotty Diftinctions out of the plain Word of God, and making them of equal Importance with it.

Thus unhappy has the greateft Part of the World been, and is, in its Ghoftly Government ; two Words which are a Contradiction to each other ;

fince

CATO's LETTERS. 107

since the Mind and Underſtanding, in which alone
all Religion that is rational doth reſide, can never
be altered or controuled by any other Means than
that of Counſel, Reaſoning, and Exhortation ;
which Method is utterly inconſiſtent with Force
and poſitive Authority, as the ſame are implied in
the Idea of Government.

Nor can I ſay, that Mankind have been more
happy in their Civil Lot, and in the Adminiſtration of their Temporal Affairs ; which are almoſt
every where in a wretched Situation, and they
themſelves under the Iron Hand of the Oppreſſor.
The whole terraqueous Globe cannot ſhew Five
free Kingdoms; nor perhaps half ſo many Kings,
who make the Eaſe and Proſperity of their People
their Care.

In enſlaved Countries (that is, in all Countries,
except our own, and a very few more) the Good
of the Governed is ſo far from entering into the
Hearts and Counſels of the Governors, that it is
oppoſite to the Genius of their Politicks, either to
do them Good, or to ſuffer them to acquire it for
themſelves. Their Happineſs and Security, which
are the very Ends of Magiſtracy, would be terrible to their Magiſtrates ; who, being the publick
Enemies of their Country, are forced, for their
own Safety, to leave their People none.

How vile is that Government, and thoſe Governors, whoſe only Strength lies in Whips and
Chains ; a ſort of Inſtrument of Servitude, which
it would much better become the Baſeneſs of theſo
Mens Natures to wear themſelves, than to inflict
upon others ! A Prince of Slaves is a Slave; he
is only the biggeſt and the worſt ; juſt as the Chief
of the Banditti is one of them. Such a Prince is
but

but a National Executioner, and for a Scepter he carries a bloody Knife.

Such, for the moſt part, by far the moſt part, are the Governors of the World: They derive their whole Greatneſs, Plenty, Splendor, and Security, from the Miſery, Poverty, Peril, and Deſtruction of the Governed. Whoever makes juſt, equal, and impartial Laws, does, by doing ſo, but declare to the People, *Be wicked at your Peril:* But he who rules them by Terrors and Standing Armies, does, in Effect, tell them in a terrible Tone, *Be happy if you dare.*

Who, that has human Compaſſion, can help feeling the Sorrows of his wretched Race, and behold, unconcerned, the forlorn and abject State of Mankind? Monks deceiving, alarming, and ſpunging them; their Governors taxing, mulcting, and ſqueezing them! Soldiers harraſſing, oppreſſing, and butchering them! And, in ſhort, all the bitter Evils and crying Miſeries in human Power to inflict, deliberately and daily inflicted upon them! Nor do Things mend; on the contrary, the Miſchiefs and Misfortunes of the World grow hourly greater, and its Inhabitants thinner.

All theſe black Conſiderations would lead a Man, who had no other Spirit or Guide but that of Nature, to think that Providence, tempted by the Sins of Men, had long ago renounced them, or ſigned a Decree of Vengeance againſt them, which has ever ſince been dreadfully executed, and continues to be.

If one was to conſider Mankind in Theory only, his own Species would make no ſmall Figure in his Imagination; he would ſee them formed by a divine Hand, and according to a di-

vine

vine Model; poffeffed of all the Advantages of
Strength and Contrivance, guided by Reafon,
made wife by Obfervation, and cautious by their
own Forefight and the Experience of others; directed by Laws and human Conftitutions; rendered difcerning by the frequent Trials of Good
and Evil, and many of them enlightened by divine
Revelation : He would fee them Lords of the Creation, Arbiters of their own Condition and Felicity, invefted with the Ufe and Property of Sea
and Land, and with Dominion over every other
Creature.

Thus Mankind appear in Speculation, powerful, wife, juft, equal, and happy. But viewed in
another Light, they make another Appearance.
They ufe one another worfe than they do the
Beafts of the Field ; and, by the wretched and
monftrous Œconomy and Government, almoft
every where found amongft them, they would
feem not to have more Underftanding, as they
have certainly lefs Happinefs. The Beafts no
where appoint or fuffer one of their own Herd to
monopolize the whole Soil, to engrofs every Advantage to himfelf, to deprive them of all, to kill
and deftroy, to difperfe and to ftarve them at his
Pleafure. Every one of them equally enjoys the
Shelter and Pafture, the Air and the Water, which
Nature makes common to them all.

But Men, their Mafters, cannot boaft fuch Security and Juftice : they generally live at the mere
Mercy of One, one of themfelves, whofe Views
fuffer him to have no Mercy. He is often a Madman, often an Idiot, often a Deftroyer ; and the
whole Art of his Government confifting in oppreffing

preffing and terrifying, no other Talent is required but a mercilefs Spirit and brutal Force.

Such is an Arbitrary Prince, and the Defcen-
dants of *Adam* know few others. Sometimes a
Creature is feen to ftart into Imperial Power,
whom the World never knew before, or knew
only for his Infamy : Taken out of the Stews or
out of a Dungeon, into a Throne ; and without
knowing how to rule himfelf, he rules an Empire ;
living a Reclufe, and feen by nobody, he governs
all but the Women or Parafites, who govern
him : Millions of Men, and their Properties, are
at the fole Difcretion of one who has none ; and a
Creature void of Humanity difpofes wantonly of a
great Part of human Kind.

This is the difmal State of all *Afia* and of all
Africa, except a few free Towns. The Spirit of
their Monarchs, which is generally alike, may be
feen in a Story (among many others) which *Knox*
tells us of the King of *Ceilon*, who, being in Danger of drowning, was faved by the officious Affection or Ambition of one of his Slaves, who leaped
into the Water, and ventured his own Life to preferve his Mafter's. This, one would think, was
the greateft and moft heroick Kindnefs that one
Man could do another. But mark how the Monarch requites it ! why, the firft Thing he did
after he came to himfelf, was to order the Belly
of his Preferver to be ripped up, for daring to touch
the Perfon of his facred Majefty.

Nature has prepared many Advantages and Pleafures for the Ufe of Mankind, given them Tafte
to enjoy them, and Sagacity to improve them :
But their Governors, almoft univerfally, fruftrate
the

the kind Purpofes of Nature, render her Bene-
ficence abortive, and marr all human Happinefs.
They have fuccefsfully ftudied the Arts of Mifery,
and propagated the Practice.

It is a melancholy Reflection, that when human Affairs are put into a bad Way, where they
do not fpeedily recover, they never recover, or
rarely ever. One great Reafon is, that Power is
always on the worft Side, either promoting Mifchief, or preventing its Removal ; and the Champions of Difhonefty and Oppreffion are more artful
and better paid than the Patrons of Juftice and Innocence.

It has hitherto been the good Fortune of *England* (and I hope always will be) when Attempts
have been made upon its Liberty, to recover it
before it was gone, at leaft before the Senfe of it
was gone. And therefore it ftill fubfifts in fpite of
all the powerful, popular, and fanctified Attacks
that have been made, and frequently made, upon
it. Let us make much of it ; while it remains, it
will make us Amends for all the Loffes and Mifcarriages which we have fallen under, or may fall
under, and will enable us to get the better of them.
It is the Root of our Felicity, and all our Civil
Advantages grow from it. By it we exceed almoft all other Nations, many more Degrees than
fome of them exceed us in Sun and Soil: We are
Men, and they are Slaves. Only Government
founded upon Liberty, is a publick Bleffing ; without Liberty, it is a publick Curfe, and a publick
Warrant for Depredation and Slaughter.

Let us therefore remember the mighty Difference between ourfelves and other Nationt, and the
glorious Caufe of it, and always dearly cherifh it.

We

We are not the Prey of Monks, or Janizaries, or Dragoons, nor the blind Slaves of unaccountable Will and Pleasure.   Our Lives and Properties are secured by the best Bulwark in the World, that of Laws made by ourselves, and executed by our Magistrates, who are likewise made by us; and when they are dishonestly executed, or wilfully neglected, our Constitution affords a Remedy, a tried and a practicable Remedy.   And as no Nation ever lost its Liberty but by the Force of Foreign Invaders, or the domestick Treachery of its own Magistrates; we have the Sea and a great Navy for our Defenders against the former; and Exorbitancies of the other are prevented or restrained by an excellent Counterpoise, in the Frame of our Legislature.

That we may be for ever able to boast of all these Blessings, these glorious and uncommon Blessings, is the cordial Wish and passionate Prayer of

G

Your's, &c.

Of the Power of Prejudice.

S I R,

MEN boast of their Reason, and might justly, if they used it freely, and applied it properly; but considering that generally in their moral Conduct they are guided by such Reasons as are a Shame and a Contradiction to Reason, it seems to be thrown away upon them : Indeed so little, or so wrong, is the Use which they make of it, that

it

it would be really for their Reputation if they had none.

But though the Many scarce use it all, and none so much as they ought; yet every Man thinks he does, and never wants something which he calls Reason, for the Justification of his Folly or Wickedness. Prejudice or Passion steps into its Room, takes its Name; and, under the Appearance of Reason, does Things which Reason abhors. And thus Reason, as well as Religion, is forced to furnish its Enemies with Arms against itself; and the Abuse of it is worse and more dangerous than the absolute Want of it; as an Idiot is less terrible and less odious than a Knave, and as a harmless *Pagan* is a much more amiable Character than an outrageous persecuting Bigot. So that as no Religion at all is better than a mischievious Religion; that is to say, any Religion that prompts Men to hurt one another; so the Absence or Inactivity of the Faculties is better than the Quickness of Faculties wickedly applied.

Of all the many false Lights that mislead Men from their Reason, Prejudice is one of the foremost and most successful; and though no two Things upon Earth are more opposite in their Natures, or more destructive of each other, than Reason and Prejudice are; yet they are often made to pass for each other: And as some Men will give you very good Reasons for their being in the wrong themselves, there are those too, who will give you as good, why others should not be in the right; that is, the Prejudices of some would be thought Wisdom, and the Wisdom of others is miscalled Prejudice. The worst Things that Men do, called by a good Name, pass for the best; and the

best

beft, blackened by an ill Name, pafs for the worft. Such is the Force of Prejudice in the World, and fo fuccefsfully does this Foe to Reafon ape Reafon !

Prejudice is an obftinate and unreafonable Attachment to an Opinion, fupported only by a Wilfulnefs to maintain it, whether regarding Men or Things: It links the good with the bad, the bad with the good, and hates or loves by the Lump. Thus if a Man be called a Saint, his worft Actions are fainted with him; his very Ignorance and Cruelty, and even his Dirtinefs and his Dreams, are made facred and meritorious ; as may be feen at large in the *Romifh* Legends, where the principal Qualification for Saintfhip feems to have confifted in ftark raving Madnefs, and in an implacable and bloody Fury towards all Senfe and Sobriety. And thus, even with us, if a Man paffes for a good Man, his bad Deeds are often thought good ones, by thofe that think him fo, and only becaufe they think him fo.

On the other Side, if a Man be called an *Atheift*, the Odium of that Name, where it is believed true, is made a Blot upon his beft Actions and greateft Virtues, and to defeat them as well as foil them. That there are fuch Men as *Atheifts*, can only be imagined by thofe, who, doubting of a Deity themfelves, may naturally enough fuppofe that there are others who quite difbelieve One : For my own particular, I cannot think that there are any fuch Men ; but if there were, I cannot think that Truth and Sobriety in an *Atheift* are worfe than in another Man. That Black is not White, and that Two and Two make Four, is as true out of the Mouth of an *Atheift*, as out of the

the Mouth of an Apostle : A Penny given by an *Atheist* to a Beggar, is better Alms than a Half-penny given by a Believer; and the good Sense of an *Atheist* is preferable to the Mistakes of a good Christian : In short, whatever reputed *Atheists* do well, or speak truly, is more to be imitated and credited, than what the greatest Believers do wickedly, or say falsly ; and even in the Business of bearing Testimony, or making a Report, in which Cases the Credit and Reputation of the Witness gives some Weight, or none, to what he says, more Regard is to be had to the Word of an Unbeliever who has no Interest on either Side, than than to the Word of a Believer who has.

So that as no Man is to be believed an Atheist, unless he be evidently proved one; which, where he himself denies it, can be done by God only : So neither are the good or bad Actions of an *Atheist* worse, with respect to the World at least, for his being one; though the Sin of a Saint is more sinful than that of a *Pagan*. As it is therefore the blackest and most barbarous Villainy to charge any Man with Atheism, who is no *Atheist*; it is the greatest Folly to think that any Man's Crimes are the less for the Name of him that commits them ; or that Truth is less or more Truth, for the ill or good Name of him that speaks it.

Prejudice has long taught Men, contrary to all Reason, to think otherwise ; and to consider, not what was done or said, but who were the Men that said or did it. —— A happy Expedient, I must own, to acquire Dominion, and to exercise it , and to keep, for that End; Mankind ignorant and base, as their Teachers and Governors too generally keep them ! And therefore, in most Parts
of

of the World, Truth is a capital Crime ; and the
Pope and *Mahomet*, the *Alcoran* and the *Mafs-Book*,
and the like Sounds, with a competent Affiftance
of Fire and Sword, are fufficient to convince and
govern all true *Catholicks* and *Muffulmen*.

But we live in a Land of Liberty ; and have,
I hope, well-nigh wiped off the Scandal of being
led or animated by Noife or Names, as were many
of our Forefathers ; whofe Reafon, being in other
Mens keeping, was generally turned upon them,
and co-operated with other Caufes towards keeping them in Bondage. They were decoyed or
frightened into Folly and Chains ; fome faw not
their Condition, others wanted Courage or Power
to mend it. But with Liberty Light has fprung
in, and we have got rid of the Terror and Delufion occafioned by folemn and ill founding Names ;
a fort of Bugbears that frighten only in the Dark :
We have learned, that we are as fit to ufe our
own Underftandings, as they are whofe Underftandings are no better than ours ; and that there
is no Merit in Sounds, nor in thofe Actions which
a wicked Man may practife as well as a good Man,
without departing from his Character.

True Learning and Prejudices cannot fubfift together ; and therefore, though in Societies of Pedants, little elfe is to be found but Prejudices, Bitternefs, Ignorance, and Ill-Breeding ; I am amazed to hear, that in Societies of Gentlemen, formed for the promoting of Knowledge, and Liberty
of Enquiry, a Province utterly inconfiftent with
the narrow Spirit of Prejudice, there are yet found
Inftances of the greateft. I hope, however, that
it is not true, what I am told, That the *Royal
Society* refufed admitting Mr. *Whifton* and another
                                        ingenious

ingenious Gentleman as Members, becaufe the one was an *Arian*, and the other a *Black*. Who would imagine, that natural Complexion, or religious Opinions, could any way affect the Difcovery of Foffils and Cocklefhels, or the Improvement of Muftard and Pickles? But I dare fay, that this is only a Story raifed, to bring that learned Body into Ridicule and Contempt: If it were true, it would juftify the Jeft made upon them by a Gentleman, who, being afked by fome of them, Whether he had a mind to be a Member? told them, *No, Gentlemen, 'tis impoffible; you fee I have a Mole on my Upper Lip, and I am fubject to talk in my Sleep.*

It is fcarce credible, but that wee fee it, how violently and fhamefully Prejudice flies in the Face of Reafon, and often gets the better of it, in Inftances too where Reafon feems to be ftrongeft and moft obvious. I fhall mention a remarkable one.

Alexander and *Cæfar* are never mentioned but with Applaufe, or thought of but as amiable Characters, and the true Patterns of Princes and Heroes, though it is certain that there never lived more wicked Men; they turned the World upfide down, and ufurped its Power; they paved their Way to Dominion with dead Bodies, and were the Oppreffors and Butchers of human Race. Here is Fact, plain undeniable Fact, againft Prejudice and Opinion-

Oliver Cromwell, on the contrary, is fcarce ever mentioned but with Deteftation, or thought of but as a Monfter; though it is as certain that he never did the hundredth Part of the Mifchief that was done by either of the other Two. He had at leaft
as

as good a Right to *Great Britain* as they had to the Globe, and ruled it with more Equity and lefs Blood. He was, doubtlefs, an Ufurper, but a little one; and though wicked enough, really an innocent Man compared to them. Nor was he at all below them in Parts and Courage. What therefore is the Caufe of this mighty and unjuft Difference, where the leffer Wickednefs is moft magnified, and leaft excufed; and where the blackeft Criminals and the higheft Ufurpers are admired and extolled?

There is yet one Effect of Prejudice more impious than all the reft; I mean, the daring Prefumption of thofe Men who wantonly apply the Judgments of God to others, and of calling thofe Things Judgments which are not fo. Probably nothing ever yet happened to one Man, but has happened to another, and a different Man: The Wicked live in as much Profperity, and die with as few Agonies, as do the Righteous; who, I think, are allowed to be here below much the more unhappy of the Two. Who has told us, what God can only tell, that Misfortunes are Judgments, or that Death is one? That Death which is common to all Men? And as to the different and difaftrous Manners of Dying; have not Fire and Sword, Famine and Peftilence, Poifon and Torture, wild Beafts and Accidents, deftroyed as many good Men as evil Men?

How foolifh and infolent are we! When we are angry, unreafonably angry with one another, we prefumptuoufly think that God, the good and all-wife God, is fo too; by which we profanely fuggeft, that he is a Being as weak, ridiculous, and paffionate as ourfelves. Whereas that often

pleafes

pleafes God, which is hated by Man; and that which is really a Bleffing, is often thought a Curfe: and therefore fome wickedly think the Judgment of God due to others for Things that entitle them rather to God's Favour. So wickedly do Men differ in their Sentiments and Affections !

They who call the Misfortunes of others Judgments upon them, plainly enough own, though not in Words, that they wifh for Judgments upon others, or are glad when they happen. What can we fay of fuch an antichriftian Spirit as this ?

When the Heathens were uppermoft, they charged the Chriftians with being the Caufe of all the Evils and Misfortunes that befel the *Roman* Empire, fuch as Inundations, Plagues, Earthquakes, and the like ; and one of the Fathers writ a Book, to prove, that all thofe Things had been from the Beginning ; and whoever makes the like Charge now againft any Man, or Body of Men, may be filenced, if he has Modefty, Senfe, or Shame, in him, by the fame Anfwer.

G   *I am,* &c.

SATUR-

SATURDAY, *October* 28, 1721.   No. 50.

An Idea of the Turkifh *Government, taken from Sir* Paul Ricaut.

S I R,

SIR *Paul Ricaut*'s *State of the* Ottoman *Empire*, is what I have quoted before in thefe Letters : It is written with Fidelity and Judgment, and gives us a good Idea of that horrible and deftroying Government ; a Government fierce and inhuman, founded in Blood, fupported by Barbarity ; and a Government that has a declared Enmity to all that is good and lovely in the Eyes of Mankind.

I have therefore tranfcribed the following Paffage from him, to fhew my Countrymen the abject, the deplorable Condition of that People, and the brutifh and deftructive Genius of their Government, and I do it with a benevolent View, to make them more and more in love with their own, and paffionate for its Prefervation.

No Man's Authority is, or ought to be, of any Weight for or againft Truth, when every Man fees it, or may fee it : But fince weak Men, and they that are worfe, make a Difficulty of crediting the Reafonings and Relations of any Men about any Thing, unlefs they know and approve his Opinions in every Thing ; I think it not amifs to acquaint my Readers, that Sir *Paul* was a fincere Monarchy-man, and an unqueftionable Friend to our Civil and Religious Eftablifhment; but having long feen the difmal Terrors and Defolations

of

of abfolute Monarchy, he could not help obferve-
ing the infinite Diftance between that and a limited one ; as may be feen in the following Quotation.

For my own particular, I think it contrary to
common Senfe to concern myfelf with the Character of a Writer, in thofe Writings which do
not concern his Character : And therefore in Matters of Reafon or Fact, *Cicero* is as much regarded
by me as Dr. *Tillotfon* ; and I credit *Livy* as much
as I do Dr. *Prideaux*. For this Reafon, in reading Authors, Chriftian or Heathen, Monarchical
or Republican, I do not confider their Syftem,
but their Senfe ; which I fhall therefore, as often
as I fee neceffary, give in their own Words, where
I cannot mend them : And as often as they fpeak
my Thoughts as well, or better than I could fpeak
them myfelf, I fhall not fcruple being beholden to
them.

G   *I am,* &c.

" HE that is an Eye-witnefs and ftrict Obfer-
" ver of the various Changes and Chances
" in the Greatnefs, Honours, and Riches of the
" *Turks,* hath a lively Emblem before him of the
" Unconftancy and Mutability of human Affairs.
" Fortune fo ftrangely fports with this People,
" that a Comedy or a Tragedy on the Stage,
" with all its Scenes, is fcarce fooner opened or
" ended, than the Fate of divers great Men, who
" in the Day-time being exhaled into high Sub-
" limity by the powerful Rays of the *Sultan*'s
" Favour, fall or vanifh in the Night, like a Me-
" teor. The Reafon hereof, if duly confidered,
" may be of great Ufe as Things ftand here ;
                                    " that

" that is, the Power of the *Grand Seignior* ; for in
" this Conftitution, the Benefit of the Emperor
" is confulted before the Welfare of the People.

* * * * * * * * * * * * * *

" And this Courfe does not only evidence the
" Power of the *Grand Seignior* ; but likewife en-
" creafes it : For none are advanced in thefe
" Times to Office, but pay the *Grand Seignior*
" vaft Sums of Money for it, according to the
" Riches and Expectations of Profit from the
" Charge. Some pay, as the *Bafhaws* of *Grand*
" *Cairo* and *Babylon*, Three or Four Hundred
" Thoufand Dollars upon paffing the Commif-
" fion ; others One, others Two Hundred Thou-
" fand ; fome Fifty Thoufand, as their Places are
" more or lefs confiderable ; and the Money is
" moft commonly taken up at Intereft at 40 or
" 50 *per Cent.* for the Year, and fometimes at
" double, when they are conftrained to become
" Debtors to the covetous Eunuchs of the *Seraglio.*
" So that every one, at his firft Entrance into
" Office, looks upon himfelf (as indeed he is)
" greatly indebted, and obliged, by Juftice or In-
" juftice, right or wrong, fpeedily to difburthen
" himfelf of the Debts, and improve his own
" Principal in the World ; and this Defign muft
" not be long in Performance, left the hafty Edict
" overtake him before the Work is done, and call
" him to an Account for the Improvement of his
" Talent.

" Taking then all Circumftances together, the
" covetous Difpofition of a *Turk*, the Cruelty
" and Narrownefs of Soul in thofe Men com-
" monly that are born and educated in Want ;
" think what Oppreffion, what Rapine and Vio-
" lence

" lence muſt be exerciſed, to ſatisfy the Appetite
" of theſe Men, who come famiſhed with im-
" menſe Deſires and ſtrange Conſiderations to
" ſatisfy ! *Diu ſordidus, repente dives mutationem*
" *fortunæ male regit, accenſis ageſtate longa cupidi-*
" *nibus immoderatus.* Tacit. So that Juſtice in its
" common Courſe is ſet to Sale ; and it is very
" rare, when any Law-Suit is in Hand, but Bar-
" gains are made for the Sentence ; and he hath
" moſt Right, who hath moſt Money to make
" him *rectus in curia*, and advance his Cauſe ;
" and it is the common Courſe for both Parties at
" Difference, before they appear together in Pre-
" ſence of the Judge, to apply themſelves ſingly
" to him, and try whoſe Donative and Preſent
" hath the moſt in it of Temptation ; and it is
" no Wonder if corrupt Men exerciſe this Kind
" of Trafficking with Juſtice, for having before
" bought the Office, of Conſequence they muſt
" ſell the Fruit.

" Add hereunto a ſtrange Kind of Facility in
" the *Turks*, for a Trifle or ſmall Hire, to give
" falſe Witneſs in any Caſe, eſpecially (and that
" with a Word) when the Controverſy happens
" between a Chriſtian and a *Turk* ; and then the
" Pretence is for the *Muſſulmanleek*, as they call
" it ; the Cauſe is religious, and hallows all Falſe-
" neſs and Forgery in the Teſtimony. * * *
* * * * * * * * * * * * * * * *

" This Conſideration and Practice made an
" *Engliſh* Embaſſador, upon renewing the Capi-
" tulations, to inſert an Article of Caution againſt
" the Teſtimony of *Turks*, as never to be admit-
" ted or pleaded in any Court of *Turkiſh* Juſtice,
" againſt the *Engliſh* Intereſt. * * * * *

" In

" In the Times of the beft Emperors, when
" Virtue and Deferts were confidered, and the
" Empire flourifhed and encreafed, Men had Of-
" fices conferred upon them for their Merits, and
" good Services were rewarded freely and with
" Bounty, without Sums of Money and Payments.
" ——But now it is quite contrary, and all
" Matters run out of Courfe ; a manifeft Token,
" in my Opinion, of the Declenfion and Decay
" of the Empire !——However, this ferves in
" part the great End of the Empire ; for *Bafhaws*
" and great Men, having a kind of a Neceffity
" upon them to opprefs their Subjects, the People
" thereby lofe their Courage ; and by continual
" Taxes and Seizures upon what they gain, Po-
" verty fubdues their Spirits, and makes them
" more patiently fuffer all kind of Injuftice and
" Violence that can be offered them, without
" Thoughts or Motion to Rebellion : And fo the
" Lord *Verulam* fays in his Effays, That it is im-
" poffible for a People overladen with Taxes ever
" to become martial or valiant ; for no Nation
" can be the Lion's Whelp, and the Afs between
" two Burthens.

" By this Means the *Turk* preferves fo many
" different Sorts of People, as he hath conquered,
" in due Obedience, ufing no other Help than a
" fevere Hand, joined to all kind of Oppreffion :
" But fuch as are *Turks*, and bear any Name of
" Office or Degree in the Service of the Empire,
" feel but Part of this Oppreffion, and live with
" all Freedom, having their Spirits raifed by a
" Licence they attain to infult over others that
" dare not refift them.

" But

" But the Iſſue and Concluſion of the Spoils
" that theſe great Men make on Subjects is very
" remarkable : For, as if God were pleaſed to
" evidence his juſt Puniſhment more evidently and
" plainly here than in other Sins, ſcarce any of
" all theſe *Baſhaws* that have made haſte to be
" rich, have eſcaped the *Grand Seignior*'s Hands ;
" but he either wholly diveſts them of All, or
" will ſhare the beſt Part of the Prey with them.
" Amongſt whom I have obſerved none paſſes ſo
" hardly as the *Baſhaws* of *Grand Cairo*, becauſe
" it is the richeſt and moſt powerful of all the
" Governments of this Empire ; and ſo, either
" in his Journey Home, or after his Return, he
" loſes his Life by publick Command, or at leaſt
" is rifled of his Goods as ill got, which are con-
" demned to the *Grand Seignior*'s Treaſury : And
" it is ſtrange yet to ſee with what Heat theſe
" Men-labour to amaſs Riches, which they know
" by often Experiences have proved but Collec-
" tions for their Maſter ; and only the Odium
" and Curſes which the oppreſſed Wretches have
" vented againſt their Rapine, remain to them-
" ſelves. *Rebus ſecundis avidi, adverſis autem in-*
" *cauti.* Tacit. * * * * * * * * *
* * * * * * * * * * * *

" The *Turk* underſtands well how profitable it
" is for the Conſtitution of his Eſtate, to uſe evil
" Inſtruments, who may oppreſs and poll his
" People, intending afterwards for himſelf the
" whole Harveſt of their Labours ; they remain-
" ing with their Hatred, while the Prince, under
" Colour of performing Juſtice, procures both
" Riches and Fame together.

" If

" If it be fufpected that any great Man intends
" to make Combuftion or Mutiny in his Govern-
" ment, or that his Wealth or natural Abilities
" render him formidable, without further Inquifi-
" tion or Scrutiny, all Difcontent of the *Grand*
" *Seignior* is diffembled, and perhaps a Horfe, or
" Sword, or Sable Veft, is reported to be pre-
" fented, and all fair Treatment is counterfeited,
" till the Executioner gets the Bow-ftring about
" his Neck, and then they care not how rudely
" they deal with him : Juft like the Birds in *Plu-*
" *tarch*, that beat the Cuckow, for fear that in
" Time he fhould become a Hawk.

" And to make more Room for the Multitude
" of Officers that crowd for Preferments, and to
" act the cruel Edicts of the Empire with the
" leaft Noife ; oftentimes when a great Perfonage
" is removed from his Place of Truft, and fent
" with a new Commiffion to the Charge, per-
" haps, of a greater Government ; and though
" he depart from the Regal Seat with all fair
" Demonftrations of Favour, yet before he hath
" advanced Three Days in his Journey, triumph-
" ing in the Multitude of his Servants and his late
" Hopes, the fatal Command overtakes him, and,
" without any Accufation or Caufe, other than
" the Will of the *Sultan*, he is barbaroufly put to
" Death, and his Body thrown into the Dirt of
" a foreign and unknown Country, without So-
" lemnity of Funeral or Monument ; and he is
" no fooner in his Grave, than his Memory is
" forgotten.

" Hence are apparent the Caufes of the Decay
" of Arts amongft the *Turks* ; and of the Neglect
" and Want of Care in manuring and cultivating
" their

" their Lands; why their Houfes and private
" Buildings are made flight, and not durable for
" more than Ten or Twenty Years; why you
" find there no delightful Orchards, and pleafant
" Gardens and Plantations; and why, in thofe
" Countries where Nature hath contributed fo
" much on her Part, there are no additional La-
" bours of Art to complete all, and turn it into
" a Paradife: For Men, knowing no certain
" Heir, nor who fhall fucceed them in their La-
" bours, contrive only for a few Years Enjoy-
" ment. And moreover, Men are afraid of fhew-
" ing too much Oftentation or Magnificence in
" their Palaces, or Ingenuity in the Pleafures of
" their Gardens, left they fhould bring on them
" the fame Fate that *Naboth*'s Vineyard occa-
" fioned to its Mafter. And therefore Men neg-
" lect all Applications to the Studies of Arts and
" Sciences, but only fuch as are neceffary to the
" mere Courfe of Living: For the Fear and
" Crime of being known to be rich, makes them
" appear outwardly poor; and fo become natu-
" rally *Stoicks* and Philofophers in all the Points of
" a referved and cautious Life.

" And here I am at a Stand, and cannot con-
" clude, without contemplating a while, and
" pleafing myfelf with the Thoughts of the Blef-
" fednefs, the Happinefs, the Liberty of my own
" Country; where Men, under the Protection
" and fafe Influence of a gracious and the beft
" Prince in the World," (*He might with more
Propriety have faid, the beft Conftitution in the
World*) " enjoy and eat of the Fruit of their
" own Labour; and purchafe to themfelves,
" with Security, Fields and Manors, and dare
" acknow-

" acknowledge and glory in their Wealth and
" Pomp, and yet leave the Inheritance to their
" Pofterity."

SATURDAY, *November* 4, 1721.   No. 51.

Popularity no Proof of Merit.

S I R,

POpularity is the Fondnefs and Applaufe of
many, following the Perfon of one, who, in
their Opinion, deferves well of them ; and it
muft doubtlefs be a fenfible Pleafure to him who
enjoys it, if he enjoy it upon good Terms, and
from reputable Caufes : But where it is only to
be acquired by deceiving Men with Words, or in-
toxicating them with Liquors, or purchafing their
Hearts with Bribes, a virtuous Man would rather
be without it ; and therefore virtuous Men have
been rarely popular, except in the Beginning, or
near the firft Rife of States, while they yet preferved their Innocence.

Where Parties prevail, a principal Way to gain
Popularity is, to act foolifhly for one Side, and
wickedly againft the other : And therefore fome
publick Talkers have grown popular, by calling
thofe whom they difliked by bitter and ill-bred
Names ; or by rioting and making a Noife for
fome Sounds, which they had taken a Liking to ;
or by infulting and abufing thofe that affronted
them, by being more fober and fenfible than themfelves : And fome, to be revenged on thofe that

never

never hurt them, have given themfelves up a blind Prey to certain Leaders, who deluded them, and fold them, and yet earned popular Applaufe of them for fo ferving them.

So that Popularity is often but the Price which the People pay to their Chiefs, for deceiving and felling them : And this Price is fo implicitly paid, that the very Vices and Fooleries of a popular Chief become popular too, and were perhaps amongft the firft Caufes that made him fo. Some Gentlemen of this Caft owe their Figure to the Weaknefs of their Heads, or the Strength of their Barrels ; and grow confiderable by their having fmall Parts, or by drinking away thofe that they have.

Thefe are the Inftruments that cunning Men work with ; and therefore fometimes a Knave, who is not popular, fhall get a weak Man, who is fo, to do thofe Things with Applaufe, for which he himfelf would be hated and condemned : And the Hand that executes fhall be bleffed, when the Head that contrives would be curfed, for one and the fame Thing.

This fhews that Names are principal Reafons to determine the Multitude to popular Love and Hatred ; and it proceeds not fo much from their being untaught as ill taught : When they are inftructed not to reafon but to rage, not to judge but to miftake, a better Difcernment and wifer Behaviour are not to be hoped from them.

Demetrius, and the other Craftfmen, Shrinemakers to *Diana*, at *Ephefus*, were more popular Men than St. *Paul*, and raifed a Mob to confute his Arguments for Chriftianity : For it had not yet entered into the Heads of the People, that Religion

ligion and Rage were contradictory Things, and that Antiquity and Reverence could not sanctify Impiety, Falshood, and Folly.

In like Manner, *Barabbas*, a Rioter and a Murderer, had more Votes to save him than our blessed Saviour had ; who was thought by that zealous, deluded, and outrageous People, to be the greater Criminal of the Two, for having told them sober, and saving Truth, which was new to them, though everlasting in itself ; and therefore condemned because it was new.

Now, in neither of these Instances were the People, though they acted thus impiously and madly, originally in the Fault ; but those who taught them ; and who, having for Religion taught them Trifles, Folly, and Fury, were alarmed by the rational and prevailing Doctrines of Mercy, Wisdom, and Truth. They therefore blaspheme against the Author of Truth, yet charge him with Blasphemy. As to the Populace, they did as they were taught, and uttered the Cry which was put into their Mouths.

The People, when they are left to themselves, and their own Understandings and Observation, will judge of Men by their good or bad Actions, and are capable of separating Vice from Virtue, and the Just from the Unjust : And therefore, when their Government is not corrupted, the best and most virtuous Men will always be the most popular, and he who does best will be esteemed best : But when strong Liquor, or Money, or false Terrors intervene, and Government is turned into Faction ; the Judgment of the People is vitiated, and worse than none. They then prefer the worst Men to the best, if they have stronger

Drink,

Drink, or more Money, or are covered with any other falfe Merit, by thofe whofe Word they take, and whofe Authority they fubmit to; and the moft popular Man is he who bribes higheft, or impofes upon them beft.

That thefe Things are common, and almoft univerfal, is not ftrange: Generally fpeaking, where-ever there is Power, there will be Faction; and where-ever there is Money, there will be Corruption: So that the Heads of Faction, and the Promoters of Corruption, have from their very Characters, which ought to render them deteftable, the Means of Popularity.

Who was better beloved at *Rome* than *Spurius Melius*, while he was meditating the Slavery of the *Roman* People? Who could ever boaft fuch potent Parties, fuch numerous Followers, fuch high Applaufe and Regard, fuch Trophies and Statues, as *Marius* and *Sylla*, *Pompey* and *Cæfar*, *Auguftus* and *Anthony* could boaft; while they were overturning the State, oppreffing Mankind, butchering one Half of the World, and putting Shackles upon the other? And, in fine, who was ever a greater Impoftor, and a more admired Prophet, than *Mahomet* was? All thefe Men were Enemies to Liberty, Truth, and Peace; the Plagues and Scourges of the Earth: But they deceived and deftroyed their People with their own Confent, and by the higheft Wickednefs gained the higheft Popularity.

The Two Dukes of *Guife*, *Francis* and *Henry*, Father and Son, were the Two moft popular Men that ever *France* faw, and grew fo by doing it more Mifchief than ever Two Men till then had done. They were perpetually, during a Courfe

of

of many Years, deftroying its Peace, violating its
Laws, ufurping its Authority, pufhing at the
Crown, raifing and carrying on Rebellions, committing Maffacres, and filling it with Blood and
Defolation : They had no one publick End, and
did no one publick Thing, but what was pernicious
to *France* ; yet *France* adored them.

Whoever is the Author of a Civil War, is Author of all its cruel Confequences ; Plunders, Devaftations, Burnings, Rapes, Slaughters, Oppreffion and Famine.——A frightful Catalogue of
Crimes to lie at one Man's Door ! yet both thefe
Dukes had them all to anfwer for over and over,
yet were vaftly beloved. Even when they were
dead, they continued the Authors of long publick
Miferies, by leaving their deftructive Schemes and
their Party behind them ; a fierce, lawlefs, and
powerful Party, that maintained the Civil War
long after them ; and having deftroyed *Henry* III.
was like to prove too hard even for the great
Henry IV. nor did he overcome it but by infinite
Courage, Induftry, and Patience, and the renouncing of his Religion : Nay, at laft, his Murder
was owing to the Spirit of the League, firft concerted, and afterwards conftantly headed and animated, by thefe two Dukes fucceffively.

Had ever any Country two greater Foes ? yet
were ever two Men greater Darlings of any Country ? For *Henry* Duke of *Guife* particularly, he
had fo much the Hearts of the People, that their
Paffion for him ran not only to Dotage, but Idolatry ; and they blafphemed God, to do the Duke
Honour : They worfhipped his Image ; they in-
voked him in their Prayers ; they touched religioufly the Hem of his Garment, and with the
                                        fame

2222

same Spirit and Design rubbed their Beads upon his Clothes ; nay, following him in Multitudes as he passed their Streets, saluted him with *Hosannas to the Son of* David.

Thus they treated and adored this Idol.; a lewd Man, a publick Incendiary and Destroyer, but represented to them as their Saviour.——He had for the Ends of Ambition put himself at the Head of the *Catholick* Cause ; the surest Warrant in the World for Mischief and Homage !

Our good Fortune, or our better Constitution, has hitherto restrained us against our Will from running into all these ·Excesses of Distraction and Folly. But we have had our popular Idols too ; wretched Idols, who could not furnish us from their Parts or Reputation with one Reason for our Stupidity in admiring them. Sometimes paltry and turbulent Priests, destitute of all Virtue and Good-breeding, weak and immoral Patricians, or loud and ignorant Plebeians, have run away with our Reverence, without being able to merit our Esteem ; without Religion they have been popular in the Cause of Religion, and contended popularly for Loyalty by Faction and Rebellion.

To every Reader, Instances of this Nature will occur within his own Memory and Observation. To name them with the other great Names above-mentioned, would be an Honour too mighty for them, who were but small wicked Men, though greatly popular.

I have often remembered, with Compassion, an unfortunate Great Man still living, but utterly ruined by his Popularity and false Friends. His Good-nature has been often mentioned, and is grown almost proverbial : Nor do I deny it ; though
by

by it he never ferved himfelf, his Family, or the
Publick. On the contrary, it has proved his Fail-
ing and his Crime. If one were to enquire for
the Caufes of his Popularity in the Probity of his
Life, the Piety of his Mind, his publick Abilities,
private Œconomy, or conjugal or domeftick Virtues, thefe are Topicks upon which his Friends
do not extol him : And for his Loyalty, take
Loyalty in what Senfe you will, he will be found
to have given prepofterous Proofs of it, and to
have been engaged in all the Depths of Rebellion
and Perjury, and is ftill engaged.

From what has been faid, it will not feem
ftrange that fome of the moft popular Men in the
World have been the moft mifchievous in their
Behaviour and Opinions. What Fighting and
Burning has there been for Tranfubftantiation !
what Declaiming, Damning, and Rebelling, for
Paffive Obedience ! what fierce Contention, and
how many foolifh Arguments for Perfecution ! All
which Opinions are a Contradiction to Religion
and Scripture, an Affront to Common-Senfe, and
utterly deftructive of all Civil and Religious Liberty, and of all human Happinefs : Nor would any of
them, or any like them, have ever entered into
the Heart of any Man, unlefs he were firft deceived, or found his Account in deceiving. But even
Crimes, Contradictions, and Folly, will be popular
in a State, when they bring Gain or felfifh Gratifications to thofe who are in Poffeffion of a Power
to render Folly, Contradiction, and Crimes, advantageous to the pernicious Purfuits which they
are engaged in.

G   *I am,* &c.

S A T U R-

SATURDAY, *November* 11, 1721. No. 52.

Of Divine Judgments; the Wickedness and Absurdity of applying them to Men and Events.

SIR,

I Have in a former Letter to you, not long since, shewn the Rashness of Men in applying to one another the Judgments of God. I shall in this consider that Subject farther, and endeavour to cure that prevailing and uncharitable Spirit.

Almost all Sorts of Men pretend, in some Instances, to be in the Secrets of the Almighty, and will be finding out the unsearchable Purposes of his Providence ; they will be prying into the hidden Things of God, and assigning such Ends and Motives for his all-wife Dispensations, as are only suitable to their own Weakness, or Prejudices, or Malice : They give him the same Passions that they themselves possess, and then make him love and hate what and whom they themselves love and hate : They are pleased with Flattery and Sounds, and provoked by Trifles and Names ; and so they think is he. And as they thus sanctify all their own Doings, Affections, and Fancies, with a *Fiat* and Approbation from Heaven, and belie and provoke God, to make him their Friend ; so they take it for granted that he is an Enemy to all their Enemies ; and that therefore every Evil, or seeming Evil, that befals their Enemies, or those whom they dislike, is a manifest Judgment from God, and a Justification of whatever they can do against them :

them : So that God is often made the Author of every Mifchief which they themfelves commit ; but they that feel it, think more rationally that they are animated by a contrary Spirit.

God made Man after his own Likenefs, perfect, amiable, merciful, and upright ; and Men are bold and foolifh enough to make God after theirs ; and almoft every one has his own God, one fafhioned according to his own Temper, Imaginations, and Prejudices. In this Senfe they worfhip as many falfe Gods, as they have wrong Notions of the true one; and fo in fome fort *Polytheifm* does yet remain even in the Chriftian World. They only agree in calling what they worfhip by the fame Name ; but they conceive him in fuch a different Manner, they differ fo widely about his Nature and Will, and either give him fuch contradictory Attributes, or fo contradict one another in explaining thefe Attributes, that it is plain they do not mean one and the fame Being. Some make God hate what he certainly loves, others make him love what he certainly hates ; and all take it amifs if you think that they own and adore any God but the true God. But let them think what they will, many of them ftill worfhip the old Gods of the Heathens, Gods that were delighted with Baubles, Shew, and Grimace, and with Cruelty, Revenge, and human Sacrifices.

From this miftaken and impious Spirit it proceeds, that when Calamities and Difafters befal others, efpecially thofe that differ from us, we call them Judgments, and fay that the Hand of God is againft them : But when the fame Evils or worfe befal ourfelves, the Stile is changed, and them *whom God loveth he chafteneth* ; or if we own them

to

to be Judgments, yet ftill they are Judgments upon us for other People's Sins.

Thus all the Misfortunes that happened to *Spain* for many hundred Years, whether they came from the Enemy, or the Elements, were divine Judgments upon them for fuffering the idolatrous *Moors* to inhabit that good Catholick Country ; and therefore, like true Catholicks, they brought the greateft Judgment of all upon it, by deftroying and banifhing that numerous and induftrious People. Thus the bigotted *Pagans*, when *Alarick* King of the *Huns* facked *Rome*, charged the Chriftians with being the Caufe of that and of every other Calamity that befel the Empire : The Chriftians defpifed their Gods, and therefore their Gods, out of a particular Spite to the Chriftians, afflicted the whole World with Miferies ; and fo Plagues, Wars, Hurricanes, and Earthquakes, which were Evils that had been in the World from the Beginning of it, and will be to the End, were, notwithftanding, all fo many Judgments, occafioned by the poor Chriftians !——Hence the Beginning of Penalties, Severities, and Perfecutions againft them ; and thus the Chriftians came in Time to return the Charge upon the Heathens, to ufe the fame Way of Reafoning, and to make the like Reprifals, and with as little Equity, Truth, or Clemency : And thus, laftly, all Parties in Religion have ever dealt with one another.

We are commanded *not to judge, left we be judged* ; and we are told that *Vengeance is the Lord's,* and that *Judgments are in his Hand :* All which are to convince us, that we have no certain or probable Rule to apply God's Judgments by ; and that the fureft Rule is the Rule of Charity, *which wifheth*

wisheth all Things, hopeth all Things. The Good
and Evil that happen to Man in this World, are
no sure Marks of the Approbation and Displeasure
of Almighty God, who makes his Sun to shine
and his Rain to fall upon the Just and the Unjust :
Good-Fortune and Calamities are the Portion of
the Good and of the Bad ; and if there be any Inequality, the Wicked seem to have the Advantage.
The World had more People and Temporal Prosperity in the Times of Heathenism, than since its
Abolishment ; *Mahometanism* possesses much more
of the Globe than Christianity possesses ; the Pa-
pists are more numerous than the Protestants are,
and have greater and better Countries. The Apostles and Saints were the poorest Men in the World,
and debauched Men are often uppermost, and
thrive best ; and as the Righteous are at least as
subject to Distempers and Affliction while they live,
as the Wicked are, so the Wicked die with as little
Pain and as few Pangs as the Righteous die.

That there is a Providence, and a gracious Providence presiding over the World, is manifest and
undeniable ; but how it works, and from what
particular Motives, in a thousand Instances, none
but the Author of it can tell ; though almost all
pretend to tell, and are for ever diving into the
secret Counsels of the most High, with as much
Temerity as ill Success.

To the Discredit of this Practice, it is observe-
able, that none but the fierce and uncharitable,
none but ignorant and narrow-spirited Bigots and
Barbarians come into it or encourage it. Men of
charitable and benevolent Minds, enlarged by Reason and Observation, condemn it as irreligious ;
they know that it is often malicious and dishonest,
always.

always ridiculous and dangerous ; they know the
Ways of God to be paſt finding out ; they ſee
human Affairs ſo perplexed and unaccountable ;
Men ſometimes riſing and ſometimes falling, both
by Virtue and Vice ; ſuch Viciſſitudes and Revolutions in the Fortunes of Men and of Nations,
often without any Change in theſe Men and Nations from Virtue to Vice, or from Vice to Virtue ;
People growing greater without becoming better,
and poorer without growing worſe : They behold
Good and Evil ſo promiſcuouſly diſpenſed ; ſometimes Thouſands of Men, Women, and Children,
of different Spirits, Merit, and Morals, ſuffering
equally under the ſame publick Calamity, and deriving equally the like Advantages from publick
Proſperity ; they hehold the Adverſity of ſome to
be the viſible Cauſe of the Proſperity of others,
who are no better than them ; and the Proſperity
of ſome the viſible Cauſe of the Adverſity of others,
who are no worſe than the former ; and one and
the ſame Thing producing Good and Evil to thoſe
who alike deſerve or do not deſerve Good and
Evil : They ſee ſo little Equity or Conſiſtency in
the Proceedings of Men ; ſometimes good Men
exalted, without any Regard had to their Virtue ;
ſometimes wicked Men caſt down, without any
Reſentment of their Crimes ; ſometimes gocd
Men puniſhed for being good, and wicked Men
raiſed and rewarded for being wicked ; ſometimes
both Good and Bad ſuffering or proſpering alike ;
ſometimes Good-Fortunes following the Good, and
Ill-Fortune the Bad, often taking a contrary
Freak.——I ſay, wiſe and honeſt Men, ſeeing
all theſe Things in this great Confuſion and Uncertainty, find ſufficient Reaſon to be afraid of
                                        making

making bold with Heaven, and of chriftening by the Name of its Judgments any of thefe Events and Evils that afflict any Part of Mankind.

But Bigots, and they, who, to ferve ill Ends, intereft Heaven in all that they do, deal more freely and profanely with their great Maker and Judge, whofe Counfels and Judgments being incomprehenfible, it is Impiety and a Contradiction to go about to explain and apply them. The *Turks* make God the Author of every Thing that they do, and of every Evil that others fuffer from them. They meafure his Will by the Event ; and, with them, whatever is fuccefsful, is lawful and juft : The Murder of a Prince, or his murdering of others, is never finful if it fucceed : God, they fay, bleffes and approves the Event, elfe he would prevent it. So that, upon this Principle, there can be no fuch Thing as Wickednefs and Villainy amongft them ; for who knows but it may fucceed, and then it is good ? or if it do not fucceed, who could forefee but it would ? This impious Tenet of that brutifh People arms them with Fiercenefs and Outrage againft one another, and all the World ; it animates them to commit Rapine and Butcheries, and then fears their Confciences, and prevents all Remorfe. Nay, they glory in executing Cruelty, becaufe it is the Judgment of God, and they are his Agents.

I wifh I could keep this dreadful Principle out of *Chriftendom* ; but I am forry to fay, that it is common amongft us. Whoever applies the Judgment of God to others, has this *Turkifh* Spirit in him : And all Men that make fuch Applications, reafon fo foolifhly, fo falfly, and often fo malicioufly in their Defence, that every Inftance which

I

I have ever yet met with in all my Reading and Obfervation (except the declared Inftances in facred Writ) expofes them.

Upon the Murder of *Henry* III. of *France*, by *Jaques Clement*, a *Dominican* Friar, the Deputy of the famous *French* League, then at *Rome*, tells the Pope, in an Audience given upon that Occafion, That the Affaffin was chofen by God, and divinely infpired to murder his Prince, and calls it a glorious Exploit : And though that execrable and bloody Monk ufed all the Methods of Falfhood, Lies, and Forgeries, to get Accefs to the King, in order to deftroy him ; yet the Deputy folemnly tells his Holinefs, that it was notorious that the Thing came not from Men. The League diftreffed, refifted, and at laft murdered their Prince : And all thefe their own wicked Doings were, forfooth, the Judgments of God upon him, for fuffering Herefy in the Land.

The *Hugonots*, on the other hand, made a Judgment of that Murder too ; but a Judgment on their Side, for his frequent Breach of Faith and Edicts with them, and for his Barbarities towards them. They faid, it was a remarkable Providence of God, that he was affaffinated in the fame Chamber where he had concerted the furious Maffacre of St. *Bartholomew*————in the very Chamber, nay, on the fame Day, the fame Hour, and on the fame Spot ! Here are Judgments encountering Judgments ! let who will reconcile them. I think both Sides fufficiently rafh and ridiculous in making them, as are all thofe that do, whatever Side they are of.

The Conqueft of the *Greeks* by *Mahomet* II. and their flavifh Subjection to the *Turks*, is afcribed

by

by the Jesuit *Maimbourg* to the Schism, which he says they were guilty of in withdrawing their Obedience from the See of *Rome*. Here, according to him, was the Judgment and the Cause of the Judgment. *Bayle* observes upon this Occasion, that *Rome* being taken by *Charles* V. in 1527, was as barbarously pillaged by his Troops, as was *Constantinople* by the *Turks*, when they took it: And he asks, Whether *Maimbourg* would take it well to be told by the *Greeks* that that Desolation of *Rome* was a Judgment upon her for her Pride and Ambition, in demanding, imperiously, of the *Greek* Church an absolute Uniformity and Obedience to her Discipline and Dictates? He says, that *Maimbourg*, since he was dealing in Judgments, might as well have given this another Turn, with which *Chalcondylis* would have furnished him. That Historian relates, that when *Mahomet* invaded and subdued *Greece*, the then Inhabitants of *Rome*, who thought themselves the Descendants of the old *Romans*, who came from *Æneas*, who came from *Troy*, asserted positively, that all the Destruction brought upon the *Greeks* by the *Barbarians*, was but a Judgment upon them for all the Ravages which their *Greek* Ancestors had committed against the Subjects of *Priamus*, and in the Destruction of *Troy* some Thousand Years before.

The Death of *Oliver Cromwell* was, it seems, attended or followed by a very high Wind; which was nothing strange: But as *Oliver* had been a Usurper, and a great Deceiver, and was greatly hated; most of the Vulgar, and many that would be thought much wiser took it into their Heads, that that same Storm was a loud Judgment and

Declara-

Declaration of the Wrath of Heaven againft him, and that *Satan* was fetching away his Soul in a Whirlwind. But his Friends turned it quite another Way; particularly Mr. *Waller*, who made all that Tumult and Bellowing in the Elements, to be partly the Call of Heaven, fummoning away fo great a Man; partly the Sighs and Sympathy of Nature for his laft Agonies and Departure. The Copy of Verfes that *Waller* made on that Occafion is one of the nobleft in our Language; I fhall conclude with a few Lines out of it.——

We muft refign; Heav'n his great Soul does claim,
In Storms as loud as his immortal Fame.
His dying Groans, his laft Breath fhakes our Ifle;
And Trees, uncut, fall for his Fun'ral Pile.
New Rome in fuch a Tempeft loft her King,
And, from obeying, fell to worfhipping.
Nature herfelf took Notice of his Death,
And, fighing, fwell'd the Sea with fuch a Breath,
That, to remoteft Shores, her Billows roll'd,
Th' approaching Fate of their great Ruler told.
G

I am, &c.

SATURDAY, *November* 18, 1721.   No. 53.

Dr. Prideaux's *Reasoning about the Death of* Cam-
byses, *examined; whether the same was a Judgment for his killing the* Egyptian *God* Apis.

S I R,

THE Talent of writing History is so rare on
this Side the *Alps*, and more on this Side the
Channel, that I think most of our Southern Neighbours have far exceeded us in it ; as much, perhaps, as some of the Antients have exceeded them.
By far the most Part of our *English* Histories are
pitiful Performances, unworthy of a free, polite,
and learned Nation.   But though many of our
Neighbours excel us in the Histories of their own
Countries, we can boast of two universal Histories,
which do Honour to the Authors, and their Country.   The first is Sir *Walter Raleigh* ; one of the
worthiest and ablest Men that this or any other
Country ever produced.   He had a Soul as vast as
the Work which he undertook, and his Work re-
sembles him ; for though it has much in it that is
foreign to History, it is noble, nervous, and in-
structive ; its Spirit, Clearness, and Stile, are admirable ; and for Narration, Penetration, Knowledge, Sentences, and Observation, he has few
Competitors in Antiquity.

The other is the very reverend, learned, and
aged Dr. *Prideaux*, Dean of *Norwich* ; who has
given us a Body of universal History, written with
such Capacity, Accuracy, Industry, and Honesty,
as

as make it one of the beſt Books that ever came
into the World, and ſhew him to be one of the
greateſt Men in it. No Book was ever more
univerſally read and approved. It is indeed a great
publick Service done to Mankind, and entitles the
Author to the higheſt publick Gratitude and Honour.

But though I never ſaw any great Work to
which I found fewer Objeƈtions ; yet, as a memorable Proof how inſeparably Miſtakes and Prejudices cleave to the Mind of Man, the great and
candid Dr. *Prideaux* is not without them ; I therefore do not upbraid him with them, but rather
admire him for having ſo few. There are however ſome of his Theological Obſervations, which
ſeem to me not only ill-grounded, but to have a
Tendency to create in his Readers wrong Notions
of the Deity, and to encourage them to miſtake
the common Accidents of Life, and the common
Events of Nature, for the Judgments of God,
and to apply them ſuperſtitiouſly as ſuch.

Of this Kind is the Obſervation which he makes
upon the Death of *Cambyſes*, the *Perſian* Emperor,
who had ſlain the *Egyptian Apis*. For the better
underſtanding of this, we muſt know, that *the chief
God of the* Egyptians *was* Oſiris ; *him they worſhipped in the Shape of a Bull, and that not only in Ima-
gery, but alſo in Reality ; for they kept a Bull in the
Temple of* Oſiris, *which they worſhipped in his ſtead.*
The Doƈtor adds, That *in Imitation of this Idolatry was it that* Aaron *made the Golden Calf in the
Wilderneſs, and* Jeroboam *thoſe in* Dan *and* Bethel,
*and did ſet them up thereto be worſhipped by the Chil-
dren of Iſrael, as the Gods that had brought them
out of the Land of* Egypt.

When

When this the God and Bull of the *Egyptians*
died, they looked out for another, with such proper Marks and Spots as were certain Indications
of his Divinity ; and when they found one, they
expreſſed their Joy in great and publick Feſtivity.
In ſuch a Fit of Rejoicing *Cambyſes* found the
City of *Memphis*, when he returned to it from
his unproſperous Expedition into *Æthiopia*. The
Egyptians had juſt then found a new God amongſt
the Cattle, and had lodged him at his Crib in his
Temple with great Solemnity. *Cambyſes* had a
Mind to ſee this Deity of theirs : " And, *ſays*
" *Dr*. Prideaux, this *Apis* being brought to him,
" he fell into a Rage, as well he might, at the
" Sight of ſuch a God ; and, drawing out his
" Dagger, run it into the Thigh of the Beaſt ;
" and then reproaching the Prieſts for their Stu-
" pidity and Wretchedneſs in worſhipping a Brute
" for a God, ordered them to be ſeverely whipped,
" and all the *Egyptians* in *Memphis* to be ſlain,
" who ſhould be found any more rejoicing there
" on this Occaſion. The *Apis* being carried back
" to the Temple, languiſhed of his Wounds, and
" died.

As to the Death of *Cambyſes*, and the Manner
of it, take it alſo in the Doctor's Words. " As
" he mounted his Horſe, his Sword falling out of
" the Scabbard, gave him a Wound in the Thigh,
" of which he died : The *Egyptians* remarking,
" that it was in the ſame Part of the Body where
" he had afore wounded the *Apis*, reckoned it as
" an eſpecial Judgment from Heaven upon him
" for that Fact ; and perchance they were not
" much out in it : For it ſeldom happening in an
" Affront given to any particular Mode of Wor-
" ſhip,

" fhip, how erroneous foever it may be, but that
" Religion in general is wounded thereby ; there
" are many Inftances in Hiftory, wherein God
" had very fignally punifhed the Profanations of
" Religion in the worft of Times, ard under the
" worft Modes of Heathen Idolatry.

Without inquiring whether this be any Compliment to Truth and Religion, I freely own,
that the diftreffing or difturbing of any Sort of People in any Sort of Worfhip, however falfe and ridiculous, where the fame does not violate Property or human Society, is an Invafion of the
Rights of Nature and Confcience, and no Man
can do it with a wife and honeft Defign : And
what Men do of this Kind, out of Bitternefs of
Spirit or Self-Ends, no one will juftify. If People
will play the Fool in their Devotion, they only
expofe themfelves, but hurt not others ; and whoever does Hurt to them, does but warrant them to
return it : And hence is the fure Beginning of Tyranny, and of eternal Civil and Religious War.
Every Man reckons every Religion falfe or foolifh,
which he does not embrace ; and his own the beft,
though it be the worft. And if in this univerfal
Obftinacy of every Man in every religious Opinion
which he has imbibed, a Difpute by the Sword,
and Arguments of Authority and Force, were encouraged, or but permitted, Confufion and Slaughter would be their chief Employment. Or if one
Man's Will were to be a Law to other Mens
Thoughts, the Effects would be every where
alike; that is, the Stupidity and Slavery of *Turks*
would be the Portion and Character of *Englifhmen.*

But,

But I cannot think that the wounding of a
Bull, even of a confecrated Bull, and the whip-
ping of his Priefts, were fuch Crimes as, beyond
all the other Crimes of *Cambyfes*, called for the
avenging Judgments of God upon him. He had
others to anfwer for of a far more black, malignant, and deteftable Nature : He put his Brother
to Death for his Merit, and for a Dream that he
had concerning him. He killed, by a Kick in
the Belly, his beloved Wife *Meroe*, who was alfo
his Sifter, and then with Child by him, for la-
menting the Death of her murdered Brother.
" He caufed feveral of his principal Followers to
" be buried alive, without any Caufe deferving of
" it, and daily facrificed fome or other of them
" to his wild Fury. And when *Crœfus* (formerly
" King of *Lydia*, the old and faithful Friend and
" Counfellor of his Father *Cyrus*) advifed him
" againft thofe Proceedings, and laid before him
" the ill Confequences which they would lead to,
" he ordered him to be put to Death ; and when
" thofe who received his Orders, knowing he
" would repent of it next Day, did therefore de-
" fer the Execution, he caufed them all to be
" executed for *it*, though at the fame time he
" expreffed great Joy that *Crœfus* was alive : And
" out of a mere Humour, only to fhew his Skill
" in Archery, he fhot to Death the Son of *Prex-*
" *afpes*, who was the Chief of his Favourites."
He caufed the Magiftrates of *Memphis* to be put to
Death, for anfwering truly to a Queftion which
he afked them. In his mad March over the *Ly-*
bian Sands, to invade a People that had done him
no Harm, he deftroyed moft of his vaft Army,

Fifty

Fifty Thoufand in one Place: The reft were reduced by Famine to feed on each other.

Which now is moft likely, and moft becoming the divine Wifdom and Goodnefs, that the great God of Heaven and Earth fhould be more offended with this black Catalogue of Cruelties and Crimes, than with a hafty Blow given to a Brute worfhipped as God; which the Doctor owns had juftly provoked the Rage of *Cambyfes?* And is the Almighty more provoked at an Affront put upon an Idol, and upon the Attendants of an Idol, which falfly and impudently is made to reprefent him, than at a terrible and raging Tyranny, that fpreads Blood and Defolation over the Face of the Earth?

Cambyfes, upon his invading *Egypt,* did another Thing as bad as the wounding of *Apis;* I fhall relate it in the Doctor's own Words: " Finding
" that the Garrifon of *Pelufium,* a ftrong Fron-
" tier Town, were all *Egyptians,* in an Affault
" which he made upon the City, he placed a
" great Number of Cats, Dogs, Sheep, and
" others of thofe Animals which the *Egyptians*
" reckoned facred, in the Front of the Army;
" and therefore the Soldiers not daring to throw
" a Dart, or fhoot an Arrow, that Way, for fear
" of killing fome of thofe Animals, *Cambyfes,*
" made himfelf Mafter of the Place without any
" Oppofition. For thefe being the Gods which
" the *Egyptians* then adored, it was reckoned the
" higheft Impiety to kill any of them; and when
" they died of themfelves, they buried them with
" great Solemnity.

The Doctor makes no Reflection upon this; though, upon the fame Principle, it muft have
been

been an Affront to Religion ; and if none of thefe facred Creatures were killed, it was owing to no Tendernefs in *Cambyfes*, who expofed them to fo much Danger. But if true Religion be hurt by putting an Affront upon a falfe one, how came it to be a Merit in the primitive Chriftians to pull down the Heathen Temples, and to deftroy the Idols of the Heathen, as they almoft every where did where they had Power, often in Oppofition to Power ? And upon what Foot and Motive is it that Penalties and Incapacities are put upon any Sect of Religion in any Country ? And how came the *Jews* to exercife fuch Fury upon the Gods and Worfhip of the *Gentiles*, as many of the *Jewifh* Leaders, efpecially the *Maccabees*, did, often out of their own Country, often without Provocation ?

The primitive Fathers are every where full of Sarcafms againft the Heathenifh Worfhip, which they treat conftantly with Ridicule and Reproach, with Contempt and Bitternefs : Did Chriftianity fuffer by this Behaviour of theirs ; or did not Chriftianity rather gain Advantage and new Beauties, by comparing it with the Abfurdities, the Fopperies, Nonfenfe, Corruptions, and Vanities of the *Pagans ?* Truth cannot fuffer by expofing Falfhoods, which can no more bear the Face of Truth, than Darknefs can the Face of the Sun. No two Things are more unlike than true and falfe Religion ; and the fame Treatment can never affect both in any Refpect, as the fame Arguments cannot defend Truth and Error. Indeed, true Religion is defended and recommended by the very Means that expofe and deftroy a falfe one. I have therefore often wondered at a Saying of Mr. *Collier's*, though not that it was faid by him ; namely,

namely, That the Tranfition is eafy from ridiculing a falfe Religion to the ridiculing a true one ; or Words to that Effect. Than which nothing could be more unjuftly faid : They are as oppofite as Law and the Violation of Law ; as unlike as Juftice and Oppreffion , and as different as *Chrift* and *Belial.* How fhould the Worfhip of Dæmons refemble the Worfhip of the true God ? And if they cannot be miftaken for each other, how can they be annoyed by the fame Weapons ? The Fathers were fo far from fuch an Imagination, that in their Railleries and Reafonings upon the devout Fooleries of the *Gentiles*, they did not treat them with a bit the more Reverence or Regard for their being eftab ifhed by a Law.

So much may ferve to fhew, that the true Religion can have no Sympathy with the falfe, nor fuffer in its Sufferings. As to the Death of *Cambyfes*, I do not fee any Sign of a Judgment in it, unlefs every Death occafioned by an Accident, or an Inftrument, is a Judgment. Indeed every Difafter, before it can be called a Judgment in this Senfe of the Word, muft be proved a Miracle ; and common Effects from vifible and common Caufes, as they are no Miracles, fo neither can they be called Judgments, unlefs God, the Author of Judgments, declares them fo, as he did not in the Cafe before us. Many a good Man has been killed in a more terrible Manner, as were all the Saints and Martyrs.

Now where is the Miracle of a Sword falling out of the Sheath, when a Man is mounting his Horfe ? And where was it more likely to fall than on his Leg or his Thigh ? If indeed it had got out of the Scabbard of its own Accord, and
mounted

mounted up to his Head and cut it off, it might have looked like a Judgment; but yet I fhould have looked out rather for any Caufe of it, than the killing of a deified Bull.

G   *I am, &c.*

SATURDAY, *November* 25, 1721.   No. 54.

The Reafoning of Dr. Prideaux *about the Fate of* Brennus *the Gaul, and of his Followers, examined; whether the fame were a Judgment for an Intention to plunder the Temple of* Delphos.

SIR,

I Shall beftow this Paper in confidering what Dr. *Prideaux* fays of *Brennus* the *Gaul*, his Expedition, Death, and Crime. This Man, at the Head of a great Number of his Countrymen, fent Abroad to feek new Habitations, paffing through *Hungary*, *Illyrium*, and *Macedonia*, plundering, ravaging, and deftroying as they went, at laft invaded *Greece*, and " marched on towards *Delphos*,
" to plunder the Temple in that City of the vaft
" Riches which were there laid up. But he there
" met a wonderful Defeat : For on his approach-
" ing the Place, there happened a terrible Storm
" of Thunder, Lightning, and Hail, which de-
" ftroyed great Numbers of his Men ; and at the
" fame Time there was as terrible an Earthquake,
" which rending the Mountains in Pieces, threw
" down whole Rocks upon them, which over-
" whelmed them by Hundreds at a Time ; by
" which the whole Army being much difmayed,
                                            " they

" they were the following Night feized with fuch
" a pannick Fear, that every Man fuppofing him
" that was next to him to be a *Grecian* Enemy,
" they fell upon each other ; fo that before there
" was Day-light enough to make them fee the
" Miftake, one half of the Army had deftroyed
" the other. By all this the *Greeks*, who were
" now come together from all Parts to defend their
" Temple, being much animated, fell furioufly
" on them ; and although now *Acichorus* was come
" up with *Brennus*, yet both their Forces to-
" gether could not ftand the Affault ; but great
" Numbers of them were flain, and great Num-
" bers were wounded ; and amongft thefe laft was
" *Brennus* himfelf, who had received feveral
" Wounds ; and although none of them were
" mortal, yet feeing all now loft, and the whole
" Expedition, which he had been the Author of,
" thus ended in a difmal Ruin, he was fo con-
" founded at the Mifcarriage, that he refolved
" not to outlive it : And therefore calling to him
" as many of the chief Leaders as he could get
" together amidft that calamitous Hurry, he ad-
" vifed them to flay all the wounded, and with
" the Remainder make as good a Retreat back-
" ward as they could ; and then having guzzled
" down as much Wine as he could drink, he
" ran himfelf through and died. — The reft being
" to march through Enemies Countries, they
" were, as they paffed, fo diftreffed for want of
" Provifions, which they were every where to
" fight for, fo incommoded at Night by lodging
" moftly upon the Ground in a Winter Seafon,
" and in fuch a Manner harraffed and fallen upon
" where-ever they came by the People of thofe

Countries

" Countries through which they paffed, that
" what with Famine, Cold, and Sicknefs, and
" what with the Sword of their Enemies, they
" were all cut off and deftroyed : So that of the
" numerous Company which did firft fet out on
" this Expedition, not fo much as one Man efca-
" ped the calamitous Fate of miferably perifhing
" in it.

This is the Story of *Brennus*, which I have told
in the Doctor's own Words : Now follows his Reflection upon it : " Thus God was pleafed in a
" very extraordinary Manner to execute his Ven-
" geance upon thofe facrilegious Wretches, for
" the Sake of Religion in general, how falfe and
" idolatrous foever that particular Religion was,
" for which that Temple at *Delphos* was erected.
" For, to believe a Religion true, and offer facri-
" legious Violences to the Places confecrated to
" the Devotions of that Religion, is abfolute Im-
" piety, and a Sin againft all Religion ; and there
" are many Inftances of very fignal Judgments
" with which God hath punifhed it even amongft
" the worft of Heathens and Infidels ; and much
" more may they expect it, who, having the
" Truth of God eftablifhed among them, fhall
" become guilty hereof.

If this unhappy End of *Brennus* and his Followers was a Judgment, as doubtlefs this reverend and
worthy Author thinks, I cannot fee why an Intention to pillage a ftupid Idol of his ufelefs Wealth
and devout Bawbles, given and ufed for the Ends
of Idolatry and Delufion, fhould be reckoned the
Caufe of it. I would be glad to know how any
Part of Mankind would have fuffered in their Religion and Fortune, though the Shrine and Temple
of

of *Apollo* had been ftripped of all their fuperftitious and ill-got Finery ; or how God Almighty came to fhew himfelf thus miraculoufly the Guardian of an Idol, fet up to rival him, and to deceive the World by uttering oraculous Lies ; or, how the taking away thofe Riches that were acquired by belying God and deceiving Man, and employed for the Ornament and Support of a blafphemous Impofture, could be called Sacrilege or robbing of God, who was really robbed by an Idol of That only which he can be robbed of, divine Worfhip and Homage.

But becaufe People are apt to be mifguided and terrified by Words, efpecially by fuch as are applied to Devotion and holy Things, I fhall here beftow fome Refleaions npon the awful Word *Sacrilege*, and fhew that it is ill underftood.

Sacrilege, we are told by fome, fignifies the robbing or ftealing from God any Thing which is peculiarly his. Now nothing can be ftolen from God, nor can any Thing be concealed from him. Every Thing being his, it is as much his in the Hands of one Man as in the Hands of another ; for, let who will have the Ufe of it, the Property cannot be altered : God, who has all Things, can never be put out of Poffeffion of any Thing ; and as nothing can be taken from him, fo neither can any Thing be given to him, becaufe all the World and every Thing in it is already his ; and it is abfurd to imagine that any Form of Words, or Change of Place or Pofition, can enlarge or leffen his Property in any Thing. All that we have, we have from him ; and to return him his own Gifts back again, which we want, and he does not, is no Compliment nor any Part of Religion or of Reafon: It is fhewing ourfelves wifer than him, in fetting apart for his Ufe thofe Things which he has gracioufly created and fet apart for ours. Can we feed him ? Or can we clothe, adorn, or enrich him ? Can we build him a City to dwell in, or furnifh him with Guards for the Security of his Perfon ?

Sacrilege therefore is either the robbing of Men, or no Robbery at all. And this Crime is greater or lefs, according to the Meafure or Mifchief done. To rob a poor Man of his Loaf, is a greater Crime, *in foro confcientiæ*, than to rob a rich Man of an Ox : To rob a Man of a fmall Part of a Thing that is neceffary to him, is a greater Crime, than the robbing him of a great Superfluity; and if I rob a Man of a Thing that will do him Hurt, I hope I do him lefs an Injury, than if I robbed him of a Thing which does him Good. But if I take a Thing which no Man has a Right to, I myfelf have a Right to it, by poffeffing it.

To apply all this to the Bufinefs of Sacrilege; if a Man take away any of the Books, Veft-ments, or Utenfils, made ufe of in Devotion, he only robs the Congregation, who muft buy more; and many being more able than one to bear this Lofs, the Offence, as to its Effects, is lefs than if he robbed but one Man. But if he take away from a Heathen Temple, Plate, or hidden Trea-fure, laid up there, but not ufed, he indeed does an Action that he has no Right to do, but an Action that however does Good to the World, by turning into Ufe that which was of none, or of bad Ufe.

Dead Treafure, firft drawn from the People in fuperftitious Offerings, and then laid up in a Heathen Temple, and kept and ufed for impious and idolatrous Ends, but never to return again into the World, for the neceflary Purpofes of Life and Commerce, is the Plunder of Mankind; and the worft of all Plunders, becaufe it never circulates; and People are greatly the worfe for it, in refpect both of Soul and Body, but never can be the better. It is firft taking from them, and afterwards denying them, the great and chief Means of Life and Convenience. He therefore, whoever he be, that takes it from thence, let him take it in what Manner he will, does a better and more publick Thing than he who keeps it there.

No Man can be robbed of a Thing in which he has no Property. Of this Sort was *Apollo*'s Wealth; and no body was robbed in taking it away. So that whoever takes away golden Images, or other dead Wealth, the Means and Objects of falfe Adoration, is guilty of no other Crime, than that of difturbing erroneous Confciences: Nor need fuch Confciences be much difturbed, fince the Crime being committed without their Confent, they have no Share in it. And therefore if fuch idolatrous Images, and fuch fuperftitious, ufelefs, and pernicious Riches, be taken away by a lawful Authority, or in a lawful War, it is no Crime at all. So that in every Senfe *Brennus* committed a greater Crime in plundering one Village, than he could have committed, had he plundered, as he intended, the Temple of *Delphos*.

If *Brennus* had believed in *Apollo*, he finned againft his Confcience, in defigning to rob him. But we do not know that *Brennus*, or thofe that followed him, believed thus. I do not remember that *Apollo* wes the God of the *Gauls*, or that the

Druids

Druids owned him: All Nations agreed not in
worſhipping the ſame Gods, but often diſputed
about the Quality, Birth, and Precedence of their
Gods. And if *Brennus* deſpiſed or diſregarded
Apollo, he committed no Sacrilege; at leaſt with
reſpect to himſelf, it was no Sacrilege, but only
Rapine ; but if, believing in him, though an Idol,
he would have ſinned in pillaging him, as doubtleſs he would, here is an Argument, that a good
Conſcience may be an erroneous Conſcience ; and
that if no Man muſt act againſt his own Conſcience, though it be erroneous, as doubtleſs he muſt
not, then much leſs has any other Man whatſoever a Right to puniſh or diſtreſs him for it. If
God approve, who is it that condemns ? And none
but God knows the Heart of another.

If *Brennus* had worſhipped *Apollo*, he was guilty
of Idolatry, in the Opinion of all Chriſtians: And
if he had robbed him, he was guilty of Sacrilege in
the Opinion of moſt. Now we hear of no Judgment falling upon thoſe that worſhipped *Apollo*, and
ſupported that Idol with ſuperſtitious Donations ;
all which was Idolatry. And is Idolatry, which
God has declared abominable in his Eyes, a leſs
Sin than robbing an idolatrous Temple, which
Action God has no where declared a Sin ? The
good Kings of the *Jews* deſtroyed all Idols and
idolatrous Temples, where-ever they had Power ;
and the Wrath of God was kindled againſt all that
did not. If it was therefore a Sin againſt the true
God, not to deſtroy them ; how came it to be Sin
only to rob them ?

I think all this is enough to ſhew, that an Intention to plunder *Apollo* of his idle and unhal-
lowed Wealth, was not the probable Cauſe of any
Judgment

Judgment upon *Brennus* and his Followers: But if there muft be a Judgment in the Cafe, there were Reafons for it much more powerful, and much more likely to provoke God to fend it. He was a wild and barbarous Robber, at the Head of an Army of Savages, who cruelly ravaged many Nations, made Spoil of all Mens Property, and inhumanly maffacred thofe that defended their own. They were Invaders, Plunderers, and Murderers, who, by Numbers, Barbarity, Rapine, and Slaughter, laid wafte whole Countries, and deftroyed, unprovoked, Men and Property. In this general Pillage, they had already paffed through and defolated *Hungary*, *Illyrium*, *Macedonia*, and were now got into *Greece*. Was not here Guilt enough to call down a Thoufand Judgments? And after all this bloody and brutifh Violence done to the World, and to the Laws of God and Man; can we imagine that thefe *Gauls* fuffered that terrible Doom for barely intending a Thing, in which neither God would have been difhonoured, nor Man injured? At leaft in any Degree of Comparifon, with the leaft of the other great and terrible Calamities, which they fuffered from thefe deftroying *Barbarians*?

I fhall now add fomething more particularly concerning the wretched End of thefe *Gauls*, and enquire how far it can be reckoned a Judgment. And here I am of Opinion, that either every Calamity, publick or private, muft be accounted a Judgment; which Doctrine, I believe, no Man holds; or elfe we muft determine, by what Means we can know a Judgment from a Calamity: Nor do I know of any fufficient Marks to direct us in this Matter, but an immediate Miracle, and Declaration

claration from Almighty God, that he means it fo : And in fuch a miraculous Declaration, the Crime muft be exprefly fpecified, for which fuch Judgment is inflicted ; becaufe for every Crime Judgments are not inflicted, nor always for the lateft Crimes ; but fometimes overtake the Sinner, long after the Sin is committed.   All this I take to be felf-evident. We muft remember that Men, biaffed by Paffions and Prejudices, do often confound Good and Evil, and miftake the greateft Wickednefs for the greateft Merit, and the higheft Merit for the higheft Wickednefs : Publick Maffacres have been applauded, publick Incendiaries have been fainted, publick Tyrants deified. While on the other Side, publick Virtue has paffed for a publick Crime, Truth for Blafphemy, and Chriftianity has been rewarded with Fire and Sword.   So that Men thus blind and perverfe do frequently entitle Vice to the Bleffing and Favour of God, and Virtue and Merit to his fevereft Judgments.

Where-ever therefore there is a great Complication of Crimes, and fometimes of great Crimes, how can we diftinguifh for which of them the Judgment is fent, unlefs he that fends it declare the fame ? If he fend it for more Crimes than one, how fhall we diftinguifh where he, who only can, does not ? And if the Judgment be fent for one Sin only, by what certain Token can we difcover it ? If one Man hurt or difoblige Twenty, in Twenty different Ways ; rob One, fteal from Another, deceive a Third, calumniate a Fourth, wound a Fifth, bear falfe Witnefs againft a Sixth, and fo on till he has as many Enemies as Crimes, and afterwards die by a Difafter or the Law ; every one of the Twenty will be apt to

call

call it a Judgment, and a particular Judgment,
for the particular Offence done to himself. Now
where is the Rule, by which certainly to know
either that this Man's Death was a Judgment, or
to find out the certain Crime that brought it upon
him? Or is ever such a Rule like to be found,
as long as all Sorts of Evils befall all Sorts of
Men?

As to the Thunder, Lightning, Hail, and
Earthquakes, that destroyed so many of the *Gauls*,
were they not the usual Operations and Effects of
Nature? And have they not been from the Beginning? Have not whole Cities and Countries
been destroyed by them? And has not their impartial Fury been felt by the Good and the Bad,
without Distinction? In destroying Storms by
Land and Sea, are the Wicked only overtaken?
And do not the Virtuous perish undistinguished
with the latter? And are not just Men, going
upon just Expeditions, frequently overwhelmed by
them? And do not wicked Men, in wicked En-
terprizes, often escape them? When an impetuous
Shock of an Earthquake overturns a City, or opens
a devouring Chasm to swallow it up; do the Dwel-
lings of the Righteous remain unmoved, and their
Persons unhurt!

Nor is it at all wonderful and uncommon, that
this ignorant Multitude, dismayed by so many and
so alarming Misfortunes, thus suddenly checked in
their Progress, at a great Distance from Home,
beset with Enemies in an Enemy's Country, un-
skilled in the Phænomena of Nature, suffering
many Calamities, and dreading more, fell into a
Pannick; and, having lost their Senses, attacked
one another, by a Mistake, in the Dark. Wicked
Armies

Armies have fallen into the like Terror upon the Sight of an Eclipfe : And the fame unaccountable Fear, but without the fame Effect, feized the victorious *Macedonian* Army of *Alexander* the Great, the very Night before they fought one of their greateft and moft fuccefsful Battles.   And we have ftill a much later Inftance at Home : At the Battle of *Nafeby*, King *Charles* I. who was in it, being preffed by fome of his own People that were behind them, bid them keep back ; which Words being repeated by others to thofe next them, and by thefe to others, the Word *back* was catched up, and running from Man to Man through all the Ranks, was underftood as a Sign to fly ; and accordingly the Royal Army fled, and the Field was loft.   And thus a Chance Word threw a whole Army into a Pannick. None of the Royal Party have yet told us, that this was a Judgment upon that King and his Caufe ; nor, I dare fay, would they have believed the other Party, had the other Party alledged that it was.

Confidering all thefe Calamities and Loffes fuffered by the *Gauls*, and the Confternation which they were in, I fuppofe there was no great Miracle in their being vanquifhed by the *Greeks*, who were now come together from all Parts, to fall furioufly on a defeated Enemy.   And as fmall is the Wonder of *Brennus*'s killing himfelf : He was a refolute Man, and took this Method to cure himfelf of that Grief and Difappointment which he could not bear, and to preferve himfelf from falling alive into the Hands of his Enemies, to whom he had given a Right of ufing him very ill.

Neither is it any thing furprizing that the reft, *being to march through Enemies Countries, were, as*
                                                        they

they paſſed, ſo diſtreſſed for want of Proviſions, which they were every where to fight for ; *ſo incommoded at Night by lodging moſtly on the Ground in a Winter Seaſon, and in ſuch a Manner haraſſed and fallen upon where-ever they came by the People of thoſe Countries through which they paſſed, that what with Famine, Cold, and Sickneſs, and what with the Sword of their Enemies, they were all cut off and deſtroyed.* All this Misfortune is thus fairly accounted for, and the Thing is not uncommon. The whole Nation of the *Cimbrians* were deſtroyed in much greater Numbers, when they left their old Habitations in queſt of new ; though it does not appear that they intended to rob Temples. And yet *Xerxes* deſtroyed and plunder'd all the idolatrous Temples in the *Eaſt*, except that of *Diana* at *Epheſus*, without thriving the worſe for it.

They were all cut off and deſtroyed! for which plain, natural, and neceſſary Cauſes are aſſigned ; and yet it was a Judgment ! Surely this is ſtrange and unaccountable ! Doubtleſs there were Degrees and great Differences of Guilt and Innocence amongſt *Brennus*'s Followers ; and why ſhould they, who were not all equally guilty, all equally ſuffer ? Why ſhould Subjects and Soldiers be puniſhed for the Sins of a Prince or a General ? Soldiers are often preſſed into the Service, and rarely or never know the Reaſons of the Commander's Orders ; and it is Mutiny and Death to diſobey him. And Princes often run into wild Wars, without the Conſent of their Subjects, and againſt their Intereſt ; and yet if their Subjects oppoſe them in it, they are guilty of Reſiſtance, which is reckoned Rebellion ; a very terrible and crying Crime, to
which

which the Judgment of God has been pronounced
due: And yet the Judgments of God, which
fometimes fall upon Princes for an unjuft War,
fall alfo upon their Subjects, who were utterly
guiltlefs of it. What ftrange Doctrine is this?
that every Man in a Nation fhall fuffer for the
Sins of one Man, whom they could not reftrain;
or that any Man fhall fuffer for the Crimes of
another? And that the beft Men in an Army or
a Nation fhall bear the Calamities inflicted upon
them for the Sins of the worft; as if it were a
Crime in a good Man to live where his Lot has
caft him, without his own Confent, next Door to
a wicked Man, or within Ten Miles of him?

This Paper, which I could make much longer,
grows already too long. I fhall conclude with obferving, that we either apply God's Judgments at
Random, without his Authority, always in Oppofition to his Commands, and, for aught we know,
as often contrary to his Ends and Intention; or
we do it out of Prejudices to Men and Opinions:
And by this we give Advantage to Infidels and
Men of no Religion, to reproach us with Prefumption upon our own Principles, in meddling
with the fecret Councils of God, in confounding
his Mercy and Juftice, in making him act capricioufly, and in confounding one Religion with another, the Good with the Bad, as if we thought
them all alike. Let us give no more ground for
this Reproach; and as a Specimen of our Candour and equitable Judgment, let us own, in the
Inftance before us, that the Liberty, Profperity,
and Peace of the World, and, amongft the reft,
the Liberty of *Greece*, were Things fomewhat

more

more facred and inviolable than *Apollo*'s confecrated
Bawbles.

I am, &c.

P. S. The Story about King *Charles* I relate
upon Memory, and may miftake in Names or
Circumftances.

G

Saturday, *December* 2, 1721. No. 55.

The Lawfulnefs of killing Julius Cæfar *confidered,
and defended, againft Dr.* Prideaux.

S I R,

I Shall, in this Paper, confider and difcufs a great
Point ; namely, Whether the Killing of *Julius
Cæfar* was a Virtue, or a Crime ? And becaufe
Dr. *Prideaux,* who condemns it, does not only
fpeak his own Senfe, but that of a great Party, I
fhall here tranfcribe what he fays of it.

" He was murdered in the Senate-Houfe, by a
" Confpiracy of Senators. This was a moft bafe
" and villainous Act ; and was the more fo, in that
" the prime Authors of it, *Marcus Brutus, Deci-*
" *mus Brutus, Caffius,* and *Trebonius,* and fome
" others of them, were fuch as *Cæfar* had in the
" higheft Manner obliged ; yet it was executed
" under the Notion of an high heroick Virtue,
" in thus freeing their Country from one whom
" they called a Tyrant ; and there are not wanting
" fuch as are ready, even in our Days, to applaud
" the Act. But divine Juftice declared itfelf
                                        " other-

" otherwise in this Matter : For it purfued every
" one of them that were concerned herein with
" fuch a juft and remarkable Revenge, that they
" were every Man of them cut off in a fhort Time
" after, in a violent Manner, either by their own
" or other Mens Hands."

Thefe are the Doctor's Words, and this his Judgment, which is roundly paffed ; but how juftly, I hope to make appear before I have ended this Letter. He has not told us what it was, that, in his Opinion, rendered the Perfon of *Cæfar* fo very inviolable. That *Cæfar* had for his Title, only Power and Succefs gained by Violence, and all wicked Means, is moft certain. That the acquiring and exercifing of Power by Force, is Tyranny, is as certain; nor did ever any reafonable Man fay, that Succefs was a Proof of Right. They who make the Perfon of *Cæfar* facred, declare the Perfon of a Tyrant, and an Ufurper to be facred ; for no Man ever lived, to whom thofe two Characters do more notoriously belong. And if all the Privileges and Impunity belonging to a lawful Magiftrate, who protects his People, and rules himfelf and them by Law, and their own Confent, do alfo appertain to a lawlefs Intruder, who is ftronger than all, by being worfe than all ; and under the mock Name of a publick Magiftrate, is a publick Oppreffor, Scourge, Ufurper, Executioner, and Plunderer ; then all thefe bleffed Confequences follow : That there is an utter End of all publick and private Right and Wrong, every Magiftrate may be a Tyrant, every Tyrant is a lawful Magiftrate ; it is unlawful to refift the greateft human Evil ; the neceffary Means of Self-Prefervation are unlawful ; though it be lawful

and

and expedient to deftroy little Robbers, who have
as much Right, and more Innocence, than great
Ones, and who are only fo for Subfiftence ; yet
it is impious and unlawful to oppofe great Robbers, who, out of Luft, Avarice, Cruelty, or
Wantonnefs, take away Life and Property, and
deftroy Nations at Pleafure : That real, great, and
general Mifchief, is defended by giving it a good
Name, by which he who commits it is protected;
Violence, Fraud, and Oppreffion, may be committed with Security, if they be but called Magiftracy ; and the execrable Authors of them are not
only fafe, but facred, if they be but called Magiftrates : Though it be unlawful to be a publick
Deftroyer and Murderer, yet it is unlawful to deftroy him ; that is, it is unlawful to prevent or
punifh that which is moft impious and unlawful :
And, finally, that any Man who can opprefs and
enflave the World, and deftroy Nations, with the
moft and beft Men in them, may do all this with
Impunity.

If *Julius Cæfar* was a lawful Magiftrate, then
every Man who has Force and Villainy enough,
may make himfelf a lawful Magiftrate ; and lawful Magiftrates are, or may be made by Force and
Villainy. But if Magiftracy is not acquired by
overturning with the Sword all Law and Magiftracy, then *Julius Cæfar* was no Magiftrate ; and
if he was not, how came he by the Rights and
Impunity with which lawful Magiftrates only are
vefted ?

Againft any Man ufing unlawful Force, every
Man has a Right to ufe Force. What Crime
would it have been in any *Roman*, or Body of
Romans, even without any Commiffion from *Rome*,
to

to have flain *Alarick*, or *Attila*, or *Brennus*, when they invaded the *Roman* Territories? And what more Right had *Cæfar* than they? In Truth, his Crime was infinitely greater than theirs, as he added the Sins of Ingratitude, Treachery, and Parricide, to that of Ufurpation. The *Goths* and *Gauls* did indeed violate the Laws of Nations, in molefting and invading a Country, that owed them neither Subjection nor Homage: But *Cæfar* violated the Laws of Nature, and of his Country, by enflaving thofe whom he was entrufted and bound to defend.

Every body, I believe, will own, that when he firft made War upon his Country, his Country had a Right to make War upon him; and to deftroy him, who fought to deftroy them. How came that Right to ceafe, after he had, by his Succefs in Villainy and Ufurpation, added to his Crimes, and made Death ftill more his Due? Or, is it lawful to refift and kill a Robber before he has taken away your Money, but not after he has done it? And does a Villain grow facred and inviolable, by the mere Merit of completing his Villainy? If *Cæfar* had forfeited his Life, as he certainly had by all the Laws of *Rome*; why was it not lawful to take it away by the Hands of Thirty Men, as by the Arms of Thirty Thoufand, and in the Senate as well as in the Field?

The Reafon why one private Man muft not kill another in Society, even when he does that which deferves Death, is, that in Society no Man muft be his own Judge, or take his own Revenge; but the more equitable Law muft give it him, and there are Judges eftablifhed for that Purpofe. But if the Offender fet himfelf above the Law and the

Judges,

Judges, he leaves a Right to the Perfon injured to feek Redrefs his own Way, and as he can get it. Whoever puts himfelf in a State of War againft me, gives me a Right of War againft him ; and Violence is a proper Remedy for Violence, when no other is left.

That Right which, in the State of Nature, every Man had, of repelling and revenging Injuries, in fuch a Manner as every Man thought beft, is transferred to the Magiftrate, when Political Societies are formed, and Magiftracy eftablifhed ; but muft return to private Men again, when the Society is diffolved : Which Diffolution may happen either through the natural Demife of the Perfons entrufted with the publick Authority, where there is no Provifion made in the Conftitution for others to fucceed them ; or when, by a fuperior unlawful Force, they are reftrained from anfwering the great End of their Truft, in protecting the Innocent ; an End for which alone Men part with their natural Rights, and become the Members and Subjects of Society.

It is a moft wicked and abfurd Pofition, to fay, that a whole People can ever be in fuch a Situation, as not to have a Right to defend and preferve themfelves, when there is no other Power in Being to protect and defend them ; and much more, that they muft not oppofe a Tyrant, a Traytor, an univerfal Robber, who, by Violence, Treachery, Rapine, infinite Murders and Devaftations, has deprived them of their legal Protection.

Now, that all thefe black Characters belonged to *Cæfar*, is indifputable Fact ; nor was there ever a Traytor and a Tyrant in the World, if he was not one. He broke, outrageoufly broke, every

Tye

Tye that can bind a human Soul ; Honour, Virtue, Religion, Law, Truft, Humanity, and every
Thing that is facred and valuable amongft Men.
He was a Subject and Servant of the *Roman* Commonwealth, greatly honoured and trufted by it ;
he was a Senator and High Prieft ; he had been
Conful ; he was General of one of its greateft Armies, Governor of one of its greateft and beft Provinces. All this Power and Credit, all thefe
Offices and Forces, he turned, ungratefully, barbaroufly, and traiteroufly, upon his Mafters, and
made a Prey of his Country with its own Money
and Arms.

The Means by which he did this mighty and
confummate Evil, were fuitable to the End. He
ftuck at nothing ; nor was any Pitch of Bafenefs
too high or too low for him. He even fubmitted
his Perfon to infamous and unnatural Proftitution,
for the Ends of Ambition ; and from a Boy was
in every Faction for embroiling and overturning
the State ; firft in the bloody Meafures of *Marius* ;
afterwards in the more terrible Confpiracy of *Catiline*, to murder the Confuls and the Senate, to
burn *Rome*, and to enflave the Commonwealth :
And though he failed in that Confpiracy, he went
on confpiring ; he corrupted the People, and
headed Parties of Defperadoes, to frighten thofe
whom he could not bribe : He oppreffed the Provinces, and deftroyed their Inhabitants ; he robbed
the publick Temples ; he flaughtered the Armies
of the Republick ; he feized the publick Treafure ;
at laft, he feized the World, and extinguifhed its
Liberty. Hear the difmal Dread of the *Roman*
Senate and People, upon that dreadful Occafion,
as the fame is defcribed by *Lucan*.

———*Fuit*

——*Fuit hæc menfura timoris,*
Velle putant quodcunque poteft——
Omnia Cæfar erat ; privatæ curia vocis
Teftis adeft. Sedere patres, cenfere parati,
Si regnum, fi templa fibi, jugulumque fenatus,
Exiliumque petat.——
Lucan. Pharfal. l. 3. v. 108.

Thus fell *Rome*, the Glory and Miftrefs of the
Earth, and the Earth with it, under the Yoke of
a Tyrant, whofe Parts encreafed his Guilt, and
made him the more dreadful. From the numberlefs Mifchiefs which he had done to get Power,
the higheft were apprehended from him now he
was poffeffed of it ; and it was not doubted, but he
would have proceeded to Maffacre and Conflagra-
tion, had he been provoked by Oppofition.

——*Namque ignibus atris*
Creditur ut captæ rapturus mœnia Romæ.
Lucan. ut fupra, v. 99.

And therefore moft of the Senators were fled with
Pompey, and *Rome* was left defencelefs to the Sword
of the Ufurper.

What now had the *Romans* to do in this calamitous Cafe, under this enormous Oppreffor ; owing them Duty and Allegiance as one of their own
Citizens, but, like a barbarous Conqueror and an
Alien, holding them in Bonds with his Sword at
their Throats ? Law, Liberty, and Appeals, were
no more ! A Tyrant was their chief Magiftrate ;
his Will their only Law. Becaufe he had murdered one half of the People, had he therefore a
Right to govern the reft ? And becaufe he had
robbed them of moft of their Property, were they
obliged

obliged to give him the Remainder ? Does the
Succefs of a Criminal fanctify his Crime, or are
Crimes fanctified by their Greatnefs ? If only an
Intention to deftroy the State, was High Treafon
and Death ; how did the executing of that execrable Intention become lawful Government, and
acquire a Right of Allegiance ?

I fay, what remained now to the *Romans* to be
done for Relief ? As to legal Procefs againft *Cæfar*,
there could be none ; *omnia Cæfar erat !* Nor was
there any publick Force great enough to oppofe
him : He had before deftroyed or corrupted the
Armies of the Commonwealth. Or, if a new
Army could have been drawn together, ought an
Opportunity to have been given him to have deftroyed that too ? Or, was it lawful to kill him, and
Twenty or Thirty Thoufand Men with him, and
perhaps with the like Slaughter on the other Side,
and with the Lofs of the beft and braveft *Romans*
whom his Ambition had left unmurdered ; and
yet was it unlawful to kill him, without all this
Apparatus, Expence, and Mifchief ? Strange !
that the killing by Surprize a fingle Traytor and
Parricide, who had forfeited his Life by all the
Laws of God and Man, fhould be efteemed a
heinous and crying Crime ; and yet that the furprizing and cutting to Pieces a whole Army fhould
be reckoned heroick Virtue !

It was a known Maxim of Liberty amongft
the great, the wife, the free Antients, that a
Tyrant was a Beaft of Prey, which might be killed by the Spear as well as by a fair Chace, in his
Court as well as in his Camp ; that every Man
had a Right to deftroy one who would deftroy all
Men ; that no Law ought to be given him who
took

took away all Law ; and that, like *Hercules*'s
Monsters, it was glorious to rid the World of him,
whenever, and by what Means soever, it could be
done.

If we read the Stories of the most celebrated
Heroes of Antiquity (Men of whom the present
World is not worthy) and consider the Actions
that gained them their highest Reverence and Renown, and recommended their Names to Posterity with the most Advantage ; we shall find those
in the first Rank of Glory, who have resisted,
destroyed, or expelled Tyrants and Usurpers, the
Pests, the Burthens, and the Butchers of Mankind. What can be more meritorious, what
more beneficent to the World, than the saving
of Millions of Men at the Expence of one grand
Murderer, one merciless and universal Plunderer ?
And can there be any better or other Reason
given for the killing of any guilty Man, but the
preserving of the Innocent ? Indeed, an Action
so glorious to those that did it, and so benevolent
and advantageous to those for whom it was done,
could never have been censured in the World, if
there had not lived in all Ages abject Flatterers,
and servile Creatures of Power, always prepared
to sanctify and abet any the most enormous Wickedness, if it were gainful : And these are they
who have often misled good Men in the worst
Prejudices.

Timoleon, one of the wisest and most virtuous
Men that ever blessed this Earth, spent a long and
glorious Life in destroying Tyrants ; he killed, or
caused to be killed, his own Brother, when he
could not persuade him to lay down an usurped
Power, and no other Means were left to save his
Country

Country. And if this Action coft him afterwards much Grief and Melancholy, it was owing to his own tender Heart, and the Curfes and Reproaches of a Mother otherwife indulgent. He was even cenfured for this his Sorrow, as if it had got the better of his Love to Mankind; and when he at laft overcame it, he fhewed that it was not oc-cafioned for having flain a Tyrant, but his Bro-ther; for he immortalized the reft of his Life in doing nothing elfe but deftroying Tyrants, and re-ftoring Liberty.

But if the Killing *Cæfar* were fo great a Crime, how comes *Catiline* to be ftill fo univerfally deteft-ed, for only intending what *Cæfar* accomplifhed! It is true, *Cæfar* did not burn *Rome*; nor did he fave it out of any Tendernefs to it, but faved it for himfelf: He fpared Fire, only becaufe the Sword was fuff.cient. I would here afk another Queftion :——If *Oliver Cromwell* had died by any of the numerous Confpiracies formed to take away his Life; would Pofterity have condemned the Action for this Reafon alone, that it was done the only Way that it could be done ?

But there is an Inftance in the *Roman* Hiftory, that will fet this Matter yet in a fuller Light ;—it is the Story of *Spartacus*, a *Thracian* Slave and Gladiator, who bid fair for being Lord of the *Roman* World. He feems to me to have had per-fonal Qualifications and Abilities, as great as thofe of *Cæfar*, without *Cæfar*'s Birth and Education, and without the Meafure of *Cæfar*'s Guilt. For I hope all Mankind will allow it a lefs Crime in any Man to attempt to recover his own Liberty, than wantonly and cruelly to deftroy the Liberty of his Country.

It

It is aftonifhing to confider, how a poor Slave, from the Whip and the Chain, followed only by about Seventy fugitive Gladiators, fhould begin a Revolt from the moft powerful State that ever the World faw ; fhould gather and form, by his Courage and Dexterity, a formidable Army ; fhould infpire Refolution and Fidelity into the very Dregs of Mankind ; fhould qualify his fudden Soldiers, compofed of Thieves and Vagabonds, to face and defeat the *Roman* Legions, that were a Terror to the World, and had conquered it ; fhould keep together, without Pay or Authority, a raw and lawlefs Rabble, till he had vanquifhed two *Roman* Armies, and one of them a *Prætorian* Army : And even when *Crixius*, his Fellow-Commander, envying his Glory and Succefs, had withdrawn from him, and carried with him a great Number of his Forces, and was cut to Pieces with Twenty Thoufand of his Men, by *Q. Arrius* the Prætor, yet he ftill continued to conquer. He beat that very *Arrius* that had killed *Crixius* ; he defeated *Lentulus* the Conful ; he overcame *L. Gellius*, another Conful ; and in all likelihood, had he not been weakened by the above Defection of *Crixius*, he had beat *Craffus* too, and feen himfelf Lord of *Rome*.

Now I would afk the Advocates of lawlefs Power, the Friends to the Life and Name of *Cæfar*, Whether *Spartacus*, if he had fucceeded in his laft Battle againft *Craffus*, had been lawful and irrefiftible King of *Rome ?* And whether the Senate and People of *Rome*, with the greateft Part of the known World, would have owed him Duty and Allegiance ? Or, would he not have continued ftill a Thief and a Robber ? And if he had continued

nued fo, then, by all the Laws of Nature and Self-Prefervation, as well as by the municipal Laws of every Country in the World, every Man was at Liberty to feize him how he could, and to kill him, if he refifted, or ran away.

Tell me, O ye unlimited Slaves, ye Beafts of lawlefs Power, ye loyal Levellers of Right and Wrong! how came *Cæfar* by a better Title to Dominion than *Spartacus* had, whofe Sword was as good, though not quite fo profperous and deftructive, as *Cæfar's* ? Tell me where lav the Difference between them, unlefs in their different Succefs ; and that *Spartacus* was as great a Man, but *Cæfar* a greater Traytor and Tyrant?

Indeed, had Sir *Robert Filmer*, or any other of the honeft and fage Difcoverers of *Adam's* right Heir, lived in thofe Days (as they have done fince, and plainly pointed him out) and complimented *Cæfar*, as doubtlefs they would, with a lineal and hereditary Title from *Æneas, wandering Prince of Troy* ; he might have been called the Lord's A-nointed, as well as others, and his Affaffination been accounted Rebellion, and worfe than the Sin of Witchcraft. But as I do not find that *Cæfar,* though he valued himfelf upon his Defcent from the pious *Trojan* Hero, did yet claim any dictatorial Right by Virtue of his illuftrious Parentage ; I have therefore taken Liberty to treat him as a mere Traytor, an Ufurper, and a Tyrant.

G

I am, &c.

SATURDAY, *December* 9, 1721.   No. 56.

A Vindication of Brutus *for having killed* Cæsar.

S I R,

HAVING proved in my laft, I think unan-
fwerably, that *Cæfar* was rightly killed ; I
will here enquire, whether *Brutus* and the other
Tyrannicides did right in killing him ? And methinks, if it has been fhewn that he ought to have
been flain, as an Enemy to every *Roman* Citizen,
and virtuous Man ; every *Roman* Citizen, and
every virtuous Man, had a Right to flay him.

But fince there are in our World fo many little
and cramped Spirits, who dare not think out of
the vulgar Path, though ever fo crooked and dark,
and perhaps firft ftruck out by Ignorance or
Fraud : Narrow Minds, which, locked up in received Syftems, fee all Things through falfe Mir-
rors, and as they are reprefented by ftrong Prejudices, prevailing Cuftoms, and very often by Corruption and Party-Intereft : I fhall, as I have Occafion, endeavour to difperfe thefe thick and deceitful Mifts from before weak Eyes ; and fhall
confider the prefent Queftion, as well as all others
that come before me, as they appear in their own
Nature, independent on the Quirks of Pedants,
and the narrow Jurifdiction of inferior Tribunals :
I fhall bring them before the great Tribunal of
Heaven ; and affert the Caufe of Liberty and
Truth, by Arguments deduced from Common-
Senfe, and the common Good of Mankind.

It

It is generally alledged againſt *Brutus*, and ſome of thoſe who joined with him in this great Action, that they were highly obliged by *Cæſar* ; which is a ſtrange Objection.   How were they obliged ? He gave *Brutus* a Life, which he could not take from him without Murder ; and did a mighty generous Thing in not murdering *Brutus* for defending his Country, animated by his own virtuous Spirit, and the known Laws of *Rome !* This is the Obligation of a Highwayman, who, taking away your Money, which is all he wants, kindly leaves you your Life. Are you obliged in Honour, Conſcience, or Common-Senſe, to ſpare the Robber, becauſe he was not a Murderer ? Or are you obliged not to purſue and take him, and to kill him, if he refuſe to ſubmit ? In Truth, *Cæſar* was one of the greateſt Robbers and Murderers that ever lived: Every Man ſlain in that unjuſt, bloody, and unnatural War, which he wantonly and maliciouſly made upon his Country, was murdered : And the World was the mighty Spoil which he gained by univerſal Murder and Rapine. He was, in ſhort, a Man ſo conſummately wicked, that the ſtrongeſt Words which you can uſe, and the bittereſt Inſtances which you can bring, to paint out him and his Actions, will be but faint, compared to him and his Actions.

As to the Places and Favours conferred upon *Brutus*, by *Cæſar*; they were not *Cæſar's*, but *Rome's*. He was only *rapti largitor. Cæſar* had no Right to the Publick, nor to diſpoſe of it, or its Emoluments.   It was all barefaced Uſurpation. Beſides, when Favours of this, or any kind, with-hold a Man from his Duty, they are miſchievous Baits and Corruptions, and ought to

bind

bind no Man, as they never will a virtuous Man : And we fee how *Brutus*, who was the moft virtuous Man upon Earth, underftood and difregarded them.

They were only the artful Shackles of a Tyrant, intended to bind the bold and free Mind of *Brutus* to his Intereft : But he, who owed no Allegiance but to the Commonwealth, fcorned the deceitful Smiles and Generofity of its Oppreffor ; who was bribing him to be his Slave, with the Gifts and Offices of his Country, to which he himfelf had no Title, but *Brutus* had every Title. This therefore was a Piece of impudent Civility, which *Brutus* could not but deteft, as it was a fhameful and melancholy Proof of *Cæfar*'s Tyranny, and of his own and *Rome*'s Vaffalage. They were hollow and deftructive Favours ; it was High-Treafon to be the Author of them : And was not Death fignally due to fuch High-Treafon ? *Brutus* therefore made the propereft Return.

Cæfar had ufurped the *Roman* World, and was cantoning it out to his Creatures as became a Tyrant, and paying his perfonal Creatures with the publick Bounty. As the worft Tyrants muft have fome Friend ; and as the beft Men do them the moft Credit, and bring them the moft Support, if fuch can be got ; *Cæfar* had Senfe enough to know, that he could never buy *Brutus* too dear ; and fo paid him great Court. But *Brutus* faw the Tyrant's Defign, and his own Shame ; and every Civility was a frefh Provocation. It was as if a Thief breaking into a Houfe to rob a Lady of her Jewels, fpoke thus to her Son ; *Sir, pray permit me, or affift me, to cut your Mother's Throat, and feize*
her

her Treasure, and I will generously reward you with your Life, and lend you one or two of her Diamonds to sparkle in as long as I think fit. Could such a villainous Civility as this engage the Son, especially a virtuous Son, to any thing but Revenge? And would not the only Way that he could take it, be the best Way?

Cæsar took from *Brutus* his Liberty, and his legal Title to his Life and his Estate, and gave him in lieu of it a precarious one during his own arbitrary Will and Pleasure: Upon the same Terms he gave him some mercenary Employments, as Hire for that great good Man's Assistance to support his Tyranny. Could the great and free Soul of *Brutus* brook this? Could *Brutus* be the Instrument or Confederate of lawless Lust? *Brutus* receive Wages from an Oppressor! That great, virtuous, and popular *Brutus*; who, if the Commonwealth had subsisted, might, from his Reputation, Birth, Abilities, and his excellent Worth, have challenged the most honourable and advantageous Offices in it, without owing Thanks to *Cæsar*.

So that the Injuries done by *Cæsar* to *Brutus* were great, heinous, and many; and the Favours none. All the Mercy shewn by *Cæsar* was Art and Affectation, and pure Self-Love. He had found in the *Roman* People so universal a Detestation of the bloody Measures of *Marius*, *Cinna*, and *Sylla*: He saw the whole Empire so reduced and enervated by repeated Proscriptions and Massacres, that he thought it his Interest to establish his new-erected Dominion by different Measures; and to reconcile, by a false and hypocrital Shew of Clemency, the Minds of Men, yet bleeding with their late and former Wounds, to his Usurpation,

pation. That *Cæfar*, the ufurping and deftructive *Cæfar*, who had flaughtered Millions, and wantonly made Havock of the human Race, had any other Sort of Mercy, than the Mercy of Policy and Deceit, will not be pretended by any Man, that knows his and the *Roman* Story. *Brutus* therefore being the moft reverenced and popular Man in *Rome*, it became the Craft of the Tyrant to make *Brutus* his Friend ; it was adding a Sort of Sanctity to a wicked Caufe : Whereas the Death of *Brutus* by *Cæfar*, would have made *Cæfar* odious and dreadful even amongft his own Followers.

But it is faid, that *Brutus* fubmitted to *Cæfar*, and was bound by his own Act. Here the Allegation is true, but the Confequence falfe. Did not *Brutus* fubmit to *Cæfar*, as innocent Men are often forced to fubmit to the Galleys, the Wheel, and the Gibbet ? He fubmitted, as a Man robbed and bound fubmits to a Houfe-breaker, who, with a Piftol at his Heart, forces from him a Difcovery of his Treafure, and a Promife not to profecute him. Such Engagements are not only void in themfelves, but aggravate the Injury, and become themfelves frefh Injuries. By the Law of Nature and Reafon, as well as by the pofitive Inftitutions of every Country, all Promifes, Bonds, or Oaths, extorted by Durefs, that is, by unlawful Imprifonments or Menaces, are not obligatory : It is, on the contrary, a Crime to fulfil them ! becaufe an Acquiefcence in the Impofitions of lawlefs Villains, is abetting lawlefs Villains.

Befides, it was not in the Power of *Brutus* to alter his Allegiance, which he had already engaged to the Commonwealth, which had done nothing
to

to forfeit the fame. For how lawful foever it be for Subjects to transfer their Obedience to a Conqueror, in a foreign War, when the former Civil Power can no longer protect them ; or to a new Magiftrate made by Confent, when the old had forfeited or refigned : It is ridiculous to fuppofe, that they can transfer it to a domeftick Traytor and Robber, who is under the fame Ties and Allegiance with themfelves, and, by all Acts of Violence, Treafon, and Ufurpation, extorts a Submiffion from his oppreffed Mafters and Fellow-Subjects.—At leaft fuch Allegiance can never be pre-engaged, whilft any Means in Nature are left to rid the World of fuch a Monfter.

It is a poor Charge againft *Brutus*, that *Cæfar* intended him for his Heir and Succeffor. *Brutus* fcorned to fucceed a Tyrant : And what more glorious for *Brutus*, than thus to own that the dangerous and bewitching Profpect of the greateft Power that ever mortal Man poffeffed, could not fhake the firm and virtuous Heart of *Brutus*, nor corrupt his Integrity ? To own that no perfonal Confiderations, even the higheft upon Earth, could reconcile him to a Tyrant ; and that he preferred the Liberty of the World to the Empire of the World !

The above Charges therefore againft *Brutus* can hardly come from any but thofe, who, like the profane and flavifh *Efau*, would fell their Birthright for a Mefs of Pottage ; would facrifice their Duty to their Intereft ; and, unconcerned what becomes of the reft of Mankind, would promote Tyranny, if they might but fhine in its Trappings. But an honeft Mind, a Mind great and virtuous, fcorns and hates all Ambition, but that

of

of doing Good to Men, and to all Men; it despises momentary Riches, and ill-gotten Power; it enjoys no vicious and hard-hearted Pleasures, arising from the Miseries of others: But it wishes and endeavours to procure impartial, diffusive, and universal Happiness to the whole Earth.

This is the Character of a great and good Mind; and this was the great and sublime Soul of the immortal *Brutus.*

From this Mention of the slippery and dangerous Favours of Tyrants, I would just observe, as I go along, that, to any Man who values Virtue or Liberty, Twenty Pounds a Year in a free Country, is preferable to the being First Minister to the *Great Turk*; whose Ministers, by their Station and Allegiance, are obliged to be Oppressors, and are often rewarded with the Bow-string for their most faithful Services to their Master, and for Services perhaps performed by his Command.

But to return to *Brutus:* He had on his Side the Law of Self-Preservation, the Spirit of the *Roman* Constitutions, and of those Laws of Liberty, which had subsisted near Five Hundred Years, but were now destroyed by the Usurper. And during all those long and renowned Ages of Liberty, the destroying of Tyrants was ever accounted Glory and Heroism. And, as every Law of the Commonwealth was against *Cæsar*, who was an open Enemy to the Commonwealth; the Commonwealth, and all its Laws, were for *Brutus*, its greatest and best Subject. *Cæsar's* Laws were none, and worse than none; but the whole Life and Actions of *Brutus* were agreeable to the Constitution of his Country.

Suppose

Suppose *Brutus*, having killed *Cæsar*, had succeeded him : He could not have been a greater Usurper than *Cæsar* was. And yet would he, in that Case, have been less sacred and inviolable than *Cæsar?* I hope the oppressing of Mankind is not a less Crime than the killing of their Oppressor.

Our *Brutus* could not have greater Ties of Affection to the Tyrant *Cæsar*, who usurped *Rome*, and destroyed its Liberties, than the elder *Brutus* had to his own Sons, whom he put to Death, for a Plot to restore the Tyrant *Tarquin*, a thousand times more innocent than *Cæsar :* And as to the sudden Manner of putting him to Death, *Mutius Scævola* is immortalized for a bold Attempt, to kill by Surprize the *Tuscan* King *Porsenna*, who was a foreign Enemy, making unjust War upon *Rome*, to restore *Tarquin :* And the like Immortality is bestowed upon *Judith*, for killing *Holofernes* deceitfully, when it could be done no other Way. Now both these Men were publick Enemies ; but neither of them a publick Traytor : *Cæsar* was both ; and *dolus an virtus quis in hoste requirat?* Was ever *Aratus* mentioned with Reproach, or does Dr. *Prideaux* mention him with Reproach, for surprizing and expelling *Nicocles*, Tyrant of *Sicyon* ; or has he not gained deathless Fame by that worthy Action ? And how comes the little Tyrant *Nicocles* to be less sacred than the great Tyrant *Cæsar*, who did Millions of Mischiefs more than *Nicocles?*

Let us now see what Dr. *Prideaux* says of *Cæsar* After having told us, that *he was excited by Ambition and Malice*; that he *justly had for the Reward thereof* that Destruction by which he fell ;

the

the Doctor adds thefe Words : " He is faid to
" have flain Eleven Hundred and Ninety-Two
" Thoufand Men ; which proves him to have
" been a terrible Scourge in the Hand of God, for
" the Punifhment of the Wickednefs of that Age.
" —And, confequently, he is to be reputed the
" greateft Peft and Plague that Mankind had
" therein : But notwithftanding this, his Actions
" have with many acquired great Glory to his
" Name : Whereas true Glory is due only to
" thofe who benefit, not to thofe who deftroy,
" Mankind."

All this is honeftly and juftly faid ; but I cannot
reconcile it to what he has faid before, about the
Death of that Deftroyer. Sure, upon his own
Principles, never was true Glory more due to any
mortal Man, than to *Brutus !* His Life and Studies were laid out in doing Good to Mankind ;
whereas *Cæfar* was indeed the greateft Peft and
Plague that Mankind had. For, befides all the
Wickednefs that he did with his own wicked
Hands and Counfels, he fruftrated all the Purpofes,
Virtue, and Bravery, of the old *Romans*, in eftablifhing Liberty, and in conquering, polifhing,
and fetting free great Part of the barbarous World.
All the Battles that they fought, were fought for
him ; all the Blood that they fpilt, was fpilt for
him. *Cæfar* took all, and overturned all. Befides, all the numberlefs and heavy Mifchiefs that
the *Roman* World fuffered from fucceeding Tyrants, were, in a great Meafure, owing to *Cæfar*,
who eftablifhed a Government by Tyrants. He
was in this Senfe the Author of all the Barbarity,
Rapine, and Butcheries, brought upon the Empire, by the *Goths*, *Huns*, *Vandals*, and other Barbarians,

barians, who eafily maftered an Empire, weakened, and already almoft deftroyed, by the Folly, Madnefs, Cruelty, and Prodigality, of the Imperial Tyrants, his Succeffors.

The Doctor takes Notice, that *Caffius Parmenfis*, being the only remaining Tyrannicide, was put to Death by the Command of *Auguftus*. And he obferves upon it, that Murder feldom efcapes the vindictive Hand of God, and efpecially the Murder of Princes. All this may be true ; and yet, What is all this to *Julius Cæfar ?* If *Cæfar* was a Prince, any Robber or Murderer that has Force and Villainy enough, may be a Prince ; and Blood, and Wounds, and Treafon, conftitute a Prince. Every Soldier in *Cæfar's* Army had as good a Right to the Government of *Rome*, as *Cæfar* had. Was his Style like that of a Prince, or the Father of his Country, when he told his Soldiers, according to *Petronius*, and agreeably to what he did afterwards ;

> ———— *Ite furentes,*
> *Ite mei comites, & caufam dicite ferro.*
> *Judice fortuna cadat alea : Sumite bellum ;*
> *Inter tot fortes armatus nefcio vinci.*

Was not this fetting up open Violence and the Sword for a Title ? If *Rob Roy* had conquered *Scotland*, with his barbarous Highland Hoft ; would he have been a Prince, Prince of *Scotland*? Was *Cromwell* a Prince ? And would *Maffianello* and *Jack Straw*, had they fucceeded, have been Princes ?

As to *Cæfar's* Parts, they added vaftly to his Crimes, and were, as he applied them, only a great Capacity to do great Mifchief. *Curfe on his Virtues,*

Virtues, they have undone his Country! Befides, there
were doubtlefs many Men in *Rome* who had equal
Parts, and infinitely more Merit. *Brutus* particularly had.—The Devil has much greater Abilities
than *Cæfar* had, and is alfo a Prince, a very great
Prince; the Executioner of God's Vengeance too,
the greateft Executioner: And yet are we not exprefly commanded to refift him? The Plague is
often the Inftrument of God's Judgment; are we
therefore not to refift the Plague, by proper Diet
and Antidotes? The Bite of an Adder may be the
Judgment of God; Is it therefore a Sin to tread
upon the Adder's Head, and kill him? Or are Antidotes againft all other Plagues lawful; but none
lawful againft the worft, the moft lafting and de-
ftruâive of all Plagues, the Plague of Tyranny?
Or is an Adder lefs facred that a Tyrant? And
why? I hope God made Adders as well as *Cæfar*.
A Storm may be a Judgment; muft we not therefore difcharge a great Gun againft it, in order to
difperfe it? Or pray how comes one Sort of the
Inftruments of God's Judgment to be more facred
than another? I am fure, God detefts Tyrants;
and if they be God's Minifters, fo are Plagues and
Serpents, and fo is *Satan* himfelf.

   Brutus was one of the propereft Perfons to kill
Cæfar; as he was of all the Men in *Rome* the
moft reverenced and popular. His Wifdom, and
Virtue, and Publick Spirit, were known and adored: The Confent of the Senate, and of all good
Men, was with him; none but the proftitute
Creatures of Power, and thofe that ambitioufly
fought it, with their deceived and hireling Followers, condemned him; nor durft even they at
firft. But *Brutus*, out of his too great Goodnefs
            ·nd

and Generofity, fpared *Anthony*, who ought to have accompanied *Cæfar*. But while the wild *Anthony* remained, the Root of the Evil was not quite pluckcd up. He began a new War upon his Country. The Senate, however, declared for the Tyrannicides ; declared *Mark Anthony* a publick Enemy for making War upon *Decimus Brutus*, who was one of them ; and fent both the Confuls with an Army againft *Anthony*, in Defence of *Brutus* : And had it not been for the treacherous and ungrateful young *Cæfar*, the Commonwealth would have been, in all Likelihood, thoroughly eftablifhed. But this young Traytor, like his Uncle *Julius*, turned the Arms of the Commonwealth upon the Commonwealth, and joined with its Enemy *Mark Anthony* to opprefs it.

The terrible Proceedings and bloody Profcriptions that followed this Agreement are well known. Nor is it at all ftrange, that not one of the Tyrannicides furvived the Civil War, or died a natural Death. They were almoft all Soldiers and Commanders, and were either moftly flain in Battle, or by the Command of the Conquerors : Their Enemies got the better, and they had no where to fly to. The World was poffeffed by the Ufurpers. If *Brutus* and *Caffius* killed themfelves, rather than fall into their Enemies Hands, and adorn the Triumphs of fuccefsful Traytors ; feveral of the Chiefs of the other Party did alfo kill themfelves during the War ; particularly *Dolabella*, and many of the Principals of his Party at *Antioch*, when *Caffius* befieged them there. Was this alfo a Judgment ?

Brutus and *Caffius* killed themfelves ! What then ? Was it not done like *Romans*, like virtuous
old

old *Romans*, thus to prefer Death to Slavery ? It
was a *Roman* Spirit ; and thofe who poffeffed it,
did as much difdain to be Tyrants, as to fubmit
to Tyranny ; a Spirit that fcorned an ignominious
Life, held only at the Mercy of an Ufurper, or
by flattering his Villainy, and abetting his Ufurpations ; and a Spirit, which thofe that want it can
never admire. Great Souls are not comprehended
by Small ! It is undoubtedly true, that by the
Precepts of Chriftianity we are not at Liberty to
difpofe of our own Lives ; but are to wait for the
Call of Heaven to alleviate or end our Calamities :
But the *Romans* had no other Laws to act by, but
the natural Dictates of uncorrupted Reafon. I
call upon the great Pretenders to Philofophy and
refined Morals, to affign one fair Reafon, why a
Roman, why *Brutus* and *Caffius*, fhould prefer a
miferable Life to an honourable Death ; fhould
bear Vaffalage, Chains, and Tortures of Body or
Mind, when all thofe Evils were to be avoided by
doing only that, which, by the Courfe of Nature,
every Man muft foon do. It is better not to be,
than to be unhappy ; and the fevereft Judgment
on the Wicked is, that they fhall live for ever,
and can never end their Miferies : Much lefs can
it be any Service to Society, to keep alive by Art
or Force a melancholy, miferable, and ufelefs
Member, grown perhaps burthenfome too by Age
and Infirmities.

In this Light we muft view the Actions of the
old *Romans*, guided only by Nature, and unreftrained from Suicide by any Principles of their
Religion. We find, on the contrary, in Hiftory,
many Examples of the great and magnanimous
Heroes of Antiquity, choofing voluntary Death,

often

often in the midft of Health, with the greateft Calmnefs of Mind ; fometimes from Satiety of Life and Glory, either when they could gain no more, or apprehending that the future Caprices of unconftant Fortune might fully the paft ; and oftener ftill, to avoid fubmitting to Difgrace and Servitude.

A voluntary Death from fuch Motives as thefe, was, among the Antients, one of the Paths to Immortality ; and, under certain Circumftances, none but mean and abject Minds declined it. *Roman* Ladies often chofe it. *Cleopatra*, Queen of *Egypt*, chofe a long premeditated Death, rather than be led Captive to *Rome*. And when *Perfeus* fent to P. *Æmilius*, befeeching him with all Earneftnefs, That fo great a Prince, late Lord of *Macedon*, and good Part of *Greece*, might not be led, like a Slave, in Chains at his Chariot Wheel, to grace his Triumph ; he received this fhort Anfwer, That *it was in his own Power to prevent it :* Thus fignifying to him, that he deferved the Difgrace, if he would live to bear it.

Even under the Difpenfations of a new Religion, which God Almighty condefcended perfonally to teach Mankind ; Human Nature has prevailed fo far over revealed Truths, that in Multitudes of Inftances a voluntary Death is approved, at leaft not condemned, by almoft the greateft Part of the World. Men in extreme Pain and Agonies do often refufe Phyfick, and the Means of preferving their Lives, Days, Weeks, and Months longer. Men in lingering and defperate Diftempers go, uncalled, to mount a Breach in a Siege, or into the midft of the Battle, to meet certain Death. Great Commanders have done
the

the fame, when the Day went againſt them, rather than furvive being beaten. Commanders of
Ships have blown up themſelves and their Ships,
rather than be the Prey of the Conqueror. Towns
beſieged, when they could defend themſelves no
longer, have firſt burnt their Town, then preci-
pitated themſelves deſperately amongſt their Enemies, to procure an honourable Death and Revenge. Even common Malefactors often chooſe
to die, rather than diſcover their Accomplices; and
always get Credit by doing ſo. And the Stories
of the *Decii*, of *Celanus*, of the Great *Cato*, and
even of *Otho*, and many other of the great Examples of Antiquity, made immortal by this Act
of antient Heroiſm, are ſtill read with Admiration.

I ſhall, for a Concluſion of this long Paper, give
my Readers the Sentiments of the excellent Mr.
Cowley, concerning *Brutus* and *Cæſar*, in his Ode
intitled *B R U T U S*.

> *Can we ſtand by and ſee*
> *Our Mother robb'd, and bound, and raviſh'd be,*
>   *Yet not to her Aſſiſtance ſtir,*
> *Pleas'd with the Strength and Beauty of the Raviſher?*
> *Or ſhall we fear to kill him, if before*
>   *The cancell'd Name of Friend he bore?*
> *Ingrateful* Brutus *do they call?*
> *Ingrateful* Cæſar, *who could* Rome *inthral!*
> *An Act more barbarous and unnatural*
> *(In th' exact Balance of true Virtue try'd)*
> *Than his Succeſſor* Nero's *Parricide!*
> * * * * * * * * *
> *What Mercy could the Tyrant's Life deſerve*
>   *From him who kill'd himſelf rather than ſerve?*
>   * * *

* * * * * * * * * *

What Joy can human Things to us afford,
When we see perish thus by odd Events,
By ill Men and wretched Accidents,
The best Cause, and best Man that ever drew a Sword?
When we see
The false Octavius *and wild* Anthony,
God-like Brutus ! *conquer Thee ?*

G   I am, &c.

SATURDAY, *December* 16, 1721. No. 57.

Of false Honour, publick and private.

SIR,

I Have more than once complained in these Letters, that the best Things being most abused are
capable of doing the greatest Harm : Nor is it a
new Observation, whatever new Occasion there
may be, at all Times, to repeat it. Men have
been ever deceived by good Names into an Approbation of ill Things, sanctified by these Names.
Imposture and Delusion have been called Religion,
and thought so ; Oppression and Rapine have been
called Government, and esteemed Government.
Teachers have degenerated into Deceivers, Sub-
mission into Slavery, Taxation into Plundering,
Protection into Destruction, and Magistrates into
Murderers, without changing their Names : Power
and Right have been ever confounded ; and Success, or the want of Success, has turned Villainy
into Virtue, and Virtue into Villainy.

Hence

Hence it is that little Crimes and fmall Criminals have been detefted and punifhed, while great Malefactors have been generally reverenced and obeyed : and that little Rogues have been called Thieves, and hanged ; and great Thieves have been ftiled Conquerors and Princes, and fometimes deified.   Your *Alexanders* and *Cæfars* were only Felons above the Gallows; and fo have been many others of much lefs Figure than they.   Great Crimes protect themfelves, and one another ; fo that, in effect, Crimes are not always punifhed becaufe they are Crimes, but becaufe they are not mighty Crimes : Nor, in the inflicting of Punifhments, has the Offence or the Offender been confidered, but only the Figure of the Offender ; who, if he were poor and neceffitous, has been put to Death ; if great and ambitious, has been protected or preferred.   And thus it is, that Halters and Garters, Axes and White Staves, Palaces and Dungeons, have been often miferably confounded and mifplaced.

Thus are the Boundaries and Diftinction between Good and Evil almoft loft in the World. To illuftrate this in every Inftance that deferves Illuftration, would be to write a Folio inftead of a Letter ; at prefent I fhall confine myfelf to the Confideration of falfe Honour, which has done much more Mifchief to Mankind than ever real Honour did Good, as it is more conducing to the little perfonal Gratifications, and the crooked Self-Ends of particular Men.

True Honour is an Attachment to honeft and beneficent Principles, and a good Reputation ; and prompts a Man to do Good to others, and indeed to all Men, at his own Coft, Pains, or Peril.

Falfe

Falfe Honour is a Pretence to this Character, but does Things that deftroy it: And the Abufe of Honour is called Honour, by thofe who from that good Word borrow Credit to act bafely, rafhly, or foolifhly.

A Man cannot act honourably in a bad Caufe. That he thinks it a good Caufe, is not a good Excufe; for Folly and Miftake is not Honour: Nor is it a better Excufe, that he is engaged in it, and has pledged his Faith to fupport it, and act for it; for this is to engage his Honour againft Honour, and to lift his Faith in a War againft Truth. To fay that he is afhamed to defert it, is to fay that he is afhamed to do an honeft Thing; and that he prefers falfe Shame to true Honour, which engages the Man that poffeffes it to hate and break all criminal Engagements. If a Man enter into a Party or Society, becaufe he thinks it an honeft Society; is he obliged to continue in it, when he finds it a Society of Knaves? And does his Honour oblige him to be a Knave too, or to defert thofe that are Knaves? Or, does a Robber, who leaves the Gang, violate his Honour, which was only an Obligation to rob?

A good Confcience, an honeft Heart, and clean Hands, are infeparable from true Honour; nor does true Honour teach any Man to act againft his Judgment. It muft be convinced before it acts, and mere Authority has no Weight with it. In human Matters, it does not confider what is commanded, but what ought to be commanded; and before it executes an Injunction, enquires whether the fame be rational and juft. When fuperior Orders are unjuft, the Honour of Obedience is taken away; for Honour is not the Inftrument

of

of Evil ; it is therefore falfe and pretended Honour, to execute and vindicate a bad Action by an unjuft Command.   Indeed, no Command of any Confequence ought to be obeyed, but what is or ought to be Law, and is not forbidden by any Law.

But this is only Reafoning, which has but little Force with Men when it combats their Intereft and worft Paffions.   To them therefore who follow the Guides of Gain and Ambition, what I have here faid is not addreffed ; but to thofe who, contrary to their Intereft, follow and approve others whofe only Principle is Intereft.

Falfe Honour has more Power over Men than Laws have ; and thofe who defpife all the Ties of Laws, and of Religion and Humanity, are often very exact in obferving all the fantaftical and wicked Rules of falfe Honour.   There are no Debts fo punctually paid as thofe contracted at Play : though there are exprefs Laws againft Play, and againft paying of Money won at Play ; nay, 'tis penal to pay fuch Debts.   And yet thofe that are thus exact in paying to their own Ruin, and in Defiance of Law, whatever Debts they contract to avowed Sharpers, who live by cheating and picking Pockets, and are the Deftruction of Families, and a publick Nuifance : I fay, thofe Men thus exact in Unrighteoufnefs and their own Wrong, fhall run in Debt to honeft Tradefmen, without any Purpofe of paying them, and, unconcerned, fee them broke, imprifoned, and undone, for want of fuch Payment.   So lawlefly juft are they to Rogues that ruin them, and fo barbaroufly unjuft to induftrious and credulous Men, who feed and clothe them !

Is

Is this Honour! What Dupes are we to Words
and to our own Vice and Folly! It is but fmall
Comfort to us, that this voluntary Madnefs prevailed of old amongft our barbarous *German* Anceftors; of whofe diftracted Propenfity to Gaming
Tacitus gives us this aftonifhing Account: *Aleam
fobrii inter feria exercent, tanta lucrandi perdendive
temeritate, ut cum omnia defecerunt, extremo ac no-
viffimo jactu, de libertate & de corpore contendant.
Victus voluntariam fervitutem adit, quamvis junior,
quamvis robuftior, adligari fe ac venire patitur. Ea
eft in re prava pervicacia: ipfi fidem vocant.*

    " Gaming is one of their moft ferious Employ-
" ments, and even fober they are Gamefters!
" To this rafh Vice they are fo violently addict-
" ed, that when they have wantonly loft all,
" they have not done, but defperately ftake their
" Liberty and their Perfons upon the laft Throw.
" The Lofer goes calmly into Bondage; and
" though the younger and the ftronger, fuffers
" himfelf tamely to be bound and fold by him that
" wins. Such is their vicious Perfeverance in
" Folly! they themfelves call it Honour.

Our modern Gamefters do not indeed go quite
this Length; they only fell themfelves, with their
Families and Pofterity, to Beggary: For as to their
Bodies, no body will ftake any Thing againft them.
But in Point of Honour, in Gaming, we ftill re-
tain the Strictnefs of thefe our polite Anceftors at
Play, and generoufly pay to the laft Morfel of
Bread, and venture Famine rather than a Dun
from one that has foiled us at the Art of picking
Pockets.——— As to other Duns, honeft and necef-
fitous Duns, we matter them not; and Debts of

real

real Honour and Confcienc, do not at all touch
our Honour.

Thus is Honour fet up againft Virtue and Law.
Good Laws not executed are worfe than none,
and only teach Men to defpife Law: whereas
Reverence and Obedience go together. No Law
will or can ever be executed by inferior Magiftrates, while the Breach of it is openly encouraged
by the Example of fuperior. Does any Man
think that the beft Laws, even infpired Laws,
againft Duelling, would have any Effect, if there
was at the fame Time a Duelling-Office kept
open at St. *James*'s ? The Example of thofe that
fhould execute Laws, or fee them executed, is
ftronger than the Authority of thofe that make
them. The Example of *Vefpafian* did more towards the Reftraint of Luxury, than all the fump-
tuary Laws of *Rome* could do till his Time. *Præ-
cipuus adftricti moris auctor Vefpafianus fuit. Obfe-
quium inde in principem, & æmulandi amor, validior
quam pœna ex legibus & metus.* " *Vefpafian* was
" himfelf a fpecial Inftance and Author of Tem-
" perance and Frugality. From hence grew in
" the People a Reverence for the Example of
" the Prince, and an Emulation to conform
" their Manners to his ; —a Tie much ftronger
" than the Dread of Laws and all their Penal-
" ties.

It is moreover become a mighty Piece of Honour to repair one Crime by another, and a worfe;
and when one has done you an Injury, he muft,
by the Rules of Honour, fight to defend it. Having affronted or harmed you, contrary to Juftice
and Honour, he makes you Satisfaction by taking
away your Life, according to the Impulfes of true
Honour;

Honour ; fo here is a War of Honour againft Honour and Juftice and common Senfe.

Another Piece of Honour is an Adherence to Error, after Conviction, and not to change a bad Religion for a better. To have been born in a certain Faith, is juft as good Senfe as to have been born a Lawyer or Mathematician ; and yet that fame is often the beft and trueft Reafon againft Change ! And therefore we often adhere againft all our Reafon, to what others faid or did for us without our Confent, and when we had no Reafon. Becaufe perhaps fome People promifed for us when we were a Day old, that we fhould Forty Years afterwards, and all our Life, count Beads, worfhip unfavoury Bones, be governed by Deceivers, and believe Contradictions ; are we therefore obliged to do all this, though we find it to be againft all Religion ? Muft we be Hypocrites, becaufe our Anceftors were Fools ? Are old Falfhoods and Fooleries the Standard of our Honour ? Are we never to mend a wretched Condition, and never to make ufe of our Confcience ? If fo, then here is a War of Honour againft Confcience, a War of Faith againft Belief, and a War of Religion againft Perfuafion !

Another Piece of falfe Honour has fometimes been that of ferving a Prince at the Expence of one's Country, though the ferving of that Country was the only Duty and only Bufinefs of the Prince, and of every Man in Office under him. But this, though a Truth as felf-evident as any in the Bible, has been fo little underftood or practifed, that the wicked Execution of impious Engagements made to a Tyrant, againft thofe made to Society, has been called Honour. And it has frequently

quently been the Honour of a Courtier, to execute
all the ill Purpofes of a Court againſt his Country.   And here was the War of Honour againſt
Duty.

The Honour of a Party is to adhere to one another, right or wrong ; and though their Chief
be a Knave and a Traytor, their Honour is engaged to be honeſt to him in all his Rogueries and
Treaſon.   And this is a War of Honour againſt
Honeſty.

The Honour and *bona fide* of ſome Princes have
been of that odd and unprincely Contexture, that
they were never once reſtrained by the ſame, from
deceiving, plaguing, invading, robbing, and uſurping upon their Neighbours, and doing Things
which would have entitled a plain Subject to the
Gibbet.   Their Honour ſeems to have been deeply
concerned to have no Honour :   And though their
Faith was engaged to protect their Subjects ; yet
their Honour, on the other Side, was engaged to
pillage and enſlave them.   And here grew the
Royal War of Honour againſt Faith and Equity !

How many peaceable Nations have been robbed,
how many Millions of Innocents butchered, out
of mere Honour, princely Honour ?   This Honour is indeed ſo wild, miſchievous, and extravagant, that Words, the moſt warm and ſignificant
Words, fail in deſcribing it.   I ſhall therefore ſub-
join a few Inſtances of its Spirit, and conclude.

His Grace, *Villiers*, firſt Duke of *Buckingham*,
engaged his Country in Two mad Wars at once
with the Two greateſt Powers in *Europe*, becauſe
his Honour had ſuffered a Rebuff in his Attempts
to debauch Two great foreign Ladies.   *Europe* was
to be embroiled ; Lives, Treaſure, and the Safety
oF

of Kingdoms to be rifqued and thrown away, to vindicate, forfooth, his Grace's debauched Honour.

Cambyfes, to revenge an Affront put upon his Father many Years before by an *Egyptian* King, in the Bufinefs of fending him a Wife, involved the World in a Flame of War; and at the Expence of perhaps a Million of Lives, and the Deftruction of Kingdoms, did at laft heroically vindicate his Father's Honour and his own, upon the Bones of a dead King, whom he caufed to be dug up, and, after many Indignities, caft into the Fire.

White Elephants are rare in Nature, and fo greatly valued in the *Indies*, that the King of *Pegu* hearing that the King of *Siam* had got Two, fent an Embaffy in Form, to defire one of them of his Royal Brother, at any Price: But being refufed, he thought his Honour concerned to wage War for fo great an Affront. So he entered *Siam* with a vaft Army, and with the Lofs of Five Hundred Thoufand of his own Men, and the Deftruction of as many of the *Siamefes*, he made himfelf Mafter of the Elephant, and retrieved his Honour.

Darius (I think it was *Darius* the *Mede*) found his Honour concerned to chaftife the *Scythians* for having invaded *Afia* a Hundred and Thirty Years before; and loft a great Army to vindicate his Honour, which yet was not vindicated; that is, he miffed the white Elephant. For,

In fhort, Honour and Victory are generally no more than white Elephants; and for white Elephants the moft deftructive Wars have been often made. What Man free, either by Birth or Spirit,
                                                          could,

could, without Pity and Contempt, behold, as in a late *French* Reign he frequently might behold, a Swarm of flavifh *Frenchmen*, in wooden Shoes, with hungry Bellies, and no Cloaths, dancing round a Maypole, becaufe their *Grand Monarque*, at the Expence of a Million of their Money, and Thirty or Forty Thoufand Lives, had acquired a white Elephant, or, in other Words, gained a Town or Victory?

Inftances are endlefs, or elfe I could name other People, who have employed themfelves feveral Years in catching white Elephants by Sea and Land; but I am in hafte to conclude.

G

I am, &c.

SATURDAY, *December* 23, 1721. No. 58.

Letter from a Lady, with an Anfwer, about Love, Marriage, and Settlements.

To CATO.

SIR,

THOUGH Love, abftracted from Marriage, is a Subject too low for a Statefman, a Politician, and I might add a Philofopher; yet as it relates to that Holy State (as our Church is pleafed to call it) it is worthy the greateft Notice; for though many take upon them to ridicule all lawful and honourable Love, and Marriage, which crowns and proves it, yet I will venture to affirm, that hardly any Perfon lives a long Life without
defiring

desiring at some Part of it to enter into that State: It is like Religion, implanted in our Natures ; and all Men have a Notion that 'tis the Way to Happiness, though all do not practise it : The Reasons of this Want of Practice are many ; besides the Degeneracy of human Nature, the Imperfections of both Sexes make them afraid of so close an Affinity ; the Want of Constancy in the Male Sex, and, above all, the Love of Money in both, is the greatest Scandal and Hindrance to this most Honourable State in Life.

I cannot excuse either Sex (though by this Time, both from my Subject and handling of it, you will guess me to be of the weakest) from this last Vice, the Love of Money ; and I might add to it Ambition ; for it seems to me grown the Rule of Marriage, there being few Alliances contracted of late Years, but where this is the chief Motive on the Man's Side, and almost so on the Woman's : No Wonder the Ladies should have catched the Vice ; for when a Woman finds herself slighted for no other Want but that of a large Fortune, she must needs think it worth purchasing at any Rate, and neglect all other Merit as useless.

I do not pretend to say that Virtue and Merit, in our Sex, is to be met with in every Corner of the Streets, as I am too sensible the contrary is ; but sure I am it is to be found, and Judgment was given to the Men in order to distinguish it. But, say your Sex, is Money then to be despised ? Must the contrary be sought ? And has a Lady less Merit for having a large Fortune ? Not always, but indeed too often ; nay, nothing can hinder it but natural good Sense and Temper, joined to great

Care

Care taken in the Education; without that a fuperior Fortune makes a worfe Woman, confequently a worfe Wife.

I was led into this Thought, and which occafioned this Letter, bv a Difappointment that a
young Lady I had a Friendfhip for met with lately,
with relation to this Subject, which coft her her
Life.

She was addreffed to by a Gentleman, whofe
good Senfe and Agreeablenefs would, fhe thought,
attone for fome natural Defects and Infirmities,
which fhe had Penetration enough to find out in
his Temper and Difpofition ; among which his
Love of Money was not the leaft : He was fuperior to her in Fortune ; but fhe was a Gentlewo-
man born, and bred fo, and in every Refpect,
but Money, his Equal : She refolved to fuit herfelf to his Humour ; and fancied herfelf cut out to
pleafe and make him happy, not out of Vanity,
but Inclination to do fo. She had Pride, and did
not greatly care to be obliged, even by the Man
whom fhe loved ; but fanfied fhe could fave up a
Fortune to him in a few Years, and, with the refufing of Prefents, and refigning of Settlements,
attone in great Meafure for the want of it. He
thought it worth while to deceive her for a confiderable Length of Time, for what Reafon I cannot guefs, fhe being a Woman of undoubted Character, which he had known for fome Years before, and all her Actions anfwered : But in fhort
he left her, and that in fo abrupt and rude a Manner, as made her bear it worfe ; not fhewing the
leaft Abatement of his Paffion the laft Time he
faw her, more than at the firft. I wifh that he
had trufted her with the Secret of forfaking her ;
for

for I dare fay fhe would have taken it handfomely, and (for his Advantage) given him up.

The Difappointment met her under an Indifpo-fition of Body, elfe I believe fhe had good Senfe, Reafon, and Refentment enough, to have got the better of it. But fhe died, and without reproach-ing of him, or behaving herfelf unhandfomely; fhe faid fhe was inclined to believe that there was a Fate in Things of that Nature, and wifhed him happier than (fhe doubted) he deferved.

He is now upon the Brink of Marriage to a Lady, that I dare fay he does not like half fo well as this Lady whom he left for her; but fhe has more Money abundantly, which he does not want; and then, though, as I faid before, Money is no Objection, nor need a Woman be fought out that wants it, yet I would not have a Man venture to leave a Woman for no other. Reafon, left he (as too probably he may) chance to repent it.

Sir, if you think this Subject, or our Sex, wor-thy your Notice, we fhall be obliged to you; you are an Author, I might fay it to your Face, capa-ble of ferving any Caufe that you undertake; ours is a charitable one: I am out of the Queftion my-felf, with relation to making my Fortune, or it might not have been fo proper for me to have ftart-ed this Subject, though obfcure; but I have a ge-neral Love for Mankind, and particularly for my own Sex; whofe Caufe I commit to you, as into the Hands of a moft powerful Advocate, and (I hope) a willing Patron. My Sincerity on this Subject cannot be doubted, when I moft humbly fubfcribe myfelf of that Sex whofe Caufe I recom-mend; *viz.*

A WOMAN.
To

To the Lady who wrote the Foregoing.

M A D A M,

YOU will eafily believe me, when I acquaint
you, that I am not a little proud of the Honour you have done me, in thinking me worthy
of the Correfpondence of a Lady, to whom Nature has fhewn herfelf fo indulgent. She feldom
leaves her own Work imperfect; and therefore I
doubt not but fhe has been propitious to you more
Ways than one: And I am perfuaded, that if you
had been the firft Object of the inconftant *Stre-
phon*'s Adoration, he had never worfhipped any
falfe Goddefs.

I can affure you, Madam, you could never
have recommended yourfelf fo much to me, or
have obliged me more, than in engaging me in
this agreeable Manner in the Caufe of helplefs Innocence, and diftreffed Virtue; and in giving me
an Opportunity to confider the greater and better Half of the World in their neareft and moft
engaging Relation. I am, by Profeffion, a Knight-
Errant: It is my Bufinefs to right Wrongs, and
redrefs Injuries; and none more than thofe done
to your tender Sex.

It is a Subject which employs my fofteft and
moft delicate Thoughts and Inclinations; which I
can in nothing gratify fo much, as by contributing
to the Eafe and Happinefs of that Sex, to whom
we owe moft of our own.

That Cordial Drop Heav'n in our Cup has thrown,
To make the naufeous Draught of Life go down;

And

And to attone for the Thousands, Ten Thousands of Evils, to which human Condition is subject.

Hercules himself laid down his Club, and took up a Distaff: And,

> ———*furious* Mars,
> *The only Governor and God of Wars,*
> *When tir'd with Heat and Toil, does oft resort*
> *To taste the Pleasures of the* Paphian *Court.*

I do not therefore depart from my Character, or desert my Duty, in considering this Subject, and attending upon the Concerns of the Fair: With their Cause the Cause of Liberty is blended; and scarce any Man will be much concerned for publick Happiness, unless he enjoys domestick: Publick Happiness being nothing else but the Magistrate's protecting of private Men in their Property, and their Enjoyments. It is certain, that a Man's Interest, in Point of Happiness and Pleasures, is in no Instance so much concerned as in that of Marriage; which being the happiest or unhappiest State in the World, must mostly contribute to his Happiness or Misery.

The Beauty, the Vigour, the Wit, and consequently the Preferment of his Posterity, do much depend upon the Choice of his Wife, and possibly upon his Inclinations to her, and hers to him. We are very careful of the Breed of our Horses, of our Cocks, and our Dogs, and as remarkably neglectful of the Education of our Children; and yet we dedicate Two Thirds of our Substance to our Posterity: For so much is the Difference between the Purchase of Estates of Inheritance, and of Estates only for our own Lives.

Our

Our Wealth does alfo depend in a great Meafure upon domeftick Sympathy and Concord ; and
it is a true Proverb, that *A Man muft afk Leave of
his Wife to be rich :* So great a Share of his Subftance and Profperity muft remain in her Power,
and at her Difcretion, and under her Management,
that if he would thrive and be happy himfelf, he
muft make her fo.

In order to this, he ought to choofe one whofe
Temper, good Senfe, and Agreeablenefs, fhall
make him find his Pleafure in obliging her ; and
by Conftancy and endearing Actions make her
wholly his own, and to do all in her Power to
oblige him.   No Man can live in a conftant State
of Hypocrify in his own Family ; but if he has
Diftaftes, they will certainly break out ; or at leaft
be found out by one who is always about him, and
whofe conftant Bufinefs it is to obferve him, and
his Humours and Affections.   And therefore it is
his beft and only Way to find out fuch a one as he
need not counterfeit a Kindnefs to.

In all my Obfervation, a good Hufband rarely
miffes to make a good Wife.   The Hearts of
Women are naturally fo tender, their Paffions towards their Hufbands fo ftrong, their Happinefs
and the Refpect which they meet with in the
World are fo much owing to their Hufbands, that
we feldom find a married Woman who will not,
with a little real, and often with but a feeming
Kindnefs, do whatever a prudent Hufband will defire of her ; and often, to oblige him, more than
he defires.   And what can be more barbarous, than
to ufe one ill who throws herfelf into his Power,
and depends upon his Protection ; who gives up all
that

that fhe has to his Mercy, and receives it afterwards at his Pleafure ?

It is miferable Folly, to put yourfelf in a Circumftance of being uneafy in your own Houfe,
which ought to be a Retreat from all the Ruffles
and Difappointments that you meet with elfewhere :
In Confequence of this, you muft feek your Pleafures abroad at great Expence, and the Hazard of
your Health, and to the Neglect of your Affairs.
Your Wife too, when fhe finds herfelf neglected
by one in whom fhe had fixed her whole Happinefs, will not bear the Place and Manfion of her
Mifery, but will fall into a Defpondency, and an
Indifference to your Intereft ; and will be apt to
look out in her Turn for Pleafures abroad, when
fhe can have none at home. Women for the moft
part place their Felicity in their Hufbands, and in
their Families ; and generally purfue thofe Views,
till the Unkindnefs, Neglect, and Folly of their
Hufbands render them impracticable.

Whatever Excufe there may be for Men over-
run with Debts, or otherwife very neceffitous, to
aim only at Money in Marriage, and thereby to
throw themfelves into a miferable and naufeous
Imprifonment for Life, to prevent falling into one
but little worfe ; I cannot find one tolerable Reafon in Nature, why any Man in eafy Circumftances, and who does not want the common Neceffaries of Life, fhould purchafe the Superfluities
at fo dear a Price. But it is ftupendous that Men
of Figure and Fortune, who have in their Power
the Means of enjoying not only the Convenien-
cies, but the Luxury and Vices of Life, (if fuch
can be called Enjoyments) fhould yet barter away
all

all their Happiness for a little seeming additional Wealth, which for the most part produces real Poverty.

It is certain, that Ten Men of Birth and Estates have been undone by marrying great Fortunes, for One who has been enriched by it. Most Men pay Twenty *per Cent.* for such Portions, as long as they have any thing to pay. Ten Thousand Pounds additional Fortune, when laid out in Land, will not produce Three Hundred Pounds a Year clear; which Sum will scarce maintain the Tea-Table, and keep the supernumerary Bawbles in Repair; and it will cost as much more to shew them. Besides, when the usual Presents are made, and an expensive Marriage is solemnized, gaudy Clothes and Equipage are bought, and perhaps a *London* House furnished; a considerable Part of this Portion will be disbursed, and the forlorn Hero of this shewy, noisy Farce, will discover, too late, how much more eligible it had been to have married a Lady well born, of a discreet, modest, and frugal Education, and an agreeable Person, with less Money, than a haughty Dame with all her Quality Airs about her, or Mr. *Thimbleman*'s Daughter, though bedecked with as many Trinkets as *Tallboy* or *Jerry Blackacre* upon the Stage.

But before we can complete this Account, we must balance what must be given in lieu of this Lady's Wealth, besides the entire Loss of conjugal and domestick Happiness. It is truly said, that *Gold may be bought too dear*; and I may safely say, that the dearest Purchase now in *England*, is a Wife with a great Fortune, not excepting that of *South-Sea* Stock last Year.

For

For every Thousand Pounds the Lady brings, she must have a Hundred Pounds a Year, at least during her own Life, and often a Rent-Charge, which alone is worth the Purchase Money which she brings, if she outlives her Husband ; and then she brings nothing towards the Issue, which, modestly speaking, are as much her's as her Husband's ; and it is certain, that during her living with him, she spends more than the Interest of it : For (besides her private Expence) the Gay Furniture, the Rich Beds, the *China* Ware, the Tea-Table, the Visiting-Rooms, Rich Coaches, &c. must be chiefly placed to her Account ; and she shares equally in the Table Expence, and in that of the Children and Gardens : And yet, over and above all this, a Man must settle the Remainder of his Estate and Substance out of his own Power, and intail it upon whatever Heir Chance and his Wife bring him ; perhaps upon an ungrateful and disobedient One, made so by his Independency upon his Father ; often upon a foolish and unimprovable One ; sometimes, perhaps, upon a spurious One.

I do not complain of this usual Method of Settlement, as thinking it reasonable that any Man should give a large Sum of Money in Dowry with his Daughter, without taking proper Precautions to provide for her and his own Posterity : But I censure the present great Abuse of giving and demanding such Fortunes, which have inverted the very Ends of Marriage, and made Wives independent on their Husbands, and Sons on their Fathers ; Fortunes, which make Men bargain for their Wives, as they would for Cattle ; and, instead of creating conjugal Friendship and Affection, and all Sorts of domestick Happiness, have produced nothing

thing but Strife, Averfion, and Contention, where
there ought to be perfect Sympathy and Unanimi-
ty ; and have brought into the World a Race of
Monkeys and Baboons, inftead of Creatures with
human Shape and Souls.

Why fhould Men of Fortune and Underftanding bring themfelves, without any Motive from
Reafon or Intereft, into thefe unhappy Circumftances ? Why fhould any Man, without any
Confideration, at leaft any valuable Confideration,
diveft himfelf of the greateft Part of the Property
of his own Eftate ? Why make himfelf only Tenant for Life, when he is in Poffeffion of an Inheritance ; and render himfelf by that Means un-
able to provide againft the many Emergencies of
Life ? Why fubject himfelf to the Infolence of
an ungrateful Heir, or be forced to leave it to an
unworthy One ? Why be obliged to bear the Caprices and Difhonour of a wanton and peevifh
Wife, perhaps made fo by his Neglect, arifing
from his Averfion, the ordinary Effect of Marriage againft Inclination ? when he might have
chofen one every Way fuited to the fame ; and,
by contenting himfelf with lefs Fortune, have kept
the greateft Part of his Eftate in his own Power,
and with it the further Means of obliging her, and
of making her future Fortune and Expectations to
depend upon her own Conduct, Complaifance, and
affectionate Behaviour ?

T

You have given me, Madam, a very pregnant
and affecting Inftance of a Gentleman, who, made
falfe by Avarice, has loft, and wickedly loft, a
virtuous, prudent, and fond Wife, while he fought
Money more than Merit ; and cruelly broke his
Faith,

Faith, and with it a tender Heart, for the infamous Sake of Lucre ; which may deservedly prove a Canker in his Soul and his Substance, and bring him a Lady with Qualities proper to revenge the other's just Quarrel and barbarous Wrongs. And I, on my part, can give you an Instance of a Gentleman of great Fortune and Figure, who, by acting according to the former wiser Rules, has made himself happy in an amiable, discreet, and observant Lady, and enjoys with her all the Blessings of mutual Confidence and tender Affection. He is complaisant without Art, and she without Fear. I am,

G   *With perfect Respect,*

M A D A M,

Your most humble

And most obedient Servant,

C A T O.

P O S T S C R I P T.

I Have, in several of my late Letters, observed some Slips that have escaped from the Pen of the great and learned Dr. *Prideaux* ; but as I have done this with no Design of blemishing a Character which cannot be blemished, I think myself obliged to own once more, his great Merit, the Service done by him to Mankind, the Honour to his Country, and the Pleasure and Information which I in particular have received from his worthy Labours.

It

It is poffible, that out of Deteftation to Principles which fubvert and tear up by the Roots all Liberty and civil Happinefs, I may have ufed fome warm Expreffions againft thofe that maintain them. Such Expreffions therefore can be applied only to thofe who have been ever the avowed and active Enemies of every thing lovely, valuable, or praifeworthy amongft Men. But as to Dr. *Prideaux*, however he is fallen into Prejudice, perhaps early imbibed, and not fince examined by him with his ufual Accuracy; or however he might intend to ferve a pious Caufe with adventitious Helps and precarious Supports, which it wanted not : Certain it is, from the whole Courfe of his excellent Performance, that he had fincerely at Heart the Intereft of true Religion and Liberty. A Spirit of Virtue, Piety, good Senfe, and Integrity, and an Averfion to Oppreffion, Cruelty, and Tyranny, fhine through his whole Hiftory, and animate the fame; and neither he nor his Hiftory can be too much commended.

But the Doctor is an eminent Inftance, how little any Man ought to be guided by the mere Authority of another; fince one of the greateft and worthieft Men living is capable of falling into fuch obvious Errors. From the Greatnefs of his Name and Credit alone I was led to thefe Animadverfions, and with Reluctance I made them. Falcons do not prey upon Flies. Other Writers, whofe Characters add no Weight to their Miftakes, are fafe from any Cenfure of mine. For this Reafon I fhall not trouble myfelf with the Party-Falfhoods, and pious Ribaldry, and Blunders, of a modern voluminous Writer of *Englifh* Hiftory. His Contract and Dialogue between
Oliver

Oliver Cromwell and the Devil, is a harmless Piece
of Hiſtory, and as entertaining as the reſt.
    T

                                I am, &c.

SATURDAY, *December* 30, 1721. No. 59.

*Liberty proved to be the unalienable Right of all
Mankind.*

S I R,

I Intend to entertain my Readers with Diſſerta-
tions upon *Liberty*, in ſome of my ſucceeding
Letters; and ſhall, as a Preface to that Deſign,
endeavour to prove in this, that Liberty is the unalienable Right of all Mankind.

All Governments, under whatſoever Form they
are adminiſtered, ought to be adminiſtered for the
Good of the Society; when they are otherwiſe
adminiſtered, they ceaſe to be Government, and
become Uſurpation. This being the End of all
Government, even the moſt deſpotick have this
Limitation to their Authority: In this Reſpeĉt,
the only Difference between the moſt abſolute
Princes and limited Magiſtrates, is, that in free
Governments there are Checks and Reſtraints appointed and expreſſed in the Conſtitution itſelf:
In deſpotick Governments, the People ſubmit
themſelves to the Prudence and Diſcretion of the
Prince alone: But there is ſtill this tacit Condition
annexed to his Power, that he muſt aĉt by the
unwritten Laws of Diſcretion and Prudence, and
employ it for the ſole Intereſt of the People, who
                                                give

give it to him, or fuffer him to enjoy it, which they ever do for their own Sakes.

Even in the moft free Governments, fingle Men are often trufted with difcretionary Power : But they muft anfwer for that Difcretion to thofe that truft them. Generals of Armies and Admirals of Fleets have often unlimited Commiffions ; and yet are they not anfwerable for the prudent Execution of thofe Commiffions ? The Council of Ten, in *Venice*, have abfolute Power over the Liberty and Life of every Man in the State: But if they fhould make ufe of that Power to flaughter, abolifh, or enflave the Senate; and, like the *Decemviri* of *Rome*, to fet up themfelves ; would it not be lawful for thofe, who gave them that Authority for other Ends, to put thofe Ten unlimited Traytors to Death, any Way that they could ? The Crown of *England* has been for the moft part entrufted with the fole Difpofal of the Money given for the Civil Lift, often with the Application of great Sums raifed for other publick Ufes ; yet, if the Lord-Treafurer had applied this Money to the Difhonour of the King, and Ruin of the People (though by the private Direction of the Crown itfelf) will any Man fay that he ought not to have compenfated for his Crime, by the Lofs of his Head and his Eftate ?

I have faid thus much, to fhew that no Government can be abfolute in the Senfe, or rather Nonfenfe, of our modern Dogmatizers, and indeed in the Senfe too commonly practifed. No barbarous Conqueft ; no extorted Confent of miferable People, fubmitting to the Chain to efcape the Sword ; no repeated and hereditary Acts of Cruelty, though called Succeffion, no Continua-
tion

tion of Violence, though named Prefcription; can alter, much lefs abrogate, thefe fundamental Principles of Government itfelf, or make the Means of Prefervation the Means of Deftruction, and render the Condition of Mankind infinitely more miferable than that of the Beafts of the Field, by the fole Privilege of that Reafon which diftinguifhes them from the Brute Creation.

Force can give no Title but to Revenge, and to the Ufe of Force again; nor could it ever enter into the Heart of any Man, to give to another Power over him, for any other End but to be exercifed for his own Advantage: And if there are any Men mad or foolifh enough to pretend to do otherwife, they ought to be treated as Idiots or Lunaticks; and the Reafon of their Conduct muft be derived from their Folly and Frenzy.

All Men are born free; Liberty is a Gift which they receive from God himfelf; nor can they alienate the fame by Confent, though poffibly they may forfeit it by Crimes. No Man has Power over his own Life, or to difpofe of his own Religion; and cannot confequently transfer the Power of either to any body elfe: Much lefs can he give away the Lives and Liberties, Religion or acquired Property of his Pofterity, who will be born as free as he himfelf was born, and can never be bound by his wicked and ridiculous Bargain.

The Right of the Magiftrate arifes only from the Right of private Men to defend themfelves, to repel Injuries, and to punifh thofe who commit them: That Right being conveyed by the Society to their publick Reprefentative, he can execute the fame no further than the Benefit and Security of that Society requires he fhould. When he exceeds

his

his Commiſſion, his Acts are as extrajudicial as are thoſe of any private Officer uſurping an unlawful Authority, that is, they are void ; and every Man is anſwerable for the Wrong which he does. A Power to do Good can never become a Warrant for doing Evil.

But here ariſes a grand Queſtion, which has perplexed and puzzled the greateſt Part of Mankind: Yet, I think, the Anſwer to it eaſy and obvious. The Queſtion is, who ſhall be Judge whether the Magiſtrate acts juſtly, and purſues his Truſt ? To this it is juſtly ſaid, That if thoſe who complain of him are to judge him, then there is a ſettled Authority above the Chief Magiſtrate, which Authority muſt be itſelf the Chief Magiſtrate ; which is contrary to the Suppoſition ; and the ſame Queſtion and Difficulty will recur again upon this new Magiſtracy. All this I own to be abſurd ; and I aver it to be at leaſt as abſurd to affirm, That the Perſon accuſed is to be the deciſive Judge of his own Actions, when it is certain that he will always judge and determine in his own Favour ; and thus the whole Race of Mankind will be left helpleſs under the heavieſt Injuſtice, Oppreſſion, and Miſery, that can afflict human Nature.

But if neither Magiſtrates, nor they who complain of Magiſtrates, and are aggrieved by them, have a Right to determine deciſively, the one for the other; and if there be no common eſtabliſhed Power, to which both are ſubject ; then every Man intereſted in the Succeſs of the Conteſt, muſt act according to the Light and Dictates of his own Conſcience, and inform it as well as he can. Where no Judge is nor can be appointed, every

Man

Man muſt be his own; that is, when there is no
ſtated Judge upon Earth, we muſt have Recourſe
to Heaven, and obey the Will of Heaven, by declaring ourſelves on that which we think the juſter
Side.

If the Senate and People of *Rome* had differed
irreconcileably, there could have been no common
Judge in the World between them; and conſequently no Remedy but the laſt: For that Government conſiſting in the Union of the Nobles and
the People, when they differed, no Man could determine between them; and therefore every Man
muſt have been at Liberty to provide for his own
Security, and the general Good, in the beſt Manner he was able. In that Caſe the common Judge
ceaſing, every one was his own: The Government becoming incapable of acting, ſuffered a political Demiſe: The Conſtitution was diſſolved; and
there being no Government in Being, the People
were in the State of Nature again.

The ſame muſt be true, where two abſolute
Princes, governing a Country, come to quarrel,
as ſometimes two *Cæſars* in Partnerſhip did, eſpecially towards the latter End of the *Roman* Empire; or where a Sovereign Council govern a
Country, and their Votes come equally to be divided. In ſuch a Circumſtance, every Man muſt
take that Side which he thinks moſt for the publick Good, or chooſe any proper Meaſures for his
own Security: For, if I owe my Allegiance to
two Princes agreeing, or to the Majority of a
Council; when between theſe Princes there is no
longer any Union, nor in that Council any Majority, no Submiſſion can be due to that which is
not;

not; and the Laws of Nature and Self-Preferva-tion muft take place, where there are no other.

The Cafe is ftill the fame, when there is any Difpute about the Titles of abfolute Princes, who govern independently on the States of a Country, and call none. Here too every Man muft judge for himfelf what Party he will take, to which of the Titles he will adhere; and the like private Judgment muft guide him, whenever a Queftion arifes whether the faid Prince be an Idiot or a Lu-natick, and confequently whether he be capable or incapable of Government. Where there are no States, there can be no other Way of judging; but by the Judgment of private Men the Capacity of the Prince muft be judged, and his Fate deter-mined. Lunacy and Idiotifm are, I think, allowed by all to be certain Difqualifications for Govern-ment; indeed they are as much fo, as if he were deaf, blind, and dumb, or even dead. He who can neither execute an Office, nor appoint a De-puty, is not fit for one.

Now I would fain know, why private Men may not as well ufe their Judgment in an Inftance that concerns them more; I mean that of a ty-rannical Government, of which they hourly feel the fad Effeets, and forrowful Proofs; whereas they have not by far the equal Means of coming to a Certainty about the natural Incapacity of their Governor. The Perfons of great Princes are known but to few of their Subjeets, and their Parts to much fewer; and feveral Princes have, by the Management of their Wives, or Minifters, or Murderers, reigned a good while after they were dead. In Truth, I think it is as much the

Bufinefs

Bufinefs and Right of the People to judge whether their Prince be good or bad, whether a Father or an Enemy, as to judge whether he be dead or alive ; unlefs it be faid (as many fuch wife Things have been faid) that they may judge whether he can govern them, but not whether he does ; and that it behoves them to put the Adminiftration in wifer Hands, if he be a harmlefs Fool, but it is impious to do it, if he be only a deftructive Tyrant ; that Want of Speech is a Difqualification, but Want of Humanity, none.

That Subjects were not to judge of their Governors, or rather for themfelves in the Bufinefs of Government, which of all human Things concerns them moft, was an Abfurdity that never entered into the Imagination of the wife and honeft Ancients : Who, following for their Guide that everlafting Reafon, which is the beft and only Guide in human Affairs, carried Liberty, and human Happinefs, the legitimate Offspring and Work of Liberty, to the higheft Pitch that they were capable of arriving at. But the above Abfurdity, with many others as monftrous and mifchievous, were referved for the Difcovery of a few wretched and dreaming *Mahometan* and Chriftian Monks, who, ignorant of all Things, were made, or made themfelves, the Directors of all Things ; and bewitching the World with holy Lies and unaccountable Ravings, dreffed up in barbarous Words and uncouth Phrafes, bent all their Fairy Force againft common Senfe and common Liberty and Truth, and founded a pernicious, abfurd, and vifionary Empire upon their Ruins. Syftems without Senfe, Propofitions without Truth, Religion

without Reafon, a rampant Church without Charity, Severity without Juftice, and Government
without Liberty or Mercy, were all the blefled
Handy-works of thefe religious Mad-men, and
godly Pedants ; who, by pretending to know the
other World, cheated and confounded this. Their
Enmity to common Senfe, and Want of it, were
their Warrants for governing the Senfe of all Mankind : By Lying, they were thought the Champions of the Truth ; and by their Fooleries, Impieties, and Cruelty, were efteemed the Favourites
and Confidents of the God of Wifdom, Mercy,
and Peace.

Thefe were the Men, who, having demolifhed
all Senfe and human Judgment, firft made it a
Principle, that People were not to judge of their
Governor and Government, nor to meddle with
it ; nor to preferve themfelves from publick Deftroyers, falfly calling themfelves Governors : Yet
thefe Men, who thus fet up for the Support and
Defenders of Government, without the common
Honefty of diftinguifhing the Good from the Bad,
and Protection from Murder and Depredation,
were at the fame Time themfelves the conftant
and avowed Troublers of every Government which
they could not direct and command ; and every
Government, however excellent, which did not
make their Reveries its own Rules, and themfelves
alone its peculiar Care, has been honoured with
their profeffed Hatred ; whilft Tyrants and publick Butchers, who flattered them, have been deified. This was the poor State of *Chriftendom* before the *Reformation* ; and I wifh I could fay, of
no Parts of it fince.

This

This barbarous Anarchy in Reasoning and Politicks, has made it necessary to prove Propositions which the Light of Nature had demonstrated. And, as the Apostles were forced to prove to the misled *Gentiles*, that they were no Gods which were made with Hands ; I am put to prove, that the People have a Right to judge, whether their Governors were made for them, or they for their Governors ? Whether their Governors have necessary and natural Qualifications ? Whether they have any Governors or no ? And whether, when they have none, every Man must not be his own ? I therefore return to Instances and Illustrations from Facts which cannot be denied ; though Propositions as true as Facts may, by those especially who are defective in Point of Modesty or Discernment.

In *Poland*, according to the Constitution of that Country, it is necessary, we are told, that, in their Diets, the Consent of every Man present must be had to make a Resolve effectual : And therefore, to prevent the cutting of People's Throats, they have no Remedy but to cut the Throats of one another ; that is, they must pull out their Sabres, and force the refractory Members (who are always the Minority) to submit. And amongst us in *England*, where a Jury cannot agree, there can be no Verdict ; and so they must fast till they do, or till one of them is dead, and then the Jury is dissolved.

This, from the Nature of Things themselves, must be the constant Case in all Disputes between Dominion and Property. Where the Interest of the Governors and that of the Governed clash,

there

there can be no ftated Judge between them : To
appeal to a foreign Power, is to give up the Sovereignty ; for either Side to fubmit, is to give up
the Queftion : And therefore, if they themfelves
do not amicably determine the Difpute between
themfelves, Heaven alone muft. In fuch Cafe,
Recourfe muft be had to the firft Principles of
Government itfelf ; which being a Departure from
the State of Nature, and a Union of many Families forming themfelves into a political Machine
for mutual Protection and Defence, it is evident,
that this formed Relation can continue no longer
than the Machine fubfifts and can act ; and when
it does not, the Individuals muft return to their
former State again. No Conftitution can provide
againft what will happen, when that Conftitution
is diffolved. Government is only an Appointment
of one or more Perfons, to do certain Actions for
the Good and Emolument of the Society ; and if
the Perfons thus interefted will not act at all, or
act contrary to their Truft, their Power muft return of Courfe to thofe who gave it.

Suppofe, for Example, the Grand Monarch,
as he was called, had bought a neighbouring Kingdom, and all the Lands in it, from the Courtiers,
and the Majority of the People's Deputies ; and
amongft the reft, the Church-Lands, into the Bargain, with the Confent of their Convocation or
Synod, or by what other Name that Affembly
was called ; would the People and Clergy have
thought themfelves obliged to have made good this
Bargain, if they could have helped it ? I dare fay
that neither would ; but, on the contrary, that
the People would have had the Countenance of
                                        thefe

thefe reverend Patriots to have told their Reprefentatives in round Terms, that they were chofen
to act for the Intereft of thofe that fent them, and
not for their own; that their Power was given
them to protect and defend their Country, and not
to fell and enflave it.

This Suppofition, as wild as it feems, yet is not
abfolutely and univerfally impoffible. King *John*
actually fold the Kingdom of *England* to his Holinefs: And there are People in all Nations ready to
fell their Country at Home; and fuch can never
have any Principles to with-hold them from felling
it Abroad.

It is foolifh to fay, that this Doctrine can be
mifchievous to Society, at leaft in any Proportion
to the wild Ruin and fatal Calamities which muft
befal, and do befal the World, where the contrary
Doctrine is maintained: For, all Bodies of Men
fubfifting upon their own Subftance, or upon the
Profits of their Trade and Induftry, find their
Account fo much in Eafe and Peace, and have
juftly fuch terrible Apprehenfions of Civil Diforders, which deftroy every thing that they enjoy;
that they always bear a Thoufand Injuries before
they return One, and ftand under the Burthens as
long as they can bear them; as I have in another
Letter obferved.

What with the Force of Education, and the
Reverence which People are taught, and have
been always ufed to pay to Princes; what with
the perpetual Harangues of Flatterers, the gaudy
Pageantry and Outfide of Power, and its gilded
Enfigns, always glittering in their Eyes; what
with the Execution of the Laws in the fole Power
of

of the Prince ; what with all the regular Magiftrates, pompous Guards and ftanding Troops,
with the fortified Towns, the Artillery, and all
the Magazines of War, at his Difpofal ; befides
large Revenues, and Multitudes of Followers and
Dependants, to fupport and abet all that he does :
Obedience to Authority is fo well fecured, that it
is wild to imagine, that any Number of Men, formidable enough to difturb a fettled State, can unite
together and hope to overturn it, till the publick
Grievances are fo enormous, the Oppreffion fo
great, and the Difaffection fo univerfal, that there
can be no Queftion remaining, whether their Calamities be real or imaginary, and whether the
Magiftrate has protected or endeavoured to deftroy
his People.

This was the Cafe of *Richard* II. *Edward* II.
and *James* II. and will ever be the Cafe under the
fame Circumftances. No Society of Men will
groan under Oppreffions longer than they know
how to throw them off ; whatever unnatural
Whimfies and Fairy Notions idle and fedentary
Babblers may utter from Colleges and Cloifters ;
and teach to others, for vile Self-Ends, Doctrines,
which they themfelves are famous for not practifing.

Upon this Principle of People's judging for themfelves, and refifting lawlefs Force, ftands our late
happy *Revolution,* and with it the juft and rightful
Title of our moft excellent Sovereign King *George,*
to the Scepter of thefe Realms ; a Scepter which
he has, and I doubt not will ever fway, to his
own Honour, and the Honour, Protection, and
Profperity of us his People.

T   *I am,* &c.

SATUR-

All Government proved to be inftituted by Men, and
only to intend the general Good of Men.

S I R,

THERE is no Government now upon Earth,
which owes its Formation or Beginning to
the immediate Revelation of God, or can derive
its Exiftence from fuch Revelation: It is certain,
on the contrary, that the Rife and Inftitution or
Variation of Government, from Time to Time,
is within the Memory of Men or of Hiftories; and
that every Government, which we know at this
Day in the World, was eftablifhed by the Wifdom and Force of mere Men, and by the Concurrence of Means and Caufes evidently human.
Government therefore can have no Power, but
fuch as Men can give, and fuch as they actually
did give, or permit for their own Sakes: Nor
can any Government be in Fact framed but by
Confent, if not of every Subject, yet of as many
as can compel the reft; fince no Man, or Council of Men, can have perfonal Strength enough to
govern Multitudes by Force, or can claim to themfelves and their Families any Superiority, or natural
Sovereignty over their Fellow-Creatures naturally
as good as them. Such Strength, therefore, where-
ever it is, is civil and accumulative Strength, derived from the Laws and Conftitutions of the Society,

ciety, of which the Governors themfelves are but Members.

So that to know the Jurifdiction of Governors, and its Limits, we muft have Recourfe to the Inftitution of Government, and afcertain thofe Limits by the Meafure of Power, which Men in the State of Nature have over themfelves and one another : And as no Man can take from many, who are ftronger than him, what they have no Mind to give him ; and he who has not Confent muft have Force, which is itfelf the Confent of the Stronger ; fo no Man can give to another either what is none of his own, or what in its own Nature is infeparable from himfelf ; as his Religion particularly is.

Every Man's Religion is his own ; nor can the Religion of any Man, of what Nature or Figure foever, be the Religion of another Man, unlefs he alfo choofes it ; which Action utterly excludes all Force, Power, or Government.   Religion can never come without Conviction, nor can Conviction come from Civil Authority ; Religion, which is the Fear of God, cannot be fubject to Power, which is the Fear of Man.   It is a Relation between God and our own Souls only, and confifts in a Difpofition of Mind to obey the Will of our great Creator, in the Manner which we think moft acceptable to him.   It is independent upon all human Directions, and fuperior to them ; and confequently uncontroulable by external Force, which cannot reach the free Faculties of the Mind, or inform the Underftanding, much lefs convince it.   Religion therefore, which can never be fubject to the Jurifdiction of another, can never be alienated to another, or put in his Power.

Nor

Nor has any Man in the State of Nature Power over his own Life, or to take away the Life of another, unless to defend his own, or what is as much his own, namely, his Property. This Power therefore, which no Man has, no Man can transfer to another.

Nor could any Man in the State of Nature, have a Right to violate the Property of another; that is, what another had acquired by his Art or Labour; or to interrupt him in his Industry and Enjoyments, as long as he himself was not injured by that Industry and those Enjoyments. No Man therefore could transfer to the Magistrate that Right which he had not himself.

No Man in his Senses was ever so wild as to give an unlimited Power to another to take away his Life, or the Means of Living, according to the Caprice, Passion, and unreasonable Pleasure of that other: But if any Man restrained himself from any Part of his Pleasures, or parted with any Portion of his Acquisitions, he did it with the honest Purpose of enjoying the rest with the greater Security, and always in Subserviency to his own Happiness, which no Man will or can willingly and intentionally give away to any other whatsoever.

And if any one, through his own Inadvertence, or by the Fraud or Violence of another, can be drawn into so foolish a Contract, he is relievable by the eternal Laws of God and Reason. No Engagement that is wicked and unjust can be executed without Injustice and Wickedness: This is so true, that I question whether there be a Constitution in the World which does not afford, or pretend

tend to afford, a Remedy for relieving ignorant, diftreffed, and unwary Men, trepanned into fuch Engagements by artful Knaves, or frightened into them by imperious ones. So that here the Laws of Nature and general Reafon fuperfede the muni-cipal and pofitive Laws of Nations ; and no where oftner than in *England.* What elfe was the De-fign, and ought to be the Bufinefs, of our Courts of Equity ? And I hope whole Countries and So-cieties are no more exempted from the Privileges and Protection of Reafon and Equity, than are private Particulars.

Here then is the natural Limitation of the Ma-giftrate's Authority : He ought not to take what no Man ought to give ; nor exact what no Man ought to perform : All he has is given him, and thofe that gave it muft judge of the Application. In Government there is no fuch Relation as Lord and Slave, lawlefs Will and blind Submiffion ; nor ought to be amongft Men : But the only Re-lation is that of Father and Children, Patron and Client, Protection and Allegiance, Benefaction and Gratitude, mutual Affection and mutual Af-fiftance.

So that the Nature of Government does not al-ter the natural Right of Men to Liberty, which in all political Societies is alike their Due : But fome Governments provide better than others for the Security and impartial Diftribution of that Right. There has been always fuch a conftant and certain Fund of Corruption and Malignity in human Nature, that it has been rare to find that Man, whofe Views and Happinefs did not center in the Gratification of his Appetites, and worft
Appetites,

Appetites, his Luxury, his Pride, his Avarice, and Luft of Power ; and who confidered any publick Truft repofed in him, with any other View, than as the Means to fatiate fuch unruly and dangerous Defires ! And this has been moft eminently true of Great Men, and thofe who afpired to Dominion. They were firft made Great for the Sake of the Publick, and afterwards at its Expence. And if they had been content to have been moderate Traytors, Mankind would have been ftill moderately happy ; but their Ambition and Treafon obferving no Degrees, there was no Degree of Vilenefs and Mifery which the poor People did not often feel.

The Appetites therefore of Men, efpecially of Great Men, are carefully to be obferved and ftayed, or elfe they will never ftay themfelves. The Experience of every Age convinces us, that we muft not judge of Men by what they ought to do, but by what they will do ; and all Hiftory affords but few Inftances of Men trufted with great Power without abufing it, when with Security they could. The Servants of Society, that is to fay, its Magiftrates, did almoft univerfally ferve it by feizing it, felling it, or plundering it ; efpecially when they were left by the Society unlimited as to their Duty and Wages. In that Cafe thefe faithful Stewards generally took all ; and, being Servants, made Slaves of their Mafters.

For thefe Reafons, and convinced by woful and eternal Experience, Societies found it neceffary to lay Reftraints upon their Magiftrates or publick Servants, and to put Checks upon thofe who would otherwife put Chains upon them ; and therefore
thefe

thefe Societies fet themfelves to model and form
national Conftitutions with fuch Wifdom and Art,
that the publick Intereft fhould be confulted and
carried at the fame Time, when thofe entrufted
with the Adminiftration of it were confulting and
purfuing their own.

Hence grew the Diftinction between Arbitrary
and Free Governments: Not that more or lefs
Power was vefted in the one than in the other;
nor that either of them lay under lefs or more
Obligations, in Juftice, to protect their Subjects,
and ftudy their Eafe, Profperity, and Security, and
to watch for the fame. But the Power and Sovereignty of Magiftrates in free Countries was fo qualified, and fo divided into different Channels, and
committed to the Direction of fo many different
Men, with different Interefts and Views, that the
Majority of them could feldom or never find their
Account in betraying their Truft in fundamental
Inftances. Their Emulation, Envy, Fear, or
Intereft, always made them Spies and Checks upon one another. By all which Means the People
have often come at the Heads of thofe who forfeited their Heads, by betraying the People.

In defpotick Governments Things went far
otherwife, thofe Governments having been framed
otherwife; if the fame could be called Governments, where the Rules of publick Power were
dictated by private and lawlefs Luft; where Folly
and Madnefs often fwayed the Scepter, and blind
Rage weilded the Sword. The whole Weath of
the State, with its Civil or Military Power, being
in the Prince, the People could have no Remedy
but Death and Patience, while he oppreffed them
by

by the Lump, and butchered them by Thoufands: Unlefs perhaps the Ambition or perfonal Refentments of fome of the Inftruments of his Tyranny procured a Revolt, which rarely mended their Condition.

The only Secret therefore in forming a Free Government, is to make the Interefts of the Governors and of the Governed the fame, as far as human Policy can contrive. Liberty cannot be preferved any other Way. Men have long found, from the Weaknefs and Depravity of themfelves and one another, that moft Men will act for Intereft againft Duty, as often as they dare. So that to engage them to their Duty, Intereft muft be linked to the Obfervance of it, and Danger to the Breach of it. Perfonal Advantages and Security, muft be the Rewards of Duty and Obedience; and Difgrace, Torture, and Death, the Punifhment of Treachery and Corruption.

Human Wifdom has yet found out but one certain Expedient to effect this ; and that is, to have the Concerns of all directed by all, as far as poffibly can be : And where the Perfons interefted are too numerous, or live too diftant to meet together on all Emergencies, they muft moderate Neceffity by Prudence, and act by Deputies, whofe Intereft is the fame with their own, and whofe Property is fo intermingled with theirs, and fo engaged upon the fame Bottom, that Principals and Deputies muft ftand and fall together. When the Deputies thus act for their own Intereft, by acting for the Intereft of their Principals ; when they can make no Law but what they themfelves, and their Pofterity, muft be fubject to ; when they
can

can give no Money, but what they muft pay their
Share of; when they can' do no Mifchief, but
what muft fall upon their own Heads in common
with their Countrymen ; their Principals may then
expect good Laws, little Mifchief, and much Frugality.

Here therefore lies the great Point of Nicety and
Care in forming the Conftitution, that the Perfons entrufted and reprefenting, fhall either never
have any Intereft detached from the Perfons en-
trufting and reprefented, or never the Means to
purfue it. Now to compafs this great Point effectually, no other Way is left, but one of thefe two,
or rather both ; namely, to make the Deputies fo
numerous, that there may be no Poffibility of corrupting the Majority ; or, by changing them fo
often, that there is no fufficient Time to corrupt
them, and to carry the Ends of that Corruption.
The People may be very fure, that the major Part
of their Deputies being honeft, will keep the reft
fo ; and that they will all be honeft, when they
have no Temptations to be Knaves.

We have fome Sketch of this Policy in the
Conftitution of our feveral great Companies, where
the General Court, compofed of all its Members,
conftitutes the Legiflature, and the Confent of
that Court is the Sanction of their Laws ; and
where the Adminiftration of their Affairs is put
under the Conduct of a certain Number chofen
by the Whole. Here every Man concerned faw
the Neceffity of fecuring Part of their Property,
by putting the Perfons entrufted under proper
Regulations ; however remifs they may be in take-
ing Care of the Whole. And if Provifion had
been

been made, That, as a Third Part of the Directors are to go out every Year, so none should stay in above Three, (as I am told was at first promised) all Juggling with Courtiers, and raising great Estates by Confederacy, at the Expence of the Company, had, in a great Measure, been prevented; though there were still wanting other Limitations, which might have effectually obviated all those Evils.

This was the ancient Constitution of *England:* Our Kings had neither Revenues large enough, nor Offices gainful and numerous enough in their Disposal, to corrupt any considerable Number of Members; nor any Force to frighten them. Besides, the same Parliament seldom or never met twice: For, the serving in it being found an Office of Burthen, and not of Profit, it was thought reasonable that all Men qualified should, in their Turns, leave their Families and domestick Concerns, to serve the Publick; and their Boroughs bore their Charges. The only Grievance then was, that they were not called together often enough, to redress the Grievances which the People suffered from the Court during their Intermission: And therefore a Law was made in *Edward* the IIId's Time, That Parliaments should be holden once a Year.

But this Law, like the late Queen's Peace, did not execute itself; and therefore the Court seldom convened them, but when they wanted Money, or had other Purposes of their own to serve; and sometimes raised Money without them: Which arbitrary Proceeding brought upon the Publick numerous Mischiefs; and, in the Reign of King
Charles

Charles the Ift, a long and bloody Civil War. In
that Reign an Act was paffed, That they fhould
meet of themfelves, if they were not called according to the Direction of that Law; which was
worthily repealed upon the Reftoration of King
Charles the IId: And in the fame kind Fit, a
great Revenue was given him for Life, and continued to his Brother. By which Means thefe
Princes were enabled to keep ftanding Troops, to
corrupt Parliaments, or to live without them; and
to commit fuch Acts of Power as brought about,
and indeed forced the People upon the late happy
Revolution. Soon after which a new Act was
paffed, That Parliaments fhould be rechofen once
in three Years: Which Law was alfo repealed,
upon his Majefty's Acceffion to the Throne, that
the prefent Parliament might have Time to rectify
thofe Abufes which we labour under, and to
make Regulations proper to prevent them *All* for
the future. *All* which has fince been happily ef-
fected; and, I blefs God, we are told, that the
People will have the Opportunity to thank them,
in another Election, for their great Services to
their Country. I fhall be always ready, on my
Part, to do them Honour, and pay them my
Acknowledgments, in the moft effectual Manner
in my Power. —— But more of this in the fucceeding Papers.

T   *I am,* &c.

SATURDAY, *January* 13, 1721.   No. 61.

*How free Governments are to be framed so as to last,
and how they differ from such as are arbitrary.*

S I R,

THE moft reafonable Meaning that can be put
upon this Apothegm, that *Virtue is its own
Reward*, is, that it feldom meets with any other.
God himfelf, who having made us, beft knows
our Natures, does not truft to the intrinfick Excellence and native Beauty of Holinefs alone, to
engage us in its Interefts and Purfuits, but recommends it to us by the ftronger and more affecting
Motives of Rewards and Punifhments.   No wife
Man, therefore, will in any Inftance of Moment
truft to the mere Integrity of another.   The Experience of all Ages may convince us, that Men,
when they are above Fear, grow for the moft
part above Honefty and Shame : And this is particularly and certainly true of Societies of Men,
when they are numerous enough to keep one another in Countenance ; for when the Weight of
Infamy is divided amongft many, no one finks
under his own Burthen.

Great Bodies of Men have feldom judged what
they ought to do, by any other Rule than what
they could do.   What Nation is there that has
not oppreffed any other, when the fame could
be done with Advantage and Security ?   What
Party

Party has ever had Regard to the Principles which they profeſſed, or ever reformed the Errors which they condemned ? What Company, or particular Society of Merchants or Tradeſmen, has ever acted for the Intereſt of general Trade, though it always filled their Mouths in private Converſation ?

And yet Men, thus formed and qualified, are the Materials for Government. For the Sake of Men it is inſtituted, by the Prudence of Men it muſt be conducted ; and the Art of political Mechaniſm is, to erect a firm Building with ſuch crazy and corrupt Materials. The ſtrongeſt Cabies are made out of looſe Hemp and Flax ; the World itſelf may, with the Help of proper Machines, be moved by the Force of a ſingle Hair ; and ſo may the. Government of the World, as well as the World itſelf. But whatever Diſcourſes I ſhall hereafter make upon this great and uſeful Subject, I ſhall confine myſelf in this Letter to free monarchical Conſtitutions alone, and to the Application of ſome of the Principles laid down in my laſt.

It is there ſaid, that when the Society conſiſts of too many, or when they live too far apart to be able to meet together, to take Care of their own Affairs, they can no otherwiſe preſerve their Liberties, than by chooſing Deputies to repreſent them, and to act for them ; and that theſe Deputies muſt be either ſo numerous, that there can be no Means of corrupting the Majority ; or ſo often changed, that there ſhall be no Time to do it ſo as to anſwer any End by doing it. Without one of theſe Regulations, or both, I lay it down as a
certain

certain Maxim in Politicks, that it is impoffible to preferve a free Government long.

I think I may with great Modefty affirm, that in former Reigns the People of *England* found no fufficient Security in the Number of their Reprefentatives. What with the Crowd of Offices in the Gift of the Crown, which were poffeffed by Men of no other Merit, nor held by any other Tenure, but merely a Capacity to get into the Houfe of Commons, and the Differvice which they could and would do their Country there : What with the Promifes and Expectations given to others, who by Court-Influence, and often by Court-Money, carried their Elections: What by artful Careffes, and the familiar and deceitful Addreffes of great Men to weak Men : What with luxurious Dinners, and Rivers of *Burgundy*, *Champaign*, and *Tokay*, thrown down the Throats of Gluttons ; and what with Penfions, and other perfonal Gratifications, beftowed where Wind and Smoke would not pafs for current Coin : What with Party Watch-Words and imaginary Terrors, fpread amongft the drunken 'Squires, and the deluded and enthufiaftick Bigots, of dreadful Defigns in *Embrio*, to blow up the Church, and the Proteftant Intereft ; and fometimes with the Dread of mighty Invafions juft ready to break upon us from the Man in the Moon : I fay, by all thefe corrupt Arts, the Reprefentatives of the *Englifh* People, in former Reigns, have been brought to betray the People, and to join with their Oppreffors. So much are Men governed by artful Applications to their private Paffions and Intereft. And it is evident to me, that if ever we have a weak or an
ambitious

ambitious Prince, with a Miniftry like him, we muft find out fome other Refources, or acquiefce in the Lofs of our Liberties. The Courfe and Tranfiency of human Affairs will not fuffer us to live always under the prefent righteous Adminiftration.

So that I can fee no Means in human Policy to preferve the publick Liberty and a monarchical Form of Government together, but by the frequent frefh Elections of the People's Deputies : This is what the Writers in Politicks call Rotation of Magiftracy. Men, when they firft enter into Magiftracy, have often their former Condition before their Eyes : They remember what they themfelves fuffered, with their Fellow-Subjects, from the Abufe of Power, and how much they blamed it ; and fo their firft Purpofes are to be humble, modeft, and juft ; and probably, for fome Time, they continue fo. But the Poffeffion of Power foon alters and viciates their Hearts, which are at the fame time fure to be leavened, and puffed up to an unnatural Size, by the deceitful Incenfe of falfe Friends, and by the proftrate Submiffion of Parafites. Firft, they grow indifferent to all their good Defigns, then drop them : Next, they lofe their Moderation ; afterwards, they renounce all Meafures with their old Acquaintance and old Principles ; and feeing themfelves in magnifying Glaffes, grow, in Conceit, a different Species from their Fellow-Subjects ; and fo by too fudden Degrees become infolent, rapacious and tyrannical, ready to catch at all Means, often the vileft and moft oppreffive, to raife their Fortunes as high as their imaginary Greatnefs. So that the

only

only Way to put them in mind of their former Condition, and confequently of the Condition of other People, is often to reduce them to it ; and to let others of equal Capacities fhare of Power in their Turn : This alfo is the only Way to qualify Men, and make them equally fit for Dominion and Subjection.

A Rotation therefore, in Power and Magiftracy, is effentially neceffary to a free Government : It is indeed the Thing itfelf; and conftitutes, animates, and informs it, as much as the Soul conftitutes the Man. It is a Thing facred and inviolable, where-ever Liberty is thought facred ; nor can it ever be committed to the Difpofal of thofe who are trufted with the Prefervation of National Conftitutions : For though they may have the Power to model it for the publick Advantage, and for the more effectual Security of that Right ; yet they can have none to give it up, or, which is the fame Thing, to make it ufelefs.

The Conftitution of a limited Monarchy, is the joint Concurrence of the Crown and of the Nobles (without whom it cannot fubfift) and of the Body of the People, to make Laws for the common Benefit of the Subject ; and where the People, through Number or Diftance, cannot meet, they muft fend Deputies to fpeak in their Names, and to attend upon their Intereft : Thefe Deputies therefore act by, under, and in Subferviency to the Conftitution, and have not a Power above it and over it.

In *Holland*, and fome other free Countries, the States are often obliged to confult their Principals ; and, in fome Inftances, our own Parliaments have declined entering upon Queftions of Importance,

tance, till they had gone into the Country, and known the Sentiments of thofe that fent them ; as in all Cafes they ought to confult their Inclinations as well as their Intereft. Who will fay, that the Rump, or Fag-end of the Long Parliament of Forty-One, had any Right to expel fuch Members as they did not like ? Or to watch for their Abfence, that they might feize to themfelves, or give up to any body elfe, the Right of thofe from whofe Confidence and Credulity they derived the Authority which they acted by ?

With Thanks to God, I own, that we have a Prince fo fenfible of this Right, and who owes his Crown fo intirely to the Principles laid down, and I think fully proved in thefe Letters ; that it is impoffible to fufpect, either from his Inclinations, his Intereft, or his known Juftice, that he fhould ever fall into any Meafures to deftroy that People, who have given him his Crown, and fupported him in it with fo much Generofity and Expence ; or that he fhould undermine, by that Means, the Ground upon which he ftands. I do therefore the lefs regard the idle Sufpicions and Calumnies of difaffected Men, who would furmife, that a Defign is yet on Foot to continue this Parliament ; —— a Reflection the moft impudent and invidious that can be thrown upon his Majefty, his Minifters, or his Two Houfes ; and a Reflection that can come from none but profeffed, or at leaft from concealed, *Jacobites*.

It is no lefs than an Infinuation, that our moft excellent Sovereign King *George* has a Diftruft of his faithful Subjects ; that he will refufe them the Means of their own Prefervation, and the Prefervation

vation of that Conftitution which they chofe him
to preferve ; that he will fhut his Ears againft their
modeft, juft, and dutiful Complaints ; and that he
apprehends Danger from meeting them in a New
and Free-chofen Parliament. This is contrary to
the Tenor of his whole Life and Actions ; who,
as he has received Three Crowns from their Gift,
fo he lies under all the Ties of Generofity, Gratitude, and Duty, to cherifh and protect them, and
to make them always great, free, and happy.

It is a moft fcandalous Calumny upon his faithful Servants, to fuggeft that any of them, confcious of Guilt and Crimes, feared any thing from
the moft ftrict and rigorous Infpection into their
Proceedings. Some of them have already ftood
the fiery Trial, and come off triumphant with general Approbation. They have, befides, the Advantage of his Majefty's moft gracious Pardon,
which they did not want, and which was not paffed for their Sakes. Who therefore can fufpect, that
Patriots fo uncorrupt, fo prudent, and fo popular,
will difhonour their Mafter, give up the Conftitution, ruin their Country, and render themfelves
the Objects of univerfal Scorn, Deteftation, and
Curfing, by advifing the moft odious, dangerous,
and deftructive Meafures, that ever Counfellors
gave a Prince ?

It is a moft ungrateful Return to our illuftrious
Reprefentatives, to fuggeft, that Men who have
left their domeftick Concerns to ferve their Country at their own Expence, and without any perfonal Advantages, and have beftowed their Labours upon the Publick for a much longer Time
than their Principals had at firft a Right to expect
from

from them ; and have, during all that Time,
been rectifying the Abuses which have crept into
our Constitution ; and have assisted his Majesty in
going through two very useful and necessary Wars,
and have regulated our Finances, and the Expence
of our Guards and Garisons, and corrected many
Abuses in the Fleet and the Civil Administration ;
and have taken effectual Vengeance of all those
who were concerned in promoting, procuring,
aiding, or assisting the late dreadful *South-Sea* Project :——I say, after so many Things done by
them for the publick Honour and Prosperity, it is
the basest Ingratitude to surmise, that any of them
would give up that Constitution which they were
chosen, and have taken so much Pains, to preserve.

I do indeed confess, if any Invasion were to be
feared from *Muscovy, Mecklenburg, Spain,* or *Civita Vecchia* ; if new Provinces were to be obtained
Abroad, new Armies to be raised, or new Fleets
to be equipped, upon warlike Expeditions ; if new
Provision were wanting for the Civil List, and
new Taxes to be levied, or new Companies to be
erected to pay off the publick Debts ; if the Uni-
versities were to be farther regulated, or any In-
spection were necessary into the Increase of Fees
and Exactions of Civil Officers ; if there were
the least Ground to suspect Bribery or Corruption
in a Place where it should not be ; or if there
were any new Project on Foot to banish tyrannical and popish Principles far out of the Land : I
say, that in such a Scene of Affairs, I dare not be
altogether so positive in my Assertion, that we
ought to venture, and at all Events to leave to
Chance,

Chance, that which we are in Poffeffion of already.
—But as we are at prefent in the happy State of
Indolence and Security, at Peace with all the
World and our own Confciences ; as little more
Money can be raifed from the People, moft of it
being already in Hands, which, according to the
Rules of good Policy, unite Dominion and Property ; as our Benefactors too are generous and
honourable, our Boroughs not infenfible or ungrateful, nor the Counties themfelves inexorable to
fhining Merit : So it is much to be hoped, that
another Parliament may be chofen equally deferve-
ing, and as zealous for the publick Intereft ; or, at
worft, there are honeft and tried Meafures at Hand,
which will undoubtedly make them fo. And I
offer this as a conclufive, and I think a moft con-
vincing, Argument, that the Kingdom will be
obliged with a new Election.

T   *I am,* &c.

SATURDAY, *January* 20, 1721.   No. 62.

*An Enquiry into the Nature and Extent of Liberty ;
with its Lovelinefs and Advantages, and the vile
Effects of Slavery.*

S I R,

I Have fhewn, in a late Paper, wherein confifts
the Difference between Free and Arbitrary Governments, as to their Frame and Conftitution ;
and in this and the following, I fhall fhew their
different Spirit and Effects. But firft I fhall fhew
wherein Liberty itfelf confifts.   By

By Liberty, I underſtand the Power which every Man has over his own Actions, and his Right to enjoy the Fruit of his Labour, Art, and Induſtry, as far as by it he hurts not the Society, or any Members of it, by taking from any Member, or by hindering him from enjoying what he himſelf enjoys. The Fruits of a Man's honeſt Induſtry are the juſt Rewards of it, aſcertained to him by natural and eternal Equity, as is his Title to uſe them in the Manner which he thinks fit : And thus, with the above Limitations, every Man is ſole Lord and Arbiter of his own private Actions and Property.——A Character of which no Man living can diveſt him but by Uſurpation, or his own Conſent.

The entering into political Society, is ſo far from a Departure from his natural Right, that to preſerve it was the ſole Reaſon why Men did ſo ; and mutual Protection and Aſſiſtance is the only reaſonable Purpoſe of all reaſonable Societies. To make ſuch Protection practicable, Magiſtracy was formed, with Power to defend the Innocent from Violence, and to puniſh thoſe that offered it ; nor can there be any other Pretence for Magiſtracy in the World. In order to this good End, the Magiſtrate is intruſted with conducting and applying the united Force of the Community ; and with exacting ſuch a Share of every Man's Property, as is neceſſary to preſerve the Whole, and to defend every Man and his Property from foreign and domeſtick Injuries. Theſe are the Boundaries of the Power of the Magiſtrate, who deſerts his Function whenever he breaks them. By the Laws of Society, he is more limited and
reſtrained

reftrained than any Man amongft them ; fince,
while they are abfolutely free in all their Actions,
which purely concern themfelves ; all his Actions,
as a publick Perfon, being for the Sake of Society, muft refer to it, and anfwer the Ends of
it.

It is a miftaken Notion in Government, that
the Intereft of the Majority is only to be confulted,
fince in Society every Man has a Right to every
Man's Affiftance in the Enjoyment and Defence
of his private Property ; otherwife the greater
Number may fell the leffer, and divide their Eftates
amongft themfelves ; and fo, inftead of a Society,
where all peaceable Men are protected, become
a Confpiracy of the Many againft the Minority.
With as much Equity may one Man wantonly
difpofe of all, and Violence may be fanctified by
mere Power.

And it is as foolifh to fay, that Government
is concerned to meddle with the private Thoughts
and Actions of Men, while they injure neither
the Society, nor any of its Members.   Every Man
is, in Nature and Reafon, the Judge and Difpofer of his own domeftick Affairs ; and, according to the Rules of Religion and Equity, every
Man muft carry his own Confcience.   So that
neither has the Magiftrate a Right to direct the
private Behaviour of Men ; nor has the Magiftrate, or any body elfe, any Manner of Power to
model People's Speculations, no more than their
Dreams.   Government being intended to protect
Men from the Injuries of one another, and not to
direct them in their own Affairs, in which no one
is interefted but themfelves ; it is plain, that their
                                            Thoughts

Thoughts and domeftick Concerns are exempted intirely from its Jurifdiction : In Truth, Mens Thoughts are not fubject to their own Jurifdiction.

Idiots aud Lunaticks indeed, who cannot take Care of themfelves, muft be taken Care of by others : But whilft Men have their five Senfes, I cannot fee what the Magiftrate has to do with Actions by which the Society cannot be affected ; and where he meddles with fuch, he meddles impertinently or tyrannically. Muft the Magiftrate tie up every Man's Legs, becaufe fome Men fall into Ditches ? Or, muft he put out their Eyes, becaufe with them they fee lying Vanities ? Or, would it become the Wifdom and Care of Governors to eftablifh a travelling Society, to prevent People, by a proper Confinement, from throwing themfelves into Wells, or over Precipices ; Or to endow a Fraternity of Phyficians and Surgeons all over the Nation, to take Care of their Subjects Health, without being confulted ; and to vomit, bleed, purge, and fcarify them at Pleafure, whether they would or no, juft as thefe eftablifhed Judges of Health fhould think fit ? If this were the Cafe, what a Stir and Hubbub fhould we foon fee kept about the eftablifhed Potions and Lancets? Every Man, Woman, or Child, though ever fo healthy, muft be a Patient, or woe be to them ! The beft Diet and Medicines would foon grow pernicious from any other Hand ; and their Pills alone, however ridiculous, infufficient, or diftafteful, would be attended with a Bleffing.

Let People alone, and they will take Care of themfelves, and do it beft ; and if they do not, a

fufficient

fufficient Punifhment will follow their Neglect,
without the Magiftrate's Interpofition and Penalties. It is plain, that fuch bufy Care and officious
Intrufion into the perfonal Affairs, or private
Actions, Thoughts, and Imaginations of Men,
has in it more Craft than Kindnefs; and is only
a Device to miflead People, and pick their Pockets, under the falfe Pretence of the publick and
their private Good. To quarrel with any Man
for his Opinions, Humours, or the Fafhion of his
Clothes, is an Offence taken without being given.
What is it to a Magiftrate how I wafh my Hands,
or cut my Corns; what Fafhion or Colours I
wear, or what Notions I entertain, or what Ge-
ftures I ufe, or what Words I pronounce, when
they pleafe me, and do him and my Neighbour
no Hurt? As well may he determine the Colour of my Hair, and controul my Shape and Features.

True and impartial Liberty is therefore the
Right of every Man to purfue the natural, reafonable, and religious Dictates of his own Mind;
to think what he will, and act as he thinks, provided he acts not to the Prejudice of another; to
fpend his own Money himfelf, and lay out the
Produce of his Labour his own Way; and to labour for his own Pleafure and Profit, and not for
others who are idle, and would live and riot by
pillaging and oppreffing him, and thofe that are
like him.

So that Civil Government is only a partial Reftraint put by the Laws of Agreement and Society
upon natural and abfolute Liberty, which might
otherwife grow licentious: And Tyranny is an
unlimited

unlimited Reftraint put upon natural Liberty, by the Will of one or a few. Magiftracy, amongft a free People, is the Exercife of Power for the Sake of the People ; and Tyrants abufe the People, for the Sake of Power. Free Government is the protecting the People in their Liberties by ftated Rules : Tyranny is a brutifh Struggle for unlimited Liberty to one or a few, who would rob all others of their Liberty, and act by no Rule but lawlefs Luft.

So much for an Idea of Civil Liberty. I will now add a Word or two, to fhew how much it is the Delight and Paffion of Mankind ; and then fhew its Advantages.

The Love of Liberty is an Apperite fo ftrongly implanted in the Nature of all Living Creatures, that even the Appetite of Self-prefervation, which is allowed to be the ftrongeft, feems to be contained in it ; fince by the Means of Liberty they enjoy the Means of preferving themfelves, and of fatisfying their Defires in the Manner which they themfelves choofe and like beft. Many Animals can never be tamed, but feel the Bitternefs of Reftraint in the midft of the kindeft Ufage ; and rather than bear it, grieve and ftarve themfelves to Death ; and fome beat out their Brains againft their Prifons.

Where Liberty is loft, Life grows precarious, always miferable, often intolerable. Liberty is, to live upon one's own Terms ; Slavery is, to live at the mere Mercy of another ; and a Life of Slavery is, to thofe who can bear it, a continual State of Uncertainty and Wretchednefs, often an Apprehenfion of Violence, often the lingering Dread of
a violent

a violent Death: But by others, when no other Remedy is to be had, Death is reckoned a good one. And thus, to many Men, and to many other Creatures, as well as Men, the Love of Liberty is beyond the Love of Life.

This Paffion for Liberty in Men, and their Poffeffion of it, is of that Efficacy and Importance, that it feems the Parent of all the Virtues: And therefore in free Countries there feems to be another Species of Mankind, than is to be found under Tyrants. Small Armies of *Greeks* and *Romans* defpifed the greateft Hofts of Slaves; and a Million of Slaves have been fometimes beaten and conquered by a few Thoufand Freemen. Infomuch that the Difference feemed greater between them than between Men and Sheep. It was therefore well faid by *Lucullus*, when, being about to engage the great King *Tigranes*'s Army, he was told by fome of his Officers, how prodigious great the fame was, confifting of between Three and Four Hundred Thoufand Men: *No matter*, faid that brave *Roman*, drawing up his little Army of Fourteen Thoufand, but Fourteen Thoufand *Romans: No matter*; *the Lion never enquires into the Number of the Sheep.* And thefe Royal Troops proved no better; for the *Romans* had little elfe to do but to kill and purfue; which yet they could fcarce do for laughing; fo much more were they diverted than animated by the ridiculous Dread and fudden Flight of thefe Imperial Slaves and Royal Cowards.

Men eternally cowed and oppreffed by haughty and infolent Governors, made bafe themfelves by the Bafenefs of that Sort of Government, and be-
                                                            come

come Slaves by ruling over Slaves, want Spirit and
Souls to meet in the Field Freemen, who fcorn Oppreffors, and are their own Governors, or at leaft
meafure and direct the Power of their Governors.

Education alters Nature, and becomes ftronger.
Slavery, while it continues, being a perpetual Awe
upon the Spirits, depreffes them, and finks natural
Courage ; and Want and Fear, the Concomitants
of Bondage, always produce Defpondency and
Bafenefs ; nor will Men in Bonds ever fight bravely, but to be free. Indeed, what elfe fhould they
fight for ; fince every Victory that they gain for a
Tyrant, makes them poorer and fewer ; and, increafing his Pride, increafes his Cruelty, with their
own Mifery and Chains ?

Thofe, who, from Terror and Delufion, the
frequent Caufes and certain Effects of Servitude,
come to think their Governors greater than Men,
as they find them worfe, will be as apt to think
themfelves lefs : And when the Head and the
Heart are thus both gone, the Hands will fignify
little. They who are ufed like Beafts, will be
apt to degenerate into Beafts. But thofe, on the
contrary, who, by the Freedom of their Government and Education, are taught and accuftomed
to think freely of Men and Things, find, by comparing one Man with another, that all Men are
naturally alike ; and that their Governors, as they
have the fame Face, Conftitution, and Shape with
themfelves, and are fubject to the fame Sicknefs,
Accidents, and Death, with the meaneft of their
People ; fo they poffefs the fame Paffions and Faculties of the Mind which their Subjects poffefs,
and not better. They therefore fcorn to degrade

and proftrate themfelves, to adore thofe of their
own Species, however covered with Titles, and
difguifed by Power : They confider them as their
own Creatures ; and, as far as they furmount
themfelves, the Work of their own Hands, and
only the chief Servants of the State, who have no
more Power to do Evil than one of themfelves,
and are void of every Privilege and Superiority,
but to ferve them and the State. They know it
to be a Contradiction in Religion and Reafon, for
any Man to have a Right to do Evil ; that not to
refift any Man's Wickednefs, is to encourage it ;
and that they have the leaft Reafon to bear Evil
and Oppreffion from their Governors, who of all
Men are the moft obliged to do them Good. They
therefore deteft Slavery, and defpife or pity Slaves ;
and, adoring Liberty alone, as they who fee its
Beauty and feel its Advantages always will, it is
no Wonder that they are brave for it.

Indeed Liberty is the divine Source of all human
Happinefs. To poffefs, in Security, the Effects
of our Induftry, is the moft powerful and reafonable Incitement te be induftrious : And to be able
to provide for our Children, and to leave them all
that we have, is the beft Motive to beget them.
But where Property is precarious, Labour will
languifh. The Privileges of thinking, faying,
and doing what we pleafe, and of growing as
rich as we can, without any other Reftriction,
than that by all this we hurt not the Publick, nor
one another, are the glorious Privileges of Liberty ;
and its Effects, to live in Freedom, Plenty, and
Safety.

Thefe are Privileges that increafe Mankind,
and

and the Hppinefs of Mankind. And therefore
Countries are generally peopled in Proportion as
they are free, and are certainly happy in that Proportion : And upon the fame Tract of Land that
would maintain a Hundred Thoufand Freemen in
Plenty, Five Thoufand Slaves would ftarve. In
Italy, fertile *Italy*, Men die fometimes of Hunger
amongft the Sheaves, and in a plentiful Harveft ; for what they fow and reap is none of their
own ; and their cruel and greedy Governors,
who live by the Labour of their wretched Vaffals,
do not fuffer them to eat the Bread of their own
Earning, nor to fuftain their Lives with their own
Hands.

Liberty naturally draws new People to it, as
well as increafes the old Stock ; and Men as naturally run when they dare from Slavery and Wretchednefs, whitherfoever they can help themfelves.
Hence great Cities lofing their Liberty become
Defarts, and little Towns by Liberty grow great
Cities ; as will be fully proved before I have gone
through this Argument. I will not deny, but that
there are fome great Cities of Slaves : But fuch are
only Imperial Cities, and the Seats of great Princes,
who draw the Wealth of a Continent to their Capital, the Center of their Treafure and Luxury.
Babylon, *Antioch*, *Seleucia*, and *Alexandria*, were great
Cities peopled by Tyrants ; but peopled partly by
Force, partly by the above Reafon, and partly by
Grants and Indulgencies. Their Power, great and
boundlefs as it was, could not alone people their
Cities; but they were forced to foften Authority by
Kindnefs ; and having brought the Inhabitants to-
gether by Force, and by driving them Captive like
Cattle,

Cattle, could not keep them together, without be-
ftowing on them many Privileges, to encourage
the firft Inhabitants to ftay, and to invite more to
come.

This was a Confeffion in thofe Tyrants, that
their Power was mifchievous and unjuft ; fince they
could not erect one great City, and make it flourifh, without renouncing in a great meafure their
Power over it ; which, by granting it thefe Privileges, in Effect they did. Thefe Privileges were
fixed Laws, by which the Trade and Induftry of
the Citizens were encouraged, and their Lives and
Properties afcertained and protected, and no longer
fubjected to the Laws of mere Will and Pleafure :
And therefore, while thefe free Cities, enjoying their
own Liberties and Laws, flourifhed under them,
the Provinces were miferably harraffed, pillaged,
difpeopled, and impoverifhed, and the Inhabitants
exhaufted, ftarved, butchered, and carried away
captive.

This fhews that all Civil Happinefs and Profperity is infeparable from Liberty ; and that Tyranny
cannot make Men, or Societies of Men, happy,
without departing from its Nature, and giving them
Privileges inconfiftent with Tyranny. And here is
an unanfwerable Argument, amongft a Thoufand
others, againft abfolute Power in a fingle Man.
Nor is there one Way in the World to give Happinefs to Communities, but by fheltering them
under certain and exprefs Laws, irrevocable at
any Man's Pleafure.

There is not, nor can be, any Security for a
People to truft to the mere Will of one, who,
while his Will is his Law, cannot protect them

if

if he would. The Number of Sycophants and wicked Counsellors, that he will always and necessarily have about him, will defeat all his good Intentions, by representing Things falsly, and Persons maliciously ; by suggesting Danger where it is not, and urging Necessity where there is none; by filling their own Coffers, under Colour of filling his, and by raising Money for themselves, pretending the publick Exigencies of the State ; by sacrificing particular Men to their own Revenge, under Pretence of publick Security ; and by engaging him and his People in dangerous and destructive Wars, for their own Profit or Fame ; by throwing publick Affairs into perpetual Confusion, to prevent an Enquiry into their own Behaviour ; and by making him jealous of his People, and his People of him, on purpose to manage and mislead both Sides.

By all these, and many more wicked Arts, they will be constantly leading him into cruel and oppressive Measures, destructive to his People, scandalous and dangerous to himself ; but entirely agreeable to their own Spirit and Designs. Thus will they commit all Wickedness by their Master's Authority, against his Inclinations, and grow rich by the People's Poverty, without his Knowledge ; and the Royal Authority will be first a Warrant for Oppression, afterwards a Protection from the Punishment due to it. For, in short, the Power of Princes is often little else but a Stalking-Horse to the Intrigues and Ambition of their Minister.

But if the Disposition of such a Prince be evil, what must be the forlorn Condition of his People, and what Door of Hope can remain for common
Protection !

Protection! The best Princes have often evil Counsellors, the Bad will have no other : And in such a
Case, what Bounds can be set to their Fury, and
to the Havock they will make ? The Instruments
and Advisers of Tyranny and Depredation always
thrive best and are nearest their Ends, when Depredation and Tyranny run highest : When most
is plundered from the People, their Share is greatest ; we may therefore suppose every Evil will befal
such a People, without supposing extravagantly. No
Happiness, no Security, but certain Misery, and a
vile and precarious Life, are the blessed Terms of
such a Government—A Government which necessarily introduces all Evils, and from the same
Necessity neither must nor can redress any.

The Nature of his Education, bred up as he
ever is in perpetual Flattery, makes him haughty
and ignorant ; and the Nature of his Government,
which subsists by brutish Severity and Oppression,
makes him cruel. He is inaccessible, but by his
Ministers, whose Study and Interest will be to keep
him from knowing or helping the State of his miserable People. Their Master's Knowledge in his
own Affairs, would break in upon their Scheme
and Power ; they are not likely to lay before him
Representations of Grievances caused by themselves ; nor, if they be the Effects of his own Barbarity and Command, will he hear them.

Even where absolute Princes are not Tyrants,
there Ministers will be Tyrants. But it is indeed
impossible for an arbitrary Prince to be otherwise,
since Oppression is absolutely necessary to his being
so. Without giving his People Liberty, he cannot
make them happy ; and by giving them Liberty,
                                                    he

he gives up his own Power. So that to be and continue arbitrary, he is doomed to be a Tyrant in his own Defence. The Oppreſſion of the People, Corruption, wicked Counſellors, and perniꞏ cious Maxims in the Court, and every where Baſeneſs, Ignorance, and Chains, muſt ſupport Tyranny, or it cannot be ſupported. So that in ſuch Governments there are inevitable Grievances, without poſſible Redreſs; Miſery, without Mitigation or Remedy; whatever is good for the People, is bad for their Governors; and what is good for the Governors, is pernicious to the People.

G

I am, &c.

Saturday, *January* 27, 1721.   No. 63.

Civil Liberty produces all Civil Bleſſings, and how ; with the baneful Nature of Tyranny.

S I R,

I Go on with my Conſiderations upon Liberty, to ſhew that all Civil Virtue and Happineſs, every moral Excellency, all Politeneſs, all good Arts and Sciences, are produced by Liberty ; and that all Wickedneſs, Baſeneſs, and Miſery, are immediately and neceſſarily produced by Tyranny ; which being founded upon the Deſtruction of every thing that is valuable, deſireable, and noble, muſt ſubſiſt upon Means ſuitable to its Nature, and remain in everlaſting Enmity to all Goodneſs and every human Bleſſing.

By

By the Eftablifhment of Liberty, a due Diftribution of Property and an equal Diftaibution of
Juftice is eftablifhed and fecured. As Rapine is
the Child of Oppreffion, Juftice is the Offspring
of Liberty, and her Handmaid ; it is the Guardian
of Innocence, and the Terror of Vice : And when
Fame, Honour, and Advantages, are the Rewards of Virtue, fhe will be courted for the Dower
which fhe brings ; otherwife, like Beauty without
Wealth, fhe may be praifed, but more probably
will be calumniated, envied, and very often perfecuted ; while Vice, when it is gainful, like rich
Deformity and profperous Folly, will be admired
and purfued. Where Virtue is all its own Reward, fhe will be feldom thought any ; and few
will buy That for a great Price, which will fell for
none. So that Virtue, to be followed, muft be
endowed, and her Credit is beft fecured by her Intereft ; that is, fhe muft be ftrengthened and recommended by the publick Laws, and embellifhed
by publick Encouragements, or elfe fhe will be
flighted and fhunned.

Now the Laws which encourage and increafe
Virtue, are the fixed Laws of general and impartial Liberty ; Laws, which being the Rule of
every Man's Actions, and the Meafures of every
Man's Power, make Honefty and Equity their
Intereft. Where Liberty is thoroughly eftablifhed,
and its Laws equally executed, every Man will
find his Account in doing as he would be done unto, and no Man will take from another what he
would not part with himfelf : Honour and Advantage will follow the Upright, Punifhment overtake the Oppreffor. The Property of the Poor
will

will be as facred as the Privileges of the Prince, and the Law will be the only Bulwark of both. Every Man's honeft Induftry and ufeful Talents, while they are employed for the Publick, will be employed for himfelf; and while he ferves himfelf, he will ferve the Pyblick: Publick and private Intereft will fecure each other; all will chearfully give a Part to fecure the Whole, and be brave to defend it.

Thefe certain Laws therefore are the only certain Beginnings and Caufes of Honefty and Virtue amongft Men. There may be other Motives, I own; but fuch as only fway particular Men, few enough, God knows: And univerfal Experience has fhewn us, that they are not generally prevailing, and never to be depended upon. Now thefe Laws are to be produced by Liberty alone, and only by fuch Laws can Liberty be fecured and increafed: And to make Laws certainly good, they muft be made by mutual Agreement, and have for their End the general Intereft.

But Tyranny muft ftand upon Force; and the Laws of Tyranny being only the fickle Will and unfteady Appetite of one Man, which may vary every Hour; there can be no fettled Rule of Right or Wrong in the variable Humours and fudden Paffions of a Tyrant, who, though he may fometimes punifh Crimes, perhaps more out of Rage than Juftice, will be much more likely to perfecute and opprefs Innocence, and to deftroy Thoufands cruelly, for one that he protects juftly. There are Inftances of Princes, who, being out of Humour with a Favourite, have put to Death all that fpoke well of him, and afterwards all that
did

did not : Of Princes, who put fome of their Minifters to Death, for ufing one or two of their
Barbers and Buffoons ill ; as they did others of
their Minifters, for ufing a whole Country well :
Of Princes, who have deftroyed, a whole People,
for the Crimes or Virtues of one Man ; and who,
having killed a Minion in a Paffion, have, to revenge themfelves upon thofe who had not provoked them, deftroyed in the fame unreafonable
Fury, a Hundred of their Servants who had no
Hand in it, as well as all that had ; who yet
would have been deftroyed, had they not done it :
Of Princes, who have deftroyed Millions in fingle mad Projects and Expeditions : Of Princes,
who have given up Cities and Provinces to the
Revenge or Avarice of a vile Woman or Eunuch,
to be plundered, or maffacred, or burned, as he
or fhe thought fit to direct : Of Princes, who, to
gratify the Ambition and Rapine of a few forry
Servants, have loft the Hearts of their whole
People, and detached themfelves from their good
Subjects, to protect thefe Men in their Iniquity,
who yet had done them no other Service? but that
of deftroying their Reputation, and fhaking their
Throne.

Such are arbitrary Princes, whofe Laws are
nothing but fudden Fury, or lafting Folly and
Wickednefs in uncertain Shapes.————Hopeful
Rules thefe, for the governing of Mankind, and
making them happy ! Rules which are none, fince
they cannot be depended upon for a Moment ;
and generally change for the worfe, if that can be.
A Subject worth Twenty Thoufand Pounds to
Day, may, by a fudden Edict iffued by the dark
Counfel

Counfel of a Traytor, be a Beggar to Morrow, and lofe his Life without forfeiting the fame. The Property of the whole Kingdom fhall be great, or little, or none, juft at the Mercy of a Secretary's Pen, guided by a Child, or a Dotard, or a foolifh Woman, or a favourite Buffoon, or a Gamefter, or whoever is uppermoft for the Day ; the next Day fhall alter entirely the Yefterday's Scheme, though not for the better; and the fame Men, in different Humours, fhall be the Authors of both. Thus in arbitrary Countries, a Law aged Two Days is an old Law ; and no Law is fuffered to be a ftanding Law, but fuch as are found by long Experience to be fo very bad, and fo thoroughly deftructive, that human Malice, and all the Arts of a Tyrant's Court, cannot make them worfe. ——A Court which never ceafeth to fqueeze, kill, and opprefs, till it has wound up human Mifery fo high, that it will go no further. This is fo much Fact, that I appeal to all Hiftory and Travels, and to thofe that read them, whether in arbitrary Countries, both in *Europe* and out of it, the People do not grow daily thinner, and their Mifery greater ; and whether Countries are not peopled and rich, in Proportion to the Liberty which they enjoy and allow.

It has been long my Opinion, and is more and more fo, that in flavifh Countries the People muft either throw off their cruel and deftroying Government, and fet up another in its Room, or in fome Ages the Race of Mankind there will be extinct. Indeed, if it had not been for free States, that have repaired and prevented in many Places the Mifchiefs done by Tyrants, the Earth
had

had been long fince a Defart, as the fineft Countries in it are at this Day by that Means. The Gardens of the World, the fruitful and lovely Countries of the lower *Afia*, filled formerly by Liberty with People, Politenefs, and Plenty, are now glorioufly peopled with Owls and Grafhoppers ; and perhaps here and there, at vaft Diftances, with Inhabitants not more valuable, and lefs happy ; a few dirty Huts of Slaves groaning, ftarvving, and perifhing, under the fatherly Protection of the *Sultan*, a Prince of the moft Orthodox Standard.

The Laws therefore of Tyrants are not Laws, but wild Acts of Will, counfelled by Rage or Folly, and executed by Dragoons. And as thefe Laws are evil, all Sorts of Evil muft concur to fupport them. While the People have Common-Senfe left, they will eafily fee whether they are juftly governed, and well or ill ufed ; whether they are protected or plundered : They will know that no Man ought to be the Director of the Affairs of All, without their Confent ; that no Confent can give him unlimited Power over their Bodies and Minds ; and that the Laws of Nature can never be entirely abrogated by pofitive Laws ; but that, on the contrary, the entering into Society, and becoming fubject to Government, is only the parting with natural Liberty, in fome Inftances, to be protected in the Enjoyment of it in others.

So that for any Man to have arbitrary Power, he muft have it without Confent ; or if it be unadvifedly given at firft, they who gave it foon repent when they find its Effects. In Truth, all thofe Princes that have fuch Power, by keeping up

great

great Armies in Time of Peace, effectually confefs that they rule without Confent, and dread
their People, whofe worft Enemies they undoubtedly are.   An arbitrary Prince therefore muft preferve and execute his Power by Force and Terror ;
which yet will not do, without calling in the auxiliary Aids and ftrict Allies of Tyranny, Impofture,
and conftant Oppreffion.   Let this People be ever
fo low and miferable, if they be not alfo blind,
he is not fafe.   He muft have eftablifhed Deceivers to miflead them with Lyes, to terrify them
with the Wrath of God, in cafe they ftir Hand
or Foot, or fo much as a Thought, to mend their
doleful Condition ; as if the good God was the
Sanctifier of all Villainy, the Patron of the worft
of all Villains ! He muft have a Band of ftanding
Cut-throats to murder all Men who would facri-
legioufly defend their own.   And both his Cut-
throats and his Deceivers muft go Shares with him
in his Tyranny.

Men will naturally fee their Interefts, feel their
Condition ; will quickly find that the Sword, the
Rack, and the Spunge, are not Government, but
the Height of Cruelty and Robbery ; and will never fubmit to them, but by the united Powers of
Violence and Delufion : Their Bodies muft be
chained, their Minds enchanted and deceived ;
the Sword kept conftantly over their Heads, and
their Spirits kept low with Poverty, before they
can be brought to be ufed at the wanton and brutifh Pleafure of the moft dignified and lofty Oppreffor. So that God muft be belied, his Creatures muft be fettered, frightened, deceived, and
ftarved, and Mankind made bafe and undone,
                                                    that

that one of the worft of them may live rio-
toufly and fafely amongft his Whores, Butchers,
and Buffoons.

Men, therefore, muft ceafe to be Men, and
in Stupidity and Tamenefs grow Cattle, before
they can become quiet Subjects to fuch a Government ; which is a Complication of all the Villainies, Falfhood, Oppreffion, Cruelty, and Depredation, upon the Face of the Earth : Nor can
there be a more provoking, impudent, fhocking,
and blafpemous Pofition, than to affert all this
Groupe of Horrors, or the Author of them, to be
of God's Appointment.

> *If fuch Kings are by God appointed,*
> *Satan may be the Lord's Anointed.*

And whoever fcatters fuch Doctrine, ought, by all
the Laws of God, Reafon, and Self-prefervation,
to be put to Death as a general Poifoner, and Advocate for publick Deftruction.

All Men own, that it is the Duty of a Prince
to protect his People : And fome have faid, that it
is their Duty to obey him, when he butchers them.
—An admirable Confequence, and full of fweet
Confolation ! His whole Bufinefs and Office is to
defend them, and to do them Good ; therefore
they are bound to let him deftroy them.—Was
ever fuch Impudence in an enlightened Country ?
It is perfectly agreeable to the Doctrines and Followers of *Mahomet :* But fhall *Englifhmen,* who
make their own Laws, be told, that they have no
Right to the common Air, to the Life and Fortune which God has given them, but by the Permiffion

miffion of an Officer of their own making; who is what he is only for their Sakes and Security, and has no more Right to thefe Bleffings, nor to do Evil, than one of themfelves ? And fhall we be told this by Men, who are eternally the firft to violate their own Doctrines? Or fhall they after this have the Front to teach us any Doctrine, or to recommend to us any one Virtue, when they have thus given up all Virtue and Truth, and every Bleffing that Life affords ? For there is no Evil, Mifery, and Wickednefs, which arbitrary Monarchies do not produce, and muft produce ; nor do they, nor can they, produce any certain, general, or diffufive Good.

I have fhewn, in my laft, that an arbitrary Prince cannot protect his People if he would ; and I add here, that he dares not. It would dif- guft the Inftruments of his Power, and the Sharers in his Oppreffion, who will confider the Property of the People as the Perquifites of their Office, and claim a Privilege of being little Tyrants, for making him a great one : So that every Kindnefs to his Subjects will be a Grievance to his Servants ; and he muft affert and exercife his Tyranny to the Height for their Sakes, or they will do it for him. And the Inftances are rare, if any, of any abfolute Monarch's protecting in earneft his People againft the Depredations of his Minifters and Sol- diers, but it has coft him his Life ; as may be fhewn by many Examples in the *Roman* Hiftory : For this the Emperor *Pertinax* was murdered, and fo was *Galba*.

Machiavel has told us, that it is impoffible for fuch a Prince to pleafe both the People and his

Soldiers :

Soldiers: The one will not be satisfied without Protection, nor the other without Rapine: To comply with the People, he must give up his Power; to comply with his Soldiers, he must give up his People. So that to continue what he is, and to preserve himself from the Violence of his Followers, he must countenance all their Villainies and Oppression, and be himself no more than an Imperial Thief at the Head of a Band of Thieves; for which Character he is generally well qualified by the base and cruel Maxims of that Sort of Power, and by the vile Education always given to such a Prince by the worst and most infamous of all Men, their supple and lying Sycophants.

Even the Christian Religion can do but little or no Good in Lands of Tyranny, since Miracles have ceased; but is made to do infinite Harm, by being corrupted and perverted into a deadly Engine in the Hands of a Tyrant and his Impostors, to rivet his Subjects Chains, and to confirm them thorough Wretches, Slaves, and Ignorants. I cannot indeed say, that they have the Christian Religion at all amongst them, but only use its amiable Name to countenance abominable Falshoods, Nonsense, and heavy Oppression; to defend furious and implacable Bigotry, which is the direct Characteristick and Spirit of *Mahometism*, and destroys the very Genius and first Principles of Christianity. All this will be further shewn hereafter. I shall conclude with observing, that arbitrary Monarchy is a constant War upon Heaven and Earth, against the Souls as well as Bodies and Properties of Men.

G   *I am,* &c.

Saturday, *February* 3, 1721.   No. 64.

Trade and Naval Power the Offspring of Civil Liberty only, and cannot subsist without it.

SIR,

I HAVE in former Letters begun to shew, by an Induction of Particulars, and shall hereafter more fully shew, that Population, Riches, true Religion, Virtue, Magnanimity, Arts, Sciences, and Learning, are the necessary Effects and Productions of Liberty; and shall spend this Paper in proving, that an extensive Trade, Navigation, and Naval Power, entirely flow from the same Source: In this Case, if natural Advantage and Encouragements be wanting, Art, Expence, and Violence, are lost and thrown away. Nothing is more certain, than that Trade cannot be forced; she is a coy and humorous Dame, who must be won by Flattery and Allurements, and always flies Force and Power; she is not confined to Nations, Sects, or Climates, but travels and wanders about the Earth, till she fixes her Residence where she finds the best Welcome and kindest Reception; her Contexture is so nice and delicate, that she cannot breathe in a tyrannical Air; Will and Pleasure are so opposite to her Nature, that but touch her with the Sword, and she dies: But if you give her gentle and kind Entertainment, she is a grateful and beneficent Mistress; she will turn Deserts into fruitful Fields, Villages into great Cities, Cottages into Palaces,

Beggars

Beggars into Princes, convert Cowards into Heroes, Blockheads into Philofophers ; will change the Coverings of little Worms into the richeft Brocades, the Fleeces of harmlefs Sheep into the Pride and Ornaments of Kings, and by a further Metamorphofis will tranfmute them again into armed Hofts and haughty Fleets.

Now it is abfolutely impoffible, from the Nature of an arbitrary Government, that fhe fhould enjoy Security and Protection, or indeed be free from Violence, under it. There is not One Man in a Thoufand that has the Endowments and Abilities neceffary to govern a State, and much fewer yet that have juft Notions how to make Trade and Commerce ufeful and advantageous to it ; and, amongft thefe, it is rare to find one who will forego all perfonal Advantages, and devote himfelf and his Labours wholly to his Country's Intereft : But if fuch a Phœnix fhould arife in any Country, he will find it hard to get Accefs to an arbitrary Court, and much harder yet to grapple with and ftem the raging Corruptions in it, where Virtue has nothing to do, and Vice rides triumphant ; where Bribery, fervile Flattery, blind Submiffion, riotous Expence, and very often Luft and unnatural Proftitutions, are the Ladders to Greatnefs ; which will certainly be fupported by the fame Methods by which it is obtained.

What has a virtuous Man to do, or what can he do, in fuch Company ? If he pity the People's Calamities, he fhall be called feditious ; if he recommend any publick Good, he fhall be called preaching Fool ; if he fhould live foberly and virtuoufly himfelf, they will think him fit only to be

fent to a Cloyfter ; if he do not flatter the Prince
and his Superiors, he will be thought to envy their
Profperity ; if he prefume to advife his Prince to
purfue his true Intereft, he will be efteemed a formidable Enemy to the whole Court, who will
unite to deftroy him : In fine, his Virtues will be
Crimes, Reproaches, and of dangerous Confequence to thofe who have none. As Jails pick up
all the little pilfering Rogues of a Country, fo
fuch Courts engrofs all the great Ones ; who have
no Bufinefs there but to grow rich, and to riot
upon the publick Calamities, to ufe all the Means
of Oppreffion and Rapine, to make hafty Fortunes before the Bow-ftring overtakes them, or a
fudden Favourite fupplants them.

Now what Encouragement or Security can
Trade and Induftry receive from fuch a Crew
of Banditti ? No Privileges and Immunities, or
even Protection, can be obtained but for Money,
and are always granted to fuch who give moft ;
and thefe again fhall be curtailed, altered, abrogated, and cancelled, upon the Change of a Minifter, or of his Inclinations, Intereft, and Caprices : Monopolies, exclufive Companies, Liberties of Pre-emption, &c. fhall be obtained for
Bribes or Favour, or in Truft for Great Men, or
vile and worthlefs Women. Some Merchants
fhall be openly encouraged and protected, and get
Exemptions from Searches and Duties, or fhall be
connived at in efcaping them ; others fhall be
burthened, oppreffed, manacled, ftopped, and de-
layed, to extort Prefents, to wreak Revenge, or
to give Preference of Markets to Favourites. Governors of Port-Towns, or of Colonies, who have
purchafed

purchafed their Employments at Court, fhall be indulged and countenanced in making Reprifals upon the Traders, and to enable them to fatisfy the yearly Prefents due to Minions : Admirals and Commanders of Men of War fhall prefs their Sailors, to be paid for not doing it ; and Military Officers and Soldiers fhall moleft and interrupt them in the Courfe of their Commerce and honeft Induftry.

Nor fhall it be in the Power of the moft vigilant, active and virtuous Prince, to prevent thefe and a Thoufand other daily Oppreffions ; he muft fee with his Minifters Eyes, and hear with their Ears ; nor can there be any Accefs to him but by their Means, and by their Leave : Conftant Spies fhall watch and obferve the firft Intentions, or leaft Approaches to a Complaint ; and the Perfon injured fhall be threatened, way-laid, imprifoned, perhaps murdered ; but if he efcape all their Treacheries, and can get to the Ear of his Prince, it is great odds but he will be treated and punifhed as a Calumniator, a falfe Accufer, and a feditious Difturber of his Majefty's Government : No Witnefs will dare to appear for him, many falfe ones will be fuborned againft him ; and the whole Poffe of Minifters, Officers, Favourites, Parafites, Pathicks, Strumpets, Buffoons, Fidlers, and Pimps, will confpire to ruin him, as a common Enemy to their common Interefts.

But if all thefe Mifchiefs could be avoided, the Neceffities of fuch a Prince, arifing from the Profufion and vaft Expence of his Court, from his foolifh Wars, and the Depredations, Embezzlements, and various Thefts of his Minifters and

Servants,

Servants, will be always calling for new Supplies, for new Extortions, which muft be raifed by all the Means by which they can be raifed: New and fudden Impofitions fhall be put upon Trade, new Loans be exacted from Merchants ; Commodities of general ufe fhall be bought up by the Prince's Order, perhaps upon Truft, and afterwards retailed again at extravagant Advantages : Merchants fhall be encouraged to import their Goods, upon Promifes of eafy and gentle Ufage ; thefe Goods when imported fhall be fubjected to exorbitant Impofitions and Cuftoms, perhaps confifcated upon frivolous Pretences. But if thefe, and infinite other Oppreffions, could be prevented for fome time, by the Vigilance of a wife Prince, or the Care of an able Minifter ; yet there can be no probable Security, or even Hopes of the Continuance of honeft and prudent Meafures in fuch a Government: For One wife Prince fo educated, there will be Twenty foolifh ones ; and for One honeft Minifter, there will be a Thoufand corrupt ones.

Under fuch natural Difadvantages, perpetual Uncertainties, or rather certain Oppreffions, no Men will embark large Stocks and extenfive Talents for Bufinefs, breed up their Children to precarious Employments, build Forts, or plant Colonies, when the Breath of a weak Prince, or the Caprice of a corrupt Favourite, fhall dafh at once all their Labours and their Hopes ; and therefore it is impoffible that any Trade can fubfift long in fuch a Government, but what is neceffary to fupport the Luxury and Vices of a Court ; and even fuch Trade is, for the moft part, carried on by

the

the Stocks, and for the Advantage of free Countries, and their own petty Merchants are only Factors to the others. True Merchants are Citizens of the World, and that is their Country where they can live beft and moft fecure; and whatever they can pick up and gather together in tyrannical Governments, they remove to free ones. *Tavernier* invefted all the Riches he had amaffed by his long Ramble over the World, in the barren Rocks of *Switzerland:* And being afked by the laft King of *France*, how it came to pafs that he, who had feen the fineft Countries on the Globe, came to lay out his Fortune in the worft ? He gave his haughty Majefty this fhort Anfwer, That he was willing to have fomething which he could call his own.

As I think it is evident, by what I have faid before, that Trade cannot long fubfift, much lefs flourifh, in arbitrary Governments ; fo there is fo clofe and infeparable a Connexion between that and Naval Power, that I dare boldly affirm, that the latter can never arrive to any formidable Height, and continue long in that Situation, under fuch a State. Where there is an extenfive Trade ; great Numbers of able-bodied and courageous Sailors, Men bred up to Fatigues, Hardfhips, and Hazards, and confequently Soldiers by Profeffion, are kept in conftant Pay ; not only without any Charge to the Publick, but greatly to its Benefit ; not only by daily adding to its Wealth and Power, but by venting and employing Abroad, to their Country's Honour and Safety, thofe turbulent and unruly Spirits that would be Fuel for Factions, and the Tools and Inftruments

of

of ambitious or difcontented Great Men at Home. Thefe Men are always ready at their Country's Call, to defend the Profeffion which they live by, and with it the publick Happinefs : They are, and ever muft be, in the publick Intereft, with which their own is fo clofely united ; for they fubfift by exporting the Productions of the People's Induftry, which they conftantly increafe by fo doing : They receive their Pay from the Merchants, a Sort of Men always in the Interefts of Liberty, from which alone they can receive Protection and En-couragement. And as this Race of Men contri-bute vaftly to the publick Security and Wealth, fo they take nothing from it : They are not quartered up and down their native Country, like the Bands of defpotick Princes, to opprefs their Subjects, in-terrupt their Induftry, debauch their Wives and Daughters, infult their Perfons, to be Examples of Lewdnefs and Prodigality, and to be always ready at Hand to execute the bloody Commands of a Tyrant.

No Monarch was ever yet powerful enough to keep as many Seamen in conftant Pay at his own Expence, as fingle Cities have been able to do without any at all : The Pay of a Sailor, with his Provifion, is equal to that of a Trooper in ar-bitrary Governments ; nor can they learn their Trade, by taking the Sea-Air for a few Summer Months, and wafting about the Coafts of their own Country : They gain Experience and Bold-nefs, by various and difficult Voyages, by being conftantly inured to Hardfhips and Dangers. Nor is it poffible for fingle Princes, with all their Power and Vigilance, to have fuch regular Sup-plies

plies of Naval Provisions, as trading Countries muft have always in Store. There muft be a regular and conftant Intercourfe with the Nations from whom thefe Supplies come ; a certain and regular Method of paying for them ; and conftant Demands will produce conftant Supplies. There are always numerous Magazines in the Hands of private Merchants, ready for their own Ufe or Sale. There muft be great Numbers of Shipwrights, Anchor-Smiths, Rope and Sail-Makers, and infinite other Artificers, fure always of conftant Employment ; and who, if they are oppreffed by one Mafter, may go to another. There muft be Numbers of Ships ufed for Trade, that, upon Occafions, may be employed for Men of War, for Tranfports, for Firefhips, and Tenders. Now all thefe Things, or fcarce any of them, can ever be brought about by arbitrary Courts ; Stores will be embezzled, exhaufted, and worn out, before new ones are fupplied ; Payments will not be punctually made ; Artificers will be difcouraged, oppreffed, and often left without Employ : Every thing will be done at an exorbitant Expence, and often not done when it is paid for ; and when Payments are made, the greateft Part fhall go in Fees, or for Bribes, or in fecret Trufts.

For thefe Reafons, and many others, defpotick Monarchs, though infinitely powerful at Land, yet could never rival *Neptune*, and extend their Empire over the liquid World ; for though great and vigorous Efforts have been often made by thefe haughty Tyrants of Mankind, to fubject that Element to their Ambition and their Power, being

taught

taught by woful Experience, arising from perpetual Losses and Disappointments, of what vast Importance that Dominion was to unlimited and universal Sovereignty; yet all their Riches, Application, and Pride, have never been able, in one Instance, to effect it. Sometimes, indeed, Trade, like a Phantom, has made a faint Appearance at an arbitrary Court, but disappeared again at the first Approach of the Morning Light: She is the Portion of free States, is married to Liberty, and ever flies the foul and polluted Embraces of a Tyrant.

The little State of *Athens* was always able to humble the Pride, and put a Check to the growing Greatness, of the towering *Persian* Monarchs, by their Naval Power; and when stripped of all their Territories by Land, and even their capital City, the Seat of their Commonwealth, yet had Strength enough left to vanquish numerous Fleets, which almost covered the Sea, and to defeat an Expedition carried on by Armies that drank up Rivers, and exhausted all the Stores of the Land.

The single City of *Venice* has proved itself an Over-match in Naval Power to the great *Ottoman* Empire, though possessed of so many Islands, useful Ports, environed with so many Sea-Coasts, and abounding with all Sorts of Stores necessary to Navigation; and in the Year Fifty-six gave the *Turks* so signal an Overthrow at the *Dardanels*, as put that State in such a Consternation, that they believed their Empire at an End; and it is thought if the *Venetians* had pursued their Victory, they had driven them out of *Constantinople*, and even out of *Europe*; for the Grand Seignior himself was
preparing

preparing to fly into *Asia.* The little Island of *Rhodes* defended itself for some Ages against the whole Power of the *Sultan,* though encompassed by his Dominions; and it was with great Difficulty, Hazard, and Expence, that he at last overcame them, and drove the Inhabitants to *Malta,* where they have ever since braved his Pride, and live upon the Plunder of his Subjects: And notwithstanding all his numerous and expensive Efforts to share with the Christians the Dominion of the Sea; yet there are no other Seeds or Traces of it left through his great and extensive Territories, but what are found in the free pyratical States of *Algiers, Tunis,* and *Tripoli.*

Neither the *Sophi* of *Persia,* the *Great Mogul,* the many Kings who command the Banks of the *Ganges,* nor all the haughty Potentates of *Asia* and *Africk,* are able to contend at Sea with the *English* or *Dutch East-India* Companies, or even to defend their Subjects against but a few Pyrates, with all their Population, and their Mines of Gold and Diamonds.

Spain in all her Pride, with the Wealth of both *Indies,* with Dominions so vast and extensive, that the Sun rises and sets within them, and a Sea-Line, which if extended would inviron the Earth, yet was not able to dispute their Title to that Element with a few revolted Provinces, who grew up through the Course of an expensive War to that amazing Greatness, that in less than a Century they saw themselves, from a few Fisher-Towns encompassed with Bogs and Morasses, become a most formidable State, equal to the greatest Potentates at Sea, and to most at Land; to have great
Kings

Kings in a diftant World fubmit to be their Vaffals ; and, in fine, to be Protectors of that mighty
Nation from whom they revolted. Here is a
ftupendous Inftance of the Effects of Liberty,
which neighbouring Monarchs with Twenty times
the Territory tremble at, and Pofterity will hardly
believe.

France, with all its Œconomy, Addrefs, and
Power, with its utmoft and moft expenfive Efforts, and the Affiftance of neighbouring and even
rival Kings, has not been able to eftablifh an Empire upon that coy Element. She faw it, like a
Mufhroom, rife in a Night, and wither again the
next Day. It is true, that at an immenfe Expence
and infinite Labour, fhe got together a formidable
Fleet, and with it got Victories, and took Thoufands of rival Ships ; yet every Day grew weaker
as her Enemies grew ftronger, and could never
recover a fingle Defeat, which in *Holland* would
have been repaired in a few more Weeks than the
Battle was Days in fighting : So impoffible is it for
Art to contend with Nature, and Slavery to difpute the Naval Prize with Liberty.

Sweden and *Denmark*, though poffeffed of the
Naval Stores of *Europe*, Nations who fubfift by
that Commerce, and are conftantly employed to
build Ships for their Neighbours ; yet are not able,
with their united Force, to equip, man out, and
keep upon the Sea for any confiderable Time, a
Fleet large enough to difpute with an *Englifh* or
Dutch Squadron : And I dare venture my Reputation and Skill in Politicks, by boldly afferting, that
another vain and unnatural Northern Apparition
will foon vanifh and difappear again, like the Morn-
ing-

ing-Star at the Glimmering of the Sun, and every one shall aſk, *Where is it?*

T

I am, &c.

SATURDAY, *February* 10, 1721. No. 65

Military Virtue produced and ſupported by Civil Liberty only.

SIR,

I HAVE ſhewn in my laſt, that Trade and Naval Power are produced by Liberty only; and ſhall ſhew in this, that Military Virtue can proceed from nothing elſe, as I have in a good Meaſure ſhewn already.

In free Countries, as People work for themſelves, ſo they fight for themſelves: But in arbitrary Countries, it is all one to the People, in Point of Intereſt, who conquers them; they cannot be worſe uſed; and when a Tyrant's Army is beaten, his Country is conquered: He has no Reſource; his Subjects having neither Arms, nor Courage, nor Reaſon to fight for him: He has no Support but his ſtanding Forces; who, for enabling him to oppreſs, are Sharers in his Oppreſſion; and fighting for themſelves while they fight for him, do ſometimes fight well: But his poor People, who are oppreſſed by him, can have no other Concern for his Fate, than to wiſh him the worſt.

In

In Attacks upon a free State, every Man will fight to defend it, becaufe every Man has fomething to defend in it. He is in love with his Condition, his Eafe, and Property, and will venture his Life rather than lofe them; becaufe with them he lofes all the Bleffings of Life. When thefe Bleffings are gone, it is Madnefs to think that any Man will fpill his Blood for him who took them away, and is doubtlefs his Enemy, though he may call himfelf his Prince. It is much more natural to wifh his Deftruction, and help to procure it.

For thefe Reafons, fmall free States have conquered the greateft Princes; and the greateft Princes have never been able to conquer free States, but either by furprizing them bafely, or by corrupting them, or by Forces almoft infinitely fuperior, or when they were diftracted and weakened by domeftick Divifions and Treachery.

The *Greeks* thought fcarce any Number of *Perfians* too great for their own fmall Armies, or any Army of their own too fmall for the greateft Number of *Perfians*. *Agefilaus* invaded the great *Perfian* Empire, the greateft then in the World, at the Head of no more than Ten Thoufand Foot, and Four Thoufand Horfe, and carried all before him; he defeated the *Afiatick* Forces with fo much Eafe, that they fcarce interrupted his March; he fubdued their Provinces as faft as he entered them, and took their Cities without fitting down before them: And had he not been recalled by his Countrymen to defend his own City againft a Confederacy of other *Greek* Cities, much more terrible Foes than the greateft Armies of the

great

great King, it is very probable that that brave old *Spartan* would have foon robbed him of his Empire.

And not long before this, when *Cyrus* made War upon his Brother *Artaxerxes* for the Crown, Thirteen Thoufand auxiliary *Greeks* entertained by him for that End, routed the Emperor's Army of Nine Hundred Thoufand Men, and got the Victory for *Cyrus*, had he outlived the Battle to enjoy it. And though they had now loft the Prince they fought for, and afterwards *Clearchus* their General, who with other of their Officers was treacheroufly murdered by the *Perfians* when they had brought him to a Parley; though they were in great Streights, deftitute of Horfes, Money, and Provifions, far from Home, in the Heart of an Enemy's Country, watched, and diftreffed by a great Army of Four Hundred Thoufand Men, who waited for an Occafion to cut them off in their Retreat, if they attempted it; yet thefe excellent Soldiers, excellent by being Freemen, commanded by the famous *Xenophon*, made good that Retreat of Two Thoufand Three Hundred Miles over the Bellies of their Enemies, through Provinces of *Perfians*, and in fpite of a vaft Hoft of *Perfians*, who coafted and haraffed them all the Way.

Alexander of *Macedon*, with his free *Greeks*, attacked the *Perfians*, and beat them at all Difadvantages in the open Fields, when they were five, ten, nay, twenty times his Number; and having, paffed the *Hellefpont*, with not Fifteen Thoufand Pounds in his Treafury, and not above Thirty-five Thoufand Men in his Army, he made him-

felf

felf Mafter of that great and overgrown Empire, with as much Expedition as he could travel over it ; and though he fought three Battles for it, he fcarce loft in them all one Regiment of his Men.

Leonidas, at the Head of Four Thoufand *Greeks*, fought *Xerxes* at the Head of Six and Twenty Hundred Thoufand *Perfians*, according to *Herodotus*, in the Streights of *Thermopylæ* for two Days together, and repulfed them at every Affault with vaft Slaughter ; nor did they at laft get the better of him, till being led by a treacherous *Greek* a fecret Way over the Mountains, they fell upon him in the Rear, and furrounded him with their Numbers ; neither did he then defert his Poft, though all his Men retreated, except Three Hundred *Spartans*, who refolutely ftood by him, and were all flain with him upon the Spot, with Twenty Thoufand *Perfians* round them.

The *Romans*, enjoying the fame Liberty, and animated by it, vanquifhed all the enflaved Nations of the known World, with the fame Eafe, and upon the fame unequal Terms.   The fubduing of free Countries coft them long Labour and Patience, great Difficulty, and a World of Blood; and they fuffered many Defeats before they got a decifive Victory :   The Inhabitants being all Freemen, were all brave, all Soldiers, and were exhaufted before their States could be conquered : And the *Volfcians*, *Æquians*, *Tufcans*, and *Samnites*, preferved their Liberties, as long as they had Men left to defend them.   The *Samnites* particularly declared in their Embaffy to *Hannibal*, that having often brought great Numbers of Men into the Field againft the *Romans*, and fometimes defeated the

Roman

Roman Armies, they were at laft fo wafted, that they could not refift one *Roman* Legion.

But when the *Romans* came to war againft great and arbitrary Kings, they had little elfe to do but to fhew their Swords; they gained Battles almoft without fighting, and Two or Three Legions have routed Three or Four Hundred Thoufand Men. One Battle generally won a Kingdom, and fometimes two or three. *Antiochus* was fo frightened with one Skirmifh with *Acilius* at *Thermopylæ*, that he ran away out of *Greece*, and left all that he poffeffed there to the *Romans*; and being beaten afterwards by *Scipio*, the Brother of *Africanus*, he quitted to them all his Kingdoms and Territories on this Side Mount *Taurus*. And *Paulus Æmilius*, by one Battle with *Perfeus*, became Mafter of *Macedonia*. *Tigranes*, *Ptolomy*, and *Syphax*, all Monarchs of mighty Territories, were ftill more eafily vanquifhed. So that the great Kingdoms of *Afia*, *Ægypt*, *Numidia*, and *Macedon*, were all of them much more eafily overcome, and fuffered much fewer Defeats, than the *Samnites* alone, though inhabiting a fmall barren Province.

The only dreadful Foes which the *Romans* ever found, were People as free as themfelves; and the moft dreadful of all were the *Carthaginians*. *Hannibal* alone beat them oftener, and flew more of their Men in Battle, than all the Kings in the World ever did, or could do. But for all the great and repeated Defeats which he gave them; though he had deftroyed Two Hundred Thoufand of their Men, and many of their excellent Commanders; though, at the fame Time, their

Armies

Armies were cut off in *Spain*, and with them the two brave *Scipios*; and though they had suffered great Losses in *Sicily*, and at Sea, yet they never sunk nor wanted Soldiers, nor their Soldiers Courage; and as to great Commanders, they had more and better than ever they had before: And having conquered *Hannibal*, they quickly conquered the World.

This vast Virtue of theirs, and this unconquerable Spirit, was not owing to Climate or Complexion, but to Liberty alone, and to the Equality of their Government, in which every *Roman* had a Share: They were nursed up in the Principles of Liberty; in their Infancy they were instructed to love it; Experience afterwards confirmed their Affections, and shewed them its glorious Advantages: Their own happy Condition taught them a Contempt and Indignation for those wretched and barbarous Governments, which could neither afford their Subjects Happiness nor Protection: And when they attacked such Governments and their wretched People, they found themselves like Lions amongst Sheep.

It is therefore Government alone that makes Men cowardly or brave: And *Boccalini* well ridicules the absurd Complaint of the Princes of his Time, that their Subjects wanted that Love for their Country which was found in free States, when he makes *Apollo* tell them, that no People were ever in Love with Rapine, Fraud, and Oppression; that they must mend their own Administration, and their People's Condition; and that People will then love their Country, when they live happily in it. The old *Romans* were Masters

of

of Mankind; but the prefent Race of People in
Rome are not a Match for one of the *Swifs* Cantons; nor could thefe Cantons ever be conquered,
even by the united Forces of the Houfe of *Auftria*.
Charles Duke of *Burgundy* was the laft that durft
invade them; but though he had been long a
Terror and conftant Rival to *Louis* the Eleventh
of *France*, a crafty, politick, and powerful Monarch, and often too hard for him; he paid dear
for his Bravery in attacking the *Switzers*, and loft
by doing it Three Armies, and his own Life.
They were a free People, and fought in their own
Quarrel; the greateft Incitement upon Earth to
Boldnefs and Magnanimity.   The *Switzers* had a
Property, though in Rocks; and were Freemen,
though amongft Mountains.   This gives them the
Figure which they make in *Europe*; fuch a Figure, that they are courted by the greateft Princes
in it, and have fupported fome of them in their
Wars, when their own native Slaves could not
fupport them.

The *Dutch*, having revolted from the greateft
Potentate then in *Europe*, defended themfelves
againft all his Power for near a Hundred Years,
and grew rich all the Time, while he grew poor;
fo poor, that *Spain* has never yet recovered its
Loffes in that War: Aud though they are in their
Conftitution more formed for Trade than War,
yet their own Bravery in their own Defence is
aftonifhing to thofe that know not what the Spirit
of Liberty can do in any People: Even their Women joined to defend their Walls; as the Women
of *Sparta* once did, and as the Women of *Barcelona* more lately did, though the united Force of
                                                    the

the Two Monarchies of *France* and *Spain* had at
laft the Honour to take that City, efpecially when
We, who had engaged them in the War, had
alfo given them up.

Thefe fame *Dutch* in that War, when they were
clofely befieged in one of their Towns by the
Spanifh Army, let in the Sea upon their Country,
trufting rather to the Mercy of that Element,
than to the Mercy of an invading Tyrant; and
the Sea faved them. It muft be remembered too,
that they had the Power of the Emperor, as well
as that of *Spain*, to contend with; both thefe
mighty Monarchs having joined their Counfels
and Arms to fubdue Seven little Provinces, which
yet they never were able to fubdue: The City of
Oftend alone coft them a Three Years Siege, and
an Hundred and Thirty Thoufand Men; and
when they took it, they only took a Heap of Rub-
bifh, to which it was reduced before it was furrendered.

In free States, every Man being a Soldier, or
quickly made fo, they improve in a War, and
every Campaign fight better and better. Whereas
the Armies of an abfolute Prince grow every
Campaign worfe; efpecially if they be compofed
of his own Subjects, who, being Slaves, are with
great Difficulty and long Difcipline made Soldiers,
and fcarce ever made good ones; and when his
old Troops are gone, his new ones fignify little.
This was eminently fhewn in the late War with
France, which degenerated in Arms every Year;
while the *Englifh* and *Dutch* did as evidently mend.
And doubtlefs, if the *French* Barrier of fortified
Towns had been quite broken through, as it was

very

very near, One Battle would have completed the Conqueſt of *France*, and perhaps it would not have coſt a Battle.

And if free States ſupport themſelves better in a War than an abſolute Prince, they do likewiſe much ſooner retrieve their Loſſes by it. The *Dutch*, when they had been beaten twice at Sea by *Cromwell's* Admirals and *Engliſh* Seamen, with great Slaughter and Loſs of Ships, did notwith-ſtanding, in Two Months Time, after the ſecond great Defeat, fit out a Third Fleet of a Hundred and Forty Men of War, under the famous *Van Trump:* Upon this Lord *Clarendon* obſerves, that " there cannot be a greater Inſtance of the Opu- " lency of that People, than that they ſhould be " able, after ſo many Loſſes, and ſo late a great " Defeat, in ſo ſhort a Time, to ſet out a Fleet " ſtrong enough to viſit thoſe who had ſo lately " overcome them." This is what no arbitrary Prince in *Europe*, or upon the Face of the Earth, could have done ; nor do I believe, that all the arbitrary Monarchs in *Europe*, *Africa*, and *Aſia*, with all their united Powers together, could do it at this Day. The whole Strength of the *Spaniſh* Monarchy could not fit out their famous *Armada*, without the Aſſiſtance of Money from the little free State of *Genoa* ; and that invincible *Armada*, being beaten by the *Engliſh*, and quite deſtroyed, *Spain* has never been able, with all her *Indies*, and her Mountains of Silver and Gold, to make any Figure at Sea ſince, nor been able to pay that very Money which equipped that its laſt great Fleet.

The little City of *Tyre* gave *Alexander* the Great more Reſiſtance, and coſt him more Labour

bour to take it, than to conquer the great Monarchy of *Afia* ; and though, when with Infinite Labour and Courage he had taken it, he burnt it to the Ground, flew Eight Thoufand *Tyrians* in the Sackage of their Town, crucified Two Thoufand more, and fold all the reft for Slaves ; yet fome of the Citizens, with their Wives and Children, having efcaped to *Carthage*, (a Colony of their own) and others being conveyed away and faved by their Neighbours the *Sidonians* during the Siege, they returned and rebuilt their defolated City ; and in fo fmall a Time as Nineteen Years afterwards, endured another Siege of Fifteen Months from *Antigonus*, the moft powerful of all *Alexander*'s Succeffors ; nor could he take it at laft, but upon honourable Terms. What an Inftance of the Bleffings and Power of Liberty and Trade !

From the Moment that the *Romans* loft their Liberty, their Spirit was gone, and their Valour fcarce ever after appeared. In the Beginning of *Auguftus*'s Reign, the beft and braveft of them perifhed by the Sword, either in the Civil War, where, *Romans* fighting againft *Romans*, Multitudes were flain, with *Brutus* and *Caffius*, the laft brave Men that ever drew a Sword for the Commonwealth ; or in the bloody Profcriptions that followed, in which all the excellent Men and Affertors of Liberty, who efcaped the Battle, were gleaned up and murdered by Soldiers and Informers, and, amongft the reft, the divine *Cicero*. Afterwards, when *Auguftus* had got the World to himfelf, *jura omnium in fe traxit*; Flatterers were his only Favourites, and none were preferred to
Magiftracy,

Magiftracy, but the fervile Creatures of his Power ; Liberty was extinct, and its Spirit gone ; and though there was a univerfal Peace, yet the Power of the Empire continually decayed. *Auguftus* himfelf was fo fenfible of this, that the Lofs of two or three Legions under *Varus* in *Germany*, frightened him, and had almoft broke his Heart ; not from any Tendernefs in it, for he had butchered Myriads, and enflaved all ; but he knew that now *Roman* Legions were hard to be got, and fcarce worth getting. Having deftroyed fo many brave *Romans*, and made the reft bafe by Slavery, and by the Corruptions which fupport it, he knew the Difficulty of forming a *Roman* Army.

His Succeffors were worfe ; they went on in a perpetual Series of Slaughters, dreading and deftroying every Thing that had the Appearance of Virtue or Goodnefs ; and even fo early as *Tiberius*'s Reign, That Emperor, fays *Tacitus*, knew *magis fama quam vi ftare res fuas*, that his Empire was fupported more by the Reputation of *Roman* Greatnefs, than by the real Strength of the *Romans*, who grew every Day more and more weak and wretched ; and though they had now and then a little Sun-fhine in the Reign of a good Emperor, yet the Root of the Evil remained : They were no longer Freemen, and for far the moft part, their Government was nothing elfe but a conftant State of Oppreffion, and a continual Succeffion of Maffacres. Tyrants governed them, and Soldiers created and governed the Tyrants, or butchered them if they would not be Butchers.

As to Military Virtue, it was no more : The Prætorian Bands were only a Band of Hangmen

with

with an Emperor at their Head ; *Italy* and the Provinces were exhaufted ; the *Roman* People were nothing but an idle and debauched Mob, that cared not who was uppermoft, fo they had but a little Victuals, and faw Shews : The provincial Armies were foreign Hirelings, and there was not a *Roman* Army in the *Roman* Empire. *Inops Italia, plebs urbana imbellis nihil in exercitibus validum præter externum.* This was faid not long after the Death of *Auguftus* ; nor do I remember an Inftance of one great *Roman* Captain after *Germanicus* and *Corbulo* ; the firft murdered by *Tiberius*, his Uncle and Father by Adoption ; and the other by *Nero*, for whom he reconquered and fettled the *Eaft* ; and after *Vefpafian* and *Titus*, every *Roman* Emperor of remarkable Bravery was a Foreigner, and every Victory gained by them, was gained by Foreigners ; who, being all Mercenaries, were perpetually fetting up and pulling down their own Monarchs. At length, being poffeffed of the whole Power of the Empire, they took it to themfelves ; and thus it ended, and became difmembered by feveral Nations, and into feveral Governments, according to their Fortune ; and it is remarkable, that though thofe Nations had frequent Wars amongft themfelves about the Countries which they invaded, yet they had nothing to apprehend from the *Romans* while they were feizing *Roman* Provinces.

Tyrants are fo fenfible, that when they have loft their Army, they have loft all, that amongft their other deftructive Expedients to preferve themfelves, whatever becomes of their People, one of their Methods is, to lay whole Countries wafte, and to

keep

keep them wafte, to prevent an Invader from fubfifting ; and their beft Provinces are by this Means
turned often into Wilderneffes. For this Reafon
a March to *Conftantinople* is fcarce practicable to an
Enemy from any Quarter.

I will conclude with anfwering an Objection :
It may be faid, that the Armies of Tyrants often
fight bravely, and are brave ; and I own it to be
true in many Inftances : But I defire it may be
remembered, that in arbitrary Countries nothing
flourifhes except the Court and the Army. A Tyrant muft give his Spoilers Part of the Spoil, or
elfe they will fight but faintly for it, or perhaps
put him to Death.if he do not.   The moft abfolute Princes muft therefore ufe their Soldiers like
Freemen, as they tender their own Power and
their Lives ; and under the greateft Tyrants the
Men of War enjoy great Privileges, even greater
than in free States.   The Privileges and Immunities which they enjoy, conftitute a Sort of Liberty, dear to themfelves, but terrible always to
the Subject, and often pernicious to the Prince : It
being the certain Condition of a Tyrant, that to
be able to opprefs his People, or plague his Neighbours, he muft empower his Soldiers to deftroy
himfelf.

The chief Forces therefore of an arbitrary
Prince confift of Freemen : Such were the Prætorian Bands of the *Roman* Emperors, and fuch
are the *Turkifh* Janizaries ; and both of them,
though they maintained the Tyranny, have frequently killed the Tyrants ; and fuch are the
Grand Seignior's *Zaims, Timariots,* or Horfemen,
who have Lands given them in the Provinces,
                                                    and

and are the only Nobility and Gentry there : And such too were the *Mamalukes* of *Egypt*, which Country at laft they ufurped for themfelves, haveing put the King their Mafter to Death.   I might mention here the *Swifs* Guards, and *Gens d'Armes* of a neighbouring Prince, which are his Janizaries.   As to the *Turkifh* Janizaries, I own the Sultan may put particular Men of them to Death, but no Sultan dares touch their Privileges as a Body ; and two or three of their greateft Emperors were depofed and deftroyed by them for attempting it.

Mere Slaves can defend no Prince, nor enable him even to rule over Slaves : So that by giving Liberty, or rather Licentioufnefs, to a Few, the Slavery of All is maintained.

All this does, I think, fully prove, that where there is no Liberty, there can be no Magnanimity. It is true, Enthufiafm has infpired Armies, and moft remarkably of all the *Saracen* Armies, with amazing Refolution and Fury ; but even that was Fiercenefs for Liberty of Opinion to themfelves, and for fubduing all Men to it ; and befides, this Courage of Enthufiafm is rarely eminent, except in the firft Rife of States and Empires.

G

I am, &c.

SATURDAY, *February* 17, 1721.   No. 66.

Arbitrary Government proved incompatible with true Religion, whether Natural or Revealed.

S I R,

I SHALL fhew, in this Paper, that neither the Chriftian Religion, nor Natural Religion, nor any Thing elfe that ought to be called Religion, can fubfift under tyrannical Governments, now that Miracles are ceafed. I readily confefs, that fuch Governments are fertile in Superftition, in wild Whimfies, delufive Phantoms, and ridiculous Dreams; proper to terrify the human Soul, degrade its Dignity, deface its Beauty, and fetter it with flavifh and unmanly Fears, to render it a proper Object of Fraud, Grimace, and Impofition; and to make Mankind the ready Dupes of gloomy Impoftors, and the tame Slaves of raging Tyrants. For, Servitude eftablifhed in the Mind, is beft eftablifhed.

But all thefe bewildered Imaginations, thefe dark and dreadful Horrors, which banifh Reafon, and contract and imbitter the Heart, what have they to do with true Religion, unlefs to deftroy it? —That Religion, which improves and enlarges the Faculties of Men, exalts their Spirits, and makes them brave for God and themfelves; that Religion, which gives them great and worthy Conceptions of the Deity; and that Religion which

infpires

infpires them with generous and beneficent Affections to one another, and with univerfal Love and Benevolence to the whole Creation ? No Man can love God, if he love not his Neighbour ; and whoever loves his Neighbour, will neither injure, revile, nor opprefs him : Nor can we otherwife fhew our Love to God, than by kind, humane, and affectionate Actions to his Creatures : *A new Commandment*, fays our blefled Saviour, *I give unto you, that ye love one another.*

Almighty God, the great Author of our Nature, and of all Things, who has the Heavens for his Throne, and the Earth for his Footftool, is raifed far above the Reach of our Kindnefs, our Malice, or our Flattery. He derives infinite Happinefs from his own infinite Perfections ; nor can any frail Power or Actions of ours leflen or improve it : Religion therefore, from which he can reap no Advantage, was inftituted by him for the Sake of Men, as the beft Means and the ftrongeft Motive to their own Happinefs, and mutual Happinefs ; and by it Men are taught and animated to be ufeful, affifting, forgiving, kind and merciful one to another. But to hurt, calumniate, or hate one another, for his Sake, and in Defence of any Religion, is a flat Contradiction to *his* Religion, and an open Defiance of the Author of Religion : And to quarrel about Belief and Opinions, which do not immediately and necefſarily produce practical Virtue and focial Duties, is equally wicked and abfurd. This is to be wicked in behalf of Righteoufnefs, and to be cruel out of Piety. A Religion which begets Selfifhnefs and Partiality only to a few, and its own Followers, and which infpires
Hatred

Hatred and Outrage towards all the reft of the World, can never be the Religion of the merciful and impartial Maker and Judge of the World. Speculations are only fo far a Part of Religion, as they produce the moral Duties of Religion, general Peace, and unlimited Charity, publick Spirit, Equity, Forbearance, and good Deeds to all Men : And the Worfhip of God is no longer the Worfhip of God, than as it warms our Minds with the Remembrance of his gracious Condefcenfions, his indulgent Care, Bounty, and Providence, exercifed towards us ; and as it raifes and forms our Affections to an Imitation of fuch his divine and unreftrained Goodnefs, and to ufe one another kindly by his great Example, who ufes us all fo. So that our worthy, tender, and beneficent Behaviour to one another, is the beft Way to acknowledge his to us : It is the moft acceptable Way that we can worfhip him, and the Way which he will beft accept our Worfhip : And whatever Devotion has not this Effect, or a contrary Effect, is the dry or mad Freaks of an Enthufiaft, and ought to be called by another and a properer Name.

This is a general Idea of true Religion ; thefe are the certain and only Marks of it : All which, as they are oppofite to the Effence and Spirit of an arbitrary Government ; fo every arbitrary Government is an Enemy to the Spirit of true Religion, and defeats its Ends. In thefe Governments, in Defiance of Religion, Humanity, and common Senfe, Millions muft be miferable to exalt and embellifh One or a Few, and to make them proud, arrogant, and great : Protection and Security
rity

rity are no more ; the Spirit of the People is funk,
their Induftry difcouraged and loft, or only employed to feed Luxury and Pride ; and Multitudes
ftarve, that a few may riot and abound. All Love
to Mankind is extinct, and Virtue and publick
Spirit are dangerous or unknown ; while Vice,
Falfhood, and fervile Sycophancy, become neceffary to maintain precarious Safety and an ignominious Life : And, in fine, Men live upon the
Spoils of one another, like ravenous Fifhes and
Beafts of Prey : They become rapacious, brutifh,
and favage to one another, as their cruel Governors are to them all ; and, as a furth:r Imitation
of fuch Mafters, their Souls are abject, mean, and
villainous. To live upon Prey, and worry human
Race, is the Genius and Support of Tyrants, as
well as of Wolves and Tygers ; and it is the Spirit
and Practice of Men to refemble their Governors,
and to act like them. Virtue and Vice, in Courts,
run like Water in a continual Defcent, and quickly
overflow the inferior Soil.

Torva Leæna lupum, &c.

Now, what can be found here to anfwer the
Spirit and Precepts of the Chriftian Religion,
which is all Love, Charity, Meeknefs, mutual
Affiftance, and mutual Indulgence ; and muft either deftroy Tyranny, which deftroys all thefe,
or be deftroyed by it ? A Religion given by God,
to infpire Men with every focial Virtue, and to
furnifh them with every Argument for focial Happinefs, will never find Quarter, much lefs Protection, from a Government, which fubfifts by an
unrelenting War againft every Virtue, and all human

man Felicity. On the contrary, all its divine
Doctrines fhall be perverted, all its divine Principles mangled, and both its Principles and its Precepts corrupted, difguifed, and wrefted, to be
made free of the Court : Truth will be made to
patronize Impofture, and Meeknefs to fupport Tyranny : Obedience to equal Laws, and Submiffion
to juft Authority, fhall be turned into a fervile and
crouching Subjection to blind Rage and inhuman
Fury ; complaifant and refpective Behaviour into
flavifh Flattery, and fupple Homage to Power ;
Meeknefs and Humility into Dejection, Poornefs
of Spirit, and bodily Proftrations ; Charity, Benevolence, and Humanity, into a fiery and outrageous Zeal to propagate fafhionable and gainful
Opinions : Chriftian Courage fhall be changed
into Cruelty and brutifh Violence ; impartial Juftice into favage Severity ; Protection into Oppreffion and Plundering : the Fear of God into the
Fear of Man ; and the Worfhip of the Deity into
an idolatrous Adoration of a Tyrant.

Though God Almighty fent his only Son into
the World to teach his Will to Men, and to confirm his Miffion by Wonders and Miracles ; yet,
having once fully manifefted himfelf and his Law,
he has left it to be propagated and carried on by
human Means only, according to the Holy Writings infpired by him ; and if the Powers of the
World will not fubmit to thofe Directions, and
will neither purfue them themfelves, nor fuffer their
Subjects to purfue them, nor leave them the Means
of doing it ; then the Chriftian Religion muft take
the Fate of all fublunary Things, and be loft from
amongft Men, unlefs Heaven interpofe again miraculoufly

raculoufly in its Favour. Now the Experience of all Ages will convince us, that all tyrannical Princes will be againſt the Religion which is againſt them; and either aboliſh it, or, which is much worſe, pervert it into a deadly and unnatural Engine, to increaſe and defend that Pride and Power, which Chriſtianity abhors; and to promote thoſe Evils and Miſeries, which Chriſtianity forbids, and, were it left to itſelf, would prevent or relieve. A Religion modelled by uſurped Power, to countenance Uſurpation and Oppreſſion, is as oppoſite to the Chriſtian Religion, as Tyranny is to Liberty, and Wickedneſs to Virtue. When Religion is taught to ſpeak Court-Language, and none are ſuffered to preach it, but ſuch as ſpeak the ſame Dialect; when thoſe who are Miniſters of the Goſpel, muſt be alſo the Miniſters of Ambition, and either ſanctify Falſhood and Violence, by the Word of Mercy and Truth, or hold their Tongues; when Preferments and worldly Honours are on the Side of Impoſture, and Galleys, Racks and Dungeons, are the Rewards of Conſcience and Piety; the Good and Efficacy of Chriſtianity will be as effectually gone, as if it were formally exchanged for *Mahometaniſm*; and under thoſe Circumſtances, if its Name be retained, it is only retained to do Evil, and might be as innocently baniſhed with the Thing.

The Chriſtian Religion has as rarely gained by Courts, as Courts have improved by the Chriſtian Religion; and arbitrary Courts have ſeldom meddled with it, but either to perſecute it, or debaſe and corrupt it; nor could the Power and Fury of Tyrants ever hurt or weaken it ſo much, as their

pretended

pretended Favours and Countenance have done:
By appearing for it, they turn their Power moſt
effectually againſt it.   Their avowed Perſecution
of Chriſtianity, did only deſtroy Chriſtians; but
afterwards, while they ſet up for protecting none
but the true Chriſtians, that is, thoſe that were
as bad as themſelves, and having no Religion of
their own, adopted blindly the Religion of their
Prince; and whilſt they were for puniſhing all
who were not true Chriſtians, that is, all that
were better than themſelves, and would take their
Religion from no Man's Word, but only from
the Word of God; they liſted Chriſtians againſt
Chriſtians, and disfigured, and undermined, and baniſhed Chriſtianity itſelf, by falſe Friendſhip to its
Profeſſors: And theſe Profeſſors thus corrupted,
joining a holy Title to an impious Cauſe, concurred in the Conſpiracy, and contended fiercely in
the Name of Chriſt for ſecular Advantages, which
Chriſt never gave nor took, and for a ſecular Sovereignty, which he rejected, and his Goſpel forbids.   Thus one Sort of Tyranny was artfully
made to ſupport another, and both by a Union of
Intereſts maintained a War againſt Religion, under Colour of defending it, and fought the Author
of it under his own Banner; that is, as Dr. *Til-
lotſon* finely ſays, *They lied for the Truth, and killed
for God's Sake.*
    The many various and contradictory Opinions
of weak Enthuſiaſts, or of deſigning Men, and
all the different and repugnant Interpretations of
Scripture, publiſhed and contended for by them,
could have done but ſmall Prejudice to Religion
and Society, if human Authority had not inter-
poſed

pofed with its Penalties and Rewards annexed to
the believing or not believing fortuitous Speculations, ufelefs Notions, dry Ideas, and the inconfiftent Reveries of difordered Brains ; or the felfifh
Inventions of ufurping Popes, ambitious Synods,
and turbulent and afpiring Doctors, or the crafty
Schemes of difcontented or oppreffive Statefmen :
For all thefe have been the important Caufes,
and the wicked Fuel, of religious Wars and Perfecutions.

It is fo much the general Intereft of Society to
perform and to encourage all its Members to perform the practical Duties of Religion, that if a
ftronger and more prevailing Intereft were not
thrown by Power into the contrary Scale, there
would be no Difference amongft Men about the
Nature and Extent of their Duties to Magiftrates,
to Parents, Children, and to Friends and Neighbours : And if thefe focial Duties (the only Duties
which human Society, as fuch, is concerned to
promote) were agreed upon and practifed, the Magiftrate would have no more to do with their Opinions than with their Shape and Complexion ; nor
could he know, if he would, by what Method to
alter them. No Man's Belief is in his own Power,
or can be in the Power of another.

The utmoft Length that the Power of the
Magiftrate can in this Matter extend, beyond that
of Exhortation, which is in every Man's Power,
can be only to make Hypocrites, Slaves, Fools,
or Atheifts. When he has forced his Subjects to
belye their Confciences, or to act againft them,
he has in Effect driven them out of all Religion,
to bring them into his own ; and when they thus

see and feel the professed Defender of Religion
overturning all its Precepts, exhorting by Bribes,
rebuking by Stripes, Confiscations and Dungeons,
and making Christianity the Instrument of Fury,
Ambition, Rapine, and Tyranny ; what can they
think, but either that he is no Christian, or that
Christianity is not true ? If they come to suspect
it of Imposture, they grow Infidels ; if they grow
into a Belief that Religion countenances Bitterness,
Outrage, and Severities, nay, commands all these,
they become Bigots ; the worst and most mischievous Character of the Two : For, Unbelievers,
guided by the Rules of Prudence or Good Nature, may be good Neighbours and inoffensive
Men ; but Bigotry, standing upon the Ruins of
Reason, and being conducted by no Light but
that of an inflamed Imagination, and a sour, bitter, and narrow Spirit, there is no Violence nor
Barbarity which it is not capable of wishing or
acting.

Happiness is the chief End of Man, and the
saving of his Soul is his chief Happiness ; so that
every Man is most concerned for his own Soul,
and more than any other can be : And if no Ob-
struction be thrown in his Way, he will for the
most part do all in his Power for his own Salva-
tion, and will certainly do it best ; and when he
has done all that he can, he has done all that he
ought : People cannot be saved by Force ; nor can
all the Powers in the World together make one
true Christian, or convince one Man.   Conviction is the Province and Effect of Reason ; when
that fails, nothing but the Grace of God can supply it : And what has the Power and Penalties of
Men

Men to do either with Reafon or Grace ; which being both the Gifts of God, are not to be conquered by Chains, though they may be weakened, and even banifhed, by worldly Allurements blended with Chriftianity, and by the worldly Pride of its Profeffors ?

The Methods of Power are repugnant to the Nature of Conviction, which muft either be promoted by Exhortation, Kindnefs, Example, and Arguments, or can never be promoted at all : Violence does, on the contrary, but provoke Men, and confirm them in Error ; nor will they ever be brought to believe, that thofe who barbaroufly rob them of their prefent Happinefs, can be charitably concerned for their future.

It is evident in Fact, that moft of the different religious Inftitutions now fubfifting in the World, have been founded upon Ambition and Pride ; and were advanced, propagated, and eftablifhed, by Ufurpation, Faction, and Oppreffion : They were begun for the moft part by Enthufiafts, or by defigning and unpreferred Churchmen ; or at leaft occafioned by the continued Ufurpations and Infults of cruel and oppreffive ones, and always in Times of Faction and general Difcontent. Turbulent and afpiring Men, difcarded and difcontented Courtiers, or ambitious and defigning Statefmen, have taken Advantage from thefe general Diforders, or from the hot and giddy Spirits of an enthufiaftical or oppreffed People, and from thence have formed Parties ; and fetting themfelves at the Head, formed National Eftablifhments, with the Concurrence of weak Princes, fometimes in Oppofition to them, by the Affiftance of factious

Clergy-

Clergymen and factious Affemblies, often by Tu-
mults and popular Infurrections ; and at laft, under Pretence of faving Mens Souls, they feized
their Property. A fmall Acquaintance with Ecclefiaftical Hiftory, and the Hiftory of the *Turks*
and *Saracens*, will fhew fuch Caufes as thefe to
have given Rife to moft of the National Religious
Eftablifhments upon Earth : Nor can I fee how
any future one can arife by other Means, whilft
Violence and worldly Intereft have any thing to
do with them.

Such therefore as is the Government of a Country, fuch will be made its Religion ; and no body,
I hope, is now to learn what is, and ever will be,
the Religion of moft Statefmen ; even a Religion
of Power, to do as little Good and as much Mifchief as they pleafe. Nor have Churchmen, when
they ruled States, had ever any other View ; but
having double Authority, had generally double
Infolence, and remarkably lefs Mercy and Regard
to Confcience or Property, than others who had
fewer Ties to be merciful and juft : And therefore the foreft Tyrants have been they, who united
in one Perfon the Royalty and Priefthood. The
Pope's Yoke is more grievous than that of any
Chriftian Prince upon Earth ; nor is there a Trace
of Property, or Felicity, or of the Religion of
Jefus Chrift, found in the Dominions of this Father of *Chriftendom* ; all is Ignorance, Bigotry,
Idolatry, Barbarity, Hunger, Chains, and every
Species of Mifery. The *Caliphs* of *Egypt*, who
founded the *Saracen* Empire there, and maintained
it for a great while, were at once Kings and
Priefts ; and there never lived more raging Bigots,

or

or more furious and oppreffive Barbarians. The Monarchy of *Perfia,* which is alfo a fevere Tyranny, has the Priefthood annexed to it; and the *Sophy* is at the fame time the *Caliph.* The *Turkifh* Religion is founded on Impofture, blended with outrageous and avowed Violence; and by their Religion, the Imperial Executioner is, next to their *Alcoran,* the moft facred Thing amongft them : And though he be not himfelf Chief Prieft, yet he creates and uncreates him at Pleafure, and is, without the Name of *Mufti,* the Chief Doctor, or rather Author of their Religion; and we all know what Sort of a Religion it is.

In Fact, as arbitrary Princes want a Religion fuited to the Genius of their Power, they model their Religion fo as to ferve all the Purpofes of Tyranny; and debafe, corrupt, difcourage, or perfecute all Religion which is againft Tyranny, as all true Religion is : For this Reafon, not one of the great abfolute Princes in *Europe* embraced the *Reformation,* nor would fuffer his People to embrace it, but they were all bitter and profefled Enemies to it : Whereas all the great free States, except *Poland,* and moft of the fmall free States, became *Proteftants.* Thus the *Englifh, Scotch,* the *Dutch,* the *Bohemians,* and *Sweden* and *Denmark,* (which were then free Kingdoms) the greateft Part of *Swifferland,* with *Geneva,* and all the *Hans-Towns,* which were not awed by the Emperor, threw off the *Popifh* Yoke : And not one of the free *Popifh* States, out of *Italy,* could be ever brought to receive the *Inquifition* ; and the State of *Venice,* the greateft free State there, to fhew that they received it againft their Will, have taken

wife

wife Care to render it ineffectual : And many of
the *Popiſh* free States would never come into Perfecution, which they knew would impoveriſh and
difpeople them ; and therefore the States of *Arra-
gon, Valencia,* and *Catalonia,* oppofed, as much as
they were able, the Expulfion of the *Moors,* which
was a pure Act of Regal Power, to the Undoing
of *Spain* ; and therefore a deſtructive and barbarous
Act of Tyranny.   As to the *Proteſtant* Countries,
which have fince loft their Liberties, there is much
miferable Ignorance, and much bitter and implacable Bigotry, but little Religion, and no Charity,
amongſt them.

We look upon *Montezuma,* and other Tyrants,
who worſhipped God with human Sacrifice, as fo
many Monſters, and hug ourfelves that we have
no fuch Sons of *Moloch* here in *Europe* ; not confidering, that every Man put to Death for his Religion, by the *Inquiſition* and elfewhere, is a real human Sacrifice, as it is burning and butchering Men
for God's Sake.

I think no body will deny, but that in King
James's Time, we owed the Prefervation of our
Religion to our Liberties, which both our Clergy
and People almoſt unanimoufly concurred to defend, with a Refolution and Boldnefs worthy of
Britons and Freemen.   And as the Caufe and
Bleſſings of Liberty are ſtill better underſtood, its
Spirit and Intereſt daily increafe.   Moſt of the Biſhops, and many of the inferior Clergy, are pro-
feſſedly in the Principles of Civil and Religious Liberty, notwithſtanding the ſtrong and early Prejudices of Education.   And I hope foon to fee them
all as thorough Advocates for publick Liberty, as
their

their Predeceffors were, upon Grounds lefs juft, in the Times of *Popery*; and then there will be an End of the pernicious and knavifh Diftinction of *Whig* and *Tory*; and all the World will unite in paying them that Refpect which is due to their holy Office.

I fhall conclude with this fhort Application; That as we love Religion, and the Author of it, we ought to love and preferve our Liberties.

    G

                I am, &c.

SATURDAY, *February* 24, 1721. No. 67.

Arts and Sciences the Effects of Civil Liberty only, and ever deftroyed or oppreffed by Tyranny.

S I R,

HAVING already fhewn, that Naval Trade and Power cannot fubfift but in free Countries alone, I will now fhew, that the fame is true of domeftick Arts and Sciences; and that both thefe, and Population, which is their conftant Concomitant, and their chief Caufe as well as their certain Effect, are born of Liberty, and nurfed, educated, encouraged, and endowed, by Liberty alone.

Men will not fpontaneoufly toil and labour but for their own Advantage, for their Pleafure or their Profit, and to obtain fomething which they want or defire, and which, for the moft part, is not to be obtained but by Force or Confent.

                         Force

Force is often dangerous ; and when employed to acquire what is not ours, it is always unjuft ; and therefore Men, to procure from others what they had not before, muft gain their Confent ; which is not to be gained, but by getting them in lieu of the Thing defired, fomething which they want and value more than what they part with. This is what we call Trade ; which is the Exchange of one Commodity for another, or for that which purchafes all Commodities, Silver and Gold.

Men, in their firft State, content themfelves with the fpontaneous Productions of Nature, the Fruits of the Field and the liquid Stream, and fuch occafional Supplies as they now and then receive from the Deftruction of other Animals. But when thofe Supplies become infufficient to fupport their Numbers, their next Refource is to open the Bofom of the Earth, and, by proper Application and Culture, to extort her hidden Stores : And thus were invented Tillage and Planting. And an Hundred Men thus employed can fetch from the Bowels of our common Mother, Food and Suftenance enough for Ten Times their own Number ; and one Tenth part more may poffibly be able to fupply all the Inftruments of Hufbandry, and whatever is barely neceffary to fupport thefe Hufbandmen : So that all the reft of the People muft rob or ftarve, unlefs either the Proprietors of the Land will give them the Produce of their Eftates for nothing, or they can find fomething wherewithal to purchafe it.

Now in Countries where no other Arts are in Ufe, but only Hufbandry and the Profeffions neceffary

ceffary to it, and to fupport thofe who are employed about it ; all the other Inhabitants have no
Means of purchafing Food and Raiment, but by
felling their Perfons, and becoming vile Slaves and
Vaffals to their Princes, Lords, or other Proprietors of the Land ; and are obliged, for neceffary
Suftenance, to follow them in their wild Wars,
and their perfonal and factious Quarrels, and to
become the bafe Inftruments of their Ambition
and Pride. Great Men will rather throw their
Eftates into Forefts and Chaces, for the Support
of wild Beafts, and for their own Pleafure in hunting them, than into Farms, Gardens, and fruitful
Fields, if they can get nothing from the Productions of them.

This is the forlorn Condition of Mankind, in
moft of the wild Empires of the *Eaft* ; this was
their Condition in all the *Gothick* Governments ;
and this is the Condition of *Poland* and of the
Highlands of *Scotland*; where a few have Liberty,
and all the reft are Slaves. And nothing can free
Mankind from this abject and forlorn Condition,
but the Invention of Arts and Sciences ; that is,
the finding out of more Materials and Expedients
to make Life eafy and pleafant ; and the inducing
People to believe, what they will readily believe,
that other Things are neceffary to their Happinefs,
befides thofe which Nature has made neceffary.
Thus the Luxury of the Rich becomes the Bread
of the Poor.

As foon as Men are freed from the Importuni-
ties of Hunger and Cold ; the Thoughts and Defire of Conveniency, Plenty, Ornament, and Politenefs, do prefently fucceed: And then follow
after,

after, in very quick Progreffion, Emulation, Ambition, Profufion, and the Love of Power : And all thefe, under proper Regulations, contribute to the Happinefs, Wealth, and Security of Societies. It is natural to Men and Societies, to be fetting their Wits and their Hands to work, to find out all Means to fatisfy their Wants and Defires, and to enable them to live in Credit and Comfort, and to make fuitable Provifion that their Pofterity may live fo after them.

Neceffity is the Mother of Invention ; and fo is the Opinion of Neceffity. Whilft Things are in their own Nature neceffary to us, or, from Cuftom and Fancy, made neceffary ; we will be turning every Thought, and trying every Method, how to come at them ; and where they cannot be got by Violence and Rapine, Recourfe will be had to Invention and Induftry. And here is the Source of Arts and Sciences ; which alone can fupport Multitudes of People, who will never be wanting to the Means which bring them Support.

Where-ever there is Employment for People, there will be People ; and People, in moft Countries, are forced, for want of other Employment, to cut the Throats of one another, or of their Neighbours ; and to ramble after their Princes in all their mad Conquefts, ridiculous Contentions, and other mifchievous Maggots ; and all to get, with great Labour, Hazard, and often with great Hunger and Slaughter, a poor, precarious, and momentary Subfiftence.

And therefore whatever State gives more Encouragement to its Subjects than the neighbouring

States do, and finds them more Work, and gives them greater Rewards for that Work ; and by all thefe laudable Ways makes human Condition eafier than it is elfewhere, and fecures Life and Property better ; that State will draw the Inhabitants from the neighbouring Countries to its own ; and when they are there, they will, by being richer and fafer, multiply fafter. Men will naturally fly from Danger to Security, from Poverty to Plenty, and from a Life of Mifery to a Life of Felicity.

And as there will be always Induftry where-ever there is Protection ; fo where-ever there is Induftry and Labour, there will be the Silver, the Gold, the Jewels, the Power, and the Empire. It does not import who they are that have con-quered, or inhabit the Countries where Silver and Gold are Natives, or who they are that toil for them in the Mines ; fince they will be the Poffef-fors of the Coin, who can purchafe it afterwards with the Goods and Manufactures which the Pro-prietors of the Mine and their People want. One Artificer in *England*, or *Holland*, can make Ma-nufacture enough in a Week to buy as much Silver and Gold at the Mine, as a Labourer there can dig and prepare in a Month, or perhaps Two ; and all the while that *Spain* and *Portugal* leffen their Inhabitants, we encreafe ours : They lofe their People by fending them away to dig in the Mines ; and we, by making the Manufactures which they want, and the Inftruments which they ufe, multiply ours. By this Means every Man that they fend out of their Country is a Lofs to it, becaufe the Reafon and Produce of their Labour goes to enrich rival Nations ; whereas
every

every Man that we fend to our Plantations, adds
to the Number of our Inhabitants here at Home,
by maintaining fo many of them employed in fo
many Manufactures which they take off there ;
befides fo many Artificers in Shipping, and all the
numerous Traders and Agents concerned in ma-
naging and venting the Produce of the Plantations,
when it is brought hither, and in bringing it hither : So that the *Englifh* Planters in *America*, befides maintaining themfelves and Ten times as
many *Negroes*, maintain likewife great Numbers
of their Countrymen in *England*.

Such are the Bleffings of Liberty, and fuch is
the Difference which it makes between Country
and Country ! The *Spanifh* Nation loft much more
by the Lofs of their Liberties, followed with the
Expulfion of the *Moors*, than ever they got by the
Gold and Silver Mountains of *Mexico* and *Peru*,
or could get by all the Mines of Gold, Silver, and
Diamonds upon Earth.

Where there is Liberty, there are Encouragements to Labour, beaufe People labour for themfelves : and no one can take from them the Acquifitions which they make by their Labour :
There will be the greateft Numbers of People,
becaufe they find Employment and Protection ;
there will be the greateft Stocks, becaufe moft is
to be got, and eafieft to be got, and fafeft when
it is got ; and thofe Stocks will be always encreafing by a new Aceeffion of Money acquired elfewhere, where there is no Security of enjoying it ;
there People will be able to work cheapeft, becaufe
lefs Taxes will be put upon their Work, and upon
the Neceffaries which muft fupport them whilft
they

they are about it : There People will dare to own
their being rich ; there will be moft People bred
up to Trade, and Trade and Traders will be
moft refpected ; and there the Intereft of Money
will be lower, and the Security of poffeffing it
greater, than it ever can be in tyrannical Governments, where Life and Property and all Things
muft depend upon the Humour of a Prince, the
Caprice of a Minifter, or the Demand of a Har-
lot. Under thofe Governments few People can
have Money, and they that have muft lock it up,
or bury it to keep it ; and dare not engage in large
Defigns, when the Advantages may be reaped by
their rapacious Governors, or given up by them
in a fenfelefs and wicked Treaty : Befides, fuch
Governors contemn Trade and Artificers ; and
only Men of the Sword, who have an Intereft
incompatible with Trade, are encouraged by
them.

For thefe Reafons, Trade cannot be carried
on fo cheap as in free Countries ; and whoever
fupplies the Commodity cheapeft, will command
the Market. In free Countries, Men bring out
their Money for their Ufe, Pleafure, and Profit,
and think of all Ways to employ it for their Intereft and Advantage. New Projects are every
Day invented, new Trades fearched after, new
Manufactures fet up ; and when Tradefmen have
nothing to fear but from thofe whom they truft,
Credit will run high, and they will venture in
Trade for many times as much as they are worth :
But in arbitrary Countries, Men in Trade are
every Moment liable to be undone, without the
Guilt of Sea or Wind, without the Folly or
Treachery

Treachery of their Correfpondents, or their own want of Care or Induftry : Their Wealth fhall be their Snare ; and their Abilities, Vigilance, and their Succefs, fhall either be their undoing, or nothing to their Advantage : Nor can they truft any one elfe, or any one elfe them, when Payment and Performance muft depend upon the Honefty and Wifdom of thofe who often have none.

T

Ignorance of Arts and Sciences, and of every Thing that is good, together with Poverty, Mifery, and Defolation, are found for the moft part all together, and are all certainly produced by Tyranny. In all the great Empires of *Morocco*, *Abyffinia*, *Perfia*, and *India*, there is not amongft the Natives fuch a Thing as a tolerable Architect ; nor one good Building, unlefs we except a Palace built by a *Portugueze* for the *Abyffinian* Emperor ; and perhaps there may be in all thefe vaft Continents a few more good Houfes built by *Europeans*. The *Æthiopians* have fcarce fuch a Thing as an Artificer among them ; their only Weavers are the *Jews*, who are likewife their Smiths, whofe higheft Employment in Iron is to make Heads for their Spears ; and for Artifts of their own, their wretched Trumpeters and Horn-winders feem to be the higheft. When the *Jefuits* built a few Churches and Chapels in their Country, the whole Nation were alarmed, taking them for fo many Caftles and Fortreffes. The reft of their Condition is of a-piece ; they are abjectly miferable, in fpite of their Soil, which in many Places is luxuriant, and yields Three Crops a Year : Of fuch fmall Effect are the Gifts of God to his

Creatures,

Creatures, when the Breath of a Tyrant can blaft them !

In *Perfia*, the Carpenters and Joiners have but four Tools for all their Work, and we may guefs what fort of Work they make ; they have a Hatchet, a Saw, and a Chizzel, and one fort of Plainer, brought thither not long fince by a *Frenchman*. As to Printing, they have none ; nor any Paper but coarfe brown Stuff, which cannot be folded without breaking to Pieces. In Painting, they do not go beyond Birds and Flowers, and are utterly ignorant of Figures and Hiftory.

Egypt was once the Mother of Arts and Sciences, and from thence *Greece* had them : But *Egypt* lofing its Liberties, loft with them all Politenefs, as all Nations do ; and the Pyramids were built by the firft *Egyptian* Tyrants, while the Knowledge of Arts was not yet loft in Barbarifm, and before the Country was difpeopled, elfe they never had been built. Nor could all the Power of the *Ottoman* Empire build fuch in the Place now, though the *Turks* were not Savages in the Sciences, as they are. " Till the Time of *Ramphfinitus*, " *fays Herodotus*, the *Egyptians* report, that Li- " berty flourifhed, and the Laws were the high- " eft Power." Then he tells us, that *Cheops*, the Succeffor of that King, falling into all Debauchery and Tyranny, employed a Hundred Thoufand of his People in drawing of Stone ; *Diodorus Siculus* fays, Three Hundred and Sixty Thoufand were employed in this inhuman Drudgery ; —— and then he began a Pyramid. The *Egyptians* grew afterwards in Ignorance, Barbarity, and Vilenefs, and almoft any body that invaded
them,

them, maftered them ; and when they were defended, the free *Greeks* defended them, a Band of
them being generally entertained for that End by
the *Egyptian* Kings. It is true, One or Two of
the *Ptolomeys*, particularly the Firft, attempted to
revive Arts and Learning amongft them ; but the
Attempt came to nothing : They were Slaves,
incapable either of tafting or producing the Em-
bellifhments and Excellencies of Liberty, of which
they had been long deprived ; and therefore the
Greek Artifts, and the *Greek* Profeffors in *Egypt*,
had the Glory of every Improvement to themfelves, as indeed they were the Authors of all.
The *Romans* afterwards left there many Monuments of their Grandeur and Politenefs : But when
their free Government ended, as Tyranny fucceeded, fo did Barbarity all over the Empire, and
no where more than in *Egypt*, which is at this
Day the Prey of robbing and thieving *Arabs*, and
of oppreffive and devouring *Turks*.

I fhall here fubjoin a fummary Account given
us by that judicious Traveller Monfieur *Bernier*,
concerning the Condition of the Three great Eaftern Empires, beft known to us. It is in his laft
Chapter of *The Hiftory of the Great Mogul*.

There is, fays he, almoft no Perfon fecure
from the Violence of the Governors, *Timariots*,
and Farmers of the Royal Rents ; nor can the
Princes, though they were difpofed, hinder thefe
Violences, nor prevent the Tyranny of their Servants over their People ; which fhould be the
chief Employment of a King. This Tyranny is
often fo extenfive, that it leaves to the Peafant
and Tradefman neither Food nor Raiment, but
robs

robs them of the common Neceffaries of Life,
and they live in Mifery, and die with Hunger :
They either beget no Children ; or, if they do,
fee them perifh in their Infancy, for want of
Food : Sometimes they defert their Huts and
Land, to become Lacqueys to the Soldiers, or fly
to neighbouring Nations (*where their Condition is
not mended.*) In fhort, the Land is not tilled but
by Force, and therefore wretchedly tilled ; and
great Part of it lies wafte and is loft: There is
no body to clear the Ditches and Water-Courfes ;
no body to build Houfes, or to repair thofe that
are ruinous. The *Timariot* will not improve the
Ground for his Succeffor, not knowing how foon
he may come ; nor will the Peafant work for a
Tyrant, and ftarve while he does it : And neither
Timariot nor Peafant will labour for Bread which
others are to eat. So the Peafant is left to ftarve,
and the Land to become a Defart.

Hence it is, that we fee thofe vaft States in *Afia*
run and running to wretched Ruin : Moft of their
Towns a e raifed with Dirt and Earth ; and you
fee nothing but ruinous Towns, and deferted Villages : And hence it is, that thofe celebrated Re-
gions of *Mefopotamia, Anatolia, Paleftine,* with
thofe admirable Plains of *Antioch,* and fo many
other Countries, antiently fo well manured, fo
fertile, and fo full of People, are all at prefent half
deferted, abandoned, and untilled, or become peftilent and uninhabitable Bogs. *Egypt* is in the
like Condition ; and within thefe fourfcore Years,
above the tenth Part of its incomparable Soil is
loft by Poverty, and want of Hands to fcour the
Channels of the *Nile,* and remove the Sand which
covers their Fields.

From

From the fame Caufes, Arts languifh and ftarve in thofe Countries : For with what Heart can an Artizan labour and ftudy for ignorant Beggars, who are not Judges of his Work, and cannot pay him for it, or for Grandees who will not ? He is fo far from any Profpect of Reward, that he is not only without all Hopes of Wealth, Office or Lands ; but, to avoid being thought rich, muft live poorly : He muft never eat a good Meal, never wear a decent Coat, never appear to be worth Sixpence. Nay, he is happy if he can efcape the *Korrah*, a terrible Whip exercifed by the great Lords upon the Artifts ; proper Encouragement of Ingenuity !

Indeed, the Knowledge and Beauty of Arts had been loft in thofe Countries long fince, were it not that the Kings and Grandees give Wages to certain Handicraftfmen, who work in their Houfes, and, to efcape the Whip, do their beft : Befides, the rich Merchants, who fhare their Gains with Men in Power, to be protected by them, give thefe Handicraftfmen a little more Pay, and but a little. We muft not therefore think, upon feeing rich *Eaftern* Stuffs here, that the Workman there is in any Condition or Efteem : He works not for himfelf : Only Neceffity and the Cudgel makes him work ; and let him work how he will, he is doomed to live miferably, to clothe himfelf meanly, to eat poorly.

Traffick alfo in thofe Countries is faint and decaying : For how many are there that care to take much Pains ; to make dangerous Voyages, and take long Journeys ; to be conftantly running up and down ; to write much, to live in perpetual

tual Anxiety and Care, and to rifque all Hazards and Chances ; and all for a precarious Gain, which is at the Mercy of the next greedy Governor ?

This whole Chapter of *Bernier* deferves every Man's reading : I have only Room to add Part of another Paragraph. Talking of the *Turkiſh* Empire : We have travelled, *ſays he*, through almoſt all the Parts of it ; we have feen how wofully it is ruined and difpeopled ; and how in the Capital City the raifing of five or fix thoufand Men requires three whole Months : And we know what a Fall it muſt have had before now, had it not been for the Supplies of Chriſtian Slaves and Captives brought thither every Year from all Parts. Without doubt, if the fame Sort of Government continue, that State will deſtroy itſelf : It is at this Day maintained by its own Weakneſs, and muſt at laſt fall by it. The Governors are frequently changed, to make Room for new Oppreſſors ; but neither has any one Governor, or one Subjeĉt in the whole Empire, a Penny that he can call his own, to maintain the leaſt Party ; nor, if he had Money, are there any Men to be had in thefe wide defolate Provinces. A bleſſed Expedient this, to make a State fubfiſt ! An Expedient, much like that of a *Brama* of *Pegu*, who, to prevent Sedition, commanded that no Land ſhould be tilled for fome Years together ; and having thus deſtroyed half the Kingdom with Hunger, he turned it into Foreſts : Which Method, however, did not anſwer his End, nor prevent Divifions in that State, which was reduced fo low, that a Handful of *Chineſe* Fugitives were like to have taken and maſtered the Capital City *Ava*.

Thu

Thus far *Bernier*. Sir *Paul Ricaut* tells us, that it is a reigning Maxim in the *Turkish* Policy, to lay a great Part of their Empire waste.——A Maxim, which they need take no Pains to practise ; since, without destroying deliberately their People and Provinces, which yet they do, the dreadful Spirit of their Government creates Desolation fast enough in all Conscience.

The whole City of *Dhili*, the Capital of *India*, is obliged to follow the Great Mogul their Emperor, when he takes a Journey, their whole Dependence being upon the Court and the Soldiery ; for they cannot support themselves: Nor is the Country round them, which is either waste, or its Inhabitants starving, able to support them. So that the Citizens of this mighty Metropolis, are only the wretched Suttlers to a Camp : They are forced to leave their Houses empty, and stroll after their Monarch, whenever he is graciously disposed to take a Jaunt; and are absent sometimes from home a Year and a half together.

The Jesuit *Nicholas Pimenta*, who was in *Pegu* about an hundred and twenty Years ago, gives this Account of it : The last King, *says he*, was a mighty King, and could bring into the Field a Million and sixty thousand Men, taking one out of ten : But his Son had, by his Wars, his Oppressions, his Murders, and other Cruelties, made such quick Dispatch of his Subjects, that all that were left did not exceed seven thousand, including Men, Women, and Children. What an affecting Instance is here of the pestilential Nature of Tyranny !

It is not unlikely that some of these fatal Wars were made by this inhuman Prince, for White Elephants ;

Elephants ; and that he either made or provoked
Invafions upon that Score, as I have inftanced in
another Paper : And here I fhall add fomething
to make this Conjecture ftill more probable. Mr.
Ralph Fitch, a Merchant of *London*, was at *Pegu*
thirteen or fourteen Years before *Pimenta*, in the
Reign of the above potent King ; and he fays,
" Such is the Efteem that this King has for an
" Elephant of this Colour, that amongft his other
" Titles, he is called *King of the White Elephants* ;
" a Title, which to him feems as lofty as any of
" the reft.   And that no other Prince round
" about him may wear this glorious Title, there-
" fore none of them muft keep a White Ele-
" phant, though Nature gave it them ; but muft
" fend it to him, or an Army fhall fetch it ; for
" rather than not have it, he will make War
" for it."

He fays, that the Houfes of thefe Creatures are
fplendidly gilt, and fo are the Silver Veffels out of
which they are fed.   When they go to the River
to be wafhed, which they do every Day, fix or
feven Men bear up a Canopy of Cloth of Gold or
Silk over them ; and as many more march with
Drums and mufical Inftruments before them ; and
when they come out of the Water, their Feet
are wafhed in great Silver Bafons by Perfons of
Quality, whofe Office it is thus to ferve them.
Bernier fays, the Great Mogul allows fixed Penfions (fometimes very large ones) to every Elephant, with proper Attendance ; nay, two Men
are employed in the fultry Months, to ftand, one
on each Side, to fan them.

I

I only mention this, to fhew how much more Care thefe Tyrants take of their Beafts, than of their People. And it is too true of all arbitrary Princes; their Stable of Horfes is dearer to them than their Subjects, and live infinitely better.

This is almoft univerfally true where-ever there are fuch. Nay, they value their Dogs more than they do the Lives of Men. When the Grand Seignior goes a hunting, a great Number of Peafants muft enclofe the Ground for feveral Leagues round, and keep in the Game; this they muft often do for many Days together, fometimes in Ice and Snow, with hungry Bellies. By which Means their Work is neglected, their Grounds are deftroyed, and they themfelves are many times killed in the Sport, or ftarved in attending it; and it often happens, that forty or fifty of his own Followers perifh in a Day. *Sultan Mahomet's* grand Falconer had once the Honefty and Boldnefs to reprefent to his Mafter all this Deftruction and Carnage which attended his endlefs Paffion for Hunting; but all the Anfwer which he received from this Father of the Faithful, was, *By all Means take Care of the Dogs, let them have Clothing and other Accommodations.*

This Paper upon Arts and Population grows too long: I fhall therefore referve to another what I have to fay further upon this Subject.

G

I am, &c.

SATUR-

SATURDAY, *March* 3, 1721. No. 68.

Property and Commerce secure in a free Government only ; with the consuming Miseries under simple Monarchies.

S I R,

I HERE send you what I have to say further upon Arts, Industry, and Population. To live securely, happily, and independently, is the End and Effect of Liberty ; and it is the Ambition of all Men to live agreeably to their own Humours and Discretion. Nor did ever any Man that could live satisfactorily without a Master, desire to live under one ; and real or fancied Necessity alone makes Men the Servants, Followers, and Creatures of one another. And therefore all Men are animated by the Passion of acquiring and defending Property, because Property is the best Support of that Independency, so passionately desired by all Men. Even Men the most dependent have it constantly in their Heads and their Wishes, to become independent one Time or other ; and the Property which they are acquiring, or mean to acquire by that Dependency, is intended to bring them out of it, and to procure them an agreeable Independency. And as Happiness is the Effect of Independency, and Independency the Effect of Property ; so certain Property is the Effect of Liberty alone, and can only be secured by the Laws

of

of Liberty ; Laws which are made by Confent, and cannot be repealed without it.

All thefe Bleffings, therefore, are only the Gifts and Confequences of Liberty, and only to be found in free Countries, where Power is fixed on one Side, and Property fecured on the other ; where the one cannot break Bounds without Check, Penalties or Forfeiture, nor the other fuffer Diminution without Redrefs ; where the People have no Mafters but the Laws, and fuch as the Laws appoint ; where both Laws and Magiftracy are formed by the People or their Deputies ; and no Demands are made upon them, but what are made by the Law, and they know to a Penny what to pay before it is afked ; where they that exact from them more than the Law allows, are punifhable by the Law ; and where the Legiflators are equally bound by their own Acts, equally involved in the Confequences.

There can be no Good, where there are none of the Caufes of Good ; and confequently all the Advantages of Liberty muft be' loft with Liberty, and all the Evils of Tyranny muft accompany Tyranny. I have in my laft taken a View of the *Eaftern* Monarchies, with regard to the miferable Decay of their People and Arts ; I fhall in this confine myfelf, for Inftances, to *Europe*, and begin with *Mufcovy*, by far the grenteft Empire for Territory in *Chriftendom :* And becaufe the beft fhort Account that I have feen of that Government, is given by *Giles Fletcher*, who was there in the latter End of Queen *Elizabeth*'s Time, I fhall here recite Part of that Account.

Talking

Talking of the many wicked and barbarous Arts used by the late *Czars* of *Ruffia*, to drain and opprefs their People, he fays; " They would fuffer " their People to give freely to the Monafteries, " (as many do, efpecially in their laft Wills) and " this they do, becaufe they may have the Money " of the Realm more ready at Hand, when they " lift to take it, which is many Times done ; " the Friars parting freely with fome, rather than " lofe all.

" *John Bafilowitz* pretended to refign the Crown " to the Prince of *Cazan*, and to retire for the " reft of his Life to a Monaftery : He then caufed " this new King to call in all the Ecclefiaftical " Charters, and to cancel them. Then pretend- " ing to diflike this Fact, and the Mifrule of the " new King, he refumed the Sceptre, poffeffed " as he was of all the Church Lands ; of which " he kept what he would, and gave new Char- " ters for the reft. By this he wrung from the " Ecclefiafticks a vaft Sum ; and yet hoped to " abate the ill Opinion of his Government, by " fhewing a worfe.

" When they want to levy a new Tax, they " make a Shew of Want, as was done by Duke " *Theodore* ; who, though left very rich by his " Father, yet fold moft of his Plate, and coined " the reft, that he might feem in Neceffity : " Whereupon prefently came out a new Tax up- " on his People.

" They would fometimes fend their Meffengers " into the Provinces to foreftall and engrofs the " Commodities of the Country, taking them at " fmall Prices, what they themfelves lifted, and
" felling

" felling them again at exceffive Prices to their
" own Merchants, or to Strangers. If they re-
" fufe to buy them, then they force them into it :
" The like they do, when any Commodity thus
" engroffed, Foreign or Native, fuch as Cloth of
" Gold, Broad Cloth, and the like, happens to
" decay, by lying upon Hand ; it is forced upon
" the Merchants at the Emperor's Price, whether
" they will or no.

" Befides the engroffing of foreign Commodi-
" ties, and forcing them upon the Merchants,
" they make a Monopoly for a Seafon of all fuch
" Commodities as are paid the Prince for Rent or
" Cuftom ; and this they do to enhance the Price
" of them : Thus they monopolize Furs, Corn,
" Wood, &c. during all which Time none muft
" fell of the fame Commodity, till the Emperor's
" be all fold.

" The above-mentioned *John Bafilowitz* fent
" into *Permia* (a Country of the poor *Samoides*)
" for certain Loads of *Cedar*, though he well
" knew that none grew there ; and the Inhabi-
" tants returned Anfwer, that they could find
" none. Whereupon he taxed the Country in
" Twelve Thoufand Rubles.————Again, he
" fent to the City of *Mofcow* to provide for him a
" Meafure full of Fleas, for a Medicine. They
" anfwered, that the Thing was impoffible ; and
" if they could get them, yet they could not mea-
" fure them, becaufe of their leaping out. Upon
" which he fet a Mulct upon them of Seven Thou-
" fand Rubles.

" To thefe may be added, their Seizures and
" Confifcations upon fuch as are under Difplea-
                                    " fure,

" fure, and the Connivance at the Oppreſſion
" and Extortions of the Governors of the Pro-
" vinces, till their Time be expired; and then
" turning all their wicked Plunder into the Em-
" peror's Treaſury, but never a Penny back again
" to the right Owner, how great or evident ſo-
" ever the Injury be.

" As to the People, they are of no Rank or
" Account, and eſteemed no better than Villains;
" and ſo they ſubſcribe themſelves in all their
" Writings to any of the Nobility, as they of the
" Nobility do to the Emperor: And indeed, no
" Bond Slaves are kept more in Awe and Subjec-
" tion, than the common People are, by the
" Nobility, Officers, and Soldiers; ſo that when
" a poor *Mouſick* (one of the Commonalty) meets
" any of them upon the Highway, he muſt turn
" himſelf about, as not daring to look them in
" the Face, and fall down with his Head to the
" very Ground.

" And as to the Lands and Goods of theſe mi-
" ſerable People, they are ſo expoſed to the Rapine
" of the Nobility and Soldiers, beſides the Taxes,
" Cuſtoms, and Seizures, and other publick Ex-
" actions laid upon them by the Emperor, that
" they are utterly diſcouraged from following their
" Trades and Profeſſions; becauſe the more they
" have, the more Danger they are in, not only
" of their Goods, but even of their Lives: And
" if they happen to have any thing, they convey
" it into Monaſteries, or hide it in Woods or un-
" der Ground, as Men do when they are in Fear
" of a Foreign Iavaſion. So that many Villages
" and Towns are intirely without Inhabitants;
" and

" and in the Way towards *Mofcow*, betwixt *Vo-*
" *laghda* and *Yareflave*, for about an Hundred *Eng-*
" *lifh* Miles, there are at leaft Fifty Villages, fome
" half a Mile long, fome a whole Mile long, that
" ftand wholly defolate, without a fingle Inha-
" bitant. The like Defolation is feen in all other
" Places of the Realm, as I have been told by
" thofe that travelled the Country.

" In every great Town the Emperor hath a
" Drinking-Houfe, which he rents out : Here the
" Labouring Man and Artificer many Times
" fpends all from his Wife and Children. Some
" drink away all that they wear about them, to
" their very Shirts, and fo walk naked ; and all
" for the Honour of the Emperor. Nay, while
" they are thus drinking themfelves naked, and
" ftarving their Families, no body muft call them
" away, upon any Account, becaufe he would
" hinder the Emperor's Revenue.

" The capital Punifhments upon the People are
" very cruel ; but if Theft or Murder be com-
" mitted upon them by one of the Nobility, he
" is feldom punifhed, or fo much as called to Ac-
" count for it, becaufe the People are the Slaves
" of the Nobility : Or if thefe Crimes are com-
" mitted by a Gentleman Soldier, perhaps he may
" be imprifoned at the Emperor's Pleafure, or
" perhaps fined ———and that is all."

I make this Quotation chiefly upon Memory,
having only taken down fome Hints when I read
it ; but I can affert it to be a juft one, and almoft
wholly in the Doctor's Words.

I know much has been faid of the Improvements made by the prefent *Czar,* and of his many
Projects

Projects in Favour of Arts and Trade : And it is
very true, that he is a Prince of a very active and
inquifitive Genius. But though he has made himfelf a more powerful Prince than any of his Predeceffors were, I do not find that the Numbers of
his People are increafed, or their general wretched
Condition much mended. He has a vaft Army
conftantly on Foot ; he keeps vaft Numbers of his
poor Subjects conftantly employed in making Ha-
vens and Canals ; great Taxes are raifed, great
and daily Wafte is made of his People, who are
likewife miferably oppreffed by his *Boyars*, to whom
he ftill leaves the raifing of Money, and the Direction of Trade : So that the general Oppreffion
remains ; Trade is deadned and diftreffed ; the
People burdened beyond Meafure ; fudden and arbitrary Duties are laid upon Commodities imported ; the old Way of Monopolies is continued ; the
State of the Exchange, and the Allay and uncertain Value of the current Coin, are as bad as they
can be ; Arts and Ingenuity are really difcouraged,
and thofe who have Skill in any Art muft conceal
it, to avoid working for nothing ; there are Grievances without Number, and like to be, for he
who complains is certainly undone, and Petitions
are anfwered with Stripes, fometimes with Death
itfelf. In fhort, the Condition of the *Ruffian* People is much upon the fame Foot as it was in Dr.
Fletcher's Time ; and whoever doubts it, may find
full Conviction from Captain *Perry*'s State of *Ruffia*, under the prefent *Czar*.

In *Poland*, nothing can be more miferable than
the Condition of the Peafants, who are fubject to
the mere Mercy of the great Lords, as to Life
and

and Death and Property ; and muſt labour Five
Days in a Week, nay ſometimes Six, for theſe
Lords ; and if they cannot ſubſiſt themſelves and
their Families upon One Day's Labour in Seven,
they muſt famiſh. The State of the other Northern Kingdoms is, with reſpect to the People, as
wretched as any yet named : They have many
Soldiers, endleſs Taxes, dreadful Poverty, few
People, and gaudy Courts. It is indeed ſaid of
ſome arbitrary Princes in ſome Parts of *Europe*,
that they are merciful to their Subjects, and do not
uſe them barbarouſly ; that is, they do not deliberately butcher them, but only take all that they
have, and leave them to ſtarve peaceably upon the
reſt : All the Riches of the Country are to be ſeen
at Court, and the People are wretchedly poor.
Contabit vacuus.——A Countryman once complained to General *Kirk*, that his Soldiers had
plundered him of all that he had in the World :
Thou art a happy Man, ſays the General, *for then
they will plunder thee no more.*

The woful Decay of People and Plenty in many States in *Italy* is ſo aſtoniſhing, that were it
not obvious to every Eye that ſees it, and ſo well
atteſted to thoſe who have not ſeen it, by thoſe
who have, it would ſeem beyond all Belief.
" When I came into the Pope's Territories at
" *Pont Centino*, (ſays Dr. *Burnet*) there was a
" rich Bottom all uncultivated, and not ſo much
" as ſtocked with Cattle : But as I paſſed from
" *Montifiaſcone* to *Viterbo*, this appeared yet more
" amazing ; for a vaſt champain Country lay
" almoſt quite deſerted. And that wide Town,
" which is of ſo great Compaſs, hath few Inha-
" bitants,

" bitants, and thofe looked poor and miferable.
" When I was within a Day's Journey of *Rome*,
" I fanfied the Neighbourhood of fo great a
" City muft mend the Matter; but I was much
" difappointed : For a Soil that was fo rich, and
" lay fo fweetly, that it far exceeded any Thing
" I ever faw out of *Italy*, had neither Inhabi-
" tants in it, nor Cattle upon it, to the Tenth
" Part of what it could bear. The Surprize this
" gave me increafed upon me, as I went out of
" *Rome* on its other Side, chiefly all the Way to
" *Naples*, and on the Way to *Civita Vecchia* ; for
" that vaft and rich Champain Country, which
" runs all along to *Terracina*, which from *Civita*
" *Vecchia* is a Hundred Miles long, and is in many
" Places 'Twelve or Twenty Miles broad, is aban-
" doned to fuch a Degree, that as far as one's
" Eye can carry one, there is often not fo much
" as a Houfe to be feen. The Severity of the
" Government hath driven away the Inhabitants ;
" and their being driven away hath reduced it to
" fuch a Pafs, that it is hardly poffible to people
" it." He adds, that in *Rome* itfelf, " it is not
" poffible for the People to live and pay Taxes ;
" which has driven, as it is believed, almoft a
" Fourth Part of the People out of *Rome* during
" this Pontificate."

He tells us elfewhere, that the *Pope* buys in all
the Corn of St. *Peter's* Patrimony. " He buys
" it at Five Crowns their Meafure, and even that
" is flowly and ill paid. So that there was Eight
" Hundred Thoufand Crowns owing upon that
" Score when I was at *Rome*. In felling this out,
" the Meafure is leffened a Fifth Part, and the
                                          " Price

" Price of the Whole is doubled ; fo that what
" was bought at Five Crowns, is fold out at
" Twelve ; and if the Bankers, who are obliged
" to take a determined Quantity of Corn from
" the Chamber, cannot retail out all that is im-
" pofed upon them, but are forced to return fome
" Part of it back, the Chamber difcounts to them
" only the firft Price of Five Crowns."

It is obferved by another noble Author of our
Country, that *Mario Chigi*, Brother to Pope *Alex-*
ander the Seventh, by one fordid Cheat upon the
Sale of Corn, is faid within Eight Years to have
deftroyed above the Third Part of the People in
the Ecclefiaftical State ; and that that Country,
which was the Strength of the *Romans* in the *Car-*
thaginian Wars, fuffered more by the Covetoufnefs and Fraud of that Villain, than by all the Defeats received from *Hannibal.*

The Country of *Ferrara* was formerly very populous, and the Lands being fertile, were well
cultivated ; but fince the Pope has got Poffeffion
of it, it is almoft depopulated ; the Lands are
nigh defolate ; and, for want of People, it is like
the reft of the Ecclefiaftical State, unhealthy to
live in. His Holinefs has reduced the Inhabitants
from above an Hundred Thoufand, to about
Twelve Thoufand. In the City itfelf, Grafs
grows in the Streets, and moft of the Houfes are
empty.

The Great Duke's Dominions lie much in the
fame difmal Solitude. When *Sienna* and *Pifa* were
free States, they fwarmed with People, and were
rich in Trade and Territory : *Sienna* alone was
computed to have had above half a Million of Subjects ;

jects; but in a matter of an Hundred and Fourscore
Years, during which Time it has been in the Poffeffion of his Highnefs of *Tufcany*, they are funk
below Twenty Thoufand, and thefe miferably
poor. The fame is the abject Condition of *Pifa*,
Piftoja, *Arezzo*, *Cortona*, and many other great
Towns. *Florence*, his Capital particularly, which,
in the Days of Liberty, could, by the Ringing of
a Bell, bring together, of its own Citizens and the
Inhabitants of the Valley *Arno*, a Hundred and
Thirty-five Thoufand well armed Men in a few
Hours Time, is now fo poor and low, that it
could not bring together Three tolerable Regiments in Thirteen Months.

The City of *Pifa* alone was reckoned, when it
was free, to have had a Hundred and Fifty Thoufand Inhabitants, all happy in Liberty and Commerce; and now they are about Ten Thoufand,
without Liberty, and Commerce, and Bread.
Formerly an Hundred of its Citizens could fit out
an Hundred Galleys, and maintain them during a
War, at their own Charge; and now the whole
City could not furnifh out nor maintain one.
Their ftately Palaces are defolate, like their Territory; or let out for Stables, or any other forry
Ufe, at Three or Four Pounds a Year Rent.
Their Streets are covered with Grafs; their Territory, by being wafte, is grown unwholfome; and
their few Remains of People are ftarving. And
that great State, which the Great Duke could not
mafter without the Armies of *Spain*, are not now
able to contend with his infamous Crew of Tax-
gatherers. The People are famifhed Slaves, their
Houfes are Ruins, their Trade is gone, their Land
unma-

unmanured, and yet their Taxes are not leſſened; and if there be any Plenty amongſt them, 'tis only Plenty of Beggars.

The ſame is the Condition of the *Milaneze*, and other Countries under the ſame Sort of Government; the People ſtarve in the beſt Soils: Whereas in *Switzerland*, and in the Territories of *Genoa*, *Lucca*, and the *Griſons*, they are numerous, and live happily in the worſt. " The People " in *France*, (ſays the Author of the Supplement " to Dr. *Burnet*'s Travels) eſpecially the Peaſants, " are very poor, and moſt of them reduced to " great Want and Miſery; and yet *France* is an " extraordinary good Country. The People of " *Switzerland* (*which is a Country of Mountains*) " cannot be ſaid to be very rich, but there are " very few, even of the Peaſants, that are miſe- " rably poor.——The moſt Part of them have " enough to live on. Every where in *France*, " even in the beſt Cities, there are Swarms of " Beggars; and yet ſcarce any to be ſeen through- " out all *Switzerland*. The Houſes of the Coun- " try People in *France* are extremely mean; and " in them no other Furniture is to be found, but " poor naſty Beds, Straw Chairs, with Plates and " Diſhes of Wood and Earth. In *Switzerland*, " the Peaſants have their Houſes furniſhed with " good Feather-Beds, good Chairs, and other " convenient Houſhold-Stuffs; their Windows " are all of Glaſs, always kept mended and " whole; and their Linnen, both for Bedding and " their Tables, is very neat and white."

This was written above Thirty Years ago, when *France* was in a much better Condition than
it

it has been fince.   The Glory of their late Grand
Monarch coft them much Mifery, and many Myriads of People.   And yet even Thirty Years ago
their Miferies were great and affecting !   " As I
" came from *Paris* to *Lyons*, (fays Dr. *Burnet*)
" I was amazed to fee fo much Mifery as ap-
" peared not only in Villages, but even in big
" Towns ; where all the Marks of an extreme
" Poverty fhewed themfelves, both in the Build-
" ings, the Clothes, and almoft in the Looks of
" the Inhabitants. And a general difpeopling in
" all the Towns, was a very vifible Effect of the
" Hardfhips under which they lay."   What bleffed Circumftances that great Kingdom is in now,
Mr. *Law*, who is amongft us, can beft tell ;
though we all pretty well know.   It is really a
Science, and no eafy one, to know the Names,
Numbers, and Quality of their Taxes ; which
are fo many, fo various, and fo heavy, that one
of their own Writers calls them, *Inventions proper*
to impoverifh the People, and to enrich the Dictiona-
ries.   Bulion, Treafurer to *Lewis* the Thirteenth,
told his Mafter, that *his Subjects were too happy,*
they were not yet reduced to eat Grafs.   And the
cruel Spirit and Politicks of that Minifter were
afterwards fo well improved, that I am apt to
think their prefent Felicity is no Part of their
Misfortunes.

   Such Inftances fhew what hopeful Methods fuch
Governors take to increafe People, Trade, and
Riches.

   As to the politer Arts, I own feveral of them
have flourifhed under fome of the Popes themfelves, and fome other arbitrary Princes ; fuch as
                                        Painting,

Painting, Architecture, Sculpture, and Mufick. But thefe Arts, and the Improvements of them, were fo far from owing any Thing to that Sort of Government, that by Liberty alone, and the Privileges given to the Profeffors of them, they came to excel in them ; nor would they ever have excelled upon the common Foot and Condition of their other Subjects : So that to make them Excellent, they made them Free. And thus even Tyrants, the Enemies of Liberty, were, for their Furniture, Luxury, Pomp, Pleafure, and Entertainment, forced to be beholden to Liberty ; and for thofe particular Purpofes, they gave it to particular Men. But for the reft of their Subjects, they were left by them in the Condition of Brutes, both in Point of Livelihood and Knowledge : For it is Liberty more than Shape, that makes the Difference ; fince Reafon without Liberty proves little better, and fometimes worfe, than none. Servitude mars all Genius ; nor is either a Pen or a Pencil of any Ufe in a Hand that is manacled.

G   *I am,* &c.

The End of the SECOND VOLUME.